A Microeconomics Reader

T0300564

This book draws together the key contributions to the major areas of microeconomic theory from the last few decades. It is intended to provide both undergraduate and graduate students with an essential guide to the current state of the discipline. The articles have been carefully selected not only for the role they have played in the progress of microeconomics, but also for their usefulness and potential to inspire future research.

The main themes covered include consumer theory, the theory of the firm, the theory of markets, pricing theory, and labor compensation theory, with the common threads of transaction costs, strategic decisions, and information imperfections. Unlike similar anthologies, this Reader also draws attention to methodological issues and heterodox approaches to microeconomics. Amongst those whose works appear here are Gary Becker, George Stigler, Harvey Leibenstein, Ronald Coase, Oliver Williamson, George Akerlof, Joseph Stiglitz, Avinash Dixit, and Paul Klemperer.

This Reader will be an invaluable resource for advanced undergraduate and graduate students in economics, as well as casual readers interested in an "insider's view" of the discipline. It serves not only to collect in a single place the most significant papers in economics that have been published in recent decades but also, with several introduction chapters, to give the literature a coherent structure.

Tran Huu Dung is Associate Professor of Economics at Wright State University in Dayton, Ohio, USA. He is a specialist in the economies of East Asia, particularly Vietnam. He is also the Managing Editor of the popular web portal *Arts & Letters Daily*.

A Microeconomics Reader

Edited by Tran Huu Dung

Routledge
Taylor & Francis Group

LONDON AND NEW YORK

First published 2013
by Routledge
2 Park Square, Milton Park, Abingdon, Oxon, OX14 4RN

Simultaneously published in the USA and Canada
by Routledge
711 Third Avenue, New York, NY 10017

Routledge is an imprint of the Taylor & Francis Group, an informa business

British Library Cataloguing in Publication Data
A catalogue record for this book is available from the British Library

Library of Congress Cataloging in Publication Data

A microeconomics reader/edited by Tran Huu Dung.
p. cm.
Includes bibliographical references and index.
1. Microeconomics. I. Dung, Tran Huu.
HB172.M5995 2013
338.5–dc23
2012038372

ISBN: 978-0-415-77193-1 (hbk)
ISBN: 978-0-415-77192-4 (pbk)

Typeset in Times New Roman
by Sunrise Setting Ltd, Paignton, UK

Contents

List of figures

List of tables

Preface

Why this *Reader*?

Nothwithstanding the growing accessibility of scholarly articles online, it is a widely shared sentiment that seeing the most noteworthy works in close physical proximity, between the covers of a printed volume, is still the best guide to a subject. Accompanied by a "user friendly" introduction, such a collection would give the subject a structure and cohesiveness that are not easy for most readers to get on their own. This *Reader* is intended to meet this need for microeconomics, mainly for advanced undergraduate and graduate students in economics. Casual readers might also use this collection for an "insider's view" of the state of the subject.

This book contains twenty-nine articles which, in my opinion, have made signal contributions to the recent progress in microeconomics. They are valuable for their insights, or have been proven useful (for example, by introducing a particular modeling technique) in later works by others. They are all deemed seminal in our understanding of various problems in microeconomics. Although these works are well known within the profession, and their main ideas can be found in most textbooks, reading the original papers is still worthwhile for the nuggets of insights that might have been overlooked. Originals often contain observations that are personal and inspiring. As convenient shortcuts to other works, several surveys are also included. To maintain accessibility, super-technical articles are avoided (although, admittedly, the mathematics in economics is increasingly demanding).

In contrast to frequent "paradigmatic shifts" that behooved macroeconomics (from classical economics, to Keynesianism, and back), microeconomic evolution has been relatively smooth.[1] One reason is, perhaps, that the stake in microeconomics is not as high as in macroeconomics, at least for public policy making, where disagreements are often highly charged. In microeconomics, a good idea almost always inspires further research, and a sizable literature would soon emerge. Pioneering works are sometimes questioned, but rarely rejected with rancor. There has been no "counterrevolution" in microeconomics.[2]

Articles included in this *Reader* are divided into five Parts, each with its own brief introduction: Part I: Consumer theory, Part II: Theory of the firm, Part III: Theory of the market, Part IV: Pricing theory, and Part V: Labor compensation theory.

Given the breadth of the subject, many topics have had to be left out of this *Reader*, most notably applied and empirical papers (including experimental microeconomics). Fortunately, there are in existence several "niche" collections that might complement the *Reader* in this regard.[3]

An anthology like this offers the editor an opportunity to reflect on his or her academic discipline, and truth be told, this editor is rather proud of his. It is hoped that the excitement shown by the authors of the articles selected herein will be contagious to the readers. For those about to join the economics profession, we hope that this collection will spark much inspiration for their own future research.

Last but not least, the editor would like to thank all the authors whose works are presented here for their kind permission, Robert Langham for suggesting this project and for being so incredibly understanding through countless delays, and the editorial staff at Routledge for their patience, promptness, and efficiency.

Tran Huu Dung

Notes

1 Arguably, the macroeconomic tension has its mirror image in microeconomics in the debate between predictivism and instrumentalism. See, for example, Caldwell (1994).
2 Backhouse (2010) makes an interesting point: "It also seems clear that economics is most successful where problems are narrowly defined and that its application is most problematic when wider issues, involving politics or social phenomena, need to be considered."
3 "The International Library of Critical Writings in Economics" published by Elgar is a fine example.

References

Backhouse, R. (2010) *The Puzzle of Modern Economics: Science or Ideology*, N.Y.: Cambridge University Press.
Caldwell, B. (1994) *Beyond Positivism* (rev. edn), London: Routledge.

Acknowledgements

The editor and publisher would like to thank the following for their kind permission to reproduce copyright material.

Part I

2 "De gustibus non est disputandum" by George J. Stigler and Gary S. Becker is reproduced with permission from the American Economic Association. The text appearing in this volume first appeared in *The American Economic Review* (1977) volume 67(2), pp. 139–47.

3 "Bandwagon, snob, and Veblen effects in the theory of consumers' demand" by Harvey Leibenstein is reproduced with permission from the Oxford University Press. This text was published in *The Quarterly Journal of Economics* (1950) volume 64(2), pp. 183–207.

4 "A theory of the allocation of time" by Gary Becker is reproduced by permission of Blackwell Publishing Ltd. This text first appeared in *The Economic Journal* © Royal Economic Society (1965) 73, September, pp. 493–517.

5 "A new approach to consumer theory" by Kelvin Lancaster is reproduced by permission of the University of Chicago Press. It first appeared in *The Journal of Political Economy* (1966) 74, pp. 132–57.

6 "Rationality in psychology and economics" by Herbert A. Simon is reproduced by permission of The University of Chicago Press. The text first appeared in *The Journal of Business*, Vol. 59. No. 4, Part 2: The Behavioural Foundations of Economic Theory (Oct. 1986) pp. S209–S224.

Part II

7 "The nature of the firm" by Ronald Coase is reproduced by permission of Blackwell Publishing. The text first appeared in *Economica* (November 1937) New Series 4, issue 16, pp. 386–405.

8 "Production, information costs, and economic organization" by Armen Alchian and Harold Demsetz is reproduced by permission of the American Economic Association. The article first appeared in *The American Economic Review* (1972) 62, December, pp. 777–95.

9 "An economist's perspective on the theory of the firm" by Oliver Hart is reproduced by permission of the Copyright Clearance Center, Inc. The article first appeared in the *Columbia Law Review* (1989) 89(7) published by the Columbia Law Review Association, Inc., November, pp. 1757–74.

10 "The firm in Illyria: market syndicalism" by Benjamin Ward is reproduced by permission of the American Economic Association. It first appeared in *The American Economic Review* (1958) 48, pp. 566–89.

11 "The theory of the firm as governance structure: from choice to contract" by Oliver Williamson is reproduced by permission of the American Economic Association. It first appeared in *The Journal of Economic Perspectives* (Summer 2002) 16(3), pp. 171–95.

12 "Vertical integration, appropriable rents, and the competitive contracting process" by Benjamin Klein, Robert G. Crawford, and Armen A. Alchian is reproduced by permission of the University of Chicago, © 1978 The University of Chicago. It first appeared in *The Journal of Law and Economics* (1978) 21(2), pp. 297–326.

13 "Agency problems and the theory of the firm" by Eugene Fama is reproduced by permission of the University of Chicago, © 1980 The University of Chicago Press. It first appeared in the *Journal of Political Economy* 88(2), (April 1980), pp. 288–307.

Part III

14 "The use of knowledge in society" by Friedrich Hayek is reproduced by permission of the American Economic Association. It first appeared in *The American Economic Review* (1945) 35(4), September, pp. 519–30.

15 "The market for 'lemons': quality uncertainty and the market mechanism" by George A. Akerlof appears by permission of Oxford University Press and first appeared in *The Quarterly Journal of Economics* (August 1970) 84(3), pp. 488–500.

16 "Information and the change in the paradigm of economics" by Joseph Stiglitz was the Nobel Prize Lecture, December 8, 2001, © The Nobel Foundation 2001. It is reproduced with the permission of the Nobel Foundation.

17 "Duopoly models with consistent conjectures" by Timothy Bresnahan is reproduced with the permission of the American Economic Association. It first appeared in *The American Economic Review* (December 1981) volume 71(5), 1981, pp. 934–45.

18 "Games economists play: a noncooperative view" by Franklin M. Fisher is reproduced by permission of Blackwell Publishing. It first appeared in *The RAND Journal of Economics* published by Wiley/Blackwell (1989) 20(1), pp. 113–24.

19 "The approach of institutional economics" by Geoffrey Hodgson is reproduced by permission of the American Economic Association. It first appeared in the *Journal of Economic Literature* (1998) 36, March, pp. 166–92.

Part IV

20 "Monopolistic competition and optimal product diversity" by Avinash Dixit and Joseph Stiglitz is reproduced by permission of the American Economic Association. It first appeared in *The American Economic Review* (1977) 67, 297–308.

21 "A Disneyland dilemma: two-part tariffs for a Mickey Mouse monopoly" by Walter Oi is reproduced by permission of Oxford University Press. It first appeared in the *Quarterly Journal of Economics* (1971) 85(1), pp. 77–96.

22 "Commodity bundling and the burden of monopoly" by Walter Adams and Janet Yellen is reproduced by permission of Oxford University Press. It first appeared in the *Quarterly Journal of Economics* (1976) 90(3), pp. 475–98.

23 "Peak loads and efficient pricing" by Peter Steiner is reproduced by permission of Oxford University Press. It first appeared in the *Quarterly Journal of Economics* (1957) 71(4), pp. 585–610.

24 "Bundling as an entry barrier" by Barry Nalebuff is reproduced by permission of Oxford University Press. It first appeared in *The Quarterly Journal of Economics* (2004) 119(1), pp. 159–87.

25 "What really matters in auction design" by Paul Klemperer is reproduced by permission of the American Economic Association. The text appearing in this volume first appeared in *The Journal of Economic Perspectives* (2002) 16, pp. 169–89.

26 "Network externalities (effects)" by Stan Liebowitz and Stephen Margolis is reproduced by permission of Palgrave Macmillan. The text here appears in *The New Palgrave Dictionary of Economics and the Law* (1998).

Part V

27 "The economics of superstars" by Sherwin Rosen is reproduced by permission of the American Economic Association. The article first appeared in *The American Economic Review* (1981) 71, pp. 845–58.

28 "Strategic behavior in contests" by Avinash Dixit is reproduced by permission of the American Economic Association. The article first appeared in *The American Economic Review* (1987) 77, pp. 891–98.

29 "Job Market Signaling" by Michael Spence is reproduced by permission of Oxford University Press. It first appeared in the *Quarterly Journal of Economics* (August 1973) 87(3), pp. 355–74.

30 "The causes and consequences of the dependence of quality on price" by Joseph Stiglitz is reproduced by permission of the American Economic Association. It first appeared in the *Journal of Economic Literature* (1987) 25, pp. 1–48.

Every effort has been made to contact copyright holders for their permission to reprint selections in this volume. The publisher would be grateful to hear from any copyright holder who is not here acknowledged and will undertake to rectify any errors or omissions in future editions.

1 A brief guide to contemporary microeconomics

Tran Huu Dung

It is a widely recognized fact that, until recently, microeconomics has been dominated (for better or for worse) by the *neoclassical paradigm*. As a bare-bones summary, this paradigm can be described as a mode of thought where the firm is viewed as a "black box" (with little attention paid to its internal structure) represented by a "production function." This function is presumed to embody all that the (solitary) owner-cum-manager should know about the manufacturing techniques available. As for the consumer, he/she is routinely described as a utility-maximizing entity, at least for modeling purposes. These producers and consumers meet in frictionless markets where no one has any actionable influence (with some exceptions) on anyone else. Everybody has perfect information. Within this set-up, the focus of most *theoretical* economic analyses (*empirical* studies have other objectives) is to identify some kind of "equilibrium," and to determine whether this equilibrium is "efficient" in some sense.

In the last few decades, however, microeconomics has grown out of its neoclassical mold. The range of topics under its penumbra has expanded considerably, and interesting new ways have been found to examine familiar problems. Many reasons can be cited for this progress. First, there is now a stronger connection between microeconomics and business practices: Unlike the earlier days when most academic economists tended to look down on matters of commerce, contemporary microeconomics has a newfound fascination with business decisions, including the behavior of constituents within a firm.[1] Second, microeconomics has become more integrated. For example, consumption and production no longer seem so fundamentally different (many authors regard consumption as a form of production, with its own inputs and technology). Likewise, the similarity between internal (inside a firm) and external labor markets is increasingly noted, and so on. Somewhat surprisingly, this integration has not come about, as many economists of a generation ago had perhaps expected, by an ever more elaborate general equilibrium set-up (whose focus is the interdependence among markets), probably augmented with a dose of economies of scale and assorted externalities. Rather, the links among these different issues have emerged through the identification of a few elements common to almost all economic activities: transaction costs, the role of information, and strategic interactions among economic agents (i.e., interactions in which at least one decision maker takes into consideration the reaction of other(s)). These elements, and methods suggested for their analyses, have reframed many familiar problems, and indeed have brought into economics quite a few novel and fascinating topics to study.

Transaction costs

We are all familiar with production costs – the costs of *making* a product. Since the early 1930s, following the seminal work of Ronald Coase, more attention has been given to non-production costs, which could be broadly defined as the expenses of executing a transaction (such as selling and buying). These have come to be known as *transaction costs*.

Transaction costs have been invoked to explain the (sometime) superiority of firms over markets as institutions for resource allocation. These explanations postulate that decision-makers always minimize costs, which include transaction costs. For this purpose, a hierarchical structure (such as the firm) is preferred if it helps avoid costs that are often associated with arm's length transactions.

Given their pervasiveness, the inclusion of transaction costs in a model almost always makes the analysis more realistic. It might even suggest new ways to view an economic phenomenon. For example, interpreting transaction costs to include the costs of monitoring and enforcement could explain the necessity as well as the limitations of contracts. With additional ingredients (for instance, the impossibility of designing a "complete" contract, and the nontransferability of some assets among uses) transaction costs could also be invoked to explain why some firms choose to "outsource" (i.e., acquire certain inputs from other firms) rather than to make these inputs themselves. Further, considering switching cost as a type of transaction costs could explain a variety of oligopolistic behavior, among other things. Some authors make a useful distinction between *ex ante* and *ex post* transaction costs, i.e., transaction costs that exist before or after the activation of a contract. Indeed, the multiplicity and nebulousness of transaction costs have caused some concern among those who wish for a more succinct concept.

Rivalry

Until a few decades ago, the main focus of microeconomics had been on price-taking agents. While this research has resulted in a theoretical edifice that appeared to be quite elegant, it was rather unconcerned with the fact that most economic interactions are antagonistic or rivalrous, not harmonious or even neutral. In reality, economic units compete (to various degrees) among themselves, and only coordinate or assist each other when it is in their interests to do so. (Even altruism could be treated as a special kind of self-interest.) Furthermore, when the group is not very large, one person's pursuing of his/her goals usually depends on some conjecture regarding others' behavior. The recognition of this dependency opens up myriad complications: actions depend on anticipated reactions, and repeatedly so.

Take for example the competition among firms. The effects of a firm's price cut, say, depend not only on the timing and size of the cut but also on how other firms will react to that cut. In the canonical neoclassical model of perfect competition, each firm is assumed to be just one among many, producing an identical product, so other firms' "reaction" is arguably inconsequential as it would hardly have any effect. However, the mutual dependency among firms cannot be ignored if, for instance, the number of firms is not large, or if this number is large but only a few firms are dominant. Clearly, the presumption of price-taking behavior, while enabling an elegant theoretical construct, does not do justice to reality.

Rivalries among firms are, of course, for all to see, but the relationship between shareholders and a company's executives (usually thought of as being "on the same side") is unlikely to be harmonious either. "Rivalry" might also be the lens through which one explains the decisions of a firm, not as a hierarchy of decision-makers with a common objective, but as a coalition of competing interest groups (the workers, the stockholders, the managers . . .). Rivalries also arise when a firm must deal with its retailers at one end, and suppliers at the other, as well as with its employees, especially when these employees are unionized. (And, surely, each labor union has within itself its own set of rivalrous interactions – between, say, the leadership and the rank and file.)

Still, even the recognition of strategic decisions could not have shaped modern microeconomics as much as it has without the concomitant development of *game theory*. With its transparent logic and potent analytics, this branch of applied mathematics has deeply influenced the way economists[2] formalize circumstances in which the outcome of a decision depends not only on that decision but also on the reactions of others, both simultaneously and sequentially. In game-theoretic parlance, an agent is said to engage in "strategic thinking" when she chooses an action, taking into consideration the anticipated reactions of others that might, intentionally or not, affect the result of her action. "Non-strategic thinking" is when such consideration is absent.

The heavy use of game theory in economics, however, is not without its skeptics.[3] Some have argued that the game-theoretic approach would take us down the wrong path. More specifically, to be amenable to this approach, an economic problem might be too restrictively framed, or the mathematics of game theory gives the analysis a false rigor. Time will tell whether this suspicion is justified. But surely, one way or another, the strategic thinking behind most decisions must be accounted for.

Information imperfections

Recent microeconomics progress has also been driven by a third engine: the recognition of the crucial role of *information* in all economic activities. People seldom, if ever, know everything relevant to every decision they make. Producers are often unaware of all available techniques, and sellers and buyers are usually ignorant of each other's whereabouts, among many other useful attributes. Indeed, not only is it impossible for anyone to foresee what will happen, it is rarely possible to conceive all that *could* happen.

But insufficiency is not the only problem with information; there is also the "asymmetry" of information among participants in a transaction: some might have more and/or better information than others. This asymmetry could be of two kinds. In one, participants might have unequal knowledge about something (for instance, the quality of a product) germane to the transaction. In the second, the required action of one party (for instance, to fulfill a contract) cannot be accurately gauged by others (including the judge, if the case should ever come to court) due to the lack of information. For example, it is difficult for an insurance company to know how well a policy-holder takes care of the insured object.

These two aspects of information (incompleteness and asymmetry) could explain many phenomena, from problems between buyers and sellers, to contracts between employers and employees.[4] Indeed, further thinking along this line has inspired whole new research areas. For instance, there is a burgeoning literature on "signals," i.e., the information (embedded in certain action) purposefully sent by one party to other(s), implicitly or explicitly, and attendant problems (noise, credibility, etc.)

Interest in information has also benefited from the phenomenal progress in information technology (computers, telecommunications, and such). Works pioneered by Hal Varian, in particular, have brought forth a plethora of insights. Other problems, such as the nature of innovation and invention, however, remain under-explored.

Viewed through the triple lens of transaction costs, strategic behavior, and information imperfections, the variety of topics taken on by contemporary microeconomics comes into sharper focus. The connection between different approaches becomes clearer. Unmistakable patterns emerge. Post-1970s theories do not break with the tradition of neoclassical economics, however. Rather, most of the advances are grounded in refinements of the units of decision-making ("the firm," for example, is now more realistically seen as a complex network of employer(s) and employees rather than a unitary owner/manager), incorporating whenever possible the role of information. The new "market analysis," on the other hand, has moved away from the assumption that every agent is a price-taker, and slowly subsumed into the emerging field of industrial organization, where strategic decisions are front and center. Broadly speaking, then, despite their shortcomings, neoclassical models remain the workhorse to study industries and markets, i.e., to trace the consequences of the behavior of groups of sellers and buyers (and not what led to that behavior).

While these three themes have garnered increasing attention, general equilibrium theory, once the crown jewel of economics, has been slowly losing its place as the core interest of professional economists. The notion of equilibrium itself, however, is still very much economics' center of gravity. Indeed, information, and related issues (such as heterogeneity, incentives, and risks) have led to new concepts such as "pooling" and "separating" equilibrium. In some areas, in the "new" personnel economics for example, the determination of "equilibrium" is posited to be the key to new insights. In addition, the interest in welfare theory (that has gone hand-in-hand with general equilibrium theory) has found a second life in public economics, especially in the theory of regulation (which is enriched by the recognition of the regulators' lack of information). Also, the trend toward issues that are closer to managerial and business economics is particularly pronounced in pricing theory and labor economics.

Transaction costs, strategic decisions, and information imperfections can also be combined in various ways. An example is the so-called *agency theory*. This theory concerns the problem associated with, say, the design of a compensation package for a hired employee.[5] Such a package must address three facts, two of which involve information. First, the employer and the employee are likely to have different, even conflicting, objectives (the employer wants the employee to work hard, the employee wants to work as little as possible). This means the employee's compensation must reflect the effort applied by the employee to his or her job. Second, it takes up resources for the employer to constantly monitor each and every employee. Hence the compensation scheme should not require constant, close monitoring. And third, it is impossible to design a contract that is not only enforceable but also (1) not open to different interpretations, and (2) anticipative of every contingency. The severity of each of these problems relative to others determines which compensation scheme should be chosen.

Auction (where one seller faces a few buyers) also lends itself to studies through the dual lens of strategic behavior and information imperfection: evidently auctioneer(s) and bidders make their decisions from what they perceive to be the possible reaction of others, and on the information they have. The new twist here is that the sequence of actions is critical.

Needless to say, this *Reader* offers only a minuscule number of noteworthy articles. Most of the articles not found here have long been integrated into the canon, or otherwise left no singular influence. Interested readers could easily track them down by consulting the references in the articles in this collection.

Notes

1 Conversely, many authors suggest that some areas of economics, such as industrial organizaition, have become independent disciplines (see Cabral, 2000).
2 Political scientists, evolutionary economists…also find game theory useful.

3 Hay (1991, 60): "it is perhaps true that game theory has never quite lived up to the potential which its initial development appeared to offer. One recent text on the subject (Rasmussen, 1989) describes it as the Argentina of economics, in terms of the gap between potential and achievement. . ." See also Fisher (1989), Sutton (1990).
4 The Zeitgeist was captured by Spence (2001) thus: "What did blossom at that time (about 1970) was a serious attempt by many talented economists to capture in applied microeconomic theory a whole variety of aspects of market structure and performance. That work produced a partial melding of theory, industrial organization, labor economics, finance and other fields. An important early part of that effort was the attempt to capture informational aspects of market structure to study the ways in which markets adapt, and the consequences of informational gaps for market performance" (p. 403).
5 Or, to take another example, a landlord and his tenant.

References

Cabral, L. M. B. (2000) *Introduction to Industrial Organization*, Cambridge, MA: MIT Press.
Fisher, F. (1989) "Game Economists Play: A Non-Cooperative View," *The Rand Journal of Economics* 30, pp. 113–24.
Rasmussen, E. (1989) *Game and Information*, Oxford: Blackwell.
Spence, A. M. (2001) "Signaling in Retrospect and the Informational Structure of Markets," Nobel Lecture.
Sutton, J. (1990) "Explaining everything, explaining nothing? Game theoretic models in industrial economics," *European Economic Review* 34, pp. 505–12.
Thaler, R. H. and Sunstein, C. R. (2008) *Nudge: Improving Decisions About Health, Wealth, and Happiness*, New Haven: Yale University Press.

Part I

Consumer theory

Introduction

The current state of consumer theory could be broadly viewed in two ways. One is to see it as being evolved from its axiomatic formulation dated back to the 1960s, grounded in works such as Debreu's magisterial "Theory of Value," exploring the logical structure and consistency of choices, and their ramifications. To its critics, this view is almost a branch of applied logic, not economics per se. Anyhow, this tradition of consumer theory has waned noticeably, except in social welfare theory (as in works by Kenneth Arrow[1] and Amartya Sen[2]), analysis of economic justice in particular, where the logic of preferences, both individual and social, remains the focus of analysis.

In recent years, attention has shifted to different research agenda. Here, starting with Simon (1947) and especially Leibenstein (1980), each in his own way, the focus on the logic of decision making has given way to interests in the connection between psychology and economic behavior.[3] While this transition has been lauded by those who believe that economics should address observed human behavior, messy as it is, rather than sticking to an austere agenda, it has also been met with vigorous resistance, not from the logicians themselves, but by those who insist on adhering to the utility maximization model, regardless.

Within the framework of utility maximization theory, the fundamental question is: what should be taken as the irreducible building block in a model of consumer behavior? At first look, "tastes" appear to be the obvious answer. Tastes are the ground on which utility maximization takes place, generating predictions about individual decisions. Two questions then arise: (1) Could a person's tastes be regarded as time-invariant, unaffected by the group of which the person is a member? (2) Does an individual consumer always maximize "utility"? The answers depend on what the term "tastes" means. Do "tastes" in consumer theory have the same meaning as in ordinary language, or are they a meta-construct ("deep preferences") suggestive of, but not quite synonymous with, the concept of "tastes" in everyday parlance?

These questions are critical in judging the success of a consumer theory. If "deep preferences" are identical across individuals and time-invariant, the task of economics would be relatively simple. This view is implicit in most works in the Chicago tradition, especially those by George Stigler and Gary Becker. Their position exemplifies how the dominant – and controversial – economic methodology, that of Friedman's predictivism (1953), is brought to bear on a problem.[4] Indeed, the standard assumption in most mainstream articles is that preferences are exogenous and unchanging. However, this assumption puts decisions that are commonly thought of as resulting from "addiction"[5] outside the purview of economics. This exclusion does not go well with those who suggest that these kinds of behavior violate the neoclassical maximization hypothesis. Of course, critics would say that a "preference structure" could always be constructed to generate any kind of consumer behavior. The problem is that this "preference structure" is unlike anything familiar to most people. The disagreement between predictivists and instrumentalists, though rather quiet of late, is still lurking behind many disputes in economics.[6]

If, as in the second view, the word "tastes" is used as it is understood in the common language, preferences are allowed to be changeable and not immune to external (social or peer) pressure, then the results could be quite messy, and unambiguous predictions are few.

The five articles in Part I are chosen to reflect the broad methodological spectrum described above.

Leibenstein (1950) allowed more "real world" concepts (e.g., addiction, passion) to enter consumer theory. He also identified phenomena such as the way an individual could derive more satisfaction by conforming to a group (the *bandwagon effect*), or when an individual takes extra pleasure in the presumed "uniqueness" of his choice (the *snob effect*). Although Leibenstein's analysis has been praised for its common sense, it is the kind of theorizing that hardcore neoclassical theorists regard as ad hoc, unscientific.

Becker (1965) formulated an individual's labor supply decision as a resource (namely, time) allocation problem.[7] This paper is a landmark in consumer theory.

Lancaster (1966) expanded the neoclassical maximization model in a new direction to deal with the problem of new products. His ingenious suggestion is to consider a product, existing or yet to be invented, as a "bundle of attributes," all of which are well known to the consumer. The consumer, then, is to choose among these bundles, rather than among the products as usually perceived. This approach has the advantage of incorporating "new" products (including those yet to be invented) into the analysis: they are not "new" in the sense of having been completely unknown, but only new ways of bundling attributes already known. This model might also be added to the Chicago *repertoire* in which every aspect of individual behavior can be explained on an invariant foundation. In Lancaster formulation, that foundation is the space of known characteristics that are desired by the consumer.

Defending the strict version of neoclassical economics, Stigler and Becker (1977) argued that the "abnormal" behavior suggested by Leibenstein (and others) could be viewed as the result of a *normal* maximization process carried out on *some* invariant preference structure. In other words, Stigler and Becker made the case for using the hypothesis of utility maximization, and utility maximization alone, as the predictor of individual decisions.

The final paper in this group, Simon (1986), is an authoritative and critical review of criticisms of the rationality assumption in economics.

Certainly, not all strands of consumer theory are represented by the five articles included here. In empirical research especially, increasingly sophisticated techniques have been brought to bear on consumer studies. New conceptual trends have also been developed, among the most interesting is *behavioral economics*, in which the "context" of choice does matter.[8] For instance, given three options, A, B, and C, an individual's choice would depend on the order in which these options were shown, and on the environment in which they exist. Unlike traditional choice theory, which is elegant in its abstractness at the expense of realism, behavioral economics is rich in anecdotal evidence and policy implications. At present, however, it is still a work in progress, awaiting a more complete theoretical foundation.

Notes

1 Arrow (1963).
2 Sen (1970).

3 For a scholarly survey, see Rubin (1998); for a popular exposition, see Thaler and Sunstein (2008).

4 For an excellent account of this debate, see Caldwell (1994).

5 Whereupon an individual's desire for a product becomes stronger with uses, over time.

6 Richard Posner (2008) suggests that behavioral economics makes use of concepts (such as passion) that are imprecise and, furthermore, unnecessary to explain many phenomena that behavioral economists claim to be able to explain.

7 Becker (1976) was also influential but his role in the methodological debate is much clearer after reading Stigler and Becker.

8 For an excellent introduction, see Thaler and Sunstein (2008), also Tversky and Kahneman (1986).

References

Arrow, K. J. (1963) *Social Choice and Individual Values* (2nd edn) New Haven: Yale University Press.

Becker, G. (1965) "A Theory of the Allocation of Time," *Economic Journal* 75(299), pp. 493–517.

Becker, G. (1976) *The Economic Approach to Human Behavior*, Chicago: University of Chicago Press.

Caldwell, B. (1994) *Beyond Positivism* (rev. edn), London: Routledge.

Debreu, G. (1972) *Theory of Value*, New Haven: Yale University Press.

Friedman, M. (1953) "The Methodology of Positive Economics," in *Essays in Positive Economics*, Chicago: University of Chicago Press, pp. 3–45.

Lancaster, K. (1966) "A New Approach to Consumer Theory," *Journal of Political Economy* 74(2), pp. 122–57.

Leibenstein, H. (1950) "Bandwagon, Snob and Veblen Effects in the Theory of Consumer Demand," *Quarterly Journal of Economics* 64(2), pp. 183–207.

Leibenstein, H. (1980) "Issues in Development Economics: An Introduction," *Social Research* 47(2), pp. 204–12.

Posner, R. (2008) "Treating Financial Consumers as Consenting Adults," *Wall Street Journal*, July 22.

Rubin, M. (1998) "Psychology and Economics," *Journal of Economic Literature* 36, March, pp. 11–46.

Sen, A. K. (1970) *Collective Choice and Social Welfare*, New York: Holden-Day.

Simon, H. A. (1947) *Administrative Behavior: A Study of Decision-making Processes in Administrative Organization*, New York: Macmillan.

Simon, H. A. (1978), *Rational Decision-making in Business Organizations*, Nobel Memorial Lecture.

Simon, H. A. (1986) "Rationality in Psychology and Economics," *Journal of Business* 56(4), pp. S209–S224.

Thaler, R. H. and Sunstein, C. R. (2008) *Nudge: Improving Decisions About Health, Wealth, and Happiness*, New Haven: Yale University Press.

Tversky, A. D. and Kahneman, D. (1986) "Rational Choice and the Framing of Decisions," *Journal of Business* 56, pp. S251–S278.

2   De gustibus non est disputandum

George J. Stigler and Gary S. Becker

The venerable admonition not to quarrel over tastes is commonly interpreted as advice to terminate a dispute when it has been resolved into a difference of tastes, presumably because there is no further room for rational persuasion. Tastes are the unchallengeable axioms of a man's behavior: he may properly (usefully) be criticized for inefficiency in satisfying his desires, but the desires themselves are *data*. Deplorable tastes – say, for arson – may be countered by coercive and punitive action, but these deplorable tastes, at least when held by an adult, are not capable of being changed by persuasion.

Our title seems to us to be capable of another and preferable interpretation: that tastes neither change capriciously nor differ importantly between people. On this interpretation one does not argue over tastes for the same reason that one does not argue over the Rocky Mountains – both are there, will be there next year, too, and are the same to all men.

The difference between these two viewpoints of tastes is fundamental. On the traditional view, an explanation of economic phenomena that reaches a difference in tastes between people or times is the terminus of the argument: the problem is abandoned *at this point* to whoever studies and explains tastes (psychologists? anthropologists? phrenologists? socio-biologists?). On our preferred interpretation, one never reaches this impasse: the economist continues to search for differences in prices or incomes to explain any differences or changes in behavior.

The choice between these two views of the role of tastes in economic theory must ultimately be made on the basis of their comparative analytical productivities. On the conventional view of inscrutable, often capricious tastes, one drops the discussion as soon as the behavior of tastes becomes important – and turns his energies to other problems. On our view, one searches, often long and frustratingly, for the subtle forms that prices and incomes take in explaining differences among men and periods. If the latter approach yields more useful results, it is the proper choice. The establishment of the proposition that one may usefully treat tastes as stable over time and similar among people is the central task of this essay.

The ambitiousness of our agenda deserves emphasis: we are proposing the hypothesis that widespread and/or persistent human behavior can be explained by a generalized calculus of utility-maximizing behavior, without introducing the qualification "tastes remaining the same." It is a thesis that does not permit of direct proof because it is an assertion about the world, not a proposition in logic. Moreover, it is possible almost at random to throw up examples of phenomena that presently defy explanation by this hypothesis: Why do we have inflation? Why are there few Jews in farming?[1] Why are societies with polygynous families so rare in the modern era? Why aren't blood banks responsible for the quality of their product? If we could answer these questions to your satisfaction, you would quickly produce a dozen more.

What we assert is not that we are clever enough to make illuminating applications of utility-maximizing theory to all important phenomena – not even our entire generation of economists is clever enough to do that. Rather, we assert that this traditional approach of the economist offers guidance in tackling these problems – and that no other approach of remotely comparable generality and power is available.

To support our thesis we could offer samples of phenomena we believe to be usefully explained on the assumption of stable, well-behaved preference functions. Ultimately, this is indeed the only persuasive method of supporting the assumption, and it is legitimate to cite in support all of the existing corpus of successful economic theory. Here we shall undertake to give this proof by accomplishment a special and limited interpretation. We take categories of behavior commonly held to demonstrate changes in tastes or to be explicable only in terms of such changes, and show both that they are reconcilable with our assumption of stable preferences and that the reformulation is illuminating.

The new theory of consumer choice

The power of stable preferences and utility maximization in explaining a wide range of behavior has been significantly enhanced by a recent reformulation of consumer theory.[2] This reformulation transforms the family from a passive maximizer of the utility from market purchases into an active maximizer also engaged in extensive production and investment activities. In the traditional theory, households maximize a utility function of the goods and services bought in the marketplace, whereas in the reformulation they maximize a utility function of objects of choice, called commodities, that they produce with market goods, their own time, their skills, training and other human capital, and other inputs. Stated formally, a household seeks to maximize

$$U = U(Z_i, \ldots Z_m) \tag{2.1}$$

with

$$Z_i = f_i(X_{1i}, \ldots X_{ki}, t_{1i}, \ldots t_{\ell i}, S_1, \ldots S_\ell, Y_i), \quad i = 1 \ldots m \tag{2.2}$$

where Z_i are the commodity objects of choice entering the utility function, f_i is the production function for the ith commodity, X_{ji} is the quantity of the jth market good or service used in the production of the ith commodity, t_{ji} is the jth person's own time input, S_j the jth person's human capital, and Y_i represents all other inputs.

The Z_i have no market prices since they are not purchased or sold, but do have "shadow" prices determined by their costs of production. If f_i were homogeneous of the first degree in the X_{ji} and t_{ji}, marginal and average costs would be the same and the shadow price of Z_i would be

$$\pi_i = \sum_{j=1}^{k} \alpha_{ji} \left(\frac{p}{w_1}, \frac{w}{w_1}, S, Y_i \right) p_j + \sum_{j=1}^{l} \beta_{ji} \left(\frac{p}{w_1}, \frac{w}{w_1}, S, Y_i \right) w_j \tag{2.3}$$

where p_j is the cost of X_j, w_j is the cost of t_j, and α_{ji}, and β_{ji} are input-output coefficients that depend on the (relative) set of p and w, S, and Y_i. The numerous and varied determinants of these shadow prices give concrete expression to our earlier statement about the subtle forms that prices take in explaining differences among men and periods.

The real income of a household does not simply equal its money income deflated by an index of the prices of market goods, but equals its full income (which includes the value of "time" to the household)[3] deflated by an index of the prices, π_i, of the produced commodities. Since full income and commodity prices depend on a variety of factors, incomes also take subtle forms. Our task in this paper is to spell out some of the forms prices and full income take.

Stability of tastes and "addiction"

Tastes are frequently said to change as a result of consuming certain "addictive" goods. For example, smoking of cigarettes, drinking of alcohol, injection of heroin, or close contact with some persons over an appreciable period of time, often increases the desire (creates a craving) for these goods or persons, and thereby cause their consumption to grow over time. In utility language, their marginal utility is said to rise over time because tastes shift in their favor. This argument has been clearly stated by Alfred Marshall when discussing the taste for "good" music:

> There is however an implicit condition in this law [of diminishing marginal utility] which should be made clear. It is that we do not suppose time to be allowed for any alteration in the character or tastes of the man himself. It is therefore no exception to the law that the more good music a man hears, the stronger is his taste for it likely to become... [p. 94]

We believe that the phenomenon Marshall is trying to explain, namely that exposure to good music increases the subsequent demand for good music (for some persons!), can be explained with some gain in insight by assuming constant tastes, whereas to assume a change in tastes has been an unilluminating "explanation." The essence of our explanation lies in the accumulation of what might be termed "consumption capital" by the consumer, and we distinguish "beneficial" addiction like Marshall's good music from "harmful" addiction like heroin.

Consider first beneficial addiction, and an unchanging utility function that depends on two produced commodities:

$$U = U(M, Z) \tag{2.4}$$

where M measures the amount of music "appreciation" produced and consumed, and Z the production and consumption of other commodities. Music appreciation is produced by a function that depends on the time allocated to music (t_m), and the training and other human capital conducive to music appreciation (S_m) (other inputs are ignored):

$$M = M_m(t_m, S_m) \tag{2.5}$$

We assume that

$$\frac{\partial M_m}{\partial t_m} > 0, \quad \frac{\partial M_m}{\partial S_m} > 0$$

and also that

$$\frac{\partial^2 M_m}{\partial t_m \partial S_m} > 0$$

An increase in this music capital increases the productivity of time spent listening to or devoted in other ways to music.

In order to analyze the consequences for its consumption of "the more good music a man hears," the production and consumption of music appreciation has to be dated. The amount of appreciation produced at any moment j, M_j, would depend on the time allocated to music and the music human capital at j: t_{m_j} and S_{m_j}, respectively. The latter in turn is produced partly through "on-the-job" training or "learning by doing" by accumulating the effects of earlier music appreciation:

$$S_{m_j} = h(M_{j-1}, M_{j-2}, \ldots, E_j) \tag{2.6}$$

By definition, the addiction is beneficial if

$$\frac{\partial S_{m_j}}{\partial M_{j-v}} > 0, \quad \text{all } v \text{ in (2.6)}$$

The term E_j measures the effect of education and other human capital on music appreciation skill, where

$$\frac{\partial S_{m_j}}{\partial E_j} > 0$$

and probably

$$\frac{\partial^2 S_{m_j}}{\partial M_{j-v} \partial E_j} > 0$$

We assume for simplicity a utility function that is a discounted sum of functions like the one in equation (2.4), where the M and Z commodities are dated, and the discount rate determined by time preference.[4] The optimal allocation of consumption is determined from the equality between the ratio of their marginal utilities and the ratio of their shadow prices:

$$\frac{MU_{m_j}}{MU_{z_j}} = \frac{\partial U}{\partial M_j} \bigg/ \frac{\partial U}{\partial Z_j} = \frac{\pi_{m_j}}{\pi_{z_j}} \tag{2.7}$$

The shadow price equals the marginal cost of adding a unit of commodity output. The marginal cost is complicated for music appreciation M by the positive effect on subsequent music human capital of the production of music appreciation at any moment j. This effect on subsequent capital is an investment return from producing appreciation at j

that reduces the cost of production at j. It can be shown that the marginal cost at j equals[5]

$$\pi_{m_j} = \frac{w \partial t_{m_j}}{\partial M_j} - w \sum_{i=1}^{n-j} \frac{\partial M_{j+i}}{\partial S_{m_{j+i}}} \bigg/ \frac{\partial M_{j+i}}{\partial t_{m_{j+i}}}$$

$$\cdot \frac{dS_{m_{j+i}}}{dM_j} \cdot \frac{1}{(i+r)^i}$$

$$= \frac{w \partial t_{m_j}}{\partial M_j} - A_j = \frac{w}{MPt_{m_j}} - A_j \tag{2.8}$$

where w is the wage rate (assumed to be the same at all ages), r the interest rate, n the length of life, and A_j the effect of addiction, measures the value of the saving in future time inputs from the effect of the production of M in j on subsequent music capital.

With no addiction, $A_j = 0$ and equation (2.8) reduces to the familiar marginal cost formula. Moreover, A_j is positive as long as music is beneficially addictive, and tends to decline as j increases, approaching zero as j approaches n. The term w/MP_{t_m} declines with age for a given time input as long as music capital grows with age. The term A_j may not change so much with age at young ages because the percentage decline in the number of remaining years is small at these ages. Therefore, π_m would tend to decline with age at young ages because the effect on the marginal product of the time input would tend to dominate the effect on A. Although π_m might not always decline at other ages, for the present we assume that π_m declines continuously with age.

If π_z does not depend on age, the relative price of music appreciation would decline with age; then by equation (2.7), the relative consumption of music appreciation would rise with age. On this interpretation, the (relative) consumption of music appreciation rises with exposure not because tastes shift in favor of music, but because its shadow price falls as skill and experience in the appreciation of music are acquired with exposure.

An alternative way to state the same analysis is that the marginal utility of time allocated to music is increased by an increase in the stock of music capital.[6] Then the consumption of music appreciation could be said to rise with exposure because the marginal utility of the time spent on music rose with exposure, even though tastes were unchanged.

The effect of exposure on the accumulation of music capital might well depend on the level of education and other human capital, as indicated by equation (2.6). This would explain why educated persons consume more "good" music (i.e., music that educated people like!) than other persons do.

Addiction lowers the price of music appreciation at younger ages without any comparable effect on the productivity of the time spent on music at these ages. Therefore, addiction would increase the time spent on music at younger ages: some of the time would be considered an investment that increases future music capital. Although the price of music tends to fall with age, and the consumption of music tends to rise, the time spent on music need not rise with age because the growth in music capital means that the consumption of music could rise even when the time spent fell with age. The time spent would be more likely to rise, the more elastic the demand curve for music appreciation. We can express this result in a form that will strike many readers as surprising; namely, that the time (or other inputs) spent on music appreciation is more likely to be addictive – that is, to rise with exposure to music – the more, not less, elastic is the demand curve for music appreciation.

The stock of music capital might fall and the price of music appreciation rise at older ages because the incentive to invest in future capital would decline as the number of remaining years declined, whereas the investment required simply to maintain the capital stock intact would increase as the stock increased. If the price rose, the time spent on music would fall if the demand curve for music were elastic. Consequently, our analysis indicates that the observed addiction to music may be stronger at younger than at older ages.

These results for music also apply to other commodities that are beneficially addictive. Their prices fall at younger ages and their consumption rises because consumption capital is accumulated with exposure and age. The time and goods used to produce an addictive commodity need not rise with exposure, even though consumption of the commodity does; they are more likely to rise with exposure, the more elastic is the demand curve for the commodity. Even if they rose at younger ages, they might decline eventually as the stock of consumption capital fell at older ages.

Using the same arguments developed for beneficial addiction, we can show that all the results are reversed for harmful addiction,[7] which is defined by a negative sign of the derivatives in equation (2.6):

$$\frac{\partial S_j}{\partial H_{j-v}} < 0, \quad \text{all vin (2.6)} \tag{2.9}$$

where H is a harmfully addictive commodity. An increase in consumption at any age reduces the stock of consumption capital available subsequently, and this raises the shadow price at all ages.[8] The shadow price would rise with age and exposure, at least at younger ages, which would induce consumption to fall with age and exposure. The inputs of goods and time need not fall with exposure, however, because consumption capital falls with exposure; indeed, the inputs are likely to rise with exposure if the commodity's demand curve were inelastic.

To illustrate these conclusions, consider the commodity "euphoria" produced with input of heroin (or alcohol or amphetamines.) An increase in the consumption of current euphoria raises the cost of producing euphoria in the future by reducing the future stock of "euphoric capital." The effect of exposure to euphoria on the cost of producing future euphoria reduces the consumption of euphoria as exposure continues. If the demand curve for euphoria were sufficiently inelastic, however, the use of heroin would grow with exposure at the same time that euphoria fell.

Note that the amount of heroin used at younger ages would be reduced because of the negative effect on later euphoric capital. Indeed, no heroin at all might be used only because the harmfully addictive effects are anticipated, and discourage any use. Note further that if heroin were used even though the subsequent adverse consequences were accurately anticipated, the utility of the user would be greater than it would be if he were prevented from using heroin. Of course, his utility would be still greater if technologies developed (methadone?) to reduce the harmfully addictive effects of euphoria.[9]

Most interestingly, note that the use of heroin would grow with exposure at the same time that the amount of euphoria fell, if the demand curve for euphoria and thus for heroin were sufficiently inelastic. That is, addiction to heroin – a growth in use with exposure – is the *result* of an inelastic demand for heroin, *not*, as commonly argued, the *cause* of an inelastic demand. In the same way, listening to music or playing tennis would be addictive if the demand curves for music or tennis appreciation were sufficiently elastic; the addiction again is the result, not the cause, of the particular elasticity. Put differently, if addiction were surmised (partly because the input of goods or time rose with age), but if it were not clear whether the addiction were harmful or beneficial, the elasticity of demand could be used to distinguish between them: a high elasticity suggests beneficial and a low elasticity suggests harmful addiction.[10]

We do not have to assume that exposure to euphoria changes tastes in order to understand why the use of heroin grows with exposure, or why the amount used is insensitive to changes in its price. Even with constant tastes, the amount used would grow with exposure, and heroin is addictive precisely *because* of the insensitivity to price changes.

An exogenous rise in the price of addictive goods or time, perhaps due to an excise tax, such as the tax on cigarettes and alcohol, or to restrictions on their sale, such as the imprisonment of dealers in heroin, would have a relatively small effect on their use by addicts if these are harmfully addictive goods, and a relatively large effect if they are beneficially addictive. That is, excise taxes and imprisonment mainly transfer resources away from addicts if the goods are harmfully addictive, and mainly reduce the consumption of addicts if the goods are beneficially addictive.

The extension of the capital concept to investment in the capacity to consume more efficiently has numerous other potential applications. For example, there is a fertile field in consumption capital for the application of the theory of division of labor among family members.

Stability of tastes and custom and tradition

A "traditional" qualification to the scope of economic theory is the alleged powerful hold over human behavior of custom and tradition. An excellent statement in the context of the behavior of rulers is that of John Stuart Mill:

> It is not true that the actions even of average rulers are wholly, or anything approaching to wholly, determined by their personal interest, or even by their own opinion of their personal interest... I insist only on what is true of all rulers, viz., that the character and course of their actions is largely influenced (independently of personal calculations) by the habitual sentiments and feelings, the general modes of thinking and acting, which prevail throughout the community of which they are members; as well as by the feelings, habits, and modes of thought which characterize the particular class in that community to which they themselves belong... They are also much influenced by the maxims and traditions which have descended to them from other rulers, their predecessors; which maxims and traditions have been known to retain an ascendancy during long periods, even in opposition to the private interests of the rulers for the time being. [p. 484]

The specific political behavior that contradicts "personal interest" theories is not clear from Mill's statement, nor is it much clearer in similar statements by others applied to firms or households. Obviously, stable behavior by (say) households faced with stable prices and incomes – or more generally a stable environment – is no contradiction since stability then is implied as much by personal interest theories as by custom and tradition. On the other hand, stable behavior in the face of changing prices and incomes might contradict the approach taken in this essay that assumes utility maximizing with stable tastes.

Nevertheless, we believe that our approach better explains when behavior is stable than do approaches based on custom and tradition, and can at the same time explain how and when behavior does change. Mill's "habits and modes of thought," or his "maxims and traditions which have descended," in our analysis result from investment of time and other resources in the accumulation of knowledge about the environment, and of skills with which to cope with it.

The making of decisions is costly, and not simply because it is an activity which some people find unpleasant. In order to make a decision one requires information, and the information must be analyzed. The costs of searching for information and of applying the information to a new situation are such that habit is often a more efficient way to deal with moderate or temporary changes in the environment than would be a full, apparently utility-maximizing decision. This is precisely the avoidance of what J. M. Clark termed the irrational passion for dispassionate rationality.

A simple example of economizing on information by the habitual purchase from one source will illustrate the logic. A consumer buys one unit of commodity X in each unit of time. He pays a price p_t at a time t. The choices he faces are:

1. To search at the time of an act of purchase to obtain the lowest possible price $\hat{p}_t$ consistent with the cost of search. Then $\hat{p}_t$ is a function of the amount of search s (assumed to be the same at each act of purchase):

$$\hat{p}_t = f(s), \quad f'(s) < 0 \qquad (2.10)$$

   where the total cost of s is $C(s)$.
2. To search less frequently (but usually more intensively), relying between searches upon the outcome of the previous search in choosing a supplier. Then the price p_t will be higher (relative to the average market price), the longer the period since the previous search (at time t_0),

$$p_t = g(t - t_0), \quad g' > 0$$

Ignoring interest, the latter method of purchase will have a total cost over period T determined by

(1) K searches (all of equal intensity) at cost $KC(s)$.
(2) Each search lasts for a period T/K, within which $r = T/K$ purchases are made, at cost $r\bar{p}$, where $\bar{p}$ is the average price. Assume that the results of search "depreciate" (prices appreciate) at rate δ. A consumer minimizes his combined cost of the commodity and search over the total time period; the minimizing condition is[11]

$$r = \sqrt{\frac{2C}{\delta \hat{p}}} \qquad (2.11)$$

In this simple model with r purchases between successive searches, r is larger the larger the amount spent on search per dollar spent on the commodity $(C/\hat{p})$, and the lower the rate of appreciation of prices (δ). If there were full search on each individual act of purchase, the total cost could not be less than the cost when the optimal frequency of search was chosen, and might be much greater.

When a temporary change takes place in the environment, perhaps in prices or income, it generally would not pay to disinvest the capital embodied in knowledge or skills, or to accumulate different types of capital. As a result, behavior will be relatively stable in the face of temporary changes.

A related situation arises when an unexpected change in the environment does not induce a major response immediately because time is required to accumulate the appropriate knowledge and skills. Therefore, stable preferences combined with investment in "specific" knowledge and skills can explain the small or "inelastic" responses that figure so prominently in short-run demand and supply curves.

A permanent change in the environment, perhaps due to economic development, usually causes a greater change in the behavior of young than of old persons. The common interpretation is that young persons are more readily seduced away from their customs and traditions by the glitter of the new (Western?) environment. On our interpretation, young and old persons respond differently, even if they have the same preferences and motivation. To change their behavior drastically, older persons have to either disinvest their capital that was attuned to the old environment, or invest in capital attuned to the new environment. Their incentive to do so may be quite weak, however, because relatively few years remain for them to collect the returns on new investments, and much human capital can only be disinvested slowly.

Young persons, on the other hand, are not so encumbered by accumulations of capital attuned to the old environment. Consequently, they need not have different preferences or motivation or be intrinsically more flexible in order to be more affected by a change in the environment: they simply have greater incentive to invest in knowledge and skills attuned to the new environment.

Note that this analysis is similar to that used in the previous section to explain addictive behavior: utility maximization with stable preferences, conditioned by the accumulation of specific knowledge and skills. One does not need one kind of theory to explain addictive behavior and another kind to explain habitual or customary behavior. The same theory based on stable preferences can explain both types of behavior, and can accommodate both habitual behavior and the departures therefrom.

Stability of tastes and advertising

Perhaps the most important class of cases in which "change of tastes" is invoked as an explanation for economic phenomena is that involving advertising. The advertiser "persuades" the consumer to prefer his product, and often a distinction is drawn between "persuasive" and "informative" advertising.[12] John Kenneth Galbraith is the most famous of the economists who argue that advertising molds consumer tastes:

> These [institutions of modern advertising and salesmanship] cannot be reconciled with the notion of independently determined desires for their central function is to create desires – to bring into being wants that previously did not exist. This is accomplished by the producer of the goods or at his behest. – Outlays for the manufacturing of a product are not more important in the strategy of modern business enterprise than outlays for the manufacturing of demand for the product. [pp. 155–56]

We shall argue, in direct opposition to this view, that it is neither necessary nor useful to attribute to advertising the function of changing tastes.

A consumer may indirectly receive utility from a market good, yet the utility depends not only on the quantity of the good but also the consumer's knowledge of its true or alleged properties. If he does not know whether the berries are poisonous, they are not food; if he does not know that they contain vitamin C, they are not consumed to prevent scurvy. The quantity of information is a complex notion: its degree of accuracy, its multidimensional properties, its variable obsolescence with time are all qualities that make direct measurement of information extremely difficult.

How can this elusive variable be incorporated into the theory of demand while preserving the stability of tastes? Our approach is to continue to assume, as in the previous sections, that the ultimate objects of choice are commodities produced by each household with market goods, own time, *knowledge*, and perhaps other inputs. We now assume, in addition, that the knowledge, whether real or fancied, is produced by the advertising of producers and perhaps also the own search of households.

Our approach can be presented through a detailed analysis of the simple case where the output x of a particular firm and its advertising A are the inputs into a commodity produced and consumed by households; for a given household:

$$Z = f(x, A, E, y) \tag{2.12}$$

where $\partial Z/\partial x > 0$, $\partial Z/\partial A > 0$, E is the human capital of the houshold that affects these marginal products, and y are other variables, possibly including advertising by other firms. Still more simply,

$$Z = g(A, E, y)x \tag{2.13}$$

where $\partial g/\partial A = g' > 0$ and $\partial^2 g/\partial A^2 = < 0$. With A, E, and y held constant, the amount of the commodity produced and consumed by any household is assumed to be proportional to the amount of the firm's output used by that household.[13] If the advertising reaching any household were independent of its behavior, the shadow price of Z, the marginal cost of x, would simply be the expenditure on x required to change Z by one unit. From equation (2.13), that equals

$$\pi_z = \frac{p_x}{g} \tag{2.14}$$

where p_x is the price of x.

An increase in advertising may lower the commodity price to the household (by raising g), and thereby increase its demand for the commodity and change its demand for the firm's output, because the household is made to believe – correctly or incorrectly – that it gets a greater output of the commodity from a given input of the advertised product. Consequently, advertising affects consumption in this formulation not by changing tastes, but by changing prices. That is, a movement along a stable demand curve for commodities is seen as generating the apparently unstable demand curves of market goods and other inputs.

More than a simple change in language is involved: our formulation has quite different implications from the conventional ones. To develop these implications, consider a firm that is determining its optimal advertising along with its optimal output. We assume initially that the commodity indirectly produced by this firm (equation (2.12)) is a perfect substitute to consumers for commodities indirectly produced by many other firms. Therefore, the firm is perfectly competitive in the commodity market, and could (indirectly) sell an unlimited amount of this commodity at a fixed commodity price. Observe that a firm can have many perfect substitutes in the commodity market even though few other firms produce the same physical product. For example, a firm may be the sole designer of jewelry that contributes to the social prestige of consumers, and yet compete fully with many other products that also contribute to prestige: large automobiles, expensive furs, fashionable clothing, elaborate parties, a respected occupation, etc.

If the level of advertising were fixed, there would be a one-to-one correspondence between the price of the commodity and the price of the firm's output (see equation (2.14)). If π_z were given by the competitive market, p_x would then also be given, and the firm would find its optimal output in the conventional way by equating marginal cost to the given product price. There is no longer such a one-to-one correspondence between π_z and p_x, however, when the level of advertising is also a variable, and even a firm faced with a fixed commodity price in a perfectly competitive commodity market could sell its product at different prices by varying the level of advertising. Since an increase in advertising would increase the commodity output that consumers receive from a given amount of this firm's product, the price of its product would then be increased relative to the fixed commodity price.

The optimal advertising, product price, and output of the firm can be found by maximizing its income

$$I = p_x X - TC(X) - A p_a \qquad (2.15)$$

where X is the firm's total output, TC its costs of production other than advertising, and p_a the (constant) cost of a unit of advertising. By substituting from equation (2.14), I can be written as

$$I = \pi_z^0 g(A) X - TC(X) - A p_a \qquad (2.15')$$

where π_z^0 is the given market commodity price, the advertising-effectiveness function (g) is assumed to be the same for all consumers,[14] and the variables E and y in g are suppressed. The first-order maximum conditions with respect to X and A are

$$p_x = \pi_z^0 g = MC(X) \qquad (2.16)$$

$$\frac{\partial p_x}{\partial A} X = \pi_z^0 X g' = p_a \qquad (2.17)$$

Equation (2.16) is the usual equality between price and marginal cost for a competitive firm, which continues to hold when advertising exists and is a decision variable. Not surprisingly, equation (2.17) says that marginal revenue and marginal cost of advertising are equal, where marginal revenue is determined by the level of output and the increase in product price "induced" by an increase in advertising. Although the commodity price is fixed, an increase in advertising increases the firm's product price by an amount that is proportional to the increased capacity (measured by g') of its product to contribute (at least in the minds of consumers) to commodity output.

In the conventional analysis, firms in perfectly competitive markets gain nothing from advertising and thus have no incentive to advertise because they are assumed to be unable to differentiate their products to consumers who have perfect knowledge. In our analysis, on the other hand, consumers have imperfect information, including misinformation, and a skilled advertiser might well be able to differentiate his product from other apparently similar products. Put differently, advertisers could increase the value of their output to consumers without increasing to the same extent the value of the output even of perfect competitors in the *commodity* market. To simplify, we assume that the value of competitors' output is unaffected, in the sense that the commodity price (more generally, the commodity demand curve) to any firm is not affected by its advertising. Note that when firms in perfectly competitive commodity markets differentiate their products by advertising, they still preserve the perfect competition in these markets. Note moreover, that if different firms were producing the same physical product in the same competitive commodity market, and had the same marginal cost and advertising-effectiveness functions, they would produce the same output, charge the same product price, and advertise at the same rate. If, however, either their marginal costs or advertising-effectiveness differed, they would charge different product prices, advertise at different rates, and yet still be perfect competitors (although not of one another)!

Not only can firms in perfectly competitive commodity markets – that is, firms faced with infinitely elastic commodity demand curves – have an incentive to advertise, but the incentive may actually be greater, the more competitive the commodity market is. Let us consider the case of a finite commodity demand elasticity.

The necessary conditions to maximize income given by equation (2.15′), if π_z varies as a function of Z, are

$$\frac{\partial I}{\partial X} = \pi_z g + X \frac{\partial \pi_z}{\partial Z} \frac{\partial Z}{\partial X} g - MC(X) = 0, \tag{2.18}$$

or since $Z = gX$, and $\partial Z/\partial X = g$,

$$\pi_z g \left(1 + \frac{1}{\epsilon_{\pi_z}}\right) = p_x \left(1 + \frac{1}{\epsilon_{\pi_z}}\right) = MC(X) \tag{2.18′}$$

where ϵ_{π_z}, is the elasticity of the firm's commodity demand curve. Also

$$\frac{\partial I}{\partial A} = X \frac{\partial p_x}{\partial A} - p_a = \pi_z \frac{\partial Z}{\partial A} + \frac{\partial \pi_z}{\partial Z} \cdot \frac{\partial Z}{\partial A} \cdot Z - p_a = 0 \tag{2.19}$$

or

$$X \frac{\partial p_x}{\partial A} = \pi_z g' X \left(1 + \frac{1}{\epsilon_{\pi_z}}\right) = p_a \tag{2.19′}$$

Equation (2.18′) is simply the usual maximizing condition for a monopolist that continues to hold when there is advertising.[15] Equation (2.19′) clearly shows that, given $\pi_z g' X$, the marginal revenue from additional advertising is greater, the greater is the elasticity of the commodity demand curve; therefore, the optimal level of advertising would be positively related to the commodity elasticity.

This important result can be made intuitive by considering Figure 2.1. The curve DD gives the firm's commodity demand curve, where π_z is measured along the vertical and commodity output Z along the horizontal axis. The firm's production of X is held fixed so that Z varies only because of variations in the level of advertising. At point e^0, the level of advertising is A_0, the product price is p_x^0, and commodity output and price are Z_0 and π_z^0, respectively. An increase in advertising to A_1 would increase Z to Z_1, (the increase in Z is determined by the given g' function). The decline in π_z induced by the increase in Z would be negatively related to the elasticity of the commodity demand curve: it would be less, for example, if the demand curve were $D'D'$ rather than DD. Since the increase in p_x is negatively related to the decline in π_z,[16] the increase in p_a, and thus the marginal revenue from the increase in A, is directly related to the elasticity of the commodity demand curve.[17]

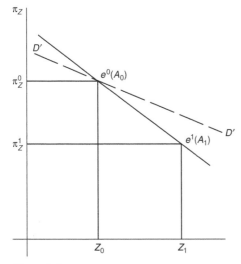

Figure 2.1

The same result is illustrated with a more conventional diagram in Figure 2.2: the firm's product output and price are shown along the horizontal and vertical axes. The demand curve for its product with a given level of advertising is given by *dd*. We proved earlier (Note 15) that with advertising constant, the elasticity of the product demand curve is the same as the elasticity of its commodity demand curve. An increase in advertising "shifts" the product demand curve upward to *d'd'*, and the marginal revenue from additional advertising is directly related to the size of the shift; that is, to the increase in product price for any given product output. Our basic result is that the shift is itself directly related to the elasticity of the demand curve. For example, with the same increase in advertising, the shift is larger from *dd* to *d'd'* than from *ee* to *e'e'* because *dd* is more elastic than *ee*.

This role of information in consumer demand is capable of extension in various directions. For example, the demand for knowledge is affected by the formal education of a person, so systematic variations of demand for advertisements with formal education can be explored. The stock of information possessed by the individual is a function of his age, period of residence in a community, and other variables, so systematic patterns of purchase of heavily and lightly advertised goods are implied by the theory.

Fashions and fads

The existence of fashions and fads (short episodes or cycles in the consumption habits of people) seems an especially striking contradiction of our thesis of the stability of tastes. We find fashions in dress, food, automobiles, furniture, books, and even scientific doctrines.[18] Some are modest in amplitude, or few in their followers, but others are of violent amplitude: who now buys an ouija board, or a bustle? The rise and fall of fashions is often attributed to the fickleness of people's tastes. Herbert Blumer, the distinguished sociologist, gave a characteristic expression of this view:

> Tastes are themselves a product of experience, they usually develop from an initial state of vagueness to a state of refinement and stability, but once formed they may decay and disintegrate....

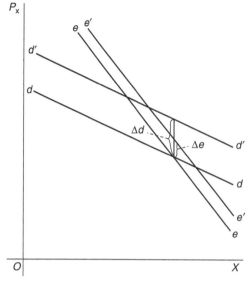

Figure 2.2

The fashion process involves both a formation and an expression of collective taste in the given area of fashion. The taste is intially a loose fusion of vague inclinations and dissatisfactions that are aroused by new experience in the field of fashion and in the larger surrounding world. In this initial state, collective taste is amorphous, inarticulate, and awaiting specific direction. Through models and proposals, fashion innovators sketch possible lines along which the incipient taste may gain objective expression and take definite form. [p. 344]

The obvious method of reconciling fashion with our thesis is to resort again to the now familiar argument that people consume commodities, and only indirectly do they consume market goods, so fashions in market goods are compatible with stability in the utility function of commodities. The task here, as elsewhere, is to show that this formulation helps to illuminate our understanding of the phenomena under discussion; we have some tentative comments in this direction.

The commodity apparently produced by fashion goods is social distinction: the demonstration of alert leadership, or at least not lethargy, in recognizing and adopting that which will in due time be widely approved. This commodity – it might be termed style – sounds somewhat circular, because new things appear to be chosen simply because they are new. Such circularity is no more peculiar than that which is literally displayed in a race – the runners obviously do not run around a track in order to reach a new destination. Moreover, it is a commendation of a style good that it be superior to previous goods, and style will not be sought intentionally through less functional goods. Indeed, if the stylish soon becomes inferior to the unstylish, it would lose its attractiveness.

Style, moreover, is not achieved simply by change: the newness must be of a special sort that requires a subtle prediction of what will be approved novelty, and a trained person can make better predictions than an untrained person. Style is social rivalry, and it is, like all rivalry, both an incentive to individuality and a source of conformity.

The areas in which the rivalry of fashion takes place are characterized by public exposure and reasonably short life. An unexposed good (automobile pistons) cannot be judged as to its fashionableness, and fashions in a good whose efficient life is long would be expensive. Hence fashion generally concentrates on the cheaper classes of garments and reading matter, and there is more fashion in furniture than in housing.

Fashion can be pursued with the purse or with the expenditure of time. A person may be well-read (i.e., have read the recent books generally believed to be important), but if his time is valuable in the market place, it is much more likely that his spouse will be the well-read member of the family. (So the ratio of the literacy of wife to that of husband is positively related to the husband's earning power, and inversely related to her earning power.)

The demand for fashion can be formalized by assuming that the distinction available to any person depends on his social environment, and his own efforts: he can be fashionable, give to approved charities, choose prestigious occupations, and do other things that affect his distinction. Following recent work on social interactions, we can write the social distinction of the ith person as

$$R_i = D_i + h_i \tag{2.20}$$

where D_i is the contribution to his distinction of his social environment, and h_i is his own contribution. Each person maximizes a utility function of R and other commodities subject to a budget constraint that depends on his own income and the exogenously given social environment.[19] A number of general results have been developed with this approach (see Becker), and a few are mentioned here to indicate that the demand for fashion (and other determinants of social distinction) can be systematically analyzed without assuming that tastes shift.

An increase in i's own income, prices held constant, would increase his demand for social distinction and other commodities. If his social environment were unchanged, the whole increase in his distinction would be produced by an increase in his own contributions to fashion and other distinction-producing goods. Therefore, even an average income elasticity of demand for distinction would imply a high income elasticity of demand for fashion (and these other distinction-producing) goods, which is consistent with the common judgement that fashion is a luxury good.[20]

If other persons increase their contributions to their own distinction, this may lower i's distinction by reducing his social environment. For distinction is scarce and is to a large extent simply redistributed among persons: an increase in one person's distinction generally requires a reduction in that of other persons. This is why people are often "forced" to conform to new fashions. When some gain distinction by paying attention to (say) new fashions, they lower the social environment of others. The latter are induced to increase their own efforts to achieve distinction, including a demand for these new fashions, because an exogenous decline in their social environment induces them to increase their own contributions to their distinction.

Therefore, an increase in all incomes induces an even greater increase in i's contribution to his distinction than does an increase in his own income alone. For an increase in the income of others lowers i's social environment because they spend more on their own distinction; the reduction in his environment induces a further increase in i's contribution to his distinction. Consequently, we expect wealthy countries like the United States to pay more attention to fashion than poor countries like India, even if tastes were the same in wealthy and poor countries.

Conclusion

We have surveyed four classes of phenomena widely believed to be inconsistent with the stability of tastes: addiction, habitual behavior, advertising, and fashions, and in each case offered an alternative explanation. That alternative explanation did not simply reconcile the phenomena in question with the stability of tastes, but also sought to show that the hypothesis of stable tastes yielded more useful predictions about observable behavior.

Of course, this short list of categories is far from comprehensive: for example, we have not entered into the literature of risk aversion and risk preference, one of the richest sources of *ad hoc* assumptions concerning tastes. Nor have we considered the extensive literature on time preference, which often alleges that people "systematically undervalue...future wants."[21]

The taste for consumption in say 1984 is alleged to continue to shift upward as 1984 gets closer to the present. In spite of the importance frequently attached to time preference, we do not know of any significant behavior that has been illuminated by this assumption. Indeed, given additional space, we would argue that the assumption of time preference impedes the explanation of life cycle variations in the allocation of resources, the secular growth in real incomes, and other phenomena.

Moreover, we have not considered systematic differences in tastes by wealth or other classifications. We also claim, however, that no significant behavior has been illuminated by assumptions of differences in tastes. Instead, they, along with assumptions of unstable tastes, have been a convenient crutch to lean on when the analysis has bogged down. They give the appearance of considered judgement, yet really have only been *ad hoc* arguments that disguise analytical failures.

We have partly translated "unstable tastes" into variables in the household production functions for commodities. The great advantage, however, of relying only on changes in the arguments entering household production functions is that *all* changes in behavior are explained by changes in prices and incomes, precisely the variables that organize and give power to economic analysis. Addiction, advertising, etc. affect not tastes with the endless degrees of freedom they provide, but prices and incomes, and are subject therefore to the constraints imposed by the theorem on negatively inclined demand curves, and other results. Needless to say, we would welcome explanations of why some people become addicted to alcohol and others to Mozart, whether the explanation was a development of our approach or a contribution from some other behavioral discipline.

As we remarked at the outset, no conceivable expenditure of effort on our part could begin to exhaust the possible tests of the hypothesis of stable and uniform preferences. Our task has been oddly two-sided. Our hypothesis is trivial, for it merely asserts that we should apply standard economic logic as extensively as possible. But the self-same hypothesis is also a demanding challenge, for it urges us not to abandon opaque and complicated problems with the easy suggestion that the further explanation will perhaps someday be produced by one of our sister behavioral sciences.

Acknowledgment

We have had helpful comments from Michael Bozdarich, Gilbert Ghez, James Heckman, Peter Pashigian, Sam Peltzman, Donald Wittman, and participants in the Workshop on Industrial Organization, University of Chicago.

Notes

1 Our lamented friend Reuben Kessel offered an attractive explanation: since Jews have been perse-
cuted so often and forced to flee to other countries, they have not invested in immobile land, but in
mobile human capital – business skills, education, etc. – that would automatically go with them. Of
course, someone might counter with the more basic query: but why are they Jews, and not Christians
or Moslems?
2 An exposition of this reformulation can be found in Robert Michael and Becker. This exposition
emphasizes the capacity of the reformulation to generate many implications about behavior that are
consistent with stable tastes.
3 Full income is the maximum money income that a household could achieve by an appropriate
allocation of its time and other resources.
4 A consistent application of the assumption of stable preferences implies that the discount rate is
zero; that is, the absence of time preference (see the brief discussion the Conclusion.)
5 The utility function

$$V = \sum_{j=1}^{a} a^j U(M_j, Z_j)$$

is maximized subject to the constraints

$$M_j = M(t_{m_j}, S_{m_j}); \quad Z_j = Z(x_j, t_{z_j})$$

$$S_{m_j} = h(M_{j-1}, M_{j-2}, \ldots, E_j)$$

$$\sum \frac{px_j}{(1+r)^j} = \sum \frac{wt_{wj} + b_j}{(1+r)^j}$$

and $t_{w_j} + t_{m_j} + t_{z_j} = t$, where t_{w_j} is hours worked in the jth period, and b_j is property income in
that period. By substitution one derives the full wealth constraint:

$$\sum \frac{px_j + w(t_{m_j} + t_{z_j})}{(1+r)^j} = \sum \frac{wt + b_j}{(1+r)^j} = W$$

Maximization of V with respect to M_j and Z_j subject to the production functions and the full wealth
constraint gives the first-order conditions

$$a^j \frac{\partial U}{\partial Z_j} = \frac{\lambda}{(1+r)^j} \left(\frac{pdx_j}{dZ_j} + \frac{wdt_{z_j}}{dZ_j} \right) = \frac{\lambda}{(1+r)^j} \pi_{z_j}$$

$$a^j \frac{\partial U}{\partial M_j} = \frac{\lambda}{(1+r)^j} \cdot \left(\frac{w\partial t_{m_j}}{\partial M_j} + \sum_{i=1}^{n-j} \frac{wdt_{m_{j+1}}}{dM_j} \cdot \frac{1}{(1+r)^i} \right)$$

$$= \frac{\lambda}{(1+r)^j} \pi_{m_j}$$

Since, however,

$$\frac{dM_{j+i}}{dM_j} = 0 = \frac{\partial M_{j+i}}{\partial S_{m_{j+i}}} \frac{dS_{m_{j+i}}}{dM_j} + \frac{\partial M_{j+i}}{\partial tm_{j+i}} \frac{dt_{m_{j+i}}}{dM_j}$$

then

$$\frac{dt_{m_{j+i}}}{dM_j} = -\frac{\partial M_{j+i}}{\partial S_{m_{j+i}}} \bigg/ \frac{\partial M_{j+i}}{\partial t_{m_{j+i}}} \cdot \frac{dS_{m_{j+i}}}{dM_j}$$

28   *George J. Stigler & Gary S. Becker*

By substitution into the definition of π_{mj} equation (2.8) follows immediately.

6 The marginal utility of time allocated to music at j includes the utility from the increase in the future stock of music capital that results from an increase in the time allocated at j. An argument similar to the one developed for the price of music appreciation shows that the marginal utility of time would tend to rise with age, at least at younger ages.

7 In some ways, our analysis of beneficial and harmful addiction is a special case of the analysis of beneficial and detrimental joint production in Michael Grossman.

8 Instead of equation (2.8), one has

$$\pi_{h_j} = \frac{w}{MP_{t_j}} + A_j$$

where $A_j \leq 0$.

9 That is, if new technology reduced and perhaps even changed the sign of the derivatives in equation (2.9). We should state explicitly, to avoid any misunderstanding, that "harmful" means only that the derivatives in (2.9) are negative, and not that the addiction harms others, nor, as we have just indicated, that it is unwise for addicts to consume such commodities.

10 The elasticity of demand can he estimated from the effects of changes in the prices of inputs. For example, if a commodity's production function were homogeneous of degree one, and if all its future as well as present input prices rose by the same known percentage, the elasticity of demand for the commodity could he estimated from the decline in the inputs. Therefore the distinction between beneficial and harmful addiction is operational: these independently estimated commodity elasticities could be used, as in the text, to determine whether an addiction was harmful or beneficial.

11 The price of the ith purchase within one of the K search periods is $p_i = \hat{p}(1+\delta)^{i-1}$. Hence

$$\bar{p} = \frac{1}{r}\sum_{i=1}^{r}\hat{p}(1+\delta)^{i-1} = \hat{p}\frac{(1+\delta)^r - 1}{r\delta}$$

The total cost to he minimized is

$$TC = Kr\bar{p} + KC(s) = k\hat{p}\frac{(1+\delta)^r - 1}{\delta} + KC$$

By taking a second-order approximation to $(1+\delta)^r$, we get

$$TC = T\left\{\hat{p}\left[1 + \frac{(r-1)\delta}{2}\right] + \frac{c}{r}\right\}$$

Minimizing with respect to r gives

$$\frac{\partial TC}{\partial r} = 0 = T\left(\frac{\hat{p}\delta}{2} - \frac{C}{r^2}\right)$$

$$\text{or} \quad r = \sqrt{\frac{2C}{\delta\hat{p}}}.$$

12 The distinction, if in fact one exists, between persuasive and informative advertising must be one of purpose or effect, not of content. A simple, accurately stated fact ("I otter you this genuine $1 bill for 10 cents") can be highly persuasive; the most bizarre claim ("If Napoleon could have bought our machine gun, he would have defeated Wellington") contains some information (machine guns were not available in 1814).

13 Stated differently, Z is homogeneous of the first degree in x alone.

14 Therefore,

$$p_x X = \pi_z^0 g \sum_{i=1}^{n} x_i$$

where n is the number of households.

15 If the level of advertising is held constant, Z is proportional to X, so

$$\epsilon_{\pi_z} = \frac{dZ}{Z} \bigg/ \frac{d\pi_z}{\pi_z} = \epsilon_{ps} = \frac{dX}{X} \bigg/ \frac{d p_x}{p_x}$$

16 Since $\pi_z g = p_x$,

$$\frac{\partial p_x}{\partial A} = \pi_z g' + g \frac{\partial \pi_z}{\partial A} > 0$$

The first term on the right is positive and the second term is negative. If g, g', and π_z, are given, $\partial p_x / \partial A$ is linearly and negatively related to $\partial \pi_z / \partial A$.

17 Recall again our assumption, however, that even firms in perfectly competitive markets can fully differentiate their products. If the capacity of a firm to differentiate itself were inversely related to the elasticity of its commodity demand curve, that is, to the amount of competition in the commodity market, the increase in its product price generated by its advertising might not be directly related to the elasticity of its commodity demand curve.

18 "Fashion" indeed, does not necessarily refer only to the shorter term preferences. Adam Smith says that the influence of fashion "over dress and furniture is not more absolute than over architecture, poetry, and music" (p. 283).

19 The budget constraint for i can be written as

$$\prod_{R_i} R + \prod_{z} Z = I_i + \prod_{R_i} D_i = S_i$$

where Z are other commodities, $\prod_{R_i}$ is his marginal cost of changing R, I_i is his own full income, and S_i is his "social income."

20 Marshall believed that the desire for distinction was the most powerful of passions and a major source of the demand for luxury expenditures (see pp. 87–88, 106).

21 This quote is taken from the following longer passage in Böhm-Bawerk:

We must now consider a *second* phenomenon of human experience – one that is heavily fraught with consequence. That is the fact that we feel less concerned about future sensations of joy and sorrow simply because they do lie in the future, and the lessening of our concern is in proportion to the remoteness of that future. Consequently we accord to goods which are intended to serve future ends a value which falls short of the true intensity of their future marginal utility. We *systematically undervalue our future wants and also the means which serve to satisfy them.* [p. 268]

References

G. S. Becker, "A Theory of Social Interaction," *J. Polit. Econ.*, Nov./Dec. 1974, *82*, 1063–93.

H. C. Blumer, "Fashion," in Vol. V, *Int. Encyclo. Soc. Sci.*, New York 1968.

Eugen von Böhm-Bawerk, *Capital and Interest*, Vol. 2, South Holland, IL 1959.

John K. Galbraith, *The Affluent Society*, Boston 1958.

M. Grossman, "The Economics of Joint Production in the Household," rep. 7145, Center Math. Stud. Bus. Econ., Univ. Chicago 1971.

Alfred Marshall, *Principles of Economics*, 8th ed., London 1923.
R. T. Michael and G. S. Becker, "On the New Theory of Consumer Behavior," *Swedish J. Econ.*, Dec. 1973, *75*, 378–96.
John S. Mill, *A System of Logic*, 8th ed., London 1972.
Adam Smith, *Theory of Moral Sentiments*, New Rochelle 1969.

3 Bandwagon, snob, and Veblen effects in the theory of consumers' demand

Harvey Leibenstein

The nature of the problem[1]

The desire of some consumers to be "in style," the attempts by others to attain exclusiveness, and the phenomena of "conspicuous consumption," have as yet not been incorporated into the current theory of consumers' demand. My purpose, in this paper, is to take a step or two in that direction.

"Non-additivity" in consumers' demand theory

This enquiry was suggested by some provocative observations made by Professor Oskar Morgenstern in his article, "Demand Theory Reconsidered."[2] After examining various aspects of the relationship between individual demand curves and collective market demand curves Professor Morgenstern points out that in some cases the market demand curve is not the lateral summation of the individual demand curves. The following brief quotation may indicate the nature of what he calls "non-additivity" and give some indication of the problem involved. "Non-additivity in this simple sense is given, for example, in the case of fashions, where one person buys because another is buying the same thing, or vice versa. The collective demand curve of snobs is most likely not additive. But the phenomenon of non-additivity is in fact much deeper; since virtually all collective supply curves are non-additive it follows that the demand of the firms for their labor, raw materials, etc. is also non-additive. This expands the field of non-additivity enormously."[3]

Since the purpose of Professor Morgenstern's article is immanent criticism he does not present solutions to the problems he raises. He does clearly imply, however, that since coalitions are bound to be important in this area only the "Theory of Games" (developed by Von Neumann and Morgenstern) is likely to give an adequate solution to this problem.[4] The present writer is not competent to judge whether this is or is not the case, but he does believe that there are many markets where coalitions among consumers are not widespread or of significance, and hence abstracting from the possibility of such coalitions may not be unreasonable. Should this be the case we may be able to make some headway through the use of conventional analytical methods.

What we shall therefore be concerned with substantially is a reformulation of some aspects of the static theory of consumers' demand while permitting the relaxation of one of the basic implicit assumptions of the current theory – namely, that the consumption behaviour of any individual is independent of the consumption of others. This will permit us to take account of consumers' motivations not heretofore incorporated into the theory. To be more specific, the proposed analysis is designed to take account of the desire of people to wear, buy, do, consume, and behave like their fellows; the desire to join the crowd, be "one of the boys," etc. – phenomena of mob motivations and mass psychology either in their grosser or more delicate aspects. This is the type of behaviour involved in what we shall call the "bandwagon effect." On the other hand, we shall also attempt to take account of the search for exclusiveness by individuals through the purchase of distinctive clothing, foods, automobiles, houses, or anything else that individuals may believe will in some way set them off from the mass of mankind – or add to their prestige, dignity, and social status. In other words, we shall be concerned with the impact on the theory created by the potential nonfunctional utilities inherent in many commodities.

The past literature

The past literature on the interpersonal aspects of utility and demand can be divided into three categories: sociology, welfare economics, and pure theory. The sociological writings deal with the phenomena of fashions and conspicuous consumption and their relationship to social status and human behaviour. This treatment of the subject was made famous by Veblen – although Veblen, contrary to the notions of many, was neither the discoverer nor the first to elaborate upon the theory of conspicuous consumption. John Rae, writing before 1834, has quite an extensive treatment of conspicuous consumption, fashions, and related matters pretty much along Veblenian lines.[5] Rae attributes many of these ideas to earlier writers, going so far as to find the notion of conspicuous consumption in the Roman poet Horace; and a clear statement of the "keeping up with the Joneses" idea in the verse of Alexander Pope.[6] An excellent account of how eighteenth and nineteenth century philosophers and economists handled the problem of fashion is given in Norine Foley's article "Fashion."[7] For the most part, these treatments are of a "sociological" nature.

The economist concerned with public policy will probably find the "economic welfare" treatment of the problem most interesting. Here, if we examine the more recent contributions first and then go backward, we find examples of current writers believing they have stumbled upon something new, although they had only rediscovered what had been said many years before. Thus, Professor Melvin Reder in his recent treatment of the theory of welfare economics claims that "...there is another type of external repercussion which is rarely, *if ever*, recognized in discussions of welfare economics. It occurs where the utility function of one individual contains, as variables, the quantities of goods consumed by other persons."[8] It can only be lack of awareness of the past literature that causes Reder to imply that this consideration has not been taken up before. Among those who considered the problem earlier are J. E. Meade,[9] A. C. Pigou,[10] Henry Cunynghame,[11] and John Rae.[12]

The similarity in the treatment of this matter by Reder and Rae is at times striking. For example, Reder suggests that legislation forbidding "invidious expenditure" may result in an increase in welfare by freeing resources from "competitive consumption" to other uses.[13] In a similar vein Rae argued that restrictions on the trade of "pure luxuries" can only be a gain to some and a loss to none, in view of the labor saved in avoiding the production of "pure luxuries." It is quite clear from the context that what Rae calls. "pure luxuries" is exactly the same as Reder's commodities that enter into "competitive consumption."[14]

One reason why the interpersonal effects on demand have been ignored in current texts may be the fact that Marshall did not consider the matter in his *Principles*. We know, however, from Marshall's correspondence,[15] that he was aware of the problem. Both Cunynghame and Pigou pointed out that Marshall's treatment of consumers' surplus did not take into account interpersonal effects on utility. Marshall seemed to feel that this would make the diagrammatical treatment too complex. Recently, Reder[16] and Samuelson[17] noticed that external economies and diseconomies of consumption may vitiate (or, at best, greatly complicate) their "new" welfare analysis, and hence, in true academic fashion, they assume the problem away. This, however, is not the place to examine the question in detail.

The only attack on the problem from the point of view of pure theory that the writer could find[18] is a short article by Professor Pigou.[19] In this article Pigou sets out to inquire under what circumstances the assumption of the additivity of the individual demand curves "adequately conforms to the facts, and, when it does not so conform, what alternative assumption ought to be substituted for it."[20] It is obvious that the particular choice of alternative assumptions will determine (a) whether a solution can, given the existing analytical tools, be obtained, and (b) whether such a solution is relevant to the real world. Pigou's treatment of the problem is, unfortunately, exceedingly brief. He attempts to deal with non-additivity in both supply and demand curves within the confines of six pages. In examining the additivity assumption he points out that it is warranted when (1) the demand for the commodity is wholly for the direct satisfaction yielded by it or, (2) where disturbances to equilibrium are so small that aggregate output is not greatly changed.

After briefly suggesting some of the complexities of non-additivity he concludes that the "...problems, for the investigation of which it is necessary to go behind the demand schedule of the market as a whole, are still, theoretically, soluble; there are a sufficient number of equations to determine the unknowns."[21] This last point, which is not demonstrated in Pigou's article, is hardly satisfying since it has been shown that the equality of equations and unknowns is not a sufficient condition for a determinate solution, or indeed for any solution, to exist.[22]

The approach and limits of the ensuing analysis

It should, perhaps, be pointed out at the outset that the ensuing exposition is limited to statics. In all probability, the most interesting parts of the problem, and also those most relevant to real problems, are its dynamic aspects. However, a static analysis is probably necessary, and may be of significance, in order to lay a foundation for a dynamic analysis. In view of the limitations to be set on the following analysis, it becomes necessary to demarcate clearly the conceptual borderline between statics and dynamics.

There are, unfortunately, numerous definitions of statics and there seems to be some confusion on the matter. In view of this it will not be possible to give *the* definition of statics. All that we can hope to do is to choose a definition that will be consistent with and useful for our purposes – and also one that at the same time does not stray too far from some of the generally accepted notions about statics. Because of the fact that we live in a dynamic world most definitions of statics will imply a state of affairs that contradicts our general experience. But this is of necessity the case. What we must insist on is internal consistency but we need not, at this stage, require "realism."

Our task, then, is to define a static situation – a situation in which static economics is applicable. Ordinarily, it is thought that statics is in some way "timeless." This need not be the case. For our purposes, a static situation is not a "timeless" situation, nor is static economics timeless economics. It is, however, "temporally orderless" economics. That is, we shall define a static situation as one in which the order of events is of no significance. We, therefore, abstract from the consequences of the temporal order of events.[23] The above definition is similar to, but perhaps on a slightly higher level of generality than, Hicks's notion that statics deals with "those parts of economic theory where we do not have to trouble about dating."[24]

In order to preserve internal consistency, it is necessary to assume that the period of reference is one in which the consumer's income and expenditure pattern is synchronized. And, we have to assume also that this holds true for all consumers. In other words, we assume that both the income patterns and the expenditure patterns repeat themselves *every* period. There is thus no overlapping of expenditures from one period into the next. This implies, of course, that the demand curve reconstitutes itself every period.[25] The above implies also that only one price can exist during any unit period and that price can change only from period to period. A disequilibrium can, therefore, be corrected only over two or more periods.

Functional and nonfunctional demand

At the outset it is probably best to define clearly some of the basic terms we are going to use and to indicate those aspects of demand that we are going to treat. The demand for consumers' goods and services may be classified according to motivation. The following classification, which we shall find useful, is on a level of abstraction which, it is hoped, includes most of the motivations behind consumers' demand.

A. Functional
B. Nonfunctional

    1. External effects on utility

        (a) Bandwagon effect
        (b) Snob effect
        (c) Veblen effect

    2. Speculative
    3. Irrational

By functional demand is meant that part of the demand for a commodity which is due to the qualities inherent in the commodity itself. By nonfunctional demand is meant that portion of the demand for a consumers' good which is due to factors other than the qualities inherent in the commodity. Probably the most important kind of nonfunctional demand is due to external effects on utility. That is, the utility derived from the commodity is enhanced or decreased owing to the fact that others are purchasing and consuming the same commodity, or owing to the fact that the commodity bears a higher rather than a lower price tag. We differentiate this type of demand into what we shall call the "bandwagon" effect, the "snob" effect, and the "Veblen" effect.[26] By the bandwagon effect, we refer to the extent to which the demand for a commodity is *increased* due to the fact that others are also consuming the same commodity. It represents the desire of people to purchase a commodity in order to get into "the swim of things"; in order to conform with the people they wish to be associated with; in order to be fashionable or stylish; or, in order to appear to be "one of the boys." By the snob effect we refer to the extent to which the demand for a consumers' good is *decreased* owing to the fact that others are also consuming the same commodity (or that others are increasing their consumption of that commodity). This represents the desire of people to be exclusive; to be different; to dissociate themselves from the "common herd." By the Veblen effect we refer to the phenomenon of conspicuous consumption; to the extent to which the demand for a consumers' good is increased because it bears a higher rather than a lower price. We should perhaps emphasize the distinction made between the snob and the Veblen effect – the former is a function of the consumption of others, the latter is a function of price.[27] This paper will deal almost exclusively with these three types of nonfunctional demand.

For the sake of completeness there should perhaps be some explanation as to what is meant by speculative and irrational demand. Speculative demand refers to the fact that people will often "lay in" a supply of a commodity because they expect its price to rise. Irrational demand is, in a sense, a catchall category. It refers to purchases that are neither planned nor calculated but are due to sudden urges, whims, etc., and that serve no rational purpose but that of satisfying sudden whims and desires.

In the above it was assumed throughout that income is a parameter. If income is not given but allowed to vary, then the income effect on demand may in most cases be the most important effect of all. Also, it may be well to point out that the above is only one of a large number of possible classifications of the types of consumers' demand – classifications that for some purposes may be superior to the one here employed. We therefore suggest the above classification only for the purposes at hand and make no claims about its desirableness, or effectiveness, in any other use.

The bandwagon effect

A conceptual experiment

Our immediate task is to obtain aggregate demand curves of various kinds in those cases where the individual demand curves are non-additive. First we shall examine the case where the bandwagon effect is important. In its pure form this is the case where an individual will demand more (less) of a commodity at a given price because some or all other individuals in the market also demand more (less) of the commodity.

One of the difficulties in analyzing this type of demand involves the choice of assumptions about the knowledge that each individual possesses. This implies that everyone knows the quantity that will be demanded by every individual separately, or the quantity demanded by all individuals collectively at any given price – after all the reactions and adjustments that individuals make to each other's demand has taken place. On the other hand, if we assume ignorance on the part of consumers about the demand of others, we have to make assumptions as to the nature and extent of the ignorance – ignorance is a relative concept. A third possibility, and the one that will be employed at first, is to devise some mechanism whereby the consumers obtain accurate information.

Another problem involves the choice of assumptions to be made about the demand behaviour of individual consumers. Three possibilities suggest themselves: (1) The demand of consumer A (at given prices) may be a function of the total demand of all others in the market collectively. Or, (2) the demand of consumer A may be a function of the demand of all other consumers both separately and collectively. In other words, A's demand may be more influenced by the demand of some than by the demand of others. (3) A third possibility is that A's demand is a function of the number of people that demand the commodity rather than the number of units demanded. More complex demand behaviour patterns that combine some of the elements of the above are conceivable. For present purposes it is best that we assume the simplest one as a first approximation.[28] Initially, therefore, we assume that A's demand is a function of the units demanded by all others collectively. This is the same as saying that A's demand is a function of total market demand at given prices, since A always knows his own demand, and he could always subtract his own demand from the total market demand to get the quantity demanded by all others.

In order to bring out the central principle involved in the ensuing analysis, consider the following *gedankenexperiment*. A known product is to be introduced into a well-defined market at a certain date. The nature of the product is such that its demand depends partially on the functional qualities of the commodity, and partially on whether many or few units are demanded. Our technical problem is to compound the nonadditive individual demand curves into a total market demand curve, given sufficient information about the individual demand functions. Now, suppose that it is possible to obtain an accurate knowledge of the demand function of an individual through a series of questionnaires. Since an individual's demand is, in part, a function of the total market demand, it is necessary to take care of this difficulty in our questionnaires. We can have a potential consumer fill out the first questionnaire by having him assume that the total market demand, at all prices, is a given very small amount – say 400 units. On the basis of this assumption the consumer would tell us the quantities he demands over a reasonable range of prices. Subjecting every consumer to the same questionnaire, we add the results across and obtain a market demand curve that would reflect the demand situation if every consumer believed the total demand were only 400 units. This, however, is not the real market demand function under the assumption of the possession of accurate market information by consumers, since the total demand (at each price) upon which consumers based their replies was not the actual market demand (at each price) as revealed by the results of the survey. Let us call the results of the first survey "schedule No. 1."

We can now carry out a second survey, that is, subject each consumer to a second questionnaire in which each one is told that schedule No. 1 reflects the total quantities demanded, at each price.

Aggregating the replies we obtain schedule No. 2. Schedule No. 1 then becomes a parameter upon which schedule No. 2 is based. In a similar manner we can obtain schedules No. 3, No. 4, ..., No. n, in which each schedule is the result of adding the quantities demanded by each consumer (at each price), *if each consumer believes that the total quantities demanded (at each price) are shown by the previous schedule*. Now, the quantities demanded in schedule No. 2 will be greater than or equal to the quantities demanded in schedule No. 1 for the same prices. Some consumers may increase the quantity they demand when they note that the total quantity demanded, at given prices, is greater than they thought it would be. As long as some consumers or potential consumers continue to react positively to increases in the total quantity demanded the results of successive surveys will be different. That is, some or all of the quantities demanded in schedule No. 1 will be less than the quantities demanded at the same prices, in schedule No. 2, which in turn will be equal to or less than the quantities demanded, at the same prices, in schedule No. 3, and so on.

At this point it is appropriate to introduce a new principle with the intention of showing that this process cannot go on indefinitely. Sooner or later two successive schedules will be identical. If two successive surveys yield the same market demand schedules, then an equilibrium situation exists since the total quantities demanded, at each price, upon which individual consumers based their demand, turns out to be correct. Thus, if schedule No. n is identical with schedule No. $n-1$, then schedule No. n is the actual market demand function for the product on the assumption that consumers have accurate information of market conditions.

The question that arises is whether there is any reason to suppose that sooner or later two successive surveys will yield exactly the same result. This would indeed be the case if we could find good reason to posit a principle to the effect that for every individual there is some point at which he will cease to increase the quantities demanded for a commodity, at given prices, in response to incremental increases in total market demand. Such a principle would imply that beyond a point incremental increases in the demand for the commodity by others have a decreasing influence on a consumer's own demand; and, further, that a point is reached at which these increases in demand by others have no influence whatsoever on his own demand. It would, of course, also be necessary to establish that such a principle holds true for every consumer. It would not be inappropriate to call this the principle of diminishing marginal external consumption effect. Does such a principle really exist? There are some good reasons for believing that it does. First, the reader may note that the principle is analogous to the principle of diminishing marginal utility. As the total market demand grows larger, incremental increases in total demand become smaller and smaller proportions of the demand. It sounds reasonable, and probably appeals to us intuitively that an individual would be less influenced, and indeed take less notice of, a one per cent increase in total demand, than of a ten per cent increase in total demand, though these percentage increases be the same in absolute amount. Second, we can probably appeal effectively to general experience. There are no cases in which an individual's demand for a consumers' good increases end-lessly with increases in total demand. If there were two or more such individuals in a market then the demand for the commodity would increase in an endless spiral. Last but not least, the income constraint is sufficient to establish that there must be a point at which increases in a consumer's demand must fail to respond to increases in demand by others. Since every consumer is subject to the income constraint, it must follow that the principle holds for all consumers.[29]

Now, to get back to our conceptual experiment, we would find that after administering a sufficient number of surveys, we would sooner or later get two surveys that yield identical demand schedules. The result of the last survey would then represent the true demand sit-uation that would manifest itself on the market when the commodity was offered for sale. We may perhaps justly call such a demand function the equilibrium demand function – or demand curve. The equilibrium demand curve is the curve that exists when the marginal external consumption effect for every consumer, but one,[30] at all alternate prices is equal to zero. All other demand curves may be conceived as disequilibrium curves that can exist only because of temporarily imperfect knowledge by consumers of other people's demand. Once the errors in market information were discovered such a curve would move to a new position.

The bandwagon effect – diagrammatical method

The major purpose of going through the conceptual experiment with its successive surveys was to illustrate the diminishing marginal external consumption effect and to indicate its role in obtaining a determinate demand curve. There is, however, a relatively simple method for obtaining the market demand function in those cases where external consumption effects are significant. This method will allow us to compare some of the properties of the "bandwagon demand curve" with the usual "functional" demand curve; and, it will also allow us to sep-arate the extent to which a change in demand is due to a change in price, and the extent to which it is due to the bandwagon effect.

Given a certain total demand for a commodity as a parameter,[31] every individual will have a demand function based on this total market demand. Let the alternative total market demands that will serve as parameters for alternate individual demand functions be indicated as superscripts $a, b, \ldots n$ (where $a < b < \cdots < n$). Let the individual demand functions be $d_1, d_2, \ldots d_n$; where every subscript indicates a different consumer. Thus d_3^a is the individual

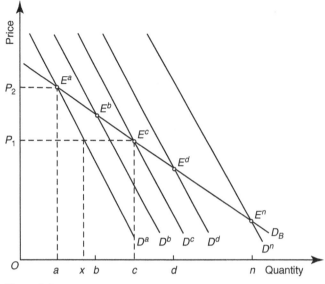

Figure 3.1

demand curve for consumer 3 if the consumer believes that the total market demand is a units. Similarly d_{500}^m is the individual demand curve for the 500th consumer if he believes that the total market demand will be m units. We could now add across $d_1^a, d_2^a, d_3^a, \ldots, d_n^a$ which will give us the market demand curve D^a, which indicates the quantities demanded at alternate prices if all consumers believed that the total demand was a units. In the same manner we can obtain $D^b, D^c, \ldots, D^n$. These hypothetical market demand curves $D^a, D^b, D^c, \ldots, D^n$ are shown in Figure 3.1. Now, if we assume that buyers have accurate knowledge of market conditions (i.e., of the total quantities demanded at every price) then only one point on any of the curves $D^a, D^b, \ldots, D^n$ could be on the real or equilibrium demand curve. These are the points on each curve $D^a, D^b, \ldots, D^n$ that represent the amounts on which the consumers based their individual demand curves; that is, the amounts that consumers expected to be the total market demand. These points are labeled in Figure 1 as $E^a, E^b, \ldots, E^n$. They are a series of virtual equilibrium points. Given that consumers possess accurate market information, $E^a, E^b, \ldots, E^n$, are the only points that can become actual quantities demanded. The locus of all these points DB is therefore the actual demand curve for the commodity.

It may be of interest, at this point, to break up changes in the quantity demanded due to changes in price into a price effect and a bandwagon effect; that is, the extent of the change that is due to the change in price, and the extent of the change in demand that is due to consumers adjusting to each other's changed consumption.[32] With an eye on Figure 3.1 consider the effects of a reduction in price from P_2 to P_1. The increase in demand after the change in price is *ac*. Only part of that increase, however, is due to the reduction in price. To measure the amount due to the reduction in price we go along the demand curve D^a to P_1 which tells us the quantity that would be demanded at P_1 if consumers did not adjust to each other's demand. This would result in an increase in demand of *ax*. Due to the bandwagon effect, however, an additional number of consumers are induced to enter the market or to increase their demands. There is now an additional increase in demand of *xc* after consumers have adjusted to each other's increases in consumption. Exactly the same type of analysis can, of course, be carried out for increases as well as for decreases in price.

We may note another thing from Figure 3.1. The demand curve D_B is more elastic than any of the other demand curves shown in the diagram. This would suggest that, other things being equal, the demand curve will be more elastic if there is a bandwagon effect than if the demand is based only on the functional attributes of the commodity. This, of course, follows from the fact that reactions to price changes are followed by additional reactions, *in the same direction*, to each other's changed consumption.

Social taboos and the bandwagon effect

Social taboos, to the extent that they affect consumption, are, in a sense, bandwagon effects in reverse gear. That is to say, some people will not buy and consume certain things because other people are not buying and consuming these things. Thus, there may not be any demand for a commodity even though it has a functional utility, although, apart from the taboo, it would be purchased. Individual A will not buy the commodity because individuals B, C, and D do not, while individuals B, C, and D may refrain from consumption for the same reasons. It is not within the competence of the economist to investigate the psychology of this kind of behaviour. For our purposes we need only note that such behaviour exists and attempt to analyze how such behaviour affects the demand function.

We can proceed as follows. Let d_1^x be the demand curve of the least inhibited individual in the market, where the superscript x is the total quantity demanded in the market upon which he bases his individual demand. Suppose that at market demand x consumer 1 will demand at some range of prices one unit of the commodity, but at no price will he demand more. If he believes, however, that the total market demand is less than x units he will refrain from making any purchases. Since, *ex hypothesi*, consumer 1 is the least inhibited consumer, he will, at best, be the only one who will demand one unit of the commodity if consumers expect the total market demand to be x units. It must be clear, then, that x units cannot be a virtual equilibrium point, since only points where the total expected quantity demanded is equal to the actual quantity demanded can be points on the real demand curve, and the quantity x cannot at any price be a point where expected total demand is equal to actual total demand. Now, if the total expected demand were $x + 1$ the actual demand might increase, say, to 2 units. At expected total demands $x + 2$ and $x + 3$, more would enter the market and the actual demand would be still greater since the fear of being different is considerably reduced as the expected demand is increased. With given increases in the expected total demand there must, at some point, he more than equal increases in the actual demand, because, if a real demand curve exists at all, there must be some point where the expected demand is equal to the actual demand. That point may exist, say, at $x + 10$. That is, at an expected total demand of $x + 10$ units a sufficient number of people have overcome their inhibitions to being different so that, at some prices, they will actually demand $x + 10$ units of the commodity. Let us call this point "T" – it is really the "taboo breaking point." The maximum bid (the point T in Figure 3.2) of the marginal unit demanded if the total demand were T units now gives us the first point on the real demand curve (the curve D_B.).

How social taboos may affect the demand curve is shown in Figure 3.2. It will be noted that the price axis shows both positive and negative "prices." A negative price may be thought of as the price it would be necessary to pay individuals in order to induce them to consume in public a given amount of the commodity; that is, the price that it would be necessary to pay the consumers in order to induce them to disregard their aversion to be looked upon as odd or peculiar.

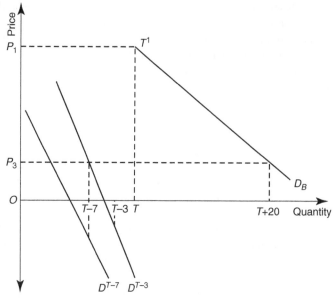

Figure 3.2

As we have already indicated, the point T in Figure 3.2 is the "taboo breaking point." T represents the number of units at which an *expected* total quantity demanded of T units would result in an *actual* quantity demanded of T units at some *real* price. Now, what has to be explained is why an expected demand of less than T units, say $T - 3$ units, would not yield an actual demand of $T - 3$ units at a positive price but only at a "negative price." Let the curve D^{T-3} be the demand curve that would exist if consumers thought the total demand was $T - 3$. Now, at any positive price, say P_3, the amount demanded would be less than $T - 3$, say $T - 7$. The price P_3 can therefore exist only if there is inaccurate information of the total quantity demanded. Once consumers discovered that at P_3 only $T - 7$ was purchased, and believed that this was the demand that would be sustained, their demand would shift to the D^{T-7} curve. At P_3 the amount purchased would now be less than $T - 7$ and demand would now shift to a curve to the left of the D^{T-7} curve. This procedure would go on until the demand was zero at P_3. We thus introduce a gap into our demand function and focus attention on an interesting psychological phenomenon that may affect demand. What we are suggesting, essentially, is that given "accurate expectations" of the total quantity demanded on the part of consumers, there is a quantity less than which there will not be any quantity demanded at any real price. In other words, this is a case in which a commodity will either "go over big" or not "go over" at all. It will be noted that at P_3 zero units or $T + 20$ units (Figure 3.2) may be taken off the market given "accurate expectations" of the total quantity demanded. It would seem, therefore, that "accurate expectations" of the total quantity demanded at P_3 can have two values depending upon whether people are generally pessimistic or optimistic about other consumers' demands for the commodity in question. If everybody expects that everybody else would not care much for the commodity, then zero units would be the accurate expectation of the total quantity demanded; if everybody, on the other hand, expects others to take up the commodity with some degree of enthusiasm,[33] then $T + 20$ units would be the accurate expectation of the total quantity demanded. The factors that would determine one set of expectations rather than the other are matters of empirical investigation in the field of social psychology. The factors involved may be the history of the community, the people's conservatism or lack of conservatism, the type and quantity of advertising about the commodity under consideration, etc.

The really significant point in Figure 3.2 is T', the first point on the real demand curve D_B. As already indicated, it is the point at which the maximum bid of the marginal unit demanded is P_t and the total market demand is T units. If the price were higher than P_t, the Tth unit would not be demanded and all buyers would leave the market because of the effect of the taboo at less than a consumption of T units.[34] By way of summary we might say that the whole point of this section is an attempt to show that in cases where social taboos affect demand the real demand curve may not start at the price-axis but that the smallest possible quantity demanded may be some distance to the right of the price-axis.

The snob effect

Thus far, in our conceptual experiment and diagrammatic analysis, we have considered only the bandwagon effect. We now consider the reverse effect – the demand behaviour for those commodities with regard to which the individual consumer acts like a snob. Here, too, we assume at first that the quantity demanded by a consumer is a function of price and of the total market demand, but that the individual consumer's demand is negatively correlated with the total market demand. In the snob case it is rather obvious that the external consumption effect must reach a limit although the limit may be where one snob constitutes the only buyer. For most commodities and most buyers, however, the motivation for exclusiveness is not that great; hence the marginal external consumption effect reaches zero before that point. If the commodity is to be purchased at all, the external consumption effect must reach a limit, at some price, where the quantity demanded has a positive value. From this it follows that after a point the principle of the diminishing marginal external consumption effect must manifest itself. We thus have in the snob effect an opposite but completely symmetrical relationship to the bandwagon effect.

The analysis of markets in which all consumers behave as snobs follows along the same lines as our analysis of the bandwagon effect. Because of the similarity we will be able to get through our analysis of the snob effect in short order. We begin, as before, by letting the alternate total market demands that serve as parameters for alternate individual demand curves be indicated by the superscripts $a, b, \ldots, n$ (where $a < b < n$). Let the individual demand functions be $d_1, d_2, \ldots, d$, where there are n consumers in the market. Again, d_3^a signifies the individual demand curve for consumer 3 on the assumption that he expects the total market demand to be "a" units. By adding

$$d_1^a + d_2^a + \cdots + d_n^a = D^a$$
$$d_1^b + d_2^b + \cdots + d_n^b = D^b$$
$$\vdots \qquad \vdots$$
$$d_1^n + d_2^n + \cdots + d_n^n = D^n$$

we obtain the market demand functions on the alternate assumptions of consumers expecting the total market demands to be $a, b, \ldots, n$. Due to snob behaviour the curves $D^a, D^b, \ldots, D^n$ move to the left as the expected total market demand increases. This is shown in Figure 3.3. Using the same procedure as before we obtain the virtual equilibrium points $E^a, E^b, \ldots, E^n$.

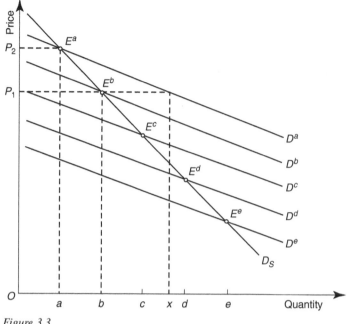

Figure 3.3

They represent the only points on the curves $D^a, D^b, \ldots, D^n$ that are consistent with consumers' expectations (and hence with the assumption of accurate information). The locus of these virtual equilibrium points is the demand curve D_s.

Now, given a price change from P_2 to P_1 we can separate the effect of the price change into a price effect and a snob effect. In Figure 3.3 we see that the net increase in the quantity demanded due to the reduction in price is ab. The price effect, however, is *ax*. That is, if every consumer expected no increase in the total quantity demanded then the total quantity demanded at P_1 would be Ox. The more extreme snobs will react to this increase in the total quantity demanded and will leave the market.[35] The total quantity demanded will hence be reduced by *bx*. The net result is therefore an increase in demand of only *ab*.

It may be of interest to examine some of the characteristics of the curves in Figure 3.3. First we may note that all the points on the curves other than D_s (except $E_a, E^b, \ldots, E^n$) are theoretical points that have significance only under conditions of imperfect knowledge.

Second, we may note from the diagram that the demand curve for snobs is less elastic than the demand curves where there are no snob effects. The reason for this, of course, is that the increase in demand due to a reduction in price is counterbalanced, in part, by some snobs leaving the market because of the increase in total consumption (i.e., the decrease in the snob value of the commodity). It should be clear, however, that the snob effect, as defined, can never be in excess of the price effect since this would lead to a basic contradiction. If the snob effect were greater than the price effect, then the quantity demanded at a lower price would be less than the quantity demanded at a higher price. This implies that some of the snobs in the market at the higher price leave the market when there is a reduction in the total quantity demanded; which, of course, is patently inconsistent with our definition of snob behaviour. It therefore follows that the snob effect is never greater than the price effect. It follows, also, that D_s is monotonically decreasing if $D^a, D^b, \ldots, D^n$ are monotonically decreasing.[36]

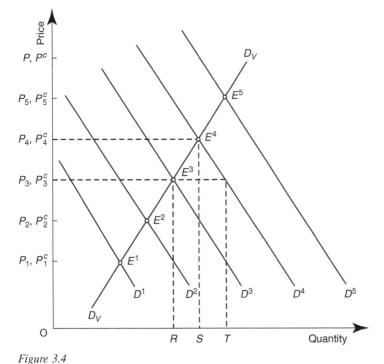

Figure 3.4

Note: Price effect = ST; Veblen effect = −TR; Net effect = −SR.

Finally, it may be interesting to note another difference between the usual functional demand curve and the D_s curve. In the usual demand curve the buyers at higher prices always remain in the market at lower prices. That is, from the price point of view, the bids to buy are cumulative downward. This is clearly not the case in the D_s curve. Such terms as intramarginal buyers may be meaningless in snob markets.

The Veblen effect

Although the theory of conspicuous consumption as developed Veblen and others is quite a complex and subtle sociological construct we can, for our purposes, quite legitimately abstract from the psychological and sociological elements and address our attention exclusively to the effects that conspicuous consumption has on the demand function. The essential economic characteristic with which we are concerned is the fact that the utility derived from a unit of a commodity employed for purposes of conspicuous consumption depends not only on the inherent qualities of that unit, but also on the price paid for it. It may, therefore, be helpful to divide the price of a commodity into two categories: the real price and the conspicuous price. By the real price we refer to the price the consumer paid for the commodity in terms of money. The conspicuous price is the price other people think the consumer paid for the commodity[37] and which therefore determines its conspicuous consumption utility. These two prices would probably be identical in highly organized markets where price information is common knowledge. In other markets, where some can get "bargains" or special discounts, the real price or conspicuous price need not be identical. In any case, the quantity demanded by a consumer will be a function of both the real price and the conspicuous price.

The market demand curve for commodities subject to conspicuous consumption can be derived through a similar diagrammatical method (summarized in Figure 3.4). This time we let the superscripts $1, 2, \ldots, n$ stand for the expected conspicuous prices. The real prices are $P_1, P_2, \ldots, P_n$. The individual demand functions are $d_1, d_2, \ldots, d_n$. In this way d_6^3 stands for the demand curve of consumer number 6 if he expects a conspicuous price of P_1^c.[38] We can now add across $d_1^1, d_2^1, \ldots, d_n^1$ and get the market demand curve D^1 which indicates the quantities demanded at alternate prices if all consumers expected a conspicuous price of P_1^c. In a similar manner we obtain $D^2, D^3, \ldots, D^n$. The market demand curves will, of course, up to a point, shift to the right as the expected conspicuous price increases. Now on every curve $D^1, D^2, \ldots, D^n$ in Figure 3.4 only one point can be a virtual equilibrium point if we assume that consumers possess accurate market information – the point where the real price is equal to the conspicuous price (that is, where $P_1 = P_1^c, P_2 = P_2^c, \ldots, P_n = P_n^c$). The locus of these virtual equilibrium points $E^1, E^2, \ldots, E^n$ gives us the demand curve D_V.

As before, we can separate the effects of a change in price into two effects – the price effect, and, what we shall call for want of a better term, the Veblen effect. In Figure 3.4 it will be seen that a change in price from P_4 to P_3 will reduce the quantity demanded by RS. The price effect is to increase the quantity demanded by ST; that is, the amount that would be demanded if there were no change in the expected conspicuous price would be OT. However, at the lower price a number of buyers would leave the market because of the reduced utility derived from the commodity at that lower conspicuous price. The Veblen effect is therefore RT.

It should be noted that unlike the D_s curve, the D_v curve can be positively inclined, negatively inclined or a mixture of both. It all depends on whether at alternate price changes the Veblen effect is greater or less than the price effect. It is possible that in one portion of the curve one effect may predominate while in another portion another may predominate. It is to be expected, however, that in most cases, if the curve is not monotonically decreasing it will be shaped like a backward S, as illustrated in Figure 3.5(a). The reasons for this are as follows: First, there must be a price so high that no units of the commodity will be purchased at that price owing to the income constraint (among other reasons). This is the price P_n in Figure 5(a), and it implies that there must be some point at which the curve shifts from being positively inclined to being negatively inclined as price increases. Second, there must be some point of satiety for the good. This is the point T in Figure 5(a). It therefore follows that some portion of the curve must be monotonically decreasing to reach T if there exists some minimum price at which the Veblen effect is zero. It is of course reasonable to assume that there is some low price at which the commodity would cease to have any value for purposes of conspicuous consumption. If this last assumption does not hold, which is unlikely, then the curve could have the shape indicated in Figure 5(c). Otherwise, it would have the general shape indicated in Figure 5(a), or it might be in two segments as illustrated in Figure 5(b).

Mixed effects

Any real market for semidurable or durable goods will most likely contain consumers that are subject to one or a combination of the effects discussed heretofore. Combining these effects presents no new formal difficulties with respect to the determination of the market demand curve, although it complicates the diagrammatic analysis considerably. The major principle, however, still holds. For any price there is a quantity demanded such that the marginal external consumption effect (or the marginal Veblen effect) for all buyers but one, is zero. This implies that for every price change there is a point at which people cease reacting

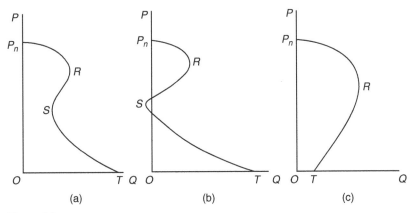

Figure 3.5

to each other's quantity changes, regardless of the direction of these reactions. If this is so, then for every price there is a determinate quantity demanded, and hence the demand curve is determinate.

Now, for every price change we have distinguished between the price effect and some other, such as the snob, the Veblen, or the bandwagon effect. In markets where all four effects are present we should be able to separate out and indicate the direction of each of them that will result from a price change. That is, every price change will result in two positive and two negative effects – two which, other things being equal, will increase the quantity demanded, and two which, other things being equal, will decrease it. Which effects will be positive and which will be negative will depend on the relative strength of the Veblen effect as against the price effect. The Veblen and the price effects will depend directly on the direction of the price change. An increase in price will therefore result in price and bandwagon effects that are negative, and in Veblen and snob effects that are positive, provided that the price effect is greater than the Veblen effect; that is, if the net result is a decrease in the quantity demanded at the higher price. If, on the other hand, the Veblen effect is more powerful than the price effect, given a price increase, then the bandwagon effect would be positive and the snob effect negative. The reverse would of course be true for price declines.

The market demand curve for a commodity where different consumers are subject to different types of effects can be obtained diagrammatically through employing the methods developed above – although the diagrams would be quite complicated. There is no point in adding still more diagrams to illustrate this. Briefly, the method would be somewhat as follows: (1) Given the demand curves for every individual, in which the expected total quantity demanded is a parameter for each curve, we can add these curves laterally and obtain a map of aggregate demand curves, in which each aggregate curve is based on a given total quantity demanded. (2) The locus of the equilibrium points on each aggregate demand curve (as derived in Figure 3.1) gives us a market demand curve that accounts for both bandwagon and snob effects. This last curve assumes that only one conspicuous price exists. For every conspicuous price there exists a separate map of aggregate demand curves from which different market demand curves are obtained. (3) This procedure yields a map of market demand curves in which each curve is based on a different conspicuous price. Employing the method used in Figure 4 we obtain our final market demand curve which accounts for bandwagon, snob, and Veblen effects simultaneously.

Conclusion

It is not unusual for a writer in pure theory to end his treatise by pointing out that the science is really very young; that there is a great deal more to be done; that the formulations presented are really of a very tentative nature; and that the best that can be hoped for is that his treatise may in some small way pave the road for future formulations that are more directly applicable to problems in the real world.[39] This is another way of saying that work in pure theory is an investment in the future state of the science where the returns in terms of applications to real problems are really very uncertain. This is probably especially true of value theory where the investment in time and effort is more akin to the purchase of highly speculative stocks rather than the purchase of government bonds. Since this was only a brief essay on one aspect of value theory, the reader will hardly be surprised if the conclusions reached are somewhat less than revolutionary.

Essentially, we have attempted to do two things. First, we have tried to demonstrate that non-additivity is not necessarily an insurmountable obstacle in effecting a transition from individual to collective demand curves. Second, we attempted to take a step or two in the direction of incorporating various kinds of external consumption effects into the theory of consumers' demand. In order to solve our problem, we have introduced what we have called the principle of the diminishing marginal external consumption effect. We indicated some reasons for believing that for every individual, there is some point at which the marginal external consumption effect is zero. We have attempted to show that if this principle is admitted, then there are various ways of effecting a transition from individual to collective demand curves. The major conclusion reached is that under conditions of perfect knowledge (or accurate expectations) any point on the demand curve, for any given price, will be at that total quantity demanded where the marginal external consumption effect for all consumers but one, is equal to zero.

In comparing the demand curve in those situations where external consumption effects are present with the demand curve as it would be where these external consumption effects are absent, we made three basic points. (1) If the bandwagon effect is the most significant effect, the demand curve is more elastic than it would be if this external consumption effect were absent. (2) If the snob effect is the predominant effect, the demand curve is less elastic than otherwise. (3) If the Veblen effect is the predominant one, the demand curve is less elastic than otherwise, and some portions of it may even be positively inclined; whereas, if the Veblen effect is absent, the curve will be negatively inclined regardless of the importance of the snob effect in the market.

Notes

1 The writer wishes to take this opportunity to thank Professor Ansley Coale and Messrs. Carey P. Modlin and Norman B. Ryder for their painstaking criticism of an earlier draft of this paper.
2 This *Journal*, February 1948, pp. 165–201.
3 *Ibid.*, p. 175 n.
4 *Ibid.*, p. 201.
5 John Rae, *The Sociological Theory of Capital* (London: The Macmillan Co., 1905), especially Chap. XIII, "Of Economic Stratification," and Appendix I, "Of Luxury," pp. 218–76.
6 *Ibid.*, pp. 249 and 253.
7 *Economic Journal*, 1893, pp. 458–74.
8 *Studies in the Theory of Welfare Economics* (New York: Columbia University Press, 1947), p. 64. Italics mine.
9 "Mr. Lerner on the Economics of Control," *Economic Journal*, 1945, pp. 51–6.
10 *The Economics of Welfare* (4th Edition, 1929), pp. 190–2, 225–6, 808.

11 "Some Improvements in Simple Geometrical Methods of Treating Exchange Value, Monopoly, and Rent," *Economic Journal*, 1892, pp. 35–9.

12 Rae, *op. cit.*, pp. 277–96.

13 Reder, *op. cit.*, pp. 65–6.

14 Rae, *op. cit.*, pp. 282–8.

15 Pigou, *Memorials of Alfred Marshall*, pp. 433 and 450. These are Marshall's letters to Pigou and Cunynghame which indicate that Marshall had read the articles (*E.J.* 1892, and *E.J.* 1903), where Pigou and Cunynghame consider the matter.

16 Reder, *op. cit.*, p. 67. "We shall assume, throughout its remainder, that the satisfaction of one individual does not depend on the consumption of another."

17 *Foundations of Economic Analysis*, p. 224.

18 James S. Duesenberry, in his recent book, *Income, Saving, and the Theory of Consumer Behavior* (Harvard University Press, 1949), considers problems of a somewhat similar nature but handles them in quite a different manner. Chapter VI on interdependent preferences and the "new" welfare analysis is especially worthy of mention. Duesenberry's treatment of the problem helps considerably to fill an important gap in the current theory. Unfortunately, Mr. Duesenberry's work came to the attention of the writer too late to be given the detailed consideration it deserves.

19 "The Interdependence of Different Sources of Demand and Supply in a Market," *Economic Journal*, 1913, pp. 18–24.

20 *Ibid.*, p. 18.

21 *Ibid.*, p. 24.

22 On this point cf. Morgenstern, "Professor Hicks on Value and Capital," *Journal of Political Economy*, June 1941, pp. 368–76. See also part of an article by Don Patinkin, "The Indeterminacy of Absolute Prices in Classical Economic Theory," *Econometrica*, January 1949, pp. 310–11, which sets out the conditions under which systems of homogeneous equations will possess no solution.

23 An excellent discussion of the above problem, the relationship between the notions of time in economics and various definitions of statics and dynamics, can be found in W. C. Hood, "Some Aspects of the Treatment of Time in Economic Theory," *The Canadian Journal of Economics and Political Science*, 1948, pp. 453–68.

24 *Value and Capital*, p. 115.

25 The above assumptions are necessary in order to take care of some of the difficulties raised by Professor Morgenstern in "Demand Theory Reconsidered."

26 It is assumed from here on that the reader will be aware that these terms will be used in the special sense here defined, and hence the quotation marks will hereafter be deleted.

27 Some writers have not made the above distinction but have combined the two effects into what they termed "snob behaviour" (see Morgenstern, *op. cit.*, p. 190). The above does not imply that our distinction is necessarily the "correct" one, but only that it is found useful in our analysis.

28 As is customary in economic theory the ensuing analysis is carried out on the basis of a number of simplifying assumptions. The relaxation of some of the simplifying assumptions and the analysis of more complex situations must await some other occasion. The present writer has attempted these with respect to some of the simplifying assumptions but the results cannot be included within the confines of an article of the usual length.

29 If the reader should object to our dignifying the diminishing marginal external consumption effect by calling it a principle or a law, we could point out that if it is not a "law," then it must be an equilibrium condition.

30 The fact that the marginal external consumption effect of one consumer is greater than zero can have no effect on the demand schedule since total market demand, at any given price, cannot increase unless there are at least two consumers who would react on each other's demand.

31 The reader should note that the analysis in the following pages is based on a somewhat different assumption than the *gedankenexperiment*. In the diagrams that follow each demand curve (other than the equilibrium demand curve) is based on the assumption that consumers believe that a fixed amount will be taken off the market at all prices. There is more than one way of deriving the equilibrium demand curve. The earlier method helped to bring out the nature of the central principle that is involved, while the method which follows will enable us to separate price effects from bandwagon effects and snob effects, etc.

32 We are now really in the area of "comparative statics." It may be recalled that we defined statics and our unit period in such a way that only *one* price holds within any unit period. Thus, when we

examine the effects of a change in price we are really examining the reasons for the differences in the quantities demanded at one price in one unit period and another price in the succeeding unit period.

33 If consumers have accurate expectations of the degree of enthusiasm with which others will take up the product, then they will expect demand to be $T + 20$ units.

34 This is a "pure" case where *all* buyers are governed by taboo considerations.

35 The other snobs will, of course, reduce their demand but not by an amount large enough to leave the market.

36 We shall see below however that the snob effect plus the Veblen effect combined can be greater than the price effect.

37 More accurately, the conspicuous price should be the price that the consumer thinks other people think he paid for the commodity.

38 The expected conspicuous prices are distinguished from the real prices by adding the superscript c to the P's. Thus, to the range of real prices $P_1, P_2, \ldots, P_n$, we have a corresponding range of conspicuous prices denoted by $P_1^c, P_2^c, \ldots, P_n^c$.

39 See, for example, Samuelson, *Foundations of Economic Analysis*, p. 350, and Joan Robinson, *Economics of Imperfect Competition*, p. 327.

4 A theory of the allocation of time

Gary S. Becker

I Introduction

Throughout history the amount of time spent at work has never consistently been much greater than that spent at other activities. Even a work week of fourteen hours a day for six days still leaves half the total time for sleeping, eating and other activities. Economic development has led to a large secular decline in the work week, so that whatever may have been true of the past, to-day it is below fifty hours in most countries, less than a third of the total time available. Consequently the allocation and efficiency of non-working time may now be more important to economic welfare than that of working time; yet the attention paid by economists to the latter dwarfs any paid to the former.

Fortunately, there is a movement under way to redress the balance. The time spent at work declined secularly, partly because young persons increasingly delayed entering the labour market by lengthening their period of schooling. In recent years many economists have stressed that the time of students is one of the inputs into the educational process, that this time could be used to participate more fully in the labour market and therefore that one of the costs of education is the forgone earnings of students. Indeed, various estimates clearly indicate that forgone earnings is the dominant private and an important social cost of both high-school and college education in the United States.[1] The increased awareness of the importance of forgone earnings has resulted in several attempts to economise on students' time, as manifested, say, by the spread of the quarterly and tri-mester systems.[2]

Most economists have now fully grasped the importance of forgone earnings in the educational process and, more generally, in all investments in human capital, and criticise educationalists and others for neglecting them. In the light of this it is perhaps surprising that economists have not been equally sophisticated about other non-working uses of time. For example, the cost of a service like the theatre or a good like meat is generally simply said to equal their market prices, yet everyone would agree that the theatre and even dining take time, just as schooling does, time that often could have been used productively. If so, the full costs of these activities would equal the sum of market prices and the forgone value of the time used up. In other words, indirect costs should be treated on the same footing when discussing all non-work uses of time, as they are now in discussions of schooling.

In the last few years a group of us at Columbia University have been occupied, perhaps initially independently but then increasingly less so, with introducing the cost of time systematically into decisions about non-work activities. J. Mincer has shown with several empirical examples how estimates of the income elasticity of demand for different commodities are biased when the cost of time is ignored;[3] J. Owen has analysed how the demand for leisure can be affected;[4] E. Dean has considered the allocation of time between subsistence work and market participation in some African economies;[5] while, as already mentioned, I have been concerned with the use of time in education, training and other kinds of human capital. Here I attempt to develop a general treatment of the allocation of time in all other non-work activities. Although under my name alone, much of any credit it merits belongs to the stimulus received from Mincer, Owen, Dean and other past and present participants in the Labor Workshop at Columbia.[6]

The plan of the discussion is as follows. The first section sets out a basic theoretical analysis of choice that includes the cost of time on the same footing as the cost of market goods, while the remaining sections treat various empirical implications of the theory. These include a new approach to changes in hours of work and "leisure," the full integration of so-called "productive "consumption into economic analysis, a new analysis of the effect of income on the quantity and "quality" of commodities consumed, some suggestions on the measurement of productivity, an economic analysis of queues and a few others as well. Although I refer to relevant empirical work that has come to my attention, little systematic testing of the theory has been attempted.

II A revised theory of choice

According to traditional theory, households maximise utility functions of the form

$$U = U(y_1, y_2, \ldots, y_n) \tag{4.1}$$

subject to the resource constraint

$$\sum p_i' y_i = I = W + V \tag{4.2}$$

where y_i are goods purchased on the market, p_i' are their prices, I is money income, W is earnings and V is other income. As the introduction suggests, the point of departure here is the systematic incorporation of non-working time. Households will be assumed to combine time and market goods to produce more basic commodities that directly enter their utility functions. One such commodity is the seeing of a play, which depends on the input of actors, script, theatre and the playgoer's time; another is sleeping, which depends on the input of a bed, house (pills ?) and time. These commodities will be called Z_i and written as

$$Z_i = f_i(x_i, T_i) \tag{4.3}$$

where x_i is a vector of market goods and T_i a vector of time inputs used in producing the ith commodity.[7] Note that, when capital goods such as refrigerators or automobiles are used, x refers to the services yielded by the goods. Also note that T_i is a vector because, e.g., the hours used during the day or on weekdays may be distinguished from those used at night or on week-ends. Each dimension of T_i refers to a different aspect of time. Generally, the partial derivatives of z_i with respect to both x_i and T_i are non-negative.[8]

In this formulation households are both producing units and utility maximisers. They combine time and market goods via the "production functions" f_i to produce the basic commodities Z_i, and they choose the best combination of these commodities in the conventional way by maximising a utility function

$$U = U(Z_i, \ldots Z_m) \equiv U(f_1, \ldots f_m) \equiv U(x_1, \ldots x_m; T_1, \ldots T_m) \tag{4.4}$$

subject to a budget constraint

$$g(Z_i, \ldots Z_m) = Z \tag{4.5}$$

where g is an expenditure function of Z_i and Z is the bound on resources. The integration of production and consumption is at odds with the tendency for economists to separate them sharply, production occurring in firms and consumption in households. It should be pointed out, however, that in recent years economists increasingly recognise that a household is truly a "small factory":[9] it combines capital goods, raw materials and labour to clean, feed, procreate and otherwise produce useful commodities. Undoubtedly the fundamental reason for the traditional separation is that firms are usually given control over working time in exchange for market goods, while "discretionary" control over market goods and consumption time is retained by households as they create their own utility. If (presumably different) firms were also given control over market goods and consumption time in exchange for providing utility the separation would quickly fade away in analysis as well as in fact.

The basic goal of the analysis is to find measures of g and Z which facilitate the development of empirical implications. The most direct approach is to assume that the utility function in equation (4.4) is maximised subject to separate constraints on the expenditure of market goods and time, and to the production functions in equation (4.3). The goods constraint can be written as

$$\sum_1^m p_i x_i = I = V + T_w \bar{w} \tag{4.6}$$

where p_i is a vector giving the unit prices of x_i, T_w is a vector giving the hours spent at work and $\bar{w}$ is a vector giving the earnings per unit of T_w. The time constraints can be written as

$$\sum_1^m T_i = T_c = T - T_w \tag{4.7}$$

where T_c is a vector giving the total time spent at consumption and T is a vector giving the total time available. The production functions (4.3) can be written in the equivalent form

$$\left. \begin{array}{l} T_i \equiv t_i Z_i \\ x_i \equiv b_i Z_i \end{array} \right\} \tag{4.8}$$

where t_i is a vector giving the input of time per unit of Z_i and b_i is a similar vector for market goods.

The problem would appear to be to maximise the utility function (4.4) subject to the multiple constraints (4.6) and (4.7) and to the production relations (4.8). There is, however, really only one basic constraint: (4.6) is not independent of (4.7) because time can be converted into goods by using less time at consumption and more at work. Thus, substituting for T_w, in (4.6) its equivalent in (4.7) gives the single constraint[10]

$$\sum p_i x_i + \sum T_i \bar{w} = V + T \bar{w} \tag{4.9}$$

By using (4.8), (4.9) can be written as

$$\sum (p_i b_i + t_i \bar{w}) Z_i = V + T \bar{w} \tag{4.10}$$

with

$$\left.\begin{array}{l} \pi_i \equiv p_i b_i + t_i \bar{w} \\ S' \equiv V + T \bar{w} \end{array}\right\} \tag{4.11}$$

The full price of a unit of $Z_i(\pi_i)$ is the sum of the prices of the goods and of the time used per unit of Z_i. That is, the full price of consumption is the sum of direct and indirect prices in the same way that the full cost of investing in human capital is the sum of direct and indirect costs.[11] These direct and indirect prices are symmetrical determinants of total price, and there is no analytical reason to stress one rather than the other.

The resource constraint on the right side of equation (4.10), S', is easy to interpret if $\bar{w}$ were a constant, independent of the Z_i. For then S' gives the money income achieved if all the time available were devoted to work. This achievable income is "spent" on the commodities Z_i either directly through expenditures on goods, $\sum p_i b_i Z_i$, or indirectly through the forgoing of income, $\sum t_i \bar{w} Z_i$, i.e., by using time at consumption rather than at work. As long as $\bar{w}$ were constant, and if there were constant returns in producing Z_i so that b_i and t_i were fixed for given p_i and $\bar{w}$ the equilibrium condition resulting from maximising (4.4) subject to (4.10) takes a very simple form:

$$U_i = \frac{\partial U}{\partial Z_i} = \lambda \pi_i \quad i = 1, \ldots m \tag{4.12}$$

where λ is the marginal utility of money income. If $\bar{w}$ were not constant the resource constraint in equation (4.10) would not have any particularly useful interpretation : $S' = V + T\bar{w}$ would overstate the money income achievable as long as marginal wage-rates were below average ones. Moreover, the equilibrium conditions would become more complicated than (4.12) because marginal would have to replace average prices.

The total resource constraint could be given the sensible interpretation of the maximum money income achievable only in the special and unlikely case when average earnings were constant. This suggests dropping the approach based on explicitly considering separate goods and time constraints and substituting one in which the total resource constraint necessarily equalled the maximum money income achievable, which will be simply called "full income."[12] This income could in general be obtained by devoting all the time and other resources of a household to earning income, with no regard for consumption. Of course, all the time would not usually be spent "at" a job: sleep, food, even leisure are required for efficiency, and some time (and other resources) would have to be spent on these activities in order to maximise money income. The amount spent would, however, be determined solely by the effect on income and not by any effect on utility. Slaves, for example, might be permitted time "off" from work only in so far as that maximised their output, or free persons in poor environments might have to maximise money income simply to survive.[13]

Households in richer countries do, however, forfeit money income in order to obtain additional utility, i.e., they exchange money income for a greater amount of psychic income. For example, they might increase their leisure time, take a pleasant job in preference to a better-paying unpleasant one, employ unproductive nephews or eat more than is warranted by considerations of productivity. In these and other situations the amount of money income forfeited measures the cost of obtaining additional utility.

Thus the full income approach provides a meaningful resource constraint and one firmly based on the fact that goods and time can be combined into a single overall constraint because time can be converted into goods through money income. It also incorporates a unified treatment of all substitutions of non-pecuniary for pecuniary income, regardless of their nature or whether they occur on the job or in the household. The advantages of this will become clear as the analysis proceeds.

If full income is denoted by S, and if the total earnings forgone or "lost" by the interest in utility is denoted by L, the identity relating L to S and I is simply

$$L(Z_1, \ldots, Z_m) \equiv S - I(Z_1, \ldots, Z_m) \qquad (4.13)$$

I and L are functions of the Z_i because how much is earned or forgone depends on the consumption set chosen; for example, up to a point, the less leisure chosen the larger the money income and the smaller the amount forgone.[14] Using equations (4.6) and (4.8), equation (4.13) can be written as

$$\sum p_i b_i Z_i + L(Z_1, \ldots, Z_m) \equiv S \qquad (4.14)$$

This basic resource constraint states that full income is spent either directly on market goods or indirectly through the forgoing of money income. Unfortunately, there is no simple expression for the average price of Z_i as there is in equation (4.10). However, marginal, not average, prices are relevant for behaviour, and these would be identical for the constraint in (4.10) only when average earnings, $\bar{w}$, was constant. But, if so, the expression for the loss function simplifies to

$$L = \bar{w} T_c = \bar{w} \sum t_i Z_i \qquad (4.15)$$

and (4.14) reduces to (4.10). Moreover, even in the general case the total marginal prices resulting from (4.14) can always be divided into direct and indirect components: the equilibrium conditions resulting from maximising the utility function subject to (4.14)[15] are

$$U_i = T(p_i b_i + L_i), \quad i = 1, \ldots, m \qquad (4.16)$$

where $p_i b_i$ is the direct and L_i the indirect component of the total marginal price $p_i b_i + L_i$.[16]

Behind the division into direct and indirect costs is the allocation of time and goods between work-orientated and consumption-orientated activities. This suggests an alternative division of costs; namely, into those resulting from the allocation of goods and those resulting from the allocation of time. Write $L_i = \partial L / \partial Z_i$ as

$$L_i = \frac{\partial L}{\partial T_i} \frac{\partial T_i}{\partial Z_i} + \frac{\partial L}{\partial x_i} \frac{\partial x_i}{\partial Z_i} \qquad (4.17)$$

$$= l_i t_i + c_i b_i \qquad (4.18)$$

where $l_i = \frac{\partial L}{\partial T_i}$ and $c_i = \frac{\partial L}{\partial x_i}$ are the marginal forgone earnings of using more time and goods respectively on Z_i. Equation (4.16) can then be written as

$$U_i = T[b_i(p_i + c_i) + t_i l_i] \qquad (4.19)$$

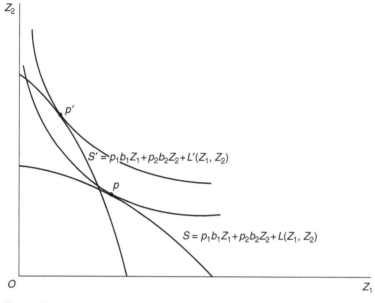

Figure 4.1

The total marginal cost of Z_i is the sum of $b_i(p_i + c_i)$, the marginal cost of using goods in producing Z_i, and $t_i l_i$, the marginal cost of using time. This division would be equivalent to that between direct and indirect costs only if $c_i = 0$ or if there were no indirect costs of using goods.

The accompanying figure shows the equilibrium given by equation (4.16) for a two-commodity world. In equilibrium the slope of the full income opportunity curve, which equals the ratio of marginal prices, would equal the slope of an indifference curve, which equals the ratio of marginal utilities. Equilibrium occurs at p and p' for the opportunity curves S and S' respectively.

The rest of the paper is concerned with developing numerous empirical implications of this theory, starting with determinants of hours worked and concluding with an economic interpretation of various queueing systems. To simplify the presentation, it is assumed that the distinction between direct and indirect costs is equivalent to that between goods and time costs; in other words, the marginal forgone cost of the use of goods, c_i, is set equal to zero. The discussion would not be much changed, but would be more cumbersome were this not assumed.[17] Finally, until Section IV goods and time are assumed to be used in fixed proportions in producing commodities; that is, the coefficients b_i and t_i in equation (4.8) are treated as constants.

III Applications

(a) Hours of work

If the effects of various changes on the time used on consumption, T_c, could be determined their effects on hours worked, T_w, could be found residually from equation (4.7). This section considers, among other things, the effects of changes in income, earnings and market prices on T_c, and thus on T_w, using as the major tool of analysis differences among commodities in the importance of forgone earnings.

The relative marginal importance of forgone earnings is defined as

$$\alpha_i = \frac{l_i t_i}{p_i b_i + l_i t_i} \qquad (4.20)$$

The importance of forgone earnings would be greater the larger l_i and t_i, the forgone earnings per hour of time and the number of hours used per unit of Z_i respectively, while it would be smaller the larger p_i and b_i, the market price of goods and the number of goods used per unit of Z_i respectively. Similarly, the relative marginal importance of time is defined as

$$\gamma_i = \frac{t_i}{p_i b_i + l_i t_i} \qquad (4.21)$$

If full income increased solely because of an increase in V (other money income) there would simply be a parallel shift of the opportunity curve to the right with no change in relative commodity prices. The consumption of most commodities would have to increase; if all did, hours worked would decrease, for the total time spent on consumption must increase if the output of all commodities did, and by equation (4.7) the time spent at work is inversely related to that spent on consumption. Hours worked could increase only if relatively time intensive commodities, those with large γ, were sufficiently inferior.[18]

A uniform percentage increase in earnings for all allocations of time would increase the cost per hour used in consumption by the same percentage for all commodities.[19] The relative prices of different commodities would, however, change as long as forgone earnings were not equally important for all; in particular, the prices of commodities having relatively important forgone earnings would rise more. Now the fundamental theorem of demand theory states that a compensated change in relative prices would induce households to consume less of commodities rising in price. The figure shows the effect of a rise in earnings fully compensated by a decline in other income: the opportunity curve would be rotated clockwise through the initial position p if Z_1 were the more earnings-intensive commodity. In the figure the new equilibrium p' must be to the left and above p, or less Z_1 and more Z_2 would be consumed.

Therefore a compensated uniform rise in earnings would lead to a shift away from earnings-intensive commodities and towards goods-intensive ones. Since earnings and time intensiveness tend to be positively correlated,[20] consumption would be shifted from time-intensive commodities. A shift away from such commodities would, however, result in a reduction in the total time spent in consumption, and thus an increase in the time spent at work.[21]

The effect of an uncompensated increase in earnings on hours worked would depend on the relative strength of the substitution and income effects. The former would increase hours, the latter reduce them; which dominates cannot be determined *a priori*.

The conclusion that a pure rise in earnings increases and a pure rise in income reduces hours of work must sound very familiar, for they are traditional results of the well-known labour–leisure analysis. What, then, is the relation between our analysis, which treats all commodities symmetrically and stresses only their differences in relative time and earning intensities, and the usual analysis, which distinguishes a commodity having special properties called "leisure" from other more commonplace commodities? It is easily shown that the usual labour–leisure analysis can be looked upon as a special case of ours in which the cost of the commodity called leisure consists entirely of forgone earnings and the cost of other commodities entirely of goods.[22]

As a description of reality such an approach, of course, is not tenable, since virtually all activities use both time and goods. Perhaps it would be defended either as an analytically necessary or extremely insightful approximation to reality. Yet the usual substitution and income effects of a change in resources on hours worked have easily been derived from a more general analysis which stresses only that the relative importance of time varies among commodities. The rest of the paper tries to go further and demonstrate that the traditional approach, with its stress on the demand for "leisure," apparently has seriously impeded the development of insights about the economy, since the more direct and general approach presented here naturally leads to a variety of implications never yet obtained.

The two determinants of the importance of forgone earnings are the amount of time used per dollar of goods and the cost per unit of time. Reading a book, taking a haircut or commuting use more time per dollar of goods than eating dinner, frequenting a night-club or sending children to private summer camps. Other things the same, forgone earnings would be more important for the former set of commodities than the latter.

The importance of forgone earnings would be determined solely by time intensity only if the cost of time was the same for all commodities. Presumably, however, it varies considerably among commodities and at different periods. For example, the cost of time is often less on week-ends and in the evenings because many firms are closed then,[23] which explains why a famous liner intentionally includes a week-end in each voyage between the United States and Europe.[24] The cost of time would also tend to be less for commodities that contribute to productive effort, traditionally called "productive consumption." A considerable amount of sleep, food and even "play" fall under this heading. The opportunity cost of the time is less because these commodities indirectly contribute to earnings. Productive consumption has had a long but bandit-like existence in economic thought; our analysis does systematically incorporate it into household decision-making.

Although the formal specification of leisure in economic models has ignored expenditures on goods, cannot one argue that a more correct specification would simply associate leisure with relatively important forgone earnings? Most conceptions of leisure do imply that it is time intensive and does not indirectly contribute to earnings,[25] two of the important characteristics of earnings-intensive commodities. On the other hand, not all of what are usually considered leisure activities do have relatively important forgone earnings: night-clubbing is generally considered leisure, and yet, at least in its more expensive forms, has a large expenditure component. Conversely, some activities have relatively large forgone earnings and are not considered leisure: haircuts or child care are examples. Consequently, the distinction between earnings-intensive and other commodities corresponds only partly to the usual distinction between leisure and other commodities. Since it has been shown that the relative importance of forgone earnings rather than any concept of leisure is more relevant for economic analysis, less attention should be paid to the latter. Indeed, although the social philosopher might have to define precisely the concept of leisure,[26] the economist can reach all his traditional results as well as many more without introducing it at all!

Not only is it difficult to distinguish leisure from other non-work[27] but also even work from non-work. Is commuting work, non-work or both? How about a business lunch, a good diet or relaxation? Indeed, the notion of productive consumption was introduced precisely to cover those commodities that contribute to work as well as to consumption. Cannot pure work then be considered simply as a limiting commodity of such joint commodities in which the contribution to consumption was nil? Similarly, pure consumption would be a limiting commodity in the opposite direction in which the contribution to work was nil, and intermediate commodities would contribute to both consumption and work. The more important the contribution to work relative to consumption, the smaller would tend to be the relative importance of forgone earnings. Consequently, the effects of changes in earnings, other income, etc., on hours worked then become assimiliated to and essentially a special case of their effects on the consumption of less earnings-intensive commodities. For example, a pure rise in earnings would reduce the relative price, and thus increase the time spent on these commodities, *including the time spent at work;* similarly, for changes in income and other variables. The generalisation wrought by our approach is even greater than may have appeared at first.

Before concluding this section a few other relevant implications of our theory might be briefly mentioned. Just as a (compensated) rise in earnings would increase the prices of commodities with relatively large forgone earnings, induce a substitution away from them and increase the hours worked, so a (compensated) fall in market prices would also induce a substitution away from them and increase the hours worked: the effects of changes in direct and indirect costs are symmetrical. Indeed, Owen presents some evidence indicating that hours of work in the United States fell somewhat more in the first thirty years of this century than in the second thirty years, not because wages rose more during the first period, but because the market prices of recreation commodities fell more then.[28]

A well-known result of the traditional labour – leisure approach is that a rise in the income tax induces at least a substitution effect away from work and towards "leisure." Our approach reaches the same result only via a substitution towards time-intensive consumption rather than leisure. A simple additional implication of our approach, however, is that if a rise in the income tax were combined with an appropriate excise on the goods used in time-intensive commodities or subsidy to the goods used in other commodities there need be no change in full relative prices, and thus no substitution away from work. The traditional approach has recently reached the same conclusion, although in a much more involved way.[29]

There is no exception in the traditional approach to the rule that a pure rise in earnings would not induce a decrease in hours worked. An exception does occur in ours, for if the time and earnings intensities (i.e., $l_i t_i$ and t_i) were negatively correlated a pure rise in earnings would induce a substitution towards time-intensive commodities, and thus away from work.[30] Although this exception does illustrate the greater power of our approach, there is no reason to believe that it is any more important empirically than the exception to the rule on income effects.

(b) The productivity of time

Most of the large secular increase in earnings, which stimulated the development of the labour – leisure analysis, resulted from an increase in the productivity of working time due to the growth in human and physical capital, technological progress and other factors. Since a rise in earnings resulting from an increase in productivity has both income and substitution effects, the secular decline in hours worked appeared to be evidence that the income effect was sufficiently strong to swamp the substitution effect.

The secular growth in capital and technology also improved the productivity of consumption time: supermarkets, automobiles, sleeping pills, safety and electric razors, and telephones are a few familiar and important examples of such developments. An improvement in the productivity of consumption time would change relative commodity prices and increase full income, which in turn would produce substitution and income effects. The interesting point is that a very different interpretation of the observed decline in hours of work is suggested because these effects are precisely the opposite of those produced by improvements in the productivity of working time.

Assume a uniform increase only in the productivity of consumption time, which is taken to mean a decline in all t_i, time required to produce a unit of Z_i, by a common percentage. The relative prices of commodities with large forgone earnings would fall, and substitution would be induced towards these and away from other commodities, causing hours of work also to fall. Since the increase in productivity would also produce an income effect,[31] the demand for commodities would increase, which, in turn, would induce an increased demand for goods. But since the productivity of working time is assumed not to change, more goods could be obtained only by an increase in work. That is, the higher real income resulting from an advance in the productivity of consumption time would cause hours of work to *increase*.

Consequently, an emphasis on the secular increase in the productivity of consumption time would lead to a very different interpretation of the secular decline in hours worked. Instead of claiming that a powerful income effect swamped a weaker substitution effect, the claim would have to be that a powerful substitution effect swamped a weaker income effect.

Of course, the productivity of both working and consumption time increased secularly, and the true interpretation is somewhere between these extremes. If both increased at the same rate there would be no change in relative prices, and thus no substitution effect, because the rise in l_i induced by one would exactly offset the decline in t_i induced by the other, marginal forgone earnings ($l_i t_i$) remaining unchanged. Although the income effects would tend to offset each other too, they would do so completely only if the income elasticity of demand for time-intensive commodities was equal to unity. Hours worked would decline if it was above and increase if it was below unity.[32] Since these commodities have probably on the whole been luxuries, such an increase in income would tend to reduce hours worked.

The productivity of working time has probably advanced more than that of consumption time, if only because of familiar reasons associated with the division of labour and economies of scale.[33] Consequently, there probably has been the traditional substitution effect towards and income effect away from work, as well as an income effect away from work because time-intensive commodities were luxuries. The secular decline in hours worked would only imply therefore that the combined income effects swamped the substitution effect, not that the income effect of an advance in the productivity of working time alone swamped its substitution effect.

Cross-sectionally, the hours worked of males have generally declined less as incomes increased than they have over time. Some of the difference between these relations is explained by the distinction between relevant and reported incomes, or by interdependencies among the hours worked by different employees;[34] some is probably also explained by the distinction between working and consumption productivity. There is a presumption that persons distinguished cross-sectionally by money incomes or earnings differ more in working than consumption productivity because they are essentially distinguished by the former. This argument does not apply to time series because persons are distinguished there by calendar time, which in principle is neutral between these productivities. Consequently, the traditional substitution effect towards work is apt to be greater cross-sectionally, which would help to explain why the relation between the income and hours worked of men is less negatively sloped there, and be additional evidence that the substitution effect for men is not weak.[35]

Productivity in the service sector in the United States appears to have advanced more slowly, at least since 1929, than productivity in the goods sector.[36] Service industries like retailing, transportation, education and health, use a good deal of the time of households that never enter into input, output and price series, or therefore into measures of productivity. Incorporation of such time into the series and consideration of changes in its productivity would contribute, I believe, to an understanding of the apparent differences in productivity advance between these sectors.

An excellent example can be found in a recent study of productivity trends in the barbering industry in the United States.[37] Conventional productivity measures show relatively little advance in barbers' shops since 1929, yet a revolution has occurred in the activities performed by these shops. In the 1920s shaves still accounted for an important part of their sales, but declined to a negligible part by the 1950s because of the spread of home safety and electric razors. Instead of travelling to a shop, waiting in line, receiving a shave and continuing to another destination, men now shave themselves at home, saving travelling, waiting and even some shaving time. This considerable advance in the productivity of shaving nowhere enters measures for barbers' shops. If, however, a productivity measure for general barbering activities, including shaving, was constructed, I suspect that it would show an advance since 1929 comparable to most goods.[38]

(c) Income elasticities

Income elasticities of demand are often estimated cross-sectionally from the behaviour of families or other units with different incomes. When these units buy in the same market-place it is natural to assume that they face the same prices of goods. If, however, incomes differ because earnings do, and cross-sectional income differences are usually dominated by earnings differences, commodities prices would differ systematically. All commodities prices would be higher to higher-income units because their forgone earnings would be higher (which means, incidentally, that differences in real income would be less than those in money income), and the prices of earnings-intensive commodities would be unusually so.

Cross-sectional relations between consumption and income would not therefore measure the effect of income alone, because they would be affected by differences in relative prices as well as in incomes.[39] The effect of income would be underestimated for earnings-intensive and overestimated for other commodities, because the higher relative prices of the former would cause a substitution away from them and towards the latter. Accordingly, the income elasticities of demand for "leisure," unproductive and time-intensive commodities would be under-stated, and for "work," productive and other goods-intensive commodities over-stated by cross-sectional estimates. Low apparent income elasticities of earnings-intensive commodities and high apparent elasticities of other commodities may simply be illusions resulting from substitution effects.[40]

Moreover, according to our theory demand depends also on the importance of earnings as a source of income. For if total income were held constant an increase in earnings would create only substitution effects: away from earnings-intensive and towards goods-intensive commodities. So one unusual implication of the analysis that can and should be tested with available budget data is that the source of income may have a significant effect on consumption patterns. An important special case is found in comparisons of the consumption of employed and unemployed workers. Unemployed workers not only have lower incomes but also lower forgone costs, and thus lower relative prices of time and other earnings-intensive commodities. The propensity of unemployed workers to go fishing, watch television, attend school and so on are simply vivid illustrations of the incentives they have to substitute such commodities for others.

One interesting application of the analysis is to the relation between family size and income.[41] The traditional view, based usually on simple correlations, has been that an increase in income leads to a reduction in the number of children per family. If, however, birth-control knowledge and other variables were held constant economic theory suggests a positive relation between family size and income, and therefore that the traditional negative correlation resulted from positive correlations between income, knowledge and some other variables. The data I put together supported this interpretation, as did those found in several subsequent studies.[42]

Although positive, the elasticity of family size with respect to income is apparently quite low, even when birth-control knowledge is held constant. Some persons have interpreted this (and other evidence) to indicate that family-size formation cannot usefully be fitted into traditional economic analysis.[43] It was pointed out, however, that the small elasticity found for children is not so inconsistent with what is found for goods as soon as quantity and quality income elasticities are distinguished.[44] Increased expenditures on many goods largely take the form of increased quality – expenditure per pound, per car, etc. – and the increase in quantity is modest. Similarly, increased expenditures on children largely take the form of increased expenditures per child, while the increase in number of children is very modest.

Nevertheless, the elasticity of demand for number of children does seem somewhat smaller than the quantity elasticities found for many goods. Perhaps the explanation is simply the shape of indifference curves; one other factor that may be more important, however, is the increase in forgone costs with income.[45] Child care would seem to be a time-intensive activity that is not "productive" (in terms of earnings) and uses many hours that could be used at work. Consequently, it would be an earnings-intensive activity, and our analysis predicts that its relative price would be higher to higher-income families.[46] There is already some evidence suggesting that the positive relation between forgone costs and income explains why the apparent quantity income elasticity of demand for children is relatively small. Mincer found that cross-sectional differences in the forgone price of children have an important effect on the number of children.[47]

(d) Transportation

Transportation is one of the few activities where the cost of time has been explicitly incorporated into economic discussions. In most benefit-cost evaluations of new transportation networks the value of the savings in transportation time has tended to overshadow other benefits.[48] The importance of the value placed on time has encouraged experiment with different methods of determination: from the simple view that the value of an hour equals average hourly earnings to sophisticated considerations of the distinction between standard and overtime hours, the internal and external margins, etc.

The transport field offers considerable opportunity to estimate the marginal productivity or value of time from actual behaviour. One could, for example, relate the ratio of the number of persons travelling by aeroplane to those travelling by slower mediums to the distance travelled (and, of course, also to market prices and incomes). Since relatively more people use faster mediums for longer distances, presumably largely because of the greater importance of the saving in time, one should be able to estimate a marginal value of time from the relation between medium and distance travelled.[49]

Another transportation problem extensively studied is the length and mode of commuting to work.[50] It is usually assumed that direct commuting costs, such as train fare, vary positively and that living costs, such as space, vary negatively with the distance commuted. These assumptions alone would imply that a rise in incomes would result in longer commutes as long as space ("housing") were a superior good.[51]

A rise in income resulting at least in part from a rise in earnings would, however, increase the cost of commuting a given distance because the forgone value of the time involved would increase. This increase in commuting costs would discourage commuting in the same way that the increased demand for space would encourage it. The outcome depends on the relative strengths of these conflicting forces: one can show with a few assumptions that the distance commuted would increase as income increased if, and only if, space had an income elasticity greater than unity.

For let Z_1 refer to the commuting commodity, Z_2 to other commodities, and let

$$Z_1 = f_1(x, t) \tag{4.22}$$

where t is the time spent commuting and x is the quantity of space used. Commuting costs are assumed to have the simple form $a + l_1 t$, where a is a constant and l_1 is the marginal forgone cost per hour spent commuting. In other words, the cost of time is the only variable commuting cost. The cost per unit of space is $p(t)$, where by assumption $p' < 0$. The problem is to maximise the utility function

$$U = U(x, t, Z_2) \tag{4.23}$$

subject to the resource constraint

$$a + l_1 t + px + h(Z_2) = S \tag{4.24}$$

If it were assumed that $U_t = 0$ – commuting was neither enjoyable nor irksome – the main equilibrium condition would reduce to

$$l_1 + p'x = 0 \tag{4.25}$$ [52]

which would be the equilibrium condition if households simply attempt to minimise the sum of transportation and space costs.[53] If $l_1 = kS$, where k is a constant, the effect of a change in full income on the time spent commuting can be found by differentiating equation (4.25) to be

$$\frac{\partial t}{\partial S} = \frac{k(\epsilon_x - 1)}{p''x} \tag{4.26}$$

where ϵ_x is the income elasticity of demand for space. Since stability requires that $p'' > 0$, an increase in income increases the time spent commuting if, and only if, $\epsilon_x > 1$.

In metropolitan areas of the United States higher-income families tend to live further from the central city,[54] which contradicts our analysis if one accepts the traditional view that the income elasticity of demand for housing is less than unity. In a definitive study of the demand for housing in the United States, however, Margaret Reid found income elasticities greater than unity.[55] Moreover, the analysis of distance commuted incorporates only a few dimensions of the demand for housing; principally the demand for outdoor space. The evidence on distances commuted would then only imply that outdoor space is a "luxury," which is rather plausible[56] and not even inconsistent with the traditional view about the total elasticity of demand for housing.

(e) The division of labour within families

Space is too limited to do more than summarise the main implications of the theory concerning the division of labour among members of the same household. Instead of simply allocating time efficiently among commodities, multi-person households also allocate the time of different members. Members who are relatively more efficient at market activities would use less of their time at consumption activities than would other members. Moreover, an increase in the relative market efficiency of any member would effect a reallocation of the time of all other members towards consumption activities in order to permit the former to spend more time at market activities. In short, the allocation of the time of any member is greatly influenced by the opportunities open to other members.

IV Substitution between time and goods

Although time and goods have been assumed to be used in fixed proportions in producing commodities, substitution could take place because different commodities used them in different proportions. The assumption of fixed proportions is now dropped in order to include many additional implications of the theory.

It is well known from the theory of variable proportions that households would minimise costs by setting the ratio of the marginal product of goods to that of time equal to the ratio of their marginal costs.[57] A rise in the cost of time relative to goods would induce a reduction in the amount of time and an increase in the amount of goods used per unit of each commodity. Thus, not only would a rise in earnings induce a substitution away from earnings-intensive commodities but also a substitution away from time and towards goods in the production of each commodity. Only the first is (implicitly) recognised in the labour – leisure analysis, although the second may well be of considerable importance. It increases one's confidence that the substitution effect of a rise in earnings is more important than is commonly believed.

The change in the input coefficients of time and goods resulting from a change in their relative costs is defined by the elasticity of substitution between them, which presumably varies from commodity to commodity. The only empirical study of this elasticity assumes that recreation goods and "leisure" time are used to produce a recreation commodity.[58] Definite evidence of substitution is found, since the ratio of leisure time to recreation goods is negatively related to the ratio of their prices. The elasticity of substitution appears to be less than unity, however, since the share of leisure in total factor costs is apparently positively related to its relative price.

The incentive to economise on time as its relative cost increases goes a long way towards explaining certain broad aspects of behaviour that have puzzled and often disturbed observers of contemporary life. Since hours worked have declined secularly in most advanced countries, and so-called "leisure" has presumably increased, a natural expectation has been that "free" time would become more abundant, and be used more "leisurely" and "luxuriously." Yet, if anything, time is used more carefully to-day than a century ago.[59] If there was a secular increase in the productivity of working time relative to consumption time (see Section III (b)) there would be an increasing incentive to economise on the latter because of its greater expense (our theory emphatically cautions against calling such time "free"). Not surprisingly, therefore, it is now kept track of and used more carefully than in the past.

Americans are supposed to be much more wasteful of food and other goods than persons in poorer countries, and much more conscious of time: they keep track of it continuously, make (and keep) appointments for specific minutes, rush about more, cook steaks and chops rather than time-consuming stews and so forth.[60] They are simultaneously supposed to be wasteful – of material goods – and overly economical – of immaterial time. Yet both allegations may be correct and not simply indicative of a strange American temperament because the market value of time is higher relative to the price of goods there than elsewhere. That is, the tendency to be economical about time and lavish about goods may be no paradox, but in part simply a reaction to a difference in relative costs.

The substitution towards goods induced by an increase in the relative cost of time would often include a substitution towards more expensive goods. For example, an increase in the value of a mother's time may induce her to enter the labour force and spend less time cooking by using pre-cooked foods and less time on child-care by using nurseries, camps or baby-sitters. Or barbers' shops in wealthier sections of town charge more and provide quicker service than those in poorer sections, because waiting by barbers is substituted for waiting by customers. These examples illustrate that a change in the quality of goods[61] resulting from a change in the relative cost of goods may simply reflect a change in the methods used to produce given commodities, and not any corresponding change in *their* quality.

Consequently, a rise in income due to a rise in earnings would increase the quality of goods purchased not only because of the effect of income on quality but also because of a substitution of goods for time; a rise in income due to a rise in property income would not cause any substitution, and should have less effect on the quality of goods. Put more dramatically, with total income held constant, a rise in earnings should increase while a rise in property income should decrease the quality chosen. Once again, the composition of income is important and provides testable implications of the theory.

One analytically interesting application of these conclusions is to the recent study by Margaret Reid of the substitution between store-bought and home-delivered milk.[62] According to our approach, the cost of inputs into the commodity "milk consumption at home" is either the sum of the price of milk in the store and the forgone value of the time used to carry it home or simply the price of delivered milk. A reduction in the price of store relative to delivered milk, the value of time remaining constant, would reduce the cost of the first method relatively to the second, and shift production towards the first. For the same reason a reduction in the value of time, market prices of milk remaining constant, would also shift production towards the first method.

Reid's finding of a very large negative relation between the ratio of store to delivered milk and the ratio of their prices, income and some other variables held constant, would be evidence both that milk costs are a large part of total production costs and that there is easy substitution between these alternative methods of production. The large, but not quite as large, negative relation with income simply confirms the easy substitution between methods, and indicates that the cost of time is less important than the cost of milk. In other words, instead of conveying separate information, her price and income elasticities both measure substitution between the two methods of producing the same commodity, and are consistent and plausible.

The importance of forgone earnings and the substitution between time and goods may be quite relevant in interpreting observed price elasticities. A given percentage increase in the price of goods would be less of an increase in commodity prices the more important forgone earnings are. Consequently, even if all commodities had the same true price elasticity, those having relatively important forgone earnings would show lower apparent elasticities in the typical analysis that relates quantities and prices of goods alone.

The importance of forgone earnings differs not only among commodities but also among households for a given commodity because of differences in income. Its importance would change in the same or opposite direction as income, depending on whether the elasticity of substitution between time and goods was less or greater than unity. Thus, even when the true price elasticity of a commodity did not vary with income, the observed price elasticity of goods would be negatively or positively related to income as the elasticity of substitution was less or greater than unity.

The importance of substitution between time and goods can be illustrated in a still different way. Suppose, for simplicity, that only good x and no time was initially required to produce commodity Z. A price ceiling is placed on x, it nominally becomes a free good, and the production of x is subsidised sufficiently to maintain the same output. The increased quantity of x and Z demanded due to the decline in the price of x has to be rationed because the output of x has not increased. Suppose that the system of rationing made the quantity obtained a positive function of the time and effort expended. For example, the quantity of price-controlled bread or medical attention obtained might depend on the time spent in a queue outside a bakery or in a physician's office. Or if an appointment system were used a literal queue would be replaced by a figurative one, in which the waiting was done at "home," as in the Broadway theatre, admissions to hospitals or air travel during peak seasons. Again, even in depressed times the likelihood of obtaining a job is positively related to the time put into job hunting.

Although x became nominally a free good, Z would not be free, because the time now required as an input into Z is not free. The demand for Z would be greater than the supply (fixed by assumption) if the cost of this time was less than the equilibrium price of Z before the price control. The scrambling by households for the limited supply would increase the time required to get a unit of Z, and thus its cost. Both would continue to increase until the average cost of time tended to the equilibrium price before price control. At that point equilibrium would be achieved because the supply and demand for Z would be equal.

Equilibrium would take different forms depending on the method of rationing. With a literal "first come first served" system the size of the queue (say outside the bakery or in the doctor's office) would grow until the expected cost of standing in line discouraged any excess demand;[63] with the figurative queues of appointment systems, the "waiting" time (say to see a play) would grow until demand was sufficiently curtailed. If the system of rationing was less formal, as in the labour market during recessions, the expected time required to ferret out a scarce job would grow until the demand for jobs was curtailed to the limited supply.

Therefore, price control of x combined with a subsidy that kept its amount constant would not change the average private equilibrium price of Z,[64] but would substitute indirect time costs for direct goods costs.[65] Since, however, indirect costs are positively related to income, the price of Z would be raised to higher-income persons and reduced to lower-income ones, thereby redistributing consumption from the former to the latter. That is, women, the poor, children, the unemployed, etc., would be more willing to spend their time in a queue or otherwise ferreting out rationed goods than would high-earning males.

V Summary and conclusions

This paper has presented a theory of the allocation of time between different activities. At the heart of the theory is an assumption that households are producers as well as consumers; they produce commodities by combining inputs of goods and time according to the cost-minimisation rules of the traditional theory of the firm. Commodities are produced in quantities determined by maximising a utility function of the commodity set subject to prices and a constraint on resources. Resources are measured by what is called full income, which is the sum of money income and that forgone or "lost" by the use of time and goods to obtain utility, while commodity prices are measured by the sum of the costs of their goods and time inputs.

The effect of changes in earnings, other income, goods prices and the productivity of working and consumption time on the allocation of time and the commodity set produced has been analysed. For example, a rise in earnings, compensated by a decline in other income so that full income would be unchanged, would induce a decline in the amount of time used at consumption activities, because time would become more expensive. Partly goods would be substituted for the more expensive time in the production of each commodity, and partly goods-intensive commodities would be substituted for the more expensive time-intensive ones. Both substitutions require less time to be used at consumption, and permit more to be used at work. Since the reallocation of time involves simultaneously a reallocation of goods and commodities, all three decisions become intimately related.

The theory has many interesting and even novel interpretations of, and implications about, empirical phenomena. A few will be summarised here.

A traditional "economic" interpretation of the secular decline in hours worked has stressed the growth in productivity of working time and the resulting income and substitution effects, with the former supposedly dominating. Ours stresses that the substitution effects of the growth in productivity of working and consumption time tended to offset each other, and that hours worked declined secularly primarily because time-intensive commodities have been luxuries. A contributing influence has been the secular decline in the relative prices of goods used in time-intensive commodities.

Since an increase in income partly due to an increase in earnings would raise the relative cost of time and of time-intensive commodities, traditional cross-sectional estimates of income elasticities do not hold either factor or commodity prices constant. Consequently, they would, among other things, be biased downward for time-intensive commodities, and give a misleading impression of the effect of income on the quality of commodities consumed. The composition of income also affects demand, for an increase in earnings, total income held constant, would shift demand away from time-intensive commodities and input combinations.

Rough estimates suggest that forgone earnings are quantitatively important and therefore that full income is substantially above money income. Since forgone earnings are primarily determined by the use of time, considerably more attention should be paid to its efficiency and allocation. In particular, agencies that collect information on the expenditure of money income might simultaneously collect information on the "expenditure" of time. The resulting time budgets, which have not been seriously investigated in most countries, including the United States and Great Britain, should be integrated with the money budgets in order to give a more accurate picture of the size and allocation of full income.

Notes

1 See T. W. Schultz, "The Formation of Human Capital by Education," *Journal of Political Economy* (December 1960), and my *Human Capital* (Columbia University Press for the N.B.E.R., 1964), Chapter IV. I argue there that the importance of forgone earnings can be directly seen, e.g., from the

failure of free tuition to eliminate impediments to college attendance or the increased enrolments that sometimes occur in depressed areas or time periods.

2 On the cause of the secular trend towards an increased school year see my comments, *ibid.*, p. 103.

3 See his "Market Prices, Opportunity Costs, and Income Effects," in *Measurement in Economics: Studies in Mathematical Economics and Econometrics in Memory of Yehuda Grunfeld* (Stanford University Press, 1963). In his well-known earlier study Mincer considered the allocation of married women between "housework" and labour force participation. (See his "Labor Force Participation of Married Women," in *Aspects of Labor Economics* (Princeton University Press, 1962).)

4 See his *The Supply of Labor and the Demand for Recreation* (unpublished Ph.D. dissertation, Columbia University, 1964).

5 See his *Economic Analysis and African Response to Price* (unpublished Ph.D. dissertation, Columbia University, 1963).

6 Let me emphasise, however, that I alone am responsible for any errors.

   I would also like to express my appreciation for the comments received when presenting these ideas to seminars at the Universities of California (Los Angeles), Chicago, Pittsburgh, Rochester and Yale, and to a session at the 1963 Meetings of the Econometric Society. Extremely helpful comments on an earlier draft were provided by Milton Friedman and by Gregory C. Chow; the latter also assisted in the mathematical formulation. Linda Kee provided useful research assistance. My research was partially supported by the IBM Corporation.

7 There are several empirical as well as conceptual advantages in assuming that households combine goods and time to produce commodities instead of simply assuming that the amount of time used at an activity is a direct function of the amount of goods consumed. For example, a change in the cost of goods relative to time could cause a significant substitution away from the one rising in relative cost. This, as well as other applications, are treated in the following sections.

8 If a good or time period was used in producing several commodities I assume that these "joint costs" could be fully and uniquely allocated among the commodities. The problems here are no different from those usually arising in the analysis of multi-product firms.

9 See, e.g., A. K. Cairncross, "Economic Schizophrenia," *Scottish Journal of Political Economy* (February 1958).

10 The dependency among constraints distinguishes this problem from many other multiple-constraint situations in economic analysis, such as those arising in the usual theory of rationing (see J. Tobin, "A Survey of the Theory of Rationing," *Econometrica* (October, 1952)). Rationing would reduce to a formally identical single-constraint situation if rations were saleable and fully convertible into money income.

11 See my *Human Capital, op. cit.*

12 This term emerged from a conversation with Milton Friedman.

13 Any utility received would only be an incidental by-product of the pursuit of money income. Perhaps this explains why utility analysis was not clearly formulated and accepted until economic development had raised incomes well above the subsistence level.

14 Full income is achieved by maximising the earnings function

$$W = W(Z_1, \ldots Z_m) \tag{1'}$$

subject to the expenditure constraint in equation (4.6), to the inequality

$$\sum_1^m T_1 \leq T \tag{2'}$$

and to the restrictions in (4.8). I assume for simplicity that the amount of each dimension of time used in producing commodities is less than the total available, so that (2') can be ignored; it is not difficult to incorporate this constraint. Maximising (1') subject to (4.6) and (4.8) yields the following conditions

$$\frac{\partial W}{\partial Z_i} = \frac{p_i b_i \sigma}{1 + \sigma} \tag{3'}$$

where σ is the marginal productivity of money income. Since the loss function $L = (S - V) - W$, the equilibrium conditions to minimise the loss is the same as (3′) except for a change in sign.

15 Households maximise their utility subject only to the single total resource constraint given by (4.14), for once the full income constraint is satisfied, there is no other restriction on the set of Z_i that can be chosen. By introducing the concept of full income the problem of maximising utility subject to the time and goods constraints is solved in two stages: first, full income is determined from the goods and time constraints, and then utility is maximised subject only to the constraint imposed by full income.

16 It can easily be shown that the equilibrium conditions of (4.16) are in fact precisely the same as those following in general from equation (4.10).

17 Elsewhere I have discussed some effects of the allocation of goods on productivity (see my "Investment in Human Capital: A Theoretical Analysis," *Journal of Political Economy*, special supplement (October 1962), Section 2); essentially the same discussion can be found in *Human Capital, op. cit.*, Chapter II.

18 The problem is: under what conditions would

$$\frac{-\partial T_w}{\partial V} = \frac{\partial T_e}{\partial V} = \sum_i t_i \frac{\partial Z_i}{\partial V} < 0 \tag{1′}$$

$$\text{when } \sum (p_i b_i + l_i t_i) \frac{\partial Z_i}{\partial V} = 1 \tag{2′}$$

If the analysis were limited to a two-commodity world where Z_1 was more time intensive, then it can easily be shown that (1′) would hold if, and only if,

$$\frac{\partial Z_1}{\partial V} < \frac{-\gamma_2}{(\gamma_1 - \gamma_2)(p_1 b_1 + l_1 t_1)} < 0 \tag{3′}$$

19 By a uniform change of β is meant

$$W_1 = (1 + \beta) W_0 (Z_1, \ldots Z_n)$$

where W_0 represents the earnings function before the change and W_1 represents it afterwards. Since the loss function is defined as

$$L = S - W - V$$
$$= W(\hat{Z}) - W(Z),$$

then $L_1 = W_1(\hat{Z}) - W_1(Z)$
$$= (1 + \beta)[W_0(\hat{Z}) - W_0(Z)] = (1 + \beta) L_0$$

Consequently, all opportunities costs also change by β.

20 According to the definitions of earning and time intensity in equations (4.20) and (4.21), they would be positively correlated unless l_i and t_i were sufficiently negatively correlated. See the further discussion later on.

21 Let it be stressed that this conclusion usually holds, even when households are irrational; sophisticated calculations about the value of time at work or in consumption, or substantial knowledge about the amount of time used by different commodities is not required. Changes in the hours of work, even of non-maximising, impulsive, habitual, etc., households would tend to be positively related to compensated changes in earnings because demand curves tend to be negatively inclined even for such households (see G. S. Becker, "Irrational Behavior and Economic Theory," *Journal of Political Economy* (February 1962)).

22 Suppose there were two commodities Z_1 and Z_2, where the cost of Z_1 depended only on the cost of market goods, while the cost of Z_2, depended only on the cost of time. The goods-budget constraint would then simply be

$$p_1 b_1 Z_1 = I = V + T_w \bar{w}$$

and the constraint on time would be

$$t_2 Z_2 = T - T_w$$

This is essentially the algebra of the analysis presented by Henderson and Quandt, and their treatment is representative. They call Z_2 "leisure," and Z_1 an average of different commodities. Their equilibrium condition that the rate of substitution between goods and leisure equals the real wage-rate is just a special case of our equation (4.19) (see *Microeconomic Theory* (McGraw-Hill, 1958), p. 23).

23 For workers receiving premium pay on the week-ends and in the evenings, however, the cost of time may be considerably greater then.

24 See the advertisement by United States Lines in various issues of the *New Yorker* magazine: "The S.S. *United States* regularly includes a week-end in its 5 days to Europe, saving [economic] time for businessmen" (my insertion).

25 For example, *Webster's Collegiate Dictionary* defines leisurely as "characterized by leisure, taking *abundant time*" (my italics); or S. de Grazia, in his recent *Of Time, Work and Leisure*, says, "Leisure is a state of being in which activity is performed for its own sake or as its own end" (New York: The Twentieth Century Fund, 1962, p. 15).

26 S. de Grazia has recently entertainingly shown the many difficulties in even reaching a reliable definition, and *a fortiori*, in quantitatively estimating the amount of leisure. See *ibid.*, Chapters III and IV; also see W. Moore, *Man, Time and Society* (New York: Wiley, 1963), Chapter II; J. N. Morgan, M. H. David, W. J. Cohen and H. E. Brazer, *Income and Welfare in the United States* (New York: McGraw-Hill, 1962), p. 322, and Owen, *op. cit.,* Chapter II.

27 Sometimes true leisure is defined as the amount of discretionary time available (see Moore, *op. cit.*, p. 18). It is always difficult to attach a rigorous meaning to the word "discretionary" when referring to economic resources. One might say that in the short run consumption time is and working time is not discretionary, because the latter is partially subject to the authoritarian control of employers. (Even this distinction would vanish if households gave certain firms authoritarian control over their consumption time; see the discussion in Section II.) In the long run this definition of discretionary time is suspect too because the availability of alternative sources of employment would make working time also discretionary.

28 See *op. cit.*, Chapter VIII. Recreation commodities presumably have relatively large forgone earnings.

29 See W. J. Corbett and D. C. Hague, "Complementarity and the Excess Burden of Taxation," *Review of Economic Studies*, Vol. XXI (1953–54); also A. C. Harberger, "Taxation, Resource Allocation and Welfare," in the *Role of Direct and Indirect Taxes in the Federal Revenue System* (Princeton University Press, 1964).

30 The effect on earnings is more difficult to determine because, by assumption, time intensive commodities have smaller costs per unit time than other commodities. A shift towards the former would, therefore, raise hourly earnings, which would partially and perhaps more than entirely offset the reduction in hours worked. Incidentally, this illustrates how the productivity of hours worked is influenced by the consumption set chosen.

31 Full money income would be unaffected if it were achieved by using all time at pure work activities. If other uses of time were also required it would tend to increase. Even if full money income were unaffected, however, full real income would increase because prices of the Z_i would fall.

32 So the "Knight" view that an increase in income would increase "leisure" is not necessarily true, even if leisure were a superior good and even aside from Robbins' emphasis on the substitution effect (see L. Robbins, "On the Elasticity of Demand for Income in Terms of Effort," *Economica* (June 1930)).

33 Wesley Mitchell's justly famous essay "The Backward Art of Spending Money" spells out some of these reasons (see the first essay in the collection, *The Backward Art of Spending Money and Other Essays* (New York: McGraw-Hill, 1932)).

34 A. Finnegan does find steeper cross-sectional relations when the average incomes and hours of different occupations are used (*see* his "A Cross-Sectional Analysis of Hours of Work," *Journal of Political Economy* (October, 1962)).

35 Note that Mincer has found a very strong substitution effect for women (see his "Labor Force Participation of Married Women," *op. cit.*).

36 See the essay by Victor Fuchs, "Productivity Trends in the Goods and Service Sectors, 1929–61: A Preliminary Survey," N.B.E.R. Occasional Paper, October 1964.

37 See J. Wilburn, "Productivity Trends in Barber and Beauty Shops," mimeographed report, N.B.E.R., September 1964.

38 The movement of shaving from barbers' shops to households illustrates how and why even in urban areas households have become "small factories." Under the impetus of a general growth in the value of time they have been encouraged to find ways of saving on travelling and waiting time by performing more activities themselves.

39 More appropriate income elasticities for several commodities are estimated in Mincer, "Market Prices...," *op. cit.*

40 In this connection note that cross-sectional data are often preferred to time-series data in estimating income elasticities precisely because they are supposed to be largely free of co-linearity between prices and incomes (see, e.g., J. Tobin, "A Statistical Demand Function for Food in the U.S.A.," *Journal of the Royal Statistical Society*, Series A (1950)).

41 Biases in cross-sectional estimates of the demand for work and leisure were considered in the last section.

42 See G. S. Becker, "An Economic Analysis of Fertility," *Demographic and Economic Change in Developed Countries* (N.B.E.R. Conference Volume, 1960); R. A. Easterlin, "The American Baby Boom in Historical Perspective," *American Economic Review* (December 1961); I. Adelman, "An Econometric Analysis of Population Growth," *American Economic Review* (June 1963); R. Weintraub, "The Birth Rate and Economic Development: An Empirical Study," *Econometrica* (October 1962); Morris Silver, *Birth Rates, Marriages, and Business Cycles* (unpublished Ph.D. dissertation, Columbia University, 1964); and several other studies; for an apparent exception, see the note by D. Freedman, "The Relation of Economic Status to Fertility," *American Economic Review* (June 1963).

43 See, for example, Duesenberry's comment on Becker, *op. cit.*

44 See Becker, *op. cit.*

45 In *Ibid.*, p. 214 fn. 8, the relation between forgone costs and income was mentioned but not elaborated.

46 Other arguments suggesting that higher-income families face a higher price of children have generally confused price with quality (see *ibid.*, pp. 214–15).

47 See Mincer, "Market Prices...," *op. cit.* He measures the price of children by the wife's potential wage-rate, and fits regressions to various cross-sectional data, where number of children is the dependent variable, and family income and the wife's potential wage-rate are among the independent variables.

48 See, for example, H. Mohring, "Land Values and the Measurement of Highway Benefits," *Journal of Political Economy* (June 1961).

49 The only quantitative estimate of the marginal value of time that I am familiar with uses the relation between the value of land and its commuting distance from employment (see *ibid.*). With many assumptions I have estimated the marginal value of time of those commuting at about 40 percent of their average hourly earnings. It is not clear whether this value is so low because of errors in these assumptions or because of severe kinks in the supply and demand functions for hours of work.

50 See L. N. Moses and H. F. Williamson, "Value of Tiine, Choice of Mode, and the Subsidy Issue in Urban Transportation," *Journal of Political Economy* (June 1963), R. Muth, "Economic Change and Rural – Urban Conversion," *Econometrica* (January 1961), and J. F. Kain, *Commuting and the Residential Decisions of Chicago and Detroit Central Business District Workers* (April 1963).

51 See Muth, *op. cit.*

52 If $U_t \neq 0$, the main equilibrium condition would be

$$\frac{U_t}{U_x} = \frac{l_1 + p'x}{p}$$

Probably the most plausible assumption is that $U_t < 0$, which would imply that $l_1 + p'x < 0$.

53 See Kain, *op. cit.,* pp. 6–12.

54 For a discussion, including many qualifications, of this proposition see L. F. Schnore, "The Socio-Economic Status of Cities and Suburbs," *American Sociological Review* (February 1963).

55 See her *Housing and Income* (University of Chicago Press, 1962), p. 6 and *passim.*

56 According to Reid, the elasticity of demand for indoor space is less than unity (*ibid.,* Chapter 12). If her total elasticity is accepted this suggests that outdoor space has an elasticity exceeding unity.

57 The cost of producing a given amount of commodity Z_i would be minimised if

$$\frac{\partial f_i / \partial x_i}{\partial f_i / \partial T_i} = \frac{P_i}{\partial L / \partial T_i}$$

If utility were considered an indirect function of goods and time rather than simply a direct function of commodities the following conditions, among others, would be required to maximise utility:

$$\frac{\partial U / \partial x_i}{\partial U / \partial T_i} \equiv \frac{\partial Z_i / \partial x_i}{\partial Z_i / \partial T_i} = \frac{p_i}{\partial L / \partial T}$$

which are exactly the same conditions as above. The ratio of the marginal utility of x_i to that of T_i depends only on f_i, x_i and T_i, and is thus independent of other production functions, goods and time. In other words, the indirect utility function is what has been called "weakly separable" (see R. Muth, "Household Production and Consumer Demand Functions," unpublished manuscript).

58 See Owen, *op. cit.,* Chapter X.

59 See, for example, de Grazia, *op. cit.,* Chapter IV.

60 For a comparison of the American concept of time with others see Edward T. Hall, *The Silent Language* (New York: Doubleday, 1959), Chapter 9.

61 Quality is usually defined empirically by the amount spent per physical unit, such as pound of food, car or child. See especially S. J. Prais and H. Houthakker, *The Analysis of Family Budgets* (Cambridge, 1955); also my "An Economic Analysis of Fertility," *op. cit.*

62 See her "Consumer Response to the Relative Price of Store versus Delivered Milk," *Journal of Political Economy* (April 1963).

63 In queueing language the cost of waiting in line is a "discouragement" factor that stabilises the queueing scheme (see, for example, D. R. Cox and W. L. Smith, *Queues* (New York: Wiley 1961)).

64 The social price, on the other hand, would double, for it is the sum of private indirect costs and subsidised direct costs.

65 Time costs can be criticised from a Pareto optimality point of view because they often result in external diseconomies: e.g., a person joining a queue would impose costs on subsequent joiners. The diseconomies are real, not simply pecuniary, because time is a cost to demanders, but is not revenue to suppliers.

5 A new approach to consumer theory

Kelvin J. Lancaster

The current status of consumer theory

The theory of consumer behavior in deterministic situations as set out by, say, Debreu (1959, 1960) or Uzawa (1960) is a thing of great aesthetic beauty, a jewel set in a glass case. The product of a long process of refinement from the nineteenth-century utility theorists through Slutsky and Hicks-Allen to the economists of the last twenty-five years,[1] it has been shorn of all irrelevant postulates so that it now stands as an example of how to extract the minimum of results from the minimum of assumptions.

To the process of slicing away with Occam's razor, the author made a small contribution (1957). This brought forth a reply by Johnson (1958) which suggested, somewhat tongue-in-cheek, that the determinateness of the sign of the substitution effect (the only substantive result of the theory of consumer behavior) could be derived from the proposition that goods are goods.

Johnson's comment, on reflection, would seem to be almost the best summary that can be given of the current state of the theory of consumer behavior. All *intrinsic* properties of particular goods, those properties that make a diamond quite obviously something different from a loaf of bread, have been omitted from the theory, so that a consumer who consumes diamonds alone is as rational as a consumer who consumes bread alone, but one who sometimes consumes bread, sometimes diamonds (*ceteris paribus*, of course), is irrational. Thus, the only property which the theory can build on is the property shared by all goods, which is simply that they are goods.

Indeed, we can continue the argument further, since goods are simply what consumers would like more of; and we must be neutral with respect to differences in consumer tastes (some consumers might like more of something that other consumers do not want), that the ultimate proposition is that *goods are what are thought of as goods*.

In spite of the denial of the relevance of intrinsic properties to the pure theory, there has always been a subversive undercurrent suggesting that economists continue to take account of these properties. Elementary textbooks bristle with substitution examples about butter and margarine, rather than about shoes and ships, as though the authors believed that there was something intrinsic to butter and margarine that made them good substitutes and about automobiles and gasoline that made them somehow intrinsically complementary. Market researchers, advertisers, and manufacturers also act as though they believe that knowledge of (or belief in) the intrinsic properties of goods is relevant to the way consumers will react toward them.

The clearest case of conflict between a belief that goods do have intrinsic properties relevant to consumer theory but that they are not taken into account has been the long search for a definition of "intrinsic complementarity." The search was successful only where Morishima

(1959) turned from traditional theory to an approach somewhat similar to that of the present paper.

Perhaps the most important aspects of consumer behavior relevant to an economy as complex as that of the United States are those of consumer reactions to new commodities and to quality variations. Traditional theory has nothing to say on these. In the case of new commodities, the theory is particularly helpless. We have to expand from a commodity space of dimension n to one of dimension $n + 1$, replacing the old utility function by a completely new one, and even a complete map of the consumer's preferences among the n goods provides absolutely no information about the new preference map. A theory which can make no use of so much information is a remarkably empty one. Even the technique of supposing the existence of a utility function for all possible goods, including those not yet invented, and regarding the prices of nonexistent goods as infinite – an incredible stretching of the consumers' powers of imagination – has no predictive value.

Finally we can note the unsuitability of traditional theory for dealing with many of the manifestly important aspects of actual relationships between goods and consumers in I. F. Pearce's (1964) recent heroic but rather unsuccessful attempts to deal with complementarity, substitution, independence, and neutral want associations within the conventional framework.

A new approach

Like many new approaches, the one set out in this paper draws upon several elements that have been utilized elsewhere. The chief technical novelty lies in breaking away from the traditional approach that goods are the direct objects of utility and, instead, supposing that it is the properties or characteristics of the goods from which utility is derived.

We assume that consumption is an activity in which goods, singly or in combination, are inputs and in which the output is a collection of characteristics. Utility or preference orderings are assumed to rank collections of characteristics and only to rank collections of goods indirectly through the characteristics that they possess. A meal (treated as a single good) possesses nutritional characteristics but it also possesses aesthetic characteristics, and different meals will possess these characteristics in different relative proportions. Furthermore, a dinner party, a combination of two goods, a meal and a social setting, may possess nutritional, aesthetic, and perhaps intellectual characteristics different from the combination obtainable from a meal and a social gathering consumed separately.

In general – and the richness of the approach springs more from this than from anything else – even a single good will possess more than one characteristic, so that the simplest consumption activity will be characterized by joint outputs. Furthermore, the same characteristic (for example, aesthetic properties) may be included among the joint outputs of many consumption activities so that goods which are apparently unrelated in certain of their characteristics may be related in others.

We shall assume that the structure we have interposed between the goods themselves and the consumer's preferences is, in principle, at least, of an objective kind. That is, the characteristics possessed by a good or a combination of goods are the same for all consumers and, given units of measurement, are in the same quantities,[2] so that the personal element in consumer choice arises in the choice between collections of characteristics only, not in the allocation of characteristics to the goods. The objective nature of the goods-characteristics relationship plays a crucial role in the analysis and enables us to distinguish between objective and private reactions to such things as changes in relative prices.

The essence of the new approach can be summarized as follows, each assumption representing a break with tradition:

1 The good, per se, does not give utility to the consumer; it possesses characteristics, and these characteristics give rise to utility.
2 In general, a good will possess more than one characteristic, and many characteristics will be shared by more than one good.
3 Goods in combination may possess characteristics different from those pertaining to the goods separately.

A move in the direction of the first assumption has already been made by various workers including Strotz (1957, 1959) and Gorman (1959), with the "utility tree" and other ideas associating a particular good with a particular type of utility. The theory set out here goes much further than these ideas. Multiple characteristics, structurally similar to those of the present paper but confined to a particular problem and a point utility function, are implicit in the classical "diet problem" of Stigler (1945), and multidimensioned utilities have been used by workers in other fields, for example, Thrall (1954). The third assumption, of activities involving complementary collections of goods, has been made by Morishima (1959) but in the context of single-dimensioned utility.

A variety of other approaches with similarities to that of the present paper occur scattered through the literature, for example, in Quandt (1956), or in Becker (1965), or in various discussions of investment-portfolio problems. These are typically set out as *ad hoc* approaches to particular problems. Perhaps the most important aspect of this paper is that the model is set out as a general replacement of the traditional analysis (which remains as a special case), rather than as a special solution to a special problem.

It is clear that only by moving to multiple characteristics can we incorporate many of the intrinsic qualities of individual goods. Consider the choice between a gray Chevrolet and a red Chevrolet. On ordinary theory these are either the same commodity (ignoring what may be a relevant aspect of the choice situation) or different commodities (in which case there is no a priori presumption that they are close substitutes). Here we regard them as goods associated with satisfaction vectors which differ in only one component, and we can proceed to look at the situation in much the same way as the consumer – or even the economist, in private life – would look at it.

Traditional theory is forever being forced to interpret quite common real-life happenings, such as the effects of advertising in terms of "change of taste," an entirely non-operational concept since there is no way of predicting the relationship between preference before and after the change. The theory outlined here, although extremely rich in useful ways of thinking about consumer behavior, may also be thought to run the danger of adding to the economist's extensive collection of non-operational concepts. If this were true, it need not, of course, inhibit the heuristic application of the theory. Even better, however, the theory implies predictions that differ from those of traditional theory, and the predictions of the new approach seem to fit better the realities of consumer behavior.

A model of consumer behavior

To obtain a working model from the ideas outlined above, we shall make some assumptions which are, on balance, neither more nor less heroic than those made elsewhere in our present economic theorizing and which are intended to be no more and no less permanent parts of the theory.

1 We shall regard an individual good or a collection of goods as a consumption activity and associate a scalar (the level of the activity) with it. We shall assume that the relationship between the level of activity k, y_k, and the goods consumed in that activity to be both linear and objective, so that, if x_j is the jth commodity we have

$$x_j = \sum_k a_{jk} y_k,$$ (5.1)

and the vector of total goods required for a given activity vector is given by

$$x = Ay.$$ (5.2)

Since the relationships are assumed objective, the equations are assumed to hold for all individuals, the coefficients a_{jk} being determined by the intrinsic properties of the goods themselves and possibly the context of technological knowledge in the society.

2 More heroically, we shall assume that each consumption activity produces a fixed vector of characteristics[3] and that the relationship is again linear, so that, if z_i is the amount of the ith characteristic

$$z_i = \sum_k b_{ik} y_k,$$ (5.3)

or

$$z = By.$$ (5.4)

Again, we shall assume that the coefficients b_{ik} are objectively determined – in principle, at least – for some arbitrary choice of the units of z.

3 We shall assume that the individual possesses an ordinal utility function on characteristics $U(z)$ and that he will choose a situation which maximizes $U(z)$. $U(z)$ is provisionally assumed to possess the ordinary convexity properties of a standard utility function. The chief purpose of making the assumption of linearity is to simplify the problem. A viable model could certainly be produced under the more general set of relationships

$$F_k(z, x) = 0, \quad k = 1 \ldots m.$$ (5.5)

The model could be analyzed in a similar way to that used by Samuelson (1953b) and others in analyzing production, although the existence of much jointness among outputs in the present model presents difficulties.

In this model, the relationship between the collections of characteristics available to the consumer – the vectors z – which are the direct ingredients of his preferences and his welfare, and the collections of goods available to him – the vectors x – which represent his relationship with the rest of the economy, is not direct and one-to-one, as in the traditional model, but indirect, through the activity vector y.

Consider the relationships which link z and x. These are the equation systems: $x = Ay$ (5.2) and $z = By$ (5.4). Suppose that there are r characteristics, m activities, and n goods. Only if $r = m = n$ will there be a one-to-one relationship between z and x. In this case both the B and A matrixes are square (the number of variables equals the number of equations in both sets of equations) and we can solve for y in terms of x, $y = A^{-1}x$, giving $z = BA^{-1}x$. $U(z)$ can be written directly and unambiguously as a function $u(x)$. Otherwise the relations are between vectors in spaces of different dimensions. Consider some x^* in the case in which $m > n$: equation (5.2) places only n restrictions on the m-vector y, so that y can still be chosen with $m - n$ degrees of freedom. If $r < m$, then there are $m - r$ degrees of freedom in choosing y, given some z, but whether the ultimate relationship gives several choices of z for a given x, or several x for a given z, and whether all vectors z are attainable, depends on the relationships between r, m, and n and the structures of the matrixes A, B. In general, we will expect that the consumer may face a choice among many paths linking goods collections with characteristics collections. The simple question asked (in principle) in the traditional analysis – does a particular consumer prefer collection x_1 or collection x_2 – no longer has a direct answer, although the question, does he prefer characteristics collection z_1 or z_2, does have such an answer.

If we take the standard choice situation facing the consumer in a free market, with a linear budget constraint, this situation, in our model, becomes:

Maximize $U(z)$

subject to $px \leqq k$

with $\quad z = By$

$\quad\quad x = Ay$

$\quad\quad x, y, z \geqq 0.$

This is a non-linear program of an intractable kind. The problem of solution need not worry us here, since we are interested only in the properties of the solution.

The simplified model

We shall simplify the model in the initial stages by supposing that there is a one-to-one correspondence between goods and activities so that we can write the consumer-choice program in the simpler form

Maximize $U(z)$

subject to $px \leqq k$

with $\quad z = Bx$

$\quad\quad z, x \geqq 0.$

This is still, of course, a non-linear program, but we now have a single step between goods and characteristics.

The model consists of four parts. There is a maximand $U(z)$ operating on characteristics, that is, U is defined on characteristics-space (C-space). The budget constraint $px \leqq k$ is defined on goods-space (G-space). The equation system $z = Bx$ represents a transformation between G-space and C-space. Finally, there are non-negativity constraints $z, x \geq 0$ which we shall assume to hold initially, although in some applications and with some sign conventions they may not always form part of the model.

In traditional consumer analysis, both the budget constraint and the utility function are defined on G-space, and we can immediately relate the two as in the ordinary textbook indifference-curve diagram. Here we can only relate the utility function to the budget constraint after both have been defined on the same space. We have two choices: (1) We can transform the utility function into G-space and relate it directly to the budget constraint; (2) we can transform the budget constraint into C-space and relate it directly to the utility function $U(z)$.

Each of these techniques is useful in different circumstances. In the case of the first, we can immediately write $U(z) = U(Bx) = u(x)$, so we have a new utility function directly in terms of goods, but the properties of the function $u(x)$ depend crucially on the structure of the matrix B and this, together with the constraints $x \geq 0$ and $z = Bx \geq 0$ give a situation much more complex than that of conventional utility maximization. The second technique again depends crucially on the structure of B and again will generally lead to a constraint of a more complex kind than in conventional analysis.

The central role in the model is, of course, played by the transformation equation $z = Bx$ and the structure and qualitative[4] properties of the matrix B. Most of the remainder of the paper will be concerned with the relationship between the properties of B, which we can call the *consumption technology*[5] of the economy, and the behavior of consumers.

Certain properties of the transformations between G- and C-space follow immediately from the fact that B is a matrix of constants, and the transformation $z = Bx$ is linear. These can be stated as follows, proof being obvious.

(a) A convex set in G-space will transform into a convex set in C-space, so that the budget constraint $px \leq k, x \geq 0$ will become a convex constraint on the z's.

(b) An inverse transformation will not necessarily exist, so that an arbitrary vector z in C-space may have no vector x in G-space corresponding to it.

(c) Where an inverse transformation does exist from C-space into G-space, it will transform convex sets into convex sets so that, for any set of z's which do have images in G-space, the convexity of the U function on the z's will be preserved in relation to the x's.

The properties are sufficient to imply that utility maximization subject to constraint will lead to determinate solutions for consumer behavior.

The structure of consumption technology

The consumption technology, which is as important a determinant of consumer behavior as the particular shape of the utility function, is described fully only by the A and B matrixes together, but certain types of behavior can be related to more generalized descriptions of the technology. We shall distinguish broadly between structural properties of the technology, such as the relationship between the number of rows and columns of B and/or A and whether A, B are decomposable, and qualitative properties, such as the signs of the elements of A and B.

The leading structural property of the consumption technology is the relationship between the number of characteristics (r) and the number of activities (m), that is, between the number of rows and columns of B. It will be assumed that B contains no linear dependence, so that its rank is the number of rows or columns, whichever is less. We shall assume, unless otherwise stated, a one-to-one relationship between goods and activities.

1 The number of characteristics is equal to the number of goods. In this case, there is a one-to-one relationship between activities vectors and characteristics vectors. We have $z = Bx, x = B^{-1}z$. If B is a permutation of a diagonal matrix then there is a one-to-one relationship between each component of z and each component of y, and the model becomes, by suitable choice of units, exactly the same as the traditional model. If B is not a diagonal permutation, the objects of utility are composite goods rather than individual goods, and the model has some important differences from the conventional analysis. Note how specialized is the traditional case in relation to our general model.

   If B is a diagonal permutation but there is not a one-to-one relationship between activities and goods so that A is not a diagonal permutation, we have a model similar to that of Morishima (1959).

2 The number of characteristics is greater than the number of goods. In this case, the relationships $Bx = z$ contain more equations than variables x_i so that we cannot, in general, find a goods vector x which gives rise to an arbitrarily specified characteristics vector z. We can take a basis of any arbitrarily chosen n characteristics and consider the reduced $n \times n$ system $\bar{B} = \bar{z}$, which gives a one-to-one relationship between n characteristics and the n goods, with the remaining $r - n$ characteristics being determined from the remaining $r - n$ equations and the goods vector x corresponding to $\bar{z}$. In this case, it is generally most useful to analyze consumer behavior by transforming the utility function into G-space, rather than the budget constraint into C-space. What does the transformed utility function look like?

   As shown in the Appendix, the utility function transformed into G-space retains its essential convexity. An intuitive way of looking at the situation is to note that all characteristics collections which are actually available are contained in an n-dimensional slice through the r-dimensional utility function, and that all slices through a convex function are themselves convex. The transformation of this n-dimensional slice into G-space preserves this convexity.

   For investigation of most aspects of consumer behavior, the case in which the number of characteristics exceeds the number of goods – a case we may often wish to associate with simple societies – can be treated along with the very special case (of which conventional analysis is a special subcase) in which the number of characteristics and goods is equal. In other words, given the consumption technology, we concern ourselves only with the particular n-dimensional slice of the r-dimensional utility function implied by that technology[6] and, since the slice of the utility function has the same general properties as any n-dimensional utility function, we can proceed as if the utility function was defined on only n characteristics.

3 In the third case, in which the number of goods exceeds the number of characteristics, a situation probably descriptive of a complex economy such as that of the United States, there are properties of the situation that are different from those of the two previous cases and from the conventional analysis.

Here, the consumption technology, $z = Bx$, has fewer equations than variables so that, for every characteristics vector there is more than one goods vector. For every point in his characteristics-space, the consumer has a choice between different goods vectors. Given a

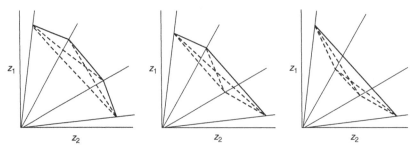

Figure 5.1

price vector, this choice is a pure efficiency choice, so that for every characteristics vector the consumer will choose the most efficient combination of goods to achieve that collection of characteristics, and the efficiency criterion will be minimum cost.

The efficiency choice for a characteristics vector z^* will be the solution of the canonical linear program

Maximize px

subject to $Bx = z^*$

$$x \geq 0.$$

Since this is a linear program, once we have the solution x^* for some z^*, with value k^*, we can apply a scalar multiple to fit the solution to any budget value k and characteristics vector $(k/k^*)z^*$. By varying z^*, the consumer, given a budget constraint $px = k$, can determine a characteristics frontier consisting of all z such that the value of the above program is just equal to k. There will be a determinate goods vector associated with each point of the characteristics frontier.

As in the previous case, it is easy to show that the set of characteristics vectors in C-space that are preferred or indifferent to z transforms into a convex set in G-space if it is a convex set in C-space; it is also easy to show that the set of z's that can be obtained from the set of x's satisfying the convex constraint $px \leq k$ is also a convex set. The characteristics frontier is, therefore, concave to the origin, like a transformation curve. For a consumption technology with four goods and two characteristics, the frontier could have any of the three shapes shown in Figure 5.1. Note that, in general, if B is a positive matrix, the positive orthant in G-space transforms into a cone which lies in the interior of the positive orthant in C-space, a point illustrated in the diagrams.

A consumer's complete choice subject to a budget constraint $px \leq k$ can be considered as consisting of two parts:

(a) An efficiency choice, determining the characteristics frontier and the associated efficient goods collections.
(b) A private choice, determining which point on the characteristics frontier is preferred by him.

The efficiency choice is an objective not a subjective choice. On the assumption that the consumption technology is objective, the characteristics frontier is also objective, and it is the same for all consumers facing the same budget constraint. Furthermore the characteristics frontier is expanded or contracted linearly and proportionally to an increase or decrease in income, so that the frontier has the same *shape* for all consumers facing the same prices, income differences simply being reflected in homogeneous expansion or contraction.

We should note that, if the consumption technology matrix has certain special structural properties, we may obtain a mixture of the above cases. For example, a matrix with the structure

$$B \equiv \begin{bmatrix} B_1 & 0 \\ 0 & B_2 \end{bmatrix},$$

where B_1 is an $(s \times k)$ matrix and B_2 is an $(r - s) \times (n - k)$ matrix, partitions the technology into two disconnected parts, one relating s of the characteristics to k of the goods, the other separately relating $r - s$ of the characteristics to $n - k$ of the goods. We can have $s \geq k$ and $r - s < n - k$ giving a mixed case.

Dropping the assumption of a one-to-one relationship between goods and activities does not add greatly to the difficulties of the analysis. We have, as part of the technology, $x = Ay$, so that the budget constraint $px \geq k$ can be written immediately as $pAy \leq k$. The goods prices transform directly into implicit activity prices $q = pA$. Interesting cases arise, of course. If the number of goods is less than the number of activities, then not all q's are attainable from the set of p's; and if the number of goods exceeds the number of activities, different p vectors will correspond to the same q vector. This implies that certain changes in relative goods prices may leave activity prices, and the consumer's choice situation, unchanged.

In most of the succeeding analysis, we will be concerned with the B matrix and the relationship between activities and characteristics, since this represents the most distinctive part of the theory.

The efficiency substitution effect and revealed preference

At this stage, it is desirable to examine the nature of the efficiency choice so that we can appreciate the role it plays in the consumer behavior implied by our model. Consider a case in which there are two characteristics, a case that can be illustrated diagrammatically, and, say, four activities.

The activities-characteristics portion of the consumption technology is defined by the two equations

$$\begin{aligned} z_1 &= b_{11}y_1 + b_{12}y_2 + b_{13}y_3 + b_{14}y_4; \\ z_2 &= b_{21}y_1 + b_{22}y_2 + b_{23}y_3 + b_{24}y_4. \end{aligned} \tag{5.6}$$

With activity 1 only, the characteristics will be obtained in proportion, b_{11}/b_{21} (the ray labeled 1 in Figure 5.2). Similarly with activities 2, 3, 4, one at a time, characteristics will be obtained in proportions b_{12}/b_{22}, b_{13}/b_{23}, b_{14}/b_{24}, respectively, corresponding to the rays 2, 3, 4 in the diagram.

We are given a budget constraint in goods space of the form $\Sigma_i p_i x_i \leq k$. If there is a one-to-one correspondence between goods and activities, the prices of the activities are given by p_i. If there is not a one-to-one relationship, but a goods-activities portion of the consumption technology

$$\begin{aligned} x_i &= a_{i1}y_1 + a_{i2}y_2 + a_{i3}y_3 + a_{i4}y_4 \\ i &= 1 \dots n, \end{aligned} \tag{5.7}$$

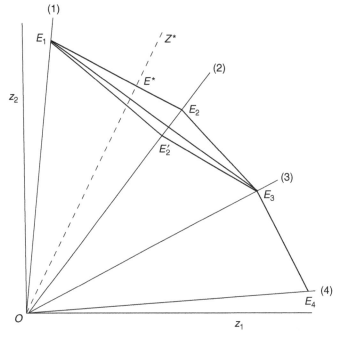

Figure 5.2

then the budget constraint can be transformed immediately into characteristics space

$$\left(\sum_i p_i a_{i1}\right) y_1 + \left(\sum_i p_i a_{i2}\right) y_2$$
$$+ \left(\sum_i p_i a_{i3}\right) y_3 + \left(\sum_i p_i a_{i4}\right) y_4 \leq k \qquad (5.8)$$

where the composite prices $q_j = \Sigma_i p_i a_{ij}$, $j = 1 \ldots 4$ represent the prices of each activity. The number of goods in relation to the number of activities is irrelevant at this stage, since each activity has a unique and completely determined price q_i, given the prices of the goods.

Given q_1, q_2, q_3, q_4, and k, the maximum attainable level of each activity in isolation can be written down (corresponding to the points E_1, E_2, E_3, E_4 in Figure 5.2,) and the lines joining these points represent combinations attainable subject to the budget constraint. In the diagram it has been assumed that prices are such that combinations of 1 and 2, 2 and 3, 3 and 4 are efficient, giving the characteristics frontier, while combinations 1 and 3, 2 and 4, or 1 and 4 are inefficient.

Suppose that the consumer chooses characteristics in the combination represented by the ray z^*, giving a point E^* on the frontier. Now suppose that relative prices change: in particular, that the price of activity 2 rises so that, with income still at k, the point E_2 moves inward on ray 2. If the movement is small enough, the characteristics frontier continues to have a corner at E_2, and the consumer will continue to obtain characteristics in proportion z^* by a combination of activities 1 and 2. If income is adjusted so that the new frontier goes through E^*, the consumer will use the same activities in the same proportions as before.

If the price of activity 2 rises sufficiently, however, the point E_2 will move inward past the line joining E_1 and E_3 to E_2'. Combinations of 1 and 2 and of 2 and 3 are now inefficient combinations of activities, their place on the efficiency frontier being taken by a combination of 1 and 3. The consumer will switch from a combination of activities 1 and 2 to a combination of activities 1 and 3.

Thus there is an efficiency substitution effect which is essentially a switching effect. If price changes are too small to cause a switch, there is no efficiency substitution effect: If they are large enough, the effect comes from a complete switch from one activity to another.

The manifestation of the efficiency substitution effect in goods space depends on the structure of the A (goods activities) matrix. There are two polar cases:

(a) If there is a one-to-one relationship between goods and activities, the efficiency substitution effect will result in a complete switch from consumption of one good to consumption of another. This might be regarded as typical of situations involving similar but differentiated products, where a sufficiently large price change in one of the products will result in widespread switching to, or away from, the product.
(b) If there is not a one-to-one relationship between goods and activities and, in particular, if all goods are used in all activities, the efficiency substitution effect will simply result in less consumption of a good whose price rises, not a complete disappearance of that good from consumption. If all cakes require eggs but in different proportions, a rise in the price of eggs will cause a switch from egg-intensive cakes to others, with a decline in the consumption of eggs, but not to zero.

The existence of an efficiency substitution effect depends, of course, on the number of activities exceeding the number of characteristics (otherwise switching of activities will not, in general, occur[7]) but does not require that the number of goods exceed the number of characteristics. In fact, with two goods, two characteristics, and three activities, the effect may occur. With two goods, two characteristics and one hundred activities (well spread over the spectrum), an almost smooth efficiency substitution effect would occur.

Since the efficiency substitution effect implies that consumers may change goods collections as a result of compensated relative price changes, simply in order to obtain the same characteristics collection in the most efficient manner, it is obvious that the existence of substitution does not of itself either require or imply convexity of the preference function on characteristics. In other words, the axiom of revealed preference may be satisfied even if the consumer always consumes characteristics in fixed proportions (and possibly even if the consumers had *concave* preferences), so that the "revelation" may be simply of efficient choice rather than convexity. A formal proof is given in the Appendix.

Objective and subjective choice and demand theory

In an economy or subeconomy with a complex consumption technology (many goods relative to characteristics), we have seen that there are two types of substitution effect:

1 Changes in relative prices may result in goods bundle I becoming an *inefficient* method of attaining a given bundle of characteristics and being replaced by goods bundle II even when the characteristics bundle is unchanged.
2 Changes in relative prices, with or without causing efficiency substitutions as in type 1, may alter the slope of the characteristics frontier in a segment relevant to a consumer's

characteristics choice. The change in the slope of the frontier is analogous to the change in the budget line slope in the traditional case and, with a convex preference function, will result in a substitution of one characteristics bundle for another and, hence, of one goods bundle for another. Note that, even with smoothly convex preferences, this effect may not occur, since the consumer may be on a corner of the polyhedral characteristics frontier, and thus his characteristics choice could be insensitive to a certain range of slope changes on the facets.

The first effect, the efficiency substitution effect, is universal and objective. Subject to consumer ignorance or inefficiency,[8] this substitution effect is independent of the shapes of individual consumers' preference functions and hence of the effects of income distribution.

The second effect, the private substitution effect, has the same properties, in general, as the substitution effect in traditional theory. In particular, an aggregately compensated relative price change combined with a redistribution of income may result in no substitution effect in the aggregate, or a perverse one.

These two substitution effects are independent – either may occur without the other in certain circumstances – but in general we will expect them both to take place and hence that their effects will be reinforcing, if we are concerned with a complex economy. Thus, the consumer model presented here, in the context of an advanced economy, has, in a sense, more substitution than the traditional model. Furthermore, since part of the total substitution effect arises from objective, predictable, and income-distribution-free efficiency considerations, our confidence in the downward slope of demand curves is increased even when income redistribution takes place.

Since it is well known that satisfaction of the revealed preference axioms *in the aggregate* (never guaranteed by traditional theory) leads to global stability in multimarket models (see, for example, Karlin, 1959), the efficiency substitution effect increases confidence in this stability.

In a simple economy, with few goods or activities relative to characteristics, the efficiency substitution effect will be generally absent. Without this reinforcement of the private substitution effect, we would have some presumption that perverse consumer effects ("Giffen goods," backward-bending supply curves) and lower elasticities of demand would characterize simple economies as compared with complex economies. This seems to be in accord with at least the mythology of the subject, but it is certainly empirically verifiable. On this model, consumption technology as well as income levels differentiate consumers in different societies, and we would not necessarily expect a poor urban American to behave in his consumption like a person at the same real-income level in a simple economy.

Commodity groups, substitutes, complements

In a complex economy, with a large number of activities and goods as well as characteristics, and with a two-matrix (A, B) consumption technology, it is obvious that taxonomy could be carried out almost without limit, an expression of the richness of the present approach. Although an elaborate taxonomy is not very useful, discussion of a few selected types of relationships between goods can be of use. One of the important features of this model is that we can discuss relationships between goods, as revealed in the structure of the technology. In the conventional approach, there are, of course, no relationships between goods as such, only properties of individual's preferences.

The simplest taxonomy is that based on the zero entries in the technology matrixes. It may be that both matrixes A, B are almost "solid," in which case there is little to be gained from a taxonomic approach. If, however, the B matrix contains sufficient zeros to be decomposable as follows,

$$B \equiv \begin{bmatrix} B_1 & 0 \\ 0 & B_2 \end{bmatrix}, \tag{5.9}$$

so that there is some set of characteristics and some set of activities such that these characteristics are derived only from these activities and these activities give rise to no other characteristics, then we can separate that set of characteristics and activities from the remainder of the technology. If, further, the activities in question require a particular set of goods which are used in no other activities (implying a decomposition of the A matrix), then we can regard the goods as forming an *intrinsic commodity group*. Goods within the group have the property that efficiency substitution effects will occur only for relative price changes within the group and will be unaffected by changes in the prices of other goods. If the utility function on characteristics has the conventional properties, there may, of course, be *private* substitution effects for goods within the group when the prices of other goods changes. For an intrinsic commodity group, the whole of the objective analysis can be carried out without reference to goods outside the group.

Goods from different intrinsic commodity groups can be regarded as *intrinsically unrelated*, goods from the same group as *intrinsically related*.

If, within a group, there are two activities, each in a one-to-one relationship with a different good, and if the bundles of characteristics derived from the two goods differ only in a scalar (that is, have identical proportions), we can regard the two goods in question as *intrinsic perfect substitutes*. If the associated characteristics bundles are similar, the goods are *close substitutes*. We can give formal respectability to that traditional butter-margarine example of our texts by considering them as two goods giving very similar combinations of characteristics.

On the other hand, if a certain activity requires more than one good and if these goods are used in no other activity we can consider them as *intrinsic total complements* and they will always be consumed in fixed proportions, if at all.

Many goods within a commodity group will have relationships to each other which are partly complementary and partly substitution. This will be true if two goods, for example, are used in different combinations in each of several activities, each activity giving rise to a similar combination of characteristics. The goods are complements within each activity, but the activities are substitutes.

Labor, leisure, and occupational choice

Within the structure of the present theory, we can regard labor as a reversed activity, using characteristics as inputs and producing commodities or a commodity as output. This is similar to the standard approach of generalized conventional theory, as in Debreu (1959).

We can add to this approach in an important way within the context of the present model by noting that a work activity may produce characteristics, as well as the commodity labor, as outputs. This is structurally equivalent to permitting some of the columns of the B matrix to have both negative and positive elements, corresponding to activities that "use up" some characteristics (or produce them in negative quantities) and produce others. In a work activity, the corresponding column of the A matrix will contain a single negative coefficient for the commodity labor, or, more differentiated, for one or more types of labor. If a work activity corresponds to a column of mixed signs in the B matrix, it is a recognition of the obvious truth that some work activities give rise to valued characteristics directly from the work itself.

Consider a very simple model of two characteristics with two commodities, labor and consumption goods. Both labor and consumption goods correspond to separate activities giving rise to the two characteristics in different proportions – perhaps negative in the case of labor. With no income other than labor, and only one good available to exchange for labor, we can collapse work and consumption into a single work–consumption activity. Given the wage rate in terms of the consumption good, the characteristics resulting from the work-consumption activity are given by a linear combination of the characteristics from work and consumption separately, the weights in the combination being given by the wage rate.

Add another activity, leisure, which gives rise to the two characteristics, and the constraint that the weighted sum of the levels of activity labor and activity leisure is a constant.

The model is illustrated in Figure 5.3. W represents a work–consumption activity giving positive levels of both characteristics, l represents a leisure activity, also giving positive levels of both characteristics. The constraint on total time (so that a linear combination of w and l is a constant) is represented by some line joining w, l.

If the constraint line has, like AB in the diagram, a negative slope, then individual consumers' utility functions will be tangent to the constraint at different points (like m, m') and we will have a neoclassical type of labor–leisure choice in which the proportions depend on individual preferences. Some consumers' preferences may be such that they will choose A (maximum work) or B (maximum leisure), but it is a private choice.

In this model, however, for a certain level of the wage, given the coefficients of the technology, the constraint may have a positive slope as in $A'B$, or AB'. If the constraint is $A'B$ (corresponding, *celeris paribus*, to a sufficiently low real wage), *all* individuals will choose B, the only efficient point on the constraint set $OA'B$. At a sufficiently high wage, giving constraint set OAB', A, the maximum labor choice, is the only efficient choice and will be chosen by *all* individuals.

The above effect, in which for some wage range there is a private labor–leisure choice between efficient points while outside the range all individuals will take maximum work or maximum leisure, can only occur if both the work-consumption and leisure activities give both characteristics in positive amounts. If the using up of characteristic 2 in labor exceeded the amount of that characteristic gained by consumption, then the work-consumption activity might lie outside the positive quadrant, like w'. In this case, a constraint like $A'B$ can exist, but not one like AB'. Furthermore, if the consumer will choose only positive characteristics vectors, no consumer will choose maximum work.

This model of the labor–leisure choice, which provides for objective and universal efficiency choices as well as private choices, may be the basis for a useful working model for an underdeveloped area. If the "leisure" be defined as "working one's own field," the work-consumption activity as entering the market economy, we see that there will be wages below which no peasant will offer himself as paid labor and that this is an *efficiency* choice and not a private choice.

We can use the same type of model also to analyze occupational choice. Suppose that we have two types of work (occupations) but otherwise the conditions are as above. If and only if the characteristics arising from the work itself are different in the two occupations, the two work-consumption activities will give rise to activities in different combinations. If the

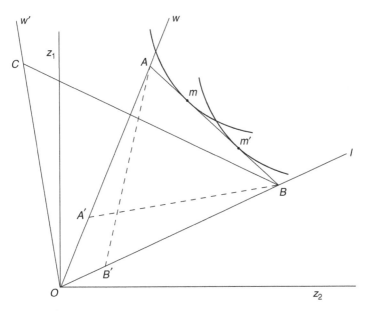

Figure 5.3

work characteristics are in the same proportion, the characteristics of the work-consumption activity will be in the same proportions and one or the other occupation will be the only efficient way to achieve this characteristics bundle.

Figure 5.4 illustrates one possible set of relationships for such a model. In the diagram, w_1, w_2 represent the characteristics combinations from work-consumption activities in occupations 1 and 2, l the characteristics combinations from leisure. The frontier consists of the lines AC (combinations of w_1 and leisure) and AB (combinations of w_2 and leisure). We shall impose the realistic restriction that an individual can have only a single occupation so that AB is not a possible combination of activities.

The choice of occupation, given the relationships in the figure, depends on personal preferences, being M_1 (combination of w_2 and leisure) for an individual with preferences skewed towards z_2 and M_2 for an individual with preferences skewed towards z_1. But note a special effect. For some individuals whose indifference curves cannot touch BC but can touch AC, the efficient choice will be the corner solution $M_3(=B)$. There is, in fact, a segment of AC to the left of w_2 (the part of AC to the right of w_2 is dominated by BC), lying below the horizontal through B which is inefficient relative to B and will never be chosen.

In a configuration like the above we have the very interesting effect, where those who choose occupation 1 will work very hard at it; leisure-lovers will choose private combinations of occupation 2 and leisure – surely a good description of effects actually observed.

The loss to certain individuals from confinement to a single occupation is obvious. Could he choose a combination of occupations 1 and 2, the individual at M_2 would do so and be better off than with a combination of occupation 1 and leisure. In a two-characteristic, three-activity model, of course, two activities will be chosen at most, so that leisure plus both occupations will not appear.

The configuration in the diagram (Figure 5.4) represents the situation for some set of technical coefficients and specific wages in the two occupations. A large number of other configurations is possible. In particular, if the wage rate in occupation 2 fell sufficiently,

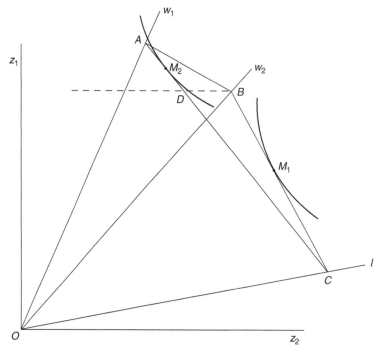

Figure 5.4

BC would lie inside *AC* and occupation 2 would cease to be chosen by any individual. All individuals, in this case, would choose their various personal combinations of occupation 1 and leisure.

Confinement to a single occupation need not result in a welfare loss, even when neither occupation dominates the other in an efficiency sense. If the technical coefficients were different, so that the characteristics vectors representing occupation 2 and leisure changed places, then the work-leisure combinations would be given by *AB* and *BC*, both efficient relative to any combination of occupations 1 and 2. In this case, all individuals would optimize by some combination of leisure and any one of the occupations.

Approaches similar to those outlined above seem to provide a better basis for analysis of occupational choice than the traditional, non-operational, catch-all "non-monetary advantages."

Consumer durables, assets, and money

Within the framework of the model, we have a scheme for dealing with durable goods and assets. A durable good can be regarded simply as giving rise to an activity in which the output consists of dated characteristics, the characteristics of different dates being regarded as different characteristics.

Given characteristics as joint outputs and two types of dimension in characteristics space – cross-section and time – any asset or durable good can be regarded as producing a combination of several characteristics at any one time, and that combination need not be regarded as continuing unchanged through time. In the decision to buy a new automobile, for example, the characteristic related to "fashion" or "style" may be present in relative strength in the first season, relatively less in later seasons, although the characteristics related to "transportation" may remain with constant coefficients over several seasons.

Elementary textbooks stress the multidimensional characteristics of money and other assets. The present model enables this multidimensionality to be appropriately incorporated. "Safety," "liquidity," and so forth become workable concepts that can be related to characteristics. We can use analysis similar to that of the preceding sections to show why efficiency effects will cause the universal disappearance of some assets (as in Gresham's Law) while other assets will be held in combinations determined by personal preferences. It would seem that development along these lines, coupled with development of some of the recent approaches to consumer preferences over time as in Koopmans (1960), Lancaster (1963), or Koopmans, Diamond, and Williamson (1964) might eventually lead to a full-blooded theory of consumer behavior with respect to assets – saving and money – which we do not have at present.

In situations involving risk, we can use multiple characteristics better to analyze individual behavior. For example, we might consider a gamble to be an activity giving rise to three characteristics – a mathematical expectation, a maximum gain, and a maximum loss. One consumer's utility function may be such that he gives more weight to the maximum gain than to the maximum loss or the expected value, another's utility function may be biased in the opposite direction. All kinds of models can be developed along these lines, and they are surely more realistic than the models (Von Neumann and Morgenstern, 1944; Friedman and Savage, 1952) in which the expected value, alone, appears in the utility-maximizing decisions.

New commodities, differentiated goods, and advertising

Perhaps the most difficult thing to do with traditional consumer theory is to introduce a new commodity – an event that occurs thousands of times in the U.S. economy, even over a generation, without any real consumers being unduly disturbed. In the theory of production, where activity-analysis methods have become widely used, a new process or product can be fitted in well enough; but in consumer theory we have traditionally had to throw away our n-dimensional preference functions and replace them by totally new $(n + 1)$ dimensional functions, with no predictable consequences.

In this model, the whole process is extraordinarily simple. A new product simply means addition of one or more activities to the consumption technology.

Given the technology (or the relevant portion of it) and given the intrinsic characteristic of the activity associated with the new good, we simply insert it in the appropriate place in the technology, *and we can predict the consequences.*

If a new good possesses characteristics in the same proportions as some existing good, it will simply fail to sell to anyone if its price is too high, or will completely replace the old good if its price is sufficiently low.

More usually, we can expect a new good to possess characteristics in somewhat different proportions to an existing good. If its price is too high, it may be dominated by some *combination* of existing goods and will fail to sell. If its price is sufficiently low, it will result in adding a new point to the efficiency frontier. In Figure 5.5, ABC represents the old efficiency frontier, on which some individuals will consume combinations of goods g_1 and g_2 in various proportions, some combinations of g_2 and g_3. If the price of the new good, g_4, is such that it represents a point, D, on the old efficiency frontier, some persons (those using combinations of g_1 and g_2) will be indifferent between their old combinations and combinations of either g_1 and g_4 or g_2 and g_4. If the price of g_4 is a little lower, it will push the efficiency frontier

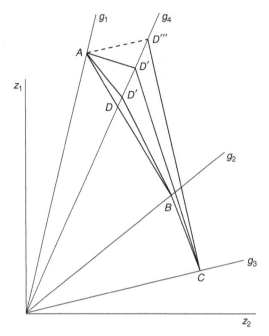

Figure 5.5

out to D'. Individuals will now replace combinations of g_1 and g_2 with combinations of g_1 and g_4 or g_2 and g_4, depending on their preferences. The new good will have taken away some of the sales from both g_1 and g_2, but completely replaced neither.

If the price of g_4 were lower, giving point D'', then combinations of g_4 and g_3 would dominate g_2, and g_2 would be replaced. At an even lower price, like D''', combinations of g_4 and g_3 would dominate g_2, and the corner solution g_4 only would dominate all combinations of g_1 and g_4 (since AD''' has a positive slope), so that g_4 would now replace both g_1 and g_2.

Differentiation of goods has presented almost as much of a problem to traditional theory as new commodities. In the present analysis, the difference is really one of degree only. We can regard a differentiated good typically as a new good within an existing intrinsic commodity group, and within that group analyze it as a new commodity. Sometimes there appear new commodities of a more fundamental kind whose characteristics cut across those of existing groups.

We may note that differentiation of goods, if successful (that is, if the differentiated goods are actually sold) represents a welfare improvement since it pushes the efficiency frontier outward an enables the consumer more efficiently to reach his preferred combination of characteristics.

Many economists take a puritanical view of commodity differentiation since their theory has induced them to believe that it is some single characteristic of a commodity that is relevant to consumer decisions (that is, automobiles are only for transportation), so that commodity variants are regarded as wicked tricks to trap the uninitiated into buying unwanted trimmings. This is not, of course, a correct deduction even from the conventional analysis, properly used, but is manifestly incorrect when account is taken of multiple characteristics.

A rather similar puritanism has also been apparent in the economist's approach to advertising. In the neoclassical analysis, advertising, if it does not represent simple information (and little information is called for in an analysis in which a good is simply a good), is an attempt to "change tastes" in the consumer. Since "tastes" are the ultimate datum in welfare judgments, the idea of changing them makes economists uncomfortable.

On the analysis presented here, there is much wider scope for informational advertising, especially as new goods appear constantly. Since the consumption technology of a modern economy is clearly very complex, consumers require a great deal of information concerning that technology. When a new version of a dishwashing detergent is produced which contains hand lotion, we have a product with characteristics different from those of the old. The consumption technology is changed, and consumers are willing to pay to be told of the change. Whether the new product pushes out the efficiency frontier (compared, say, with a combination of dishwasher and hand lotion consumed separately) is, of course, another matter.

In any case, advertising, product design, and marketing specialists, who have a heavy commitment to understanding how consumers actually do behave, themselves act as though consumers regard a commodity as having multiple characteristics and as though consumers weigh the various combinations of characteristics contained in different commodities in reaching their decisions. At this preliminary stage of presenting the model set out here, this is strong evidence in its favor.

General equilibrium, welfare, and other matters

Since the demand for goods depends on objective and universal efficiency effects as well as on private choices, we can draw some inferences relative to equilibrium in the economy.

A commodity, especially a commodity within an intrinsic commodity group, must have a price low enough relative to the prices of other commodities to be represented on the efficiency frontier, otherwise it will be purchased by no one and will not appear in the economy. This implies that if there are n viable commodities in a group, each in a one-to-one relation to an activity, the equilibrium prices will be such that the efficiency frontier has $n - 1$ facets in the two-characteristic case. In Figure 5.6, for example, where the price of commodity 3 brings it to point A on the efficiency frontier, that price could not be allowed to rise to a level bringing it inside point B, or it would disappear from the market; and if its price fell below a level corresponding to C, commodities 2 and 4 would disappear from the market. Thus the limits on prices necessary for the existence of all commodities within a group can be established (in principle) from objective data. Only the demand within that price range depends on consumer preferences.

With a large number of activities relative to characteristics, equilibrium prices would give a many-faceted efficiency frontier that would be approximated by a smooth curve having the general shape of a production possibility curve. For many purposes it may be mathematically simple to analyze the situation in terms of a smooth efficiency frontier. We can then draw on some of the analysis that exists, relating factor inputs to outputs of goods, as in Samuelson (1953*b*). Goods in our model correspond to factors in the production model, and characteristics in our model to commodities in the production model.

The welfare implications of the model set out here are quite complex and deserve a separate treatment. We might note several important aspects of the welfare problem, however, which arise directly from a many-faceted, many-cornered efficiency frontier:

1 Consumers whose choices represent a corner on the efficiency frontier are not, in general, *equating* marginal rates of substitution between characteristics to the ratio of any parameters of the situation or to marginal rates of substitution of other consumers.

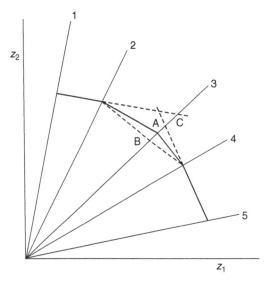

Figure 5.6

2 Consumers whose choices represent points on different facets of the efficiency frontier are equating their marginal rates of substitution between characteristics to different implicit price ratios between characteristics. If there is a one-to-one relationship between goods and activities, the consumers are reacting to relative prices between different sets of goods. The traditional marginal conditions for Paretian exchange optimum do not hold because the price ratio relevant to one consumer's decisions differs from the price ratio relevant to another's. In common-sense terms, the price ratio between a Cadillac and a Continental is irrelevant to my decisions, but the price ratio between two compact cars is relevant, while there are other individuals for whom the Cadillac/Continental ratio is the relevant datum. If the *A* matrix is strongly connected, however, the implicit price ratios between different activities can correspond to price ratios between the same sets of goods, and the Paretian conditions may be relevant.

Finally, we may note that the shape of the equilibrium efficiency frontier and the existence of the efficiency substitution effect can result in demand conditions with the traditionally assumed properties, even if the traditional, smooth, convex utility function does not exist. In particular, a simple utility function in which characteristics are consumed in constant proportions – the proportions perhaps changing with income – can be substituted for the conventional utility function.

Operational and predictive characteristics of the model

In principle, the model set out here can be made operational (that is, empirical coefficients can be assigned to the technology). In practice, the task will be more difficult than the equivalent task of determining the actual production technology of an economy.

To emphasize that the model is not simply heuristic, we can examine a simple scheme for sketching out the efficiency frontier for some commodity group. We shall assume that there is a one-to-one relationship between activities and goods, that at least one characteristic shared by the commodities is capable of independent determination, and that a great quantity of suitable market data is available.

In practice, we will attempt to operate with the minimum number of characteristics that give sufficient explanatory power. These may be combinations of fundamental characteristics (a factor-analysis situation) or fundamental characteristics themselves.

Consider some commodity group such as household detergents. We have a primary objective characteristic, cleaning power, measured in some chosen way. We wish to test whether one or more other characteristics are necessary to describe the consumer-choice situation.

We take a two-dimensional diagram with characteristic "cleaning power" along one axis. Along the axis we mark the cleaning power per dollar outlay of all detergents observed to be sold at the same time. If this is the same for all detergents, this single characteristic describes the situation, and we do not seek further. However, we shall assume this is not so. From our observed market data, we obtain cross-price elasticities between all detergents, taken two at a time. From the model, we know that cross-price elasticities will be highest between detergents with adjacent characteristics vectors, so that the order of the characteristics vectors as we rotate from one axis to the other in the positive quadrant can be established.

The ordering of "cleaning power per dollar" along one axis can be compared with the ordering of the characteristics vectors. If the orderings are the same, an equilibrium efficiency frontier can be built up with two characteristics as in Figure 5.7(a). The slopes of the facets can be determined within limits by the limiting prices at which the various detergents go off the market. If the ordering in terms of cleaning power does not agree with the ordering in terms of cross-elasticity, as in Figure 5.7(b), two characteristics do not describe the market appropriately, since detergent with cleaning power 3 in the figure cannot be on the efficiency frontier. But with a third characteristic, detergent 3 could be adjacent to detergents 2 and 1 in an extra dimension, and we could build up an efficiency frontier in three characteristics.

Other evidence could, of course, be used to determine the efficiency frontier for a given market situation. Among this evidence is that arising from ordinary activity-analysis theory, that, with r characteristics we would expect to find some consumers who used r commodities at the same time, unless all consumers were on corners or edges of the efficiency frontier.

Last, but possibly not least, simply asking consumers about the characteristics associated with various commodities may be much more productive than attempts to extract information concerning preferences within the context of conventional theory.

In general, if consumer preferences are well dispersed (so that all facets of the efficiency frontier are represented in some consumer's choice pattern), a combination of information concerning interpersonal variances in the collections of goods chosen and of the effects of price changes on both aggregate and individual choices can, in principle, be used to ferret out the nature of the consumption technology. Some of the problems that arise are similar to those met by psychologists in measuring intelligence, personality, and other multidimensional traits, so that techniques similar to those used in psychology, such as factor analysis, might prove useful.

Even without specification of the consumption technology, the present theory makes many predictions of a structural kind which may be contrasted with the predictions of conventional theory. Some of these are set out in Chart 1.

Conclusion

In this model we have extended into consumption theory activity analysis, which has proved so penetrating in its application to production theory. The crucial assumption in making this

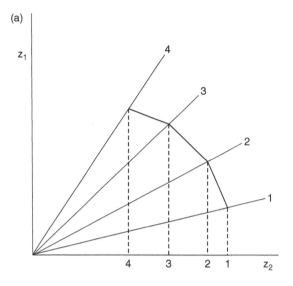

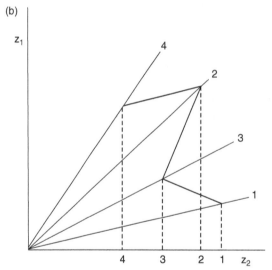

Figure 5.7

application has been the assumption that goods possess, or give rise to, multiple characteristics in fixed proportions and that it is these characteristics, not goods themselves, on which the consumer's preferences are exercised.

The result, as this brief survey of the possibilities has shown, is a model very many times richer in heuristic explanatory and predictive power than the conventional model of consumer behavior and one that deals easily with those many common-sense characteristics of actual behavior that have found no place in traditional exposition.

This paper is nothing more than a condensed presentation of some of the great number of possible ways in which the model can be used. It is hoped that a door has been opened to a new, rich treasure house of ideas for the future development of the most refined and least powerful branch of economic theory, the theory of the consumer himself.

Chart 1

This theory	*Conventional theory*
Wood will not be a close substitute for bread, since characteristics are dissimilar	No reason except "tastes" why they should not be close substitutes
A red Buick will be a close substitute for a gray Buick	No reason why they should be any closer substitutes than wood and bread
Substitution (for example, butter and margarine) is frequently intrinsic and objective, will be observed in many societies under many market conditions	No reason why close substitutes in one context should be close substitutes in another
A good may be displaced from the market by new goods or by price changes	No presumption that goods will be completely displaced
The labor–leisure choice may have a marked occupational pattern	Labor–leisure choice determined solely by individual preferences; no pattern, other than between individuals, would be predicted
(Gresham's Law) A monetary asset may cease to be on the efficiency frontier, and will disappear from the economy	No ex ante presumption that any good or asset will disappear from the economy
An individual is completely unaffected by price changes that leave unchanged the portion of the efficiency frontier on which his choice rests	An individual is affected by changes in all prices
Some commodity groups may be intrinsic, and universally so	No presumption that commodities forming a group (defined by a break in spectrum of cross-elasticities) in one context will form a group in another context

Appendix

Transformation of the utility function into G-space

Consider some characteristics vector z^* which does have an image x^* in G-space, and consider the set P of all vectors z preferred or indifferent to z^*. If U has the traditional properties, the set P is convex with an inner boundary which is the indifference surface through z^*. Now $z \geqq z^*$ implies z is in P so that every x such that $Bx \geqq z^*$, a set S, is preferred or indifferent to x^*. If we take some other z' in P, every x in S' such that $Bx \geqq z'$ is also preferred or indifferent to x'^*. Similarly for z'' in P and S'' such that that $Bx \geqq z''$, and so on. From the theory of inequalities, the sets S, S', $S'' \ldots$ are all convex, and since P is convex, a linear combination of z', z'' is in P, so that a linear combination of x's in S', S'' is also preferred or indifferent to x^*. Hence the set P of all x preferred or indifferent to x^* is the linear combination of all the sets S, S', S'', . . . and so is convex.

Thus the utility function transformed into G-space retains its essential convexity. A more intuitive way of looking at the situation is to note that all characteristics collections which are actually available are contained in an n-dimensional slice through the r-dimensional utility function and that all slices through a convex function are themselves convex. The transformation of this n-dimensional slice into G-space preserves this convexity.

"Revealed preference" in a complex economy

We shall use the structural properties of the consumption technology A, B (dropping the assumption of a one-to-one relationship between goods and activities) to show that in a complex economy with more activities than characteristics the efficiency choice always satisfies the weak axiom of revealed preference and will satisfy the strong axiom for sufficiently large price changes, so that satisfaction of even the strong axiom does not "reveal" convexity of the preference function itself.

Consider an economy with a consumption technology defined by

$$z = By,$$

$$x = Ay,$$

and a consumer subject to a budget constraint of the form $p^*x \leq k$ who has chosen goods x^* for activities y^*, giving characteristics z^*.

We know that if the consumer has made an efficient choice, y^* is the solution of the program (the value of which is k).

$$\text{Minimize } p^*Ay(= p^*x): $$
$$By = z^*, y \geq 0, \tag{5.10a}$$

which has a dual (solution v^*).

$$\text{Maximize } vz^*: vB \leq p^*A. \tag{5.10b}$$

The dual variables v can be interpreted as the implicit prices of the characteristics themselves. From the Kuh-Tucker Theorem, we can associate the vector v with the slope of the separating hyperplane between the set of attainable z's and the set of z's preferred or indifferent to z^*.

For the same satisfactions vector Z^* and a new price vector p^{**} the efficiency choice will be the solution y^{**} (giving x^{**}), v^{**}, of

$$\text{Min } p^{**}Ay : By = z^*, y \geq 0, $$
$$\text{Max } vz^* : vb \leq p^{**}A. \tag{5.11}$$

Since z^* is the same in 5.10a,b and 5.11, y^{**} is a feasible solution of (5.10a, b) and y^* of 5.11. From the fundamental theorem of linear programing we have

$$p^{**}Ay^* \geq v^{**}z^* = p^{**}Ay^{**}, \tag{5.12}$$

$$p^*Ay^{**} \geq v^*z^* = p^*Ay^*. \tag{5.13}$$

A program identical with 5.11 except that z^* is replaced by hz^* will have a solution hy^{**}, v^{**}. Choose h so that $hp^{**}Ay^{**} = p^{**}Ay^*$. From 5.12 $h \geq 1$. From 5.13,

$$hp^*Ay^{**} \geqq p^*Ay^{**} \geqq p^*Ay^*. \tag{5.14}$$

If we now write p for p^*, p' for p^{**}; $x = Ay^*$, $x' = hAy^{**}$, we have

$$p'x' = p'x \text{ implies } px' \geqq px, \tag{5.15}$$

satisfying the *weak axiom of revealed preference*.

The equality will occur on the right in 5.15 only if equalities hold in *both* 5.12 and 5.13, and these will hold only if y^{**} is optimal as well as feasible in 5.10a,b, and y^* is optimal as well as feasible in 5.11. In general, if the number of activities exceeds the number of characteristics, we can always find two prices p^*, p^{**} so related that neither of the solutions y^{**}, y^* is optimal in the other's program.

Hence, if the number of activities exceeds the number of characteristics (representing the number of primary constraints in the program), we can find prices so related that the strong axiom of revealed preference is satisfied, even though the consumer has obtained characteristics in unchanged proportions (z^*, hz^*) and has revealed nothing of his preference map.

The above effect represents an *efficiency substitution effect* which would occur even if characteristics were consumed in absolutely fixed proportions. If the consumer substitutes between different satisfactions bundles when his budget constraint changes, this private substitution effect is additional to the efficiency substitution effect.

Just as the conceptual experiment implicit in revealed preference implies "overcompensation" in the conventional analysis (see Samuelson 1948, 1953a), so the efficiency effect leads to "external overcompensation" additional to private overcompensation.

Acknowledgment

The author wishes to acknowledge helpful comments from various sources, including Gary Becker, Harry Johnson, and colleagues and students at Johns Hopkins University, especially Carl Christ, F. T. Sparrow, William Poole, C. Blackorby, T. Amemiya, and T. Tsushima.

Notes

1 The American Economic Association *Index of Economic Journals* lists 151 entries under category 2.111 (utility, demand, theory of the household) over the period 1940–63.
2 Since the units in which the characteristics are measured are arbitrary, the objectivity criterion relating goods and characteristics reduces to the requirement that the *relative* quantities of a particular characteristic between unit quantities of any pair of goods should be the same for all consumers.
3 The assumption that the consumption technology A, B is fixed is a convenience for discussing those aspects of the model (primarily static) that are the chief concern of this paper. The consequences of relaxing this particular assumption is only one of many possible extensions and expansions of the ideas presented and are discussed by the author elsewhere (Lancaster, 1966).
4 "Qualitative" is used here in a somewhat more general sense than in the author's work on the properties of qualitatively defined systems for which see Lancaster (1962, 1965).
5 If the relationship between goods and activities is not one-to-one, the consumption technology consists of the two matrixes B, A, as in the technology of the Von Neumann growth model.
6 Assuming no decomposability or singularities in the consumption technology matrix B, then, if z_n is the vector of any n components of z and B_n, the corresponding square submatrix of B, the subspace

of C-space to which the consumer is confined, is that defined by $z_{r-n} = B_{r-n}B_n^{-1}z_n$, where z_{r-n}, B_{r-n} are the vector and corresponding submatrix of B consisting of the components not included in z_n, B_n.

7 This is a somewhat imprecise statement in that, if the B matrix is partitionable into disconnected subtechnologies, for some of which the number of activities exceeds the number of characteristics and for others the reverse, an efficiency-substitution effect may exist over certain groups of activities, although the number of activities is less than the number of characteristics over-all.

8 One of the properties of this model is that it gives scope for the consumer to be more or less efficient in achieving his desired characteristics bundle, although we will usually assume he is completely efficient. This adds a realistic dimension to consumer behavior (traditional theory never permits him to be out of equilibrium) and gives a rationale for the Consumers' Union and similar institutions.

References

Becker, Gary S. "A Theory of the Allocation of Time," *Econ. J.*, September, 1965.

Debreu, Gerald. *Theory of Value.* Cowles Foundation Monograph 17, 1959.

——. "Topological Methods in Cardinal Utility Theory," in K. J. Arrow, S. Karlin, and P. Suppes (eds.). *Mathematical Methods in the Social Sciences, 1959.* Stanford, Calif.: Stanford Univ. Press, 1960.

Friedman, Milton, and Savage, L. J. "The Expected-Utility Hypothesis and the Measurability of Utility," *J.P.E.*, Vol. LX (December, 1952).

Gorman, W. M. "Separable Utility and Aggregation," *Econometrica*, Vol. XXVII (July, 1959).

Johnson, Harry G. "Demand Theory Further Revised or Goods Are Goods," *Economica*, N.S. 25 (May, 1958).

Karlin, S. *Mathematical Methods and Theory in Games, Programming and Economics.* New York: Pergamon Press, 1959.

Koopmans, T. C. "Stationary Ordinal Utility and Impatience," *Econometrica*, Vol. XXIII (April, 1960).

Koopmans, T. C. Diamond, P. A., and Williamson, R. E. "Stationary Utility and Time Perspective," *ibid.*, Vol. XXXII (January–April, 1964).

Lancaster, Kelvin J. "Revising Demand Theory," *Economica*, N.S. 24 (November, 1957).

——. "The Scope of Qualitative Economics," *Rev. Econ. Studies*, Vol. XXIX (1962).

——. "An Axiomatic Theory of Consumer Time Preference," *Internat. Econ. Rev., Vol.* IV (May, 1963).

——. "The Theory of Qualitative Linear Systems," *Econometrica*, Vol. XXXIII (April, 1965).

——. "Change and Innovation in the Technology of Consumption," *A.E.R.*, Papers and Proceedings, May, 1966 (to be published).

Morishima, M. "The Problem of Intrinsic Complementarity and Separability of Goods," *Metroeconomica*, Vol. XI (December, 1959).

Pearce, I. F. *A Contribution to Demand Analysis.* New York: Oxford Univ. Press, 1964.

Quandt, R. E. "A Probabilistic Theory of Consumer Behaviour," *Q.J.E.*, Vol. LXX (November, 1956).

Samuelson, P. A. "Consumption Theory in Terms of Revealed Preference," *Economica*, N.S. 15 (November, 1948).

——. "Consumption Theorems in Terms of Over-Compensation Rather than Indifference Comparisons," *ibid.*, N.S. 20 (February, 1953). *(a)*

——. "Prices of Factors and Goods in General Equilibrium," *Rev. Econ. Studies*, Vol. XXI (1953). *(b)*

Stigler, G. J. "The Cost of Subsistence," *J. Farm Econ.*, Vol. XXVII (1945).

Strotz, Robert, "The Empirical Implications of a Utility Tree," *Econometrica*, Vol. XXV (April, 1957).

——. "The Utility Tree: A Correction and Further Appraisal," *ibid.*, Vol. XXVII (July, 1959).

Thrall, Robert M., Coombs, C., and Davis, R. L. *Decision Processes.* New York: Wiley & Sons, 1954.

Uzawa, H. "Preference and Rational Choice in the Theory of Consumption," in K. J. Arrow, S. Karlin, and P. Suppes (eds.). *Mathematical Methods in the Social Sciences, 1959.* Stanford, Calif.: Stanford Univ. Press, 1960.

Von Neumann, J., and Morgenstern, O. *Theory of Games and Economic Behaviour.* Princeton, N.J.: Princeton Univ. Press, 1944.

6 Rationality in psychology and economics

Herbert A. Simon

The assumption that actors maximize subjective expected utility (economic rationality) supplies only a small part of the premises in economic reasoning, and that often not the essential part. The remainder of the premises are auxiliary empirical assumptions about actors' utilities, beliefs, expectations, and the like. Making these assumptions correctly requires an empirically founded theory of choice that specifies what information decision makers use and how they actually process it. This behavioral empirical base is largely lacking in contemporary economic analysis, and supplying it is essential for enhancing the explanatory and predictive power of economics.

The task I shall undertake here is to compare and contrast the concepts of rationality that are prevalent in psychology and economics, respectively. Economics has almost uniformly treated human behavior as rational. Psychology, on the other hand, has always been concerned with both the irrational and the rational aspects of behavior. In this paper, irrationality will be mentioned only obliquely; my concern is with rationality. Economics sometimes uses the term "irrationality" rather broadly (e.g., Becker 1962) and the term "rationality" correspondingly narrowly, so as to exclude from the domain of the rational many phenomena that psychology would include in it. For my purposes of comparison, I will have to use the broader conception of psychology.

One point should be set immediately outside dispute. Everyone agrees that people have reasons for what they do. They have motivations, and they use reason (well or badly) to respond to these motivations and reach their goals. Even much, or most, of the behavior that is called abnormal involves the exercise of thought and reason. Freud was most insistent that there is method in madness, that neuroses and psychoses were patients' solutions – not very satisfactory solutions in the long run – for the problems that troubled them.

I emphasize this point of agreement at the outset – that people have reasons for what they do – because it appears that economics sometimes feels called on to defend the thesis that human beings are rational. Psychology has no quarrel at all with this thesis. If there are differences in viewpoint, they must lie in conceptions of what constitutes rationality, not in the fact of rationality itself.

The judgment that certain behavior is "rational" or "reasonable" can be reached only by viewing the behavior in the context of a set of premises or "givens." These givens include the situation in which the behavior takes place, the goals it is aimed at realizing, and the computational means available for determining how the goals can be attained. In the course of this conference, many participants referred to the context of behavior as its "frame," a label that I will also use from time to time. Notice that the frame must be comprehensive enough to encompass goals, the definition of the situation, and computational resources.

In its treatment of rationality, neoclassical economics differs from the other social sciences in three main respects: (*a*) in its silence about the content of goals and values; (*b*) in its postulating global consistency of behavior; and (*c*) in its postulating "one world" – that behavior is objectively rational in relation to its total environment, including both present and future environment as the actor moves through time.

In contrast, the other social sciences, in their treatment of rationality, (*a*) seek to determine empirically the nature and origins of values and their changes with time and experience; (*b*) seek to determine the processes, individual and social, whereby selected aspects of reality are noticed and postulated as the "givens" (factual bases) for reasoning about action; (*c*) seek to determine the computational strategies that are used in reasoning, so that very limited information-processing capabilities can cope with complex realities; and (*d*) seek to describe and explain the ways in which nonrational processes (e.g., motivations, emotions, and sensory stimuli) influence the focus of attention and the definition of the situation that set the factual givens for the rational processes.

These important differences in the conceptualization of rationality rest on an even more fundamental distinction: in economics, rationality is viewed in terms of the choices it produces; in the other social sciences, it is viewed in terms of the processes it employs (Simon 1976/1982). The rationality of economics is substantive rationality, while the rationality of psychology is procedural rationality.

Substantive and procedural rationality

If we accept values as given and consistent, if we postulate an objective description of the world as it really is, and if we assume that the decision maker's computational powers are unlimited, then two important consequences follow. First, we do not need to distinguish between the real world and the decision maker's perception of it: he or she perceives the world as it really is. Second, we can predict the choices that will be made by a rational decision maker entirely from our knowledge of the real world and without a knowledge of the decision maker's perceptions or modes of calculation. (We do, of course, have to know his or her utility function.)

If, on the other hand, we accept the proposition that both the knowledge and the computational power of the decision maker are severely limited, then we must distinguish between the real world and the actor's perception of it and reasoning about it. That is to say, we must construct a theory (and test it empirically) of the processes of decision. Our theory must include not only the reasoning processes but also the processes that generate the actor's subjective representation of the decision problem, his or her frame (Simon 1978/1982).

The rational person of neoclassical economics always reaches the decision that is objectively, or substantively, best in terms of the given utility function. The rational person of cognitive psychology goes about making his or her decisions in a way that is procedurally reasonable in the light of the available knowledge and means of computation.

Embracing a substantive theory of rationality has had significant consequences for neoclassical economics and especially for its methodology. Until very recently, neoclassical economics has developed no strong empirical methodology for investigating the processes whereby values are formed, for the content of the utility function lies outside its self-defined scope. It has developed no special methodology for investigating how particular aspects of reality, rather than other aspects, come to the decision maker's attention, or for investigating how a representation of the choice situation is formed, or for investigating how reasoning processes are applied to draw out the consequences of such representations.

All these investigations call for empirical inquiry at the micro level – detailed study of decision makers engaged in the task of choice (Simon 1979b/1982, 1982). They are not questions that are easily answered by even the most sophisticated econometric analysis of aggregate data. To understand the processes that the economic actor employs in making decisions calls for observing these processes directly while they are going on, either in real world situations or in the laboratory, and/or interrogating the decision maker about beliefs, expectations, and methods of calculation and reasoning.

Securing access in order to observe decision processes in business firms or government organizations is difficult but often quite feasible – there are already a substantial number of successful studies of this kind in the literature. To extrapolate and generalize the findings requires attention to problems of sampling and aggregation; but these problems are surely easier to solve than the problem of going from the micro level of hypothetical "representative firms" or "typical consumers" to the level of markets.

Laboratory experiments on decision processes raise questions of their generalizability to real world situations. Studies that depend on interrogation of one kind or another raise questions of the veridicality of responses. There is no dearth of methodological issues but no reason to suppose that these issues are any more intractable than those encountered in standard econometric practice. But since experimental economics is well represented at this conference, I will say no more about the methodological issues it faces. They are best discussed in the context of concrete examples, a number of which will be provided here.

To move from substantive to procedural rationality requires a major extension of the empirical foundations of economics. It is not enough to add theoretical postulates about the shape of the utility function, or about the way in which actors form expectations about the future, or about their attention or inattention to particular environmental variables. These are assumptions about matters of fact, and the whole ethos of science requires such assumptions to be supported by publicly repeatable observations that are obtained and analyzed objectively.

In the following sections of this paper, I should like to illustrate, with concrete examples, the difficulties that contemporary neoclassical economics faces on a number of fronts owing to the insufficiency of its empirical foundations. These examples will also suggest the directions in which empirical work needs to go. My topics will include the shape and dimensions of the utility function, the role of attentional processes, the formation of expectations, and the sources of the empirical parameters and models that characterize cost and supply functions.

In all these examples we will see that the conclusions that are reached by neoclassical reasoning depend very much on the "auxiliary" factual assumptions that have to be made to define the situation and very little on the assumptions of substantive rationality – in particular, the utility-maximization assumptions. Indeed, in many cases, provided that the factual assumptions are retained, the conclusions reached within the utility-maximization framework could be reached as readily from much weaker assumptions of "reasonableness" in behavior (Becker 1962). Almost all the action, all the ability to reach nontrivial conclusions, comes from the factual assumptions and very little from the assumptions of optimization. Hence it becomes critically important to submit the factual assumptions to careful empirical test.

Empirical basis for the utility function

Contemporary neoclassical economics provides no theoretical basis for specifying the shape and content of the utility function, and this gap is very inadequately filled by empirical research using econometric techniques. The gap is important because many conclusions that have been drawn in the literature about the way in which the economy operates depend on assumptions about consumers' utility functions.

To illustrate this claim, I will take two examples from the work of one of my discussants, Gary Becker, at the risk, of course, of introducing circularity by discussing a discussant. Both examples are drawn from Becker's well-known *A Treatise on the Family* (1981).

The opportunities of children

My account of the first example is not original but follows an enlightening analysis that has been carried out recently by Arthur Goldberger (1985) of Becker's (1981, chs. 6, 7) theory of the opportunities of children and intergenerational mobility. On page 116 of his book, Becker follows a mathematical demonstration with the interpretation: "If parents correctly anticipate their children's luck and endowment, an increase in either would not add an equal amount to the income of children." This interpretation is later (pp. 125–26) used to question whether public compensatory education programs will achieve their goal since parents whose children participate in these programs simply reallocate elsewhere resources they would otherwise have invested in these children.

I will return in a moment to the empirical evidence for the conclusion and its application. First, however, I would like to report Goldberger's analysis of the underlying argument that leads up to it.

Goldberger shows that Becker's conclusion follows from specific assumptions that parents' utility grows positively with parents' consumption and child's income and that the child's income is an additive function of parents' investment and child's luck. If the latter function is multiplicative instead of additive, the conclusion does not follow. Moreover, the whole derivation employs a homothetic utility function. No empirical support is provided for these assumptions.

But Milton Friedman (1953) would tell us that we should concentrate our efforts on testing the conclusions, not the assumptions, and this is what Becker does. Three pieces of evidence are cited, one relating to compensatory education and two to other public "compensatory" programs. On education, Becker quotes Arthur Jensen's "famous and controversial essay" (the characterization is Becker's) to the effect that "compensatory education has been tried and it apparently has failed" (p. 125). The essay quoted is, indeed, controversial; others have subsequently reached quite different evaluations of Headstart and other compensatory education programs. Moreover, Jensen himself attributes their failure – if there was one – to causes very different from the utility functions of parents. To choose among Jensen's explanation, Becker's, and the thousand others that could be dreamed up, it would surely be important to find out directly whether families whose children participated in such programs diverted their money, nurturance, or attention away from those children. That would provide a relatively direct test of the nature of their preferences (although very far from a test either that they possessed consistent utility functions or that they were maximizing anything).

Becker's other two pieces of evidence are more to the point. It does appear that public health programs cause people to devote less of their private budgets to health matters (the programs are presumably intended to do this) and that food supplements to pregnant women are to some extent diverted by reallocation of private budgets. To that extent we can conclude that some substitutions of the sort that utility theory predicts do actually take place. But of course as Becker has pointed out elsewhere (Becker 1962), price elasticity of demand is not a very strong test of utility maximization.

What one sees in this example are matters of substantial practical as well as theoretical importance disposed of on the basis of unsupported theoretical assumptions and scanty evidence about the conclusions. Economics is too important, intellectually as well as practically, to be treated with this kind of casual empiricism.

What one also sees in this example is that the conclusions depend primarily not on the assumption of optimization but on the (untested) auxiliary assumption that the interaction of luck and endowment is additive rather than multiplicative. Utility maximization is neither a necessary nor a sufficient condition for compensatory behavior.

Finally, in this example one begins to understand the real decision making when one undertakes (as in the public health and food supplement research) to gather direct evidence about behavior through field studies or field experiments.

Labor force participation of women

Let me now turn to a second example from Becker's (1981) book. On pages 245–56 he gives us his interpretation of the evolution of the American family since World War II. The salient fact around which the analysis revolves is that there has been a steady rise in the labor force participation of married women, including those with small children. At the outset (p. 245), Becker tells us that he believes "that the major cause of these changes is the growth in the earning power of women as the American economy developed." This credo is then buttressed by the empirical observation that the weekly earnings of employed women grew substantially during this period. This, he observes, implies an increase in the opportunity cost of staying in the home and also raises the relative cost of children, thereby reducing the demand for children.

However, the question is never raised as to (*a*) whether the increase in real earnings of women was more rapid than the increase in real earnings of men during this same period or (*b*) whether the increase in women's weekly earnings might not have been in some measure due to an increase in average hours worked – itself a form rather than a consequence of greater labor force participation.

Moreover, Becker places the whole weight of explanation on an unexplained shift in the demand curve for women's labor. No account is given of why this event should have taken place at this particular moment in American history or whether it was a sudden shock or a continuing development. Nor is any evidence provided (except the circular evidence that women moved into the labor force) that the event in fact took place. In particular, the possibility is not explored that a shift in the utility function of women caused a shift in the supply of women in the labor market in the face of a highly elastic demand curve and generally rising productivity in the economy.

So in this example as in the previous one, the action comes, not from the assumption of utility maximization, but from factual assumptions about the shifting or stability of particular supply and demand curves. The true explanation will be obtained not by raising the sophistication of the economic reasoning but only by painstaking examination of occupations in manufacturing and service industries and an even more difficult empirical examination of changes in women's attitudes about where they prefer to work. Utility maximization is neither a necessary nor a sufficient condition for the conclusion that was reached. The action comes from the empirical assumptions, including assumptions about how people view their world.

Attention and representation

In a substantive theory of rationality there is no place for a variable like focus of attention. But in a procedural theory, it may be very important to know under what circumstances certain aspects of reality will be heeded and others ignored. I wish now to present two examples of situations in which focus of attention is a major determinant of behavior. The first rests on very strong empirical evidence; the second is more speculative, but I will try to make it plausible.

The purchase of flood insurance

Kunreuther et al. (1978) have studied decisions of property owners whether to purchase insurance against flood damage. Neoclassical theory would predict that an owner would buy insurance if the expected reimbursable damage from floods was greater than the premium. The actual data are in egregious conflict with this claim. Instead it appears that insurance is purchased mainly by persons who have experienced damaging floods or who are acquainted with persons who have had such experiences, more or less independently of the cost/benefit ratio of the purchaser.

If we wish to understand the insurance-buying behavior, then we must determine, as Kunreuther and his colleagues did, the circumstances that attract the attention of a property owner to this decision alternative. Utility maximization is neither a necessary nor a sufficient condition for deducing who will buy insurance. The process of deciding – in this case, the process that puts the item on the decision agenda – is the important thing.

Voting behavior

Voting behavior provides a more complex example of the role of attention in behavior. Both before and since Marx, it has been widely believed that voters respond, at least to an important extent, to their economic interests. Let us assume that is so. A substantial number of empirical studies have shown correlations between economic conditions and votes in American elections (Simon 1985). But such studies use a great variety of independent variables as measures of voters' perceptions of the economic consequences of their choices. (See, e.g., Hibbs 1982; and Weatherford 1983.) Some investigators have tried to measure the economic well-being of voters at the time of the election as compared with their well-being at some previous time. Others have measured the state of the economy – the level of the GNP, say, or of employment. Which of these (or what other measure) is the true measure of economic advantage? Quite different predictions can be made if different measures are chosen.

Consider the situation of a voter at the time of the 1984 presidential election who wished to maximize his or her economic well-being. Which of the following facts about the economy should influence the vote? (1) Real incomes of a majority have increased over the past 4 years but at less than the historical rate of a couple of decades earlier. (2) Dispersion of incomes has increased. (3) The rate of inflation has declined dramatically. (4) The rate of interest remains high compared with the historical past. (5) The national debt and deficit have increased dramatically. (6) The balance of trade has "worsened" dramatically. (7) Farm foreclosures have increased substantially. (8) Unemployment has decreased recently but is higher than it was 4 years previously. If we throw noneconomic considerations into the voter's utility function, we may add such facts as, The armament situation has changed in complex ways, et cetera, et cetera, moving into race tensions and equity to minorities, energy, the environment, creationism, abortion, and what not.

To predict how a voter, even a voter motivated solely by concern for his or her economic well-being, will vote requires much more than assuming utility maximization. A voter who attends to the rate of inflation may behave quite differently from a voter who attends to the federal deficit. Moreover, in order to predict where a voter's attention will focus, we may need to know his or her economic beliefs. A monetarist may consider different facts to be salient than the facts to which a Keynesian will attend. In any model of voting behavior that has any prospect of predicting behavior, almost all the action will lie in these auxiliary assumptions about attention and belief that define the decision maker's frame.

Expectations

Neoclassical theory, either with or without the assumption of rational expectations, cannot explain the phenomenon of the business cycle. In previous papers (e.g., Simon 1984) I have shown that auxiliary assumptions, which in this case amount to departures from objective rationality, must be annexed to the neoclassical model before a business cycle can be made to appear. I will repeat the argument here very briefly.

If we examine Keynes's reasoning in *The General Theory of Employment, Interest and Money* (1936), we see that, at most points, it fits perfectly the neoclassical mold of substantive rationality. Auxiliary assumptions (it does not matter whether we view them as "irrationalities" or simply as expectations) are introduced, however, at points that are critical to the explanation of the business cycle. One of these auxiliary assumptions is the postulate that labor suffers from the money illusion – that unions cannot distinguish between changes in real and money wages, respectively. The addition of this postulate is sufficient to produce underemployment stagnation in the Keynesian theory.

Remarkably enough, when we move from Keynes to the other end of the spectrum of economic theories – for example, to Lucas's (1981) rational expectations models – the same picture presents itself. The business cycle in these models derives, not from the assumptions of rationality, but from the appearance of money illusion in an erstwhile Eden. Only, in Lucas's theory, the illusion is suffered by businessmen, who cannot distinguish between general price movements and price changes in their industry, instead of by workers.

The action in business-cycle theories appears to reside not in the rationality assumptions but in auxiliary assumptions about the processes that people use to form expectations about future events. A theory of procedural rationality would have to employ empirical research to investigate these expectation-forming processes. Again, the assumption of utility or profit maximization provides neither a necessary nor a sufficient condition for the existence of business cycles.

We already have experience in using direct methods to learn how people form expectations about the future. Direct inquiries into people's expectations about business conditions, pioneered by George Katona (1951) at the University of Michigan, have for many years supplied inputs to econometric models of the economy. Studies have been made of planning methods and investment decision processes of business firms (for examples, see Eliasson 1976; and Bromiley 1986) that give us considerable information about what the forecasting firms do and whether and how forecasting enters into the process of choosing investments. This kind of information, which could easily be multiplied, provides us with powerful means for testing the rational expectations theory or other theories about how expectations are formed. There is no need to fall back on casual empiricism or on dubious indirect inferences from econometric data.

Other empirical parameters

My two final examples of the role of facts in economic reasoning are a little different from the previous ones. There are important cases in which not only are assumptions of substantive rationality insufficient to account for the observed phenomena but also parsimonious alternative explanations can be provided with only a minimal reference to rationality. The two examples I will discuss are the distribution of business firm sizes and the magnitudes of executive salaries.

Distribution of business firm sizes

There is no unequivocal neoclassical theory of the distribution of business firm sizes. The traditional theory of the determinants of firm size was expounded by Jacob Viner (1931) and, by some kind of intellectual Gresham's Law, has survived to this day in elementary economics textbooks and books on intermediate price theory. It postulates a family of U-shaped short-run cost curves; a U-shaped long-run cost curve that is the envelope of the short-run curves; and a firm whose size corresponds to the scale of minimum cost on the long-run curve.

There are innumerable difficulties with this account. The most serious is that empirical studies very often show cost curves to be J shaped, without a recognizable minimum, rather than U shaped. With a J-shaped curve, that is, decreasing costs at all sizes, there is no upper bound on firm size. Nearly as serious is that the theory says nothing about parameter values of the cost curves, hence nothing about what sizes of firms will actually be observed. In particular, no conclusions can be drawn about the distribution of firm sizes.

If the theory is interpreted to mean that all firms in an industry have identical cost curves (which, in the absence of rents, should be the case), then, in equilibrium, all firms will be the same size. But this prediction is contradicted by the facts as squarely as any prediction could be. The actual distributions are highly skewed, with many small firms and a few that are very large.

If, on the contrary, each firm has its own cost curve, bearing no relation to the curves of the others, then the theory predicts too little: any size distribution whatsoever can be accommodated. But the fact is that the actual distributions are quite regular and similar, approximating the Pareto distribution in the upper tail. The traditional theory is therefore a total failure in predicting actual firm size distributions and should be banished from the textbooks.

But here we face the difficulty that nature abhors a vacuum, that a bad theory is preferred to none. However, in this case, a wholly satisfactory alternative is available. It rests on plausible (although not well-tested) premises, and these premises are even consistent with possible behaviors of reasonable men and women. The key premise (Ijiri and Simon 1977) is that the expected rate of growth of a firm during any period is proportionate to the size it had attained at the beginning of that period – the so-called Gibrat assumption. With this assumption and a little attention to boundary conditions, the Pareto distribution can be deduced as the steady-state equilibrium of the system.

Such tests as have been made of the Gibrat assumption have had generally positive results. But even if we were satisfied that the assumption is empirically valid, we might wish to probe deeper. In a world in which people have reasons for their actions, why would such a relation hold? This is not the place for a full discussion of the matter, and I limit myself to two comments. First, if average rate of return on capital is independent of size of firm (as seems to be true to a first approximation), it is rather easy to think of reasons why access to internal or external capital for expansion should be, on average, roughly commensurate with present size. Second, we really do not need to do this kind of armchair guessing. We can undertake to study business firms to determine how growth comes about. What we should not do is to cling to a theory that predicts very little and that little incorrectly.

Distribution of executive salaries

My second example of a failure of classical theory that can be remedied within a framework of procedural rationality is the prediction of the distribution of the salaries of top executives.

Neoclassical theory would, of course, explain the salaries of executives in terms of individual abilities for managerial work. Moreover, a very able executive would presumably have greater productivity when engaged in large affairs, as in managing a large business firm. Hence the combined forces of supply and demand would produce a strong correlation of executive ability with firm size. Rees (1973, p. 201), in his textbook exposition of the theory, puts it this way: "The person who alone among hundreds of competing junior executives in a large corporation eventually rises to the presidency must surely have special qualities that account for this rise, although they differ from the qualities that make a successful scientist or a successful salesperson. In any event, a business that is not a monopoly would soon run at a loss if it selected executives without any regard to those kinds of ability relevant in managing a business well."

The claim is moderate and plausible. It does not require any assumption of maximization, only the assumption that those who select executives will behave reasonably, by taking ability into account. It leaves open the question of the processes of selection: how ability is judged and how accurately it can be estimated. It also leaves open the question of whether the characteristics that allow a person to compete successfully for advancement are closely correlated with the characteristics that make for effective management. But we will ignore the Peter Principle and other postulates that have been put forward challenging the close relation between managerial ability and selectability.

Difficulty arises, however, when we try to move from these premises to an account of the observed salary distribution function. A number of studies (e.g., Roberts 1959) have shown that the average compensation of top executives increases with the cube root of the size of the firm. I have been told, though I have not seen the data, that this relation continues to hold when executive bonuses and fringe benefits are included in salary. How shall we explain this very regular and persistent distribution?

Neoclassical theory, without strong auxiliary assumptions, is helpless. As Lucas (1978) has pointed out, what are needed are an assumption about the marginal product of managerial work as a function of firm size and managerial ability and an assumption about the distribution of managerial ability measured in the same units as in the previously mentioned function. Since there are no empirical data either on the marginal productivity of managers (except the salary data themselves) or on the distribution of ability, it is easy to manufacture functions that will produce the desired distribution of salaries. However, it should be noted that certain "obvious" choices of function will not work – for example, the Gibrat assumption that the marginal productivity of a manager is proportional to the size of the firm. If a function is found that fits the data, it is, of course, not refutable and hence profoundly uninteresting as a theoretical premise.

As an alternative route to an explanation of the observed salary distribution (Simon 1979a/1982), we can introduce two factual assumptions that can be verified (and for one of which we already have sufficient empirical data). The first assumption is that business organizations have a pyramidal form and that the number of subordinates reporting directly to an executive does not vary much from one organization to another or from one organizational level to another – that the span of control is relatively constant. This is a well-known fact about business organizations. The second assumption is that, by some generally accepted norm of "fairness," the ratio of the salary of an executive to the salaries of his or her immediate subordinates is a constant over organizations and over levels.

With these two assumptions, it follows immediately that the log of the salary of the top executive will vary linearly with the log of company size; and with reasonable assumptions, fitting observed facts, about the sizes of the two parameters of the theory (the span of control and the "fair" ratio of salaries), the coefficient in this linear relation can be predicted to be in the neighborhood of 0.3 – very close to the observed value.

Of course, we will be more confident that this is the correct explanation when we have more direct evidence that the postulated norm of fairness really exists in people's minds. My only claim at the moment is that here we have an explanation that takes process into account, that does not rely on any assumption of utility or profit maximization, and that does describe a realizable decision process that is not dependent on quantities that are unobservable by the actors and by economists studying the phenomena. Of course this explanation does make the correct prediction – quantitatively as well as qualitatively.

Neoclassical economists have raised several objections to the explanation I have just outlined. Rees (1973, p. 201) argues that the theory "is too special, since it applies only to hierarchical organizations." He points out that the salary distributions of such professionals as architects and attorneys, who typically work in small organizations, also are highly skewed. Of course, there is no reason to suppose that salaries in all occupations are fixed in the same way. A procedural theory of rationality would predict that the method of salary determination would depend on what kinds of information were available for assessing worth.

Position in hierarchy provides such information in large organizations. In the case of architectural and legal firms, direct measures are generally available of the magnitude of the revenues associated with an associate's work and the magnitude of the contracts he or she is able to attract. Moreover, the sizes of jobs have a highly skewed distribution for a variety of reasons that we could explore empirically. Hence the fact that the salaries of professionals other than executives of business firms are skewed hardly seems a reason for rejecting the theory of executive compensation I have proposed.

Recently, new information has been gained about bonuses and other nonsalary awards that make up an increasing part of executive compensation. This information shows that bonuses vary strongly with profits and other statistics that might be taken as measures of the effectiveness of executive performance. But such evidence merely shows that companies try to motivate their executives to make profits (often, alas, with excessive attention to short-run profits, as has been pointed out in the literature). It does not show that the incentives bear any close relation to the marginal worth of the executives or even that the fluctuations in profits are the result of the incentive compensation.

The evidence that incentives are offered to executives to increase profits is just what a procedural theory would predict. It would predict also that the rewards would be related to available statistics of company performance, even in the absence of reliable information about the exact relation between performance and managerial behavior. It would make no assumption that profits are maximized since the observable evidence provides no basis for that assumption. It would assume only that executives (and corporate boards) believe that executives can influence profits through their behavior and that a bonus plan would thereby motivate them to try harder.

A procedural theory would assume that people have reasons for what they do when they set executive salaries and that these reasons take account of the highly imperfect and incomplete information available to them. However, it would be essential, in order to predict behavior more precisely, to have good empirical information both about the kinds of information to which the decision makers have ready access and about their beliefs and opinions on the mechanisms of the world on which their decisions operate. The most likely sources of such information are direct studies of the behaviors, values, beliefs, and opinions of the actors.

Summing up

Between supporters of substantive and procedural theories of rationality there are fundamental differences about what constitutes a principled, parsimonious, scientific theory. We may put the matter in Bayesian terms. Neoclassical economists attach a very large prior probability (0.9944?) to the proposition that people have consistent utility functions and in fact maximize utilities in an objective sense. As my examples show, they are prepared to make whatever auxiliary empirical assumptions are necessary in order to preserve the utility-maximization postulate, even when the empirical assumptions are unverified. When verification is demanded, they tend to look for evidence that the theory makes correct predictions and resist advice that they should look instead directly at the decision mechanisms.

Given the magnitude of the Bayesian prior that expresses confidence in the theory and the weakness of the kinds of indirect evidence that are allowed for testing it, neoclassical economics becomes, as has been observed more than once, essentially tautological and irrefutable. Because of its preoccupation with utility maximization, it fails to observe that most of its "action" – the force of its predictions – derives from the, usually untested, auxiliary assumptions that describe the environment in which decisions are made. The examples show that the important conclusions it draws can usually also be drawn, with the aid of the auxiliary assumptions, from the postulate that people are procedurally rational and without assuming that they maximize utility.

It is too easy, within the neoclassical methodological framework, to save the theory from unpleasant evidence by modifying the auxiliary assumptions and providing a new framework within which the actor "must have been operating." Hence neoclassical theory, as usually applied, is an exceedingly weak theory, as shown by the difficulty of finding sets of facts, actual or hypothetical, that cannot be rationalized and made consistent with it.

Behavioral theories of rationality attach a high prior probability (0.9944?) to the assumption that economic actors use the same basic processes in making their decisions as have been observed in other human cognitive activities and that these processes are indeed observable. In situations that are complex and in which information is very incomplete (i.e., virtually all real world situations), the behavioral theories deny that there is any magic for producing behavior even approximating an objective maximization of profits or utilities. They therefore seek to determine what the actual frame of the decision is, how that frame arises from the decision situation, and how, within that frame, reason operates.

In this kind of complexity, there is no single sovereign principle for deductive prediction. The emerging laws of procedural rationality have much more the complexity of molecular biology than the simplicity of classical mechanics. As a consequence, they call for a very high ratio of empirical investigation to theory building. They require painstaking factual study of the decision-making process itself.

What is to be done? What prescription for economic research derives from my analysis?

First, I would recommend that we stop debating whether a theory of substantive rationality and the assumptions of utility maximization provide a sufficient base for explaining and predicting economic behavior. The evidence is overwhelming that they do not.

We already have in psychology a substantial body of empirically tested theory about the processes people actually use to make boundedly rational, or "reasonable," decisions. This body of theory asserts that the processes are sensitive to the complexity of decision-making contexts and to learning processes as well.

The application of this procedural theory of rationality to economics requires extensive empirical research, much of it at micro-micro levels, to determine specifically how process is molded to context in actual economic environments and the consequences of this interaction for the economic outcomes of these processes. Economics without psychological and sociological research to determine the givens of the decision-making situation, the focus of attention, the problem representation, and the processes used to identify alternatives, estimate consequences, and choose among possibilities-such economics is a one-bladed scissors. Let us replace it with an instrument capable of cutting through our ignorance about rational human behavior.

References

Becker, G. S. 1962. Irrational behavior and economic theory. *Journal of Political Economy* 70:1–13.

Becker, G. S. 1981. *A Treatise on the Family.* Cambridge, Mass.: Harvard University Press.

Bromiley, P. 1986. Corporate planning and capital investment. *Journal of Economic Behavior and Organization* 7:147–70.

Eliasson, G. 1976. *Business Economic Planning.* New York: Wiley.

Friedman, M. 1953. *Essays in Positive Economics.* Chicago: University of Chicago Press.

Goldberger, A. S. In press. *Modeling the Economic Family.* Ann Arbor: University of Michigan Press.

Hibbs, D. A., Jr. 1982. Economic outcomes and political support for British governments among occupational classes. *American Political Science Review* 76:259–79.

Ijiri, Y., and Simon, H. A. 1977. *Skew Distributions and the Sizes of Business Firms.* Amsterdam: North-Holland.

Katona, G. 1951. *Psychological Analysis of Economic Behavior.* New York: McGraw-Hill.

Keynes, J. M. 1936. *The General Theory of Employment, Interest and Money.* London: Macmillan.

Kunreuther, H., with Ginsberg, R.; Miller, L.; Sagi, P.; Slovic, P.; Borkan, B.; and Katz, N. 1978. *Disaster Insurance Protection: Public Policy Lessons.* New York: Wiley.

Lucas, R. E., Jr. 1978. On the size distribution of business firms. *Bell Journal of Economics* 9:508–23.

Lucas, R. E., Jr. 1981. *Studies in Business Cycle Theory.* Cambridge, Mass.: MIT Press.

Rees, A. 1973. *The Economics of Work and Pay.* New York: Harper & Row.

Roberts, D. R. 1959. *Executive Compensation.* Glencoe, Ill.: Free Press.

Simon, H. A. 1976. From substantive to procedural rationality. In S. J. Latsis (ed.), *Method and Appraisal in Economics.* Cambridge: Cambridge University Press. Reprinted in *Models of Bounded Rationality.* 2 vols. Cambridge, Mass.: MIT Press, 1982.

Simon, H. A. 1978. Rationality as process and product of thought. *American Economic Review: Proceedings* 68:1–16. Reprinted in *Models of Bounded Rationality.* 2 vols. Cambridge, Mass.: MIT Press, 1982.

Simon, H. A. 1979a. On parsimonious explanations of production relations. *Scandinavian Journal of Economics* 81:459–74. Reprinted in *Models of Bounded Rationality.* 2 vols. Cambridge, Mass.: MIT Press, 1982.

Simon, H. A. 1979b. Rational decision making in business organizations. *American Economic Review* 69:493–513. Reprinted in *Models of Bounded Rationality.* 2 vols. Cambridge, Mass.: MIT Press, 1982.

Simon, H. A. 1982. *Models of Bounded Rationality.* 2 vols. Cambridge, Mass.: MIT Press.

Simon, H. A. 1984. On the behavioral and rational foundations of economic dynamics. *Journal of Economic Behavior and Organization* 5:35–55.

Simon, H. A. 1985. Human nature in politics: The dialogue of psychology with political science. *American Political Science Review* 79:293–304.

Viner, J. 1931. Cost curves and supply curves. *Zeitschrift für Nationalökonomie* 3:23–46.

Weatherford, M. S. 1983. Economic voting and the "symbolic politics" argument. *American Political Science Review* 77:158–74.

Part II

Theory of the firm

Introduction

More than any other subject in microeconomics, the contemporary theory of the firm could be directly attributed to the dissatisfaction with the neoclassical model of the-firm-as-production-function, especially in view of the increasing complexity of modern business. While the neoclassical model is highly popular for its malleability, its limitations are becoming harder to accept.[1]

Coase (1937) set the agenda with a series of questions: Why do firms exist? If arm's length (market) transactions are the default mode of transactions, then what are the advantages of firms over other methods of organizing production activities? What determines the scope of a firm? As Coase succinctly put it: "Our task is to attempt to discover why a firm emerges at all in a specialized exchange economy."[2]

Transaction costs and monitoring costs

Coase's insight (that firms are organized to minimize transaction costs[3]) was followed by others (Oliver Williamson in particular) who have elaborated on the nature of these costs and suggest further implications. In Williamson's scheme, it is *haggling* cost (i.e., a kind of transaction cost) that is lower within firms than in markets. Thus firms, compared to markets, provide a more efficient way to resolve the conflicts pervasive in all kinds of economic interactions.

Differing slightly from Coase's view, Alchian and Demsetz (Demsetz, 2001) theorized that *monitoring* cost reduction is the source of the advantage of firms over markets. Since many activities require teamwork, they pointed out, monitoring costs required to coordinate individuals working independently (in a market) would be enormously more expensive than when these workers belong to a firm with its established hierarchy.

Monitoring costs also helps answer another question: Within a firm, what is the difference between owners and employers? The hired monitor must be given the incentive to do his job in a way that benefits the firm's owner. One possible incentive, according to this hypothesis, is by giving the monitor what's left after the (contractual) employees are paid, i.e., making him the *residual claimant* of the team's earnings. Thus, "residual claimancy" is the difference between the owners and the employees.

The contractual view of the firm could be traced to Cheung (1983), among others. As Cheung put it, the word "firm" in Coase's theory is "simply a short-hand description of a way to organize activities under contractual arrangements that differ from those of ordinary product markets" (Cheung 1983, p. 3). In other words, Coase's firm "relates to the choice of contracts."

Current attempts to explain the difference between firms and markets make two common assumptions: (a) contracts can never address every contingency, and (b) it is costly to change trading partners once the contract has started, i.e., "lock-in" could develop. These theories can be divided into two groups.[4] The first group revolves around transaction costs. These are the theories pioneered by Coase, expanded by Williamson (1975, 1979, 1985), and Klein *et al.* (1978). The second group sees "property cost" as the key. In these theories, the difference between employer and employers lies in "rights of control." Almost by definition, the owner is whoever has the residual rights of control over the physical assets. Foremost proponents of this view are Grossman and Hart (1986), and Hart and Moore (1990).[5]

Vertical integration

A comprehensive theory of the firm should also explain why some firms choose to merge, or inversely, to split. After all, these decisions are about where to draw a firm's boundary, which is one of its basic properties. Based on Coase, recent contributions (Williamson (1975, 1979, 1985), Arrow (1975), Crocker (1983) and others) have offered a more constructive view of the firm,[6] suggesting the firm has better access to information, greater managerial control and more flexibility. If this is true then vertical integration is simply a way to expand these advantages. Note that this view is related to the opportunism made possible by the unobservability of aspects of contracts. In the cases (where assets are specific) examined by these authors, "the cost of vertical contracting will generally increase more than the cost of vertical integration" (p. 298). This view, however, was criticized by by Alchian and Demsetz (1972).[7]

Variants

The neoclassical profit-maximization model of the firm is not the only one discussed in the literature. There are two major groups of alternative theories.

In the first group are models that replace the neoclassical "total profit" with an alternative maximand,[8] still with the assumption of the firm-as-a-black-box.[9] This variant is very popular in comparative economics, as it is thought to represent socialist firms, as in China and the former Yugoslavia, where these firms were supposedly run for the workers' benefit. The "labor-managed firm" introduced by Ward (1958) is representative of this type of model. A generalized setup was offered in Meade (1972). In a similar vein, Weitzman (1984) showed that profit-sharing firms, by their nature, could alleviate macroeconomic stagflation.

The second group consists a more diverse types of models that deviate more radically from the neoclassical canon. These include Nelson and Winter's evolutionary theory and W. B. Arthur's (1989) theory which highlights increasing returns and "lock-in effects."

Part II has seven articles. Coase (1937) must be read for its historical significance. Alchian and Demsetz (1972) is the pioneering article that highlights the role of information in the formation of the firm. Hart (1989), written primarily for legal scholars, was a superb survey of the theory of the firm. This author is also a major proponent of the "contract approach" to this theory. Ward (1958) modified the neoclassical maximand, replacing profit maximization with a different objective, for example, wage maximization, to study behavior of many types of non profit-maximizing firms. This paper is extremely influential in comparative economics in analyses of firms presumably found in socialist countries. Williamson (2002) was a useful introductory survey of the institutional approach pioneered by this author. Klein *et al.* (1978) considered vertical integration as a problem of expanding the firm's boundary.

This paper also offered a particularly clear explanation of what came to be known as "the hold up problem." Fama (1980) is the path-breaking work on agency theory, which highlights problems caused by the divergence of interests between a "contractor" (broadly defined) and his contracted agent.

Notes

1 Some authors, e.g., Spence (1975), prefer the "economics of internal organization" to "the theory of the firm". In their view, "the theory of the firm" would lead to a narrower, even misleading set of questions, such as "what do firms really maximize?". That question, Spence contended, has no compelling answer because of "the diversity and complexity of the environment within which firms operate and of the decisions that they make."
2 It is also worth noting that another work of Coase (1960), on the problem of "social cost," is seminal in the development of economics. In this article, Coase used the concept of transaction costs to show how the legal system could affect the working of the economic system.
3 There are other reasons for the emergence of the firm, e.g., division of labor, risk, and the coordination of production activities (see Cheung, 1983).
4 Whinston (2001).
5 As suggested by Demsetz, as resource allocation mechanisms, the former are "management guided", the latter are "price guided". This comparison is somewhat misleading, since the neoclassical ("firm-as-a black-box") view is not strictly a deliberate choice away from the "management-guided" view. The neoclassical formulation is a necessity given the limited tools and conceptualization available at the time.
6 "Constructive" in the sense that it is not a mere reaction to market imperfections.
7 See all of this in Masten (1993).
8 As Spence (1975) suggests, however, the question "What do firms really maximize?" lacks a compelling answer because of "the diversity and complexity of the environment within which firms operate and of the decisions that they make".
9 This has a long tradition (see Koutsoyannis, 1979).

Bibliography

Alchian, A. and Demsetz, H. (1972) "Production, Information Cost, and Economic Organization," *American Economic Review* 62, December, pp. 777–95.
Arrow, K. J. (1975) "Vertical Integration and Communication," *Bell Journal of Eonomics* 6, pp. 173–83.
Arthur, W. B. (1989) "Competing Technologies, Increasing Returns, and Lock-in by Historical Events," *The Economic Journal* 99, pp. 116–31.
Cheung, S. (1983) "The Contractual Nature of the Firm," *Journal of Law and Economics* 26, pp. 1–21.
Coase, R. (1937) "The Nature of Firm," *Economica*, November, 4(4), pp. 386–405.
Coase, R. (1960) "The Problem of Social Cost," *Journal of Law and Economics*, pp. 1–40.
Crocker, K. J. (1983) "Vertical Integration and the Private Use of Information," *Bell Journal of Economics* 14(1), pp. 236–48.
Demsetz, H. (2001) "The Firm in Economic Theory," *American Economic Review* 87, pp. 426–29.
Fama, E. (1980) "Agency Problems and the Theory of the Firm," *Journal of Political Economy* 88, pp. 288–307.
Gibbons, R. (2005) "Four Formal (izable) Theories of the Firm," *Journal of Economic Behavior and Organization*, pp. 200–45.
Grossman, S. J. and Hart, O. D. (1986) "The Costs and Benefits of Ownership: A Theory of Vertical and Lateral Integration," *Journal of Political Economy*, 94(4), pp. 691–719.
Hart, O. D. (1989) "An Economist's Perspective on the Theory of the Firm," *Columbia Law Journal* 89, pp. 1757–74.
Hart, O. D. (1995), *Firms, Contracts, and Financial Structure*, Oxford: Clarendon, Press.
Hart, O. D. and Moore, J. (1990) "Property Rights and the Nature of the Firm," *Journal of Political Economy* 98(6), pp. 1119–58.

Holmstrom, B. and Roberts, J. (1998) "The Boundaries of the Firm Revisited," *Journal of Economic Perspectives*, 12(4), pp. 73–94.

Klein, B., Crawford, R. G. and Alchian, A. A. (1978) "Vertical Integration, Appropriable Rents, and the Competitive Contracting Process," *Journal of Law and Economics*, 21(2), pp. 297–326.

Koutsoyiannis, A. (1979) *Modern Microeconomics*, New York: Macmillan.

Masten, S. (1993), "The Legal Basis for the Firm," in Williamson, O.E. and Winter, S. G. (ed.) *The Nature of the Firm*, New York: Oxford University Press.

Meade, J. E. (1972) "The Theory of Labour-Managed Firms and of Profit Sharing," *The Economic Journal* 82, pp. 402–28.

Miyazaki, H. and Neary H. M. (1983) "The Illyrian Firm Revisited," *The Bell Journal of Economics* 14, pp. 259–70.

Nelson, R. R. and Winter, S. (1982) *The Evolutionary Theory of Economic Change*, Cambridge, MA: Harvard University Press.

Shelanski, H. A. and Klein, P. G. (1975) "Empirical Research in Transaction Cost Economics: A Review and Assessment," *Journal of Law, Economics, and Organization*, 11(2), pp. 335–61.

Spence, A. M. (1975) "The Economics of Internal Organization," *Bell Journal of Economics* 6, pp. 163–72.

Ward, B. (1958) "The Firm in Illyria: Market Syndicalism," *American Economic Review* 48, pp. 566–89.

Weitzman, M. (1984) *The Share Economy: Conquering Stagflation*, Cambridge, MA: Harvard University Press.

Whinston, M. (2001) "Assessing Property Rights and Transaction-Cost Theories of the Firm," *American Economic Review* 91, pp. 184–99.

Williamson, O. E. (1975) *Markets and Hierarchies: Analysis and Antitrust Implications,* New York: Free Press.

Williamson, O. E. (1979) "Transaction Cost Economics: The Governance of Contractual Relations," *Journal of Law and Economics* 22, pp. 233–62.

Williamson, O. E. (1981) "The Economics of Organization: The Transaction Cost Approach," *American Journal of Sociology* 87, pp. 548–77.

Williamson, O. E. (1985) *The Economic Institutions of Capitalism*, New York: Free Press.

Williamson, O. E. (2002) "The Theory of the Firm as Governance Structure," *Journal of Economic Perspectives* 16(3), pp. 171–95.

7 The nature of the firm

R. H. Coase

Economic theory has suffered in the past from a failure to state clearly its assumptions. Economists in building up a theory have often omitted to examine the foundations on which it was erected. This examination is, however, essential not only to prevent the misunderstanding and needless controversy which arise from a lack of knowledge of the assumptions on which a theory is based, but also because of the extreme importance for economics of good judgment in choosing between rival sets of assumptions. For instance, it is suggested that the use of the word "firm" in economics may be different from the use of the term by the "plain man."[1] Since there is apparently a trend in economic theory towards starting analysis with the individual firm and not with the industry,[2] it is all the more necessary not only that a clear definition of the word "firm" should be given but that its difference from a firm in the "real world," if it exists, should be made clear. Mrs. Robinson has said that "the two questions to be asked of a set of assumptions in economics are: Are they tractable? and: Do they correspond with the real world?"[3] Though, as Mrs. Robinson points out, "more often one set will be manageable and the other realistic," yet there may well be branches of theory where assumptions may be both manageable and realistic. It is hoped to show in the following paper that a definition of a firm may be obtained which is not only realistic in that it corresponds to what is meant by a firm in the real world, but is tractable by two of the most powerful instruments of economic analysis developed by Marshall, the idea of the margin and that of substitution, together giving the idea of substitution at the margin.[4] Our definition must, of course, "relate to formal relations which are capable of being *conceived* exactly."[5]

I

It is convenient if, in searching for a definition of a firm, we first consider the economic system as it is normally treated by the economist. Let us consider the description of the economic system given by Sir Arthur Salter.[6] "The normal economic system works itself. For its current operation it is under no central control, it needs no central survey. Over the whole range of human activity and human need, supply is adjusted to demand, and production to consumption, by a process that is automatic, elastic and responsive." An economist thinks of the economic system as being co-ordinated by the price mechanism and society becomes not an organisation but an organism.[7] The economic system "works itself." This does not mean that there is no planning by individuals. These exercise foresight and choose between alternatives. This is necessarily so if there is to be order in the system. But this theory assumes that the direction of resources is dependent directly on the price mechanism. Indeed, it is often considered to be an objection to economic planning that it merely tries to do what is already done by the price mechanism.[8] Sir Arthur Salter's description, however, gives a very incomplete picture of our economic system. Within a firm, the description does not fit at all. For instance, in economic theory we find that the allocation of factors of production between different uses is determined by the price mechanism. The price of factor A becomes higher in X than in Y. As a result, A moves from Y to X until the difference between the prices in X and Y, except in so far as it compensates for other differential advantages, disappears. Yet in the real world, we find that there are many areas where this does not apply. If a workman moves from department Y to department X, he does not go because of a change in relative prices, but because he is ordered to do so. Those who object to economic planning on the grounds that the problem is solved by price movements can be answered by pointing out that there is planning within our economic system which is quite different from the individual planning mentioned above and which is akin to what is normally called economic planning. The example given above is typical of a large sphere in our modern economic system. Of course, this fact has not been ignored by economists. Marshall introduces organisation as a fourth factor of production; J. B. Clark gives the co-ordinating function to the entrepreneur Professor Knight introduces managers who co-ordinate. As D. H. Robertson points out, we find "islands of conscious power in this ocean of unconscious co-operation like lumps of butter coagulating in a pail of buttermilk."[9] But in view of the fact that it is usually argued that co-ordination will be done by the price mechanism, why is such organisation necessary? Why are there these "islands of conscious power?" Outside the firm, price movements direct production, which is co-ordinated through a series of exchange transactions on the market. Within a firm, these market transactions are eliminated and in place of the complicated market structure with exchange transactions is substituted the entrepreneur-co-ordinator, who directs production.[10] It is clear that these are alternative methods of co-ordinating production. Yet, having regard to the fact that if production is regulated by price movements, production could be carried on without any organisation at all, well might we ask, why is there any organisation?

Of course, the degree to which the price mechanism is superseded varies greatly. In a department store, the allocation of the different sections to the various locations in the building may be done by the controlling authority or it may be the result of competitive price bidding for space. In the Lancashire cotton industry, a weaver can rent power and shop-room and can obtain looms and yarn on credit.[11] This co-ordination of the various factors of production is, however, normally carried out without the intervention of the price mechanism. As is evident, the amount of "vertical" integration, involving as it does the supersession of the price mechanism, varies greatly from industry to industry and from firm to firm.

It can, I think, be assumed that the distinguishing mark of the firm is the supersession of the price mechanism. It is, of course, as Professor Robbins points out, "related to an outside network of relative prices and costs,"[12] but it is important to discover the exact nature of this relationship. This distinction between the allocation of resources in a firm and the allocation in the economic system has been very vividly described by Mr. Maurice Dobb when discussing Adam Smith's conception of the capitalist: "It began to be seen that there was something more important than the relations inside each factory or unit captained by an undertaker; there were the relations of the undertaker with the rest of the economic world outside his immediate sphere... the undertaker busies himself with the division of labour inside each firm and he plans and organises consciously," but "he is related to the much larger economic specialisation, of which he himself is merely one specialised unit. Here, he plays his part as a single cell in a larger organism, mainly unconscious of the wider rôle he fills."[13]

In view of the fact that while economists treat the price mechanism as a co-ordinating instrument, they also admit the co-ordinating function of the "entrepreneur," it is surely important to enquire why co-ordination is the work of the price mechanism in one case and of the entrepreneur in another. The purpose of this paper is to bridge what appears to be a gap in economic theory between the assumption (made for some purposes) that resources are allocated by means of the price mechanism and the assumption (made for other purposes) that this allocation is dependent on the entrepreneur-co-ordinator. We have to explain the basis on which, in practice, this choice between alternatives is effected.[14]

II

Our task is to attempt to discover why a firm emerges at all in a specialised exchange economy. The price mechanism (considered purely from the side of the direction of resources) might be superseded if the relationship which replaced it was desired for its own sake. This would be the case, for example, if some people preferred to work under the direction of some other person. Such individuals would accept less in order to work under someone, and firms would arise naturally from this. But it would appear that this cannot be a very important reason, for it would rather seem that the opposite tendency is operating if one judges from the stress normally laid on the advantage of "being one's own master."[15] Of course, if the desire was not to be controlled but to control, to exercise power over others, then people might be willing to give up something in order to direct others; that is, they would be willing to pay others more than they could get under the price mechanism in order to be able to direct them. But this implies that those who direct pay in order to be able to do this and are not paid to direct, which is clearly not true in the majority of cases.[16] Firms might also exist if purchasers preferred commodities which are produced by firms to those not so produced; but even in spheres where one would expect such preferences (if they exist) to be of negligible importance, firms are to be found in the real world.[17] Therefore there must be other elements involved.

The main reason why it is profitable to establish a firm would seem to be that there is a cost of using the price mechanism. The most obvious cost of "organising" production through the price mechanism is that of discovering what the relevant prices are.[18] This cost may be reduced but it will not be eliminated by the emergence of specialists who will sell this information. The costs of negotiating and concluding a separate contract for each exchange transaction which takes place on a market must also be taken into account.[19] Again, in certain markets, e.g., produce exchanges, a technique is devised for minimising these contract costs; but they are not eliminated. It is true that contracts are not eliminated when there is a firm but they are greatly reduced. A factor of production (or the owner thereof) does not have to make a series of contracts with the factors with whom he is co-operating within the firm, as would be necessary, of course, if this co-operation were as a direct result of the working of the price mechanism. For this series of contracts is substituted one. At this stage, it is important to note the character of the contract into which a factor enters that is employed within a firm. The contract is one whereby the factor, for a certain remuneration (which may be fixed or fluctuating), agrees to obey the directions of an entrepreneur *within certain limits*.[20] The essence of the contract is that it should only state the limits to the powers of the entrepreneur. Within these limits, he can therefore direct the other factors of production.

There are, however, other disadvantages – or costs – of using the price mechanism. It may be desired to make a long-term contract for the supply of some article or service. This may be due to the fact that if one contract is made for a longer period, instead of several shorter ones, then certain costs of making each contract will be avoided. Or, owing to the risk attitude of the people concerned, they may prefer to make a long rather than a short-term contract. Now, owing to the difficulty of forecasting, the longer the period of the contract is for the supply of the commodity or service, the less possible, and indeed, the less desirable it is for the person purchasing to specify what the other contracting party is expected to do. It may well be a matter of indifference to the person supplying the service or commodity which of several courses of action is taken, but not to the purchaser of that service or commodity. But the purchaser will not know which of these several courses he will want the supplier to take. Therefore, the service which is being provided is expressed in general terms, the exact details being left until a later date. All that is stated in the contract is the limits to what the persons supplying the commodity or service are expected to do. The details of what the supplier is expected to do is not stated in the contract but is decided later by the purchaser. When the direction of resources (within the limits of the contract) becomes dependent on the buyer in this way, that relationship which I term a "firm" may be obtained.[21] A firm is likely therefore to emerge in those cases where a very short-term contract would be unsatisfactory. It is obviously of more importance in the case of services – labour – than it is in the case of the buying of commodities. In the case of commodities, the main items can be stated in advance and the details which will be decided later will be of minor significance.

We may sum up this section of the argument by saying that the operation of a market costs something and by forming an organisation and allowing some authority (an "entrepreneur") to direct the resources, certain marketing costs are saved. The entrepreneur has to carry out his function at less cost, taking into account the fact that he may get factors of production at a lower price than the market transactions which he supersedes, because it is always possible to revert to the open market if he fails to do this.

The question of uncertainty is one which is often considered to be very relevant to the study of the equilibrium of the firm. It seems improbable that a firm would emerge without the existence of uncertainty. But those, for instance, Professor Knight, who make the *mode of payment* the distinguishing mark of the firm – fixed incomes being guaranteed to some of those engaged in production by a person who takes the residual, and fluctuating, income – would appear to be introducing a point which is irrelevant to the problem we are considering. One entrepreneur may sell his services to another for a certain sum of money, while the payment to his employees may be mainly or wholly a share in profits.[22] The significant question would appear to be why the allocation of resources is not done directly by the price mechanism.

Another factor that should be noted is that exchange transactions on a market and the same transactions organised within a firm are often treated differently by Governments or other bodies with regulatory powers. If we consider the operation of a sales tax, it is clear that it is a tax on market transactions and not on the same transactions organised within the firm. Now since these are alternative methods of "organisation" – by the price mechanism or by the entrepreneur – such a regulation would bring into existence firms which otherwise would have no *raison d'être*. It would furnish a reason for the emergence of a firm in a specialised exchange economy. Of course, to the extent that firms already exist, such a measure as a sales tax would merely tend to make them larger than they would otherwise be. Similarly, quota schemes, and methods of price control which imply that there is rationing, and which do not apply to firms producing such products for themselves, by allowing advantages to those who organise within the firm and not through the market, necessarily encourage the growth of firms. But it is difficult to believe that it is measures such as have been mentioned in this paragraph which have brought firms into existence. Such measures would, however, tend to have this result if they did not exist for other reasons.

These, then, are the reasons why organisations such as firms exist in a specialised exchange economy in which it is generally assumed that the distribution of resources is "organised" by the price mechanism. A firm, therefore, consists of the system of relationships which comes into existence when the direction of resources is dependent on an entrepreneur.

The approach which has just been sketched would appear to offer an advantage in that it is possible to give a scientific meaning to what is meant by saying that a firm gets larger or smaller. A firm becomes larger as additional transactions (which could be exchange trans-actions co-ordinated through the price mechanism) are organised by the entrepreneur and becomes smaller as he abandons the organisation of such transactions. The question which arises is whether it is possible to study the forces which determine the size of the firm. Why does the entrepreneur not organise one less transaction or one more? It is interesting to note that Professor Knight considers that:

> the relation between efficiency and size is one of the most serious problems of theory, being, in contrast with the relation for a plant, largely a matter of personality and historical accident rather than of intelligible general principles. But the question is peculiarly vital because the possibility of monopoly gain offers a powerful incentive to *continuous and unlimited* expansion of the firm, which force must be offset by some equally powerful one making for decreased efficiency (in the production of money income) with growth in size, if even boundary competition is to exist.[23]

Professor Knight would appear to consider that it is impossible to treat scientifically the determinants of the size of the firm. On the basis of the concept of the firm developed above, this task will now be attempted.

It was suggested that the introduction of the firm was due primarily to the existence of marketing costs. A pertinent question to ask would appear to be (quite apart from the monopoly considerations raised by Professor Knight), why, if by organising one can eliminate certain costs and in fact reduce the cost of production, are there any market transactions at all?[24] Why is not all production carried on by one big firm? There would appear to be certain possible explanations.

First, as a firm gets larger, there may be decreasing returns to the entrepreneur function, that is, the costs of organising additional transactions within the firm may rise.[25] Naturally, a point must be reached where the costs of organising an extra transaction within the firm are equal to the costs involved in carrying out the transaction in the open market, or, to the costs of organising by another entrepreneur. Secondly, it may be that as the transactions which are organised increase, the entrepreneur fails to place the factors of production in the uses where their value is greatest, that is, fails to make the best use of the factors of production. Again, a point must be reached where the loss through the waste of resources is equal to the marketing costs of the exchange transaction in the open market or to the loss if the transaction was organised by another entrepreneur. Finally, the supply price of one or more of the factors of production may rise, because the "other advantages" of a small firm are greater than those of a large firm.[26] Of course, the actual point where the expansion of the firm ceases might be determined by a combination of the factors mentioned above. The first two reasons given most probably correspond to the economists' phrase of "diminishing returns to management."[27]

The point has been made in the previous paragraph that a firm will tend to expand until the costs of organising an extra transaction within the firm become equal to the costs of carrying out the same transaction by means of an exchange on the open market or the costs of organising in another firm. But if the firm stops its expansion at a point below the costs of marketing in the open market and at a point equal to the costs of organising in another firm, in most cases (excluding the case of "combination"[28]), this will imply that there is a market transaction between these two producers, each of whom could organise it at less than the actual marketing costs. How is the paradox to be resolved? If we consider an example the reason for this will become clear. Suppose A is buying a product from B and that both A and B could organise this marketing transaction at less than its present cost. B, we can assume, is not organising one process or stage of production, but several. If A therefore wishes to avoid a market transaction, he will have to take over all the processes of production controlled by B. Unless A takes over all the processes of production, a market transaction will still remain, although it is a different product that is bought. But we have previously assumed that as each producer expands he becomes less efficient; the additional costs of organising extra transactions increase. It is probable that A's cost of organising the transactions previously organised by B will be greater than B's cost of doing the same thing. A therefore will take over the whole of B's organisation only if his cost of organising B's work is not greater than B's cost by an amount equal to the costs of carrying out an exchange transaction on the open market. But once it becomes economical to have a market transaction, it also pays to divide production in such a way that the cost of organising an extra transaction in each firm is the same.

Up to now it has been assumed that the exchange transactions which take place through the price mechanism are homogeneous. In fact, nothing could be more diverse than the actual transactions which take place in our modern world. This would seem to imply that the costs of carrying out exchange transactions through the price mechanism will vary considerably as will also the costs of organising these transactions within the firm. It seems therefore possible that quite apart from the question of diminishing returns the costs of organising certain transactions within the firm may be greater than the costs of carrying out the exchange transactions in the open market. This would necessarily imply that there were exchange transactions carried out through the price mechanism, but would it mean that there would have to be more than one firm? Clearly not, for all those areas in the economic system where the direction of resources was not dependent directly on the price mechanism could be organised within one firm. The factors which were discussed earlier would seem to be the important ones, though it is difficult to say whether "diminishing returns to management" or the rising supply price of factors is likely to be the more important.

Other things being equal, therefore, a firm will tend to be larger:

(a) the less the costs of organising and the slower these costs rise with an increase in the transactions organised
(b) the less likely the entrepreneur is to make mistakes and the smaller the increase in mistakes with an increase in the transactions organised
(c) the greater the lowering (or the less the rise) in the supply price of factors of production to firms of larger size.

Apart from variations in the supply price of factors of production to firms of different sizes, it would appear that the costs of organising and the losses through mistakes will increase with an increase in the spatial distribution of the transactions organised, in the dissimilarity of the transactions, and in the probability of changes in the relevant prices.[29] As more transactions are organised by an entrepreneur, it would appear that the transactions would tend to be either different in kind or in different places. This furnishes an additional reason why efficiency will tend to decrease as the firm gets larger. Inventions which tend to bring factors of production nearer together, by lessening spatial distribution, tend to increase the size of the firm.[30] Changes like the telephone and the telegraph which tend to reduce the cost of organising spatially will tend to increase the size of the firm. All changes which improve managerial technique will tend to increase the size of the firm.[31, 32]

It should be noted that the definition of a firm which was given above can be used to give more precise meanings to the terms "combination" and "integration."[33] There is a combination when transactions which were previously organised by two or more entrepreneurs become organised by one. This becomes integration when it involves the organisation of transactions which were previously carried out between the entrepreneurs on a market. A firm can expand in either or both of these two ways. The whole of the "structure of competitive industry" becomes tractable by the ordinary technique of economic analysis.

III

The problem which has been investigated in the previous section has not been entirely neglected by economists and it is now necessary to consider why the reasons given above for the emergence of a firm in a specialised exchange economy are to be preferred to the other explanations which have been offered.

It is sometimes said that the reason for the existence of a firm is to be found in the division of labour. This is the view of Professor Usher, a view which has been adopted and expanded by Mr. Maurice Dobb. The firm becomes "the result of an increasing complexity of the division of labour.... The growth of this economic differentiation creates the need for some integrating force without which differentiation would collapse into chaos; and it is as the integrating force in a differentiated economy that industrial forms are chiefly significant."[34] The answer to this argument is an obvious one. The "integrating force in a differentiated economy" already exists in the form of the price mechanism. It is perhaps the main achievement of economic science that it has shown that there is no reason to suppose that specialisation must lead to chaos.[35] The reason given by Mr. Maurice Dobb is therefore inadmissible. What has to be explained is why one integrating force (the entrepreneur) should be substituted for another integrating force (the price mechanism).

The most interesting reasons (and probably the most widely accepted) which have been given to explain this fact are those to be found in Professor Knight's *Risk, Uncertainty and Profit*. His views will be examined in some detail.

Professor Knight starts with a system in which there is no uncertainty:

> acting as individuals under absolute freedom but without collusion men are supposed to have organised economic life with the primary and secondary division of labour, the use of capital, etc., developed to the point familiar in present-day America. The principal fact which calls for the exercise of the imagination is the internal organisation of the productive groups or establishments. With uncertainty entirely absent, every individual being in possession of perfect knowledge of the situation, there would be no occasion for anything of the nature of responsible management or control of productive activity. Even marketing transactions in any realistic sense would not be found. The flow of raw materials and productive services to the consumer would be entirely automatic.[36]

Professor Knight says that we can imagine this adjustment as being "the result of a long process of experimentation worked out by trial-and-error methods alone," while it is not necessary "to imagine every worker doing exactly the right thing at the right time in a sort of 'pre-established harmony' with the work of others. There might be managers, superintendents, etc., for the purpose of co-ordinating the activities of individuals," though these managers would be performing a purely routine function, "without responsibility of any sort."[37]

Professor Knight then continues:

> With the introduction of uncertainty – the fact of ignorance and the necessity of acting upon opinion rather than knowledge – into this Eden-like situation, its character is entirely changed. . . . With uncertainty present doing things, the actual execution of activity, becomes in a real sense a secondary part of life; the primary problem or function is deciding what to do and how to do it.[38]

This fact of uncertainty brings about the two most important characteristics of social organisation.

> In the first place, goods are produced for a market, on the basis of entirely impersonal prediction of wants, not for the satisfaction of the wants of the producers themselves. The producer takes the responsibility of forecasting the consumers' wants. In the second place, the work of forecasting and at the same time a large part of the technological direction and control of production are still further concentrated upon a very narrow class of the producers, and we meet with a new economic functionary, the entrepreneur. . . When uncertainty is present and the task of deciding what to do and how to do it takes the ascendancy over that of execution the internal organisation of the productive groups is no longer a matter of indifference or a mechanical detail. Centralisation of this deciding and controlling function is imperative, a process of "cephalisation" is inevitable.[39]

The most fundamental change is:

> the system under which the confident and venturesome assume the risk or insure the doubtful and timid by guaranteeing to the latter a specified income in return for an assignment of the actual results. . . . With human nature as we know it it would be impracticable or very unusual for one man to guarantee to another a definite result of the latter's actions without being given power to direct his work. And on the other hand the second party would not place himself under the direction of the first without such a guarantee. . . . The result of this manifold specialisation of function is the enterprise and wage system of industry. Its existence in the world is the direct result of the fact of uncertainty.[40]

These quotations give the essence of Professor Knight's theory. The fact of uncertainty means that people have to forecast future wants. Therefore, you get a special class springing up who direct the activities of others to whom they give guaranteed wages. It acts because good judgment is generally associated with confidence in one's judgment.[41]

Professor Knight would appear to leave himself open to criticism on several grounds. First of all, as he himself points out, the fact that certain people have better judgment or better knowledge does not mean that they can only get an income from it by themselves actively taking part in production. They can sell advice or knowledge. Every business buys the services of a host of advisers. We can imagine a system where all advice or knowledge was bought as required. Again, it is possible to get a reward from better knowledge or judgment not by actively taking part in production but by making contracts with people who are producing. A merchant buying for future delivery represents an example of this. But this merely illustrates the point that it is quite possible to give a guaranteed reward providing that certain acts are performed without directing the performance of those acts. Professor Knight says that "with human nature as we know it it would be impracticable or very unusual for one man to guarantee to another a definite result of the latter's actions without being given power to direct his work." This is surely incorrect. A large proportion of jobs are done to contract, that is, the contractor is guaranteed a certain sum providing he performs certain acts. But this does not involve any direction. It does mean, however, that the system of relative prices has been changed and that there will be a new arrangement of the factors of production.[42] The fact that Professor Knight mentions that the "second party would not place himself under the direction of the first without such a guarantee" is irrelevant to the problem we are considering. Finally, it seems important to notice that even in the case of an economic system where there is no uncertainty Professor Knight considers that there would be co-ordinators, though they would perform only a routine function. He immediately adds that they would be "without responsibility of any sort," which raises the question by whom are they paid and why? It seems that nowhere does Professor Knight give a reason why the price mechanism should be superseded.

IV

It would seem important to examine one further point and that is to consider the relevance of this discussion to the general question of the "cost-curve of the firm."

It has sometimes been assumed that a firm is limited in size under perfect competition if its cost curve slopes upward,[43] while under imperfect competition, it is limited in size because it will not pay to produce more than the output at which marginal cost is equal to marginal revenue.[44] But it is clear that a firm may produce more than one product and, therefore, there appears to be no *prima facie* reason why this upward slope of the cost curve in the case of perfect competition or the fact that marginal cost will not always be below marginal revenue in the case of imperfect competition should limit the size of the firm.[45] Mrs. Robinson[46] makes the simplifying assumption that only one product is being produced. But it is clearly important to investigate how the number of products produced by a firm is determined, while no theory which assumes that only one product is in fact produced can have very great practical significance.

It might be replied that under perfect competition, since everything that is produced can be sold at the prevailing price, then there is no need for any other product to be produced. But this argument ignores the fact that there may be a point where it is less costly to organise the exchange transactions of a new product than to organise further exchange transactions of the old product. This point can be illustrated in the following way. Imagine, following von Thunen, that there is a town, the consuming centre, and that industries are located around this central point in rings. These conditions are illustrated in the following diagram in which A, B and C represent different industries.

Imagine an entrepreneur who starts controlling exchange transactions from x. Now as he extends his activities in the same produce (B), the cost of organising increases until at some point it becomes equal to that of a dissimilar product which is nearer. As the firm expands, it will therefore from this point include more than one product $(A$ and $C)$. This treatment of

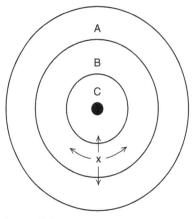

Figure 7.1

the problem is obviously incomplete,[47] but it is necessary to show that merely proving that the cost curve turns upwards does not give a limitation to the size of the firm. So far we have only considered the case of perfect competition; the case of imperfect competition would appear to be obvious.

To determine the size of the firm, we have to consider the marketing costs (that is, the costs of using the price mechanism), and the costs of organising of different entrepreneurs and then we can determine how many products will be produced by each firm and how much of each it will produce. It would, therefore, appear that Mr. Shove[48] in his article on "Imperfect Competition" was asking questions which Mrs. Robinson's cost curve apparatus cannot answer. The factors mentioned above would seem to be the relevant ones.

V

Only one task now remains; and that is, to see whether the concept of a firm which has been developed fits in with that existing in the real world. We can best approach the question of what constitutes a firm in practice by considering the legal relationship normally called that of "master and servant" or "employer and employee."[49] The essentials of this relationship have been given as follows:

(1) The servant must be under the duty of rendering personal services to the master or to others on behalf of the master, otherwise the contract is a contract for sale of goods or the like.

(2) The master must have the right to control the servant's work, either personally or by another servant or agent. It is this right of control or interference, of being entitled to tell the servant when to work (within the hours of service) and when not to work, and what work to do and how to do it (within the terms of such service) which is the dominant characteristic in this relation and marks off the servant from an independent contractor, or from one employed merely to give to his employer the fruits of his labour. In the latter case, the contractor or performer is not under the employer's control in doing the work or effecting the service; he has to shape and manage his work so as to give the result he has contracted to effect.[50]

We thus see that it is the fact of direction which is the essence of the legal concept of "employer and employee," just as it was in the economic concept which was developed above. It is interesting to note that Professor Batt says further:

> That which distinguishes an agent from a servant is not the absence or presence of a fixed wage or the payment only of commission on business done, but rather the freedom with which an agent may carry out his employment.[51]

We can therefore conclude that the definition we have given is one which approximates closely to the firm as it is considered in the real world.

Our definition is, therefore, realistic. Is it manageable? This ought to be clear. When we are considering how large a firm will be the principle of marginalism works smoothly. The question always is, will it pay to bring an extra exchange transaction under the organising authority? At the margin, the costs of organising within the firm will be equal either to the costs of organising in another firm or to the costs involved in leaving the transaction to be "organised" by the price mechanism. Business men will be constantly experimenting, controlling more or less, and in this way, equilibrium will be maintained. This gives the position of equilibrium for static analysis. But it is clear that the dynamic factors are also of considerable importance, and an investigation of the effect changes have on the cost of organising within the firm and on marketing costs generally will enable one to explain why firms get larger and smaller. We thus have a theory of moving equilibrium. The above analysis would also appear to have clarified the relationship between initiative or enterprise and management. Initiative means forecasting and operates through the price mechanism by the making of new contracts. Management proper merely reacts to price changes, rearranging the factors of production under its control. That the business man normally combines both functions is an obvious result of the marketing costs which were discussed above. Finally, this analysis enables us to state more exactly what is meant by the "marginal product" of the entrepreneur. But an elaboration of this point would take us far from our comparatively simple task of definition and clarification.

Notes

1 Joan Robinson, *Economics is a Serious Subject*, p. 12.
2 See N. Kaldor, "The Equilibrium of the Firm," *Economic Journal*, March, 1934.
3 Op. cit., p. 6.
4 J. M. Keynes, *Essays in Biography*, pp. 223–4.
5 L. Robbins, *Nature and Significance of Economic Science*, p. 63.
6 This description is quoted with approval by D. H. Robertson, Control of Industry, p. 85, and by Professor Arnold Plant, "Trends in Business Administration," *Economica*, February, 1932. It appears in *Allied Shipping Control*, pp. 16–17.
7 See F. A. Hayek, "The Trend of Economic Thinking," *Economica*, May, 1933.
8 See F. A. Hayek, op. cit.
9 Op. cit., p. 85.
10 In the rest of this paper I shall use the term entrepreneur to refer to the person or persons who, in a competitive system, takes the place of the price mechanism in the direction of resources.
11 *Survey of Textile Industries*, p. 26.
12 Op. cit., p. 71.
13 Capitalist Enterprise and Social Progress, p. 20. Cf., also, Henderson, *Supply and Demand*, pp. 3–5.
14 It is easy to see when the State takes over the direction of an industry that, in planning it, it is doing something which was previously done by the price mechanism. What is usually not realised is that any business man in organising the relations between his departments is also doing something which could be organised through the price mechanism. There is therefore point in Mr. Durbin's answer to those who emphasise the problems involved in economic planning that the same problems have to

be solved by business men in the competitive system. (See "Economic Calculus in a Planned Economy," *Economic Journal*, December, 1936.) The important difference between these two cases is that economic planning is imposed on industry while firms arise voluntarily because they represent a more efficient method of organising production. In a competitive system, there is an "optimum" amount of planning!

15 Cf. Harry Dawes, "Labour Mobility in the Steel Industry," *Economic Journal*, March, 1934, who instances "the trek to retail shopkeeping and insurance work by the better paid of skilled men due to the desire (often the main aim in life of a worker) to be independent" (p. 86).

16 None the less, this is not altogether fanciful. Some small shopkeepers are said to earn less than their assistants.

17 G. F. Shove, "The Imperfection of the Market: a Further Note," *Economic Journal*, March, 1933, p. 116, note 1, points out that such preferences may exist, although the example he gives is almost the reverse of the instance given in the text.

18 According to N. Kaldor, "A Classificatory Note of the Detenninateness of Equilibrium," *Review of Economic Studies*, February, 1934, it is one of the assumptions of static theory that "All the relevant prices are known to all individuals." But this is clearly not true of the real world.

19 This influence was noted by Professor Usher when discussing the development of capitalism. He says: "The successive buying and selling of partly finished products were sheer waste of energy." (*Introduction to the Industrial History of England*, p. 13). But he does not develop the idea nor consider why it is that buying and selling operations still exist.

20 It would be possible for no limits to the powers of the entrepreneur to be fixed. This would be voluntary slavery. According to Professor Batt, *The Law of Master and Servant*, p. 18, such a contract would be void and unenforceable.

21 Of course, it is not possible to draw a hard and fast line which determines whether there is a firm or not. There may be more or less direction. It is similar to the legal question of whether there is the relationship of master and servant or principal and agent. See the discussion of this problem below.

22 The views of Professor Knight are examined below in more detail.

23 *Risk, Uncertainty and Profit*, Preface to the Re-issue, London School of Economics Series of Reprints, No. 16, 1933.

24 There are certain marketing costs which could only be eliminated by the abolition of "consumers' choice" and these are the costs of retailing. It is conceivable that these costs might be so high that people would be willing to accept rations because the extra product obtained was worth the loss of their choice.

25 This argument assumes that exchange transactions on a market can be considered as homogeneous; which is clearly untrue in fact. This complication is taken into account below.

26 For a discussion of the variation of the supply price of factors of production to firms of varying size, see E. A. G. Robinson, *The Structure of Competitive Industry*. It is sometimes said that the supply price of organising ability increases as the size of the firm increases because men prefer to be the heads of small independent businesses rather than the heads of departments in a large business. See Jones, *The Trust Problem*, p. 530, and Macgregor, *Industrial Combination*, p. 63. This is a common argument of those who advocate Rationalisation. It is said that larger units would be more efficient, but owing to the individualistic spirit of the smaller entrepreneurs, they prefer to remain independent, apparently in spite of the higher income which their increased efficiency under Rationalisation makes possible.

27 This discussion is, of course, brief and incomplete. For a more thorough discussion of this particular problem, see N. Kaldor, "The Equilibrium of the Firm," *Economic Journal*, March, 1934, and E. A. G. Robinson, "The Problem of Management and the Size of the Firm," *Economic Journal*, June, 1934.

28 A definition of this term is given below.

29 This aspect of the problem is emphasised by N. Kaldor op. cit. Its importance in this connection had been previously noted by E. A. G. Robinson, *The Structure of Competitive Industry*, pp. 83–106. This assumes that an increase in the probability of price movements increases the costs of organising within a firm more than it increases the cost of carrying out an exchange transaction on the market – which is probable.

30 This would appear to be the importance of the treatment of the technical unit by E. A. G. Robinson, op. cit., pp. 27–33. The larger the technical unit, the greater the concentration of factors and therefore the firm is likely to be larger.

31 It should be noted that most inventions will change both the costs of organising and the costs of using the price mechanism. In such cases, whether the invention tends to make firms larger or smaller will depend on the relative effect on these two sets of costs. For instance, if the telephone reduces the costs of using the price mechanism more than it reduces the costs of organising, then it will have the effect of reducing the size of the firm.

32 An illustration of these dynamic forces is furnished by Maurice Dobb, *Russian Economic Development*, p. 68. "With the passing of bonded labour the factory, as an establishment where work was organised under the whip of the overseer, lost its *raison d'être* until this was restored to it with the introduction of power machinery after 1846." It seems important to realise that the passage from the domestic system to the factory system is not a mere historical accident, but is conditioned by economic forces. This is shown by the fact that it is possible to move from the factory system to the domestic system, as in the Russian example, as well as *vice versa*. It is the essence of serfdom that the price mechanism is not allowed to operate. Therefore, there has to be direction from some organiser. When, however, serfdom passed, the price mechanism was allowed to operate. It was not until machinery drew workers into one locality that it paid to supersede the price mechanism and the firm again emerged.

33 This is often called "vertical integration," combination being termed "lateral integration."

34 Op. cit., p. 10. Professor Usher's views are to be found in his *Introduction to the Industrial History of England*, pp. 1–18.

35 Cf. J. B. Clark, *Distribution of Wealth*, p. 19, who speaks of the theory of exchange as being the "theory of the organisation of industrial society."

36 *Risk, Uncertainty and Profit*, p. 267.

37 Op. cit., pp. 267–8.

38 Op. cit., p. 268.

39 Op. cit., pp. 268–95.

40 Op. cit., pp. 269–70.

41 Op. cit., p. 270.

42 This shows that it is possible to have a private enterprise system without the existence of firms. Though, in practice, the two functions of enterprise, which actually influences the system of relative prices by forecasting wants and acting in accordance with such forecasts, and management, which accepts the system of relative prices as being given, are normally carried out by the some persons, yet it seems important to keep them separate in theory. This point is further discussed below.

43 See Kaldor, op. cit., and Robinson, *The Problem of Management and the Size of the Firm*.

44 Mr. Robinson calls this the Imperfect Competition solution for the survival of the small firm.

45 Mr. Robinson's conclusion, op. cit., p. 249, note 1, would appear to be definitely wrong. He is followed by Horace J. White, Jr., "Monopolistic and Perfect Competition," *American Economic Review*, December, 1936, p. 645, note 27. Mr. White states "It is obvious that the size of the firm is limited in conditions of monopolistic competition."

46 *Economics of Imperfect Competition*.

47 As has been shown above, location is only one of the factors influencing the cost of organising.

48 G. F. Shove, "The Imperfection of the Market," *Economic Journal*, March, 1933, p. 115. In connection with an increase in demand in the suburbs and the effect on the price charged by suppliers, Mr. Shove asks "...why do not the old firms open branches in the suburbs?" If the argument in the text is correct, this is a question which Mrs. Robinson's apparatus cannot answer.

49 The legal concept of "employer and employee" and the economic concept of a firm are not identical, in that the firm may imply control over another person's property as well as over their labour. But the identity of these two concepts is sufficiently close for an examination of the legal concept to be of value in appraising the worth of the economic concept.

50 Batt, *The Law of Master and Servant*, p. 6.

51 Op. cit., p. 7.

8 Production, information costs, and economic organization

Armen A. Alchian and Harold Demsetz

The mark of a capitalistic society is that resources are owned and allocated by such nongovernmental organizations as firms, households, and markets. Resource owners increase productivity through cooperative specialization and this leads to the demand for economic organizations which facilitate cooperation. When a lumber mill employs a cabinetmaker, cooperation between specialists is achieved within a firm, and when a cabinetmaker purchases wood from a lumberman, the cooperation takes place across markets (or between firms). Two important problems face a theory of economic organization – to explain the conditions that determine whether the gains from specialization and cooperative production can better be obtained within an organization like the firm, or across markets, and to explain the structure of the organization.

It is common to see the firm characterized by the power to settle issues by fiat, by authority, or by disciplinary action superior to that available in the conventional market. This is delusion. The firm does not own all its inputs. It has no power of fiat, no authority, no disciplinary action any different in the slightest degree from ordinary market contracting between any two people. I can "punish" you only by withholding future business or by seeking redress in the courts for any failure to honor our exchange agreement. That is exactly all that any employer can do. He can fire or sue, just as I can fire my grocer by stopping purchases from him or sue him for delivering faulty products. What then is the content of the presumed power to manage and assign workers to various tasks? Exactly the same as one little consumer's power to manage and assign his grocer to various tasks. The single consumer can assign his grocer to the task of obtaining whatever the customer can induce the grocer to provide at a price acceptable to both parties. That is precisely all that an employer can do to an employee. To speak of managing, directing, or assigning workers to various tasks is a deceptive way of noting that the employer continually is involved in renegotiation of contracts on terms that must be acceptable to both parties. Telling an employee to type this letter rather than to file that document is like my telling a grocer to sell me this brand of tuna rather than that brand of bread. I have no contract to continue to purchase from the grocer and neither the employer nor the employee is bound by any contractual obligations to continue their relationship. Long-term contracts between employer and employee are not the essence of the organization we call a firm. My grocer can count on my returning day after day and purchasing his services and goods even with the prices not always marked on the goods – because I know what they are – and he adapts his activity to conform to my directions to him as to what I want each day . . . he is not my employee.

Wherein then is the relationship between a grocer and his employee different from that between a grocer and his customers? It is in a *team* use of inputs and a centralized position of some party in the contractual arrangements of *all* other inputs. It is the *centralized contractual agent in a team productive process* – not some superior authoritarian directive or disciplinary power. Exactly what is a team process and why does it induce the contractual form, called the firm? These problems motivate the inquiry of this paper.

The metering problem

The economic organization through which input owners cooperate will make better use of their comparative advantages to the extent that it facilitates the payment of rewards in accord with productivity. If rewards were random, and without regard to productive effort, no incentive to productive effort would be provided by the organization; and if rewards were negatively correlated with productivity the organization would be subject to sabotage. Two key demands are placed on an economic organization – metering input productivity and metering rewards.[1]

Metering problems sometimes can be resolved well through the exchange of products across competitive markets, because in many situations markets yield a high correlation between rewards and productivity. If a farmer increases his output of wheat by 10 percent at the prevailing market price, his receipts also increase by 10 percent. This method of organizing economic activity meters the *output directly*, reveals the marginal product and apportions the *rewards* to resource owners in accord with that direct measurement of their outputs. The success of this decentralized, market exchange in promoting productive specialization requires that changes in market rewards fall on those responsible for changes in *output.*[2]

The classic relationship in economics that runs from marginal productivity to the distribution of income implicitly *assumes* the existence of an organization, be it the market or the firm, that allocates rewards to resources in accord with their productivity. The problem of economic organization, the economical means of metering productivity and rewards, is not confronted directly in the classical analysis of production and distribution. Instead, that analysis tends to assume sufficiently economic – or zero cost – means, as if productivity automatically created its reward. We conjecture the direction of causation is the reverse – the specific system of rewarding which is relied upon stimulates a particular productivity response. If the economic organization meters poorly, with rewards and productivity only loosely correlated, then productivity will be smaller; but if the economic organization meters well productivity will be greater. What makes metering difficult and hence induces means of economizing on metering costs?

Team production

Two men jointly lift heavy cargo into trucks. Solely by observing the total weight loaded per day, it is impossible to determine each person's marginal productivity. With team production it is difficult, solely by observing total output, to either define or determine *each* individual's contribution to this output of the cooperating inputs. The output is yielded by a team, by definition, and it is not a *sum* of separable outputs of each of its members. Team production of Z involves at least two inputs, X_i and X_j, with $\partial^2 Z / \partial X_i, \partial X_j \neq 0$.[3] The production function is *not* separable into two functions each involving only inputs X_i or only inputs X_j. Consequently there is no *sum* of Z of two separable functions to treat as the Z of the team production function. (An example of a *separable* case is $Z = aX_i^2 + bX_j^2$ which is separable into $Z_i = aX_i^2$ and $Z_j = bX_j^2$, and $Z = Z_i + Z_j$. This is not team production.) There exist production techniques in which the Z obtained is greater than if X_i and X_j had produced separable Z. Team production will be used if it yields an output enough larger than the sum of separable production of Z to cover the costs of organizing and disciplining team members – the topics of this paper.[4]

Usual explanations of the gains from cooperative behavior rely on exchange and production in accord with the comparative advantage specialization principle with separable additive production. However, as suggested above there is a source of gain from cooperative activity involving working as a *team*, wherein individual cooperating inputs do not yield identifiable, separate products which can be *summed* to measure the total output. For this cooperative productive activity, here called "team" production, measuring *marginal* productivity and making payments in accord therewith is more expensive by an order of magnitude than for separable production functions.

Team production, to repeat, is production in which (1) several types of resources are used and (2) the product is not a sum of separable outputs of each cooperating resource. An additional factor creates a team organization problem – (3) not all resources used in team production belong to one person.

We do not inquire into why all the jointly used resources are not owned by one person, but instead into the types of organization, contracts, and informational and payment procedures used among owners of teamed inputs. With respect to the one-owner case, perhaps it is sufficient merely to note that (a) slavery is prohibited, (b) one might assume risk aversion as a reason for one person's not borrowing enough to purchase all the assets or sources of services rather than renting them, and (c) the purchase-resale spread may be so large that costs of short-term ownership exceed rental costs. Our problem is viewed basically as one of organization among different people, not of the physical goods or services, however much there must be selection and choice of combination of the latter.

How can the members of a team be rewarded and induced to work efficiently? In team production, marginal products of cooperative team members are not so directly and separably (i.e., cheaply) observable. What a team offers to the market can be taken as the marginal product of the team but not of the team members. The costs of metering or ascertaining the marginal products of the team's members is what calls forth new organizations and procedures. Clues to each input's productivity can be secured by observing *behavior* of individual inputs. When lifting cargo into the truck, how rapidly does a man move to the next piece to be loaded, how many cigarette breaks does he take, does the item being lifted tilt downward toward his side?

If detecting such behavior were costless, neither party would have an incentive to shirk, because neither could impose the cost of his shirking on the other (if their cooperation was agreed to voluntarily). But since costs must be incurred to monitor each other, each input owner will have more incentive to shirk when he works as part of a team, than if his performance could be monitored easily or if he did not work as a team. If there is a net increase in productivity available by team production, net of the metering cost associated with disciplining the team, then team production will be relied upon rather than a multitude of bilateral exchange of separable individual outputs.

Both leisure and higher income enter a person's utility function.[5] Hence, each person should adjust his work and realized reward so as to equate the marginal rate of substitution between leisure and production of real output to his marginal rate of substitution in consumption. That is, he would adjust his rate of work to bring his demand prices of leisure and output to equality with their true costs. However, with detection, policing, monitoring, measuring or metering costs, each person will be induced to take more leisure, because the effect of relaxing on *his realized* (reward) rate of substitution between output and leisure will be less than the effect on the *true* rate of substitution. His realized cost of leisure will fall more than the true cost of leisure, so he "buys" more leisure (i.e., more nonpecuniary reward).

If his relaxation cannot be detected perfectly at zero cost, part of its effects will be borne by others in the team, thus making *his* realized cost of relaxation less than the true total cost to the team. The difficulty of detecting such actions permits the private costs of his actions to be less than their full costs. Since each person responds to his private realizable rate of substitution (in production) rather than the true total (i.e., social) rate, and so long as there are costs for other people to detect his shift toward relaxation, it will not pay (them) to force him to readjust completely by making him realize the true cost. Only enough efforts will be made to equate the marginal gains of detection activity with the marginal costs of detection; and that implies a lower rate of productive effort and more shirking than in a costless monitoring, or measuring, world.

In a university, the faculty use office telephones, paper, and mail for personal uses beyond strict university productivity. The university administrators could stop such practices by iden-tifying *the* responsible person in each case, but they can do so only at higher costs than administrators are willing to incur. The extra costs of identifying each party (rather than merely identifying the presence of such activity) would exceed the savings from diminished faculty "turpitudinal peccadilloes." So the faculty is allowed some degree of "privileges, perquisites, or fringe benefits." And the total of the pecuniary wages paid is lower because of this irreducible (at acceptable costs) degree of amenity-seizing activity. Pay is lower in pecuniary terms and higher in leisure, conveniences, and ease of work. But still every person would prefer to see detection made more effective (if it were somehow possible to monitor costlessly) so that he, as part of the now more effectively producing team, could thereby realize a higher pecuniary pay and less leisure. If everyone could, at zero cost, have his reward-realized rate brought to the true production possibility real rate, all could achieve a more preferred position. But detection of the responsible parties is costly; that cost acts like a tax on work rewards.[6] Viable shirking is the result.

What forms of organizing team production will lower the cost of detecting "performance" (i.e., marginal productivity) and bring personally realized rates of substitution closer to true rates of substitution? Market competition, in principle, could monitor some team production. (It already *organizes* teams.) Input owners who are not team members can offer, in return for a smaller share of the team's rewards, to replace excessively (i.e., overpaid) shirking members. Market competition among potential team members would determine team mem-bership and individual rewards. There would be no team leader, manager, organizer, owner, or employer. For such decentralized organizational control to work, outsiders, possibly after observing each team's total output, can speculate about their capabilities as team members and, by a market competitive process, revised teams with greater productive ability will be formed and sustained. Incumbent members will be constrained by threats of replacement by outsiders offering services for lower reward shares or offering greater rewards to the other members of the team. Any team member who shirked in the expectation that the reduced out-put effect would not be attributed to him will be displaced if his activity is detected. Teams of productive inputs, like business units, would evolve in apparent spontaneity in the market – without any central organizing agent, team manager, or boss.

But completely effective control cannot be expected from individualized market competi-tion for two reasons. First, for this competition to be completely effective, new challengers for team membership must know where, and to what extent, shirking is a serious problem, i.e., know they can increase net output as compared with the inputs they replace. To the extent that this is true it is probably possible for existing fellow team members to recognize the shirking. But, by definition, the detection of shirking by observing team output is costly for team production. Secondly, assume the presence of detection costs, and assume that in order to secure a place on the team a new input owner must accept a smaller share of rewards (or a promise to produce more). Then his incentive to shirk would still be at least as great as the incentives of the inputs replaced, because he still bears less than the entire reduction in team output for which he is responsible.

The classical firm

One method of reducing shirking is for someone to specialize as a monitor to check the input performance of team members.[7] But who will monitor the monitor? One constraint on the monitor is the aforesaid market competition offered by other monitors, but for reasons already given, that is not perfectly effective. Another constraint can be imposed on the monitor: give him title to the net earnings of the team, net of payments to other inputs. If owners of cooperating inputs agree with the monitor that he is to receive any residual product above prescribed amounts (hopefully, the marginal value products of the other inputs), the monitor will have an added incentive not to shirk as a monitor. Specialization in monitoring plus reliance on a residual claimant status will reduce shirking; but additional links are needed to forge the firm of classical economic theory. How will the residual claimant monitor the other inputs?

We use the term monitor to connote several activities in addition to its disciplinary connotation. It connotes measuring output performance, apportioning rewards, observing the input behavior of inputs as means of detecting or estimating their marginal productivity and giving assignments or instructions in what to do and how to do it. (It also includes, as we shall show later, authority to terminate or revise contracts.) Perhaps the contrast between a football coach and team captain is helpful. The coach selects strategies and tactics and sends in instructions about what plays to utilize. The captain is essentially an observer and reporter of the performance at close hand of the members. The latter is an inspector-steward and the former a supervisor manager. For the present all these activities are included in the rubric "monitoring." All these tasks are, in principle, negotiable across markets, but we are presuming that such market measurement of marginal productivities and job reassignments are not so cheaply performed for team production. And in particular our analysis suggests that it is not so much the costs of spontaneously negotiating contracts in the markets among groups for team production as it is the detection of the performance of individual members of the team that calls for the organization noted here.

The specialist *who receives the residual rewards* will be the monitor of the members of the team (i.e., will manage the use of cooperative inputs). The monitor earns his residual through the reduction in shirking that he brings about, not only by the prices that he agrees to pay the owners of the inputs, but also by observing and directing the actions or uses of these inputs. *Managing or examining the ways to which inputs are used in team production is a method of metering the marginal productivity of individual inputs to the team's output.*

To discipline team members and reduce shirking, the residual claimant must have power to revise the contract terms and incentives of *individual* members without having to terminate or alter every other input's contract. Hence, team members who seek to increase their productivity will assign to the monitor not only the residual claimant right but also the right to alter individual membership and performance on the team. Each team member, of course, can terminate his own membership (i.e., quit the team), but only the monitor may unilaterally terminate the membership of any of the other members without necessarily terminating the team itself or his association with the team; and he alone can expand or reduce membership, alter the mix of membership, or sell the right to be the residual claimant-monitor of the team. It is this entire bundle of rights: (1) to be a residual claimant; (2) to observe input behavior; (3) to be the central party common to all contracts with inputs; (4) to alter the membership of the team; and 5) to sell these rights, that defines the *ownership* (or the employer) of the *classical* (capitalist, free-enterprise) firm. The coalescing of these rights has arisen, our analysis asserts, because it resolves the shirking-information problem of team production better than does the noncentralized contractual arrangement.

The relationship of each team member to the *owner* of the firm (i.e., the party common to all input contracts *and* the residual claimant) is simply a "quid pro quo" contract. Each makes a purchase and sale. The employee "orders" the owner of the team to pay him money in the same sense that the employer directs the team member to perform certain acts. The employee can terminate the contract as readily as can the employer, and longterm contracts, therefore, are not an essential attribute of the firm. Nor are "authoritarian," "dictational," or "fiat" attributes relevant to the conception of the firm or its efficiency.

In summary, two necessary conditions exist for the emergence of the firm on the prior assumption that more than pecuniary wealth enter utility functions: (1) It is possible to increase productivity through team-oriented production, a production technique for which it is costly to directly measure the marginal outputs of the cooperating inputs. This makes it more difficult to restrict shirking through simple market exchange between cooperating inputs. (2) It is economical to estimate marginal productivity by observing or specifying input behavior. The simultaneous occurrence of both these preconditions leads to the contractual organization of inputs, known as the *classical capitalist firms* with (a) joint input production, (b) several input owners, (c) one party who is common to all the contracts of the joint inputs, (d) who has rights to renegotiate any input's contract independently of contracts with other input owners, (e) who holds the residual claim, and (f) who has the right to sell his central contractual residual status.[8]

Other theories of the firm

At this juncture, as an aside, we briefly place this theory of the firm in the contexts of those offered by Ronald Coase and Frank Knight.[9] Our view of the firm is not necessarily inconsistent with Coase's; we attempt to go further and identify refutable implications. Coase's penetrating insight is to make more of the fact that markets do not operate costlessly, and he relies on the cost of using markets to *form* contracts as his basic explanation for the existence of firms. We do not disagree with the proposition that, *ceteris paribus*, the higher is the cost of transacting across markets the greater will be the comparative advantage of organizing resources within the firm; it is a difficult proposition to disagree with or to refute. We could with equal ease subscribe to a theory of the firm based on the cost of managing, for surely it is true that, *ceteris paribus*, the lower is the cost of managing the greater will be the comparative advantage of organizing resources within the firm. To move the theory forward, it is necessary to know what is meant by a firm and to explain the circumstances under which the cost of "managing" resources is low relative to the cost of allocating resources through market transaction. The conception of and rationale for the classical firm that we propose takes a step down the path pointed out by Coase toward that goal. Consideration of team production, team organization, difficulty in metering outputs, and the problem of shirking are important to our explanation but, so far as we can ascertain, not in Coase's. Coase's analysis insofar as it had heretofore been developed would suggest open-ended contracts but does not appear to imply anything more – neither the residual claimant status nor the distinction between employee and subcontractor status (nor any of the implications indicated below). And it is not true that employees are generally employed on the basis of long-term contractual arrangements any more than on a series of short-term or indefinite length contracts.

The importance of our proposed additional elements is revealed, for example, by the explanation of why the person to whom the control monitor is responsible receives the residual, and also by our later discussion of the implications about the corporation, partnerships, and profit sharing. These alternative forms for organization of the firm are difficult to resolve on the basis of market transaction costs only. Our exposition also suggests a definition of the classical firm – something crucial that was heretofore absent.

In addition, sometimes a technological development will lower the cost of market transactions while, at the same time, it expands the role of the firm. When the "putting out" system was used for weaving, inputs were organized largely through market negotiations. With the development of efficient central sources of power, it became economical to perform weaving in proximity to the power source and to engage in team production. The bringing in of weavers surely must have resulted in a reduction in the cost of negotiating (forming) contracts. Yet, what we observe is the beginning of the factory system in which inputs are organized within a firm. Why? The weavers did not simply move to a common source of power that they could tap like an electric line, purchasing power while they used their own equipment. Now team production in the joint use of equipment became more important. The measurement of marginal productivity, which now involved interactions between workers, especially through their joint use of machines, became more difficult though contract negotiating cost was reduced, while managing the *behavior* of inputs became easier because of the increased centralization of activity. The firm as an organization expanded even though the cost of transactions was reduced by the advent of centralized power. The same could be said for modern assembly lines. Hence the emergence of central power sources expanded the scope of productive activity in which the firm enjoyed a comparative advantage as an organizational form.

Some economists, following Knight, have identified the bearing of risks of wealth changes with the director or central employer without explaining why that is a viable arrangement. Presumably, the more risk-averse inputs become employees rather than owners of the classical firm. Risk averseness and uncertainty *with regard to the firm's fortunes* have little, if anything, to do with our explanation although it helps to explain why all resources in a team are not owned by one person. That is, the role of risk taken in the sense of absorbing the windfalls that buffet the firm because of unforeseen competition, technological change, or fluctuations in demand are not central to our theory, although it is true that imperfect knowledge and, therefore, risk, in *this* sense of risk, underlie the problem of monitoring team behavior. We deduce the system of paying the manager with a residual claim (the equity) from the desire to have efficient means to reduce shirking so as to make team production economical and not from the smaller aversion to the risks of enterprise in a dynamic economy. We conjecture that "distribution-of-risk" is not a valid rationale for the *existence* and organization of the *classical* firm.

Although we have emphasized team production as creating a costly metering task and have treated team production as an essential (necessary?) condition for the firm, would not other obstacles to cheap metering also call forth the same kind of contractual arrangement here denoted as a firm? For example, suppose a farmer produces wheat in an easily ascertained quantity but with subtle and difficult to detect quality variations determined by how the farmer grew the wheat. A vertical integration could allow a purchaser to control the farmer's behavior in order to more economically estimate productivity. But this is not a case of joint or team production, unless "information" can be considered part of the product. (While a good case could be made for that broader conception of production, we shall ignore it here.) Instead of forming a firm, a buyer can contract to have his inspector on the site of production, just as home builders contract with architects to supervise building contracts; that arrangement is not a firm. Still, a firm might be organized in the production of many products wherein no team production or jointness of use of separately owned resources is involved.

This possibility rather clearly indicates a broader, or complementary, approach to that which we have chosen. 1) As we do in this paper, it can be argued that the firm is the particular policing device utilized when joint team production is present. If other sources of high policing costs arise, as in the wheat case just indicated, some other form of contractual arrangement will be used. Thus to each source of informational cost there may be a different type of policing and contractual arrangement. 2) On the other hand, one can say that where policing is difficult across markets, various forms of contractual arrangements are devised, but there is no reason for that known as the firm to be uniquely related or even highly correlated with team production, as defined here. It might be used equally probably and viably for other sources of high policing cost. We have not intensively analyzed other sources, and we can only note that our current and readily revisable conjecture is that 1) is valid, and has motivated us in our current endeavor. In any event, the test of the theory advanced here is to see whether the conditions we have identified are necessary for firms to have long-run viability rather than merely births with high infant mortality. Conglomerate firms or collections of separate production agencies into one owning organization can be interpreted as an investment trust or investment diversification device – probably along the lines that motivated Knight's interpretation. A holding company can be called a firm, because of the common association of the word firm with any ownership unit that owns income sources. The term firm as commonly used is so turgid of meaning that we can not hope to explain every entity to which the name is attached in common or even technical literature. Instead, we seek to identify and explain a particular contractual arrangement induced by the cost of information factors analyzed in this paper.

Types of firms

Profit-sharing firms

Explicit in our explanation of the capitalist firm is the assumption that the cost of *managing* the team's inputs by a central monitor, who disciplines himself because he is a residual claimant, is low relative to the cost of metering the marginal outputs of team members.

If we look within a firm to see who monitors – hires, fires, changes, promotes, and renegotiates – we should find him being a residual claimant or, at least, one whose pay or reward is more than any others correlated with fluctuations in the residual value of the firm. They more likely will have options or rights or bonuses than will inputs with other tasks.

An implicit "auxiliary" assumption of our explanation of the firm is that the cost of team production is increased if the residual claim is not held entirely by the central monitor. That is, we assume that if profit sharing had to be relied upon for *all* team members, losses from the resulting increase in central monitor shirking would exceed the output gains from the increased incentives of other team members not to shirk. If the optimal team size is only two owners of inputs, then an equal division of profits and losses between them will leave each with stronger incentives to reduce shirking than if the optimal team size is large, for in the latter case only a smaller percentage of the losses occasioned by the shirker will be borne by him. Incentives to shirk are positively related to the optimal size of the team under an equal profit-sharing scheme.[10]

The preceding does not imply that profit sharing is never viable. Profit sharing to encourage self-policing is more appropriate for small teams. And, indeed, where input owners are free to make whatever contractual arrangements suit them, as generally is true in capitalist economies, profit sharing seems largely limited to partnerships with a relatively small number of *active*[11] partners. Another advantage of such arrangements for smaller teams is that it permits more effective reciprocal monitoring among inputs. Monitoring need not be entirely specialized.

Profit sharing is more viable if small team size is associated with situations where the cost of specialized management of inputs is large relative to the increased productivity potential in team effort. We conjecture that the cost of managing team inputs increases if the productivity of a team member is difficult to correlate with his behavior. In "artistic" or "professional" work, watching a man's activities is not a good clue to what he is actually thinking or doing with his mind. While it is relatively easy to manage or direct the loading of trucks by a team of dock workers where input activity is so highly related in an obvious way to output, it is more difficult to manage and direct a lawyer in the preparation and presentation of a case. Dock workers can be directed in detail without the monitor himself loading the truck, and assembly line workers can be monitored by varying the speed of the assembly line, but detailed direction in the preparation of a law case would require in much greater degree that the monitor prepare the case himself. As a result, artistic or professional inputs, such as lawyers, advertising specialists, and doctors, will be given relatively freer reign with regard to individual behavior. If the management of inputs is relatively costly, or ineffective, as it would seem to be in these cases, but, nonetheless if team effort is more productive than separable production with exchange across markets, then there will develop a tendency to use profit-sharing schemes to provide incentives to avoid shirking.[12]

Socialist firms

We have analyzed the classical proprietorship and the profit-sharing firms in the context of free association and choice of economic organization. Such organizations need not be the most viable when political constraints limit the forms of organization that can be chosen. It is one thing to have profit sharing when professional or artistic talents are used by small teams. But if political or tax or subsidy considerations induce profit-sharing techniques when these are not otherwise economically justified, then additional management techniques will be developed to help reduce the degree of shirking.

For example, most, if not all, firms in Jugoslavia are owned by the employees in the restricted sense that all share in the residual. This is true for large firms and for firms which employ nonartistic, or nonprofessional, workers as well. With a decay of political constraints, most of these firms could be expected to rely on paid wages rather than shares in the residual. This rests on our auxiliary assumption that general sharing in the residual results in losses from enhanced shirking by the monitor that exceed the gains from reduced shirking by residual-sharing employees. If this were not so, profit sharing with employees should have occurred more frequently in Western societies where such organizations are neither banned nor preferred politically. Where residual sharing by employees is politically imposed, as in Jugoslavia, we are led to expect that some management technique will arise to reduce the shirking by the central monitor, a technique that will not be found frequently in Western societies since the monitor retains all (or much) of the residual in the West and profit sharing is largely confined to small, professional-artistic team production situations. We do find in the larger scale residual-sharing firms in Jugoslavia that there are employee committees that can recommend (to the state) the termination of a manager's contract (veto his continuance) with the enterprise. We conjecture that the workers' committee is given the right to recommend the termination of the manager's contract precisely because the general sharing of the residual increases "excessively" the manager's incentive to shirk.[13]

The corporation

All firms must initially acquire command over some resources. The corporation does so primarily by selling promises of future returns to those who (as creditors or owners) provide financial capital. In some situations resources can be acquired in advance from consumers by promises of future delivery (for example, advance sale of a proposed book). Or where the firm is a few artistic or professional persons, each can "chip in" with time and talent until the sale of services brings in revenues. For the most part, capital can be acquired more cheaply if many (risk-averse) investors contribute small portions to a large investment. The economies of raising large sums of equity capital in this way suggest that modifications in the relationship among corporate inputs are required to cope with the shirking problem that arises with profit sharing among large numbers of corporate stockholders. One modification is limited liability, especially for firms that are large relative to a stockholder's wealth. It serves to protect stockholders from large losses no matter how they are caused.

If every stock owner participated in each decision in a corporation, not only would large bureaucratic costs be incurred, but many would shirk the task of becoming well informed on the issue to be decided, since the losses associated with unexpectedly bad decisions will be borne in large part by the many other corporate shareholders. More effective control of corporate activity is achieved for most purposes by transferring decision authority to a smaller group, whose main function is to negotiate with and manage (renegotiate with) the other inputs of the team. The corporate stockholders retain the authority to revise the membership of the management group and over major decisions that affect the structure of the corporation or its dissolution.

As a result a new modification of partnerships is induced – the right to sale of corporate shares without approval of any other stockholders. Any shareholder can remove his wealth from control by those with whom he has differences of opinion. Rather than try to control the decisions of the management, which is harder to do with many stockholders than with only a few, unrestricted salability provides a more acceptable escape to each stockholder from continued policies with which he disagrees.

Indeed, the policing of managerial shirking relies on across-market competition from new groups of would-be managers as well as competition from members within the firm who seek to displace existing management. In addition to competition from outside and inside managers, control is facilitated by the temporary congealing of share votes into voting blocs owned by one or a few contenders. Proxy battles or stock-purchases concentrate the votes required to displace the existing management or modify managerial policies. But it is more than a change in policy that is sought by the newly formed financial interests, whether of new stockholders or not. It is the capitalization of expected future benefits into stock prices that concentrates on the innovators the wealth gains of their actions if they own large numbers of shares. Without capitalization of future benefits, there would be less incentive to incur the costs required to exert informed decisive influence on the corporation's policies and managing personnel. Temporarily, the structure of ownership is reformed, moving away from diffused ownership into decisive power blocs, and this is a transient resurgence of the classical firm with power again concentrated in those who have title to the residual.

In assessing the significance of stockholders' power it is not the usual diffusion of voting power that is significant but instead the frequency with which voting congeals into decisive changes. Even a one-man owned company may have a long term with just one manager – continuously being approved by the owner. Similarly a dispersed voting power corporation may be also characterized by a long-lived management. The question is the probability of replacement of the management if it behaves in ways not acceptable to a majority of the stockholders. The unrestricted salability of stock and the transfer of proxies enhances the probability of decisive action in the event current stockholders or any outsider believes that management is not doing a good job with the corporation. We are not comparing the corporate responsiveness to that of a single proprietorship; instead, we are indicating features of the corporate structure that are induced by the problem of delegated authority to manager-monitors.[14]

Mutual and nonprofit firms

The benefits obtained by the new management are greater if the stock can be purchased and sold, because this enables *capitalization* of anticipated future improvements into present *wealth* of new managers who bought stock and created a larger capital by their management changes. But in nonprofit corporations, colleges, churches, country clubs, mutual savings banks, mutual insurance companies, and "coops," the future consequences of improved management are not capitalized into present wealth of stockholders. (As if to make more difficult that competition by new would-be monitors, mutiple shares of ownership in those enterprises cannot he bought by one person.) One should, therefore, find greater shirking in nonprofit, mutually owned enterprises. (This suggests that nonprofit enterprises are especially appropriate in realms of endeavor where more shirking is desired and where redirected uses of the enterprise in response to market-revealed values is less desired.)

Partnerships

Team production in artistic or professional intellectual skills will more likely he by partnerships than other types of team production. This amounts to market-organized team activity and to a non-employer status. Self-monitoring partnerships, therefore, will be used rather than employer-employee contracts, and these organizations will he small to prevent an excessive dilution of efforts through shirking. Also, partnerships are more likely to occur among relatives or long-standing acquaintances, not necessarily because they share a common utility function, but also because each knows better the other's work characteristics and tendencies to shirk.

Employee unions

Employee unions, whatever else they do, perform as monitors for employees. Employers monitor employees and similarly employees monitor an employer's performance. Are correct wages paid on time and in good currency? Usually, this is extremely easy to check. But some forms of employer performance are less easy to meter and are more subject to employer shirking. Fringe benefits often are in non-pecuniary, contingent form; medical, hospital, and accident insurance, and retirement pensions are contingent payments or performances partly in *kind* by employers to employees. Each employee cannot judge the character of such payments as easily as money wages. Insurance is a contingent payment – what the employee will get upon the contingent event may come as a disappointment. If he could easily determine what other employees had gotten upon such contingent events he could judge more accurately the performance by the employer. He could "trust" the employer not to shirk in such fringe contingent payments, but he would prefer an effective and economic monitor of those payments. We see a specialist monitor – the union employees' agent – hired by them and monitoring those aspects of employer payment most difficult for the employees to monitor. Employees should be willing to employ a specialist monitor to administer such hard-to-detect employer performance, even though their monitor has incentives to use pension and retirement funds not entirely for the benefit of employees.

Team spirit and loyalty

Every team member would prefer a team in which no one, not even himself, shirked. Then the true marginal costs and values could be equated to achieve more preferred positions. If one could enhance a common interest in nonshirking in the guise of a team loyalty or team spirit, the team would be more efficient. In those sports where team activity is most clearly exemplified, the sense of loyalty and team spirit is most strongly urged. Obviously the team is better, with team spirit and loyalty, because of the reduced shirking – not because of some other feature inherent in loyalty or spirit as such.[15]

Corporations and business firms try to instill a spirit of loyalty. This should not be viewed simply as a device to increase profits by over-working or misleading the employees, nor as an adolescent urge for belonging. It promotes a closer approximation to the employees' potentially available true rates of substitution between production and leisure and enables each team member to achieve a more preferred situation. The difficulty, of course, is to create economically that team spirit and loyalty. It can be preached with an aura of moral code of conduct – a morality with literally the same basis as the ten commandments – to restrict our conduct toward what we would choose if we bore our full costs.

Kinds of inputs owned by the firm

To this point the discussion has examined why firms, as we have defined them, exist? That is, why is there an owner-employer who is the common party to contracts with other owners of inputs in team activity? The answer to that question should also indicate the kind of the jointly used resources likely to be owned by the central-owner-monitor and the kind likely to be hired from people who are not team-owners. Can we identify characteristics or features of various inputs that lead to their being hired or to their being owned by the firm?

How can residual-claimant, central-employer-owner demonstrate ability to pay the other hired inputs the promised amount in the event of a loss? He can pay in advance or he can commit wealth sufficient to cover negative residuals. The latter will take the form of machines, land, buildings, or raw materials committed to the firm. Commitments of labor-wealth (i.e., human wealth) given the property rights in people, is less feasible. These considerations suggest that residual claimants – owners of the firm – will be investors of resalable capital equipment in the firm. The goods or inputs more likely to be invested, than rented, by the owners of the enterprise, will have higher resale values relative to the initial cost and will have longer expected use in a firm relative to the economic life of the good.

But beyond these factors are those developed above to explain the existence of the institution known as the firm – the costs of detecting output performance. When a durable resource is used it will have a marginal product and a depreciation. Its use requires payment to cover at least use-induced depreciation; unless that user cost is specifically detectable, payment for it will be demanded in accord with *expected* depreciation. And we can ascertain circumstances for each. An indestructible hammer with a readily detectable marginal product has zero user cost. But suppose the hammer were destructible and that careless (which is easier than careful) use is more abusive and causes greater depreciation of the hammer. Suppose in addition the abuse is easier to detect by observing the way it is used than by observing only the hammer after its use, or by measuring the output scored from a hammer by a laborer. If the hammer were rented and used in the absence of the owner, the depreciation would be greater than if the use were observed by the owner and the user charged in accord with the imposed depreciation. (Careless use is more likely than careful use – if one does not pay for the greater depreciation.) An absentee owner would therefore ask for a higher rental price because of the higher *expected* user cost than if the item were used by the owner. The expectation is higher because of the greater difficulty of observing specific user cost, by inspection of the hammer after use. Renting is therefore in this case more costly than owner use. This is the valid content of the misleading expressions about ownership being more economical than renting – ignoring all other factors that may work in the opposite direction, like tax provision, short-term occupancy and capital risk avoidance.

Better examples are tools of the trade. Watch repairers, engineers, and carpenters tend to own their own tools especially if they are portable. Trucks are more likely to be employee owned rather than other equally expensive team inputs because it is relatively cheap for the driver to police the care taken in using a truck. Policing the use of trucks by a nondriver owner is more likely to occur for trucks that are not specialized to one driver, like public transit busses.

The factor with which we are concerned here is one related to the costs of monitoring not only the gross product performance of an input but also the abuse or depreciation inflicted on the input in the course of its use. If depreciation or user cost is more cheaply detected when the owner can see its use than by only seeing the input before and after, there is a force toward owner use rather than renting. Resources whose user cost is harder to detect when used by someone else, tend on this count to be owner-used. Absentee ownership, in the lay language, will be less likely. Assume momentarily that labor service cannot be performed in the absence of its owner. The labor owner can more cheaply monitor any abuse of himself than if somehow labor-services could be provided without the labor owner observing its mode of use or knowing what was happening. Also his incentive to abuse himself is increased if he does not own himself.[16]

The similarity between the preceding analysis and the question of absentee landlordism and of sharecropping arrangements is no accident. The same factors which explain the contractual arrangements known as a firm help to explain the incidence of tenancy, labor hiring or sharecropping.[17]

Firms as a specialized market institution for collecting, collating, and selling input information

The firm serves as a highly specialized surrogate market. Any person contemplating a joint-input activity must search and detect the qualities of available joint inputs. He could contact an employment agency, but that agency in a small town would have little advantage over a large firm with many inputs. The employer, by virtue of monitoring many inputs, acquires special superior information about their productive talents. This aids his *directive* (i.e., market hiring) efficiency. He "sells" his information to employee-inputs as he aids them in ascertaining good input combinations for team activity. Those who work as employees or who rent services to him are using him to discern superior combinations of inputs. Not only does the director-employer "decide" what each input will produce, he also estimates which heterogeneous inputs will work together jointly more efficiently, and he does this in the context of a privately owned market for forming teams. The department store is a firm and is a superior private market. People who shop and work in one town can as well shop and work in a privately owned firm.

This marketing function is obscured in the theoretical literature by the assumption of homogeneous factors. Or it is tacitly left for individuals to do themselves via personal market search, much as if a person had to search without benefit of specialist retailers. Whether or not the firm arose because of this efficient information service, it gives the director-employer more knowledge about the productive talents of the team's inputs, and a basis for superior decisions about efficient or profitable combinations of those heterogeneous resources.

In other words, opportunities for profitable team production by inputs already within the firm may be ascertained more economically and accurately than for resources outside the firm. Superior combinations of inputs can be more economically identified and formed from resources already used in the organization than by obtaining new resources (and knowledge of them) from the outside. Promotion and revision of employee assignments (contracts) will be preferred by a firm to the hiring of new inputs. To the extent that this occurs there is reason to expect the firm to be able to operate as a conglomerate rather than persist in producing a single product. Efficient production with heterogeneous resources is a result not of having *better* resources but in *knowing more accurately* the relative productive performances of those resources. Poorer resources can be paid less in accord with their inferiority; greater accuracy of knowledge of the potential and actual productive actions of inputs rather than having high productivity resources makes a firm (or an assignment of inputs) profitable.[18]

Summary

While ordinary contracts facilitate efficient specialization according to comparative advantage, a special class of contracts among a group of joint inputs to a team production process is commonly used for team production. Instead of multilateral contracts among all the joint inputs' owners, a central common party to a set of bilateral contracts facilitates efficient organization of the joint inputs in team production. The terms of the contracts form the basis of the entity called the firm – especially appropriate for organizing team production processes.

Team productive activity is that in which a union, or joint use, of inputs yields a larger output than the sum of the products of the separately used inputs. This team production requires – like all other production processes – an assessment of marginal productivities if efficient production is to be achieved. Nonseparability of the products of several differently owned joint inputs raises the cost of assessing the marginal productivities of those resources or services of each input owner. Monitoring or metering the productivities to match marginal productivities to costs of inputs and thereby to reduce shirking can be achieved more economically (than by across market bilateral negotiations among inputs) in a firm.

The essence of the classical firm is identified here as a contractual structure with: (1) joint input production; (2) several input owners; (3) one party who is common to all the contracts of the joint inputs; (4) who has rights to renegotiate any input's contract independently of contracts with other input owners; (5) who holds the residual claim; and (6) who has the right to sell his central contractual residual status. The central agent is called the firm's owner and the employer. No authoritarian control is involved; the arrangement is simply a contractual structure subject to continuous renegotiation with the central agent. The contractual structure arises as a means of enhancing efficient organization of team production. In particular, the ability to detect shirking among owners of jointly used inputs in team production is enhanced (detection costs are reduced) by this arrangement and the discipline (by revision of contracts) of input owners is made more economic.

Testable implications are suggested by the analysis of different types of organizations – nonprofit, proprietary for profit, unions, cooperatives, partnerships, and by the kinds of inputs that tend to be owned by the firm in contrast to those employed by the firm.

We conclude with a highly conjectural but possibly significant interpretation. As a consequence of the flow of information to the central party (employer), the firm takes on the characteristic of an efficient market in that information about the productive characteristics of a large set of specific inputs is now more cheaply available. Better recombinations or new uses of resources can be more efficiently ascertained than by the conventional search through the general market. In this sense inputs compete with each other within and via a firm rather than solely across markets as conventionally conceived. Emphasis on interfirm competition obscures intrafirm competition among inputs. Conceiving competition as the *revelation and exchange* of knowledge or information about qualities, potential uses of different inputs in different potential applications indicates that the firm is a device for enchancing competition among sets of input resources as well as a device for more efficiently rewarding the inputs. In contrast to markets and cities which can be viewed as publicly or nonowned market places, the firm can be considered a privately owned market; if so, we could consider the firm and the ordinary market as competing types of markets, competition between private proprietary markets and public or communal markets. Could it be that the market suffers from the defects of communal property rights in organizing and influencing uses of valuable resources?

Acknowledgment

Acknowledgment is made for financial aid from the E. Lilly Endowment, Inc. grant to UCLA for research in the behavioral effects of property rights.

Notes

1 Meter means to measure and also to apportion. One can meter (measure) output and one can also meter (control) the output. We use the word to denote both; the context should indicate which.
2 A producer's wealth would be reduced by the present capitalized value of the future income lost by loss of reputation. Reputation, i.e., credibility, is an asset, which is another way of saying that reliable information about expected performance is both a costly and a valuable good. For acts of God that interfere with contract performance, both parties have incentives to reach a settlement akin to that which would have been reached if such events had been covered by specific contingency clauses. The reason, again, is that a reputation for "honest" dealings – i.e., for actions similar to those that would probably have been reached had the contract provided this contingency – is wealth.

Almost every contract is open-ended in that many contingencies are uncovered. For example, if a fire delays production of a promised product by A to B, and if B contends that A has not fulfilled the contract, how is the dispute settled and what recompense, if any, does A grant to B? A person uninitiated in such questions may be surprised by the extent to which contracts permit either party to escape performance or to nullify the contract. In fact, it is hard to imagine any contract, which, when taken solely in terms of its stipulations, could not be evaded by one of the parties. Yet that is the ruling, viable type of contract. Why? Undoubtedly the best discussion that we have seen on this question is by Stewart Macaulay.

There are means not only of detecting or preventing cheating, but also for deciding how to allocate the losses or gains of unpredictable events or quality of items exchanged. Sales contracts contain warranties, guarantees, collateral, return privileges and penalty clauses for specific non-performance. These are means of assignment of *risks* of losses of cheating. A lower price without warranty – an "as is" purchase – places more of the risk on the buyer while the seller buys insurance against losses of his "cheating." On the other hand, a warranty or return privilege or service contract places more risk on the seller with insurance being bought by the buyer.

3 The function is separable into additive functions if the cross partial derivative is zero, i.e., if $\partial^2 Z/\partial X_i \partial X_j = 0$.

4 With sufficient generality of notation and conception this team production function could be formulated as a case of the generalized production function interpretation given by our colleague, E. A. Thompson.

5 More precisely: "if anything other than pecuniary income enters his utility function." Leisure stands for all nonpecuniary income for simplicity of exposition.

6 Do not assume that the sole result of the cost of detecting shirking is one form of payment (more leisure and less take home money). With several members of the team, each has an incentive to cheat against each other by engaging in more than the average amount of such leisure if the employer can not tell at zero cost which employee is taking more than average. As a result the total productivity of the team is lowered. Shirking detection costs thus change the form of payment and also result in lower total rewards. Because the cross partial derivatives are positive, shirking reduces other people's marginal products.

7 What is meant by performance? Input energy, initiative, work attitude, perspiration, rate of exhaustion? Or output? It is the latter that is sought – the *effect* or output. But performance is nicely ambiguous because it suggests both input and output. It is *nicely* ambiguous because as we shall see, sometimes by inspecting a team member's input activity we can better judge his output effect, perhaps not with complete accuracy but better than by watching the output of the *team*. It is not always the case that watching input activity is the only or best means of detecting, measuring or monitoring output effects of each team member, but in some cases it is a useful way. For the moment the word performance glosses over these aspects and facilitates concentration on other issues.

8 Removal of (b) converts a capitalist proprietary firm to a socialist firm.

9 Recognition must also be made to the seminal inquiries by Morris Silver and Richard Auster, and by H. B. Malmgren.

10 While the degree to which residual claims are centralized will affect the size of the team, this will be only one of many factors that determine team size, so as an approximation, we can treat team size as exogenously determined. Under certain assumptions about the shape of the "typical" utility function, the incentive to avoid shirking with unequal profit-sharing can be measured by the Herfindahl index.

11 The use of the word active will be clarified in our discussion of the corporation, which follows below.

12 Some sharing contracts, like crop sharing, or rental payments based on gross sales in retail stores, come close to profit sharing. However, it is gross output sharing rather than profit sharing. We are unable to specify the implications of the difference. We refer the reader to S. N. Cheung.

13 Incidentally, investment activity will be changed. The inability to capitalize the investment value as "take-home" private property *wealth* of the members of the firm means that the benefits of the investment must be taken as annual income by those who are employed at the time of the income. Investment will be confined more to those with shorter life and with higher rates or pay-offs if the alternative of investing is paying out the firm's income to its employees to take home and use as private property. For a development of this proposition, see the papers by Eirik Furobotn and Svetozar Pejovich, and by Pejovich.

14 Instead of thinking of shareholders as joint *owners,* we can think of them as investors, like bondholders, except that the stockholders are more optimistic than bondholders about the enterprise prospects. Instead of buying bonds in the corporation, thus enjoying smaller risks, shareholders prefer to invest funds with a greater realizable return if the firm prospers as expected, but with smaller (possibly negative) returns if the firm performs in a manner closer to that expected by the more pessimistic investors. The pessimistic investors, in turn, regard only the bonds as likely to pay off.

If the entrepreneur-organizer is to raise capital on the best terms to him, it is to his advantage, as well as that of prospective investors, to recognize these differences in expectations. The residual claim on earnings enjoyed by shareholders does not serve the function of enhancing their efficiency as monitors in the general situation. The stockholders are "merely" the less risk-averse or the more optimistic member of the group that finances the firm. Being more optimistic than the average and seeing a higher mean value future return, they are willing to pay more for a certificate that allows them to realize gain on their expectations. One method of doing so is to buy claims to the distribution of returns that "they see" while bondholders, who are more pessimistic, purchase a claim to the distribution that they see as more likely to emerge. Stockholders are then comparable to warrant holders. They care not about the voting rights (usually not attached to warrants); they are in the same position in so far as voting rights are concerned as are bondholders. The only difference is in the probability distribution of rewards and the terms on which they can place their bets.

If we treat bondholders, preferred and convertible preferred stockholders, and common stockholders and warrant holders as simply different classes of investors – differing not only in their risk averseness but in their beliefs about the probability distribution of the firm's future earnings, why should stockholders be regarded as "owners" in any sense distinct from the other financial investors? The entrepreneur-organizer, who let us assume is the chief operating officer and sole repository of control of the corporation, does not find his authority residing in common stockholders (except in the case of a take over). Does this type of control make any difference in the way the firm is conducted? Would it make any difference in the kinds of behavior that would be tolerated by competing managers and investors (and we here deliberately refrain from thinking of them as owner-stockholders in the traditional sense)?

Investment old timers recall a significant incidence of nonvoting common stock, now prohibited in corporations whose stock is traded on listed exchanges. (Why prohibited?) The entrepreneur in those days could hold voting shares while investors held nonvoting shares, which in every other respect were identical. Nonvoting share holders were simply investors devoid of ownership connotations. The control and behavior of inside owners in such corporations has never, so far as we have ascertained, been carefully studied. For example, at the simplest level of interest, does the evidence indicate that nonvoting shareholders fared any worse because of not having voting rights? Did owners permit the nonvoting holders the normal return available to voting shareholders? Though evidence is prohibitively expensive to obtain, it is remarkable that voting and nonvoting shares sold for essentially identical prices, even during some proxy battles. However, our casual evidence deserves no more than interest-initiating weight.

One more point. The facade is deceptive. Instead of nonvoting shares, today we have warrants, convertible preferred stocks all of which are solely or partly "equity" claims without voting rights, though they could be converted into voting shares.

In sum, is it the case that the stockholder-investor relationship is one emanating from the *division* of *ownership* among several people, or is it that the collection of investment funds from people of varying anticipations is the underlying factor? If the latter, why should any of them be thought of as the owners in whom voting rights, whatever they may signify or however exercisable, should reside in order to enhance efficiency? Why voting rights in any of the outside, participating investors?

Our initial perception of this possibly significant difference in interpretation was precipitated by Henry Manne. A reading of his paper makes it clear that it is hard to understand why an investor who wishes to back and "share" in the consequences of some new business should necessarily have to acquire voting power (i.e., power to change the manager-operator) in order to invest in the venture. In fact, we invest in some ventures in the hope that no other stockholders will be so "foolish" as to try to toss out the incumbent management. We want him to have the power to stay in office, and for the prospect of sharing in his fortunes we buy nonvoting common stock. Our willingness to invest is enhanced by the knowledge that we can act legally via fraud, embezzlement and other laws to help assure that we outside investors will not be "milked" beyond our initial discounted anticipations.

15 *Sports Leagues*: Professional sports contests among teams is typically conducted by a *league* of teams. We assume that sports consumers are interested not only in absolute sporting skill but also in skills *relative* to other teams. Being slightly better than opposing teams enables one to claim a major portion of the receipts; the inferior team does not release resources and reduce costs, since they were expected in the play of contest. Hence, absolute skill is developed beyond the equality of marginal investment in sporting skill with its true social marginal value product. It follows there will be a tendency to overinvest in training athletes and developing teams. "Reverse shirking"

arises, as budding players are induced to overpractice hyperactively relative to the social marginal value of their enhanced skills. To prevent overinvestment, the teams seek an agreement with each other to restrict practice, size of teams, and even pay of the team members (which reduces incentives of young people to overinvest in developing skills). Ideally, if all the contestant teams were owned by one owner, overinvestment in sports would be avoided, much as ownership of common fisheries or underground oil or water reserve would prevent overinvestment. This hyperactivity (to suggest the opposite of shirking) is controlled by the league of teams, wherein the league adopts a common set of constraints on each team's behavior. In effect, the teams are no longer really owned by the team owners but are supervised by them, much as the franchisers of some product. They are not full-fledged owners of their business, including the brand name, and can not "do what they wish" as franchises. Comparable to the franchiser, is the league commissioner or conference president, who seeks to restrain hyperactivity, as individual team supervisors compete with each other and cause external diseconomies. Such restraints are usually regarded as anticompetitive, antisocial, collusive-cartel devices to restrain free open competition, and reduce players' salaries. However, the interpretation presented here is premised on an attempt to avoid hyperinvestment in team sports production. Of course, the team operators have an incentive, once the league is formed and restraints are placed on hyper-investment activity, to go further and obtain the private benefits of monopoly restriction. To what extent over-investment is replaced by monopoly restriction is not yet determinable; nor have we seen an empirical test of these two competing, but mutually consistent interpretations. (This interpretation of league-sports activity was proposed by Earl Thompson and formulated by Michael Canes.) Again, athletic teams clearly exemplify the specialization of monitoring with captains and coaches; a captain detects shirkers while the coach trains and selects strategies and tactics. Both functions may be centralized in one person.

16 Professional athletes in baseball, football, and basketball, where athletes having sold their source of service to the team owners upon entering into sports activity, are owned by team owners. Here the team owners must monitor the athletes' physical condition and behavior to protect the team owners' wealth. The athlete has *less* (not, *no*) incentive to protect or enhance his athletic prowess since capital value changes have less impact on his own wealth and more on the team owners. Thus, some athletes sign up for big initial bonuses (representing present capital value of future services). Future salaries are lower by the annuity value of the prepaid "bonus" and hence the athlete has *less* to lose by subsequent abuse of his athletic prowess. Any decline in his subsequent service value would in part be borne by the team owner who owns the players' future service. This does not say these losses of future salaries have no effect on preservation of athletic talent (we are not making a "sunk cost" error). Instead, we assert that the preservation is reduced, not eliminated, because the amount of loss of wealth suffered is smaller. The athlete will spend less to maintain or enhance his prowess thereafter. The effect of this revised incentive system is evidenced in comparisons of the kinds of attention and care imposed on the athletes at the "expense of the team owner" in the case where atheletes' future services are owned by the team owner with that where future labor service values are owned by the athlete himself. Why athletes' future athletic services are owned by the team owners rather than being hired is a question we should be able to answer. One presumption is cartelization and monopsony gains to team owners. Another is exactly the theory being expounded in this paper – costs of monitoring production of athletes; we know not on which to rely.

17 The analysis used by Cheung in explaining the prevalence of sharecropping and land tenancy arrangements is built squarely on the same factors – the costs of detecting output performance of jointly used inputs in team production and the costs of detecting user costs imposed on the various inputs if owner used or if rented.

18 According to our interpretation, the firm is a specialized surrogate for a market for team use of inputs; it provides superior (i.e., cheaper) collection and collation of knowledge about heterogeneous resources. The greater the set of inputs about which knowledge of performance is being collated within a firm the greater are the present costs of the collation activity. Then, the larger the firm (market) the greater the attenuation of monitor control. To counter this force, the firm will be divisionalized in ways that economize on those costs – just as will the market he specialized. So far as we can ascertain, other theories of the reasons for firms have no such implications.

In Japan, employees by custom work nearly their entire lives with one firm, and the firm agrees to that expectation. Firms will tend to be large and conglomerate to enable a broader scope of input revision. Each firm is, in effect, a small economy engaging in "intranational and international" trade. Analogously, Americans expect to spend their whole lives in the United States, and the bigger the country, in terms of variety of resources, the easier it is to adjust to changing tastes and circumstances. Japan, with its lifetime employees, should he characterized more by large, conglomerate firms. Presumably, at some size of the firm, specialized knowledge about inputs becomes as expensive to transmit across divisions of the firms as it does across markets to other firms.

References

M. Canes, "A Model of a Sports League," unpublished doctoral dissertation, UCLA 1970.

S. N. Cheung, *The Theory of Share Tenancy*, Chicago 1969.

R. H. Coase, "The Nature of the Firm," *Economics*, Nov. 1937, *4*, 386–405; reprinted in G. J. Stigler and K. Boulding, eds., *Readings in Price Theory*, Homewood 1952, 331–51.

E. Furobotn and S. Pejovich, "Property Rights and the Behavior of the Firm in a Socialist State," *Zeitschrift für Nationalökonomie*, 1970, *30*, 431–454.

F. H. Knight, *Risk, Uncertainty and Profit*, New York 1965.

S. Macaulay, "Non-Contractual Relations in Business: A Preliminary Study," *Amer. Sociological Rev.*, 1968, *28*, 55–69.

H. B. Malmgren, "Information, Expectations and the Theory of the Firm," *Quart J. Econ.*, Aug. 1961, *75*, 399–421.

H. Manne, "Our Two Corporation Systems: Law and Economics," *Virginia Law Rev.*, Mar. 1967, *53*, No. 2, 259–84.

S. Pejovich, "The Firm, Monetary Policy and Property Rights in a Planned Economy," *Western Econ. J.*, Sept. 1969, *7*, 193–200.

M. Silver and R. Auster, "Entrepreneurship, Profit, and the Limits on Firm Size," *J. Bus. Univ. Chicago*, Apr. 1969, *42*, 277–281.

E. A. Thompson, "Nonpecuniary Rewards and the Aggregate Production Function," *Rev. Econ. Statist.*, Nov. 1970, *52*, 395–404.

9 An economist's perspective on the theory of the firm

Oliver Hart

An outsider to the field of economics would probably take it for granted that economists have a highly developed theory of the firm. After all, firms are the engines of growth of modern capitalistic economies, and so economists must surely have fairly sophisticated views of how they behave. In fact, little could be further from the truth. Most formal models of the firm are extremely rudimentary, capable only of portraying hypothetical firms that bear little relation to the complex organizations we see in the world. Furthermore, theories that attempt to incorporate real world features of corporations, partnerships and the like often lack precision and rigor, and have therefore failed, by and large, to be accepted by the theoretical mainstream.

This Article attempts to give lawyers a sense of how economists think about firms. It does not pretend to offer a systematic survey of the area; rather, it highlights several ideas of particular importance, and then explores an alternative theoretical perspective from which to view the firm.[1] Part I introduces various established economic theories of the firm. Part II turns to a newer theory of the firm, based not upon human capital structures, but rather upon property rights. Part III synthesizes this property rights-based theory of the firm with more established theories.

Established theories

Neoclassical theory

Any discussion of theories of the firm must start with the neoclassical approach, the staple diet of modern economists. Developed over the last one hundred years or so, this approach can be found in any modern-day textbook; in fact, in most textbooks, it is the *only* theory of the firm presented.[2]

Neoclassical theory views the firm as a set of feasible production plans.[3] A manager presides over this production set, buying and selling inputs and outputs in a spot market and choosing the plan that maximizes owners' welfare. Welfare is usually represented by profit, or, if profit is uncertain so that profit-maximization is not well defined, by expected net present value of future profit (possibly discounted for risk) or by market value.

To many lawyers and economists, this is a caricature of the modern firm; it is rigorous but rudimentary. At least three reasons help explain its prolonged survival. First, the theory lends itself to an elegant and general mathematical formalization. Second, it is very useful for analyzing how a firm's production choices respond to exogenous change in the environment, such as an increase in wages or a sales tax.[4] Finally, the theory is also very useful for analyzing the consequences of strategic interaction between firms under conditions of imperfect competition;[5] for example, it can help us understand the relationship between the degree of concentration in an industry and that industry's output and price level.

Granted these strengths, neoclassical theory has some very clear weaknesses. It does not explain how production is organized within a firm, how conflicts of interest between the firm's various constituencies – its owners, managers, workers, and consumers – are resolved, or, more generally, how the goal of profit-maximization is achieved. More subtly, neoclassical theory begs the question of what defines a given firm or what determines its boundaries. Since the theory does not address the issue of each firm's size or extent, it does not explain the consequences of two firms choosing to merge, or of one firm splitting itself into two or more smaller firms. Neoclassical theory describes in rudimentary terms how firms function, but contributes little to any meaningful picture of their structure.

Principal-agent theory

Principal-agent theory, an important development of the last fifteen years, addresses some of the weaknesses of the neoclassical approach.[6] Principal-agent theory recognizes conflicts of interest between different economic actors, formalizing these conflicts through the inclusion of observability problems and asymmetries of information. The theory still views the firm as a production set, but now a professional manager makes production choices, such as investment or effort allocations, that the firm's owners do not observe. Because the manager deals with the day-to-day operations of the firm, she also is presumed to have information about the firm's profitability that the owners lack. In addition, the manager has other goals in mind beyond the owners' welfare, such as on-the-job perks, an easy life, empire building, and so on. Under these conditions, principal-agent theory argues that it will be impossible for the owners to implement their own profit-maximizing plan directly, through a contract with the manager – in general, the owners will not even be able to tell ex post whether the manager has chosen the right plan. Instead, the owners will try to align the manager's objectives with their own by putting the manager on an incentive scheme. Even under an optimal incentive scheme, however, the manager will put some weight on her own objectives at the expense of those of the owners, and conflicting interests remain. Hence, we have the beginnings of a managerial theory of the firm.[7]

Principal-agent theory enriches neoclassical theory significantly, but still fails to answer the vital questions of what defines a firm and where the boundaries of its structure are located. To see why, consider the example of Fisher Body, which for many years has supplied car bodies to General Motors.[8] Principal-agent theory can explain why it might make sense for GM and Fisher to write a profit-sharing agreement, whereby part of Fisher Body's reward is based on GM's profit from car sales: this encourages Fisher to supply high-quality inputs. The theory does not tell us, however, whether it matters if this profit-sharing agreement is accomplished through the merger of Fisher and GM into a single firm, with GM having authority over Fisher management; or whether GM and Fisher should remain as separate firms; or whether GM and Fisher should merge, with Fisher management having authority over GM management.[9] In other words, principal-agent theory tells us about optimal incentive schemes, but not (at least directly) about organizational form. Hence, in the absence of a parallel between the two, which turns out to be difficult to draw, principal-agent theory provides no predictions about the nature and extent of the firm.[10]

Transaction cost economics

While the neoclassical paradigm, modified by principal-agent theory, progressed along the above lines, a very different approach to the theory of the firm developed under the heading of transaction cost economics. Introduced in Coase's famous 1937 article,[11] transaction cost economics traces the existence of firms to the thinking, planning and contracting costs that accompany any transaction, costs usually ignored by the neoclassical paradigm. The idea is that in some situations these costs will be lower if a transaction is carried out within a firm rather than in the market. According to Coase, the main cost of transacting in the market is the cost of learning about and haggling over the terms of trade; this cost can be particularly large if the transaction is a long-term one in which learning and haggling must be performed repeatedly.[12] Transaction costs can be reduced by giving one party authority over the terms of trade, at least within limits. But, according to Coase, this authority is precisely what defines a firm: within a firm, transactions occur as a result of instructions or orders issued by a boss, and the price mechanism is suppressed.[13]

Such an arrangement, however, brings costs of its own. Concentrating authority in one person's hands is likely to increase the cost of errors and lead to greater administrative rigidity. In Coase's view, the boundaries of the firm occur at the point where the marginal cost savings from transacting within the firm equal these additional error and rigidity costs.[14]

Coase's ideas, although recognized as highly original, took a long time to catch on.[15] There are probably two reasons for this. First, they remain to this day very hard to formalize. Second, there is a conceptual weakness, pointed out by Alchian and Demsetz,[16] in the theory's dichotomy between the role of authority within the firm and the role of consensual trade within the market. Consider, for example, Coase's notion that an employer has authority over an employee – an employer can tell an employee what to do.[17] Alchian and Demsetz questioned this, asking what ensures that the employee obeys the employer's instructions. To put it another way, what happens to the employee if he disobeys these instructions? Will he be sued for breach of contract? Unlikely. Probably the worst that can happen is the employee will be fired. But firing is typically the sanction that one independent contractor will impose on another whose performance he does not like. To paraphrase Alchian and Demsetz's criticism, it is not clear that an employer can tell an employee what to do, any more than a consumer can tell her grocer what to do (what vegetables to sell at what prices); in either case, a refusal will likely lead to a termination of the relationship, a firing. In the case of the grocer, this means that the consumer shops at another grocer.[18] Thus, according to Alchian and Demsetz's argument, Coase's view that firms are characterized by authority relations does not really stand up.[19]

Finding Coase's characterization of the firm wanting, Alchian and Demsetz developed their own theory, based on joint production and monitoring. Transactions involving joint or team production require careful monitoring so that each actor's contribution can be assessed. According to Alchian and Demsetz, the best way to provide the monitor with appropriate incentives is to give him the following bundle of rights, which effectively define ownership of the capitalist firm: (1) to be a residual claimant; (2) to observe input behavior; (3) to be the central party common to all contracts with inputs; (4) to alter membership of the team; and, (5) to sell rights 1–4.[20] We will return to some of these ideas below, but at this stage it suffices to note that the theory suffers from the same criticism levelled at Coase: it is unclear why the problems of joint production and monitoring must be solved through the firm and cannot be solved through the market. In fact, one does not need to look far to see examples of market solutions to these problems, such as auditing between independent contractors.

At the same time that doubts were being expressed about the specifics of Coase's theory, Coase's major idea – that firms arise to economize on transaction costs – was increasingly accepted. The exact nature of these transaction costs, however, remained unclear. What lay beyond the learning and haggling costs that, according to Coase, are a major component of market transactions? Professor Oliver Williamson has offered the deepest and most far-reaching analysis of these costs.[21] Williamson recognized that transaction costs may assume particular importance in situations where economic actors make relationship-specific investments – investments to some extent specific to a particular set of individuals or assets.[22] Examples of such investments include locating an electricity generating plant adjacent to a coal mine that is going to supply it; a firm's expanding capacity to satisfy a particular customer's demands; training a worker to operate a particular set of machines or to work with a particular group of individuals; or a worker's relocating to a town where he has a new job.[23]

In situations like these, there may be plenty of competition before the investments are made – there may be many coal mines next to which an electricity generating plant could locate or many towns to which a worker could move. But once the parties sink their investments, they are to some extent locked into each other. As a result, external markets will not provide a guide to the parties' opportunity costs once the relationship is underway. This lack of information takes on great significance, since, in view of the size and degree of the specific investment, one would expect relationships like these to be long lasting.[24]

In an ideal world, the lack of ex post market signals would pose no problem, since the parties could always write a long-term contract in advance of the investment, spelling out each agent's obligations and the terms of the trade in every conceivable situation. In practice, however, thinking, negotiation and enforcement costs will usually make such a contract prohibitively expensive. As a result, parties must negotiate many of the terms of the relationship as they go along. Williamson argues that this leads to two sorts of costs. First, there will be costs associated with the ex post negotiation itself – the parties may engage in collectively wasteful activities to try to increase their own share of the ex post surplus; also, asymmetries of information may make some gains from trade difficult to realize.[25] Second, and perhaps more fundamental, since a party's bargaining power and resulting share of the ex post surplus may bear little relation to his ex ante investment, parties will have the wrong investment incentives at the ex ante stage.[26] In particular, a far-sighted agent will choose her investment inefficiently from the point of view of her contracting partners, given that she realizes that these partners could expropriate part of her investment at the ex post stage.[27]

In Williamson's view, bringing a transaction from the market into the firm – the phenomenon of integration – mitigates this opportunistic behavior and improves investment incentives. Agent *A* is less likely to hold up agent *B* if *A* is an employee of *B* than if *A* is an independent contractor. However, Williamson does not spell out in precise terms the mechanism by which this reduction in opportunism occurs. Moreover, certain costs presumably accompany integration. Otherwise, all transactions would be carried out in firms, and the market would not be used at all. Williamson, however, leaves the precise nature of these costs unclear.[28]

The firm as a nexus of contracts

All the theories discussed so far suffer from the same weakness: while they throw light on the nature of contractual failure, none explains in a convincing or rigorous manner how bringing a transaction into the firm mitigates this failure.

One reaction to this weakness is to argue that it is not really a weakness at all. According to this point of view, the firm is simply a nexus of contracts,[29] and there is therefore little point in trying to distinguish between transactions within a firm and those between firms. Rather, both categories of transactions are part of a continuum of types of contractual relations, with different firms or organizations representing different points on this continuum.[30] In other words, each type of business organization represents nothing more than a particular "standard form" contract. One such "standard form" contract is a public corporation, characterized by limited liability, indefinite life, and freely transferable shares and votes. In principle it would be possible to create a contract with these characteristics each time it is needed, but, given that these characteristics are likely to be useful in many different contexts, it is much more convenient to be able to appeal to a "standard form." Closely held corporations or partnerships are other examples of useful "standard forms."

Viewing the firm as a nexus of contracts is helpful in drawing attention to the fact that contractual relations with employees, suppliers, customers, creditors and others are an essential aspect of the firm. Also, it

> serves to make it clear that the personalization of the firm implied by asking questions such as "what should be the objective function of the firm" ... is seriously misleading. *The firm is not an individual....* The "behavior" of the firm is like the behavior of a market, i.e., the outcome of a complex equilibrium process.[31]

At the same time, the nexus of contracts approach does less to resolve the questions of what a firm is than to shift the terms of the debate. In particular, it leaves open the question of why particular "standard forms" are chosen. Perhaps more fundamentally, it begs the question of what limits the set of activities covered by a "standard form." For example, corporations are characterized by limited liability, free transferability of shares, and indefinite life. But what limits the size of a corporation – what are the economic consequences of two corporations merging or of one corporation splitting itself into two? Given that mergers and breakups occur all the time, and at considerable transaction cost, it seems unlikely that such changes are cosmetic. Presumably they have some real effects on incentives and opportunistic behavior, but these effects remain unexplained.

A property rights approach to the firm

One way to resolve the question of how integration changes incentives is spelled out in recent literature that views the firm as a set of property rights.[32] This approach is very much in the spirit of the transaction cost literature of Coase and Williamson, but differs by focusing attention on the role of physical, that is, nonhuman, assets in a contractual relationship.

Consider an economic relationship of the type analyzed by Williamson, where relationship-specific investments are important and transaction costs make it impossible to write a comprehensive longterm contract to govern the terms of the relationship. Consider also the nonhuman assets that, in the postinvestment stage, make up this relationship. Given that the initial contract has gaps, missing provisions, or ambiguities, situations will typically occur in which some aspects of the use of these assets are not specified. For example, a contract between GM and Fisher might leave open certain aspects of maintenance policy for Fisher machines, or might not specify the speed of the production line or the number of shifts per day.

Take the position that the right to choose these missing aspects of usage resides with the *owner* of the asset. That is, ownership of an asset goes together with the possession of residual rights of control over that asset; the owner has the right to use the asset in any way not inconsistent with a prior contract, custom, or any law. Thus, the owner of Fisher assets would have the right to choose maintenance policy and production line speed to the extent that the initial contract was silent about these.[33]

Finally, identify a firm with all the nonhuman assets that belong to it, assets that the firm's owners possess by virtue of being owners of the firm. Included in this category are machines, inventories, buildings or locations, cash, client lists, patents, copyrights, and the rights and obligations embodied in outstanding contracts to the extent that these are also transferred with ownership. Human assets, however, are not included. Since human assets cannot be bought or sold, management and workers presumably own their human capital both before and after any merger.

We now have the basic ingredients of a theory of the firm. In a world of transaction costs and incomplete contracts, ex post residual rights of control will be important because, through their influence on asset usage, they will affect ex post bargaining power and the division of ex post surplus in a relationship. This division in turn will affect the incentives of actors to invest in that relationship. Hence, when contracts are incomplete, the boundaries of firms matter in that these boundaries determine who owns and controls which assets.[34] In particular, a merger of two firms does not yield unambiguous benefits: to the extent that the (owner-)manager of the acquired firm loses control rights, his incentive to invest in the relationship will decrease. In addition, the shift in control may lower the investment incentives of workers in the acquired firm. In some cases these reductions in investment will be sufficiently great that nonintegration is preferable to integration.[35]

Note that, according to this theory, when assessing the effects of integration, one must know not only the characteristics of the merging firms, but also who will own the merged company. If firms A and B integrate and A becomes the owner of the merged company, then A will presumably control the residual rights in the new firm. A can then use those rights to hold up the managers and workers of firm B. Should the situation be reversed, a different set of control relations would result in B exercising control over A, and A's workers and managers would be liable to holdups by B.

It will be helpful to illustrate these ideas in the context of the Fisher Body-General Motors relationship.[36] Suppose these companies have an initial contract that requires Fisher to supply GM with a certain number of car bodies each week. Imagine that demand for GM cars now rises and GM wants Fisher to increase the quantity it supplies. Suppose also that the initial contract is silent about this possibility, perhaps because of a difficulty in predicting Fisher's costs of increasing supply. If Fisher is a separate company, GM presumably must secure Fisher's permission to increase supply. That is, the status quo point in any contract renegotiation is where Fisher does *not* provide the extra bodies. In particular, GM does not have the right to go into Fisher's factory and set the production line to supply the extra bodies; Fisher, as owner, has this residual right of control. The situation is very different if Fisher is a subdivision or subsidiary of GM, so that GM owns Fisher's factory. In this case, if Fisher management refuses to supply the extra bodies, GM always has the option to fire management and hire someone else to supervise the factory and supply extra bodies (they could even run Fisher themselves on a temporary basis). The status quo point in the contract renegotiation is therefore quite different.

To put it very simply, if Fisher is a separate firm, Fisher management can threaten to make both Fisher assets and their own labor unavailable for the uncontracted-for supply increase. In contrast, if Fisher belongs to GM, Fisher management can only threaten to make their own labor unavailable. The latter threat will generally be much weaker than the former.[37]

Although the status quo point in the contract renegotiation may depend on whether GM and Fisher are one firm rather than two, it does not follow that the outcomes after renegotiation will differ. In fact, if the benefits to GM of the extra car bodies exceed the costs to Fisher of supplying them, we might expect the parties to agree that the bodies should be supplied, regardless of the status quo point. However, the divisions of surplus in the two cases will be very different. If GM and Fisher are separate, GM may have to pay Fisher a large sum to persuade it to supply the extra bodies. In contrast, if GM owns Fisher's plant, it may be able to enforce the extra supply at much lower cost since, as we have seen in this case, Fisher management has much reduced bargaining and threat power.

Anticipating the way surplus is divided, GM will typically be much more prepared to invest in machinery that is specifically geared to Fisher bodies if it owns Fisher than if Fisher is independent, since the threat of expropriation is reduced.[38] The incentives for Fisher, however, may be quite the opposite. Fisher management will generally be much more willing to come up with cost-saving or quality-enhancing innovations if Fisher is an independent firm than if it is part of GM, because Fisher management is more likely to see a return on its activities. If Fisher is independent, it can extract some of GM's surplus by threatening to deny GM access to the assets embodying these innovations. In contrast, if GM owns the assets, Fisher management faces total expropriation of the value of the innovation to the extent that the innovation is asset-specific rather than management-specific, and GM can threaten to hire a new management team to incorporate the innovation.[39]

So far, we have discussed the effects of control changes on the incentives of top management. But workers' incentives will also be affected. Consider, for example, the incentive of someone who works with Fisher assets to improve the quality of Fisher's output by better learning some aspect of the production process. Suppose further that GM has a specific interest in this improvement in car body quality, and that none of Fisher's other customers cares about it. There are many ways in which the worker might be rewarded for this, but one important reward is likely to come from the fact that the worker's value to the Fisher-GM venture will rise in the future and, due to his additional skills, the worker will be able to extract some of these benefits through a higher wage or promotion. Note, however, that the worker's ability to do this is greater if GM controls the assets than if Fisher does. In the former case, the worker will bargain directly with GM, the party that benefits from the worker's increased skill.[40] In the latter case, the worker will bargain with Fisher, who only receives a fraction of these benefits, since it must in turn bargain with GM to parlay these benefits into dollars. In consequence, the worker will typically capture a lower share of the surplus, and his incentive to make the improvement in the first place will fall.

In other words, given that the worker may be held up no matter who owns the Fisher assets – assuming that he, himself, does not – his incentives are greater if the number of possible hold-ups is smaller rather than larger. With Fisher management in control of the assets, there are two potential hold-ups: Fisher can deny the worker access to the assets, and GM can decline to pay more for the improved product.[41] As a result, we might expect the worker to get, say, a third of his increased marginal product (supposing equal division with Fisher and GM). With GM management in control of the Fisher assets, there is only one potential hold-up, since the power to deny the worker his increased marginal product is concentrated in one agent's hands. As a result, the worker in this case might be able to capture half of his increased marginal product (supposing equal division with GM).[42]

The above reasoning applies to the case in which the improvement is specific to GM. Exactly the opposite conclusion would be reached, however, if the improvement were specific to Fisher, such as the worker learning how to reduce Fisher management's costs of making car bodies, regardless of Fisher's final customer (a cost reduction, furthermore, which could not be enjoyed by any substitute for Fisher management). In that event, the number of hold-ups is reduced by giving control of Fisher assets to Fisher management rather than GM. The reason is that with Fisher management in control, the worker bargains with the party who benefits directly from his increased productivity, whereas with GM management in control, he must bargain with an indirect recipient; GM must in turn bargain with Fisher management to benefit from the reduction in costs.

Up to this point we have assumed that GM management will control GM assets. This, however, need not be the case; in some situations it might make more sense for Fisher management to control these assets – for Fisher to buy up GM. One thing we can be sure of is that if GM and Fisher assets are sufficiently complementary, and initial contracts sufficiently incomplete, then the two sets of assets should be under common control. With extreme complementarity, no agent – whether manager or worker – can benefit from any increase in his marginal productivity unless he has access to both sets of assets (by the definition of extreme complementarity, each asset, by itself, is useless). Giving control of these assets to two different management teams is therefore bound to be detrimental to actors' incentives, since it increases the number of parties with hold-up power.[43] This result confirms the notion that when lock-in effects[44] are extreme, integration will dominate nonintegration.[45]

These ideas can be used to construct a theory of the firm's boundaries. First, as we have seen, highly complementary assets should be owned in common, which may provide a minimum size for the firm. Second, as the firm grows beyond a certain point, the manager at the center will become less and less important with regard to operations at the periphery in the sense that increases in marginal product at the periphery are unlikely to be specific either to this manager or to the assets at the center. At this stage, a new firm should be created since giving the central manager control of the periphery will increase hold-up problems without any compensating gains. It should also be clear from this line of argument that, in the absence of significant lock-in effects, nonintegration is always better than integration – it is optimal to do things through the market, for integration only increases the number of potential hold-ups without any compensating gains.[46]

Finally, it is worth noting that the property rights approach can explain how the purchase of physical assets leads to control over human assets. To see this, consider again the GM-Fisher hypothetical. We showed that someone working with Fisher assets is more likely to improve Fisher's output in a way that is specifically of value to GM if GM owns these assets than if Fisher does. This result can be expressed more informally as follows: a worker will put more weight on an actor's objectives if that actor is the worker's boss, that is, if that actor controls the assets the worker works with, than otherwise. The conclusion is quite Coasian in spirit, but the logic underlying it is very different. Coase reaches this conclusion by assuming that a boss can tell a worker what to do; in contrast, the property rights approach reaches it by showing that it is in a worker's self-interest to behave in this way, since it puts him in a stronger bargaining position with his boss later on.

To put it slightly differently, the reason an employee is likely to be more responsive to what his employer wants than a grocer is to what his customer wants is that the employer has much more leverage over his employee than the customer has over his grocer. In particular, the employer can deprive the employee of the assets he works with and hire another employee to work with these assets, while the customer can only deprive the grocer of his custom and as long as the customer is small, it is presumably not very difficult for the grocer to find another customer.

Property rights and the established theories of the firm

The property rights approach has features in common with each of the approaches described previously.[47] It is based on maximizing behavior (like the neoclassical approach); it emphasizes incentive issues (like the principal-agent approach); it emphasizes contracting costs (like the transaction cost approach); it treats the firm as a "standard form" contract (like the nexus of contracts approach);[48] and, it relies on the idea that a firm's owner has the right to alter membership of the firm: the owner has the right to decide who uses the firm's assets and who doesn't.[49] Its advantage over these other approaches, however, is its ability to explain both the costs and the benefits of integration; in particular, it shows how incentives change when one firm buys up another one.

Some react skeptically to the notion that a firm can be characterized completely by the nonhuman assets under its control.[50] That is, there is a feeling that one should be able to make sense of a firm as a mode of organization, even if there are no definable assets on the scene. In his analysis of GM's decision to acquire Fisher Body in 1926, Professor Klein argues that getting control over Fisher's organizational assets rather than their physical capital was the crucial motivating factor:

> By integrating with Fisher, General Motors acquired the Fisher Body organizational capital. This organization is embedded in the human capital of the employees at Fisher but is in some sense greater than the sum of its parts. The employees come and go but the organization maintains the memory of past trials and the knowledge of how to best do something (that is, how to make automobile bodies).[51]

Klein's conclusion is in no way inconsistent with the property rights approach. The control of physical capital can lead to control of human assets in the form of organizational capital.[52] However, Klein appears to argue that his conclusion would hold true even if physical assets were irrelevant.[53] The problem with this point of view is that, in the absence of physical assets, it is unclear how GM can get control over an intangible asset like organizational capital by purchasing Fisher. For example, what is to stop Fisher management from trying to reassert control of the organizational capital after the merger? Klein writes:

> A threat that all the individuals will simultaneously shirk or leave if their wages were not increased to reflect the quasi-rents on the organizational capital generally will not be credible. After vertical integration the Fisher brothers will not be able to hold up General Motors by telling all the employees to leave General Motors and show up on Monday morning at a new address.[54]

This conclusion is reasonable when physical capital is important since it would be difficult at best for Fisher employees to find a substitute for this capital, particularly by Monday morning. However, it is not reasonable in the absence of physical assets. In this case, to paraphrase Alchian and Demsetz, the Fisher brothers have no more ability to hold up GM by telling all the employees to leave GM or, more generally, by countermanding GM's instructions, when Fisher is separate than when Fisher belongs to GM. Their ability to do so will be determined by factors such as the motivation, talent, knowledge and charisma of the Fisher brothers; the quality of worker information;[55] and the degree of worker inertia – factors that do not seem to have anything to do with ownership structure. To put it another way, GM's response to a hold-up attempt by the Fisher brothers will be the same whether GM owns Fisher or Fisher is independent: to try to persuade Fisher workers to desert the Fisher brothers and join GM.[56]

As noted previously, one of the weaknesses of the property rights approach as described here is that it does not take account of the separation of ownership and control present in large, publicly held corporations.[57] In principle, it should be possible to extend the existing analysis to such situations. A public corporation can still be usefully considered a collection of assets, with ownership providing control rights over these assets. Now, however, the picture is more complicated. Although owners (shareholders) typically retain some control rights, such as the right to replace the board of directors, in practice they delegate many others to management, at least on a day-to-day basis.[58] In addition, some of the shareholders' rights shift to creditors during periods of financial distress. Developing a formal model of the firm that contains all these features, and that includes also an explanation of the firm's financial structure, is an important and challenging task for future research. Fortunately, recent work suggests that the task is not an impossible one.[59]

Conclusion

This Article began with the observation that the portrayal of the firm in neoclassical economics is a caricature of the modern firm. It then went on to discuss some other approaches that attempt to develop a more realistic picture. The end product to date is still, in many ways, a caricature, but perhaps not such an unreasonable one. One promising sign is that the different approaches economists have used to address this issue – neoclassical, principal-agent, transaction cost, nexus of contracts, property rights – appear to be converging. It is to be hoped that in the next few years the best aspects of each of these approaches can be drawn on to develop a more comprehensive and realistic theory of the firm. Such a theory would capture the salient features both of modern corporations and of owner-managed firms, and would illuminate the issues for economists and lawyers alike.

Acknowledgments

Helpful comments from Jeffrey Gordon, Bengt Holmstrom and Jean Tirole are gratefully acknowledged. This Article is based in part on the author's Fisher-Schultze lecture delivered to the Econometric Society in Bologna, Italy in August 1988. Some of the work was done while the author was visiting the Harvard Business School as a Marvin Bower Fellow. He would like to thank that institution for its hospitality and financial support. The author would also like to acknowledge financial assistance from the Guggenheim and Olin Foundations, the Center for Energy and Policy Research at MIT and the National Science Foundation.

Notes

1 Several recent surveys provide other perspectives on this material. See, e.g., Holmstrom & Tirole, The Theory of the Firm, *in* 1 *Handbook of Industrial Organization* (R. Schmalensee & R. Willig eds., 1989); Milgrom & Roberts, Economic Theories of the Firm: Past, Present and Future, 21 *Can. J. Econ.* 444 (1988); Williamson, The Logic of Economic Organization, 4 *J.L. Econ. & Organization* 65 (1988).

2 See, e.g., J. Henderson & R. Quandt, *Microeconomic Theory: A Mathematical Approach* 64–134 (1980); H. Varian, *Microeconomic Analysis* 6–78 (1984).

3 For example, one feasible plan might be to use 10 person-hours and one acre of land to produce one hundred pounds of wheat, while another feasible plan might be to use 12 person-hours and one and one-half acres to produce fifty pounds of corn.

4 See H. Varian, supra note 2, at 47; Bishop, *The Effects of Specific and Ad Valorem Taxes*, 82 *Q.J. Econ.* 198 (1968).

5 See J. Tirole, *The Theory of Industrial Organization* 205–301 (1988).
6 See, e.g., Holmstrom, *Moral Hazard and Observability*, 10 *Bell J. Econ.* 74 (1979); Shavell, Risk Sharing and Incentives in the Principal and Agent Relationship, 10 *Bell J. Econ.* 55 (1979). For a recent survey, see Hart & Holmstrom, The Theory of Contracts, *in Advances in Economic Theory: Fifth World Congress* 71, 75–106 (T. Bewley ed. 1987).
7 It is also possible to extend the principal-agent view of the firm to analyze conflicts of interests between managers and workers, and those between managers and consumers. See Calvo & Wellisz, Supervision, Loss of Control and the Optimum Size of the Firm, 86 *J. Pol. Econ.* 943 (1978).
8 I will discuss the GM-Fisher Body relationship at several points in the text. In doing so, I draw on material from Klein, Crawford & Alchian, Vertical Integration, Appropriable Rents, and the Competitive Contracting Process, 21 *J.L. & Econ.* 297, 308–10 (1978); Klein, Vertical Integration as Organizational Ownership: The Fisher Body-General Motors Relationship Revisited, 4 *J.L. Econ. & Organization* 199 (1988).
9 As a matter of history, GM and Fisher started off as separate firms linked by a long-term contract, but after a dispute GM bought Fisher in 1926. Klein, Crawford & Alchian, supra note 8, at 310.
10 Drawing a parallel might be possible if, say, profit- or cost-sharing arrangements were only found within a single firm. This is not the case, however. For example, consider cost-plus contracts between the United States Government and private defense contractors. See generally F. Scherer, *The Weapons Acquisition Process: Economic Incentives* 131–309 (1964) for a discussion of defense contracts.
11 Coase, The Nature of the Firm, 4 *Economica* 386 (1937).
12 One can distinguish between learning and haggling costs incurred at the beginning of the relationship when the parties reach an initial agreement and those incurred as the relationship proceeds and the parties revise their agreement. For present purposes, the latter costs are more important.
13 A related idea can be found in Simon, A Formal Theory of the Employment Relationship, 19 *Econometrica* 293 (1951) (arguing that it is efficient for an employee to accept employer's authority if employee is approximately indifferent about tasks he performs, but employer has a strict preference). It is also worth noting that the superior adaptive properties of the employment relation were emphasized by Chester Barnard at around the same time that Coase was writing. See C. Barnard, *The Functions of the Executive* 139–60 (1938) (discussing incentives necessary to induce individuals to contribute to organizations).
14 Coase, supra note 11, at 395.
15 In Coase's words, they were "much cited and little used" (until the 1970s). Coase, The Nature of the Firm: Influence, 4 *J.L. Econ. & Organization* 33, 33 (1988).
16 Alchian & Demsetz, *Production, Information Costs, and Economic Organization*, 62 *Am. Econ. Rev.* 777 (1972).
17 Coase, supra note 11, at 404.
18 Alchian & Demsetz, supra note 16, at 777–8, 783–4. But cf. Masten, A Legal Basis for the Firm, 4 *J.L. Econ. & Organization* 181, 186–7 (1988) (law makes a distinction between an employer–employee relationship and one between independent contractors, in that an employee owes her employer duties of loyalty and obedience that do not exist between independent contractors).
19 It bears noting that the second part of Coase's thesis, maintaining that firms suppress the price mechanism, is also flawed. The use of prices to allocate resources within a multidivisional firm – the phenomenon of transfer pricing, probably more common now than it was when Coase wrote – seems a fairly immediate counterexample. For a recent discussion of the use of transfer pricing, see Eccles & White, Price and Authority in Inter-Profit Center Transactions, 94 *Am. J. Soc.* S17 (Supp. 1988).
20 See Alchian & Demsetz, supra note 16, at 783.
21 See generally O. Williamson, *The Economic Institutions of Capitalism* (1985) [hereinafter Economic Institutions]; O. Williamson, *Markets and Hierarchies: Analysis and Antitrust Implications* (1975). For another significant analysis of these costs, see generally Klein, Crawford & Alchian, supra note 8.
22 See *Economic Institutions*, supra note 21, at 30.
23 Id. at 95–6.
24 Id. at 61. For empirical evidence on the importance of relationship-specific investments and lock-in effects, see Joskow, Asset Specificity and the Structure of Vertical Relationships: Empirical Evidence, 4 *J.L. Econ. & Organization* 95 (1988).

25 *Economic Institutions*, supra note 21, at 21.
26 Id. at 88–9.
27 Id. at 30–2.
28 Williamson argues that a major benefit of integration comes from the fact that the party with author-
    ity can resolve disputes by fiat (as opposed to litigation), while a major cost comes from the fact
    that the party with authority cannot commit himself to intervene selectively in the affairs of other
    parties. See id. at 76, 133–5. Williamson, however, is not very clear about what mechanisms are at
    work here. For example, a boss may try to resolve a dispute, but what guarantee is there that the
    parties will follow his edicts? To paraphrase Alchian and Demsetz, what disciplinary power does a
    boss have that an independent contractor does not? A similar issue arises with regard to selective
    intervention. In what activities will the boss intervene, and how will this intervention be enforced?
    What power to intervene does a boss have that an independent contractor does not have? See supra
    notes 16–18 and accompanying text.

     The greater powers of a boss relative to an independent contractor can be understood if one takes
    a property rights-based view of the firm – in particular, if one recognizes that a firm consists of
    nonhuman assets as well as human assets and that a boss typically has control over these nonhuman
    assets. See infra notes 33–46 and accompanying text.
29 The nexus of contract theory is often associated with Jensen and Meckling. See Jensen & Meckling,
    Theory of the Firm: Managerial Behavior, Agency Costs and Ownership Structure, 3 *J. Fin. Econ.*
    305, 310 (1976).
30 Note that lawyers' and economists' ideas of what constitutes a contract may differ. Economists tend
    to view contracts as relationships characterized by reciprocal expectations and behavior; lawyers
    consider the enforceable legal duties implicit in such relationships and look for formalization
    through the standard indicia of contract formation, such as offer and acceptance. See Gordon, The
    Mandatory Structure of Corporate Law, 89 *Colum. L. Rev.* 1549, 1549–50 (1989).
31 Jensen & Meckling, supra note 29, at 311.
32 See generally Grossman & Hart, The Costs and Benefits of Ownership: A Theory of Vertical and
    Lateral Integration, 94 *J. Pol. Econ.* 691 (1986); Holmstrom & Tirole, supra note 1; O. Hart & J.
    Moore, *Property Rights and the Nature of the Firm* (Massachusetts Institute of Technology, Dep't
    of Economics Working Paper No. 495, 1988). This literature owes much to the earlier property
    rights literature on the efficiency of private property in an externality-free world. See, e.g., Demsetz,
    Toward a Theory of Property Rights, *Am. Econ. Rev.*, May 1967, at 347.
33 This view of ownership seems consistent with the standard one adopted by lawyers:

    But what are the rights of ownership? They are substantially the same as those incident to posses-
    sion. Within the limits prescribed by policy, the owner is allowed to exercise his natural powers
    over the subject-matter uninterfered with, and is more or less protected in excluding other people
    from such interference. The owner is allowed to exclude all, and is accountable to no one.

                                                          O. Holmes, *The Common Law* 193 (1963 ed.).

34 This consolidation of ownership and control points to an important lacuna in the property rights
    approach. The approach makes no distinction between ownership and control, assuming that both
    rest with the same entity. In most of the formal models that have been developed, such an arrange-
    ment turns out to be optimal since agents are assumed to be risk-neutral and to have sufficient
    wealth to buy any asset. If managers were risk-averse and had limited wealth, however, this con-
    clusion would no longer be valid. Moreover, from a descriptive point of view, the assumption that
    owners manage is seriously inadequate; while it may apply to small firms such as partnerships or
    closed corporations, it certainly does not apply to large, publicly held corporations. For how the
    ownership/control dichotomy might affect the property rights approach, see infra notes 58–9 and
    accompanying text.
35 It is important to emphasize that the property rights approach distinguishes between ownership in
    the sense of possession of residual control rights over assets and ownership in the sense of entitle-
    ment to a firm's (verifiable) profit stream. In practice, these rights will often go together, but they
    do not have to. The property rights approach takes the point of view that the possession of control
    rights is crucial for the integration decision. That is, if firm *A* wants to acquire part of firm B's (ver-
    ifiable) profit stream, it can always do this by contract. It is only if firm *A* wants to acquire control
    over firm B's assets that it needs to integrate.

36 See supra note 8.

37 If current Fisher management is indispensable for the operation of Fisher assets, there is, of course, no difference between the two threats. It is rare, however, that current management is completely irreplaceable.

38 It should be emphasized that there is no inconsistency in assuming that an initial contract is incomplete and at the same time that the parties anticipate how the ex post surplus will be divided up as a result of this incompleteness. For example, suppose there are many individually unlikely states with similar characteristics to an uncontracted-for increase in demand. It may be prohibitively expensive for the parties to contract for each of these states, and yet they may be well aware of the average degree to which their investments will be expropriated as a result of not contracting for these states.

39 Under some conditions expropriation problems can be avoided regardless of organizational form. One possibility is for the parties to write an ex ante profit-sharing agreement. However, a profit-sharing agreement may be insufficient to encourage ex ante investments to the extent that some returns from an asset's use are unverifiable. Examples of unverifiable returns are effort costs, non-monetary rewards such as perks, and monetary returns that can be diverted so that they do not show up in the firm's accounts.

Another way the parties might overcome expropriation problems is to share investment expenditures. For example, if Fisher and GM are independent, Fisher could compensate GM for its later hold-up power by contributing towards GM's initial Fisher-specific investment. Note, however, that this strategy will work only to the extent that either GM contractually agrees to make the investment or Fisher can make part of the investment on GM's behalf. Otherwise, GM could use an up-front payment from Fisher to make a non-relationship-specific investment.

40 This is not quite correct since the worker will actually bargain with GM management rather than with GM shareholders, who are arguably the ultimate beneficiaries. However, it is approximately correct to the extent that, perhaps because GM management is on an incentive scheme, GM management benefits from an increase in GM's profit or market value. For the remainder of the discussion, we will, at a cost both in precision and realism, ignore the distinction between management and shareholders, and also treat management as a monolithic group. But see supra note 34; infra note 46 (explaining how this analysis can be generalized to include more complicated forms of group ownership); infra notes 58–9 and accompanying text.

41 We assume that no payment was specified for the improved product in the initial contract.

42 For a formal treatment of the division of surplus, see O. Hart & J. Moore, supra note 32, at 11. The numbers one-half and one-third should not be taken too seriously. The important point is that, in the context described, the worker is likely to get a larger share of his increased marginal product when GM controls the assets than when Fisher does.

43 See id. at 11, 19.

44 For examples of lock-in effects, see supra notes 22–4 and accompanying text.

45 Klein, Crawford & Alchian, supra note 8, at 300. However, Klein, Crawford and Alchian fail to provide a formal justification for this notion.

46 In the above we have concentrated on ownership by an individual or by a homogeneous and monolithic group ("management"). However, the analysis can be generalized to include more complicated forms of group ownership, such as partnerships, or worker-, manager-, or consumer-cooperatives. It turns out that these will be efficient when increases in agents' marginal products are specific to a group of individuals of variable composition, rather than to a fixed group. For example, if the increase in an agent's marginal product can be realized only if the agent has access to a majority of the members of a management team, as well as to a particular asset, then it will be optimal to give each of the managers an equal ownership share in the asset and equal voting rights, and adopt majority rule. See O. Hart & J. Moore, supra note 32, at 19.

47 See supra notes 2–31 and accompanying text.

48 In the language of the property rights approach, "firm" is shorthand for a collection of assets; "ownership" is shorthand for the possession of residual rights of control over these assets.

49 See Alchian & Demsetz, supra note 16, at 783 (manager should have right to alter membership of production team).

50 See, e.g., Klein, supra note 8, at 205–8.

51 Id. at 208.

52 See supra notes 32–46 and accompanying text. Note that the observation that the whole of organizational capital is typically greater than the sum of its parts is equivalent to the observation that the

160   *Oliver Hart*

total output of a group of workers typically exceeds the sum of the workers' individual outputs, to the extent that there are complementarities.

53 Klein, supra note 8, at 208 n. 11.

54 Id. at 208.

55 See G. Mailath & A. Postlewaite, Workers Versus Firms: Bargaining Over a Firm's Value 14 (University of Pennsylvania, Center for Analytic Research in Economics and the Social Sciences Working Paper No. 88-11, 1988).

56 This is not without qualification. It can be argued that if GM acquires Fisher, Fisher workers become liable for damages if they try to organize a new firm since, as employees, they owe GM a duty of loyalty. See Masten, supra note 18, at 189. But, in practice, employees *do* leave to form new firms. Moreover, the courts facilitate this process by sometimes hesitating to enforce covenants not to compete even when such covenants are explicit. See, e.g., E. Farnsworth, Contracts §5.3, at 337–8 (1982) (courts enforce non-compete covenants "only if...employee acquired confidential information" in course of employment). Thus, it is unclear how important this factor could have been in the GM-Fisher acquisition.

57 See supra note 34.

58 See, e.g., Clark, Agency Costs Versus Fiduciary Duties, *in Principals and Agents: The Structure of Business* 55 (J. Pratt & R. Zeckhauser eds. 1985); Easterbrook & Fischel, Voting in Corporate Law, 26 *J.L. & Econ.* 395 (1983); Fama & Jensen, Separation of Ownership and Control, 26 *J.L. & Econ.* 301 (1983).

59 See, e.g., Grossman & Hart, One Share-One Vote and the Market for Corporate Control, 20 *J. Fin. Econ.* 175 (1988); Harris & Raviv, Corporate Governance: Voting Rights and Majority Rules, 20 *J. Fin. Econ.* 203 (1988); P. Aghion & P. Bolton, An 'Incomplete Contract' Approach to Bankruptcy and the Financial Structure of the Firm (Stanford University, Institute for Mathematical Studies in the Social Sciences Technical Report No. 536, 1988); C. Kahn & G. Huberman, Default, Foreclosure, and Strategic Renegotiation (paper presented at Conference on Economics of Contract Law, Duke University, March 1988).

10 The firm in Illyria

Market syndicalism

Benjamin Ward

The discussion of the feasibility of socialism has long been closed with apparently quite general agreement that an economy will not inevitably collapse as a result of nationalization of the means of production. On the theoretical side the clinching argument was probably made by Barone shortly after the controversy began (Barone 1908). Probably the best known of the arguments on the other side of the question, that of Mises (Gligorijević 1995), was published twelve years after Barone's paper and gave rise to a new set of arguments, among them those of Taylor, Lange and Lerner (Lange and Taylor 1938; Lerner 1946). Lange in fact explicitly (though perhaps with a touch of irony) developed market socialism as a counterexample for Mises' assertions.

Today one might be inclined to take market socialism as something more than a theoretical counterexample. But as a serious proposal for social reform it leaves some important questions unanswered. For example the problem of the emergence of a bureaucracy in whose hands the economic power is largely concentrated was raised by Lange himself. Another unanswered question has to do with the behavioral response of decision-makers to such directives as the rules for determining output and changing price. Will the rules be simply obeyed or will various means of simulating compliance while serving other ends be developed?

These two questions are of special interest today as one watches some Eastern European countries groping toward a less centralized form of economic organization, and as one watches Western European socialists struggle with the implications for democracy (and efficiency) of further nationalization. In the present paper a few of the implications of one possible alternative form of industrial organization are explored. In this model the means of production are nationalized and the factories turned over to the general management of elected committees of workers who are free to set price and output policy in their own material self-interest. The nature of the resulting price and output decisions are investigated and compared with those obtained in the competitive capitalist (or market socialist) model.

The assumptions of the model bear a close resemblance to the legal status of the industrial firm in Yugoslavia in recent years. Consequently some of the organizational arrangements of a "market syndicalist" economy can be described most conveniently by citing laws on the statute books in Yugoslavia, as is done in Section I. Toward the end of the paper some comments are made as to the extent of deviations of firm behavior in Yugoslavia from that of the theorems of our model. It seems that Illyria is in fact an alternative to the existing system in Yugoslavia as well as to those in Western and the rest of Eastern Europe.

I Legal aspects of a market socialist economy

The legal framework of the Yugoslav economy has been undergoing such rapid and repeated overhaul during the past seven years that it is difficult to pin down the provisions that are relevant at any one point in time. In what follows reference is mainly to the year 1954. Of first importance in releasing the firm from its former Stalinist constraints was the new planning system.[1] Federal and republican plans no longer prescribed output norms for firms and industries. Figures in the central plan represented generalized expectations rather than explicit norms. The firm itself in its own "independent" plan set its own goals for the year and even then was not penalized for failure to fulfill these targets.

The firm was not only empowered to set its own rate of production but was also made responsible for its sales. The compulsory distribution plan was abolished (*Službeni list FNRJ*, No. 17, 1952, item 169), and the firm was permitted to enter freely into contracts for the sale of its output and the purchase of raw materials. Prices had gradually been released from central control until here too the firm had the right to price its own products "on the basis of market conditions."[2] Price controls still existed in 1954 but only for a narrow range of commodities.[3]

With output norms no longer available for the purpose, the new criterion of successful performance of the firm became profitability, that is to say, the ability to earn enough in revenue to cover costs at the existing market prices. The term "revenue" means roughly what it would mean to an American businessman. However, the term "costs" requires some discussion in view of certain aspects of the wage system and of the fact that the state retained ownership of the means of production.

Labor cost was defined by law (*Službeni list FNRJ*, No. 52, 1953, item 439) and was based on the average level of skill of workers in the industry. Industries were divided into eight groups on this basis and the labor cost per worker-month set for each group. For example, a coal mining concern, falling in Group III, was assigned a calculated (*obračunski*) wage of 8,100 dinars per worker-month. If the firm employed a staff of 100 for a full month of work, labor cost would be 810,000 dinars for the month. The calculated wage was not the same thing as the contractual wage, which was the basis on which a worker was hired. This latter could be set freely by the firm. The distinction was that the contractual wage was *not* an accounting cost and was set by the firm, while the calculated wage *was* an accounting cost and was set by the state.

Secondly, there was the problem of charging the firm for its use of the state-owned land, plant and equipment. Ground rent was to be charged industrial firms at the same rate as that charged on the "largest class of arable land in the district" (*Službeni list FNRJ*, No. 53, 1953, item 456). The latter was set on a cadastral basis in accord with the yield of the land. Capital, that is to say plant and equipment, including the more expensive tools, was revalued during 1953 on a basis which does not seem to have been described explicitly in the press.[4] The social (i.e., federal) plan was then to set each year the rate to be paid to the state as interest on fixed capital. A standard rate of depreciation on the various types of equipment was prescribed by the state and payments sufficient to maintain the value of the equipment were also charged as costs against the firm (Sirotković 1954, pp. 128–32, 165–67).

Under this system then, costs would be the sum of material costs, "regular contributions" to the state (i.e., the interest charge on fixed capital, ground rent and the excise tax on sales, where levied – a relatively insignificant item in 1954), the calculated wage fund and interest on short-term credit outstanding. Profits, i.e., revenue less costs so-defined, became the measure of success of the firm.

To lend point to this change in perspective, a bankruptcy law was promulgated.[5] Several types of receivership were defined, but in general it was provided that a firm became bankrupt if it was no longer able to make its regular payments to the state and to pay wages out of its revenues at the rate guaranteed by the state.[6] Included was a provision permitting reorganization of the firm after writing down existing debts, provided the creditors were agreeable.

The new organization was designed to increase the efficiency of the economic system via competition among firms. As Vice-President Kardelj put it, "... stimulative elements. ... appear above all through the interest of the enterprise in achieving, through free competition with other enterprises on the market, the best results as regards quality and quantity of goods, lower costs of production and good marketing" (Kardelj 1954, p. 135). The firm's incentive to participate in this competition with its fellows stemmed from two sources: workers' management and a profits-sharing scheme. The former had been established in 1950 (*Službeni list FNRJ*, No. 43, 1950) and provided for an elected council of workers in the firm which was to serve a general policy-making function. The council approved the independent plan of the firm and the wage schedule and was empowered to issue directives regarding execution of the plan and the management of the firm. These were binding upon the firm's director, providing they did not conflict with existing laws and decrees. Day-to-day supervision of operations was entrusted to the management board (*upravni odbor*),[7] a subcommittee of the workers' council which also prepared drafts of the plan and the wage schedule for the approval of the workers' council. Differential wages within the firm were thus set by the workers themselves under this law and the later planning law, the chief constraint being that no wage rate could be set below that in the state minimum wage law.[8]

The calculated wage rates were supposed to be set at levels which would add up to 90 per cent of the total contractual wages at the planned production rate and sales price. If the workers were to receive the contract wage then it was necessary for the firm to make a profit on its operation (Adašević 1954, p. 44). Furthermore, any profits achieved by the firm were placed at the disposal of the workers' council to be used either for investment or rationalization or to be paid out as a wage supplement in proportion to the contract wage received by each worker,[9] though a steeply progressive profits tax was levied on this supplementary wage fund.

While the Yugoslav economic system thus involves a considerable measure of autonomy for the firm, it should not be thought that independence of the sort possessed within the legal framework of capitalism has been acquired by the Yugoslav firm. The state reserves the right to intervene directly to alter any decisions of which it disapproves.[10] Such intervention could occur legally as a result of new decrees of the government or by means of the exertion of influence via the trade unions, the League of Communists, or the local governments, rights whose legal sanction was often based on the right of approval of the firm's decisions.[11] But intervention was now to be viewed as the exception rather than the rule.[12]

II The competitive firm: the one output-one variable input case

The Illyrian firm operates in an environment rather similar to the legal environment within which the Yuglosav firm operates. In Illyria however there will be no intervention by the state in the firm's decision-making process, nor does minimum wage legislation exist. The worker-managers are free to set firm policy under the influence of the profit incentive.

The firm to be considered in this section operates in a purely competitive market. Decision-making is concerned with the short run and is viewed as static in nature; that is, the worker-managers are interested in maximizing their individual incomes over a given period of time. The services available to the firm are labor, which is a homogeneous input, and a fixed plant, which is owned by the state and operated by the workers. The firm must pay a tax in the form of interest on the replacement cost of the plant. Ground rent, depreciation, working capital and other taxes will be ignored. The state sets the calculated wage rate w, but this is done merely to provide an accounting definition of labor cost and does not determine in fact the level of wages.[13] The workers never plough their profits back into the firm, but in each period distribute the whole amount of profits as a wage bonus. In our firm, which employs a single skill-type of worker, the distribution is made equally to each employee.

A production function will describe the technical conditions under which the firm may transform the homogeneous factor labor, x, into a salable product, y:

$$Y = f(x). \tag{10.1}$$

Over the range of the variables under consideration the marginal product of labor will be assumed to be positive but declining as output increases. Labor input will be measured in terms of the number of workers employed. By assuming that labor input can be changed only by varying the number of laborers the possibility of overtime work by the existing staff is eliminated. This is done so as to avoid introducing the marginal disutility of labor as an important constraint.[14] It is also assumed that there is no discrimination among workers, and that a decision to lay off workers on profit-maximizing grounds would not be affected by the fact that the result would be to create unemployment.[15]

The sole source of income to the firm is from the sale of its product at the parametric price p. Two costs are incurred in production: labor cost which is valued at the calculated wage w per worker,[16] and the fixed charge for the use of capital R. Profit of course is the difference between revenue and cost. The worker-managers, acting in their own material self-interest, are not necessarily interested in maximizing profits as their capitalist counterparts, the stockholders or entrepreneurs, would be. Each worker is interested in maximizing his own wage income. The workers as a group, corresponding to the group of stockholders in capitalism, are interested in adopting policies which will maximize

$$S = w + \frac{\pi}{x} \tag{10.2}$$

where π represents profits.

The last term of equation (10.2) can he divided into two parts since average profits per worker consists of the difference between average revenue per worker, U, and average cost per worker, K. The firm will then choose that output which will make the positive difference between U and K a maximum. This would be the output at which

$$dU/dy = dK/dy. \tag{10.3}$$

This is the Illyrian equivalent of the capitalist condition that price will equal marginal cost under rational management, or of the market socialist rule that managers act so as to set marginal cost equal to price. The Illyrian condition states that wages per worker (or, what amounts to the same thing, profits per worker) are maximized if the competitive firm chooses the output at which marginal revenue-per-worker equals marginal cost-per-worker.[17] This condition has more in common with the capitalist "rule" than with the Lange-Lerner rule. For the Illyrian rule represents the *result* of behavior of a specified kind (wage-maximizing behavior), as does the neoclassical rule (profit-maximizing behavior). In the market socialist economy of the Lange-Lerner type however, the managers are *directed* by the state to act in a certain way, the rule not being connected explicitly with the motivations of the managers.

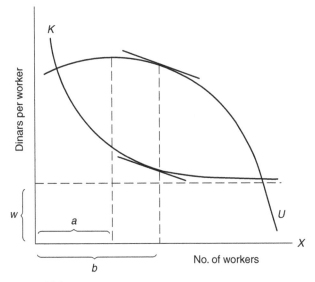

Figure 10.1

Equilibrium for the Illyrian competitive firm is described graphically in Figure 10.1, where the values of U and K are plotted against x. The solution is not altered by making x rather than y the formal choice variable. U has its maximum value at the point at which marginal and average product are equal[18] and declines as the number of workers is either increased or decreased from this value. K, representing average costs per worker, is equal to

$$w + \frac{R}{x}.$$

This curve is a rectangular hyperbola asymptotic to $x = 0$, $K = w$. Profits per worker reach a maximum when the difference between U and K is greatest, which is the value of x for which the slopes of U and K are equal. This is point b of Figure 10.1.

What is the meaning of this equilibrium? How does it compare with the equilibrium position of the traditional firm? We may consider first the effects of changes in the parameters on the Illyrian firm's behavior, and then contrast the equilibrium positions of Illyrian and capitalist firms under similar technological and market conditions.

Referring to Figure 10.2, suppose that the firm is in equilibrium producing, under revenue and cost conditions represented by U_1 and K_1, an output corresponding to the level of employment a. The state now raises the interest rate, so that R is increased. This shifts the cost curve up to K_2. But at the output corresponding to a, curve K_2 is steeper than is U_1.[19] That is to say, at employment level a the rate of decrease of average cost per worker is greater than the rate of decrease of average revenue per worker. Consequently it will be to the workers' advantage to raise output until average cost and average revenue per worker are decreasing at the same rate. In Figure 10.2 this is represented by employment level b where the slopes of U_1 and K_2 are equal. This result can be generalized into the theorem: *A change in the fixed costs of the competitive Illyrian firm leads to a change in output in the same direction.*

Further increases in R would lead to further increases in output. If K_3 were the relevant cost curve the firm would be earning zero profits. Even if R were increased beyond this point

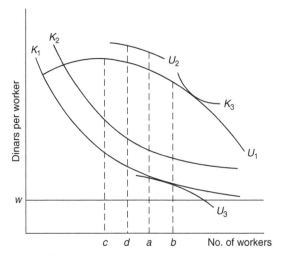

Figure 10.2

output would continue to increase, as the worker-managers strove to minimize losses. Under these circumstances the workers would be receiving less than the calculated wage w. So long as no better alternatives were available elsewhere the workers would continue to work in the given firm despite this fact, under our assumptions.[20] Decreases in R of course have the opposite effect. At $R = 0$, the cost function becomes $K_4 = w$, and output would be at the level corresponding to the maximum value of U_1. A negative interest rate would convert K into a hyperbola asymptotic to the same lines as before but located below w on Figure 10.2. Employment would be less than c and the competitive Illyrian firm would be in equilibrium with average costs falling.[21]

Price changes may be considered in a similar way. Suppose that an increase in demand for the industry's product leads to an increase in the market price p of our firm, which is currently in equilibrium at employment level a of Figure 10.2. This will shift U_1 upwards to position U_2. But at the current employment level U_2 will be steeper than K_1.[22] That is, at a the rate of decrease of average revenue per worker is greater than the rate of decrease of average cost per worker. Output and employment will contract until these rates are again equal as at employment level d. Our theorem is: *A change in price to the competitive Illyrian firm leads to a change in output in the opposite direction.*

The lower limit to a price-induced output contraction is, roughly speaking, at employment level c where average and marginal product are equal. If falling price were to shift the revenue curve down to U_3 a zero profits position would have been reached. The remarks above regarding operations at a loss would of course apply equally if falling price rather than rising fixed costs were the cause of the losses.[23]

Under the usually hypothesized market and technological conditions the Illyrian competitive firm possesses a negatively sloped supply curve. This does not mean however that Illyrian competitive markets are inherently unstable. For example, Figure 10.3 depicts the industry supply and demand curves in such a market. If demand were to shift from DD to $D'D'$ point A would no longer be an equilibrium position. If this is a "price-adjusting" market in the usual sense, the adjusting mechanism is such that the direction of movement of price over time has the same sign as the amount of excess demand. In the diagram excess demand is now positive, so price increases and eventually equilibrium is restored.

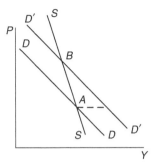

Figure 10.3

On the other hand, if the demand curve has a steeper slope than the supply curve the adjusting mechanism described above will lead away from equilibrium and the market will be unstable. To be assured of stability this possibility must be avoided, which means that some further constraint must be imposed on the structure of the firm specified above.[24] The problem of instability is most likely to arise when product demand is relatively inelastic, or when marginal product is relatively large and declining slowly as output increases.

If the state changes the calculated wage w there is no change in any of the variables relevant to the firm. The K function (*cf.* Figure 10.1) shifts vertically up or down as a result. The income of the workers is unchanged, though relatively more income is in the form of profits (if w is reduced) and relatively less in the form of wages.[25]

The Illyrian equilibrium can now be contrasted with its capitalist counterpart. Consider two firms, one in Illyria, the other in a capitalist country. They have identical production functions and are operating in purely competitive markets. In addition, market prices are equal in both cases, as are fixed costs, and the Illyrian calculated wage w_I equals the going capitalist wage w_c. In Figure 10.4 the U and K functions describe the revenue and cost positions of the Illyrian firm under alternative levels of employment. The rates of change are also drawn in. At the intersection of the latter the Illyrian firm is in equilibrium, producing the output corresponding to employment x_i.

In describing the equilibrium of the capitalist firm it will first be noted that U also expresses the value of the average product of the capitalist firm under our assumptions, since $U = py/x$. The capitalist value-of-the-marginal-product function bears the usual relation to U, and the capitalist output is found at the point x_c where *VMP* equals the wage, since output y_c is a single-valued function of labor input.[26]

In the diagram the capitalist output exceeds that of the Illyrian firm. But this need not be the case. For example, by increasing w_c it would be possible to reduce the equilibrium output level of this firm to the Illyrian level or even below. Under our assumptions a necessary and sufficient condition that the outputs of the two firms be equal is that the equilibrium marginal products be equal. The capitalist value of the marginal product is equal to w_c. In Illyria the value of the marginal product is equal to the "full" wage, i.e., the calculated wage plus the profits share to each worker.[27] Therefore the Illyrian full wage equals the capitalist wage and equality of outputs implies zero profits.[28]

Thus the Illyrian firm is capable of producing in the short run at a level equal to or even greater than that of its capitalist counterpart. And the state can affect output decisions of the firm via its ability to alter the parameter R. If it is willing to use the fixed tax for capital use as an instrument of policy in attaining desired levels of output, and consequently is willing to make discriminatory charges on this basis, it may create an environment in which it is in

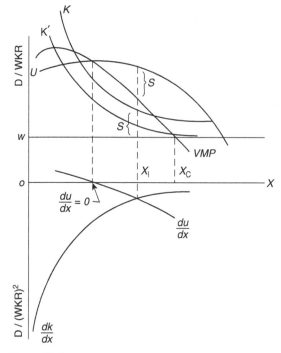

Figure 10.4

the material interests of the worker-managers to produce at the competitive capitalist output, or at some other preferred rate. Alternatively, if the industry were in longrun equilibrium in both countries and demand, labor force, etc., conditions were identical, both firms would produce the same output.

Finally, the case of constant average product y/x may be noted. In capitalism this means one of three things: (1) if $VMP > w$ the firm produces at capacity; (2) if $VMP < w$ the firm produces nothing; and (3) if $VMP = w$ output is indeterminate. In the Illyrian case this means that U is a horizontal line. The maximum positive, or minimum negative, difference between U and K consequently is at infinity whatever the position of U on the diagram. The Illyrian firm produces at capacity when marginal and average product are equal.

III The case of two variable inputs

In Illyria a single class of inputs, labor, is singled out for special treatment. The distinctive features of Illyrian behavior stem entirely from this fact. By extending our previous model to include the use by the firm of a variable nonlabor input, the special position of labor in the firm can be brought out more clearly. The production function will now have the two arguments,

$$y = f(x, z). \tag{10.4}$$

If the usual assumptions of positive marginal products and diminishing returns to the factors are made, the equilibrium condition for labor use will correspond to that in Section II, i.e., the value of the marginal product of labor will be equal to the full wage. For the nonlabor input however the value of the marginal product will be equal to the price v of the input.[29] The workers react to changes in nonlabor inputs in the same manner as do capitalists: they will increase their use of the factor as long as it contributes more to revenue than to cost. On the other hand they seem to use a different criterion in evaluating labor use. An additional laborer must contribute more to revenue per worker than to cost per worker in order for him to be employed. In fact, *only* the latter criterion is being employed in the model. It simply happens that the capitalist and Illyrian criteria lead to the same behavior with regard to non-labor inputs. Whenever one of these factors contributes more to revenue than to cost it also contributes more to revenue per worker than to cost per worker. As a result the equilibrium conditions are the same. However the two criteria do not lead to the same behavior when it comes to labor use. Because each laborer gets a share of the profits it does not follow that an additional worker who contributes more to revenue than to cost will necessarily also contribute more to revenue per worker than to cost per worker. As a result the equilibrium conditions for labor use are not the same in the two regimes.

An analysis of the effects of changes in the parameters R and p leads to less clear results in the two-input case than it did in Section II: In the case of a change in fixed costs the analysis may be illustrated by means of the factor allocation diagrams of Figure 10.5. The curves in 5A are drawn on the assumption of a fixed input of factor z and those in 5B on the assumption of a fixed level of employment. From an initial position of equilibrium in which x_1 of x and z_1 of z are being used, fixed cost is increased. This shifts K_1 upward to K_2, increasing labor input from x_1 to x_2, and consequently tending to increase output. However, there is now an additional effect which must be taken into account: namely the effect of the increase in labor use on the marginal product of the nonlabor input. If the latter is unaffected or increases, shifting VMP_1 upwards to VMP_2, the increase in output is either unaffected or magnified. However, if VMP is reduced by the increased labor use the amount of z used decreases, and the output effect of the increase in fixed cost is indeterminate by means of qualitative analysis alone. The latter, however, is a rather unlikely eventuality, since in the short run more labor will generally not decrease the usefulness of the other variable factors, and conversely. Consequently a change in fixed cost in the multifactor case will also tend to lead to a change in output in the same direction.

A more serious indeterminacy appears in the analysis of price changes. Without a good deal more information it is not possible to state the effect on output of a change in price. The possibility of a positively inclined supply curve emerges clearly however, and some presumption that the danger of instability, resulting from a negatively inclined and relatively elastic

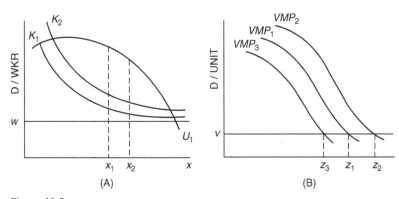

(A)   (B)

Figure 10.5

supply curve, has diminished. Whether or not a negatively sloped supply curve will result in the multifactor case depends on the relative importance of labor in the bill of inputs.[30]

Similarly, changes in the parameter v, the supply price of the nonlabor input z, have indeterminate effects on output. This is also true in the case of analysis of the capitalist firm with the same amount of information, though information sufficient to remove the indeterminacy in one case may not be sufficient in the other.

The statements made in Section I comparing competitive capitalism with competition in Illyria generally apply in the somewhat more complicated two-variable-input case. We will consider here the problem of comparative factor allocation. As before our two firms have identical production functions and are operating under identical market conditions so that:

$$p^I = p^C$$

$$w^I = w^C$$

$$v^I = v^C$$

$$R^I = R^C$$

the superscripts standing for "Illyria" and "Capitalism" respectively.

The situation is described in Figure 10.6 in which isoquants Q_i which are identical for both firms are drawn. Let us assume first that the capitalist firm is producing output Q_i. BB is the factor-cost line based on the values of w and v, so that the capitalist firm is in equilibrium at a factor mix represented by point N. Let us assume further that the capitalist firm is earning a profit at this level of operation. At the same output the Illyrian firm would be earning a profit too. But it would not be in equilibrium at point N. This is because BB is not the relevant factor cost line for the Illyrian firm. Since in Illyria the value of the marginal product of labor is equated to the full wage, i.e., including the profits share, BA, representing a larger wage "cost," is the relevant one for the Illyrian allocation decision. The Illyrian firm is in equilibrium then at point M, producing less output and using less labor than its capitalist counterpart.

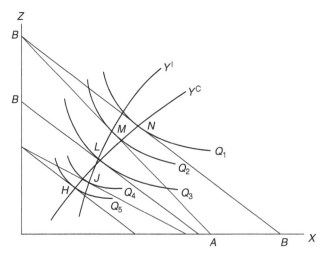

Figure 10.6

Suppose now that market price falls to the zero profits point. Capitalist output and factor mix contract along Y^C, say to point L. Illyrian output and factor mix contract along Y^I, but also to point L, since the zero-profits full wage is equal to w. If price should fall further so that both firms are incurring losses the full wage will then be less than w. For example, under conditions which would lead the capitalist firm to produce at H, the Illyrian firm would produce at J. The Illyrian firm would produce more than the capitalist firm and would use more labor, so as to spread the losses around among as many of the worker-managers as possible.

The Y^I line, like Y^C, is positively sloped in the diagram, indicating that supply responds positively to an increase in price. It is perfectly possible for Y^I to have a negative slope under suitable cost and technological conditions, but it will still intersect Y^C at the zero-profits point.[31]

As a final aspect of the multiple-input case we may consider a firm which is highly auto-mated so that labor does not enter significantly into the short-run production function as a variable input. In this case factor use and output are determined by the usual equilibrium conditions of capitalism. That is, with a fixed labor force any addition to profits is also an addition to profits per worker. Such a firm would behave in exactly the same way as its cap-italist counterpart, equating marginal cost to price and the marginal value products to the fixed input prices.

IV Market imperfections

Illyria must pay a price for its decentralized pricing system in the form of imperfect mar-kets. For the worker-managers no less than their capitalist counterparts have an incentive to profit from the negatively inclined demand schedule that must in many instances confront them. The whole congeries of market types from monopoly to monopolistic competition, including the usual forms of collusion, could emerge under Illyrian conditions. Alterations in the previous models required to take account of such market imperfections in most instances are not extensive. For example, the monopoly solution in the single-variable-input case can be discussed by means of Figure 10.2 if the U function is reinterpreted to take account of the fact that price is now a variable rather than a parameter of the sys-tem. That is, any point on U would now represent the average revenue that would accrue to the monopoly from selling the output the x workers are capable of producing at the price offered for that quantity by buyers. The result is that factors are used up to the point at which the marginal revenue product equals the (assumed perfectly elastic) supply price in the case of nonlabor inputs, and to the point at which marginal revenue product equals the "full" wage for labor inputs.[32] Output will be less than in competition under the usual conditions.

There is one factor market which exhibits a special rigidity in Illyria; namely the labor market. The situation can be illustrated by assuming away all the customary forms of rigid-ity in the labor market such as trade unions, barriers to training, imperfect knowledge, etc. If labor is a homogeneous factor well informed and concerned to better its material posi-tion as far as possible, we may assume the supply to depend solely on the wage offered. If profits figures are published or otherwise available it is the full wage that will determine the offer of labor power. Suppose that from an initial position of equilibrium the supply schedule for labor shifts up, leading to excess demand. Ignoring the influence of varying employment levels on product demand, the marginal firms are now unable to obtain labor at the going wage rate. But they are also unable to offer higher wages, since the wage rate was already at a maximum. As a result of the rigidity of the wage offer there will be no forces set in motion in the short run to correct a disequilibrium, and the shortage of workers will in itself tend to depress the wage paid by the marginal firms, since profits can no longer be maximized.

If excess supply of labor should develop, a similar rigidity would occur. Workers are willing to offer themselves at lower wage rates, but these rates cannot legally be paid. Consequently the excess supply will persist. Only entry or departure by some firms would be capable of changing the situation; i.e., by changes in the quantities demanded in each case rather than by alterations in the market price of labor.

If profit rates were kept secret it might be possible to create a supply function in which the nominal wage w_1 was the independent variable. In this case, when excess demand appeared the state could raise the nominal rate sufficiently to attract the needed number of workers into the market. This change in the wage would not affect the full wage or the product market positions.[33] That is, it would affect only the supply of labor, not the demand. However it would be rather difficult to keep all information regarding profits from the labor market when all recipients of profits or losses were also workers.

V Concluding remarks

1. The zero-profit output of the competitive Illyrian and competitive capitalist firms will be identical, given the same market and technological conditions for the two firms. This suggests that in the long run the Illyrian conditions under competition could lead to an optimal allocation of resources wherever the capitalist competitive regime would. However we have not discussed conditions of entry in Illyria. Entry could occur either by creation of new firms by the state, or by expansion of existing firms, or by some provision for individual or decentralized group initiative in starting new enterprises. All three possibilities exist in Yugoslavia but it is not possible to discuss them here. It will merely be noted that there is likely to be strong resistance by the Illyrian worker-managers to ploughing back profits, since this would involve a reduction in the current profits share. This will be true if relatively low-income entrepreneurs are likely to be more myopic than relatively high-income ones. Something additional to worker self-interest might well be necessary in the Illyrian environment to ensure entry equivalent to that under capitalism.

2. Market imperfections stemming from the ability of the seller (or buyer) to influence the market price by varying his rate of output lead generally to a lower level of output and a higher price than the competitive rates, in Illyria as in capitalism. This has been a persistent problem in Yugoslavia from the beginning of the new system (Jovanović 1952, p. 16; *Ekonomska politika*, 1953, 2, 443–44; *Ekonomska politika*, 1954, *3*, 841–42) and has led to the promulgation of an "antitrust" law.[34] The state's broad rights of intervention might seem to offer more favorable opportunities for controlling such behavior, but persistent complaints in the Yugoslav press suggest that control of monopoly has not been notably successful.[35] Of course Yugoslavia, being a rather small country with an underdeveloped industrial sector and communications network, and with a balance-of-payments problem which has led to a large number of restrictions on competitive imports, has considerable initial disadvantages to overcome in developing a purely competitive market.

3. A special stability problem arises in Illyria, since firms may react to a price change by altering the rate of output in the opposite direction (negatively sloped supply schedule), a situation which is more likely to occur the more important labor is as an input. Since

a good deal of new plant has been installed in Yugoslavia since 1952, this would be a difficult hypothesis to test. Indeed, our model does not tell us anything at all about what to expect if there is in fact instability in a market. In addition it is probable that in a large number of Yugoslav firms policy decisions are made by the director without much reference to the wage-maximizing desires of the workers. Though directors also share in the profits, it is likely that other motives also exist for them which might lead to different behavior as regards price and output and input policy.[36]

4. The beginning student of economics would undoubtedly be delighted to learn that in Illyria an increase in fixed costs would really lead to an increase in output so as to spread out the increased burden over a larger number of units. I have seen no evidence to indicate that the Yugoslav authorities have varied the interest rate on existing capital for purposes of output control, though discrimination has been practiced which is consistent with such an aim.[37]

5. The labor market possesses a rigidity which prevents adjustment of supply and demand to restore a displacement from equilibrium. It is true that in Yugoslavia there has been some excess supply of labor at least since the institution of the new economic system in 1952 (*Ekonomska politika*, 1953, 2, 182–83; Kardelj 1955), though this can be explained as well by other factors operating generally in a labor market in an underdeveloped country (and by the successive droughts) as by means of this theorem. In this excess-supply situation some incentive probably exists for the firm to practice a form of illegal discriminaton which *is* related to the specific rigidity described above. This could be done by means of an illegal contract to hire workers who would agree to work for the contractual wage rate for unskilled workers and renounce their right to profits.[38]

Finally, outside pressure by various groups, but especially by the people's committees, the organs of local government, seems to have had considerable effect on decision-making by the firm in Yugoslavia. We will note only one example. The people's committees possess the right to a portion of the profits of every firm within their territory. This has led them to influence the firms' policies and to take other steps to siphon funds from the firms into the treasury of the local government.[39] The actions of local governments and other administrative bodies, plus fears of administrative intervention, undoubtedly result in significant differences in the behavior of firms in Yugoslavia and Illyria. These factors, plus the relatively large role the director seems to play in *de facto* decision-making within the Yugoslav firm, provide the chief limitations to the application of the above analysis to current operations in Yugoslavia. The model's relevance to Yugoslavia may be somewhat increased if it is assumed that the legal framework is descriptive of an ultimate purpose on the part of the Yugoslav leadership.

In summary, market syndicalism differs from market socialism in that in the former (1) both price and output decisions are decentralized to the level of the firm; (2) the workers employed in each firm control policy making; and (3) material interest is the governing incentive. Some of the arguments in favor of market syndicalism as a non-bureaucratic alternative to other forms of socialism would bear a striking resemblance to those of the economic liberal when attacking some tendencies of contemporary capitalism; and conversely for arguments against market syndicalism. However it would not be seemly to discuss these issues until some other properties of the Illyrian economy, such as the investment decision, multiple market stability and macroeconomics, have been investigated.

Mathematical appendix

The condition for stability in a single competitive Illyrian market under the assumptions of Section II

From equations (10.2) and (10.3) in the text

$$S = \frac{py}{x} - w - \frac{R}{x} \tag{10.5}$$

so that

$$\frac{dS}{dy} = \frac{p(x - yx') + Rx'}{x^2} = 0 \tag{10.6}$$

where $x' \equiv dx/dy$. The equilibrium condition $S' = px - pyx' + Rx' = 0$ may be differentiated with respect to the parameter p:

$$\left.\frac{\partial S'}{\partial p}\right|_R = \frac{dS'}{dy}\frac{\partial y}{\partial p}\bigg|_R + \left.\frac{\partial S'}{\partial p}\right|_{y,R} \equiv 0$$

$$= (-pyx'' + Rx'')(\partial y/\partial p) + (x - yx') \equiv 0$$

or the slope of the firm's supply function:

$$\frac{\partial y}{\partial p} = \frac{yx' - x}{x''(R - py)}. \tag{10.7}$$

But $(R - py) = -pxy'$, since the equilibrium is preserved along the supply function. So supply elasticity:

$$\eta_S \equiv \frac{p}{y}\frac{\partial y}{\partial p} = \frac{x'}{xx''}\left(\frac{x}{y} - x'\right) < 0, \tag{10.8}$$

except over the relatively unimportant range in which average product is equal to or less than marginal product. Note that

$$x'' \equiv \frac{d^2x}{dy^2} = \frac{y''}{(-y')^3} > 0, \quad \text{where } y'' \equiv \frac{d^2y}{dx^2}.$$

We are assuming a price-adjusting market in which the existence of excess demand leads to price increases over time in the case of excess demand and of decreases in the case of excess supply. Such a market will be stable when the supply curve is negatively sloped provided $\eta_D > \eta_S$. If we assume that production functions of all firms are identical, elasticity is invariant under the summation from firm to industry supply function. Thinking then in terms of industry demand and firm supply conditions, we have:

$$\eta_D > \eta_S = \frac{x'}{xx''}\left(\frac{x}{y} - x'\right) \tag{10.9}$$

as a necessary and sufficient condition for stability.

Monopoly with one variable input

Equation (10.5) applies in this case, except that p is now a variable. Assume

$$p = g(y, \alpha) \tag{10.10}$$

such that $\partial p / \partial y < 0$ and α, a shift parameter, is defined so that $\partial p / \partial \alpha > 0$ and further that $\partial p / \partial y$ remains invariant under the shift. Differentiating (10.5) with respect to y and solving for the first order condition for a maximum ($y' \equiv 1/x'$):

$$y'(p + p'y) = (py - R)/x, \quad \text{where } p' = \left. \frac{\partial p}{\partial y} \right|_\alpha \tag{10.11}$$

Equation (10.11) may be differentiated with respect to R and α, respectively, and solved for:

$$\frac{\partial y}{\partial R} = -\frac{x'}{2p'x + p''xy - x''(py - R)}$$

and

$$\frac{\partial y}{\partial \alpha} = \frac{(\partial p / \partial \alpha)(x'y - x) - xy \left(\frac{\partial^2 p}{\partial y \partial \alpha} \right)}{2p'x + p''xy - x''(py - R)}.$$

Knowledge of signs tells us that, as long as the demand curve is linear or convex to the origin, a change in R leads to a change in y in the same direction. With a similar demand curve, an upward shift in demand of the hypothesized kind will lead to a decrease in output if the firm is operating beyond the point of maximum average product, but an increase in output if average product is still increasing.

The two-variable-input case

$$S = \frac{1}{x}[py - (wx + vz + R)] \tag{10.12}$$

and

$$y = f(x, z), \quad y_x > 0, \quad y_z > 0,$$
$$y_{xx} < 0, \quad y_{zz} < 0, \quad \text{and} \quad y_{xx}y_{zz} - y_{zz}^2 > 0. \tag{10.13}$$

Applying the first-order conditions for a maximum,

$$\partial S / \partial x = (1/x^2)[p(xy_x - y) + vz + R] = 0 \tag{10.14}$$

and

$$\partial S / \partial z = (1/x)(py_z - v) = 0 \tag{10.15}$$

or

$$py_x = \frac{py - (vz + R)}{x} \tag{10.16}$$

and

$$py_z = v. \tag{10.17}$$

Further differentiation of (10.14) and (10.15) gives, at the equilibrium position at which (10.16) and (10.17) are satisfied,

$$\partial^2 S/\partial x^2 = py_{xx}/x < 0,$$

$$\partial^2 S/\partial z^2 = py_{zz}/x < 0,$$

$$\partial^2 S/\partial x \partial z = py_{xz}/x$$

and

$$\frac{\partial^2 S}{\partial x^2} \frac{\partial^2 S}{\partial z^2} - \left(\frac{\partial^2 S}{\partial x \partial z}\right)^2 = \frac{p^2}{x^2}(y_{xx} y_{zz} - y_{xz^2}) > 0.$$

Therefore equations (10.16) and (10.17) determine a maximum. Both the latter equations can be differentiated with respect to R and with respect to p and solved for:

$$\frac{\partial x}{\partial R} = \frac{\begin{vmatrix} -1 & (pxy_{xz}) \\ 0 & (py_{zz}) \end{vmatrix}}{p^2 x \begin{vmatrix} y_{xx} & y_{xz} \\ y_{xz} & y_{zz} \end{vmatrix}} > 0,$$

$$\frac{\partial z}{\partial R} = \frac{\begin{vmatrix} (pxy_{xx}) & -1 \\ (py_{xz}) & 0 \end{vmatrix}}{p^2 x \begin{vmatrix} y_{xx} & y_{xz} \\ y_{xz} & y_{zz} \end{vmatrix}} \gtreqless 0,$$

$$\frac{\partial x}{\partial p} = \frac{\begin{vmatrix} (y - xy_x) & (pxy_{xz}) \\ (-y_z) & (py_{zz}) \end{vmatrix}}{p^2 x \begin{vmatrix} y_{xx} & y_{xz} \\ y_{xz} & y_{zz} \end{vmatrix}} \gtreqless 0$$

$$\frac{\partial z}{\partial P} = \frac{\begin{vmatrix} (pxy_{xx}) & (y - xy_x) \\ (py_{xz}) & (-y_z) \end{vmatrix}}{p^2 x \begin{vmatrix} y_{xx} & y_{xz} \\ y_{xz} & y_{zz} \end{vmatrix}} \gtreqless 0.$$

The slope of the supply function at the equilibrium point,

$$\frac{\partial y}{\partial p} = y_x \frac{\partial x}{\partial p} + y_z \frac{\partial z}{\partial p}$$

$$= \frac{[y_{zz}y_x(y - xy_x) - xy_z^2 y_{xx} + y_{xz}(xy_xy_z - yy_z + xy_x)]}{px(y_{xx}y_{zz} - y_{xz}^2)} \lessgtr 0 \qquad (10.18)$$

The denominator is positive, but the numerator is undetermined in sign with the specified information.

Acknowledgments

The author would like to thank Gustavo Escobar, Eberhard Fels, Arthur Goldberger, Gregory Grossman and Andreas Papandreou for critical comment on this paper, without committing them to any of the argument.

Notes

1 (*Službeni list FNRJ* 1945, No. 58, 1951). The 1954 plan is published in (*Službeni list FNRJ*, No. 13, 1954, item 146).
2 This had been carried out for certain classes of firms and industries during 1950–51 (for example price-setting in the case of textile products by the price bureaus of the Ministry for Domestic Trade was abolished by a decree published in (*Službeni list FNRJ*, No. 48, 1951, item 454)). The general statute appears in (*Službeni list FNRJ*, No. 32, 1952, item 382).
3 Prices of some industrial raw materials (e.g., pig and cast iron and sawn timber) were fixed by decree during 1954 (*Službeni list FNRJ*, No. 20, item 221; No. 26, item 295; No. 32, item 407). The Federal Price Office was re-established early in 1955 (*Službeni list FNRJ* 1945, No. 22, 1955, item 225) but there was no significant increase in the number of controlled prices at the time.
4 D. Misić (1953) says that capital was to be valued at its "real present value, taking account both of its economic obsolescence and the extent to which it is worn out."
5 (*Službeni list FNRJ*, No. 51, 1953, item 425). An earlier law (*Službeni list FNRJ*, No. 57, 1951, item 545) is much less specific and does not define the conditions under which a decree of bankruptcy against a firm will be passed.
6 In 1954 the state guaranteed up to 80 per cent of the calculated wage fund of the firm. A firm could apply to the state bank for a loan to cover up to 90 per cent of this fund, but the bank could refuse the loan if it thought the chances of repayment were not good. Guarantee of the loan by the local government (*narodni odbor* or "people's committee") was often required (*Službeni list FNRJ*, No. 5, 1954, item 57).
7 The director was a member ex officio of the management board.
8 (*Službeni list FNRJ*, No. 7, 1952, item 108) (*Službeni list FNRJ*, No. 56, 1953, item 484). Worker skills were classified in (*Službeni list FNRJ*, No. 57, 1950, item 508), and minimum compensation fixed for each grade.
9 There are several qualifications to this statement. Some portion of the profits was to be used for the building up of a reserve fund and the local government received a share as well (Adašević 1954, p. 44).
10 An official statement in vindication of the use of this right by Vice-President Kardelj can be found in (Kardelj 1954, p. 133).
11 The people's committee had the right of approval of the firm's independent plan (see planning law cited above, footnote 1) and the trade unions had some special rights of intervention in the hire–fire decision (*Službeni list FNRJ*, No. 26, 1952, item 306).
12 Such action is termed "administrative intervention" by Yugoslav economists and is asserted to have been ubiquitous under the previous Stalinist form of economic organization. A principal reason for establishing the new system was to make such actions unnecessary. See for example (Miljević 1954, pp. 95–100, 113 ff., 131–32, 224 ff.; Uvalic 1954, pp. 238 ff.).

13 In Yugoslavia the setting of the calculated wage performs an important function in determining the portion of the firm's wage bill that comes under the progressive surplus profits tax, but we are ignoring this tax in the Illyrian case.

14 The Yugoslav wage law cited above provides that time-and-a-half be paid for overtime work, but that such work cannot be paid for unless prior authorization has been obtained from the local government. Apparently there was a tendency to hog the work which, reasonably enough, was frowned upon by the authorities in a labor surplus economy.

15 The management board has the final decision in the matter of hiring and firing in the Yugoslav firm (with the exception noted above, fn. 11). If it is assumed that the board is composed of workers of relatively long tenure in their employment in the firm, so that they would not be personally affected by a decision to reduce output, aside from the favorable effect on their own income, this assumption may seem reasonable.

16 All workers and employees, including those whose wage cost to the firm would ordinarily be considered as overhead, are included in the wage cost wx, as a matter of convenience.

17 Marginal revenue-per-worker, it will be noticed, is not the same thing as marginal revenue per worker. The former measures the change in average revenue per worker brought about by a small change in output, while the latter measures the average marginal revenue per worker. In symbols, marginal revenue-per-worker is:

$$\frac{d(py/x)}{dy} = p \cdot \frac{x - yx'}{x^2}$$

while marginal revenue per worker is:

$$\frac{d(py)/dy}{x} = \frac{p}{x}.$$

18 From the preceding note it can be seen that marginal revenue-per-worker will be zero when x/y equals x'. The shape of the production function ensures that this will be a maximum value for U.

19 Since $K = w + (R/x)$, $dK/dx = -R/x^2$. Therefore, if $R_2 > R_1$, $|dK_2/dx| > |dK_1/dx|$ at $x = a$.

20 In Yugoslavia wages up to 80 per cent of the calculated wage are guaranteed by the government. If this were true of Illyria, then at outputs beyond that which yielded $0.8w$ to the workers the maximization criterion would cease to apply. Continued operation at such a level would eventually lead to bankruptcy.

21 As in capitalism this would only be true over the range in which marginal product was declining. Beyond that range the second-order condition for equilibrium would not be satisfied, so that if a solution existed it would not be a maximum. It may also be noted that over this range of values the supply curve would be positively sloped.

22 $dU/dx = (P/x)[y' - (y/x)]$. Hence if $p_2 > p_1$ then $|dU_2/dx| > |dU_1/dx|$ at $x = a$.

23 The effects of changes in p and R can perhaps be seen more clearly by considering the equilibrium condition:

$$\frac{dS}{dx} = \frac{p(xy' - y) + R}{x^2} = 0 \tag{10.19}$$

or

$$\frac{y}{x} - y' = \frac{R}{px}. \tag{10.20}$$

Thus the right-hand term of (10.20) measures the difference between average and marginal product in equilibrium, which will be positive (decreasing average product) if R is positive. But the difference between average and marginal product is a monotonic increasing function of output beyond the point of maximum average product (at which point the difference is nil). So, from equation (10.20), if R is increased, the difference between average and marginal product, and hence equilibrium output, will be increased. On the other hand an increase in p means a decrease in the difference between average and marginal product, and hence a decrease in equilibrium output.

24 See the Mathematical Appendix.

25 See note 13 above.

26 We are assuming that the capitalist firm too can vary only the number of workers employed and not the hours of work.

27 From equations (10.2) and (10.20), $S = (py - R)/x = py'$ in equilibrium.

28 We assumed at the start that $w_I = w_C$. Since the value of w_I really does not make any difference, a more significant statement would be: equality of outputs implies equal wages.

29 See the Mathematical Appendix for derivations in th e two-variable-input case.

30 *Cf.* equation (10.18) in the Appendix.

31 Figure 10.6 may also be used to contrast other comparative static changes. For example, an increase in w will increase the slope of BB without affecting that of BA. This will tend to move the capitalist equilibrium position at N closer to the Illyrian at M. An increase in R on the other hand will tend to make BA less steep without affecting the slope of BB. This will tend to move the Illyrian equilibrium position at M closer to the capitalist at N. When the equilibria coincide in either case profits will be zero.

32 See Appendix, note 2.

33 However, with a progressive profits tax, as exists in Yugoslavia, the full wage will be reduced, *ceteris paribus*, by a decrease in w, since a larger proportion of the wage bill would become taxable; and of course the full wage would increase with an increase in the calculated wage.

34 (*Službeni list FNRJ*, No. 56, 1953, item 483, esp. Article 74). The language is fully as vague as that of the Sherman Act, among other things forbidding firms from doing anything which leads to a "monopoly position in the market."

35 See however (*Ekonomska politika* 1952, 1953, 2, 1034) for a description of the refusal of a Yugoslav court to uphold a contract which was in restraint of trade.

36 See (Ward 1957) for a discussion of the relative influence of director, management board and workers' council within the firm. For example, directors are often in close contact with local government officials. One possible result of ties of this kind might be profit-maximizing behavior, as mentioned in note 38 below.

37 (Sirotković 1954, pp. 132–331. In the 1954 plan, for example, the standard rate was 6 per cent, but in some types of construction no interest at all was charged, while elsewhere a rate of 2 per cent was charged. It is certainly true that the state was specially interested in increasing output in the favored areas. It does not necessarily follow however that the planners had the mechanism operative in our model in mind in granting the favors.

38 A phenomenon known as the "dead brigades" (*mrtvi brigadi*) may have been an instance of this (*Ekonomska politika* 1952, 1953, 2, 1034; Kardelj 1955, p. 487). For example the coal mining concern mentioned on p. 568 above might hire an unskilled worker for 6000 dinars per month, which would add 8100 dinars to the calculated wage fund, i.e., to labor cost in the accounting sense. This would substantially reduce accounting profits and hence the amount of taxation under the steeply progressive profits tax law. If the firm expected to make a fairly high level of profits, this could be to the monetary advantage of the "in-group" workers even if the newly hired worker performed no work at all. From the above descriptions it seems that the dead brigades in fact had little to do. In some cases the dead brigades were in fact "dead souls," fictitious employees.

39 (Kardelj 1955, p. 159; Gligorijević 1955). The people's committee would be interested in the level of profits per se, rather than in profits per worker, so that within the framework of our model such disagreements over price-output policy could arise.

References

A. Adašević (ed.), *Novi privredni propisi* (The new economic decrees). Belgrad 1954.

E. Barone, "Il ministerio della produzione nello stato collettivista," "*Gior. d. Econ.*, 1908; English translation in reference 6.

B. P. Beckwith, *The Economic Theory of a Socialist Economy.* Stanford (Calif.) 1949. Bibliography, pp. 433–5.

Ekonomska politika (Economic Policy). Belgrad (weekly), 1952.

S. Gligorijević, "Zapazanja iz rada komunista u industriskim preduzecima" (Observations on the Work of Communists in Industrial Firms), *Komunist*, No. 4, 1955, 7, 243–47.

F. A. von Hayek, ed., *Collectivist Economic Planning.* London 1935.

B. Jovanović, "Iskustva iz primene novog privrednog sistema" (Experience with the Operation of the New Economic System), *Ekonomist*, No. 4, 1952, *5*, 12–22.

E. Kardelj, "O nekim nedostacima u radu komunista" (Certain Short-Comings in the Work of Communists), *Komunist*, No. 4, 1955, *7*, 154–70.

——, "O ulozi komunista u izgradnji našeg društvenog i državnog sistema" (The Role of the Communists in the Development of our Social System), *ibid.*, 481–511.

——, *Problemi naše socialičke izgradnje* (Problems of Our Socialist Development), Vol. 2. Belgrad 1954.

O. Lange and F. M. Taylor, *On the Economic Theory of Socialism.* Minneapolis 1938.

A. P. Lerner, *The Economics of Control.* New York 1946.

D. J. Miljević et al., *Razvoj privrednog sistema FNRJ* (The Development of Yugoslavia's Economic System). Belgrad 1954.

D. Misić, "Ekonomska zastarelost" (Economic Obsolescence), *Ekonomska politika*, 1953, *2*, 87–89.

L. von Mises, "Die Wirtschaftsrechnung im sozialen Gemeinwesen," *Archiv f. Sozialwissenschaft*, 1920, *47*; English translation in reference 6.

J. Sirotković, *Novi privredni sistem FNRJ* (Yugoslavia's New Economic System). Zagreb 1954.

Službeni list FNRJ (Official Gazette of Yugoslavia), Belgrad 1945.

R. Uvalic, "The Management of Undertakings by the Workers in Yugoslavia" (tr. from Serbo-Croatian), *Internat. Lab. Rev.*, 1954, *69*, 235–54.

B. Ward, "Workers' Management in Yugoslavia," *Jour. Pol. Econ.*, Oct. 1957, *65*, 373–86.

11 The theory of the firm as governance structure

From choice to contract

Oliver E. Williamson

The propositions that organization matters and that it is susceptible to analysis were long greeted by skepticism by economists. To be sure, there were conspicuous exceptions: Alfred Marshall in *Industry and Trade* (1932), Joseph Schumpeter in *Capitalism, Socialism, and Democracy* (1942) and Friedrich Hayek (1945) in his writings on knowledge. Institutional economists like Thorstein Veblen (1904), John R. Commons (1934) and Ronald Coase (1937) and organization theorists like Robert Michels (1915 [1962]), Chester Barnard (1938), Herbert Simon (1957a), James March (March and Simon, 1958) and Richard Scott (1992) also made the case that organization deserves greater prominence.

One reason why this message took a long time to register is that it is much easier to say that organization matters than it is to show how and why.[1] The prevalence of the science of choice approach to economics has also been an obstacle. As developed herein, the lessons of organization theory for economics are both different and more consequential when examined through the lens of contract. This paper examines economic organization from a science of contract perspective, with special emphasis on the theory of the firm.

The sciences of choice and contract

Economics throughout the twentieth century has been developed predominantly as a science of choice. As Lionel Robbins famously put it in his book, *An Essay on the Nature and Significance of Economic Science* (1932, p. 16), "Economics is the science which studies human behavior as a relationship between ends and scarce means which have alternative uses." Choice has been developed in two parallel constructions: the theory of consumer behavior, in which consumers maximize utility, and the theory of the firm as a production function, in which firms maximize profit. Economists who work out of such setups emphasize how changes in relative prices and available resources influence quantities, a project that became the "dominant paradigm" for economics throughout the twentieth century (Reder, 1999, p. 48).

But the science of choice is not the only lens for studying complex economic phenomena, nor is it always the most instructive lens. The other main approach is what James Buchanan (1964a, b, 1975) refers to as the science of contract. Indeed, Buchanan (1975, p. 225) avers that economics as a discipline went "wrong" in its preoccupation with the science of choice and the optimization apparatus associated therewith. Wrong or not, the parallel development of a science of contract was neglected.

As perceived by Buchanan (1987, p. 296), the principal needs for a science of contract were for the field of public finance and took the form of *public ordering*: "Politics is a structure of complex exchange among individuals, a structure within which persons seek to secure collectively their own privately defined objectives that cannot be efficiently secured through

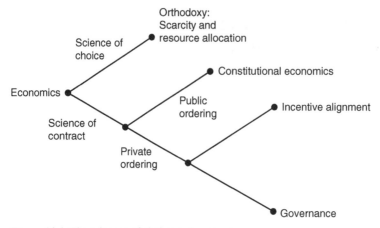

Figure 11.1 The sciences of choice and contract

simple market exchanges." Thinking contractually in the public ordering domain leads into a focus on the rules of the game. Constitutional economics issues are posed (Buchanan and Tullock, 1962; Brennan and Buchanan, 1985).

Whatever the rules of the game, the lens of contract is also usefully brought to bear on the play of the game. This latter is what I refer to as *private ordering*, which entails efforts by the immediate parties to a transaction to align incentives and to craft governance structures that are better attuned to their exchange needs. The object of such self-help efforts is to realize better the "mutuality of advantage from voluntary exchange . . . [that is] the most fundamental of all understandings in economics" (Buchanan, 2001, p. 29), due allowance being made for the mitigation of contractual hazards. Strategic issues – to which the literatures on mechanism design, agency theory and transaction cost economics/incomplete contracting all have a bearing – that had been ignored by neoclassical economists from 1870 to 1970 now make their appearance (Makowski and Ostroy, 2001, pp. 482–3, 490–1).

Figure 11.1 sets out the main distinctions. The initial divide is between the science of choice (orthodoxy) and the science of contract. The latter then divides into public ordering (constitutional economics) and private ordering parts, where the second is split into two related branches. One branch concentrates on front-end incentive alignment (mechanism design, agency theory, the formal property rights literature), while the second branch features the governance of ongoing contractual relations (contract implementation). This paper is mainly concerned with governance, especially with reference to the theory of the firm.

Organization theory through the lens of contract

Organization theory is a huge subject. Macro and micro parts are commonly distinguished, where the former is closer to sociology and the latter to social psychology. Also, it is common to distinguish among rational, natural and open systems approaches (Scott, 1992). My concern is with macro organization theory of a rational systems kind (with special reference to the contributions of Herbert Simon).

In addition to delimiting organization theory in this way, I also examine the lessons of organization theory for economics not through the lens of choice, but through the lens of contract. Whereas those who work out of the dominant paradigm have sometimes been dismissive of organization theory (Posner, 1993; Reder, 1999, pp. 46–9), the lens of contract/private ordering discloses that lessons of organization theory for economics that the dominant paradigm obscures are sometimes fundamental.

Five lessons from organization theory to the economics of contracts

A first lesson from organization theory is to describe human actors in more realistic terms. Simon (1985, p. 303) is unequivocal: "Nothing is more fundamental in setting our research agenda and informing our research methods than our view of the nature of the human beings whose behavior we are studying." Social scientists are thus invited (challenged) to name the cognitive, self-interest and other attributes of human actors on which their analyses rest.

Bounded rationality is the cognitive assumption to which Simon (1957a, p. xxiv) refers, by which he has reference to behavior that is intendedly rational, but only limitedly so. In his view, the main lesson for the science of choice is to supplant maximizing by "satisficing" (1957b, p. 204) – the quest for an alternative that is "good enough."[2]

The study of governance also appeals to bounded rationality, but the main lesson for the science of contract is different: *All complex contracts are unavoidably incomplete.* For this reason, parties will be confronted with the need to adapt to unanticipated disturbances that arise by reason of gaps, errors and omissions in the original contract. Such adaptation needs are especially consequential if, instead of describing self-interest as "frailty of motive" (Simon, 1985, p. 303), which is a comparatively benign condition, strategic considerations are entertained, as well. If human actors are not only confronted with needs to adapt to the unforeseen (by reason of bounded rationality), but are also given to strategic behavior (by reason of opportunism), then costly contractual breakdowns (refusals of cooperation, maladaptation, demands for renegotiation) may be posed. In that event, private ordering efforts to devise supportive governance structures, thereby to mitigate prospective contractual impasses and breakdowns, have merit.

To be sure, such efforts would be unneeded if common knowledge of payoffs and costless bargaining are assumed. Both of these conditions, however, are deeply problematic (Kreps and Wilson, 1982; Williamson, 1985). Moreover, because problems of nonverifiability are posed when bounded rationality, opportunism and idiosyncratic knowledge are joined (Williamson, 1975, pp. 31–3), dispute resolution by the courts in such cases is costly and unreliable. Private ordering – that is, efforts to craft governance structure supports for contractual relations during the contract implementation interval – thus makes its appearance.

A second lesson of organization theory is to be alert to all significant behavioral regularities whatsoever. For example, efforts by bosses to impose controls on workers have both intended *and* unintended consequences. Out of awareness that workers are not passive contractual agents, naïve efforts that focus entirely on intended effects will be supplanted by more sophisticated mechanisms where provision is made for consequences of both kinds. More generally, the awareness among sociologists that "organization has a life of its own" (Selznick, 1950, p. 10) serves to uncover a variety of behavioral regularities (of which bureaucratization is one) for which the student of governance should be alerted and thereafter factor into the organizational design calculus.

A third lesson of organization theory is that alternative modes of governance (markets, hybrids, firms, bureaus) differ in discrete structural ways (Simon, 1978, pp. 6–7). Not only do alternative modes of governance differ in kind, but each generic mode of governance is defined by an internally consistent syndrome of attributes – which is to say that each mode of governance possesses distinctive strengths and weaknesses. As discussed below, the challenge is to enunciate the relevant attributes for describing governance structures and thereafter to align different kinds of transactions with discrete modes of governance in an economizing way.

A fourth lesson of the theory of organizations is that much of the action resides in the microanalytics. Simon (1957a, p. xxx) nominated the "decision premise" as the unit of analysis, which has an obvious bearing on the microanalytics of choice (Newell and Simon, 1972). The unit of analysis proposed by John R. Commons, however, better engages the study of contract. According to Commons (1932, p. 4), "the ultimate unit of activity . . . must contain in itself the three principles of conflict, mutuality, and order. This unit is a transaction."

Whatever the unit of analysis, operationalization turns on naming and explicating the critical dimensions with respect to which the unit varies. Three of the key dimensions of transactions that have important ramifications for governance are asset specificity (which takes a variety of forms – physical, human, site, dedicated, brand name – and is a measure of bilateral dependency), the disturbances to which transactions are subject (and to which potential maladaptations accrue) and the frequency with which transactions recur (which bears both on the efficacy of reputation effects in the market and the incentive to incur the cost of specialized internal governance). Given that transactions differ in their attributes and that governance structures differ in their costs and competencies, the aforementioned – that transactions should be aligned with appropriate governance structures – applies.

A fifth lesson of organization theory is the importance of cooperative adaptation. Interestingly, both the economist Friedrich Hayek (1945) and the organization theorist Chester Barnard (1938) were in agreement that adaptation is the central problem of economic organization. Hayek (1945, pp. 526–7) focused on the adaptations of autonomous economic actors who adjust spontaneously to changes in the market, mainly as signaled by changes in relative prices. The marvel of the market resides in "how little the individual participants need to know to be able to take the right action." By contrast, Barnard featured coordinated adaptation among economic actors working through deep knowledge and the use of administration. In his view, the marvel of hierarchy is that coordinated adaptation is accomplished not spontaneously, but in a "conscious, deliberate, purposeful" way (p. 9).

Because a high-performance economic system will display adaptive properties of both kinds, the problem of economic organization is properly posed not as markets *or* hierarchies, bur rather as markets *and* hierarchies. A predictive theory of economic organization will recognize how and why transactions differ in their adaptive needs, whence the use of the market to supply some transactions and recourse to hierarchy for others.

Follow-on insights from the lens of contract

Examining economic organization through the lens of contract uncovers additional regularities to which governance ramifications accrue. Three such regularities are described here: the Fundamental Transformation, the impossibility of replication/selective intervention and the idea of contract laws (plural).

The Fundamental Transformation applies to that subset of transactions for which large numbers of qualified suppliers at the outset are transformed into what are, in effect, small numbers of actual suppliers during contract execution and at the contract renewal interval. The distinction to be made is between generic transactions where "faceless buyers and sellers ... meet ... for an instant to exchange standardized goods at equilibrium prices" (Ben-Porath, 1980, p. 4) and exchanges where the identities of the parties matter, in that continuity of the relation has significant cost consequences. Transactions for which *a bilateral dependency condition obtains* are those to which the Fundamental Transformation applies.

The key factor here is whether the transaction in question is supported by investments in transaction-specific assets. Such specialized investments may take the form of specialized physical assets (such as a die for stamping out distinctive metal shapes), specialized human assets (that arise from firm-specific training or learning by doing), site specificity (specialization by proximity), dedicated assets (large discrete investments made in expectation of continuing business, the premature termination of which business would result in product being sold at distress prices) or brand-name capital. Parties to transactions that are bilaterally dependent are "vulnerable," in that buyers cannot easily turn to alternative sources of supply, while suppliers can redeploy the specialized assets to their next best use or user only at a loss of productive value (Klein, Crawford and Alchian, 1978). As a result, value-preserving governance structures – to infuse order, thereby to mitigate conflict and to realize mutual gain – are sought.[3] Simple market exchange thus gives way to credible contracting, which includes penalties for premature termination, mechanisms for information disclosure and verification, specialized dispute settlement procedures and the like. Unified ownership (vertical integration) is predicted as bilateral dependency hazards build up.

The impossibility of combining replication with selective intervention is the transaction cost economics answer to an ancient puzzle: What is responsible for limits to firm size? Diseconomies of large scale is the obvious answer, but wherein do these diseconomies reside? Technology is no answer, since each plant in a multiplant firm can use the least-cost technology. Might organization provide the answer? That possibility can be examined by rephrasing the question in comparative contractual terms: Why can't a large firm do everything that a collection of small suppliers can do and more?

Were it that large firms could *replicate* a collection of small firms in all circumstances where small firms do well, then large firms would never do worse. If, moreover, large firms could always *selectively intervene* by imposing (hierarchical) order on prospective conflict, but only where expected net gains could be projected, then large firms would sometimes do better. Taken together, the combination of replication with selective intervention would permit large firms to grow without limit. Accordingly, the issue of limits to firm size turns to an examination of the mechanisms for implementing replication and selective intervention.

Examining how and why both replication and selective intervention break down is a tedious, microanalytic exercise and is beyond the scope of this paper (Williamson, 1985, chapter 6). Suffice it to observe here that the move from autonomous supply (by the collection of small firms) to unified ownership (in one large firm) is *unavoidably attended by changes* in both incentive intensity (incentives are weaker in the integrated firm) and administrative controls (controls are more extensive). Because the syndromes of attributes that define markets and hierarchies have different strengths and weaknesses, some transactions will benefit from the move from market to hierarchy while others will not.

Yet another organizational dimension that distinguishes alternative modes of governance is the regime of contract laws. Whereas economic orthodoxy often implicitly assumes that there is a single, all-purpose law of contract that is costlessly enforced by well-informed courts, the private ordering approach to governance postulates instead that each generic mode of governance is defined (in part) by a distinctive contract law regime.

The contract law of (ideal) markets is that of classical contracting, according to which disputes are costlessly settled through courts by the award of money damages. Galanter (1981, pp. 1–2) takes issue with this legal centralism tradition and observes that many disputes between firms that could under current rules be brought to a court are resolved instead by avoidance, self-help and the like. That is because in "many instances the participants can devise more satisfactory solutions to their disputes than can professionals constrained to apply general rules on the basis of limited knowledge of the dispute" (p. 4). Such a view is broadly consonant with the concept of "contract as framework" advanced by Karl Llewellyn (1931, pp. 736–7), which holds that the "major importance of legal contract is to provide...a framework which never accurately indicates real working relations, but which affords a rough indication around which such relations vary, an occasional guide in cases of doubt, and a norm of ultimate appeal when the relations cease in fact to work." This last condition is important, in that recourse to the courts for purposes of ultimate appeal serves to delimit threat positions. The more elastic concept of contract as framework nevertheless supports a (cooperative) exchange relation over a wider range of contractual disturbances.

What is furthermore noteworthy is that some disputes cannot be brought to a court at all. Specifically, except as "fraud, illegality or conflict of interest" are shown, courts will refuse to hear disputes that arise within firms – with respect, for example, to transfer pricing, overhead, accounting, the costs to be ascribed to intrafirm delays, failures of quality and the like. In effect, the contract law of internal organization is that of *forbearance*, according to which a firm becomes its own court of ultimate appeal. Firms for this reason are able to exercise fiat that the markets cannot. This, too, influences the choice of alternative modes of governance.

Not only is each generic mode of governance defined by an internally consistent syndrome of incentive intensity, administrative controls and contract law regime (Williamson, 1991a), but different strengths and weaknesses accrue to each.

The theory of the firm as governance structure

As Demsetz (1983, p. 377) observes, it is "a mistake to confuse the firm of [orthodox] economic theory with its real-world namesake. The chief mission of neoclassical economics is to understand how the price system coordinates the use of resources, not the inner workings of real firms." Suppose instead that the assigned mission of economics is to understand the organization of economic activity. In that event, it will no longer suffice to describe the firm as a black box that transforms inputs into outputs according to the laws of technology. Instead, firms must be described in relation to other modes of governance, all of which have internal structure, which structure "must arise for some reason" (Arrow, 1999, p. vii).

The contract/private ordering/governance (hereafter governance) approach maintains that structure arises mainly in the service of economizing on transaction costs. Note in this connection that the firm as governance structure is a comparative contractual construction. The firm is conceived not as a stand-alone entity, but is always to be compared with alternative modes of governance. By contrast with mechanism design (where a menu of contracts is used to elicit private information), agency theory (where risk aversion and multitasking are featured) and the property rights theory of the firm (where everything rests on asset ownership), the governance approach appeals to law and organization theory in naming incentive intensity, administrative control and contract law regime as three critical attributes.

It will be convenient to illustrate the mechanisms of governance with reference to a specific class of transactions. Because transactions in intermediate product markets avoid some of the more serious conditions of asymmetry – of information, budget, legal talent, risk aversion and the like – that beset some transactions in final product markets, I examine the "make-or-buy" decision. Should a firm make an input itself, perhaps by acquiring a firm that makes the input, or should it purchase the input from another firm?

The science of choice approach to the make-or-buy decision

The main way to examine the make-or-buy decision under the setup of firm as production function is with reference to bilateral monopoly.[4] The neoclassical analysis of bilateral monopoly reached the conclusion that while optimal quantities between the parties might be realized, the division of profits between bilateral monopolists was indeterminate (for example, Machlup and Tabor, 1960, p. 112). Vertical integration might then arise as a means by which to relieve bargaining over the indeterminacy. Alternatively, vertical integration could arise as a means by which to restore efficient factor proportions when an upstream monopolist sold intermediate product to a downstream buyer that used a variable proportions technology (McKenzie, 1951). Vertical integration has since been examined in a combined variable proportions-monopoly power context by Vernon and Graham (1971), Schmalensee (1973), Warren-Boulton (1974), Westfield (1981) and Hart and Tirole (1990).

This literature is instructive, but it is also beset by a number of loose ends or anomalies. First, since preexisting monopoly power of a durable kind is the exception in a large economy rather than the rule, what explains vertical integration for the vast array of transactions where such power is negligible? Second, why don't firms integrate everything, since under a production function setup, an integrated firm can always replicate its unintegrated rivals and can sometimes improve on them? Third, what explains hybrid modes of contracting? More generally, if many of the problems of trading are of an intertemporal kind in which successive adaptations to uncertainty are needed, do the problems of economic organization have to be recast in a larger and different framework?

Coase and the make-or-buy decision

Coase's (1937) classic article opens with a basic puzzle: Why does a firm emerge at all in a specialized exchange economy? If the answer resides in entrepreneurship, why is coordination "the work of the price mechanism in one case and the entrepreneur in the other" (p. 389)? Coase appealed to transaction cost economizing as the hitherto missing factor for explaining why markets were used in some cases and hierarchy in other cases and averred (p. 391): "The main reason why it is profitable to establish a firm would seem to be that there is a cost of using the price mechanism, the most obvious ... [being] that of discovering what the relevant prices are." This sounds plausible. But how is it that internal procurement by the firm avoids the cost of price discovery?

The "obvious" answer is that sole-source internal supply avoids the need to consult the market about prices, because internal accounting prices of a formulaic kind (say, of a cost-plus kind) can be used to transfer a good or service from one internal stage to another. If, however, that is the source of the advantage of internal organization over market procurement, the obvious lesson is to apply this same practice to outside procurement. The firm simply advises its purchasing office to turn a blind eye to the market by placing orders, period by period, with a qualified sole-source external supplier who agrees to sell on cost-plus terms. In that event, firm and market are put on a parity in price discovery respects – which is to say that the price discovery burden that Coase ascribes to the market does not survive comparative institutional scrutiny.[5]

In the end, Coase's profoundly important challenge to orthodoxy and his insistence on introducing transactional considerations does not lead to refutable implications (Alchian and Demsetz, 1972). Operationalization of these good ideas was missing (Coase, 1992, pp. 716–8). The theory of the firm as governance structure is an effort to infuse operational content. Transaction cost economizing is the unifying concept.[6]

A heuristic model of firm as governance structure

Expressed in terms of the "Commons triple" – the notion that the transaction incorporates the three aspects of conflict, mutuality and order – governance is the means by which to infuse order, thereby to mitigate conflict and to realize "the most fundamental of all understandings in economics," mutual gain from voluntary exchange. The surprise is that a concept as important as governance should have been so long neglected.

The rudiments of a model of the firm as governance structure are the attributes of transactions, the attributes of alternative modes of governance and the purposes served. Asset specificity (which gives rise to bilateral dependency) and uncertainty (which poses adaptive needs) are especially important attributes of transactions. The attributes that define a governance structure include incentive intensity, administrative control and the contract law regime. In this framework, market and hierarchy syndromes differ as follows: under hierarchy, incentive intensity is less, administrative controls are more numerous and discretionary, and internal dispute resolution supplants court ordering. Adaptation is taken to be the main purpose, where the requisite mix of autonomous adaptations and coordinated adaptations vary among transactions. Specifically, the need for coordinated adaptations builds up as asset specificity deepens.

In a heuristic way, Figure 11.2 shows the transaction cost consequences of organizing transactions in markets (M) and hierarchies (H) as a function of asset specificity (k). As shown, the bureaucratic burdens of hierarchy place it at an initial disadvantage ($k = 0$), but

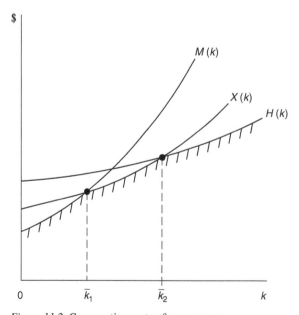

Figure 11.2 Comparative costs of governance

the cost differences between markets $M(k)$ and hierarchy $H(k)$ narrow as asset specificity builds up and eventually reverse as the need for cooperative adaptation becomes especially great $(k \gg 0)$. Provision can further be made for the hybrid mode of organization $X(k)$, where hybrids are viewed as market-preserving credible contracting modes that possess adaptive attributes located between classical markets and hierarchies. Incentive intensity and administrative control thus take on intermediate values, and Llewellyn's (1931) concept of contract as framework applies. As shown in Figure 11.2, $M(0) < X(0) < H(0)$ (by reason of bureaucratic cost differences), while $M' > X' > H'$ (which reflects the cost of coordinated adaptation).

This rudimentary setup yields refutable implications that are broadly corroborated by the data. It can be extended to include differential production costs between modes of governance, which mainly preserves the basic argument that hierarchy is favored as asset specificity builds up, ceteris paribus (Riordan and Williamson, 1985). The foregoing relations among governance structures and transactions can also be replicated with a simple stochastic model where the needs for adaptation vary with the transaction and the efficacy of adaptations of autonomous and cooperative kinds vary with the governance structures. Shift parameters can also be introduced in such a model (Williamson, 1991a). More fully formal treatments of contracting that are broadly congruent with this setup are in progress.

Whereas most theories of vertical integration do not invite empirical testing, the transaction cost theory of vertical integration invites and has been the subject of considerable empirical analysis. Empirical research in the field of industrial organization is especially noteworthy because the field has been criticized for the absence of such work. Not only did Coase once describe his 1937 article as "much cited and little used" (1972, p. 67), but others have since commented upon the paucity of empirical work on the theory of the firm (Holmstrom and Tirole, 1989, p. 126) and in the field of industrial organization (Peltzman, 1991). By contrast, empirical transaction cost economics has grown exponentially during the past 20 years. For surveys, see Shelanski and Klein (1995), Lyons (1996), Crocker and Masten (1996), Rindfleisch and Heide (1997), Masten and Saussier (2000) and Boerner and Macher (2001).[7] Added to this are numerous applications to public policy, especially antitrust and regulation, but also to economics more generally (Dixit, 1996) and to the contiguous social sciences (especially political science). The upshot is that the theory of the firm as governance structure has become a much used construction.

Variations on a theme

Vertical integration turns out to be a paradigm. Although many of the empirical tests and public policy applications have reference to the make-or-buy decision and vertical market restrictions, this same framework has application to contracting more generally. Specifically, the contractual relation between the firm and its "stakeholders" – customers, suppliers and workers along with financial investors – can be interpreted as variations on a theme.

The contractual schema

Assume that a firm can make or buy a component, and assume further that the component can be supplied by either a general purpose technology or a special purpose technology. Again, let k be a measure of asset specificity. The transactions in Figure 11.3 that use the general purpose technology are ones for which $k = 0$. In this case, no specific assets are involved, and the parties are essentially faceless. If instead, transactions use the special purpose

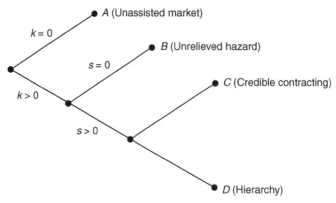

Figure 11.3 Simple contracting schema.

technology, $k > 0$. As hitherto discussed, bilaterally dependent parties have incentives to promote continuity and safeguard their specific investments. Let s denote the magnitude of any such safeguards, which include penalties, information disclosure and verification procedures, specialized dispute resolution (such as arbitration) and, in the limit, integration of the two stages under unified ownership. An $s = 0$ condition is one for which no safeguards are provided; a decision to provide safeguards is reflected by an $s > 0$ result.

Node A in Figure 11.3 corresponds to the ideal transaction in law and economics: there being an absence of dependency, governance is accomplished through competitive market prices and, in the event of disputes, by court-awarded damages. Node B poses unrelieved contractual hazards, in that specialized investments are exposed ($k > 0$) for which no safeguards ($s = 0$) have been provided. Such hazards will be recognized by farsighted players, who will price out the implied risks.

Added contractual supports ($s > 0$) are provided at nodes C and D. At node C, these contractual supports take the form of interfirm contractual safeguards. Should, however, costly breakdowns continue in the face of best bilateral efforts to craft safeguards at node C, the transaction may be taken out of the market and organized under unified ownership (vertical integration) instead. Because added bureaucratic costs accrue upon taking a transaction out of the market and organizing it internally, internal organization is usefully thought of as the organization form of last resort. That is, try markets, try hybrids and have recourse to the firm only when all else fails. Node D, the unified firm, thus comes in only as higher degrees of asset specificity and added uncertainty pose greater needs for cooperative adaptation.

Note that the price that a supplier will bid to supply under node C conditions will be less than the price that will be bid at node B. That is because the added security features serve to reduce the risk at node C, as compared with node B, so the contractual hazard premium will be reduced. One implication is that suppliers do not need to petition buyers to provide safeguards. Because buyers will receive product on better terms (lower price) when added security is provided, buyers have the incentive to offer credible commitments. Thus, although such commitments are sometimes thought of as a user-friendly way to contract, the analytical action resides in the hard-headed use of credibility to support those transactions where asset specificity and contractual hazards are an issue. Such supports are without purpose for transactions where the general purpose production technology is employed.

The foregoing schema can be applied to virtually all transactions for which the firm is in a position to own as well as to contract with an adjacent stage – backward into raw materials, laterally into components, forward into distribution.[8] But for some activities, ownership is either impossible or very rare. For example, firms cannot own their workers nor their final customers (although worker cooperatives and consumer cooperatives can be thought of in ownership terms). Also, firms rarely own their suppliers of finance. Node *D* drops out of the schema in cases where ownership is either prohibited by law or is otherwise rare. I begin with forward integration into distribution, after which relationships with other stakeholders of the firm, including labor, finance and public utility regulation, are successively considered.

Forward integration into distribution

I will set aside the case where mass marketers integrate backward into manufacturing and focus on forward integration into distribution by manufacturers of products or owners of brands. Specifically, consider the contractual relation between a manufacturer and large numbers of wholesalers or, especially, of retailers for the good or service in question.

Many such transactions are of a generic kind. Although branded goods and services are more specific, some require only shelf space, since advertising, promotion and any warranties are done by the manufacturer. Since the obvious way to trade with intermediaries for such transactions is through the market, in a node *A* fashion, what is to be inferred when such transactions are made subject to vertical market restrictions such as customer and territorial restrictions, service restrictions, tied sales and the like?

Price discrimination, to which allocative efficiency benefits were ascribed, was the usual resource allocation (science of choice) explanation for such restrictions. Such benefits, however, were problematic once the transaction costs of discovering customer valuations and deterring arbitrage were taken into account (Williamson, 1975, pp. 11–13). Moreover, price discrimination does not exhaust the possibilities. Viewed through the lens of contract, vertical market restrictions often have the purpose and effect of infusing order into a transaction where the interests of the system and the interests of the parts are in conflict. For example, the Schwinn bicycle company imposed non-resale restrictions upon franchisees. The concern was that the integrity of the brand, which was a system asset, would be compromised by franchisees who perceived local opportunities to realize individual gain by selling to discounters, who would then sell a "bike in a box" without service or support (Williamson, 1985, pp. 183–9). More generally, the argument is this: In circumstances where market power is small, where simple market exchange (at node *A*) would compromise the integrity of differentiated products and where forward integration into distribution (at node *D*) would be especially costly, the use of vertical market restrictions to effect credible commitments (at node *C*) has much to recommend it.

Relationship with labor

Because the firm is unable to own its labor, node *D* is irrelevant and the comparison comes down to nodes *A*, *B* and *C*. Node *A* corresponds to the case where labor is easily redeployed to other uses or users without loss of productive value ($k = 0$). Thus, although such labor may be highly skilled (as with many professionals), the lack of firm specificity means that, transition costs aside, neither worker nor firm has an interest in crafting penalties for unwanted quits/terminations or otherwise creating costly internal labor markets (ports of entry, promotion ladders), costly information disclosure and verification procedures, and costly firm-specific dispute settlement machinery. The mutual benefits do not warrant the costs.

Conditions change when $k > 0$, since workers who acquire firm-specific skills will lose value if prematurely terminated (and firms will incur added training costs if such employees quit). Here, as elsewhere, unrelieved hazards (as at node B) will result in demands by workers for a hazard premium, and recurrent contractual impasses, by reason of conflict, will result in inefficiency. Because continuity has value to both firm and worker, governance features that deter termination (severance pay) and quits (nonvested benefits) and that address and settle disputes in an orderly way (grievance systems) to which the parties ascribe confidence have a lot to recommend them. These can, but need not, take the form of "unions." Whatever the name, the object is to craft a collective organizational structure (at node C) in which the parties have mutual confidence and that enhances efficiency (Baron and Kreps, 1999, pp. 130–8; Williamson, 1975, pp. 27–80, 1985, pp. 250–62).[9]

Relationship with sources of finance

Viewed through the lens of contract, the board of directors is interpreted as a security feature that arises in support of the contract for equity finance (Williamson, 1988). More generally, debt and equity are not merely alternative modes of finance, which is the law and economics construction (Easterbrook and Fischel, 1986; Posner, 1986), but are also alternative modes of governance.

Suppose that a firm is seeking cost-effective finance for the following series of projects: general purpose mobile equipment, a general purpose office building located in a population center, a general purpose plant located in a manufacturing center, distribution facilities located somewhat more remotely, special purpose equipment, market and product development expenses and the like. Suppose further that debt is a governance structure that works almost entirely out of a set of rules: (1) stipulated interest payments will be made at regular intervals; (2) the business will continuously meet certain liquidity tests; (3) principal will be repaid at the loan-expiration date; and (4) in the event of default, the debtholders will exercise preemptive claims against the assets in question. In short, debt is unforgiving if things go poorly.

Such rules-based governance is well suited to investments of a generic kind ($k = 0$), since the lender can redeploy these to alternative uses and users with little loss of productive value. Debt thus corresponds to market governance at node A. But what about investment projects of more specific (less redeployable) kinds?

Because the value of holding a preemptive claim declines as the degree of asset specificity deepens, rule-based finance of the kind described above will be made on more adverse terms. In effect, using debt to finance such projects would locate the parties at node B, where a hazard premium must be charged. The firm in these circumstances has two choices: sacrifice some of the specialized investment features in favor of greater redeployability (move back to node A), or embed the specialized investment in a governance structure to which better terms of finance will be ascribed. What would the latter entail?

Suppose that a financial instrument called equity is invented, and assume that equity has the following governance properties: (1) it bears a residual claimant status to the firm in both earnings and asset liquidation respects; (2) it contracts for the duration of the life of the firm; and (3) a board of directors is created and awarded to equity that (a) is elected by the pro-rata votes of those who hold tradable shares, (b) has the power to replace the management, (c) decides on management compensation, (d) has access to internal performance measures on a timely basis, (e) can authorize audits in depth for special follow-up purposes, (f) is apprised of important investment and operating proposals before they are implemented, and

(g) in other respects bears a decision-review and monitoring relation to the firm's management (Fama and Jensen, 1983). So construed, the board of directors is awarded to the holders of equity so as to reduce the cost of capital by providing safeguards for projects that have limited redeployability (by moving them from node *B* to node *C*).

Regulation and natural monopoly

The market-oriented approach to natural monopoly is to auction off the franchise to the highest bidder (Demsetz, 1968; Posner, 1972). But whether this works well or poorly depends on the nature of the transaction and the particulars of governance. Whereas some of those who work out of the science of choice setup believe that to "expound the details of particular regulations and proposals ... would serve only to obscure the basic issues" (Posner, 1972, p. 98), the governance structure approach counsels that much of the action resides in the details.

Going beyond the initial bidding competition ("competition for the market"), the governance approach insists upon including the contract implementation stage. Transactions to which the Fundamental Transformation applies – namely, those requiring significant investments in specific assets and that are subject to considerable market and technological uncertainty – are ones for which the efficacy of simple franchise bidding is problematic.

This is not to say that franchise bidding never works. Neither is it to suggest that decisions to regulate ought not to be revisited – as witness the successful deregulation of trucking (which never should have been regulated to begin with) and more recent efforts to deregulate "network industries" (Peltzman and Winston, 2000). I would nevertheless urge that examining deregulation through the lens of contracting is instructive for both – as it is for assessing efforts to deregulate electricity in California, where too much deference was given to the (assumed) efficacy of smoothly functioning markets and insufficient attention to potential investment and contractual hazards and appropriate governance responses thereto. As Joskow (2000, p. 51) observes: "Many policy makers and fellow travelers have been surprised by how difficult it has been to create wholesale electricity markets. ... Had policy makers viewed the restructuring challenge using a TCE [transaction cost economics] framework, these potential problems are more likely to have been identified and mechanisms adopted ex ante to fix them."

Here as elsewhere, the lesson is to think contractually: Look ahead, recognize potential hazards and fold these back into the design calculus. Paraphrasing Robert Michels (1915 [1962], p. 370) on oligarchy, nothing but a serene and frank examination of the contractual hazards of deregulation will enable us to mitigate these hazards.

Recent criticisms

Many skeptics of orthodoxy have also been critics of transaction cost economics – including organization theorists (especially Simon, 1991, 1997), sociologists (for a recent survey, see Richter, 2001) and the resource-based/core competence/dynamic capabilities perspective. Having responded to these arguments elsewhere,[10] I focus here on critiques from within economics – especially those that deal with issues concerning the boundary of the firms.[11]

Property rights theory

The property rights theory of firm and market organization is unarguably a path-breaking contribution (Grossman and Hart, 1986; Hart and Moore, 1990; Hart, 1995). Prior to this work, the very idea that incomplete contracts could be formally modeled was scorned. That has all changed.

The accomplishments of the property rights theory notwithstanding, I nevertheless take exception in two related respects. First, the view that the property rights theory "builds on and formalizes the intuitions of transaction cost economics, as created by Coase and Williamson" (Salanié, 1997, p. 176) is only partly correct. To be sure, property rights theory does build on (or at least tracks) transaction cost economics in certain respects: complex contracts are incomplete (by reason of bounded rationality), contract as mere promise is not self-enforcing (by reason of opportunism), court ordering of conflicts is limited (by reason of nonverifiability) and the parties are bilaterally dependent (by reason of transaction-specific investments). But whereas transaction cost economics locates the main analytical action in the governance of ongoing contractual relations, property rights theory of the firm annihilates governance issues by assuming common knowledge of payoffs and costless bargaining. As a consequence, all of the analytical action is concentrated at the incentive alignment stage of contracting. Since the assumptions of common knowledge of payoffs (Kreps and Wilson, 1982) and costless bargaining are deeply problematic, my interpretation of property rights theory is that it is "imperfectly suited to the subject matter ... [because it] obscures the key interactions instead of spotlighting them" (Solow, 2001, p. 112).

Second, I take exception with the allegation of property rights theory that transaction cost economics offers no explanation why a bilaterally dependent transaction is subject to "less haggling and hold-up behavior in a merged firm." Hart (1995, p. 28), writes that "[t]ransaction cost theory, as it stands, does not provide the answer," evidently in the belief that property rights theory does.

Since property rights theory rests only on asset ownership, what Hart and others of this persuasion could say is that they dispute the logic of replication/selective intervention and each of the associated regularities on which transaction cost economics relies to describe why firms and markets differ in discrete structural ways. Specifically, property rights theory disputes all four of the following propositions of transaction cost economics: (1) that firms enjoy advantages over markets in cooperative adaptation respects (it being the case under property rights theory that all ownership configurations costlessly adapt in the contract implementation interval); (2) that incentive intensity is unavoidably compromised by internal organization; (3) that administrative controls are more numerous and more nuanced in firms;[12] and (4) that the implicit contract law of internal organization is that of forbearance, whence the firm is its own court for resolving disputes. Inasmuch as all four of these differences can be examined empirically, the veridicality of property rights theory in relation to transaction cost economics can be established by appealing to the data. What cannot be said is that transaction cost economics is silent or inexplicit on why firms and markets differ.

As it stands, property rights theory makes limited appeal to data, because it yields very few refutable implications and is indeed very nearly untestable (Whinston, 2001). Transaction cost economics, by contrast, yields numerous refutable implications and invites empirical testing.

Boundaries of the firm

Holmstrom and Roberts (1998, p. 91) contend, and I agree, that "the theory of the firm ... has become too narrowly focused on the hold-up problem and the role of asset specificity." Contractual complications of other (possibly related) kinds need to be admitted and the ramifications for governance worked out. But while I agree that more than asset specificity is involved, I hasten to add that asset specificity is an operational and encompassing concept.

Asset specificity is operational in that it serves to breathe content into the idea of transactional "complexity." Thus, although it is intuitively obvious that complex governance structures should be reserved for complex transactions, wherein do the contractual complexities reside? Identifying the critical dimensions with respect to which transactions differ, of which asset specificity is especially important, has been crucial for explicating contractual complexity (Williamson, 1971, 1979, p. 239) – which is not to suggest that it is exhaustive.

As for asset specificity being an encompassing concept, consider the Holmstrom and Roberts (1998, p. 87) complaint that multi-unit retail businesses (such as franchising) cannot be explained in terms of asset specificity. This complaint ignores brand name capital (Klein, 1980) as a form of asset specificity, the integrity of which can be compromised (as discussed in relation to the Schwinn case, above). Also, asset specificity would be less "overused" if other would-be explanations for complex economic organization (such as technological nonseparability or the idea that agents have different levels of risk aversion) either had wider reach and/or were not contradicted by the data. I would furthermore observe that many of the Holmstrom and Roberts (1998, p. 75) arguments and illustrations for "taking a much broader view of the firm and the determination of its boundaries" are ones with which transaction cost economics not only concurs but has actively discussed, even featured, previously.

I am puzzled, for example, by their claim (1998, p. 77) that "[i]n transaction cost economics, the functioning market is as much a black box as is the firm in neoclassical economic theory." Plainly, node C in the earlier Figure 11.3 is a market governance mode supported by conscious efforts by the parties to craft intertemporal contractual safeguards for transactions where identity matters and continuity is important. Node C is a black box only for those who refuse to take a look at the mechanisms through which hybrid governance works. Also, moving beyond the one-size-fits-all view of contract law to ascertain that contract law regimes differ systematically across modes of governance – in that contract as legal rules, contract as framework and forbearance law are the contract laws of market, hybrid and hierarchy, respectively – is not and should not be construed as a black box construction.

Holmstrom and Roberts (1998, p. 81) offer the case of Japanese subcontracting as "directly at odds with transaction cost theory." Relying in part upon the research of Banri Asanuma (1989, 1992), Holmstrom and Roberts (pp. 80–2) report that Japanese subcontracting uses "long-term close relations with a limited number of independent suppliers that mix elements of market and hierarchy ... [to protect] specific assets." These close relations are supported by careful monitoring, a two-supplier system (as at Toyota), rich information sharing and, so as to deter automakers from behaving opportunistically, a "supplier association, which facilitates communication ... and [strengthens] reputation [effects]."

As it turns out, Professor Asanuma and I visited several large Japanese auto firms (Toyota included) in the spring of 1983, and I reported on all of the above previously (Williamson, 1985, pp. 120–3, 1996, pp. 317–18). Interestingly, Baron and Kreps (1999, pp. 542–3) also interpret Toyota contracting practices as consistent with the transaction cost economics perspective.

I would nevertheless concede that the roles of organizational knowledge and learning mentioned by Holmstrom and Roberts (1998, pp. 90–1) are ones with which transaction cost economics deals with in only a limited way. This does not, however, mean that transaction cost economics does not or cannot relate to these issues. I would observe in this connection that transaction cost economics made early provision for firm-specific learning by doing and for tacit knowledge (Williamson, 1971, 1975) and that the organization of "knowledge projects" that differ in their needs for coordination are even now being examined in governance structure respects (Nickerson and Zenger, 2001). Still, the study of these and other issues to which Holmstrom and Roberts refer are usefully examined from several lenses, of which the lens of transaction cost economics is only one.

Conclusion

The application of the lens of contract/private ordering/governance leads naturally into the reconceptualization of the firm not as a production function in the science of choice tradition, but instead as a governance structure. The shift from choice to contract is attended by three crucial moves. First, human actors are described in more veridical ways with respect to both cognitive traits and selfinterestedness. Second, organization matters. The governance of contractual relations takes seriously the conceptual challenge posed by the "Commons triple" of dealing with issues of conflict, mutuality and order. Third, organization is susceptible to analysis. This last move is accomplished by naming the transaction as the basic unit of analysis, identifying governance structures (which differ in discrete structural ways) as the means by which to manage transactions, and joining these two. Specifically, transactions, which differ in their attributes, are aligned with governance structures, which differ in their cost and competencies, in an economizing way. Implementing this entails working out of the logic of efficient alignment.

Not only does the resulting theory of the firm differ significantly from the neoclassical theory of the firm, but the governance branch of contract also differs from the incentive branch, where more formal mechanism design, agency and property rights theories are located. These latter theories all concentrate the analytical action on the incentive alignment stage of contracting. Differences among governance structures with respect to adaptation in the contract implementation interval are thus suppressed. Intertemporal regularities to which organization theorists call our attention (and to which I selectively appeal) as well as the added contractual complications that I describe – the Fundamental Transformation, the impossibility of replication/selective intervention and contract law regimes – have little or no place in any of these incentive alignment literatures.

Parsimony being a virtue, such added complications need to be justified. I contend that a different and, for many purposes, richer and better understanding of firm and market organization results. Not only does the transaction cost economics theory of firm and market organization afford different interpretations of nonstandard and unfamiliar forms of contract and organization, but it yields many refutable implications. A large and growing empirical research agenda and selective reshaping of public policy toward business have resulted from supplanting the black box conception of the firm by the theory of the firm as governance structure. Dixit (1996), moreover, ascribes public policy benefits to the use of transaction cost reasoning to open up the black box of public policymaking and explain how decisions are actually made.[13]

Pluralism has much to recommend it in an area like economic organization that is beset with bewildering complexity. Such pluralism notwithstanding, the governance approach has been a productive and liberating way by which to examine economic organization. It has been productive in all of the conceptual and public policy ways described above, with more insights in prospect. It has been liberating in that it has breathed life into the science of contract and, in the process, has served to stimulate other work – part rival, part complementary. A recurrent theme is that recourse to the lens of contract, as against the lens of choice, frequently deepens our understanding of complex economic organization, with a suggestion that this same strategy can inform applied microeconomics and the contiguous social sciences more generally.

Acknowledgment

The helpful advice of Timothy Taylor and Michael Waldman in revising this manuscript is gratefully acknowledged.

Notes

1 *A Behavioral Theory of the Firm* (Cyert and March, 1963) was one obvious early candidate for an economic theory of organizations. It deals, however, with more fine-grained phenomena – such as predicting department store prices to the penny – than were of interest to most economists. For a discussion, see Williamson (1999b). The recent and growing interest in behavioral economics – which deals more with the theory of consumer behavior than with the theory of the firm – can be interpreted as a delayed response to the lessons of the "Carnegie school" associated with Cyert, March and Simon.

2 Although satisficing is an intuitively appealing concept, it is very hard to implement. Awaiting further developments, the satisficing approach is not broadly applicable (Aumann, 1985, p. 35). Indeed, there is an irony: neoclassical economists who use a mode of analysis (maximizing) that is easy to implement and often is good enough for the purposes at hand are analytical satisficers.

3 Bilateral dependency need not result from physical asset specificity if the assets are mobile, since a buyer who owns and who can repossess the assets can assign them to whichever supplier tenders the lowest bid. Also, site specific assets can sometimes be owned by a buyer and leased to a supplier. Nonetheless, such "solutions" will pose user cost problems if suppliers cannot be relied upon to exercise due care.

4 Although the bilateral monopoly explanation is the oldest explanation and the one emphasized in most microeconomics textbooks, three other price-theoretic frameworks have been used to explain the make-or-buy decision: price discrimination, barriers to entry and strategic purposes. For a summary of the arguments on these points, see Williamson (1987, pp. 808–9). For a more complete discussion, see Perry (1989).

5 It does not suffice to argue that vigilance is unneeded for trade within firms because transfer prices are a wash. For one thing, different transfer prices will induce different factor proportions in divisionalized firms where divisions are held accountable for their bottom lines (unless fixed proportions are imposed). Also, because incentives within firms are weaker, ready access to the pass-through of costs can encourage cost excesses. The overarching point is this: to focus on transfer pricing to the neglect of discrete structural differences between firm and market is to miss the forest for the trees.

6 Other purposes include choice of efficient factor proportions, specialization of labor (in both physical and cognitive respects) and knowledge acquisition and development.

7 I would note parenthetically that the GM-Fisher Body example (Klein, Crawford and Alchian, 1978) that is widely used to illustrate the contractual strains that attend bilateral dependency has come under criticism (see the exchange in the April 2000 issue of the *Journal of Law and Economics*). My responses are two. First and foremost, even if the GM-Fisher Body anecdote is factually flawed, transaction cost economics remains an empirical success story (see text and Whinston, 2001). Second, the main purpose of an anecdote is pedagogical, to provide intuition. That is what the confectioner and physician cases do for externalities (Coase, 1959), what QWERTY does for path dependency (David, 1985), what the market for lemons does for asymmetric information (Akerlof, 1970) and what the tragedy of the commons does for collective organization (Hardin, 1968). It is better, to be sure, if anecdotes are factually correct. Unless, however, the phenomenon described by the anecdote is trivial or bogus (which conditions may not be evident until an empirical research program is undertaken), an anecdote that helps to bring an abstract condition to life has served its intended purpose.

8 Closely complementary activities are commonly relegated to the "core technology" (Thompson, 1967, pp. 19–23) and are effectively exempt from comparative institutional analysis, it being "obvious" that these are done within the firm.

9 The emphasis on collective organization as a governance response is to be distinguished from the earlier work of Gary Becker, where human asset specificity is responsible for upward-sloping age-earnings profiles (Becker, 1962). Becker's treatment is more in the science of choice tradition, whereas mine views asset specificity through the lens of contract. These two are not mutually exclusive. They do, however, point to different empirical research agenda.

10 On my response to Simon, see Williamson (2002); on sociology, see Williamson (1981, 1993, 1996); on core competence, see Williamson (1999b).
11 Other criticisms include those of Fudenberg, Holmstrom and Milgrom (1990, p. 21, emphasis omitted) who contend: "If there is an optimal long-term contract, then there is a sequentially optimal contract, which can be implemented via a sequence of short-term contracts." My response is that the proof is elegant, but rests on very strong and implausible assumptions that fail the test of feasible implementation (Williamson, 1991b).
12 Grossman and Hart (1986, p. 695), for example, assume that "any audits that an employer can have done of his [wholly] owned subsidiary are also feasible when the subsidiary is a separate company." Not only does transaction cost economics hold otherwise (Williamson, 1985, pp. 154–5), but transaction cost economics also recognizes that accounting is not fully objective but can be used as a strategic instrument (chapter 6). Furthermore, accounting *will* be used as a strategic instrument if integration is as prescribed by property rights theory (directional) rather than as prescribed by transaction cost economics (unified). The upshot is that the high-powered incentives that property rights theory associates with directional integration will be compromised – in that control over accounting by the acquiring stage will be exercised to redistribute profits in its favor by manipulating transfer prices, user-cost charges, overhead rates, depreciation, amortization, inventory rules and the like. Although Hart (1995, pp. 64–6) appears to concede these effects, the basic model of the property rights theory (chapter 2) disallows them.
13 Kreps's (1999, p. 123) assessment of full formalism also signals precaution: "Most economists, and especially and most critically, new recruits in the form of graduate students, learn transaction-cost economics as translated and renamed (incomplete) contract theory. … [Awaiting new tools], we should be clear on how (in)complete the translations are, to fight misguided tendencies to put *Markets and Hierarchies* away on that semi-accessible shelf."

References

Akerlof, George A. 1970. "The Market for 'Lemons': Qualitative Uncertainty and the Market Mechanism." *Quarterly Journal of Economics.* August, 84, pp. 488–500.
Alchian, Armen and Harold Demsetz. 1972. "Production, Information Costs, and Economic Organization." *American Economic Review.* December, 62, pp. 777–95.
Arrow, Kenneth. 1999. "Forward," in *Firms, Markets and Hierarchies: The Transaction Cost Economics Perspective.* G. Carroll and D. Teece, eds. New York: New York University Press, pp. vii–viii.
Asanuma, Banri. 1989. "Manufacturer-Supplier Relationships in Japan and the Concept of Relationship-Specific Skills." *Journal of Japanese and International Economies.* 3:1, pp. 1–30.
Asanuma, Banri. 1992. "Manufacturer–Supplier Relationships in International Perspective: The Automobile Case," in *International Adjustment and the Japanese Firm.* Paul Sheard, ed. St. Leonards, NSW: Allen and Unwin, pp. 99–124.
Aumann, Robert J. 1985. "What is Game Theory Trying to Accomplish?" in *Frontiers of Economics.* K. Arrow and S. Hankapohja, eds. Oxford: Basil Blackwell, pp. 28–78.
Bajari, Patrick and Steven Tadelis. 2001. "Incentives Versus Transaction Costs: A Theory of Procurement Contracts." *Rand Journal of Economics.* Autumn, 32, pp. 387–407.
Barnard, Chester 1. 1938. *The Functions of the Executive.* Cambridge: Harvard University Press.
Baron, James N. and David M. Kreps. 1999. *Strategic Human Resources: Frameworks for General Managers.* New York: John Wiley.
Becker, Gary. 1962. "Investment in Human Capital: Effects on Earnings." *Journal of Political Economy.* October, 70, pp. 9–49.
Ben-Porath, Yoram. 1980. "The F-Connection: Families, Friends, and Firms and the Organization of Exchange." *Population and Development Review.* March, 6, pp. 1–30.
Boerner, C. S. and J. Macher. 2001. "Transaction Cost Economics: A Review and Assessment of the Empirical Literature." Unpublished Manuscript.
Brennan, Geoffrey and James Buchanan. 1985. *The Reason of Rules.* Cambridge: Cambridge University Press.
Buchanan, James M. 1964a. "What Should Economists Do?" *Southern Economic Journal.* January, 30, pp. 312–22.

Buchanan, James M. 1964b. "Is Economics the Science of Choice?" in *Roads to Freedom: Essays in Honor of F. A. Hayek.* E. Streissler, ed. London: Routledge & Kegan Paul, pp. 47–64.

Buchanan, James M. 1975. "A Contractarian Paradigm for Applying Economic Theory." *American Economic Review.* May, 65, pp. 225–30.

Buchanan, James M. 1987. "The Constitution of Economic Policy." *American Economic Review.* June, 77, pp. 243–50.

Buchanan, James M. 2001. "Game Theory, Mathematics, and Economics." *Journal of Economic Methodology.* March, 8, pp. 27–32.

Buchanan, James M. and Gordon Tullock. 1962. *The Calculus of Consent: Logical Foundations of Constitutional Democracy.* Ann Arbor: University of Michigan Press.

Coase, Ronald H. 1937. "The Nature of the Firm." *Economica.* November, 4, pp. 386–405.

Coase, Ronald H. 1959. "The Federal Communications Commission." *Journal of Law and Economics.* October, 3, pp. 1–40.

Coase, Ronald H. 1972. "Industrial Organization: A Proposal for Research," in *Policy Issues and Research Opportunities in Industrial Organization.* V. R. Fuchs, ed. New York: National Bureau of Economic Research, pp. 59–73.

Coase, Ronald H. 1992. "The Institutional Structure of Production." *American Economic Review.* September, 82, pp. 713–19.

Commons, John R. 1932. "The Problem of Correlating Law, Economics and Ethics." *Wisconsin Law Review.* 8, pp. 3–26.

Commons, John R. 1934. *Institutional Economics.* Madison: University of Wisconsin Press.

Crocker, Keith and Scott Masten. 1996. "Regulation and Administered Contracts Revisited: Lessons from Transaction-Cost Economics for Public Utility Regulation." *Journal of Regulatory Economics.* January, 9:1, pp. 5–39.

Cyert, Richard and James March. 1963. *A Behavioral Theory of the Firm.* Englewood Cliffs, NJ.: Prentice-Hall.

David, Paul. 1985. "Clio in the Economics of QWERTY." *American Economic Review.* May, 75, pp. 332–37.

Demsetz, Harold. 1968. "Why Regulate Utilities?" *Journal of Law and Economics.* April, 11, pp. 55–66.

Demsetz, Harold. 1983. "The Structure of Ownership and the Theory of the Firm." *Journal of Law and Economics.* 26:2, pp. 275–90.

Dixit, Avinash K. 1996. *The Making of Economic Policy: A Transaction-Cost Politics Perspective.* Boston, Mass.: MIT Press.

Easterbrook, Frank and Daniel Fischel. 1986. "Close Corporations and Agency Costs." *Stanford Law Review.* January, 38, pp. 271–301.

Fama, Eugene F. and Michael C. Jensen. 1983. "Separation of Ownership and Control." *Journal of Law and Economics.* June, 26, pp. 301–26.

Fudenberg, Drew, Bengt Holmstrom and Paul Milgrom. 1990. "Short-Term Contracts and Long-Term Agency Relationships." *Journal of Economic Theory.* June, 51, pp. 1–31.

Galanter, Marc. 1981. "Justice in Many Rooms: Courts, Private Ordering, and Indigenous Law." *Journal of Legal Pluralism.* 19:1, pp. 1–47.

Grossman, Sanford J. and Oliver Hart. 1986. "The Costs and Benefits of Ownership: A Theory of Vertical and Lateral Integration." *Journal of Political Economy.* August, 94, pp. 691–719.

Hardin, Garrett. 1968. "The Tragedy of the Commons." *Science.* December, 162, pp. 1243–248.

Hart, Oliver. 1995. *Firms, Contracts and Financial Structure.* New York: Oxford University Press.

Hart, Oliver and John Moore. 1990. "Property Rights and the Nature of the Firm." *Journal of Political Economy.* December, 98, pp. 1119–158.

Hart, Oliver and Jean Tirole. 1990. "Vertical Integration and Market Foreclosure," in *Brookings Papers on Economic Activity: Microeconomics.* Martin Neil Baily and Clifford Winston, eds. Washington, D.C.: Brookings Institution, pp. 205–76.

Hayek, Freidrich. 1945. "The Use of Knowledge in Society." *American Economic Review.* September, 35, pp. 519–30.

Holmstrom, Bengt and John Roberts. 1998. "The Boundaries of the Firm Revisited." *Journal of Economic Perspectives.* Fall, 12:3, pp. 73–94.

Holmstrom, Bengt and Jean Tirole. 1989. "The Theory of the Firm," in *Handbook of Industrial Organization.* R. Schmalensee and R. Willig, eds. New York: North Holland, pp. 61–133.

Joskow, Paul L. 2000. "Transaction Cost Economics and Competition Policy." Unpublished Manuscript.

Klein, Benjamin. 1980. "Transaction Cost Determinants of 'Unfair' Contractual Arrangements." *American Economic Review.* May, 70, pp. 356–62.

Klein, Benjamin, Robert A. Crawford and Armen A. Alchian. 1978. "Vertical Integration, Appropriable Rents, and the Competitive Contracting Process." *Journal of Law and Economics.* October, 21, pp. 297–326.

Kreps, David M. 1999. "Markets and Hierarchies and (Mathematical) Economic Theory," in *Firms, Markets, and Hierarchies.* G. Carroll and D. Teece, eds. New York: Oxford University Press, pp. 121–55.

Kreps, David M. and Robert Wilson. 1982. "Reputation and Imperfect Information." *Journal of Economic Theory.* August, 27:2, pp. 253–79.

Llewellyn, Karl N. 1931. "What Price Contract? An Essay in Perspective." *Yale Law Journal.* May, 40, pp. 704–51.

Lyons, Bruce R. 1996. "Empirical Relevance of Efficient Contract Theory: Inter-Firm Contracts." *Oxford Review of Economic Policy.* 12:4, pp. 27–52.

Machlup, Fritz and M. Tabor. 1960. "Bilateral Monopoly, Successive Monopoly and Vertical Integration." *Economica.* May, 27, pp. 101–19.

Makowski, Louis and Joseph Ostroy. 2001. "Perfect Competition and the Creativity of the Market." *Journal of Economic Literature.* June, 32, pp. 479–535.

March, James and Herbert Simon. 1958. *Organizations.* New York: John Wiley.

Marshall, Alfred. 1932. *Industry and Trade.* London: Macmillan.

Masten, Scott and Stephane Saussier. 2000. "Econometrics of Contracts: An Assessment of Developments in the Empirical Literature on Contracting." *Revue d'Economie Industrielle.* Second and Third Trimesters, 92, pp. 215–36.

McKenzie, L. 1951. "Ideal Output and the Interdependence of Firms." *Economic Journal.* December, 61, pp. 785–803.

Michels, Robert. 1915 [1962]. *Political Parties.* Glencoe, Ill.: Free Press.

Newell, Allen and Herbert Simon. 1972. *Human Problem Solving.* Englewood Cliffs, NJ.: Prentice-Hall.

Nickerson, Jackson and Todd Zenger. 2001. "A Knowledge-Based Theory of Governance Choice: A Problem Solving Approach." Unpublished Manuscript.

Peltzman, Sam. 1991. "The Handbook of Industrial Organization: A Review Article." *Journal of Political Economy.* February, 99:1, pp. 201–17.

Peltzman, Sam and Clifford Whinston. 2000. *Deregulation of Network Industries.* Washington, D.C.: Brookings Institution Press.

Perry, Martin. 1989. "Vertical Integration," in *Handbook of Industrial Organization.* R. Schmalensee and R. Willig, eds. Amsterdam: North-Holland, pp. 183–255.

Posner, Richard A. 1972. "The Appropriate Scope of Regulation in the Cable Television Industry." *Bell Journal of Economics.* Spring, 3, pp. 98–129.

Posner, Richard A. 1986. *Economic Analysis of Law, Third Edition.* Boston: Little Brown.

Posner, Richard A. 1993. "The New Institutional Economics Meets Law and Economics." *Journal of Institutional and Theoretical Economics.* March, 149, pp. 73–87.

Reder, Melvin W. 1999. *Economics: The Culture of a Controversial Science.* Chicago: University of Chicago Press.

Richter, Rudolph. 2001. "New Economic Sociology and New Institutional Economics." Unpublished Manuscript.

Rindfleish, Aric and Jan Heide. 1997. "Transaction Cost Analysis: Past, Present and Future Applications." *Journal of Marketing.* October, 61, pp. 30–54.

Riordan, Michael H. and Oliver E. Williamson. 1985. "Asset Specificity and Economic Organization." *International Journal of Industrial Organization.* December, 3:4, pp. 365–78.

Robbins, Lionel. 1932. *An Essay on the Nature and Significance of Economic Science.* New York: New York University Press.

Salanié, Bernard. 1997. *The Economics of Contracts.* Cambridge, Mass.: MIT Press.

Schmalensee, Richard. 1973. "A Note on the Theory of Vertical Integration." *Journal of Political Economy.* March/April, 81, pp. 442–9.

Schtunpeter, Joseph A. 1942. *Capitalism, Socialism, and Democracy.* New York: Harper & Row.

Scott, Richard W. 1992. *Organizations.* Englewood Cliffs, NJ.: Prentice-Hall.

Selznick, Philip. 1949. *TVA and the Grass Roots.* Berkeley: University of California Press.

Selznick, Philip. 1950. "The Iron Law of Bureaucracy." *Modern Review.* 3, pp. 157–65.

Shelanski, Howard A. and Peter G. Klein 1995. "Empirical Research in Transaction Cost Economics: A Review and Assessment." *Journal of Law, Economics and Organization.* October, 11, pp. 335–61.

Simon, Herbert. 1957a. *Administrative Behavior, Second Edition.* New York: Macmillan.

Simon, Herbert. 1957b. *Models of Man: Social and Rational; Mathematical Essays on Rational Human Behavior in a Social Setting.* New York: Wiley.

Simon, Herbert. 1978. "Rationality as Process and as Product of Thought." *American Economic Review.* May, 68, pp. 1–16.

Simon, Herbert. 1983. *Reason in Human Affairs.* Stanford: Stanford University Press.

Simon, Herbert. 1985. "Human Nature in Politics: The Dialogue of Psychology with Political Science." *American Political Science Review.* June, 79:2, pp. 293–304.

Simon, Herbert. 1991. "Organizations and Markets." *Journal of Economic Perspectives.* Spring, 5:2, pp. 25–44.

Simon, Herbert. 1997. *An Empirically Based Microeconomics.* New York: Cambridge University Press.

Solow, Robert. 2001. "A Native Informant Speaks." *Journal of Economic Methodology.* March, 8, pp. 111–12.

Stigler, George J. 1951. "The Division of Labor is Limited by the Extent of the Market." *Journal of Political Economy.* June, 59, pp. 185–93.

Thompson, James D. 1967. *Organizations in Action: Social Science Bases of Administrative Theory.* New York: McGraw-Hill.

Veblen, Thorstein. 1904. *The Theory of Business Enterprise.* New York: Charles Scribner's Sons.

Vernon, John M. and Daniel A. Graham. 1971. "Profitability of Monopolization by Vertical Integration." *Journal of Political Economy.* July/August, 79, pp. 924–25.

Warren-Boulton, Frederick. 1974. "Vertical Control With Variable Proportions." *Journal of Political Economy.* July/August, 82:4, pp. 783–802.

Westfield, Fred. 1981. "Vertical Integration: Does Product Price Rise or Fall?" *American Economic Review.* 71:3, pp. 334–46.

Whinston, Michael. 2001. "Assessing Property Rights and Transaction-Cost Theories of the Firm." *American Economic Review.* May, 91:2, pp. 184–99.

Williamson, Oliver E. 1971. "The Vertical Integration of Production: Market Failure Considerations." *American Economic Review.* May, 61:2, pp. 112–23.

Williamson, Oliver E. 1975. *Markets and Hierarchies: Analysis and Antitrust Implications.* New York: Free Press.

Williamson, Oliver E. 1976. "Franchise Bidding: In General and with Respect to CATV." *Bell Journal of Economics.* 7:1, pp. 73–104.

Williamson, Oliver E. 1979. "Transaction Cost Economics: The Governance of Contractual Relations." *Journal of Law and Economics.* October, 22, pp. 233–61.

Williamson, Oliver E. 1981. "The Economics of Organization: The Transaction Cost Approach." *American Journal of Sociology.* November, 87, pp. 548–77.

Williamson, Oliver E. 1983. "Credible Commitments: Using Hostages to Support Exchange." *American Economic Review.* September, 73:4, pp. 519–40.

Williamson, Oliver E. 1985. *The Economic Institutions of Capitalism.* New York: Free Press.

Williamson, Oliver E. 1987. "Vertical Integration," in *The New Palgrave: A Dictionary of Economics, Volume IV.* J. Eatwell et al., eds. London: Macmillan, pp. 807–12.

Williamson, Oliver E. 1988. "Corporate Finance and Corporate Governance." *Journal of Finance.* July, 43, pp. 567–91.

Williamson, Oliver E. 1991a. "Comparative Economic Organization: The Analysis of Discrete Structural Alternatives." *Administrative Science Quarterly.* June, 36, pp. 269–96.

Williamson, Oliver E. 1991b. "Economic Institutions: Spontaneous and Intentional Governance." *Journal of Law, Economics and Organization.* Special Issue, 7, pp. 159–87.

Williamson, Oliver E. 1993. "Calculativeness, Trust, and Economic Organization." *Journal of Law and Economics.* April, 36, pp. 453–86.

Williamson, Oliver E. 1996. *The Mechanisms of Governance.* New York: Oxford University Press.

Williamson, Oliver E. 1998. "Transaction Cost Economics: How it Works; Where it is Headed." *De Economist.* April, 146, pp. 23–58.

Williamson, Oliver E. 1999a. "Public and Private Bureaucracies: A Transaction Cost Economics Perspective." *Journal of Law, Economics and Organization.* April, 15, pp. 306–42.

Williamson, Oliver E. 1999b. "Strategy Research: Governance and Competence Perspectives." *Strategic Management Journal.* December, 20, pp. 1087–108.

Williamson, Oliver E. 2000. "The New Institutional Economics: Taking Stock, Looking Ahead." *Journal of Economic Literature.* September, 38:3, pp. 595–613.

Williamson, Oliver E. 2002. "Empirical Microeconomics: Another Perspective," in *The Economics of Choice, Change, and Organization.* Mie Augier and James March, eds. Brookfield, Vt.: Edward Elgar.

12 Vertical integration, appropriable rents, and the competitive contracting process

Benjamin Klein, Robert G. Crawford and Armen A. Alchian

More than forty years have passed since Coase's fundamental insight that transaction, coordination, and contracting costs must be considered explicitly in explaining the extent of vertical integration.[1] Starting from the truism that profit-maximizing firms will undertake those activities that they find cheaper to administer internally than to purchase in the market, Coase forced economists to begin looking for previously neglected constraints on the trading process that might efficiently lead to an intrafirm rather than an interfirm transaction. This paper attempts to add to this literature by exploring one particular cost of using the market system – the possibility of post-contractual opportunistic behavior.

Opportunistic behavior has been identified and discussed in the modern analysis of the organization of economic activity. Williamson, for example, has referred to effects on the contracting process of "*ex post* small numbers opportunism,"[2] and Teece has elaborated:

> Even when all of the relevant contingencies can be specified in a contract, contracts are still open to serious risks since they are not always honored. The 1970s are replete with examples of the risks associated with relying on contracts... [O]pen displays of opportunism are not infrequent and very often litigation turns out to be costly and ineffectual.[3]

The particular circumstance we emphasize as likely to produce a serious threat of this type of reneging on contracts is the presence of appropriable specialized quasi rents. After a specific investment is made and such quasi rents are created, the possibility of opportunistic behavior is very real. Following Coase's framework, this problem can be solved in two possible ways: vertical integration or contracts. The crucial assumption underlying the analysis of this paper is that, as assets become more specific and more appropriable quasi rents are created (and therefore the possible gains from opportunistic behavior increases), the costs of contracting will generally increase more than the costs of vertical integration. Hence, *ceteris paribus*, we are more likely to observe vertical integration.

Appropriable quasi rents of specialized assets

Assume an asset is owned by one individual and rented to another individual. The quasi-rent value of the asset is the excess of its value over its salvage value, that is, its value in its next best *use* to another renter. The potentially appropriable specialized portion of the quasi rent is that portion, if any, in excess of its value to the second highest-valuing *user*. If this seems like a distinction without a difference, consider the following example.

Imagine a printing press owned and operated by party A. Publisher B buys printing services from party A by leasing his press at a contracted rate of $5,500 per day. The

---

amortized fixed cost of the printing press is $4,000 per day and it has a current salvageable value if moved elsewhere of $1,000 (daily rental equivalent). Operating costs are $1,500 and are paid by the printing-press owner, who prints final printed pages for the publisher. Assume also that a second publisher C is willing to offer at most $3,500 for daily service. The current quasi rent on the installed machine is $3,000 (=$5,500 − $1,500 − $1,000), the revenue minus operating costs minus salvageable value. However, the daily quasi rent from publisher B relative to use of the machine for publisher C is only $2,000 (=$5,500 − $3,500). At $5,500 revenue daily from publisher B the press owner would break even on his investment. If the publisher were then able to cut his offer for the press from $5,500 down to almost $3,500, he would still have the press service available to him. He would be appropriating $2,000 of the quasi rent from the press owner. The $2,000 difference between his prior agreed-to daily rental of $5,500 and the next best revenue available to the press once the machine is purchased and installed is less than the quasi rent and therefore is potentially appropriable. If no second party were available at the present site, the entire quasi rent would be subject to threat of appropriation by an unscrupulous or opportunistic publisher.

Our primary interest concerns the means whereby this risk can be reduced or avoided. In particular, vertical integration is examined as a means of economizing on the costs of avoiding risks of appropriation of quasi rents in specialized assets by opportunistic individuals. This advantage of joint ownership of such specialized assets, namely, economizing on contracting costs necessary to insure nonopportunistic behavior, must of course be weighed against the costs of administering a broader range of assets within the firm.[4]

An appropriable quasi rent is not a monopoly rent in the usual sense, that is, the increased value of an asset protected from market entry over the value it would have had in an open market. An appropriable quasi rent can occur with no market closure or restrictions placed on rival assets. Once installed, an asset may be so expensive to remove or so specialized to a particular user that if the price paid to the owner were somehow reduced the asset's services to that user would not be reduced. Thus, even if there were free and open competition for entry to the market, the specialization of the installed asset to a particular user (or more accurately the high costs of making it available to others) creates a quasi rent, but no "monopoly" rent. At the other extreme, an asset may be costlessly transferable to some other user at no reduction in value, while at the same time, entry of similar assets is restricted. In this case, monopoly rent would exist, but no quasi rent.

We can use monopoly terminology to refer to the phenomenon we are discussing as long as we recognize that we are not referring to the usual monopoly created by government restrictions on entry or referring to a single supplier or even highly concentrated supply. One of the fundamental premises of this paper is that monopoly power, better labeled "market power," is pervasive. Because of transaction and mobility costs, "market power" will exist in many situations not commonly called monopolies. There may be many potential suppliers of a particular asset to a particular user but once the investment in the asset is made, the asset may be so specialized to a particular user that monopoly or monopsony market power, or both, is created.

A related motive for vertical integration that should not be confused with our main interest is the optimal output and pricing between two successive monopolists or bilateral monopolists (in the sense of marginal revenue less than price). A distortion arises because each sees a distorted marginal revenue or marginal cost.[5] While it is true that this successive monopoly distortion can be avoided by vertical integration, the results of the integration could, for that purpose alone, be achieved by a long-term or a more detailed contract based on the true marginal revenue and marginal costs. Integrated ownership will sometimes be utilized to economize on such precontractual bargaining costs. However, we investigate a different reason for joint ownership of vertically related assets – the avoidance of postcontractual opportunistic behavior when specialized assets and appropriable quasi rents are present. One must clearly distinguish the transaction and information costs of reaching an agreement (discovering and heeding true costs and revenues and agreeing upon the division of profits) and the enforcement costs involved in assuring compliance with an agreement, especially one in which specialized assets are involved. It is this latter situation which we here explore as a motivation for intrafirm rather than interfirm transactions.

We maintain that if an asset has a substantial portion of quasi rent which is strongly dependent upon some other particular asset, both assets will tend to be owned by one party. For example, reconsider our printing press example. Knowing that the press would exist and be operated even if its owner got as little as $1,500, publisher B could seek excuses to renege on his initial contract to get the weekly rental down from $5,500 to close to $3,500 (the potential offer from publisher C, the next highest-valuing user at its present site). If publisher B could effectively announce he was not going to pay more than, say, $4,000 per week, the press owner would seem to be stuck. This unanticipated action would be opportunistic behavior (which by definition refers to unanticipated non-fulfillment of the contract) if the press owner had installed the press at a competitive rental price of $5,500 anticipating (possibly naively) good faith by the publisher. The publisher, for example, might plead that his newspaper business is depressed and he will be unable to continue unless rental terms are revised.

Alternatively, and maybe more realistically, because the press owner may have bargaining power due to the large losses that he can easily impose on the publisher (if he has no other source of press services quickly available), the press owner might suddenly seek to get a higher rental price than $5,500 to capture some newly perceived increase in the publisher's profits. He could do this by alleging breakdowns or unusually high maintenance costs. This type of opportunistic behavior is difficult to prove and therefore litigate.

As we shall see, the costs of contractually specifying all important elements of quality varies considerably by type of asset. For some assets it may be essentially impossible to effectively specify all elements of quality and therefore vertical integration is more likely. But even for those assets used in situations where all relevant quality dimensions can be unambiguously specified in a contract, the threat of production delay during litigation may be an effective bargaining device. A contract therefore may be clearly enforceable but still subject to postcontractual opportunistic behavior. For example, the threat by the press owner to break its contract by pulling out its press is credible even though illegal and possibly subject to injunctive action. This is because such an action, even in the very short run, can impose substantial costs on the newspaper publisher.[6]

This more subtle form of opportunistic behavior is likely to result in a loss of efficiency and not just a wealth-distribution effect. For example, the publisher may decide, given this possibility, to hold or seek standby facilities otherwise not worthwhile. Even if transactors are risk neutral, the presence of possible opportunistic behavior will entail costs as real resources are devoted to the attempt to improve posttransaction bargaining positions in the event such opportunism occurs. In particular, less specific investments will be made to avoid being "locked in."[7] In addition, the increased uncertainty of quality and quantity leads to larger optimum inventories and other increased real costs of production.

This attention to appropriable specialized quasi rents is not novel. In addition to Williamson's[8] pathbreaking work in the area, Goldberg's[9] perceptive analysis of what he calls the "hold up" problem in the context of government regulation is what we are discussing in a somewhat different context. Goldberg indicates how some government regulation can usefully be considered a means of avoiding or reducing the threat of loss of quasi rent. (Goldberg treats this as the problem of providing protection for the "right to be served.") He also recognizes that this force underlies a host of other contractual and institutional arrangements such as stockpiling, insurance contracts, and vertical integration. Our analysis will similarly suggest a rationale for the existence of particular institutions and the form of governmental intervention or contractual provisions as alternatives to vertical integration in a wide variety of cases.

Contractual solutions

The primary alternative to vertical integration as a solution to the general problem of opportunistic behavior is some form of economically enforceable long-term contract. Clearly a short-term (for example, one transaction, non-repeat sale) contract will not solve the problem. The relevant question then becomes when will vertical integration be observed as a solution and when will the use of the market-contracting process occur. Some economists and lawyers have defined this extremely difficult question away by calling a long-term contract a form of vertical integration.[10] Although there is clearly a continuum here, we will attempt not to blur the distinction between a long-term rental agreement and ownership. We assume the opportunistic behavior we are concentrating on can occur only with the former.[11]

For example, if opportunism occurs by the owner-lessor of an asset failing to maintain it properly for the user-lessee and hence unexpectedly increasing the effective rental price, legal remedies (proving contract violation) may be very costly. On the other hand, if the user owned the asset, then the employee who failed to maintain the asset properly could merely be fired.[12] If the employee could still effectively cheat the owner-user of the asset because of his specific ability to maintain the asset, then the problem is that vertical integration of a relevant asset, the employee's human capital, has not occurred. For the moment, however, we will concentrate solely on the question of long-term rental versus ownership of durable physical assets.[13]

Long-term contracts used as alternatives to vertical integration can be assumed to take two forms: (1) an explicitly stated contractual guarantee legally enforced by the government or some other outside institution, or (2) an implicit contractual guarantee enforced by the market mechanism of withdrawing future business if opportunistic behavior occurs. Explicit long-term contracts can, in principle, solve opportunistic problems. but, as suggested already, they are often very costly solutions. They entail costs of specifying possible contingencies and the policing and litigation costs of detecting violations and enforcing the contract in the courts.[14] Contractual provisions specifying compulsory arbitration or more directly imposing costs on the opportunistic party (for example, via bonding) are alternatives often employed to economize on litigation costs and to create flexibility without specifying every possible contingency and quality dimension of the transaction.

Since every contingency cannot be cheaply specified in a contract or even known and because legal redress is expensive, transactors will generally also rely on an implicit type of long-term contract that employs a market rather than legal enforcement mechanism, namely, the imposition of a capital loss by the withdrawal of expected future business. This goodwill market-enforcement mechanism undoubtedly is a major element of the contractual alternative to vertical integration. Macauley provides evidence that relatively informal, legally unenforceable contractual practices predominate in business relations and that reliance on explicit legal sanctions is extremely rare.[15] Instead, business firms are said to generally rely on effective extralegal market sanctions, such as the depreciation of an opportunistic firm's general goodwill because of the anticipated loss of future business, as a means of preventing nonfulfillment of contracts.

One way in which this market mechanism of contract enforcement may operate is by offering to the potential cheater a future "premium," more precisely, a price sufficiently greater than average variable (that is, avoidable) cost to assure a quasi-rent stream that will exceed the potential gain from cheating.[16] The present-discounted value of this future premium stream must be greater than any increase in wealth that could be obtained by the potential cheater if he, in fact, cheated and were terminated. The offer of such a long-term relationship with the potential cheater will eliminate systematic opportunistic behavior.[17]

The larger the potential one-time "theft" by cheating (the longer and more costly to detect a violation, enforce the contract, switch suppliers, and so forth) and the shorter the expected continuing business relationship, the higher this premium will be in a nondeceiving equilibrium. This may therefore partially explain both the reliance by firms on long-term implicit contracts with particular suppliers and the existence of reciprocity agreements among firms. The premium can be paid in seemingly unrelated profitable reciprocal business . The threat of termination of this relationship mutually suppresses opportunistic behavior.[18]

The premium stream can be usefully thought of as insurance payments made by the firm to prevent cheating.[19] As long as both parties to the transaction make the same estimate of the potential short-run gain from cheating, the quantity of this assurance that will be demanded and supplied will be such that no opportunistic behavior will be expected to occur.[20] If postcontractual reneging is anticipated to occur, either the correct premium will be paid to optimally prevent it or, if the premium necessary to eliminate reneging is too costly, the particular transaction will not be made.

We are not implicitly assuming here that contracts are enforced costlessly and cannot be broken, but rather that given our information-cost assumptions, parties to a contract know exactly when and how much a contract will be broken. An unanticipated broken contract, that is, opportunistic behavior, is therefore not possible in this particular equilibrium. In the context of this model, expected wealth maximization will yield some opportunistic behavior only if we introduce a stochastic element. This will alter the informational equilibrium state such that the potential cheater's estimate of the short-run gain from opportunistic behavior may be at times greater than the other firm's estimate. Hence, less than an optimal premium will be paid and opportunistic behavior will occur.

The firms collecting the premium payments necessary to assure fulfillment of contractual agreements in a costly information world may appear to be earning equilibrium "profits" although they are in a competitive market. That is, there may be many, possibly identical, firms available to supply the services of nonopportunistic performance of contractual obligations yet the premium will not be competed away if transactors cannot costlessly guarantee contractual performance. The assurance services, by definition, will not be supplied unless the premium is paid and the mere payment of this premium produces the required services.

Any profits are competed away in equilibrium by competitive expenditures on fixed (sunk) assets, such as initial specific investments (for example, a sign) with low or zero salvage value if the firm cheats, necessary to enter and obtain this preferred position of collecting the premium stream.[21] These fixed (sunk) costs of supplying credibility of future performance are repaid or covered by future sales on which a premium is earned. In equilibrium, the premium stream is then merely a normal rate of return on the "reputation," or "brand-name" capital created by the firm by these initial expenditures. This brand-name capital, the value of which is highly specific to contract fulfillment by the firm, is analytically equivalent to a forfeitable collateral bond put up by the firm which is anticipated to face an opportunity to take advantage of appropriable quasi rents in specialized assets.

While these initial specific investments or collateral bonds are sometimes made as part of the normal (minimum-cost) production process and therefore at small additional cost, trans-action costs and risk considerations do make them costly.[22] We can generally say that the larger the appropriable specialized quasi rents (and therefore the larger the potential short-run gain from opportunistic behavior) and the larger the premium payments necessary to prevent contractual reneging, the more costly this implicit contractual solution will be. We can also expect the explicit contract costs to be positively related to the level of appropri-able quasi rents since it will pay to use more resources (including legal services) to specify precisely more contingencies when potential opportunities for lucrative contractual reneging exist.

Although implicit and explicit contracting and policing costs are positively related to the extent of appropriable specialized quasi rents, it is reasonable to assume, on the other hand, that any internal coordination or other ownership costs are not systematically related to the extent of the appropriable specialized quasi rent of the physical asset owned. Hence we can reasonably expect the following general empirical regularity to be true: the lower the appropriable specialized quasi rents, the more likely that transactors will rely on a contractual relationship rather than common ownership. And conversely, integration by common or joint ownership is more likely, the higher the appropriable specialized quasi rents of the assets involved.

Example of appropriable specialized quasi rent

This section presents examples of specialized quasi rents where the potential for their appro-priation serves as an important determinant of economic organization. A series of varied illustrations, some quite obvious and others rather subtle, will make the analysis more trans-parent and provide suggestive evidence for the relevance of the protection of appropriable quasi rents as an incentive to vertically integrate. It also suggests the direction of more sys-tematic empirical work that obviously is required to assess the significance of this factor relative to other factors in particular cases. Where this force towards integration (that is, the economizing on contracting costs necessary to assure nonopportunistic behavior in the presence of appropriable quasi rents) does not appear to dominate, important insights regard-ing the determinants of particular contracting costs and contract provisions are thereby provided.[23]

Automobile manufacturing

An illustrative example is the ownership by automobile-producing companies of the giant presses used for stamping body parts. The design and engineering specifications of a new automobile, for example Mustang for Ford, create value in Ford auto production. The man-ufacture of dies for stamping parts in accordance with the above specifications gives a value to these dies specialized to Ford, which implies an appropriable quasi rent in those dies. Therefore, the die owner would not want to be separate from Ford. Since an independent die owner may likely have no comparable demanders other than Ford for its product and to elicit supply requires payment to cover only the small operating costs once the large sunk fixed cost of the specific investment in the dies is made, the incentive for Ford to opportunistically renegotiate a lower price at which it will accept body parts from the independent die owner may be large. Similarly, if there is a large cost to Ford from the production delay of obtaining an alternative supplier of the specific body parts, the independent die owner may be able to capture quasi rents by demanding a revised higher price for the parts. Since the opportunity to lose the specialized quasi rent of assets is a debilitating prospect, neither party would invest in such equipment. Joint ownership of designs and dies removes this incentive to attempt appropriation.[24]

In this context, it is interesting to study in some detail the vertical merger that occurred in 1926 of General Motors with Fisher Body. The original production process for automobiles consisted of individually constructed open, largely wooden, bodies. By 1919 the production process began to shift towards largely metal closed body construction for which specific stamping machines became important. Therefore in 1919 General Motors entered a ten-year contractual agreement with Fisher Body for the supply of closed auto bodies.[25] In order to encourage Fisher Body to make the required specific investment, this contract had an exclusive dealing clause whereby General Motors agreed to buy substantially all its closed bodies from Fisher. This exclusive dealing arrangement significantly reduced the possibility of General Motors acting opportunistically by demanding a lower price for the bodies after Fisher made the specific investment in production capacity. Since exclusive dealing contractual conditions are relatively cheap to effectively specify and enforce, General Motor's postcontractual threat to purchase bodies elsewhere was effectively eliminated.

But large opportunities were created by this exclusive dealing clause for Fisher to take advantage of General Motors, namely to demand a monopoly price for the bodies. Therefore, the contract attempted to fix the price which Fisher could charge for the bodies supplied to General Motors. However, contractually setting in advance a "reasonable" price in the face of possible future changes in demand and production conditions is somewhat more difficult to effectively accomplish than merely "fixing" required suppliers. The price was set on a cost plus 17.6 per cent basis (where cost was defined exclusive of interest on invested capital). In addition, the contract included provisions that the price charged General Motors could not be greater than that charged other automobile manufacturers by Fisher for similar bodies nor greater than the average market price of similar bodies produced by companies other than Fisher and also included provisions for compulsory arbitration in the event of any disputes regarding price.

Unfortunately, however, these complex contractual pricing provisions did not work out in practice. The demand conditions facing General Motors and Fisher Body changed dramatically over the next few years. There was a large increase in the demand for automobiles and a significant shift away from open bodies to the closed body styles supplied by Fisher.[26] Meanwhile General Motors was very unhappy with the price it was being charged by its now very important supplier, Fisher. General Motors believed the price was too high because of a substantial increase in body output per unit of capital employed. This was an understandable development given the absence of a capital cost pass-through in the original contract.[27] In addition, Fisher refused to locate their body plants adjacent to General Motors assembly plants, a move General Motors claimed was necessary for production efficiency (but which required a large very specific and hence possibly appropriable investment on the part of Fisher).[28] By 1924, General Motors had found the Fisher contractual relationship intolerable and began negotiations for purchase of the remaining stock in Fisher Body, culminating in a final merger agreement in 1926.[29]

Petroleum industry

Appropriable quasi rents exist in specialized assets of oil refineries, pipelines, and oil fields. This leads to common ownership to remove the incentive for individuals to attempt to capture the rents of assets owned by someone else.

Suppose several oil wells are located along a separately owned pipeline that leads to a cluster of independently owned refineries with no alternative crude supply at comparable cost. Once all the assets are in place (the wells drilled and the pipeline and refineries constructed) the oil-producing properties and the refineries are specialized to the pipeline. The portion of their value above the value to the best alternative user is an appropriable specialized quasi rent. The extent of the appropriable quasi rent is limited, in part, by the costs of entry to a potential parallel pipeline developer. Since pipelines between particular oil-producing properties and particular refineries are essentially natural monopolies, the existing pipeline owner may have a significant degree of market power.

These specialized producing and refining assets are therefore "hostage" to the pipeline owner. At the "gathering end" of the pipeline, the monopsonist pipeline could and would purchase all its oil at the same well-head price regardless of the distance of the well from the refinery. This price could be as low as the marginal cost of getting oil out of the ground (or its reservation value for future use, if higher) and might not generate a return to the oil-well owner sufficient to recoup the initial investment of exploration and drilling. At the delivery-to-refinery end of the pipeline, the pipeline owner would be able to appropriate the "specialized-to-the-pipeline quasi rents" of the refineries. The pipeline owner could simply raise the price of crude oil at least to the price of alternative sources of supply to each refinery that are specialized to the pipeline. Given the prospects of such action, if the pipeline owner were an independent monopsonist facing the oil explorers and a monopolist to the refinery owners, everyone (explorers and refiners) would know in advance their vulnerability to rent extraction. Therefore oil-field owners and refinery owners would, through shared ownership in the pipeline, remove the possibility of subsequent rent extraction.[30]

The problem would not be completely solved if just the oil field or the refineries (but not both) were commonly owned with the pipeline, since the local monopoly (or monopsony) would persist vis-à-vis the other. Prospectively, one would expect the common ownership to extend to all three stages. If several refineries (or oil fields) were to be served by one pipeline, all the refinery (or oil field) owners would want to jointly own the pipeline. A common practice is a jointly owned company which "owns" the pipeline with the shares by producers and refiners in the pipeline company corresponding roughly to the respective shares of oil to be transported.[31]

Consider other inputs in the production process. The oil tanker, for example, is specialized to crude oil transportation. But since it is essentially equivalued by many alternative users, the appropriable quasi rent is near zero. So we would expect oil tankers not to be extensively owned by refiners or producers. Similarly, the assets used for refinery construction are not specialized to any single refiner or refinery and they should also not be commonly owned with the refinery.

Preliminary examination of the development of the American petroleum industry in the nineteenth century reveals numerous examples that appear consistent with the hypothesis that as technological change leads to assets involved in production, transportation, refining, and marketing becoming more specialized to other specific assets, joint ownership became efficient as a means of preventing opportunistic behavior.

For example, Rockefeller recognized the importance of the pending technological change implied by the substitution of highly specific long-distance pipelines for the somewhat more general capital of the railroads as the efficient mode of transporting oil and took advantage of it. First, before long-distance pipelines were clearly economical, Rockefeller used his dominant oil-refining position to obtain a price reduction on oil he shipped by rail and also rebates from the railroads on oil shipped by competitive oil producers. We conjecture that Rockefeller obtained these price reductions by threatening to build a pipeline parallel to the railroad. He was therefore able to extract the appropriable quasi rents of the railroads. This explains why the rebates were solely a function of oil shipped and not related to nonoil products such as agricultural goods. It also explains why the discount and rebate to Rockefeller were often of the same magnitude. The payment should be a function of total demand for transporting oil.

The obvious question is why some small oil producer or even a nonoil-producing firm did not similarly threaten the railroads with building a pipeline early (before it was cheaper than rail transport) and demand a payment as a function of total oil shipped. The answer, we believe, is that only a dominant oil producer would have credible bargaining power with the railroads in this situation because only a dominant producer would be able to make such a highly specific investment. If a small producer or nonoil-producing firm made such an investment, it could easily be appropriated by the oil-producing firms, especially with an alternative means of transportation available. It was therefore necessary for Rockefeller to gain a dominant oil-producing and refining position in order to make a credible threat to the railroads. Appropriating the quasi rents of the railroads by discounts and rebates not only effectively metered the demand for oil transportation but also made it easier for Rockefeller to gain a monopolistic position in the industry without being forced to buy out rivals at prices that would completely reflect future-discounted monopoly profits.[32]

Specific human capital

The previous analysis has dealt with examples of physical capital. When specific human capital is involved, the opportunism problem is often more complex and, because of laws prohibiting slavery, the solution is generally some form of explicit or implicit contract rather than vertical integration.

For example, consider the following concrete illustration from the agricultural industry. Suppose someone owns a peach orchard. The ripened peaches, ready for harvest, have a market value of about $400,000. So far costs of $300,000 have been paid and the remaining harvesting and shipping costs will be $50,000 ($5,000 transport and $45,000 labor), leaving $50,000 as the competitive return on the owner's capital. Assume the laborers become a union (one party to whom the crop is now specialized) and refuse to pick unless paid $390,000. That would leave $5,000 for transport and only $5,000 for the owner of the peach orchard, instead of the $350,000 necessary to cover incurred costs and the cost of capital. If the union had power to exclude other pickers, it could extract all the appropriable quasi rent of that year's crop specialized to that particular labor union's service. The union would be extracting not just the usual monopoly rents involved in raising wages, but also the short-run appropriable quasi rents of the farmer's specific assets represented by the ripened peaches. This gain to the union is a one-period return because obviously the farmer will not make any additional specific investments in the future if he knows it will be appropriated by the union.

To reduce this risk of appropriation, the farmer may have a large clan family (or neighbors of similar farms) do his picking. Because of diseconomies of scale, however, this "cooperative" solution is not generally the lowest-cost arrangement and some reliance on market contracting will be necessary. The individual farmer, for example, may want the labor union to put up a forfeitable bond to compensate him in the event the union under threat of strike asks for more wages at harvest time. Alternatively, but equivalently, the collateral put up by the union could be the value of the brand-name capital of the union, a value which will depreciate if its leaders engage in opportunistic behavior. The farmer would then make a continuing brand-name payment to the union (similar to the premium payment noted above) for this collateral.[33]

The market value of the union's reputation for reliability of contract observance is the present-discounted value of these brand-name payments which will be greater than any short-run opportunistic gain to the union leaders that could be obtained by threats at harvest time. These payments which increase the cost to the union of opportunistic behavior would be substantial for a perishable product with a large appropriable quasi rent. It is therefore obvious why producers of highly perishable crops are so antagonistic to unionization of field labor. They would be especially hostile to unions without established reputations regarding fulfillment of contract and with politically motivated (and possibly myopic) leaders.[34]

In addition to implicit (brand-name) contracts, opportunistic union behavior may be prevented by use of explicit contracts, often with some outside arbitration as an element of the contract-enforcement mechanism. Although it is difficult for an outsider to distinguish between opportunistic behavior and good-faith modifications of contract, impartial arbitration procedures may reduce the necessity of explicitly specifying possible contingencies and thereby reduce the rigidity of the explicit long-term contract.[35]

When the problem is reversed and quasi rents of firm-specific human capital of employees may be opportunistically appropriated by the firm, implicit and explicit long-term contracts are also used to prevent such behavior. Because of economies of scale in monitoring and enforcing such contracts, unions may arise as a contract cost-reducing institution for employees with investments in specific human capital.[36]

In addition to narrow contract-monitoring economies of scale, a union creates a continuing long-term employment relationship that eliminates the last-period (or transient employee) contract-enforcement problem and also creates bargaining power (a credible strike threat) to more cheaply punish a firm that violates the contract. Even when the specific human-capital investment is made by the firm, a union of employees may similarly reduce the contract-enforcement costs of preventing individual–worker opportunism. There are likely to be economies of scale in supply credibility of contract fulfillment, including the long-term continuing relationship aspect of a union. The existence of a union not only makes it more costly for a firm to cheat an individual worker in his last period but also makes it more costly for an individual worker in his last period to cheat the firm, because the union has the incentive (for example, withholding pension rights) to prevent such an externality on the continuing workers. Therefore unions are more likely to exist when the opportunistic cheating problem is greater, namely, when there is more specific human capital present.[37]

The first Becker analysis of the specific human-capital problem[38] ignored opportunistic bargaining difficulties and implicitly assumed arbitrary contracting costs in particular situations to determine a solution. Becker initially assumed that the firm would cheat the employee if the employee made the specific investment. He then argued that the only reason the firm would not make the entire specific investment is because the quit rate of employees, which is a negative function of wages, would then be greater than optimal. Becker did not consider the completely reciprocal nature of the possibilities for cheating. The opportunistic behavior we are emphasizing suggests the possibility of the employee threatening to quit after the firm makes the specific investment unless the wage rate is readjusted upward. Becker's solution of a sharing of the costs and benefits of the specific investment via an initial lump-sum payment by the employee and a later higher-than-market wage does not eliminate the bilateral opportunistic bargaining problem because the employer may later decrease the wage back to the competitive level (or the employee may demand a higher wage to appropriate the partial specific investment by the employer). If it is assumed that employers will not cheat or break contracts in this way, then the efficient solution would be to merely have the employee make the entire specific investment (and therefore have the optimal quit rate) because the employer can costlessly "guarantee" (by assumption) a higher wage reflecting the increased productivity of the firm. But, more generally, to obtain an equilibrium solution to the problem, the costs of creating credibility of contract fulfillment and the costs of enforcing contracts must be explicitly considered.

One of the costs of using an explicit contract which relies on governmental or other outside arbitration for enforcement – rather than on an implicit contract which relies on depreciation of the value of a firm's brand-name (that is, the loss of future premium payments) – is the likely increase in rigidity. For example, the difficulty of specifying all contingencies in labor contracts and of adjusting to unanticipated conditions is likely to lead to wage rigidity. Because contractual changes tend to create suspicion regarding the purpose of the contract alteration and, in particular, raise the question of whether a firm is using the changed conditions as an opportunity to seize some of the specific quasi rents, long-term labor contracts may consist of rigid wages and layoff provisions. If in the face of declining demand, a firm must keep wages fixed and lay off workers rather than merely reduce wages, the incentive for it to opportunistically claim a false reduction in demand is substantially reduced.[39]

The fear of opportunistic behavior leads to price (and often also output) rigidity in all kinds of long-term explicit contracts where specific capital is present. This, in turn, leads to the creation of institutions to encourage increased flexibility in the face of changing market conditions. For example, the prime-rate convention, an announced benchmark in terms of which interest rates of corporate bank loans are stated, may be partially rationalized as a cheap means by which the bank can convey information to borrowers that the bank is not opportunistically raising interest fees to a particular customer. A corporate client who has made a specific investment in the supply of information to the bank regarding its credit worthiness (including its financial record of transactions with the bank) creates some appropriable quasi rents. However, when the price of the loan is stated as, say, prime plus one per cent, unless the bank decides to cheat all customers simultaneously and thereby limit new business, an individual customer can clearly distinguish between general market movements in interest rates and any changes the bank decides to make in the particular customer's credit rating. "Price protection" clauses in contracts, where a price decrease to any customer is guaranteed to be given to all customers, may be explained on similar grounds.

These information-cost-reducing institutions, including the use of impartial arbitrators, are highly imperfect. Therefore contracts involving specific assets, even where a price is not explicitly fixed long term, will consequently involve some price rigidity. The macroeconomic implications of this observation (for example, the employment effects of aggregate nominal demand shocks) are obvious.[40] But the interaction of macroeconomic considerations and industrial organization may not be that obvious. In particular, an increase in the variance of price-level movements, which increases the expected costs to both parties of price rigidity and thereby increases the acceptable degree of price flexibility, also makes it easier for a firm to cheat by opportunistically raising its price. Increased price uncertainty is therefore likely to lead to increased vertical integration.

Where more trust is present and implicit rather than explicit contracts are used, contract prices including wages are likely to be more flexible. If the variance of the price level increases – which makes it more difficult to detect opportunistic behavior and therefore the short-run gains from such cheating – the equilibrium implicit contract will imply a larger premium stream. The interesting question is what are the economic determinants of the implicit relative to explicit contracting costs which will in turn determine the degree of price flexibility.

One determinant of implicit contracting costs is the anticipated growth of demand for the firm's product. The more rapidly demand is expected to grow, the more likely a firm will rely on an implicit contract with its customers. Creating trust is cheaper for firms facing rapid demand growth compared to firms with stable or declining demand because the loss of future business by customer termination if the firm is found to be cheating implies a relatively larger cost. Therefore a smaller current premium payment is necessary to assure nonopportanistic behavior. Hence the higher the anticipated growth in demand for a firm, the lower the contracting cost of using implicit relative to explicit contracts and the more flexible prices and other contract terms set by the firm can be expected to be.[41]

The cost to a growing firm of cheating on laborers, for example, would be higher in terms of the future increased wages (of increased employment) it would have to pay if it cheated. The penally for not relying on the firm's brand name is then more effective. This may explain why firms such as International Business Machines appear to have highly flexible labor compensation arrangements that are, in fact, quite similar to Japanese wage payments which consist of large, highly variable, biannual bonuses. Our analysis suggests that it is not because of different cultural values that Japanese labor relations rely on much trust, but because the high growth rate of future demand makes it relatively cheap for firms to behave in this way.[42]

Leasing inputs and ownership of the firm

Examination of leasing companies should reveal that leases are less common (or too expensive) for assets with specialized quasi rents that could be appropriated by the lessee or lessor. Leasing does not occur in the obvious cases of elevators or the glass of windows in an office building where postinvestment bilaterally appropriable quasi rents are enormous, while the furniture in the building is often rented. In banks, the safe is owned by the bank, but computers (though not the memory discs) are sometimes rented.[43] Though this may seem like resorting to trivialities, the fact that such leasing arrangements are taken for granted merely corroborates the prior analysis.

The standard example of leasing arrangements occurs with transportation capital, such as the planes, trucks, or cars used by a firm. This capital is generally easily movable and not very specific. But leasing arrangements are far from universal because some of this capital can be quite specific and quasi rents appropriated. For example, early American steam locomotives were specialized to operating conditions such as high speed, hill climbing, short hauls, heavy loads, sharp corners, as well as types of coal for fuel. Slight differences in engines created significant differences in operating costs. High specialization made it desirable for the rail companies to own locomotives (as well as the land on which water was available for steam). The advent of the more versatile, less specialized, diesel locomotive enabled more leasing and equipment trust financing. Similarly, Swift, the meat packer and innovator of the refrigerator car for transporting slaughtered beef, owned the specialized refrigerator cars it used.[44]

On the other hand, some capital may be quite specific to other assets in a firm's productive process and yet leased rather than owned. These cases provide useful insights into the nature of the contracting costs underlying our analysis. For example, consider the fact that agricultural land, a highly specific asset, is not always owned but often is rented. Land rented for farming purposes is typically for annual crops, like vegetables, sugar beets, cotton, or wheat, while land used for tree crops, like nuts, dates, oranges, peaches, apricots, or grape vines – assets that are highly specialized to the land – is usually owned by the party who plants the trees or vines.[45] However, long-term rental arrangements even for these "specialized asset" crops are not entirely unknown.

It is instructive to recognize why land-rental contracts, rather than vertical integration, can often be used without leading to opportunistic behavior. The primary reason is because it is rather cheap to specify and monitor the relevant contract terms (the quality of the good being purchased) and to enforce this particular rental contract. In addition, the landowner generally cannot impose a cost on the farmer by pulling the asset out or reducing the quality of the asset during the litigation process. Note the contrast with labor rental where it is essentially impossible to effectively specify and enforce quality elements (for example, all working conditions and the effort expended by workers) and where the possibility of withdrawal by strike or lockout is real and costly. Therefore, we do observe firms making highly specific investments in, for example, trees or buildings on land they do not own but only rent long term.[46] This is because credible postcontractual opportunistic threats by the landowner are not possible. However, if the landowner can vary the quality of the land, for example, by controlling the irrigation system to the crops or the electricity supply to a building, then a significant possibility of postinvestment opportunistic behavior exists and we would therefore expect vertical integration.[47]

One specific asset that is almost always owned by the firm is its trade-name or brand-name capital and, in particular, the logo it uses to communicate to consumers. If this asset were rented from a leasing company, the problems would be obvious. The firm would be extremely hesitant to make any investments to build up its goodwill, for example, by advertising or by successful performance, because such investments are highly specific to that "name." The quasi rents could be appropriated by the leasing company through increases in the rental fee for the trade name. Not only would the firm not invest in this specific asset, but there would be an incentive for the firm to depreciate a valuable rented brand name. Although these problems seem insurmountable, rental of the capital input of a firm's brand name is not entirely unknown. In fact, franchisors can be thought of as brand-name leasing companies. A franchisee is fundamentally a renter of the brand-name capital (and logo) owned by the franchisor. Because of the specific capital problems noted above, direct controls are placed on franchisee behavior. The rental payment is usually some form of profit-sharing arrangement and, although the franchisee is legally considered to be an independent firm, the situation is in reality much closer to vertical integration than to the standard contractual relationship of the independent market.

Finally, the analysis throws light on the important question of why the owners of a firm (the residual claimants) are generally also the major capitalists of the firm.[48] As we have seen, owners may rent the more generalized capital, but will own the firm's specific capital. This observation has implications for recent discussions of "industrial democracy," which fail to recognize that although employees may own and manage a firm (say, through their union), they will also have to be capitalists and own the specific capital. It will generally be too costly, for example, for the worker-owners to rent a plant because such a specific investment could be rather easily appropriated from its owners after it is constructed. Therefore it is unlikely to be built. A highly detailed contractual arrangement together with very large brand-name premium payments by the laborers would be necessary to assure nonopportunistic behavior. This is generally too expensive an alternative and explains why capitalists are usually the owners of a firm.[49]

Social institutions

Much of the previous analysis has dealt with tangible capital. Contractual arrangements involving such assets are often cheaper than complete vertical integration, even when the assets are highly specific (for example, the land-rental case.) As the discussion on human capital suggests, however, when the specific assets involved are intangible personal assets, the problems of contract enforcement become severe. In addition, when the number of individuals involved (or the extent of the specific capital) becomes very large, ownership arrangements often become extremely complex.

For example, consider country clubs. Golf country clubs are social, in addition to being golfing, organizations. Sociability of a country club involves substantial activities away from the golf course: dinners, dances, parties, cards, games, and general social activities with friends who are members of the club. However, some golf courses are operated with very few social activities for the set of members and their families. The social clubs (usually called "country clubs") are mutually owned by the members, whereas golf courses with virtually no off-course social activity often are privately owned with members paying daily golf fees without owning the golf course.

Mutual ownership is characteristic of the social country club because the specialized quasi rent of friendship is collected by each member whose friendship is specialized to the other members. The members' behavior toward one another constitutes an investment in forming valuable friendships, a congenial milieu, and rapport among the members. Each member has invested in creating that congenial milieu and atmosphere specialized to the other members. And its value could be stolen or destroyed by opportunistic behavior of a party authorized to admit new members.

To see how, suppose the club were owned by someone other than the members. Once the membership value is created by the interpersonal activities of the members, the owner of the club could then start to raise the fees for continuing members. Assuming some costs of the members moving away en masse and forming a new club, the owner could expropriate by higher fees some of the specialized quasi-rent value of the sociability created by the members' specialization to each other in their own group. Alternatively, the owner could threaten to break the implicit contract and destroy some of the sociability capital by selling admission to "undesirable" people who want to consort with the existing members.

Similarly, if the social country club were owned by the members as a corporation with each member owning a share of stock salable without prior approval of existing members (as is the case for the business corporation), a single member could, by threatening to sell to an "undesirable" potential member, extract some value of congeniality from the current members, as a payment for not selling.[50]

An extreme case of this general problem is a marriage. If each mate had a transferable share salable to a third party, there would be far fewer marriages with highly specific investments in affection and children. If a relationship is not one of specialized interest (specialized to a particular other party) or if it required no investment by any member, then the marriage relationship would be more like a corporation. As it is one of highly specific investments, marriages have historically been mutually owned entities, with permission of both parties generally required for alteration of membership. Government arbitration of this relationship to prevent postinvestment opportunistic behavior by either party can contribute toward lower bargaining costs and investments of resources (recoverable dowries) by both parties to improve their respective postinvestment bargaining positions, and, most importantly, create confidence that opportunistic behavior will not be successful. The legislative movement to "no-fault" divorce suggests that modern marriages may have less specific assets than formerly.[51]

The importance of mobility costs when many individuals in a group must jointly decide to take action, as in the case of an opportunistic country-club owner, and the importance of government intervention are clearly reflected in the case of the money-supply industry.[52] The decision regarding what is used as the dominant money (medium of exchange) in society, like many other social agreements and customs, entails a large degree of rigidity on the individual level. A decision to change a social institution, in this case what is used as money, must involve a large subset of the population to be effective. Given this natural monopoly, the cost to an individual or a new entrant of attempting change may be prohibitively costly. Therefore, once a dominant money supplier is established, the potential wealth gain that can be realized through opportunistic behavior by the money issuer (that is, by unanticipated inflation) is enormous. The private implicit contractual solution would therefore entail an extremely high brand-name "premium" payment (seigniorage return) to guarantee that a wealth-maximizing, unregulated, private, dominant money supplier will not cheat by increasing the money supply faster than anticipated. Because this premium payment and therefore the rental price of money will be so high, it is unlikely that a private, implicit contractual solution is the cheapest arrangement.[53] Traditional vertical integration would also be extremely costly in this case of a consumer asset used by so many individuals (in fact it is difficult to even understand exactly what it would mean). Some form of government intervention is obviously likely, either in the form of regulation by enforcing an explicit contractual guarantee, or in the form of outright nationalization. Government ownership of the monetary unit is actually close to what one may consider vertical integration on the part of consumers in this particular case.

Concluding comment

We should emphasize in conclusion that most business relationships are neither likely to be as simple as the standard textbook polar cases of vertical integration or market contract nor as easily explained as some of the above examples. When particular examples are examined in detail, business relationships are often structured in highly complex ways not represented by either a simple rental contract or by simple vertical integration. A timely example is the ownership rights of common services supplied in condominium or "new-town" projects. One solution often adopted is joint ownership of common assets, similar to the joint ownership by petroleum producers and refiners of oil pipeline as noted above. In the condominium case, however, the number of shareowners is sometimes equal to hundreds or even thousands of individuals and the resulting contractual arrangements are closer to a constitution for a local "government" than to the simple paradigm of a two-person market transaction. When governing costs are high, individuals have often opted for a long-term management contract (often with the builder of the housing project) for maintaining the common assets. The possible problems associated with the opportunistic appropriation by the manager of the quasi rents in specialized assets of the individual owners (including specific assets used to furnish each apartment such as carpeting and any specific "friendship capital" from association with other owner occupants) are obvious. The fact that there has been a great deal of litigation in this area is not surprising. The difficulty may be partially due to what appears to be significant economies of scale in supplying confidence concerning contract performance and diseconomies of scale in the actual production and management of housing. Some insurance or franchising arrangement may therefore evolve in this area.

There is a continuing search in this difficult area using market and governmental (regulatory, legislative, and judicial) processes to produce institutional and private contractual innovation that will lead to more economical contractual relations and ownership rights. We have little idea why one solution appears to have been efficient for one condominium project and another solution for another project. This merely indicates that as we move toward more complex ownership relationships the problem of efficiently structuring the economic relationship, either within the firm or via contracts, also becomes highly complex. Stating that the world is complicated is another way of admitting our ignorance. However, explicitly recognizing that contracting costs are not zero, as they are often implicitly assumed to be in economic analysis, and explicitly considering the determinants of these costs (such as the presence of appropriable quasi rents) is the first step in explaining the large variety of contractual and ownership arrangements we observe in the real world.

More generally, we have seen that once we attempt to add empirical detail to Coase's fundamental insight that a systematic study of transaction costs is necessary to explain particular forms of economic organization, we find that his primary distinction between transactions made within a firm and transactions made in the marketplace may often be too simplistic. Many long-term contractual relationships (such as franchising) blur the line between the market and the firm. It may be more useful to merely examine the economic rationale for different types of particular contractual relationships in particular situations, and consider the firm as a particular kind or set of interrelated contracts.[54] Firms are therefore, by definition, formed and revised in markets and the conventional sharp distinction between markets and firms may have little general analytical importance. The pertinent economic question we are faced with is "What kinds of contracts are used for what kinds of activities, and why?"

Acknowledgment

We wish to acknowledge useful comments on previous drafts by Harold Demsetz, Stephen Friedberg, Victor Goldberg, Levis Kochin, Keith Leffler, Lynne Schneider, Earl Thompson, and participants at a seminar at the Center for the Study of American Business at Washington University and at Law and Economics Workshops at UCLA and the University of Chicago. Financial assistance was provided by a grant of the Lilly Endowment Inc. for the study of property rights and by the Foundation for Research in Economics and Education. The authors are solely responsible for the views expressed and for the remaining errors.

Notes

1 R. H. Coase, The Nature of the Firm, 4 *Economica* 386 (1937), reprinted in *Readings in Price Theory* 331 (George J. Stigler & Kenneth E. Boulding eds. 1952).
2 Oliver E. Williamson, *Markets and Hierarchies: Analysis and Antitrust Implications* 26–30 (1975).
3 David J. Teece, *Vertical Integration and Divestiture in the U.S. Oil Industry* 31 (1976).
4 Vertical integration does not completely avoid contracting problems. The firm could usefully be thought of as a complex nonmarket contractual network where very similar forces are present. Frank Knight stressed the importance of this more than 50 years ago when he stated: "[T]he internal problems of the corporation, the protection of its various types of members and adherents against each

other's predatory propensities, are quite as vital as the external problem of safeguarding the public interests against exploitation by the corporation as a unit." Frank H. Knight, *Risk, Uncertainty, and Profit* 254 (1964).

5 This matter of successive and bilateral monopoly has long been known and exposited in many places. See, for example, Robert Bork, Vertical Integration and the Sherman Act: The Legal History of an Economic Misconception, 22 *U. Chi. L. Rev.* 157, 196 (1954); and the discussion in Fritz Machlup & Martha Taber, Bilateral Monopoly, Successive Monopoly, and Vertical Integration, 27 *Economica* 101 (1960), where the problem is dated back to Cournot's statement in 1838.

6 While newspaper publishers generally own their own presses, book publishers generally do not. One possible reason book publishers are less integrated may be because a book is planned further ahead in time and can economically be released with less haste. Presses located in any area of the United States can be used. No press is specialized to one publisher, in part because speed in publication and distribution to readers are generally far less important for books than newspapers, and therefore appropriable quasi rents are not created. Magazines and other periodicals can be considered somewhere between books and newspapers in terms of the importance of the time factor in distribution. In addition, because magazines are distributed nationally from at most a few plants, printing presses located in many different alternative areas are possible competitors for an existing press used at a particular location. Hence, a press owner has significantly less market power over the publisher of a magazine compared to a newspaper and we find magazines generally printed in nonpublisher-owned plants. (See W. Eric Gustafson, Periodicals and Books, in *Made in New York* 178, 190 (Max Hall ed. 1959).) But while a magazine printing press may be a relatively less specific asset compared to a newspaper printing press, appropriable quasi rents may not be trivial (as possibly they are in the case of book printing). The magazine printing contract is therefore unlikely to be of a short-term one-transaction form but will be a long-term arrangement.

7 The relevance for private investments in underdeveloped, politically unstable, that is, "opportunistic," countries is painfully obvious. The importance for economic growth of predictable government behavior regarding the definition and enforcement of property rights has frequently been noted.

8 Oliver E. Williamson, The Vertical Integration of Production: Market Failure Considerations, 61 *Am. Econ. Rev.* 112 (Papers & Proceedings, May 1971); and Oliver E. Williamson, *Markets and Hierarchies: Analysis and Antitrust Implications* (1975).

9 Victor P. Goldberg, Regulation and Administered Contracts, 7 Bell *J. Econ. & Management Sci.* 426, 439-41 (1976).

10 See, for example, Friedrich Kessler & Richard H. Stern, Competition, Contract, and Vertical Integration, 69 *Yale L.J.* 1 (1959).

11 It is commonly held that users of assets that can be damaged by careless use and for which the damage is not easy to detect immediately are more likely to own rather than rent the assets. However, these efficient maintenance considerations apply to short-term contracts and are irrelevant if the length of the long-term rental contract coincides with the economic life of the asset. Abstracting from tax considerations, the long-term contract remains less than completely equivalent to vertical integration only because of the possibility of postcontractual opportunistic reneging. These opportunistic possibilities, however, may also exist within the firm; see note 4 *supra*.

12 We are abstracting from any considerations of a firm's detection costs of determining proper maintenance. Ease of termination also analytically distinguishes between a franchisor-franchisee arrangement and a vertically integrated arrangement with a profit-sharing manager. If cheating occurs, it is generally cheaper to terminate an employee rather than a franchisee. (The law has been changing recently to make it more difficult to terminate either type of laborer.) But the more limited job-tenure rights of an employee compared to a franchisee reduce his incentive to invest in building up future business, and the firm must trade off the benefits and costs of the alternative arrangements. A profit-sharing manager with an explicit long-term employment contract would essentially be identical to a franchisee.

13 The problems involved with renting specific human capital are discussed below.

14 The recent Westinghouse case dealing with failure to fulfill uranium-supply contracts on grounds of "commercial impossibility" vividly illustrates these enforcement costs. Nearly three years after outright cancellation by Westinghouse of their contractual commitment, the lawsuits have not been adjudicated and those firms that have settled with Westinghouse have accepted substantially less than the original contracts would have entitled them to. A recent article by Paul L. Joskow, Commercial Impossibility, the Uranium Market, and the Westinghouse Case, 6 *J. Legal Stud.* 119 (1977),

analyzes the Westinghouse decision to renege on the contract as anticipated risk sharing and therefore, using our definition, would not be opportunistic behavior. However, the publicity surrounding this case and the judicial progress to date are likely to make explicit long-term contracts a less feasible alternative to vertical integration in the situations we are analyzing.

15 Stewart Macaulay, Non-Contractual Relations in Business: A Preliminary Study, 28 *Am. Soc. Rev.* 55 (Feb. 1963).

16 The following discussion of the market enforcement mechanism is based upon the analysis of competitive equilibrium under costly quality information developed in Benjamin Klein & Keith Leffler, The Role of Price in Guaranteeing Quality, *J. Pol. Econ.* (1979), which formally extends and more completely applies the analysis in Benjamin Klein, The Competitive Supply of Money, 6 *J. Money, Credit, & Banking* 423 (1974). It is similar to the analysis presented in Gary S. Becker & George J. Stigler, Law Enforcement, Malfeasance, and Compensation of Enforcers, 3 *J. Legal Stud.* 1 (1974), of insuring against malfeasance by an employer. This market-enforcement mechanism is used in Benjamin Klein & Andrew McLaughlin, *Resale Price Maintenance, Exclusive Territories, and Franchise Termination: The Coors Case* (1978) (unpublished manuscript), to explain franchising arrangements and particular contractual provisions such as resale price maintenance, exclusive territories, initial specific investments, and termination clauses.

17 Formally, this arrangement to guarantee nonopportunistic behavior unravels if there is a last period in the relationship. No matter how high the premium, cheating would occur at the start of the last period. If transactors are aware of this, no transaction relying on trust (that is, the expectation of another subsequent trial) will be made in the penultimate period, because it becomes the last period, and so on. If some large lump-sum, final-period payment such as a pension as part of the market-enforcement scheme, as outlined by Gary S. Becker & George J. Stigler, *supra* note 16, this last-period problem is obvious. One solution to this unrecognized last-period problem is the acceptance of some continuing third party (for example, escrow agents or government enforcers) to prevent reneging on the implicit contracts against reneging we are outlining. Alternatively, the potential loss of value of indefinitely long-lived saleable brand-name assets can serve as deterrents to cheating even where the contract between two parties has a last period. If one party's reputation for nonopportunistic dealings can be sold and used in later transactions in an infinite-time-horizon economy, the firm that cheats in the "last" period to any one buyer from the firm experiences a capital loss. This may partially explain the existence of conglomerates and their use of identifying (not product-descriptive) brand names.

18 Although it may not always be in one's narrow self-interest to punish the other party in such a reciprocal relationship since termination may impose a cost on both, it may be rational for one to adopt convincingly such a reaction function to optimally prevent cheating. R. L. Trivers, The Evolution of Reciprocal Altruism, 46 *Q. Rev. Bio.* 35, 49 (March 1971), discusses similar mechanisms such as "moralistic aggression" which he claims have been genetically selected to protect reciprocating altruists against cheaters. Similarly, throughout the discussion we implicitly assume that cheating individuals can only cheat once and thereafter earn the "competitive" rate of return. They may, however, be forced to earn less than the competitive wage if they are caught cheating, that is, take an extra capital loss (collusively, but rationally) imposed by other members of the group. This may explain why individuals may prefer to deal in business relations with their own group (for example, members of the same church or the same country club) where effective social sanctions can be imposed against opportunistic behavior. Reliance on such reciprocal business relationships and group enforcement mechanisms is more likely where governmental enforcement of contracts is weaker. Nathaniel H. Leff, Industrial Organization and Entrepreneurship in the Developing Countries: The Economic Groups, 26 *Econ. Dev. & Cultural Change* 661 (1978), for example, documents the importance of such groups in less-developed countries. Industries supplying illegal products and services would likely be another example.

19 It is, of course, an insurance scheme that not only pools risks but also alters them.

20 As opposed to the analysis of Michael R. Darby & Edi Karni, Free Competition and the Optimal Amount of Fraud, 16 *J. Law & Econ.* 67 (1973), the equilibrium quantity of opportunistic behavior or "fraud" will be zero under our assumptions of symmetrical information.

21 A more complete analysis of market equilibrium by the use of specific capital in guaranteeing contract enforcement is developed in Benjamin Klein & Keith Leffler, *supra* note 16.

22 An interesting example of the efficient creation of such a specific collateral investment is provided in *In re* Tastee-Freeze International, 82 F.T.C. 1195 (1973). In this case the franchisor required the

franchisee to purchase all the equipment to make soft ice cream except the final patented feeder mechanism which they would only rent at the nominal price of one dollar per month. This, we believe, served the function of substantially reducing the salvage value of the equipment upon termination and therefore was part of the enforcement mechanism to prevent cheating (for example, intentionally failing to maintain quality) by franchisees. If the feeder were sold, the equipment plus the feeder would have a substantial resale value and would not serve the purpose of assuring contract compliance. Similarly, if the equipment were rented along with the feeder the franchisee would not experience a capital loss if terminated. Since the assets of the franchisee are contractually made specific, a situation is created where the assets are now appropriable by an opportunistic franchisor. Generally, a franchisor will lose by terminating a franchisee without cause since that will produce poor incentives on the remaining franchisees to maintain quality and will make it more difficult for the franchisor to sell franchises in the future. But what prevents the franchisor from an unanticipated simultaneous termination of all franchisees, especially after growth of a chain is "complete?" This is logically equivalent to the last-period problem discussed at note 17 *supra* and is restrained in part by its effects on the salable value of the brand name of the franchisor. While we do not know of any evidence of such systematic franchisor cheating, an analysis of this problem which merely asserts that franchisees voluntarily sign contracts with knowledge of these short-term termination provisions is certainly incomplete (see, for example, Paul H. Rubin, The Theory of the Firm and the Structure of the Franchise Contract, 21 *J. Law & Econ.* 223 (1978)).

This example and much of this section of the paper is based upon a more complete theoretical and empirical analysis of actual contractual relationships developed for an ongoing study by Benjamin Klein of FTC litigation in the area of vertical-distribution arrangements.

23 It is important to recognize that not only will contracting and enforcement costs of constraining opportunistic behavior determine the form of the final economic arrangement adopted by the transacting parties, but they will also influence the firm's production function. That is, the level of specific investment and therefore the size of the potentially appropriable quasi rent is not an independent "technological" datum in each of these following cases, but is economically determined in part by transaction costs.

24 The argument also applies to die inserts which can be utilized to make slight modifications in original dies. The value of die inserts is largely an appropriable quasi rent, and so they will also be owned jointly with the designs and basic dies. Aside from the engineering design of the car, the engine blocks, the exterior shell (and possibly the crankshafts, camshafts, and gearing), no other part of the automobile would appear to possess specialized appropriable quasi rents and therefore necessarily be made exclusively by the automobile company. The integration of Ford into the manufacture of spark plugs – a part which seems to be easily standardizable among different autos – by their merger with Autolite, therefore must be explained on other grounds. See Ford Motor Co. v. United States, 405 U.S. 562 (1972).

25 The manufacturing agreement between General Motors and Fisher Body can be found in the minutes of the Board of Directors of Fisher Body Corporation for November 7, 1919.

In addition to this long-term contract General Motors also purchased a 60% interest in Fisher at this time. However, as demonstrated by future events, the Fisher brothers clearly seem to have maintained complete control of their company in spite of this purchase.

26 By 1924 more than 65% of automobiles produced by General Motors were of the closed body type. See Sixteenth Annual Report of the General Motors Corporation, year ended December 31, 1924.

27 Deposition of Alfred P. Sloan, Jr. in United States *v.* DuPont & Co., 366 U.S. 316 (1961), from complete set of briefs and trial records in custody of General Motors, 186-90 (April 28, 1952). Also see direct testimony of Alfred P. Sloan, Jr. in United States *v.* DuPont & Co., vol. 5 trial transcript, 2908-14 (March 17, 1953). (The government was attempting to demonstrate in this case that General Motors vertically integrated in order to get Fisher to purchase its glass requirements from DuPont.)

28 *Id.* It is obvious that long-term exclusive dealing contracts are necessary if such investments are to be made by nonvertically integrated firms. See *In re* Great Lakes Carbon Corp., 82 F.T.C. 1529 (1973), for an example of the government's failure to understand this. Great Lakes Carbon Corporation built plants highly specific to particular refineries to process petroleum coke (a by-product of the refining process) for these refineries and was prosecuted for requiring long-term exclusive dealing contracts with refineries.

29 United States *v.* DuPont & Co., vol. 1, defendants trial exhibits numbers GM-32, GM-33, GM-34.

30 Our argument is distinct from the traditional argument in the oil-business literature that vertical integration occurs to achieve "assurance" of supplies or of markets in the face of implicitly or explicitly assumed disequilibrium conditions. See, for example, P. H. Frankel, Integration in the Oil Industry, 1 *J. Indus. Econ.* 201 (1953); Melvin G. de Chazeau & Alfred H. Kahn, *Integration and Competition in the Petroleum Industry* 102-04 (1959); and Michael E. Canes, *A Theory of the Vertical Integration of Oil Firms* (Oct. 1976) (unpublished manuscript, Amer. Petroleum Inst.). Jerry G. Green, Vertical Integration and Assurance of Markets (Oct. 1974) (Discussion Paper No. 383, Harvard Inst. of Econ. Research), similarly argues more formally that price inflexibility in an intermediate market which causes shortages and overproduction is an incentive for vertical integration.

It is also important to distinguish between this risk-reducing reason for joint ownership (that is, the reduction in the risk of appropriation of user-associated specialized quasi rents) and the possible risk reduction from joint ownership when there is negative correlation of changes in values of nonappropriable generalized quasi rents. Joint ownership of assets whose value fluctuations are negatively correlated so that gains in one are offset by losses in the other is said to provide a form of insurance against total value changes of the resources used in the manufacturing process. These changes are not the result of any postcontractual opportunistic behavior but of general economic forces outside the control of the immediate parties. For example, a refinery and an oil-producing property fluctuate in value in opposite directions if a new oil field is discovered. The price of oil will fall but the price of refined products will not fall until additional refineries can process larger amounts of oil into more refined products at essentially constant production costs. Then, some of the oil-field owner's losses in value of crude oil are gained by his refinery. This reduces the fluctuation in values caused by factors unrelated to the efficiency of oil producing, refining, and distributing abilities.

However, diversification can also be achieved by methods other than vertical integration. One way is for the investor to buy stocks in the separate unintegrated firms – in effect integrating their ownership by joint holding of common stocks. Although individual action may not always be as cheap or effective as action through intermediaries, financial intermediaries are available such as mutual funds rather than direct diversification by integrated firms. One possible reason why negatively correlated assets could be worth more combined in a single firm is the reduction in the probability of bankruptcy and hence the probability of incurring bankruptcy costs (such as legal fees). An integrated firm with negatively correlated assets could increase its debt to equity ratio while keeping the probability of bankruptcy constant and therefore decrease the taxes on equity without any additional risk. This may be one of the gains of many conglomerate mergers.

31 Jane Atwood & Paul Kobrin, *Integration and Joint Ventures in Pipelines* (Sept. 1977) (Research Study No. 5, Am. Petroleum Inst.), find an extremely high positive correlation between a firm's crude production and its share of ownership in the pipeline. On the other hand, natural gas pipelines, although apparently economically similar in terms of potentially appropriable quasi rents, do not appear to be vertically integrated. Rather than joint-ownership arrangements with the gas producers, these pipelines are often independently owned. The difference may be due to more effective FPC (and now the Federal Energy Regulatory Commission) regulation (of the wellhead and citygate gas prices and the implied pipeline tariff) compared to the direct Interstate Commerce Commission regulation of oil pipelines as common carriers. Regulation of oil pipeline tariffs could, for example, be easily evaded by opportunistic decreases in the wellhead prices paid for oil. More complete government regulation of gas prices may effectively prevent opportunistic behavior by the natural gas pipeline owners, and thereby serve as an alternative to vertical integration. (See Victor P. Goldberg, *supra* note 9.) Edmund Kitch informs us that the evidence does indicate a much greater degree of vertical integration of natural gas pipelines in the period before FPC regulation.

32 Although our preliminary investigation indicates that control of the transportation system and vertical integration of it with the oil fields and refineries were significant, there were many other factors in Rockefeller's success. For example, the unpredictability of the life of oil fields raised the risks of a substantial investment in an integrated pipeline transportation system from one field. That Rockefeller correctly or luckily surmised that the Bradford field in 1874 would be long-lived was surely a source of his success. Also his skill in discovering consumer-preferred retailing methods, achieving lower-cost refining, and correctly assessing the ability to refine sulphurous Ohio crude undoubtedly were additional factors. See, for example, Ralph W. Hidy & Muriel E. Hidy, *History*

of Standard Oil Company (New Jersey): *Pioneering in Big Business 1882–1911* (1955); 1 & 2 Allan Nevins, John D. Rockefeller: *The Heroic Age of American Enterprise* (1940); and Harold F. Williamson & Arnold R. Daum, *The American Petroleum Industry* (1959).

This oil-pipeline analysis of appropriable specific capital may be applicable in many other situations. It should hold, for example, for ore mines and refineries which are specialized to each other. We predict that copper smelters specialized to a single mine will tend to be jointly owned, as will a cement quarry and its nearby smelter (mill). Railroad spur lines (and the land on which the track runs) from ore mines to smelters should likewise be owned by the mine-smelter owner. In addition, we would expect television program producers in an area with a single transmitter tower to be joint owners of the tower.

33 If the premium is a payment to the union per unit time, then the arrangement is identical to a collateral-bond arrangement where the union collects the interest on the bond as long as no opportunistic behavior occurs. Because of possible legal difficulties of enforcing such an arrangement, however, the premium may be reflected in the price (that is, a higher wage).

34 It is interesting to note in this context that California grape farmers preferred the established Teamsters Union to the new, untried, and apparently more politically motivated field-workers' union organized by Cesar Chavez.

Since unions are not "owned," union leaders will not have the proper incentive to maximize the union's value; they will tend more to maximize returns during their tenure. If, however, union leadership (ownership) were salable, the leaders would have the optimal incentive to invest in and conserve the union's brand-name capital. They therefore would not engage in opportunistic actions that may increase current revenue while decreasing the market value of the union. "Idealistic" union leaders that do not behave as if they own the union may, in fact, produce less wealth-maximizing action than would "corrupt" leaders, who act as if they personally own the union. Alternatively, the current members of the union may have control, not in the sense of having directly salable shares, but in the sense that the valuable union asset can be transferred to their children or relatives. If government regulations force union members to give away these rights to future rents (for example, by forcing them to admit minorities and eliminate nepotism), we can expect them to intentionally depreciate or not create the reputation capital of the union by opportunistic strikes. See Benjamin Klein, *supra* note 16, where similar problems with regard to the supply of money by nonprivately owned, nonwealth-maximizing firms are discussed.

35 An interesting legal case in this area is Publishers' Ass'n v. Newspaper & Mail Del. Union, 114 N.Y.S. 2d, 401 (1952). The union authorized and sanctioned a strike against the New York Daily News although the collective bargaining agreement had "no-strike" and arbitration clauses. The Daily News took the union to arbitration, and the arbitrator found actual damages of $2,000 and punitive damages of $5,000 if the union again violated the contract. (The court, however, overturned the punitive damages for technical reasons.) See David E. Feller, A General Theory of the Collective Bargaining Agreement, 61 *Calif. L. Rev.* 663 (1973), for a discussion of the flexibility obtained with arbitration provisions in labor contracts.

36 We should explicitly note that we are not considering unions as cartelizing devices, the usually analyzed motivation for their existence. This force is obviously present in many cases (for example, interstate trucking) but is distinct from our analysis.

37 When allowing for this "reverse" effect of employee-specific capital, and therefore higher wages, on the formation of unions, the usual positive effect of unions on wages appears to vanish. See, for example, 0. Ashenfelter & G. Johnson, Unionism, Relative Wages, and Labor Quality in U.S. Manufacturing Industries, 13 *Int'l Econ. Rev.* 488 (Oct. 1972); and Peter Schmidt & Robert P. Strauss, The Effect of Unions on Earnings and Earnings on Unions: A Mixed Logit Approach, 17 *Int'l Econ. Rev.* 204 (Feb. 1976).

38 Gary S. Becker, *Human Capital* 18–29 (1964).

39 This argument is distinct from the recent argument for the existence of rigid long-term implicit labor contracts as a means of bearing risk. See, for example, D. F. Gordon, A NeoClassical Theory of Keynesian Unemployment, 12 *Econ. Inquiry* 431 (Dec. 1974); and Costas Azariadis, Implicit Contracts and Underemployment Equilibria, 83 *J. Pol. Econ.* 1183 (1975). We should also note that although Masamori Hashimoto, Wage Reduction, Unemployment, and Specific Human Capital, 13 *Econ. Inquiry* 485 (Dec. 1975), has correctly argued that cyclically flexible wages are more likely when specific human capital is present because both workers and employers will want to

minimize the likelihood of job separation and thereby protect future returns on the specific human-capital investment, he ignores the contrary effect of increased specific human capital increasing the potential for opportunistic cheating and therefore increasing wage rigidity. The net theoretical effect is indeterminate. One possible reason that high-ranking corporate executives with a great deal of specific human capital appear to have highly flexible wages is because of the large amount of information about the firm they possess and therefore the shorter lag in detecting opportunism.

40 The recent "rational-expectations" approach to business cycles, which relies on consumer and producer uncertainty regarding whether a particular demand shock is a relative or an aggregate shift (see, for example, Robert E. Lucas, Jr., Some International Evidence on Output-Inflation Tradeoffs, 63 *Am. Econ. Rev.* 326 (1973)), implicitly assumes economic agents do not observe current movements of money supply and price level. A more realistic assumption is that economic agents are not "fooled," especially over long periods, about the nature of the shock but rather are bound, either explicitly or implicitly, by long-term contracts that have previously fixed prices.

41 A crucial determinant of economic organization is therefore the anticipated demand growth compared to the actual demand growth, or the demand growth anticipated at the time of contract and the demand growth actually experienced and therefore anticipated at some later time. For example, one possible reason for the recent movement by oil-refining companies towards vertically integrated retail-marketing operations may be the increased cost of controlling franchised dealers due to the large decrease in the anticipated growth of demand for gasoline in the period since the large OPEC-initiated price increase of crude oil. With demand growing slower than originally anticipated, the initial equilibrium "premium" earned by dealers will now be less than necessary to assure their noncheating behavior. The anticipated decrease in the total number of dealers (that is, the fact that future demand is anticipated to be zero for many dealers in the new equilibrium) will create last-period problems for particular locations that can be largely avoided by employee-operated outlets. See Benjamin Klein & Keith Leffler, *supra* note 16, for a more complete discussion of these issues.

42 Walter Galenson & Konosuke Odaka, The Japanese Labor Market, in *Asia's New Giant* 587 (Hugh Patrick & Henry Rosovsky eds. 1976); and Koji Taira, *Economic Development and the Labor Market in Japan* (1970), both documented the fact that this highly flexible wage feature of Japanese labor contracts did not become widespread until the postwar period, a time of extremely rapid growth.

43 In addition to computers being less specific and hence possessing smaller appropriable quasi rents than elevators, firms (for example, IBM) that supply computers generally possess extremely valuable brand names per unit of current sales due to a large anticipated growth in demand. Since there are some quasi rents associated with the use of a computer by a bank that could possibly be appropriated by threat of immediate removal, we would expect that if rental contracts existed they would more likely be with highly credible firms with high anticipated demand growth.

44 The great bulk of all refrigerator cars are not owned by the railroads, but rather by shipper-users such as packers and dairy companies. See Robert S. Henry, *This Fascinating Railroad Business* 247 (1942).

45 While 25% of vegetable and melon farms in California in 1974 were fully owned by the farm operator, 82% of fruit and nut tree farms were fully owned, a significantly different ownership proportion at the 99% confidence interval. Similarly, the ownership proportions of cash grain and cotton farms were 40% and 39%, respectively, both also significantly different at the 99% confidence interval from the proportions of fruit and nut tree farm ownership. See 1 U.S. Dep't of Commerce, Bureau of the Census, *1974 Census of Agriculture, State and County Data*, pt. 5, at tab. 28. Summary by Tenure of Farm Operator and Type of Organization, *id.*, 1974, California, pp. 1–29 to 1–30.

46 Rental terms may be related to sales of the firm using the land in order to share the risk of real-value changes and to reduce the risk of nominal land-value changes involved with a long-term contract.

47 Coase's example of a monopolist selling more of a durable good, say land, after initially selling a monopoly quantity at the monopoly price is analytically identical to the problem of postcontractual opportunistic behavior. Existing contractual relationships indicate, however, that the land case may be relatively easy to solve because it may not be expensive to make a credible contract regarding the remaining land. But, one of Coase's indicated solutions, the short-term rental rather than sale of the land is unlikely because it would discourage specific (to land) investments by the renter (such as building a house, developing a farm, and so forth) for fear of appropriation. See R. H. Coase, Durability and Monopoly, 15 *J. Law & Econ.* 143 (1972).

48 We are grateful to Earl Thompson for discerning this implication.

49 Armen A. Alchian & Harold Demsetz, Production, Information Costs, and Economic Organization, 62 *Am. Econ. Rev.* 777 (1972), claim that if the owner of the firm also owns the firm's capital it supplies evidence that he can pay for rented inputs, including labor. This appears to be incorrect since the owner could supply credibility by using some of his assets completely unrelated to the production process, such as treasury bonds, for collateral. Michael C. Jensen & William H. Meckling, *On the Labor-Managed Firm and the Codetermination Movement* (unpublished manuscript, Feb. 1977), emphasize the costs of monitoring managerial performance and the maintenance of rented capital, and the problems of efficiently allocating risks in a pure-rental firm. They also note that it is "impossible" for a firm to rent all the productive capital assets because many of them are intangible and therefore "it is impossible to repossess the asset if the firm refused to pay the rental fee" (*id.* at 20). This argument is similar to our analysis of opportunistic behavior. However, rather than asserting that such rentals are impossible, we would merely recognize the extremely high contracting costs generally present in such situations. More importantly, we claim that such an argument also extends to the rental of tangible specific capital.

50 The "free-rider" problems of bribing an opportunistic member to prevent sale to an "undesirable" member are obvious. This analysis could be applied to social clubs such as Elks, Masonic Order, and so forth.

51 Similarly, people whose work is highly specialized to each other will be partners (common ownership). For example, attorneys that have become highly specialized to their coattorneys will become partners, whereas new associates will at first be employees. A small team of performers (Laurel and Hardy, Sonny and Cher) who were highly specialized to each other would be "partners" (co-owners) rather than employee and employer. While it is still difficult to enforce such contracts and prevent postcontractual opportunistic behavior by either party, joint ownership creates an incentive for performance and specific investment not present in an easily terminable employer–employee contract that must rely solely on the personal brand-name reputation of contracting parties. Trust, including the reputation of certifying institutions such as theatrical agents, law schools, and so on, and the presence of social sanctions against opportunistic partners remain important.

52 The following discussion extends the analysis in Benjamin Klein, *supra* note 16.

53 The alternative cost of holding money will be significantly above the marginal cost of producing cash balances (where costs are defined exclusive of the costs necessary to guarantee nonopportunistic behavior), thereby leading to less than "the optimum" quantity of cash balances. See, for example, Milton Friedman, The Optimum Quantity of Money, in *The Optimum Quantity of Money and Other Essays* 1 (1969), for the original statement of this supposed inefficiency.

An alternative solution analytically equivalent to the "premium" solution would be the putting up by the dominant money supplier of a large forfeitable collateral bond equal to the value of the possible short-run wealth gain from cheating. This bond would be held in part by each of the demanders of the firm's money in proportion to each particular individual's money holdings and interest received on the bond by each individual would be paid to the firm if cheating did not occur. While this would not create any inefficiencies of price greater than marginal cost as implied by the premium solution, the transaction costs of enforcing such an arrangement among such a large and changing number of individuals would be extremely high. If the government acted as the consumers' agent, the solution would now be similar to a regulated industry, with the potential for opportunistic expropriation of the bond by the government.

54 If we think of firms as collections of interrelated contracts rather than the collection of goods operative in the contracts, the question of who "owns" the firm (the set of contracts) appears somewhat nonsensical. It may be useful to think solely of a set of claimants to various portions of the value consequences of the contractual coalition, with no "owner" of the firm.

13 Agency problems and the theory of the firm

Eugene F. Fama

This paper attempts to explain how the separation of security ownership and control, typical of large corporations, can be an efficient form of economic organization. We first set aside the presumption that a corporation has owners in any meaningful sense. The entrepreneur is also laid to rest, at least for the purposes of the large modern corporation. The two functions usually attributed to the entrepreneur – management and risk bearing – are treated as naturally separate factors within the set of contracts called a firm. The firm is disciplined by competition from other firms, which forces the evolution of devices for efficiently monitoring the performance of the entire team and of its individual members. Individual participants in the firm, and in particular its managers, face both the discipline and opportunities provided by the markets for their services, both within and outside the firm.

Economists have long been concerned with the incentive problems that arise when decision making in a firm is the province of managers who are not the firm's security holders.[1] One outcome has been the development of "behavioral" and "managerial" theories of the firm which reject the classical model of an entrepreneur, or ownermanager, who single-mindedly operates the firm to maximize profits, in favor of theories that focus more on the motivations of a manager who controls but does not own and who has little resemblance to the classical "economic man." Examples of this approach are Baumol (1959), Simon (1959), Cyert and March (1963), and Williamson (1964).

More recently the literature has moved toward theories that reject the classical model of the firm but assume classical forms of economic behavior on the part of agents within the firm. The firm is viewed as a set of contracts among factors of production, with each factor motivated by its self-interest. Because of its emphasis on the importance of rights in the organization established by contracts, this literature is characterized under the rubric "property rights." Alchian and Demsetz (1972) and Jensen and Meckling (1976) are the best examples. The antecedents of their work are in Coase (1937, 1960).

The striking insight of Alchian and Demsetz (1972) and Jensen and Meckling (1976) is in viewing the firm as a set of contracts among factors of production. In effect, the firm is viewed as a team whose members act from self-interest but realize that their destinies depend to some extent on the survival of the team in its competition with other teams. This insight, however, is not carried far enough. In the classical theory, the agent who personifies the firm is the entrepreneur who is taken to be both manager and residual risk bearer. Although his title sometimes changes – for example, Alchian and Demsetz call him "the employer" – the entrepreneur continues to play a central role in the firm of the property-rights literature. As a consequence, this literature fails to explain the large modern corporation in which control of the firm is in the hands of managers who are more or less separate from the firm's security holders.

The main thesis of this paper is that separation of security ownership and control can be explained as an efficient form of economic organization within the "set of contracts" perspective. We first set aside the typical presumption that a corporation has owners in any meaningful sense. The attractive concept of the entrepreneur is also laid to rest, at least for the purposes of the large modern corporation. Instead, the two functions usually attributed to the entrepreneur, management and risk bearing, are treated as naturally separate factors within the set of contracts called a firm. The firm is disciplined by competition from other firms, which forces the evolution of devices for efficiently monitoring the performance of the entire team and of its individual members. In addition, individual participants in the firm, and in particular its managers, face both the discipline and opportunities provided by the markets for their services, both within and outside of the firm.

The irrelevance of the concept of ownership of the firm

To set a framework for the analysis, let us first describe roles for management and risk bearing in the set of contracts called a firm. Management is a type of labor but with a special role – coordinating the activities of inputs and carrying out the contracts agreed among inputs, all of which can be characterized as "decision making." To explain the role of the risk bearers, assume for the moment that the firm rents all other factors of production and that rental contracts are negotiated at the beginning of each production period with payoffs at the end of the period. The risk bearers then contract to accept the uncertain and possibly negative difference between total revenues and costs at the end of each production period.

When other factors of production are paid at the end of each period, it is not necessary for the risk bearers to invest anything in the firm at the beginning of the period. Most commonly, however, the risk bearers guarantee performance of their contracts by putting up wealth ex ante, with this front money used to purchase capital and perhaps also the technology that the firm uses in its production activities. In this way the risk bearing function is combined with ownership of capital and technology. We also commonly observe that the joint functions of risk bearing and ownership of capital are repackaged and sold in different proportions to different groups of investors. For example, when front money is raised by issuing both bonds and common stock, the bonds involve a combination of risk bearing and ownership of capital with a low amount of risk bearing relative to the combination of risk bearing and ownership of capital inherent in the common stock. Unless the bonds are risk free, the risk bearing function is in part borne by the bondholders, and ownership of capital is shared by bondholders and stockholders.

However, ownership of capital should not be confused with ownership of the firm. Each factor in a firm is owned by somebody. The firm is just the set of contracts covering the way inputs are joined to create outputs and the way receipts from outputs are shared among inputs. In this "nexus of contracts" perspective, ownership of the firm is an irrelevant concept. Dispelling the tenacious notion that a firm is owned by its security holders is important because it is a first step toward understanding that control over a firm's decisions is not necessarily the province of security holders. The second step is setting aside the equally tenacious role in the firm usually attributed to the entrepreneur.

Management and risk bearing: a closer look

The entrepreneur (manager–risk bearer) is central in both the Jensen-Meckling and Alchian-Demsetz analyses of the firm. For example, Alchian-Demsetz state: "The essence of the classical firm is identified here as a contractual structure with: (1) joint input production; (2) several input owners; (3) one party who is common to all the contracts of the joint inputs; (4) who has the right to renegotiate any input's contract independently of contracts with other input owners; (5) who holds the residual claim; and (6) who has the right to sell his central contractual residual status. The central agent is called the firm's owner and the employer" (1972, p. 794).

To understand the modern corporation, it is better to separate the manager, the agents of points 3 and 4 of the Alchian-Demsetz definition of the firm, from the risk bearer described in points 5 and 6. The rationale for separating these functions is not just that the end result is more descriptive of the corporation, a point recognized in both the Alchian-Demsetz and Jensen-Meckling papers. The major loss in retaining the concept of the entrepreneur is that one is prevented from developing a perspective on management and risk bearing as separate factors of production, each faced with a market for its services that provides alternative opportunities and, in the case of management, motivation toward performance.

Thus, any given set of contracts, a particular firm, is in competition with other firms, which are likewise teams of cooperating factors of production. If there is a part of the team that has a special interest in its viability, it is not obviously the risk bearers. It is true that if the team does not prove viable factors like labor and management are protected by markets in which rights to their future services can be sold or rented to other teams. The risk bearers, as residual claimants, also seem to suffer the most direct consequences from the failings of the team. However, the risk bearers in the modern corporation also have markets for their services – capital markets – which allow them to shift among teams with relatively low transaction costs and to hedge against the failings of any given team by diversifying their holdings across teams.

Indeed, portfolio theory tells us that the optimal portfolio for any investor is likely to be diversified across the securities of many firms.[2] Since he holds the securities of many firms precisely to avoid having his wealth depend too much on any one firm, an individual security holder generally has no special interest in personally overseeing the detailed activities of any firm. In short, efficient allocation of risk bearing seems to imply a large degree of separation of security ownership from control of a firm.

On the other hand, the managers of a firm rent a substantial lump of wealth – their human capital – to the firm, and the rental rates for their human capital signaled by the managerial labor market are likely to depend on the success or failure of the firm. The function of management is to oversee the contracts among factors and to ensure the viability of the firm. For the purposes of the managerial labor market, the previous associations of a manager with success and failure are information about his talents. The manager of a firm, like the coach of any team, may not suffer any immediate gain or loss in current wages from the current performance of his team, but the success or failure of the team impacts his future wages, and this gives the manager a stake in the success of the team.

The firm's security holders provide important but indirect assistance to the managerial labor market in its task of valuing the firm's management. A security holder wants to purchase securities with confidence that the prices paid reflect the risks he is taking and that the securities will be priced in the future to allow him to reap the rewards (or punishments) of his risk bearing. Thus, although an individual security holder may not have a strong interest in directly overseeing the management of a particular firm, he has a strong interest in the existence of a capital market which efficiently prices the firm's securities. The signals provided by an efficient capital market about the values of a firm's securities are likely to be important for the managerial labor market's revaluations of the firm's management.

We come now to the central question. To what extent can the signals provided by the managerial labor market and the capital market, perhaps along with other market-induced mechanisms, discipline managers? We first discuss, still in general terms, the types of discipline imposed by managerial labor markets, both within and outside of the firm. We then analyze specific conditions under which this discipline is sufficient to resolve potential incentive problems that might be associated with the separation of security ownership and control.

The viability of separation of security ownership and control of the firm: general comments ·

The outside managerial labor market exerts many direct pressures on the firm to sort and compensate managers according to performance. One form of pressure comes from the fact that an ongoing firm is always in the market for new managers. Potential new managers are concerned with the mechanics by which their performance will be judged, and they seek information about the responsiveness of the system in rewarding performance. Moreover, given a competitive managerial labor market, when the firm's reward system is not responsive to performance the firm loses managers, and the best are the first to leave.

There is also much internal monitoring of managers by managers themselves. Part of the talent of a manager is his ability to elicit and measure the productivity of lower managers, so there is a natural process of monitoring from higher to lower levels of management. Less well appreciated, however, is the monitoring that takes place from bottom to top. Lower managers perceive that they can gain by stepping over shirking or less competent managers above them. Moreover, in the team or nexus of contracts view of the firm, each manager is concerned with the performance of managers above and below him since his marginal product is likely to be a positive function of theirs. Finally, although higher managers are affected more than lower managers, all managers realize that the managerial labor market uses the performance of the firm to determine each manager's outside opportunity wage. In short, each manager has a stake in the performance of the managers above and below him and, as a consequence, undertakes some amount of monitoring in both directions.

All managers below the very top level have an interest in seeing that the top managers choose policies for the firm which provide the most positive signals to the managerial labor market. But by what mechanism can top management be disciplined? Since the body designated for this function is the board of directors, we can ask how it might be constructed to do its job. A board dominated by security holders does not seem optimal or endowed with good survival properties. Diffuse ownership of securities is beneficial in terms of an optimal allocation of risk bearing, but its consequence is that the firm's security holders are generally too diversified across the securities of many firms to take much direct interest in a particular firm.

If there is competition among the top managers themselves (all want to be the boss of bosses), then perhaps they are the best ones to control the board of directors. They are most directly in the line of fire from lower managers when the markets for securities and managerial labor give poor signals about the performance of the firm. Because of their power over the firm's decisions, their market-determined opportunity wages are also likely to be most affected by market signals about the performance of the firm. If they are also in competition for the top places in the firm, they may be the most informed and responsive critics of the firm's performance.

Having gained control of the board, top management may decide that collusion and expropriation of security holder wealth are better than competition among themselves. The probability of such collusive arrangements might be lowered, and the viability of the board as a market-induced mechanism for low-cost internal transfer of control might be enhanced, by the inclusion of outside directors. The latter might best be regarded as professional referees whose task is to stimulate and oversee the competition among the firm's top managers. In a state of advanced evolution of the external markets that buttress the corporate firm, the outside directors are in their turn disciplined by the market for their services which prices them according to their performance as referees. Since such a system of separation of security ownership from control is consistent with the pressures applied by the managerial labor market, and since it likewise operates in the interests of the firm's security holders, it probably has good survival properties.[3]

This analysis does not imply that boards of directors are likely to be composed entirely of managers and outside directors. The board is viewed as a market-induced institution, the ultimate internal monitor of the set of contracts called a firm, whose most important role is to scrutinize the highest decision makers within the firm. In the team or nexus of contracts view of the firm, one cannot rule out the evolution of boards of directors that contain many different factors of production (or their hired representatives), whose common trait is that their marginal products are affected by those of the top decision makers. On the other hand, one also cannot conclude that all such factors will naturally show up on boards since there may be other market-induced institutions, for example, unions, that more efficiently monitor managers on behalf of specific factors. All one can say is that in a competitive environment lower-cost sets of monitoring mechanisms are likely to survive. The role of the board in this framework is to provide a relatively low-cost mechanism for replacing or reordering top managers; lower cost, for example, than the mechanism provided by an outside takeover, although, of course, the existence of an outside market for control is another force which helps to sensitize the internal managerial labor market.

The perspective suggested here owes much to, but is nevertheless different from, existing treatments of the firm in the property rights literature. Thus, Alchian (1969) and Alchian and Demsetz (1972) comment insightfully on the disciplining of management that takes place through the inside and outside markets for managers. However, they attribute the task of disciplining management primarily to the risk bearers, the firm's security holders, who are assisted to some extent by managerial labor markets and by the possibility of outside takeover. Jensen and Meckling (1976) likewise make control of management the province of the firm's risk bearers, but they do not allow for any assistance from the managerial labor market. Of all the authors in the property-rights literature, Manne (1965, 1967) is most concerned with the market for corporate control. He recognizes that with diffuse security ownership management and risk bearing are naturally separate functions. But for him, disciplining management is an "entrepreneurial job" which in the first instance falls on a firm's organizers and later on specialists in the process of outside takeover.

When management and risk bearing are viewed as naturally separate factors of production, looking at the market for risk bearing from the viewpoint of portfolio theory tells us that risk bearers are likely to spread their wealth across many firms and so not be interested in directly controlling the management of any individual firm. Thus, models of the firm, like those of

Alchian-Demsetz and Jensen-Meckling, in which the control of management falls primarily on the risk bearers, are not likely to allay the fears of those concerned with the apparent incentive problems created by the separation of security ownership and control. Likewise, Manne's approach, in which the control of management relies primarily on the expensive mechanism of an outside takeover, offers little comfort. The viability of the large corporation with diffuse security ownership is better explained in terms of a model where the primary disciplining of managers comes through managerial labor markets, both within and outside of the firm, with assistance from the panoply of internal and external monitoring devices that evolve to stimulate the ongoing efficiency of the corporate form, and with the market for outside takeovers providing discipline of last resort.

The viability of separation of security ownership and control: details

The preceding is a general discussion of how pressure from managerial labor markets helps to discipline managers. We now examine somewhat more specifically conditions under which the discipline imposed by managerial labor markets can resolve potential incentive problems associated with the separation of security ownership and control of the firm.

To focus on the problem we are trying to solve, let us first examine the situation where the manager is also the firm's sole security holder, so that there is clearly no incentive problem. When he is sole security holder, a manager consumes on the job, through shirking, perquisites, or incompetence, to the point where these yield marginal expected utility equal to that provided by an additional dollar of wealth usable for consumption or investment outside of the firm. The manager is induced to make this specific decision because he pays directly for consumption on the job; that is, as manager he cannot avoid a full ex post settling up with himself as security holder.

In contrast, when the manager is no longer sole security holder, and in the absence of some form of full ex post settling up for deviations from contract, a manager has an incentive to consume more on the job than is agreed in his contract. The manager perceives that, on an ex post basis, he can beat the game by shirking or consuming more perquisites than previously agreed. This does not necessarily mean that the manager profits at the expense of other factors. Rational managerial labor markets understand any shortcomings of available mechanisms for enforcing ex post settling up. Assessments of ex post deviations from contract will be incorporated into contracts on an ex ante basis; for example, through an adjustment of the manager's wage.

Nevertheless, a game which is fair on an ex ante basis does not induce the same behavior as a game in which there is also ex post settling up. Herein lie the potential losses from separation of security ownership and control of a firm. There are situations where, with less than complete ex post settling up, the manager is induced to consume more on the job than he would like, given that on average he pays for his consumption ex ante.

Three general conditions suffice to make the wage revaluation imposed by the managerial labor market a form of full ex post settling up which resolves the managerial incentive problem described above. The first condition is that a manager's talents and his tastes for consumption on the job are not known with certainty, are likely to change through time, and must be imputed by managerial labor markets at least in part from information about the manager's current and past performance. Since it seems to capture the essence of the task of managerial labor markets in a world of uncertainty, this assumption is no real restriction.

The second assumption is that managerial labor markets appropriately use current and past information to revise future wages and understand any enforcement power inherent in the wage revision process. In short, contrary to much of the literature on separation of security ownership and control, we impute efficiency or rationality in information processing to managerial labor markets. In defense of this assumption, we note that the problem faced by managerial labor markets in revaluing the managers of a firm is much entwined with the problem faced by the capital market in revaluing the firm itself. Although we do not understand all the details of the process, available empirical evidence (e.g., Fama 1976, chaps. 5 and 6) suggests that the capital market generally makes rational assessments of the value of the firm in the face of imprecise and uncertain information. This does not necessarily mean that information processing in managerial labor markets is equally efficient or rational, but it is a warning against strong presumptions to the contrary.

The final and key condition for full control of managerial behavior through wage changes is that the weight of the wage revision process is sufficient to resolve any potential problems with managerial incentives. In this general form, the condition amounts to assuming the desired result. More substance is provided by specific examples.

Example 1: Marketable human capital

Suppose a manager's human capital, his stream of future wages, is a marketable asset. Suppose the manager perceives that, because of the consequent revaluations of future wages, the current value of his human capital changes by at least the amount of an unbiased assessment of the wealth changes experienced by other factors, primarily the security holders, because of his current deviations from contract. Then, as long as the manager is not a risk preferrer, these revaluations of his human capital are a form of full ex post settling up. The manager need not be charged ex ante for presumed ex post deviations from contract since the weight of the wage revision process is sufficient to neutralize his incentives to deviate.

It is important to consider why the manager might perceive that the value of his human capital changes by at least the amount of an unbiased assessment of the wealth changes experienced by other factors due to his deviations from contract. Note first that the market's assessment of such wealth changes is also its assessment of the difference between the manager's ex post marginal product and the marginal product he contracted to deliver ex ante. However, any assessment of the manager's marginal product is likely to include extraneous noise which has little to do with his talents and efforts. Without specific details on what the market takes to be the statistical process governing the evolution of the manager's talents and his tastes for consumption on the job, one cannot say exactly how far it will go in adjusting his future wages to reflect its most recent measurement of his marginal product. Assuming the market uses information rationally, the adjustment is closer to complete the larger the signal in the most recent measurement relative to the noise, but as long as there is some noise in the process, the adjustment is less than complete. Specific illustrations of this point are provided later.

Although his next wage may not adjust by the full amount of an unbiased assessment of the current cost of his deviations from contract, a manager with a multiperiod horizon may perceive that the implied current wealth change, the present value of likely changes in the stream of future wages, is at least as great as the cost of his deviations from contract. In this case, the contemporaneous change in his wealth implied by an eventual adjustment of future wages is a form of full ex post settling up which results in full enforcement of his contract.

Moreover, the wage revision process resolves any potential problems about a manager's incentives even though the implied ex post settling up need not involve the firm currently employing the manager; that is, lower or higher future wages due to current deviations from contract may come from other firms.

Of course, changes in a manager's wealth as a consequence of anticipated future wage revisions are not always equivalent to full ex post settling up. When a manager does not expect to be in the labor market for many future periods, the weight of future wage revisions due to current assessments of performance may amount to substantially less than full ex post settling up. However, it is just as important to recognize that the weight of anticipations about future wages may amount to more than full ex post settling up. There may be situations where the personal wealth change perceived by the manager as a consequence of deviations from contract is greater than the wealth change experienced by other factors. Since many readers have had trouble with this point, it is well to bring it closer to home.

Economists (especially young economists) easily imagine situations where the effects of higher or lower quality of a current article or book on the market value of human capital, through enhancement or lowering of "reputation," are in excess of the effects of quality differences on the market value of the specific work to any publisher. Managers can sometimes have similar perceptions with respect to the implications of current performance for the market value of their human capital.

Example 2: Stochastic processes for marginal products

The next example of ex post settling up through the wage revision process is somewhat more formal than that described above. We make specific assumptions about the stochastic evolution of a manager's measured marginal product and about how the managerial labor market uses information from the process to adjust the manager's future wages – in a manner which amounts to precise, full ex post settling up for the results of past performance.

Suppose the manager's measured marginal product for any period t is composed of two terms: (i) an expected value, given his talents, effort exerted during t, consumption of perquisites, etc.; and (ii) random noise. The random noise may in part result from measurement error, that is, the sheer difficulty of accurately measuring marginal products when there is team production, but it may also arise in part from the fact that effort exerted and talent do not yield perfectly certain consequences. Moreover, because of the uncertain evolution of the manager's talents and tastes, the expected value of his marginal product is itself a stochastic process. Specifically, we assume that the expected value, $\bar{z}_t$, follows a random walk with steps that are independent of the random noise, ϵ_t, in the manager's measured marginal product, z_t. Thus, the measured marginal product,

$$z_t = \bar{z}_t + \epsilon_t, \tag{13.1}$$

is a random walk plus white noise. For simplicity, we also assume that this process describes the manager's marginal product both in his current employment and in the best alternative employment.

The characteristics (parameters) of the evolution of the manager's marginal product depend to some extent on endogenous variables like effort and perquisites consumed, which are not completely observable. Our purpose is to set up the managerial labor market so that the wage revision process resolves any potential incentive problems that may arise from the endogeneity of z_t in a situation where there is separation of security ownership and control of the firm.

Suppose next that risk bearers are all risk neutral and that 1-period market interest rates are always equal to zero. Suppose also that managerial wage contracts are written so that the manager's wage in any period t is the expected value of his marginal product, $\bar{z}_t$, conditional on past measured values of his marginal product, with the risk bearers accepting the noise ϵ_t, in the ex post measurement of the marginal product. We shall see below that this is an optimal arrangement for our risk-neutral risk bearers. However, it is not necessarily optimal for the manager if he is risk averse. A risk-averse manager may want to sell part of the risk inherent in the uncertain evolution of his expected marginal product to the risk bearers, for example, through a long-term wage contract.

We avoid this issue by assuming that, perhaps because of the more extreme moral hazard problems in long-term contracts (remember that $\bar{z}_t$ is in part under the control of the manager) and the contracting costs to which these moral hazard problems give rise, simple contracts in which the manager's wage is reset at the beginning of each period are dominant, at least for some nontrivial subset of firms and managers.[4] If we could also assume away any remaining moral hazard (managerial incentive) problems, then with risk-averse managers, risk-neutral risk bearers, and the presumed fixed recontracting period, the contract which specifies ex ante that the manager will be paid the current expected value of his marginal product dominates any contract where the manager also shares the ex post deviation of his measured marginal product from its ex ante expected value (see, e.g., Spence and Zeckhauser 1971).

However, contracts which specify ex ante that the manager will be paid the current expected value of his marginal product seem to leave the typical moral hazard problem that arises when there is less than complete ex post enforcement of contracts. The noise ϵ_t in the manager's marginal product is borne by the risk bearers. Once the manager's expected marginal product $\bar{z}_t$, (=his current wage) has been assessed, he seems to have an incentive to consume more perquisites and provide less effort than are implied in $\bar{z}_t$.

A mechanism for ex post enforcement is, however, built into the model. With the expected value of the manager's marginal product wandering randomly through time, future assessments of expected marginal products (and thus of wages) will be determined in part by ϵ_t, the deviation of the current measured marginal product from its ex ante expected value. In the present scenario, where $\bar{z}_t$ is assumed to follow a random walk, Muth (1960) has shown that the expected value of the marginal product evolves according to

$$\bar{z}_t = \bar{z}_{t-1} + (1-\phi)\epsilon_{t-1}, \tag{13.2}$$

where the parameter ϕ $(0<\phi<1)$ is closer to zero the smaller the variance of the noise term in the marginal product equation (13.1) relative to the variance of the steps in the random walk followed by the expected marginal product.

In fact, the process by which future expected marginal products are adjusted on the basis of past deviations of marginal products from their expected values leads to a precise form of full ex post settling up. This is best seen by writing the marginal product z_t in its inverted form, that is, in terms of past marginal products and the current noise. The inverted form for our model, a random walk embedded in random noise, is

$$z_t = (1-\phi)z_{t-1} + \phi(1-\phi)z_{t-2} + \phi^2(1-\phi)z_{t-3} + \cdots + \epsilon_t, \tag{13.3}$$

so that

$$\bar{z}_t = (1 - \phi)z_{t-1} + \phi(1 - \phi)z_{t-2} + \phi^2(1 - \phi)z_{t-3} + \cdots \tag{13.4}$$

(see, e.g., Nelson 1973, chap. 4, or Muth 1960).

For our purposes, the interesting fact is that, although he is paid his ex ante expected marginal product, the manager does not get to avoid his ex post marginal product. For example, we can infer from (13.4) that z_{t-1} has weight $1 - \phi$ in $\bar{z}_t$; then it has weight $\phi(1 - \phi)$ in $\bar{z}_{t+1}$, $\phi^2(1 - \phi)$ in $\bar{z}_{t+2}$ and so on. In the end, the sum of the contributions of z_{t-1} to future expected marginal products, and thus to future wages, is exactly z_{t-1}. With zero interest rates, this means that the risk bearers simply allow the manager to smooth his marginal product across future periods at the going opportunity cost of all such temporal wealth transfers. As a consequence, the manager has no incentive to try to bury shirking or consumption of perquisites in his ex post measured marginal product.

Since the managerial labor market is presumed to understand the weight of the wage revision process, which in this case amounts to precise full ex post settling up, any potential managerial incentive problems in the separation of risk bearing, or security ownership, from control are resolved. The manager can contract for and take an optimal amount of consumption on the job. The wage set ex ante need not include any allowance for ex post incentives to deviate from the contract since the wage revision process neutralizes any such incentives. Note, moreover, that the value of ϕ in the wage revision process described by (13.4) determines how the observed marginal product of any given period is subdivided and spread across future periods, but whatever the value of ϕ, the given marginal product is fully accounted for in the stream of future wages. Thus, it is now clear what was meant by the earlier claim that although the parameter ϕ in the process generating the manager's marginal product is to some extent under his control, this is not a matter of particular concern to the managerial labor market.

A somewhat evident qualification is in order. The smoothing process described by (13.4) contains an infinite number of terms, whereas any manager has a finite working life. For practical purposes, full ex post settling up is achieved as long as the manager's current marginal product is "very nearly" fully absorbed by the stream of wages over his future working life. This requires a value of ϕ in (13.4) which is sufficiently far from 1.0, given the number of periods remaining in the manager's working life. Recall that ϕ is closer to 1.0 the larger the variance of the noise in the manager's measured marginal product relative to the variance of the steps of the random walk taken by the expected value of his marginal product. Intuitively, when the variance of the noise term is large relative to that of the changes in the expected value, the current measured marginal product has a weak signal about any change in the expected value of the marginal product, and the current marginal product is only allocated slowly to expected future marginal products.

Some extensions

Having qualified the analysis, let us now indicate some ways in which it is robust to changes in details of the model.

MORE COMPLICATED MODELS FOR THE MANAGER'S MARGINAL PRODUCT

The critical ingredient in enforcing precise full ex post settling up through wage revisions on the basis of reassessments of expected marginal products is that when the marginal product and its expected value are expressed in inverted form, as in (13.3) and (13.4), the sum of the weights on past marginal products is exactly 1.0. This will be the case (see, e.g., Nelson 1973, chap. 4) whenever the manager's marginal product conforms to a nonstationary stochastic process, but the changes from period to period in the marginal product conform to some stationary ARMA (mixed autoregressive moving average) process. The example summarized in equations (13.1)–(13.4) is the interesting but special case where the expected marginal product follows a random walk so that the differences of the marginal product are a stationary, first-order moving average process. The general case allows the expected value of the marginal product to follow any more complicated nonstationary process which has the property that the differences of the marginal product are stationary, so that the marginal product and its expected value can be expressed in inverted form as

$$z_t = \pi_1 z_{t-1} + \pi_2 z_{t-2} + \cdots + \epsilon_t \tag{13.5}$$

$$\bar{z}_t = \pi_1 z_{t-1} + \pi_2 z_{t-2} + \cdots \tag{13.6}$$

with

$$\sum_{i=1}^{\infty} \pi_1 = 1. \tag{13.7}$$

These can be viewed as the general conditions for enforcing precise full ex post settling through the wage revision process when the manager's wage is equal to the current expected value of his marginal product.[5]

RISK-AVERSE RISK BEARERS

In the framework summarized in equations (13.5)–(13.7), if the manager switches firms, the risk bearers of his former firm are left with the remains of his measured marginal products not previously absorbed into the expected value of his marginal product. Nevertheless, in the way we have set up the world, the risk bearers realize that the manager's next firm continues to set his wage according to the same stochastic process as the last firm. Since this results in full ex post settling up on the part of the manager, the motive for switching firms cannot be to avoid perverse adjustments of future wages on the basis of past performance. On average, the switching of managers among firms does not result in gains or losses to risk bearers, which means that the switches are a matter of indifference to our presumed risk-neutral risk bearers.

It is, however, interesting to examine how the analysis might change when the risk bearers are risk averse and switching of managers among firms is not a matter of indifference. Suppose, for the moment, that the risk bearers offer managers contracts where, as before, the manager's wage tracks the expected value of his marginal product, but each period there is also a fixed discount in the wage to compensate the risk bearers for the risks of unfinished ex post settling up with the firm as a consequence of a possible future shift by the manager to another firm. Such an arrangement may satisfy the risk bearers, but it will not be acceptable to the manager. As long as his marginal product evolves according to equations (13.5)–(13.7), both in his current firm and in the best alternative, the manager is subject to full ex post settling up. Thus, any risk adjustment of his wage to reflect the fact that the settling up may not be with his current firm is an uncompensated loss which he will endeavor to avoid.

The manager can avoid any risk discount in his wage, and maintain complete freedom to switch among firms, by himself bearing all the risk of his marginal product; that is, he contracts to accept, at the end of each period, his ex post measured marginal product rather than its ex ante expected value so that there is, period by period, full ex post settling up with his current firm. There is such a presumption against the optimality of immediate, full ex post settling up in the literature on optimal contracting that it behooves us to examine how and why it works, and is optimal, in the circumstances under examination.

Contractual settling up

The literature on optimal contracting, for example, Harris and Raviv (1978, 1979), Holmstrom (1979), and Shavell (1979), suggests uniformly that when there is noise in the manager's marginal product, that is, when the deviation of measured marginal product from its expected value cannot be traced unambiguously and costlessly to the manager's actions (talents, effort exerted, and consumption on the job), then a risk-averse manager will always choose to share part of the uncertainty in the evaluation of his performance with the firm's risk bearers. He will agree to some amount of ex post settling up, but always less than 100 percent of the deviation of his measured marginal product from its ex ante expected value. In short, the contracting models suggest that we must learn to live with the incentive problems that arise when there is less than complete ex post enforcement of contracts.

The contracting literature is almost uniformly concerned with 1-period models. In a 1-period world, there can be no enforcement of contracts through a wage revision process imposed by the managerial labor market. The existence of this form of ex post settling up in a multiperiod world affects the manager's willingness to engage in explicit contractual ex post settling up.

For example, in the model summarized in equations (13.5)–(13.7), the manager's wage in any period is the expected value of his marginal product assessed at the beginning of the period, and the manager does not immediately share any of the deviation of his ex post marginal product from its ex ante expected value. However, because it contains information about future expected values of his marginal product, eventually the manager's current measured marginal product is allocated in full to future expected marginal products. Equivalently, in the wage revision process described by equations (13.5)–(13.7), the managerial labor market in effect acts as a financial intermediary. It withdraws portions of past accumulated measured marginal products to pay the manager a dividend on his human capital equal to the expected value of his marginal product, and implicitly provides the lending arrangements which allow the manager to spread his current measured marginal product over future periods in precisely the way the current marginal product will contribute to expected future marginal products.

Looked at from this perspective, however, the manager might simply contract to take the ex post measured value of his marginal product as his wage and then himself use the capital market to smooth his measured marginal product over future periods. Since the same asset (his human capital) is involved, the manager should be able to carry out these smoothing transactions via the capital market on the same terms as can be had in the managerial labor market. The advantage to the manager in smoothing through the capital market, however, is that he can then contract to accept full ex post settling up period by period (he is paid his measured marginal product), which means he can avoid any risk discount in his wage that might be imposed when he is paid the expected value of his marginal product with the possibility of unanticipated switches to other firms.[6]

It is important to recognize that using the capital market in the manner described above allows the manager to "average out" the random noise in his measured marginal product. Thus, when he is instead paid the expected value of his marginal product each period, and when the process generating his marginal product is described by equations (13.5)–(13.7), the manager's current measured marginal product is eventually allocated in full to future expected marginal products. This happily, but only coincidentally, resolves incentive problems by imposing full ex post settling up. The allocation of the current marginal product to future expected marginal products in fact occurs because the current marginal product has information about future expected marginal products. The weights π_i in equations (13.5)–(13.7) are precisely those that optimally extract this information and so optimally smooth or average out the purely random noise in the manager's measured marginal product. The manager can achieve the same result by contracting to be paid the measured value of his marginal product and then using the capital market to smooth his marginal product. This power of the capital market to reduce the terror in full contractual ex post settling up is lost in the 1-period models that dominate the contracting literature.

Conclusion

The model summarized by equations (13.5)–(13.7) is one specific scenario in which the wage revision process imposed by the managerial labor market amounts to full ex post settling up by the manager for his past performance. The important general point is that in any scenario where the weight of the wage revision process is at least equivalent to full ex post settling up, managerial incentive problems – the problems usually attributed to the separation of security ownership and control of the firm – are resolved.

No claim is made that the wage revision process always results in a full ex post settling up on the part of the manager. There are certainly situations where the weight of anticipated future wage changes is insufficient to counterbalance the gains to be had from ex post shirking, or perhaps outright theft, in excess of what was agreed ex ante in a manager's contract. On the other hand, precise full ex post settling up is not an upper bound on the force of the wage revision process. There are certainly situations where, as a consequence of anticipated future wage changes, a manager perceives that the value of his human capital changes by more than the wealth changes imposed on other factors, and especially the firm's security holders, by his current deviations from the terms of his contract.

The extent to which the wage revision process imposes ex post settling up in any particular situation is, of course, an empirical issue. But it is probably safe to say that the general phenomenon is at least one of the ingredients in the survival of the modern large corporation, characterized by diffuse security ownership and the separation of security ownership and control, as a viable form of economic organization.

Acknowledgments

This research is supported by the National Science Foundation. Roger Kormendi has contributed much, and the comments of A. Alchian, S. Bhattacharya, G. Becker, F. Black, M. Blume, M. Bradley, D. Breeden, N. Gonedes, B. Horwitz, G. Jarrell, E. H. Kim, J. Long, H. Manne, W. Meckling, M. H. Miller, M. Scholes, C. Smith, G. J. Stigler, R. Watts, T. Whisler, and J. Zimmerman are gratefully acknowledged. Presentations at the finance, labor economics, and industrial organization workshops of the University of Chicago and the workshop of the Managerial Economics Research Center of the University of Rochester have been helpful. The paper is largely an outgrowth of discussions with Michael C. Jensen.

Notes

1 Jensen and Meckling (1976) quote from Adam Smith (1776). The modern literature on the problem dates back at least to Berle and Means (1932).
2 Detailed discussions of portfolio models can be found in Fama and Miller (1972, chaps. 6 and 7), Jensen (1972), and Fama (1976, chaps. 7 and 8).
3 Watts and Zimmerman (1978) provide a similar description of the market-induced evolution of "independent" outside auditors whose function is to certify and, as a consequence, stimulate the viability of the set of contracts called the firm. Like the outside directors, the outside auditors are policed by the market for their services which prices them in large part on the basis of how well they resist perverting the interests of one set of factors (e.g., security holders) to the benefit of other factors (e.g., management). Like the professional outside director, the welfare of the outside auditor depends largely on "reputation."
4 Institutions like corporations, that are subject to rapid technological change with a large degree of uncertainty about future managerial needs, may find that long-term managerial contracts can only be negotiated at high cost. On the other hand, institutions like governments, schools, and universities may be able to forecast more reliably their future needs for managers (and other professionals) and so may be able to offer long-term contracts at relatively low cost. These institutions can then be expected to attract the relatively risk-averse members of the professional labor force, while the riskier employment offered by corporations attracts those who are willing to accept shorter-term contracts.
5 When $\bar{z}_t$, follows a stationary process, the long-run average value toward which the process always tends will eventually be known with near perfect certainty. Thus, the case of a stationary expected marginal product is of little interest, at least for the purposes of ex post settling up enforced by the wage revision process.
6 With positive interest rates, contracting to be paid his measured marginal product and then using the capital market to smooth the marginal product over future periods dominates the contract in which the manager is paid the expected value of his marginal product. Equivalence can be restored by adjusting the expected marginal product $\bar{z}_t$, in eq. (13.6) for accumulated interest on the past marginal products, $z_{t-1}, z_{t-2}, \ldots$, or by prepaying the present value of interest on the deferrals of the current marginal product over future periods. Suffice it to say, however, that either accumulation or prepayment of interest complicates the problems posed by possible shifts of the manager to other firms and so may lean the system toward contracts in which the manager is paid his measured marginal product and then uses the capital market to achieve optimal smoothing.

References

Alchian, Armen A. "Corporate Management and Property Rights." In *Economic Policy and the Regulation of Corporate Securities*, edited by Henry G. Manne. Washington: American Enterprise Inst. Public Policy Res., 1969.

Alchian, Armen A., and Demsetz, Harold. "Production, Information Costs, and Economic Organization. *A.E.R.* 62 (December 1972): 777–95.

Bautnol, William J. *Business Behavior, Value and Growth.* New York: Macmillan, 1959.

Berle, Adolph A., Jr., and Means, Gardiner C. *The Modern Corporation and Private Property.* New York: Macmillan, 1932.

Coase, Ronald H. "The Nature of the Firm." *Economica*, n.s. 4 (November 1937): 386–405.

——. "The Problem of Social Cost." *J. Law and Econ.* 3 (October 1960): 1–44.

Cyert, Richard M., and March, James G. *A Behavioral Theory of the Firm.* Englewood Cliffs, N.J.: Prentice-Hall, 1963.

Fama, Eugene F. *Foundations of Finance.* New York: Basic, 1976.

Fama, Eugene F., and Miller, Merton H. *The Theory of Finance.* New York: Holt, Rinehart & Winston, 1972.

Harris, Milton, and Raviv, Artur. "Some Results on Incentive Contracts with Applications to Education and Employment, Health Insurance, and Law Enforcement." *A.E.R.* 68 (March 1978): 20–30.

——. "Optimal Incentive Contracts with Imperfect Information." Working Paper no. 70-75-76, Carnegie-Mellon Univ., Graduate School of Indus. Admin., April 1976 (rev. January 1979), forthcoming in *J. Econ. Theory* 20(2)(1979): 231–259.

Holmström, Bengt. "Moral Hazard and Observability." *Bell J. Econ.* 10 (Spring 1979): 74–91.

Jensen, Michael C. "Capital Markets: Theory and Evidence." *Bell J. Econ. and Management Sci.* 3 (Autumn 1972): 357–98.

Jensen, Michael C., and Meckling, William H. "Theory of the Firm: Managerial Behavior, Agency Costs and Ownership Structure." *J. Financial Econ.* 3 (October 1976): 305–60.

Manne, Henry G. "Mergers and the Market for Corporate Control." *J.P.E.* 73, no. 2 (April 1965): 110–20.

——. "Our Two Corporate Systems: Law and Economics." *Virginia Law Rev.* 53 (March 1967): 259–85.

Muth, John F. "Optimal Properties of Exponentially Weighted Forecasts." *J. American Statis. Assoc.* 55 (June 1960): 299–306.

Nelson, Charles R. *Applied Time Series Analysis for Managerial Forecasting.* San Francisco: Holden-Day, 1973.

Shavell, Steven. "Risk Sharing and Incentives in the Principal and Agent Relationship." *Bell I Econ.* 10 (Spring 1979): 55–73.

Simon, Herbert A. "Theories of Decision Making in Economics and Behavioral Science." *A.E.R.* 49 (June 1959): 253–83.

Smith, Adam. *The Wealth of Nations.* 1776. Cannan ed. New York: Modern Library, 1937.

Spence, Michael, and Zeckhauser, Richard. "Insurance, Information and Individual Action." *A.E.R.* 61 (May 1971): 380–87.

Watts, Ross L., and Zimmerman, Jerold. "Auditors and the Determination of Accounting Standards, an Analysis of the Lack of Independence." Working Paper GPB 7806, Univ. Rochester, Graduate School of Management, 1978.

Williamson, Oliver E. *The Economics of Discretionary Behavior: Managerial Objectives in a Theory of the Firm.* Englewood Cliffs, N.J.: Prentice-Hall, 1964.

Part III

Theory of the market

Introduction

The contemporary theory of the market has veered away from the neoclassical classification where the degree of competition (often proxied by the number of firms), entry and exit conditions, and product homogeneity (or not) are the main criteria. The nature of the strategic decisions among firms are increasingly taken into consideration in distinguishing types of markets. In addition, with information asymmetry being a fact, more emphasis has been placed on the difference between contemporaneous and intertemporal markets: after all, it is absurd to assume that there is information symmetry among markets separated in time.

The papers chosen for this part cover four topics: (1) market and information, (2) competitiveness, (3) strategy, and (4) institutional economics and macroeconomics.

Market and information

In his classic 1945 paper, Friedrich Hayek[1] pointed out that, unlike central planning, the price system (i.e., the market) is efficient in communicating information in an environment in which "the knowledge of the relevant fact is dispersed among many people" (1945, p. 525). Although Hayek's concern was not with any specific microeconomic problem, his insight has inspired works on the role of information, especially on the possibility that ignoring information cost might not only obscure some important aspects of a problem but might also alter its very nature.[2]

Another pioneer in the economics of information is Stiglitz (2001). While Hayek pointed to the costliness of information to assert the infeasibility of central planning, Stiglitz (and like-minded authors) pointed to the need for information to argue that the notion of competitive equilibrium is untethered to reality.[3]

Dealing directly with a microeconomic phenomenon, Akerlof (1970) showed, taking the used cars market as an example, that severe information asymmetries (i.e., one side of a transaction knows a lot more than does the other) could snuff out a market.

Competitiveness

Surely the fundamental question regarding any market is how competitive it is, and one determinant of this, especially in the long run, is how easy it is for new firms to enter the industry. Hence the role of entry barriers.

The seminal work on entry barriers is Bain (1956). Bain defined an entry barrier as the set of technology or product conditions that allow incumbent firms, but not new entrants, to earn economic profits in the long run. According to Bain, these conditions are the incumbent firms' (a) economies of scale, (b) product differentiation, and (c) absolute cost advantages. Stigler (1968) objected to this view, especially the suggestion that scale economies could prevent new entrants (if the industry is profitable enough, he reckoned, new firms would enter on a large scale). In Stigler's alternative definition, an entry barrier exists if a cost of producing must be borne by an entrant but not by an incumbent.[4]

The connection between entry barriers and the degree of competition is the key in William Baumol's theory of contestable markets. Baumol made the case that entry barriers (much more so than the sheer number of firms) are the principal cause of imperfect competition. In his model, if entry is free, the industry is "contestable," then the market would be almost as "efficient" as in perfect competition, even if the actual number of firms is relatively small.

Strategy

Most readers are familiar with the oligopoly models of Cournot, Bertrand and Stackelberg. One problem with these models is that they seem to leave the firm's conjecture (about the reaction of other firm(s)) as an ad hoc exogeneous parameter. Bresnahan (1981) closed this loophole by proposing the concept of a "consistent conjecture." A conjecture is consistent if it results in an industry equilibrium when every firm has this conjecture. This model was generalized by Perry (1982), analyzed by Dixit (1986), among others.

Entry-deterrence strategy has also received considerable attention in the literature. One significant trend in modern microeconomics attempts to connect market structures with the decision of many firms in these markets, as we have seen in the case of entry barriers. There are doubts about the game-theoretic approach to oligopoly, however, as articulated by Aumann (1985), Sutton (1990), and several others.

Institutional economics and macroeconomics

It would be wrong to leave readers with the impression that the neoclassical approach, perhaps augmented with game theory, is the only economic theory of markets. In fact, the richness of "heterodox" (i.e., non-neoclassical) economics is most pronounced in its view of the markets. Williamson (2000) and Hodgson (1998) are two versions of what has become known as "institutional economics." Williamson took off from Coase's transactions-cost view and considered the economy as institutions. Hodgson, on the other hand, inherited the "old" institutionalism of Thorsten Veblen and applied it to both micro and macroeconomics. Interestingly, this area (market theory) of microeconomics has stirred up fresh attention to the microfoundation of macroeconomics, mainly due to the availability of more realistic models of labor and capital markets, whose unique characteristics had resisted fruitful analyses heretofore.

Part III has six articles. Hayek (1945) and Akerlof (1970) are two "must-read" articles. Stiglitz (2001) is a good historical survey of the role of information in economics. The references included in this paper provide a useful guide to dig further into the literature. Bresnahan (1981) introduced the concept of consistent conjectural variations. Fisher (1989) gave a skeptical view of the game-theoretic approach. Hodgson (1998) is a useful survey of the connection between microeconomics and institutional economics.

Notes

1 Not very prolific, and somewhat ideologically divisive, Fredrich Hayek was nevertheless among the most influential economists of the twentieth century. See Wapshott (2011) for a lively chronicle of Hayek and Keynes.

2 Coase (1937) also touched on the importance of information, but his conclusion was different from Hayek's: "The main reason why it is profitable to establish a firm would seem to be that there is a cost of using the price mechanism. The most obvious cost of 'organizing' production through the price mechanism is that of *discovering what the relevant prices are*" (p. 390, emphasis added). In other words, Coase suggested that information costs are what made firms superior to the market, at least in many instances.

3 As Stiglitz (2001) put it: "The (competitive) model virtually made economics a branch of engineering [...], and the participants in the economy better or worse engineers. Each was solving a maximization problem, with full information: households maximizing utility subject to budget constraints, firms maximizing profits, and the two interacting in competitive product, labor, and capital markets."

4 Again, notice Stigler's tendency to use the simplest definition possible, even by stripping some of the interesting details easily observed in reality. This is the same methodology that prompted him to dismiss Leibenstein's bandwagon effect, snob effect, addiction, etc.

Bibliography

Akerlof, G. A. (1970) "The Market for 'Lemons': Quality Uncertainty and the Market Mechanism," *The Quarterly Journal of Economics* 84(3): 488–500.

Aumann, R. (1985) "What is Game Theory Trying to Accomplish?," in *Frontiers of Economics*, edited by K. Arrow and S. Hankapohja, Oxford: Basil Blackwell, pp. 28–78.

Bain, J. (1956) *Barriers to New Competition: Their Character and Consequences in Manufacturing Industries.* Cambridge, MA: Harvard University Press, 1956.

Baumol, W., Pazar, J. and Willig, R. (1982) *Contestable Markets and the Theory of Industrial Structure.* New York: Harcourt, Brace, Jovanovich.

Bresnahan, T. F. (1981) "Duopoly Models with Consistent Conjectures," *American Economic Review*, 71: 934–45.

Carlton, D. (2004) "Why Barriers to Entry are Barriers to Understanding," *American Economic Review* 94, pp. 466–70.

Coase, R. (1937) "The Nature of the Firm," *Economica*, N.S.4, pp. 386–405.

Demsetz, H. (1982) "Barriers to Entry," *American Economic Review* 72, pp. 47–57.

Dixit, A. (1986) "Comparative Statics for Oligopoly," *International Economics Review* 27, pp. 107–22.

Fisher, F. M. (1989) "Games Economists Play. A Noncooperative View," *The Rand Journal of Economics* 20(1): 113–24.

Hayek, F. (1945) 'The Use of Knowledge in Society,' *American Economic Review* 35(4), pp. 519–30.

Hodgson, G. (1998) 'The Approach of Institutional Economics,' *Journal of Economic Literature* 36, pp. 166–92.

Nalebuff, B. (2004) "Bundling as an Entry Barrier," *Quarterly Journal of Economics* 119, pp. 159–187.

Nalebuff, B. and Stiglitz, J. (1983) "Prizes and Incentives: Toward a General Theory of Compensation and Competition," *Bell Journal of Economics* 14, pp. 21–43.

Perry, M. K. (1982) "Oligopoly and Consistent Conjectural Variations," *Bell Journal of Economics* 13, pp. 197–205.

Stigler, G. J. (1961) "The Economics of Information," *Journal of Political Economy* 69, pp. 213–235.

Stigler, G. J. (1968) *The Organization of Industry.* Homewood, Ill.: Richard D. Irwin.

Stiglitz, J. (2001) "Information and the Change in the Paradigm of Economics," Nobel Lecture.

Sutton, J. (1990) "Explaining Everything, Explaining Nothing? Game Theoretic Models in Industrial Economics," *European Economic Review* 34, pp. 505–12.

Wapshott, N. (2011) *Keynes vs. Hayek: The Clash that Defined Modern Economics*, New York: Norton.

Williamson, O. (2000) "The New Institutional Economics: Taking Stock, Looking Ahead," *Journal of Economic Literature*, 38: 595–613.

14 The use of knowledge in society

F. A. Hayek

I

What is the problem we wish to solve when we try to construct a rational economic order?

On certain familiar assumptions the answer is simple enough. *If* we possess all the relevant information, *if* we can start out from a given system of preferences and *if* we command complete knowledge of available means, the problem which remains is purely one of logic. That is, the answer to the question of what is the best use of the available means is implicit in our assumptions. The conditions which the solution of this optimum problem must satisfy have been fully worked out and can be stated best in mathematical form: put at their briefest, they are that the marginal rates of substitution between any two commodities or factors must be the same in all their different uses.

This, however, is emphatically *not* the economic problem which society faces. And the economic calculus which we have developed to solve this logical problem, though an important step toward the solution of the economic problem of society, does not yet provide an answer to it. The reason for this is that the "data" from which the economic calculus starts are never for the whole society "given" to a single mind which could work out the implications, and can never be so given.

The peculiar character of the problem of a rational economic order is determined precisely by the fact that the knowledge of the circumstances of which we must make use never exists in concentrated or integrated form, but solely as the dispersed bits of incomplete and frequently contradictory knowledge which all the separate individuals possess. The economic problem of society is thus not merely a problem of how to allocate "given" resources – if "given" is taken to mean given to a single mind which deliberately solves the problem set by these "data." It is rather a problem of how to secure the best use of resources known to any of the members of society, for ends whose relative importance only these individuals know. Or, to put it briefly, it is a problem of the utilization of knowledge not given to anyone in its totality.

This character of the fundamental problem has, I am afraid, been rather obscured than illuminated by many of the recent refinements of economic theory, particularly by many of the uses made of mathematics. Though the problem with which I want primarily to deal in this paper is the problem of a rational economic organization, I shall in its course be led again and again to point to its close connections with certain methodological questions. Many of the points I wish to make are indeed conclusions toward which diverse paths of reasoning have unexpectedly converged. But as I now see these problems, this is no accident. It seems to me that many of the current disputes with regard to both economic theory and economic policy have their common origin in a misconception about the nature of the economic problem of society. This misconception in turn is due to an erroneous transfer to social phenomena of the habits of thought we have developed in dealing with the phenomena of nature.

II

In ordinary language we describe by the word "planning" the complex of interrelated decisions about the allocation of our available resources. All economic activity is in this sense planning; and in any society in which many people collaborate, this planning, whoever does it, will in some measure have to be based on knowledge which, in the first instance, is not given to the planner but to somebody else, which somehow will have to be conveyed to the planner. The various ways in which the knowledge on which people base their plans is communicated to them is the crucial problem for any theory explaining the economic process. And the problem of what is the best way of utilizing knowledge initially dispersed among all the people is at least one of the main problems of economic policy – or of designing an efficient economic system.

The answer to this question is closely connected with that other question which arises here, that of *who* is to do the planning. It is about this question that all the dispute about "economic planning" centers. This is not a dispute about whether planning is to be done or not. It is a dispute as to whether planning is to be done centrally, by one authority for the whole economic system, or is to be divided among many individuals. Planning in the specific sense in which the term is used in contemporary controversy necessarily means central planning – direction of the whole economic system according to one unified plan. Competition, on the other hand, means decentralized planning by many separate persons. The half-way house between the two, about which many people talk but which few like when they see it, is the delegation of planning to organized industries, or, in other words, monopoly.

Which of these systems is likely to be more efficient depends mainly on the question under which of them we can expect that fuller use will be made of the existing knowledge. And this, in turn, depends on whether we are more likely to succeed in putting at the disposal of a single central authority all the knowledge which ought to be used but which is initially dispersed among many different individuals, or in conveying to the individuals such additional knowledge as they need in order to enable them to fit their plans in with those of others.

III

It will at once be evident that on this point the position will be different with respect to different kinds of knowledge; and the answer to our question will therefore largely turn on the relative importance of the different kinds of knowledge; those more likely to be at the disposal of particular individuals and those which we should with greater confidence expect to find in the possession of an authority made up of suitably chosen experts. If it is today so widely assumed that the latter will be in a better position, this is because one kind of knowledge, namely, scientific knowledge, occupies now so prominent a place in public imagination that we tend to forget that it is not the only kind that is relevant. It may be admitted that, so far as scientific knowledge is concerned, a body of suitably chosen experts may be in the best position to command all the best knowledge available – though this is of course merely shifting the difficulty to the problem of selecting the experts. What I wish to point out is that, even assuming that this problem can be readily solved, it is only a small part of the wider problem.

Today it is almost heresy to suggest that scientific knowledge is not the sum of all knowledge. But a little reflection will show that there is beyond question a body of very important but unorganized knowledge which cannot possibly be called scientific in the sense of knowledge of general rules: the knowledge of the particular circumstances of time and place. It is with respect to this that practically every individual has some advantage over all others in that he possesses unique information of which beneficial use might be made, but of which use can be made only if the decisions depending on it are left to him or are made with his active coöperation. We need to remember only how much we have to learn in any occupation after we have completed our theoretical training, how big a part of our working life we spend learning particular jobs, and how valuable an asset in all walks of life is knowledge of people, of local conditions, and special circumstances. To know of and put to use a machine not fully employed, or somebody's skill which could be better utilized, or to be aware of a surplus stock which can be drawn upon during an interruption of supplies, is socially quite as useful as the knowledge of better alternative techniques. And the shipper who earns his living from using otherwise empty or half-filled journeys of tramp-steamers, or the estate agent whose whole knowledge is almost exclusively one of temporary opportunities, or the *arbitrageur* who gains from local differences of commodity prices, are all performing eminently useful functions based on special knowledge of circumstances of the fleeting moment not known to others.

It is a curious fact that this sort of knowledge should today be generally regarded with a kind of contempt, and that anyone who by such knowledge gains an advantage over somebody better equipped with theoretical or technical knowledge is thought to have acted almost disreputably. To gain an advantage from better knowledge of facilities of communication or transport is sometimes regarded as almost dishonest, although it is quite as important that society make use of the best opportunities in this respect as in using the latest scientific discoveries. This prejudice has in a considerable measure affected the attitude toward commerce in general compared with that toward production. Even economists who regard themselves as definitely above the crude materialist fallacies of the past constantly commit the same mistake where activities directed toward the acquisition of such practical knowledge are concerned – apparently because in their scheme of things all such knowledge is supposed to be "given." The common idea now seems to be that all such knowledge should as a matter of course be readily at the command of everybody, and the reproach of irrationality leveled against the existing economic order is frequently based on the fact that it is not so available. This view disregards the fact that the method by which such knowledge can be made as widely available as possible is precisely the problem to which we have to find an answer.

IV

If it is fashionable today to minimize the importance of the knowledge of the particular circumstances of time and place, this is closely connected with the smaller importance which is now attached to change as such. Indeed, there are few points on which the assumptions made (usually only implicitly) by the "planners" differ from those of their opponents as much as with regard to the significance and frequency of changes which will make substantial alterations of production plans necessary. Of course, if detailed economic plans could be laid down for fairly long periods in advance and then closely adhered to, so that no further economic decisions of importance would be required, the task of drawing up a comprehensive plan governing all economic activity would appear much less formidable.

It is, perhaps, worth stressing that economic problems arise always and only in consequence of change. So long as things continue as before, or at least as they were expected to, there arise no new problems requiring a decision, no need to form a new plan. The belief that changes, or at least day-to-day adjustments, have become less important in modern times implies the contention that economic problems also have become less important. This belief in the decreasing importance of change is, for that reason, usually held by the same people who argue that the importance of economic considerations has been driven into the background by the growing importance of technological knowledge.

Is it true that, with the elaborate apparatus of modern production, economic decisions are required only at long intervals, as when a new factory is to be erected or a new process to be introduced? Is it true that, once a plant has been built, the rest is all more or less mechanical, determined by the character of the plant, and leaving little to be changed in adapting to the ever-changing circumstances of the moment?

The fairly widespread belief in the affirmative is not, so far as I can ascertain, borne out by the practical experience of the business man. In a competitive industry at any rate – and such an industry alone can serve as a test – the task of keeping cost from rising requires constant struggle, absorbing a great part of the energy of the manager. How easy it is for an inefficient manager to dissipate the differentials on which profitability rests, and that it is possible, with the same technical facilities, to produce with a great variety of costs, are among the commonplaces of business experience which do not seem to be equally familiar in the study of the economist. The very strength of the desire, constantly voiced by producers and engineers, to be able to proceed untrammeled by considerations of money costs, is eloquent testimony to the extent to which these factors enter into their daily work.

One reason why economists are increasingly apt to forget about the constant small changes which make up the whole economic picture is probably their growing preoccupation with statistical aggregates, which show a very much greater stability than the movements of the detail. The comparative stability of the aggregates cannot, however, be accounted for – as the statisticians seem occasionally to be inclined to do – by the "law of large numbers" or the mutual compensation of random changes. The number of elements with which we have to deal is not large enough for such accidental forces to produce stability. The continuous flow of goods and services is maintained by constant deliberate adjustments, by new dispositions made every day in the light of circumstances not known the day before, by *B* stepping in at once when *A* fails to deliver. Even the large and highly mechanized plant keeps going largely because of an environment upon which it can draw for all sorts of unexpected needs; tiles for its roof, stationery for its forms, and all the thousand and one kinds of equipment in which it cannot be self-contained and which the plans for the operation of the plant require to be readily available in the market.

This is, perhaps, also the point where I should briefly mention the fact that the sort of knowledge with which I have been concerned is knowledge of the kind which by its nature cannot enter into statistics and therefore cannot be conveyed to any central authority in statistical form. The statistics which such a central authority would have to use would have to be arrived at precisely by abstracting from minor differences between the things, by lumping together, as resources of one kind, items which differ as regards location, quality, and other particulars, in a way which may be very significant for the specific decision. It follows from this that central planning based on statistical information by its nature cannot take direct aceount of these circumstances of time and place, and that the central planner will have to find some way or other in which the decisions depending on them can be left to the "man on the spot."

V

If we can agree that the economic problem of society is mainly one of rapid adaptation to changes in the particular circumstances of time and place, it would seem to follow that the ultimate decisions must be left to the people who are familiar with these circumstances, who know directly of the relevant changes and of the resources immediately available to meet them. We cannot expect that this problem will be solved by first communicating all this knowledge to a central board which, after integrating *all* knowledge, issues its orders. We must solve it by some form of decentralization. But this answers only part of our problem. We need decentralization because only thus can we ensure that the knowledge of the particular circumstances of time and place will be promptly used. But the "man on the spot" cannot decide solely on the basis of his limited but intimate knowledge of the facts of his immediate surroundings. There still remains the problem of communicating to him such further information as he needs to fit his decisions into the whole pattern of changes of the larger economic system.

How much knowledge does he need to do so successfully? Which of the events which happen beyond the horizon of his immediate knowledge are of relevance to his immediate decision, and how much of them need he know?

There is hardly anything that happens anywhere in the world that *might* not have an effect on the decision he ought to make. But he need not know of these events as such, nor of *all* their effects. It does not matter for him *why* at the particular moment more screws of one size than of another are wanted, *why* paper bags are more readily available than canvas bags, or *why* skilled labor, or particular machine tools, have for the moment become more difficult to acquire. All that is significant for him is *how much more or less* difficult to procure they have become compared with other things with which he is also concerned, or how much more or less urgently wanted are the alternative things he produces or uses. It is always a question of the relative importance of the particular things with which he is concerned, and the causes which alter their relative importance are of no interest to him beyond the effect on those concrete things of his own environment.

It is in this connection that what I have called the economic calculus proper helps us, at least by analogy, to see how this problem can be solved, and in fact is being solved, by the price system. Even the single controlling mind, in possession of all the data for some small, self-contained economic system, would not – every time some small adjustment in the allocation of resources had to be made – go explicitly through all the relations between ends and means which might possibly be affected. It is indeed the great contribution of the pure logic of choice that it has demonstrated conclusively that even such a single mind could solve this kind of problem only by constructing and constantly using rates of equivalence (or "values," or "marginal rates of substitution"), i.e., by attaching to each kind of scarce resource a numerical index which cannot be derived from any property possessed by that particular thing, but which reflects, or in which is condensed, its significance in view of the whole means-end structure. In any small change he will have to consider only these quantitative indices (or "values") in which all the relevant information is concentrated; and by adjusting the quantities one by one, he can appropriately rearrange his dispositions without having to solve the whole puzzle *ab initio*, or without needing at any stage to survey it at once in all its ramifications.

Fundamentally, in a system where the knowledge of the relevant facts is dispersed among many people, prices can act to coördinate the separate actions of different people in the same way as subjective values help the individual to coördinate the parts of his plan. It is worth contemplating for a moment a very simple and commonplace instance of the action of the price system to see what precisely it accomplishes. Assume that somewhere in the world a new opportunity for the use of some raw material, say tin, has arisen, or that one of the sources of supply of tin has been eliminated. It does not matter for our purpose – and it is very significant that it does not matter – which of these two causes has made tin more scarce. All that the users of tin need to know is that some of the tin they used to consume is now more profitably employed elsewhere, and that in consequence they must economize tin. There is no need for the great majority of them even to know where the more urgent need has arisen, or in favor of what other needs they ought to husband the supply. If only some of them know directly of the new demand, and switch resources over to it, and if the people who are aware of the new gap thus created in turn fill it from still other sources, the effect will rapidly spread throughout the whole economic system and influence not only all the uses of tin, but also those of its substitutes and the substitutes of these substitutes, the supply of all the things made of tin, and their substitutes, and so on; and all this without the great majority of those instrumental in bringing about these substitutions knowing anything at all about the original cause of these changes. The whole acts as one market, not because any of its members survey the whole field, but because their limited individual fields of vision sufficiently overlap so that through many intermediaries the relevant information is communicated to all. The mere fact that there is one price for any commodity – or rather that local prices are connected in a manner determined by the cost of transport, etc. – brings about the solution which (it is just conceptually possible) might have been arrived at by one single mind possessing all the information which is in fact dispersed among all the people involved in the process.

VI

We must look at the price system as such a mechanism for communicating information if we want to understand its real function – a function which, of course, it fulfills less perfectly as prices grow more rigid. (Even when quoted prices have become quite rigid, however, the forces which would operate through changes in price still operate to a considerable extent through changes in the other terms of the contract.) The most significant fact about this system is the economy of knowledge with which it operates, or how little the individual participants need to know in order to be able to take the right action. In abbreviated form, by a kind of symbol, only the most essential information is passed on, and passed on only to those concerned. It is more than a metaphor to describe the price system as a kind of machinery for registering change, or a system of telecommunications which enables individual producers to watch merely the movement of a few pointers, as an engineer might watch the hands of a few dials, in order to adjust their activities to changes of which they may never know more than is reflected in the price movement.

Of course, these adjustments are probably never "perfect" in the sense in which the economist conceives of them in his equilibrium analysis. But I fear that our theoretical habits of approaching the problem with the assumption of more or less perfect knowledge on the part of almost everyone has made us somewhat blind to the true function of the price mechanism and led us to apply rather misleading standards in judging its efficiency. The marvel is that in a case like that of a scarcity of one raw material, without an order being issued, without more than perhaps a handful of people knowing the cause, tens of thousands of people whose identity could not be ascertained by months of investigation, are made to use the material or its products more sparingly; i.e., they move in the right direction. This is enough of a marvel even if, in a constantly changing world, not all will hit it off so perfectly that their profit rates will always be maintained at the same constant or "normal" level.

I have deliberately used the word "marvel" to shock the reader out of the complacency with which we often take the working of this mechanism for granted. I am convinced that if it were the result of deliberate human design, and if the people guided by the price changes understood that their decisions have significance far beyond their immediate aim, this mechanism would have been acclaimed as one of the greatest triumphs of the human mind. Its misfortune is the double one that it is not the product of human design and that the people guided by it usually do not know why they are made to do what they do. But those who clamor for "conscious direction" – and who cannot believe that anything which has evolved without design (and even without our understanding it) should solve problems which we should not be able to solve consciously – should remember this: The problem is precisely how to extend the span of our utilization of resources beyond the span of the control of any one mind; and, therefore, how to dispense with the need of conscious control and how to provide inducements which will make the individuals do the desirable things without anyone having to tell them what to do.

The problem which we meet here is by no means peculiar to economics but arises in connection with nearly all truly social phenomena, with language and most of our cultural inheritance, and constitutes really the central theoretical problem of all social science. As Alfred Whitehead has said in another connection, "It is a profoundly erroneous truism, repeated by all copy-books and by eminent people when they are making speeches, that we should cultivate the habit of thinking what we are doing. The precise opposite is the case. Civilization advances by extending the number of important operations which we can perform without thinking about them." This is of profound significance in the social field. We make constant use of formulas, symbols and rules whose meaning we do not understand and through the use of which we avail ourselves of the assistance of knowledge which individually we do not possess. We have developed these practices and institutions by building upon habits and institutions which have proved successful in their own sphere and which have in turn become the foundation of the civilization we have built up.

The price system is just one of those formations which man has learned to use (though he is still very far from having learned to make the best use of it) after he had stumbled upon it without understanding it. Through it not only a division of labor but also a coordinated utilization of resources based on an equally divided knowledge has become possible. The people who like to deride any suggestion that this may be so usually distort the argument by insinuating that it asserts that by some miracle just that sort of system has spontaneously grown up which is best suited to modern civilization. It is the other way round: man has been able to develop that division of labor on which our civilization is based because he happened to stumble upon a method which made it possible. Had he not done so he might still have developed some other, altogether different, type of civilization, something like the "state" of the termite ants, or some other altogether unimaginable type. All that we can say is that nobody has yet succeeded in designing an alternative system in which certain features of the existing one can be preserved which are dear even to those who most violently assail it – such as particularly the extent to which the individual can choose his pursuits and consequently freely use his own knowledge and skill.

VII

It is in many ways fortunate that the dispute about the indispensability of the price system for any rational calculation in a complex society is now no longer conducted entirely between camps holding different political views. The thesis that without the price system we could not preserve a society based on such extensive division of labor as ours was greeted with a howl of derision when it was first advanced by von Mises twenty-five years ago. Today the difficulties which some still find in accepting it are no longer mainly political, and this makes for an atmosphere much more conducive to reasonable discussion. When we find Leon Trotsky arguing that "economic accounting is unthinkable without market relations;" when Professor Oscar Lange promises Professor von Mises a statue in the marble halls of the future Central Planning Board; and when Professor Abba P. Lerner rediscovers Adam Smith and emphasizes that the essential utility of the price system consists in inducing the individual, while seeking his own interest, to do what is in the general interest, the differences can indeed no longer be ascribed to political prejudice. The remaining dissent seems clearly to be due to purely intellectual, and more particularly methodological, differences.

A recent statement by Professor Joseph Schumpeter in his *Capitalism, Socialism and Democracy* provides a clear illustration of one of the methodological differences which I have in mind. Its author is preeminent among those economists who approach economic phenomena in the light of a certain branch of positivism. To him these phenomena accordingly appear as objectively given quantities of commodities impinging directly upon each other, almost, it would seem, without any intervention of human minds. Only against this background can I account for the following (to me startling) pronouncement. Professor Schumpeter argues that the possibility of a rational calculation in the absence of markets for the factors of production follows for the theorist "from the elementary proposition that consumers in evaluating ('demanding') consumers' goods *ipso facto* also evaluate the means of production which enter into the production of these goods."[1]

Taken literally, this statement is simply untrue. The consumers do nothing of the kind. What Professor Schumpeter's *"ipso facto"* presumably means is that the valuation of the factors of production is implied in, or follows necessarily from, the valuation of consumers' goods. But this, too, is not correct. Implication is a logical relationship which can be meaningfully asserted only of propositions simultaneously present to one and the same mind. It is evident, however, that the values of the factors of production do not depend solely on the valuation of the consumers' goods but also on the conditions of supply of the various factors of production. Only to a mind to which all these facts were simultaneously known would the answer necessarily follow from the facts given to it. The practical problem, however, arises precisely because these facts are never so given to a single mind, and because, in consequence, it is necessary that in the solution of the problem knowledge should be used that is dispersed among many people.

The problem is thus in no way solved if we can show that all the facts, *if* they were known to a single mind (as we hypothetically assume them to be given to the observing economist), would uniquely determine the solution; instead we must show how a solution is produced by the interactions of people each of whom possesses only partial knowledge. To assume all the knowledge to be given to a single mind in the same manner in which we assume it to be given to us as the explaining economists is to assume the problem away and to disregard everything that is important and significant in the real world.

That an economist of Professor Schumpeter's standing should thus have fallen into a trap which the ambiguity of the term "datum" sets to the unwary can hardly be explained as a simple error. It suggests rather than there is something fundamentally wrong with an approach which habitually disregards an essential part of the phenomena with which we have to deal: the unavoidable imperfection of man's knowledge and the consequent need for a process by which knowledge is constantly communicated and acquired. Any approach, such as that of much of mathematical economics with its simultaneous equations, which in effect starts from the assumption that people's *knowledge* corresponds with the objective *facts* of the situation, systematically leaves out what is our main task to explain. I am far from denying that in our system equilibrium analysis has a useful function to perform. But when it comes to the point where it misleads some of our leading thinkers into believing that the situation which it describes has direct relevance to the solution of practical problems, it is time that we remember that it does not deal with the social process at all and that it is no more than a useful preliminary to the study of the main problem.

Note

1 J. Schumpeter, *Capitalism, Socialism, and Democracy* (New York, Harper, 1942), p. 175. Professor Schumpeter is, I believe, also the original author of the myth that Pareto and Barone have "solved" the problem of socialist calculation. What they, and many others, did was merely to state the conditions which a rational allocation of resources would have to satisfy, and to point out that these were essentially the same as the conditions of equilibrium of a competitive market. This is something altogether different from showing how the allocation of resources satisfying these conditions can be found in practice. Pareto himself (from whom Barone has taken practically everything he has to say), far from claiming to have solved the practical problem, in fact explicitly denies that it can be solved without the help of the market. See his *Manuel d'économie pure* (2nd ed., 1927), pp. 233–34. The relevant passage is quoted in an English translation at the beginning of my article on "Socialist Calculation: The Competitive 'Solution,'" in *Economica*, New Series, Vol. VIII, No. 26 (May, 1940), p. 125.

15 The market for "lemons"

Quality uncertainty and the market mechanism

George A. Akerlof

Introduction

This paper relates quality and uncertainty. The existence of goods of many grades poses interesting and important problems for the theory of markets. On the one hand, the interaction of quality differences and uncertainty may explain important institutions of the labor market. On the other hand, this paper presents a struggling attempt to give structure to the statement: "Business in underdeveloped countries is difficult"; in particular, a structure is given for determining the economic costs of dishonesty. Additional applications of the theory include comments on the structure of money markets, on the notion of "insurability," on the liquidity of durables, and on brand-name goods.

There are many markets in which buyers use some market statistic to judge the quality of prospective purchases. In this case there is incentive for sellers to market poor quality merchandise, since the returns for good quality accrue mainly to the entire group whose statistic is affected rather than to the individual seller. As a result there tends to be a reduction in the average quality of goods and also in the size of the market. It should also be perceived that in these markets social and private returns differ, and therefore, in some cases, governmental intervention may increase the welfare of all parties. Or private institutions may arise to take advantage of the potential increases in welfare which can accrue to all parties. By nature, however, these institutions are nonatomistic, and therefore concentrations of power – with ill consequences of their own – can develop.

The automobile market is used as a finger exercise to illustrate and develop these thoughts. It should be emphasized that this market is chosen for its concreteness and ease in understanding rather than for its importance or realism.

The model with automobiles as an example

The automobiles market

The example of used cars captures the essence of the problem. From time to time one hears either mention of or surprise at the large price difference between new cars and those which have just left the showroom. The usual lunch table justification for this phenomenon is the pure joy of owning a "new" car. We offer a different explanation. Suppose (for the sake of clarity rather than reality) that there are just four kinds of cars. There are new cars and used cars. There are good cars and bad cars (which in America are known as "lemons"). A new car may be a good car or a lemon, and of course the same is true of used cars.

The individuals in this market buy a new automobile without knowing whether the car they buy will be good or a lemon. But they do know that with probability q it is a good car and with probability $(1 - q)$ it is a lemon; by assumption, q is the proportion of good cars produced and $(1 - q)$ is the proportion of lemons.

After owning a specific car, however, for a length of time, the car owner can form a good idea of the quality of this machine; i.e., the owner assigns a new probability to the event that his car is a lemon. This estimate is more accurate than the original estimate. An asymmetry in available information has developed: for the sellers now have more knowledge about the quality of a car than the buyers. But good cars and bad cars must still sell at the same price – since it is impossible for a buyer to tell the difference between a good car and a bad car. It is apparent that a used car cannot have the same valuation as a new car – if it did have the same valuation, it would clearly be advantageous to trade a lemon at the price of new car, and buy another new car, at a higher probability q of being good and a lower probability of being bad. Thus the owner of a good machine must be locked in. Not only is it true that he cannot receive the true value of his car, but he cannot even obtain the expected value of a new car.

Gresham's law has made a modified reappearance. For most cars traded will be the "lemons," and good cars may not be traded at all. The "bad" cars tend to drive out the good (in much the same way that bad money drives out the good). But the analogy with Gresham's law is not quite complete: bad cars drive out the good because they sell at the same price as good cars; similarly, bad money drives out good because the exchange rate is even. But the bad cars sell at the same price as good cars since it is impossible for a buyer to tell the difference between a good and a bad car; only the seller knows. In Gresham's law, however, presumably both buyer and seller can tell the difference between good and bad money. So the analogy is instructive, but not complete.

Asymmetrical information

It has been seen that the good cars may be driven out of the market by the lemons. But in a more continuous case with different grades of goods, even worse pathologies can exist. For it is quite possible to have the bad driving out the not-so-bad driving out the medium driving out the not-so-good driving out the good in such a sequence of events that no market exists at all.

One can assume that the demand for used automobiles depends most strongly upon two variables – the price of the automobile p and the average quality of used cars traded, μ, or $Q^d = D(p, \mu)$. Both the supply of used cars and also the average quality μ will depend upon the price, or $\mu = \mu(p)$ and $S = S(p)$. And in equilibrium the supply must equal the demand for the given average quality, or $S(p) = D(p, \mu(p))$. As the price falls, normally the quality will also fall. And it is quite possible that no goods will be traded at any price level.

Such an example can be derived from utility theory. Assume that there are just two groups of traders: groups one and two. Give group one a utility function

$$U_1 = M + \sum_{i=1}^{n} x_4$$

where M is the consumption of goods other than automobiles, x_i is the quality of the ith automobile, and n is the number of automobiles.

Similarly, let

$$U_2 = M + \sum_{i=1}^{n} 3/2x_i$$

where M, x_i, and n are defined as before.

Three comments should be made about these utility functions: (1) Without linear utility (say with logarithmic utility) one gets needlessly mired in algebraic complication. (2) The use of linear utility allows a focus on the effects of asymmetry of information; with a concave utility function we would have to deal jointly with the usual risk-variance effects of uncertainty and the special effects we wish to discuss here. (3) U_1 and U_2 have the odd characteristic that the addition of a second car, or indeed a kth car, adds the same amount of utility as the first. Again realism is sacrificed to avoid a diversion from the proper focus.

To continue, it is assumed (1) that both type one traders and type two traders are von Neumann-Morgenstern maximizers of expected utility; (2) that group one has N cars with uniformly distributed quality x, $0 \le x \le 2$, and group two has no cars; (3) that the price of "other goods" M is unity.

Denote the income (including that derived from the sale of automobiles) of all type one traders as Y_1 and the income of all type two traders as Y_2. The demand for used cars will be the sum of the demands by both groups. When one ignores indivisibilities, the demand for automobiles by type one traders will be

$$D_1 = Y_1/p \qquad \mu/p > 1$$
$$D_1 = 0 \qquad \mu/p < 1$$

And the supply of cars offered by type one traders is

$$S_2 = pN/2 \tag{15.1}$$

with average quality

$$\mu = p/2 \tag{15.2}$$

(To derive (1) and (2), the uniform distribution of automobile quality is used.)
Similarly the demand of type two traders is

$$D_2 = Y_2/p \qquad 3\mu/2 > p$$
$$D_2 = 0 \qquad 3\mu/2 < p$$

and

$$S_2 = O$$

Thus total demand $D(p, \mu)$ is

$$D(p, \mu) = (Y_2 + Y_1)/P \qquad \text{if} \quad p < \mu$$
$$D(p, \mu) = (Y_2)/P \qquad \text{if} \quad \mu < p < 3\mu/2$$
$$D(p, \mu) = 0 \qquad \text{if} \quad p < 3\mu/2$$

However, with price p, average quality is $p/2$ and therefore at no price will any trade take place at all: in spite of the fact that *at any given price* between 0 and 3 there are traders of type one who are willing to sell their automobiles at a price which traders of type two are willing to pay.

Symmetric information

The foregoing is contrasted with the case of symmetric information. Suppose that the quality of all cars is uniformly distributed, $0 \leq x \leq 2$. Then the demand curves and supply curves can be written as follows:
Supply

$$S(p) = N \qquad p > 1$$

$$S(p) = 0 \qquad p < 1$$

And the demand curves are

$$D(p) = (Y_2 + Y_1)/p \qquad p < 1$$

$$D(p) = (Y_2/p) \qquad 1 < p < 3/2$$

$$D(p) = 0 \qquad p > 3/2$$

In equilibrium

$$P = 1 \qquad \text{if} \quad Y2 < N \qquad\qquad (15.3)$$

$$P = Y_2/N \qquad \text{if} \quad 2Y2/3 < N < V2 \qquad\qquad (15.4)$$

$$p = 3/2 \qquad \text{if} \quad N < 2Y_2/3 \qquad\qquad (15.5)$$

If $N < Y_2$ there is a gain in utility over the case of asymmetrical information of $N/2$. (If $N > Y_2$, in which case the income of type two traders is insufficient to buy all N automobiles, there is a gain in utility of $Y_2/2$ units.)

Finally, it should be mentioned that in this example, if traders of groups one and two have the same probabilistic estimates about the quality of individual automobiles – though these estimates may vary from automobile to automobile – (3), (4), and (5) will still describe equilibrium with one slight change: p will then represent the expected price of one quality unit.

Examples and applications

Insurance

It is a well-known fact that people over 65 have great difficulty in buying medical insurance. The natural question arises: why doesn't the price rise to match the risk?

Our answer is that as the price level rises the people who insure themselves will be those who are increasingly certain that they will need the insurance; for error in medical check-ups, doctors' sympathy with older patients, and so on make it much easier for the applicant to assess the risks involved than the insurance company. The result is that the average medical condition of insurance applicants deteriorates as the price level rises – with the result that no insurance sales may take place at any price.[1] This is strictly analogous to our automobiles case, where the average quality of used cars supplied fell with a corresponding fall in the price level. This agrees with the explanation in insurance textbooks:

> Generally speaking policies are not available at ages materially greater than sixty-five. ...
> The term premiums are too high for any but the most pessimistic (which is to say the least

healthy) insureds to find attractive. Thus there is a severe problem of adverse selection at these ages.[2]

The statistics do not contradict this conclusion. While demands for health insurance rise with age, a 1956 national sample survey of 2,809 families with 8,898 persons shows that hospital insurance coverage drops from 63 per cent of those aged 45 to 54, to 31 per cent for those over 65. And surprisingly, this survey also finds average medical expenses for males aged 55 to 64 of $88, while males over 65 pay an average of $77.[3] While noninsured expenditure rises from $66 to $80 in these age groups, insured expenditure declines from $105 to $70. The conclusion is tempting that insurance companies are particularly wary of giving medical insurance to older people.

The principle of "adverse selection" is potentially present in all lines of insurance. The following statement appears in an insurance textbook written at the Wharton School:

> There is potential adverse selection in the fact that healthy term insurance policy holders may decide to terminate their coverage when they become older and premiums mount. This action could leave an insurer with an undue proportion of below average risks and claims might be higher than anticipated. Adverse selection "appears (or at least is possible) whenever the individual or group insured has freedom to buy or not to buy, to choose the amount or plan of insurance, and to persist or to discontinue as a policy holder."[4]

Group insurance, which is the most common form of medical insurance in the United States, picks out the healthy, for generally adequate health is a precondition for employment. At the same time this means that medical insurance is least available to those who need it most, for the insurance companies do their own "adverse selection."

This adds one major argument in favor of medicare.[5] On a cost benefit basis medicare may pay off: for it is quite possible that every individual in the market would be willing to pay the expected cost of his medicare and buy insurance, yet no insurance company can afford to sell him a policy – for at any price it will attract too many "lemons." The welfare economics of medicare, in this view, is *exactly* analogous to the usual classroom argument for public expenditure on roads.

The employment of minorities

The Lemons Principle also casts light on the employment of minorities. Employers may refuse to hire members of minority groups for certain types of jobs. This decision may not reflect irrationality or prejudice – but profit maximization. For race may serve as a good *statistic* for the applicant's social background, quality of schooling, and general job capabilities.

Good quality schooling could serve as a substitute for this statistic; by grading students the schooling system can give a better indicator of quality than other more superficial characteristics. As T. W. Schultz writes, "The educational establishment *discovers* and cultivates potential talent. The capabilities of children and mature students can never be known until *found* and cultivated."[6] An untrained worker may have valuable natural talents, but these talents must be certified by "the educational establishment" before a company can afford to use them. The certifying establishment, however, must be credible; the unreliability of slum schools decreases the economic possibilities of their students.

This lack may be particularly disadvantageous to members of already disadvantaged minority groups. For an employer may make a rational decision not to hire any members of these groups in responsible positions – because it is difficult to distinguish those with good job qualifications from those with bad qualifications. This type of decision is clearly what George Stigler had in mind when he wrote, "in a regime of ignorance Enrico Fermi would have been a gardener, Von Neumann a checkout clerk at a drugstore."[7]

As a result, however, the rewards for work in slum schools tend to accrue to the group as a whole – in raising its average quality – rather than to the individual. Only insofar as information in addition to race is used is there any incentive for training.

An additional worry is that the Office of Economic Opportunity is going to use cost-benefit analysis to evaluate its programs. For many benefits may be external. The benefit from training minority groups may arise as much from raising the average quality of the group as from raising the quality of the individual trainee; and, likewise, the returns may be distributed over the whole group rather than to the individual.

The costs of dishonesty

The Lemons model can be used to make some comments on the costs of dishonesty. Consider a market in which goods are sold honestly or dishonestly; quality may be represented, or it may be misrepresented. The purchaser's problem, of course, is to identify quality. The presence of people in the market who are willing to offer inferior goods tends to drive the market out of existence – as in the case of our automobile "lemons." It is this possibility that represents the major costs of dishonesty – for dishonest dealings tend to drive honest dealings out of the market. There may be potential buyers of good quality products and there may be potential sellers of such products in the appropriate price range; however, the presence of people who wish to pawn bad wares as good wares tends to drive out the legitimate business. The cost of dishonesty, therefore, lies not only in the amount by which the purchaser is cheated; the cost also must include the loss incurred from driving legitimate business out of existence.

Dishonesty in business is a serious problem in underdeveloped countries. Our model gives a possible structure to this statement and delineates the nature of the "external" economies involved. In particular, in the model economy described, dishonesty, or the misrepresentation of the quality of automobiles, costs 1/2 unit of utility per automobile; furthermore, it reduces the size of the used car market from N to 0. We can, consequently, directly evaluate the costs of dishonesty – at least in theory.

There is considerable evidence that quality variation is greater in underdeveloped than in developed areas. For instance, the need for quality control of exports and State Trading Corporations can be taken as one indicator. In India, for example, under the Export Quality Control and Inspection Act of 1963, "about 85 per cent of Indian exports are covered under one or the other type of quality control."[8] Indian housewives must carefully glean the rice of the local bazaar to sort out stones of the same color and shape which have been intentionally added to the rice. Any comparison of the heterogeneity of quality in the street market and the canned qualities of the American supermarket suggests that quality variation is a greater problem in the East than in the West.

In one traditional pattern of development the merchants of the pre-industrial generation turn into the first entrepreneurs of the next. The best-documented case is Japan,[9] but this also may have been the pattern for Britain and America.[10] In *our* picture the important skill of the merchant is identifying the quality of merchandise; those who can identify used cars in our example and can guarantee the quality may profit by as much as the difference between type two traders' buying price and type one traders' selling price. These people are the merchants. In production these skills are equally necessary – both to be able to identify the quality of inputs and to certify the quality of outputs. And this is one (added) reason why the merchants may logically become the first entrepreneurs.

The problem, of course, is that entrepreneurship may be a scarce resource; no development text leaves entrepreneurship unemphasized. Some treat it as central.[11] Given, then, that entrepreneurship is scarce, there are two ways in which product variations impede development. First, the pay-off to trade is great for would-be entrepreneurs, and hence they are diverted from production; second, the amount of entrepreneurial time per unit output is greater, the greater are the quality variations.

Credit markets in underdeveloped countries

(1) Credit markets in underdeveloped countries often strongly reflect the operation of the Lemons Principle. In India a major fraction of industrial enterprise is controlled by managing agencies (according to a recent survey, these "managing agencies" controlled 65.7 per cent of the net worth of public limited companies and 66 per cent of total assets).[12] Here is a historian's account of the function and genesis of the "managing agency system":

> The management of the South Asian commercial scene remained the function of merchant houses, and a type of organization peculiar to South Asia known as the Managing Agency. When a new venture was promoted (such as a manufacturing plant, a plantation, or a trading venture), the promoters would approach an established managing agency. The promoters might be Indian or British, and they might have technical or financial resources or merely a concession. In any case they would turn to the agency because of its reputation, which would encourage confidence in the venture and stimulate investment.[13]

> In turn, a second major feature of the Indian industrial scene has been the dominance of these managing agencies by caste (or, more accurately, communal) groups. Thus firms can usually be classified according to communal origin.[14] In this environment, in which outside investors are likely to be bilked of their holdings, either (1) firms establish a reputation for "honest" dealing, which confers upon them a monopoly rent insofar as their services are limited in supply, or (2) the sources of finance are limited to local communal groups which can use communal – and possibly familial – ties to encourage honest dealing *within* the community. It is, in Indian economic history, extraordinarily difficult to discern whether the savings of rich landlords failed to be invested in the industrial sector (1) because of a fear to invest in ventures controlled by other communities, (2) because of inflated propensities to consume, or (3) because of low rates of return.[15] At the very least, however, it is clear that the British-owned managing agencies tended to have an equity holding whose communal origin was more heterogeneous than the Indian-controlled agency houses, and would usually include both Indian and British investors.

(2) A second example of the workings of the Lemons Principle concerns the extortionate rates which the local moneylender charges his clients. In India these high rates of interest have been the leading factor in landlessness; the so-called "Cooperative Movement" was

meant to counteract this growing landlessness by setting up banks to compete with the local moneylenders.[16] While the large banks in the central cities have prime interest rates of 6, 8, and 10 per cent, the local moneylender charges 15, 25, and even 50 per cent. The answer to this seeming paradox is that credit is granted only where the granter has (1) easy means of enforcing his contract or (2) personal knowledge of the character of the borrower. The middleman who tries to arbitrage between the rates of the moneylender and the central bank is apt to attract all the "lemons" and thereby make a loss.

This interpretation can be seen in Sir Malcolm Darling's interpretation of the village moneylender's power:

It is only fair to remember that in the Indian village the money-lender is often the one thrifty person amongst a generally thriftless people; and that his methods of business, though demoralizing under modern conditions, suit the happy-go-lucky ways of the peasant. He is always accessible, even at night; dispenses with troublesome formalities, asks no inconvenient questions, advances promptly, and if interest is paid, does not press for repayment of principal. He keeps in close personal touch with his clients, and in many villages shares their occasions of weal or woe. *With his intimate knowledge of those around him he is able, without serious risk, to finance those who would otherwise get no loan at all.* [Italics added.][17]

Or look at Barbara Ward's account:

A small shopkeeper in a Hong Kong fishing village told me: "I give credit to anyone who anchors regularly in our bay; but if it is someone I don't know well, then I think twice about it unless I can find out all about him."[18]

Or, a profitable sideline of cotton ginning in Iran is the loaning of money for the next season, since the ginning companies often have a line of credit from Teheran banks at the market rate of interest. But in the first years of operation large losses are expected from unpaid debts – due to poor knowledge of the local scene.[19]

Counteracting institutions

Numerous institutions arise to counteract the effects of quality uncertainty. One obvious institution is guarantees. Most consumer durables carry guarantees to ensure the buyer of some normal expected quality. One natural result of our model is that the risk is borne by the seller rather than by the buyer.

A second example of an institution which counteracts the effects of quality uncertainty is the brand-name good. Brand names not only indicate quality but also give the consumer a means of retaliation if the quality does not meet expectations. For the consumer will then curtail future purchases. Often too, new products are associated with old brand names. This ensures the prospective consumer of the quality of the product.

Chains – such as hotel chains or restaurant chains – are similar to brand names. One observation consistent with our approach is the chain restaurant. These restaurants, at least in the United States, most often appear on interurban highways. The customers are seldom local. The reason is that these well-known chains offer a better hamburger than the *average* local restaurant; at the same time, the local customer, who knows his area, can usually choose a place he prefers.

Licensing practices also reduce quality uncertainty. For instance, there is the licensing of doctors, lawyers, and barbers. Most skilled labor carries some certification indicating the attainment of certain levels of proficiency. The high school diploma, the baccalaureate degree, the Ph.D., even the Nobel Prize, to some degree, serve this function of certification. And education and labor markets themselves have their own "brand names."

Conclusion

We have been discussing economic models in which "trust" is important. Informal unwritten guarantees are preconditions for trade and production. Where these guarantees are indefinite, business will suffer – as indicated by our generalized Gresham's law. This aspect of uncertainty has been explored by game theorists, as in the Prisoner's Dilemma, but usually it has not been incorporated in the more traditional Arrow-Debreu approach to uncertainty.[20] But the difficulty of distinguishing good quality from bad is inherent in the business world; this may indeed explain many economic institutions and may in fact be one of the more important aspects of uncertainty.

Acknowledgements

The author would especially like to thank Thomas Rothenberg for invaluable comments and inspiration. In addition he is indebted to Roy Radner, Albert Fishlow, Bernard Saffran, William D. Nordhaus, Giorgio La Malfa, Charles C. Holt, John Letiche, and the referee for help and suggestions. He would also like to thank the Indian Statistical Institute and the Ford Foundation for financial support.

Notes

1 Arrow's fine article, "Uncertainty and Medical Care" *(American Economic Review*, Vol. 53, 1963), does not make this point explicitly. He emphasizes "moral hazard" rather than "adverse selection." In its strict sense, the presence of "moral hazard" is equally disadvantageous for both governmental and private programs; in its broader sense, which includes "adverse selection," "moral hazard" gives a decided advantage to government insurance programs.

2 O. D. Dickerson, *Health Insurance* (Homewood, Ill.: Irwin, 1959), p. 333.

3 O. W. Anderson (with J. J. Feldman), *Family Medical Costs and Insurance* (New York: McGraw-Hill, 1956).

4 H. S. Denenberg, R. D. Eilers, G. W. Hoffman, C. A. Kline, J. J. Melone, and H. W. Snider, *Risk and Insurance* (Englewood Cliffs, N. J.: Prentice Hall, 1964), p. 446.

5 The following quote, again taken from an insurance textbook, shows how far the medical insurance market is from perfect competition:

> insurance companies must screen their applicants. Naturally it is true that many people will voluntarily seek adequate insurance on their own initiative. But in such lines as accident and health insurance, companies are likely to give a second look to persons who voluntarily seek insurance without being approached by an agent.
> (F. J. Angell, *Insurance, Principles and Practices*, New York : The Ronald Press, 1957, pp. 8–9.)

This shows that insurance is *not* a commodity for sale on the open market.

6 T. W. Schultz, *The Economic Value of Education* (New York: Columbia University Press, 1964), p. 42.

7 G. J. Stigler, "Information and the Labor Market," *Journal of Political Economy*, Vol. 70 (Oct. 1962), Supplement, p. 104.

8 *The Times of India*, Nov. 10, (1967), p. 1.

266 *George A. Akerlof*

9 See M. J. Levy, Jr., "Contrasting Factors in the Modernization of China and Japan," in *Economic Growth: Brazil, India*, Japan, ed., S. Kuznets, *et al.*(Durham, N. C.: Duke University Press, 1955).
10 C. P. Kindleberger, *Economic Development* (New York: McGraw-Hill, 1958), p. 86.
11 For example, see W. Arthur Lewis, *The Theory of Economic Growth* (Homewood, Ill.: Irwin, 1955), p. 196.
12 *Report of the Committee on the Distribution of Income and Levels of Living*, Part I, Government of India, Planning Commission, February 1964, p. 44.
13 H. Tinker, *South Asia: A Short History* (New York: Praeger, 1966), p. 134.
14 The existence of the following table (and also the small per cent of firms under mixed control) indicates the communalization of the control of firms.

| | Distribution of industrial control by community | | |
| | *1911* | *1931* | *1951* |
		(number of firms)	
British	281	416	382
Parsis	15	25	19
Gujratis	3	11	17
Jews	5	9	3
Muslims	—	10	3
Bengalis	8	5	20
Marwaris	—	6	96
Mixed control	28	28	79
Total	341	510	619

Source: M. M. Mehta, *Structure of Indian Industries* (Bombay: Popular Book Depot, 1955), p. 314.
Note: Also, for the cotton industry see H. Fukuzawa, "Cotton Mill Industry," in V. B. Singh, editor, *Economic History of India, 1857–1956* (Bombay: Allied Publishers, 1965).

15 For the mixed record of industrial profits, see D. H. Buchanan, *The Development of Capitalist Enterprise in India* (New York: Kelley, 1966, reprinted).
16 The leading authority on this is Sir Malcolm Darling. See his *Punjabi Peasant in Prosperity and Debt.* The following table may also prove instructive:

	Secured loans (per cent)	*Commonest rates for – unsecured loans (per cent)*	*Grain loans (per cent)*
Punjab	6 to 12	12 to 24 ($18^{3/4}$ commonest)	25
United provinces	9 to 12	24 to $37^{1/2}$	25 (50 in Oudh)
Bihar		$18^{3/4}$	50
Orissa	12 to $18^{3/4}$	25	25
Bengal	8 to 12	9 to 18 for "respectable clients" $18^{3/4}$ to $37^{1/2}$ (the latter common to agriculturalists)	
Central Provinces	6 to 12	15 for proprietors 24 for occupancy tenants $37^1/2$ for ryots with no right of transfer	25
Bombay	9 to 12	12 to 25 (18 commonest)	
Sind		36	
Madras	12	15 to 18 (in insecure tracts 24	20 to 50

Source: Punjabi Peasant in Prosperity and Debt, 3rd ed., (Oxford University Press, 1932), p. 190.

17 Darling, *op. cit.,* p. 204.
18 B. Ward, "Cash or Credit Crops," *Economic Development and Cultural Change*, Vol. 8 (Jan. 1960), reprinted in *Peasant Society: A Reader*, ed., G. Foster *et al.*(Boston: Little Brown and Company,

1967). Quote on p. 142. In the same volume, see also G. W Skinner, "Marketing and Social Structure in Rural China," and S. W. Mintz, "Pratik: Haitian Personal Economic Relations."

19 Personal conversation with mill manager, April 1968.

20 R. Radner, "Equilibre de Marchés á Terme et au Comptant en Cu d'Incertitude," *in Cahiers d'Econometrie*, Vol. 12 (Nov. 1967), Centre National de la Recherche Scientifique, Paris.

16 Information and the change in the paradigm in economics

Joseph E. Stiglitz

The research for which George Akerlof, Michael Spence, and I are being recognized is part of a larger research program which today embraces a great number of researchers around the world. In this article, I want to set the particular work which was cited within this broader agenda, and that agenda within the still broader perspective of the history of economic thought. I hope to show that information economics represents a fundamental change in the prevailing paradigm within economics.

Information economics has already had a profound effect on how we think about economic policy and is likely to have an even greater influence in the future. Many of the major policy debates over the past two decades have centered around the related issues of the efficiency of the market economy and the appropriate relationship between the market and the government. The argument of Adam Smith (1776) that free markets lead to efficient outcomes, "as if by an invisible hand," has played a central role in these debates: It suggested that we could, by and large, rely on markets *without government intervention* (or, at most, with a limited role for government). The set of ideas that I will present here undermined Smith's theory and the view of the role of government that rested on it. They have suggested that the reason that the hand may be invisible is that it is simply not there – or at least that if it is there, it is palsied.

When I began the study of economics some 41 years ago, I was struck by the incongruity between the models that I was taught and the world that I had seen growing up in Gary, Indiana. Founded in 1906 by U.S. Steel, and named after its Chairman of the Board, Gary has declined to but a shadow of its former self. But even in its heyday, it was marred by poverty, periods of high unemployment, and massive racial discrimination. Yet the economic theories we were taught paid little attention to poverty, said that all markets cleared – including the labor market, so that unemployment must be nothing more than a phantasm – and claimed that the profit motive ensured that there could not be economic discrimination (Gary Becker, 1971). As a graduate student, I was determined to try to create models with assumptions – and conclusions – closer to those that accorded with the world I saw, with all of its imperfections.

My first visits to the developing world in 1967, and a more extensive stay in Kenya in 1969, made an indelible impression on me. Models of perfect markets, as badly flawed as they might seem for Europe or America, seemed truly inappropriate for these countries. While many of the key assumptions that went into the competitive equilibrium model seemed not to fit these economies well, I was particularly struck by the imperfections of information, the absence of markets, and the pervasiveness and persistence of seemingly dysfunctional institutions, such as sharecropping. I had seen cyclical unemployment – sometimes quite large – and the hardship it brought as I grew up, but I had not seen the massive unemployment that characterized African cities, unemployment that could not be explained either by unions or minimum wage laws (which, even when they existed, were regularly circumvented). Again, there was a massive discrepancy between the models we had been taught and what I saw.

In contrast, the ideas and models I will discuss here have proved useful not only in addressing broad philosophical questions, such as the appropriate role of the state, but also in analyzing concrete policy issues. For example, I believe that some of the huge mistakes which have been made in policy in the last decade, in for instance the management of the East Asian crisis or the transition of the former communist countries to the market, might have been avoided had there been a better understanding of issues – such as financial structure, bankruptcy, and corporate governance – to which the new information economics has called attention. And the so-called "Washington consensus"[1] policies, which have predominated in the policy advice of the international financial institutions over the past quarter century, have been based on market fundamentalist policies which ignored the information-theoretic concerns; this explains, at least partly, their widespread failures. Information affects decision-making in every context – not just inside firms and households. More recently, as I discuss below, I have turned my attention to some aspects of what might be called the *political economy* of information: the role of information in political processes and collective decision-making. There are asymmetries of information between those governing and those governed, and just as participants in markets strive to overcome asymmetries of information, we need to look for ways by which the asymmetries of information in political processes can be limited and their consequences mitigated.

The historical setting

I do not want here to review in detail the models that were constructed exploring the role of information; in recent years, there has been a number of survey articles and interpretive essays, even several books in this area.[2] I do want to highlight some of the dramatic impacts that information economics has had on how economics is approached today, how it has provided explanations for phenomena that were previously unexplained, how it has altered our views about how the economy functions, and, perhaps most importantly, how it has led to a rethinking of the appropriate role for government in our society. In describing the ideas, I want to trace out some of their origins. To a large extent, these ideas evolved from attempts to answer specific policy questions or to explain specific phenomena to which the standard theory provided an inadequate explanation. But any discipline has a life of its own, a prevailing paradigm, with assumptions and conventions. Much of the work was motivated by an attempt to explore the limits of that paradigm – to see how the standard models could embrace problems of information imperfections (which turned out to be not very well).

For more than 100 years, formal modeling in economics had focused on models in which information was assumed to be perfect. Of course, everyone recognized that information was in fact imperfect, but the hope, following Marshall's dictum "*Natura non facit saltum*," was that economies in which information was not too imperfect would look very much like economies in which information was perfect. One of the main results of our research was to show that this was not true; that even a small amount of information imperfection could have a profound effect on the nature of the equilibrium.

The creators of the neoclassical model, the reigning economic paradigm of the twentieth century, ignored the warnings of nineteenth-century and still earlier masters about how information concerns might alter their analyses – perhaps because they could not see how to embrace them in their seemingly precise models, perhaps because doing so would have led to uncomfortable conclusions about the efficiency of markets. For instance, Smith, in anticipating later discussions of adverse selection, wrote that as firms raise interest rates, the best borrowers drop out of the market.[3] If lenders knew perfectly the risks associated with each borrower, this would matter little; each borrower would be charged an appropriate risk premium. It is because lenders do not know the default probabilities of borrowers perfectly that this process of adverse selection has such important consequences.

I have already noted that *something* was wrong – indeed seriously wrong – with the competitive equilibrium models which represented the prevailing paradigm when we went to graduate school. The paradigm seemed to say that unemployment did not exist, and that issues of efficiency and equity could be neatly separated, so that economists could set aside problems of inequality and poverty as they went about their business of designing more efficient economic systems. But beyond these questionable conclusions there were also a host of empirical puzzles – facts that were hard to reconcile with the standard theory, institutional arrangements left unexplained. In microeconomics, there were public finance puzzles, such as why firms appear not to take actions which minimize their tax liabilities; security market paradoxes,[4] such as why asset prices are so volatile (Robert J. Shiller, 2000) and why equity plays such a limited role in the financing of new investment (Colin Mayer, 1990); and other important behavioral questions, such as why firms respond to risks in ways markedly different from those predicted by the theory. In macroeconomics, the cyclical movements of many of the key aggregate variables proved difficult to reconcile with the standard theory. For example, if labor-supply curves are highly inelastic, as most evidence suggests is the case (especially for primary workers), then falls in employment during cyclical downturns should be accompanied by large declines in the real consumption wage. This does not appear to happen. And if the perfect market assumptions were even approximately satisfied, the distress caused by cyclical movements in the economy would be much less than seems to be the case.[5]

There were, to be sure, some Ptolemaic attempts to defend and elaborate on the old model. Some authors, like George J. Stigler (1961), Nobel laureate in 1982, while recognizing the importance of information, argued that once the real costs of information were taken into account, the standard results of economics would still hold. Information was just a transactions cost. In the approach of many Chicago School economists, information economics was like any other branch of applied economics; one simply analyzed the special factors determining the demand for and supply of information, just as one might analyze the factors affecting the market for wheat. For the more mathematically inclined, information could be incorporated into production functions by inserting an I for the input "information," where I itself could be produced by inputs, like labor. Our analysis showed that this approach was wrong, as were the conclusions derived from it.

Practical economists who could not ignore the bouts of unemployment which had plagued capitalism since its inception talked of the "neoclassical synthesis": If Keynesian interventions were used to ensure that the economy remained at full employment, the story went, the standard neoclassical propositions would once again be true. But while the neoclassical synthesis (Paul A. Samuelson [1947], Nobel laureate in 1970) had enormous intellectual influence, by the 1970's and 1980's it had come under attack from two sides. One side attacked the underpinnings of Keynesian economics, its microfoundations. Why would rational actors fail to achieve equilibrium – with unemployment persisting – in the way that John Maynard Keynes (1936) had suggested? This form of the argument effectively denied the existence of the phenomena that Keynes was attempting to explain. Worse still, from this perspective some saw the unemployment that did exist as largely reflecting an interference (e.g., by government in setting minimum wages, or by trade unions using their monopoly power to set too-high wages) with the free workings of the market. The implication was that unemployment would be eliminated if markets were made more *flexible*, that is, if unions and government interventions were eliminated. Even if wages fell by a third in the Great Depression, they should have, in this view, fallen even more.

There was however an alternative perspective (articulated more fully in Bruce C. Greenwald and Stiglitz, 1987a, 1988b) which asked why we shouldn't believe that massive unemployment was just the tip of an iceberg of more pervasive market efficiencies that are harder to detect. If markets seemed to function *so* badly some of the time, they must be under-performing in more subtle ways much of the time. The economics of information bolstered this view. Indeed, given the nature of the debt contracts, falling prices in the Depression led to bankruptcy and economic disruptions, actually exacerbating the economic downturn. Had there been more wage and price flexibility, matters might have been even worse.

In a later section, I shall explain how it was not just the discrepancies between the standard competitive model and its predictions which led to its being questioned, but the model's lack of robustness – even slight departures from the underlying assumption of perfect information had large consequences. But before turning to those issues, it may be useful to describe some of the specific questions which underlay the beginnings of my research program in this area.

Sony motivating ideas

Education as a screening device

Key to my thinking on these issues was the time between 1969 and 1971 I spent at the Institute for Development Studies at the University of Nairobi with the support of the Rockefeller Foundation. The newly independent Kenyan government was asking questions that had not been raised by its former colonial masters, as it attempted to forge policies which would promote its growth and development. For example, how much should the government invest in education? It was clear that a better education got people better jobs – the credential put one at the head of the job queue. Gary S. Fields, a young scholar working at the Institute of Development Studies there, developed a simple model (published in 1972) suggesting, however, that the private returns to education – the enhanced probability of getting a good job – might differ from the social return. Indeed, it was possible that as more people got educated, the private returns got higher (it was even more necessary to get the credential) even though the social return to education might decline. From this perspective, education was performing a markedly different function than it did in the traditional economics litera-ture, where it simply added to human capital and improved productivity.[6] This analysis had important implications for Kenya's decision about how much to invest in higher education. The problem with Fields' work was that it did not provide a full *equilibrium* analysis: wages were fixed, rather than competitively determined.

This omission led me to ask what the market equilibrium would look like if wages were set equal to mean marginal products *conditional on the information that was available* (Stiglitz, 1975c). And this in turn forced me to ask: what were the *incentives* and *mechanisms* for employers and employees to acquire or transmit information? Within a group of otherwise similar job applicants (who therefore face the same wage), the employer has an incentive to identify who is the most able, to find some way of *sorting* or *screening* among them, *if he could keep that information private*. But often he cannot; and if others find out about a worker's true ability, the wage will be bid up, and the employer will be unable to appropriate the return to the information. At the very beginning of this research program we had thus identified one of the key issues in information economics: the difficulty of *appropriating* the returns to creating information.

On the other hand, if the employee knew his own ability (that is, if there were *asymmetries of information* between the employee and the employer), then a different set of incentives were at play. Someone who knows his abilities are above average has an incentive to convince his potential employer of that, but a worker at the bottom of the ability distribution has an equally strong incentive to keep the information private. Here was a second principle that was to be explored in subsequent years: there are incentives on the part of individuals for information not to be revealed, for secrecy, or, in modern parlance, for a lack of transparency. This raised questions: How did the forces for secrecy and for information disclosure get balanced? What was the equilibrium that emerged? I will postpone until the next section a description of that equilibrium.

Efficiency wage theory

That summer in Kenya I began three other research projects related to information imperfections. At the time I was working in Kenya, there was heavy urban unemployment. My colleagues at the Institute for Development Studies, Michael Todaro and John Harris, had formulated a simple model of labor migration from the rural to the urban sector which accounted for the unemployment.[7] High urban wages attracted workers, who were willing to risk unemployment for the chance at those higher wages. Here was a simple, general-equilibrium model of unemployment, but again there was one missing piece: an explanation of high urban wages, well in excess of the legal minimum wage. It did not seem as if either government or unions were *forcing* employers to pay these high wages. One needed an equilibrium theory of wage determination. I recalled discussions I had once had in Cambridge with Harvey Leibenstein, who had postulated that in very poor countries, because of nutrition, higher wages led to higher productivity (Leibenstein, 1957). The key insight was that imperfections in information and contracting might also rationalize a dependence of productivity on wages.[8] In that case, firms might find it profitable to pay a higher wage than the minimum necessary to hire labor; such wages I referred to as *efficiency wages*. With efficiency wages, unemployment could exist in equilibrium. I explored four explanations for why productivity might depend on wages (other than through nutrition). The simplest was that lower wages lead to higher turnover, and therefore higher turnover costs for the firm.[9] It was not until some years later than we were able to explain more fully – based on limitations of information – why it was that firms have to bear these turnover costs (Richard J. Arnott and Stiglitz, 1985; Arnott et al., 1988).

Another explanation for efficiency wages was related to the work I was beginning on asymmetric information. Any manager will tell you that paying higher wages attracts better workers – this is just an application of the general notion of adverse selection, which played a central role in earlier insurance literature (Kenneth J. Arrow, 1965). Firms in a market do not passively have to accept the "market wage." Even in competitive markets, firms could, if they wanted, offer higher wages than others; indeed, it might pay a firm to offer a higher wage, to attract more able workers. Again, the efficiency wage theory explained the existence of unemployment *in equilibrium*. It was thus clear that the notion that underlay much of traditional competitive equilibrium analysis – that markets *had* to clear – was simply not true if information were imperfect.

The formulation of the efficiency wage theory that has received the most attention over the years, however, has focused on problems of *incentives*. Many firms claim that paying high wages induces their workers to work harder. The problem that Carl Shapiro and I (1984) faced was to try to make sense of this claim. If all workers are identical, then if it benefited one firm to pay a high wage, it would likewise benefit all firms. But if a worker was fired for shirking, and there were full employment, he could immediately get another job at the same wage. The high wage would thus provide no incentive. Only if there were unemployment would the worker pay a price for shirking. We showed that *in equilibrium* there *had* to be unemployment: unemployment was the discipline device that forced workers to work hard (see Rey and Stiglitz [1996] for an alternative general-equilibrium formulation). The model had strong policy implications, some of which I shall describe below. Our work illustrated the use of highly simplified models to help clarify thinking about quite complicated matters. In practice, of course, workers are not identical, so problems of adverse selection become intertwined with those of incentives. For example, being fired usually does convey information – there is typically a stigma.

There was a fourth version of the efficiency wage, where productivity was related to *morale* effects, perceptions about how *fairly* they were being treated. While I briefly discussed this version in my earlier work (see in particular Stiglitz, 1974d), it was not until almost 20 years later that the idea was fully developed in the important work of Akerlof and Yellen (1990).

Sharecropping and the general theory of incentives

This work on the economics of incentives in labor markets was closely related to the third research project that I began in Kenya. In traditional economic theory, while considerable lip service was paid to incentives, there was little serious attention to issues of incentives, motivation, and monitoring. With perfect information, individuals are paid to perform a particular service. If they perform the service they receive the contracted amount; and if not, they do not. With *imperfect* information, firms have to motivate and monitor, rewarding workers for observed good performance and punishing them for bad. My interest in these issues was first aroused by thinking about sharecropping, a common form of land tenancy in developing countries. Under sharecropping, the worker surrenders half (sometimes two-thirds) of the produce to the landlord in return for the use of his land. At first blush, this seemed a highly inefficient arrangement, equivalent to a 50-percent tax on workers' labor. But what were the alternatives? The worker could rent the land. He would have full incentives but then he would have to bear all the risk of fluctuations in output; and beside, he often did not have the requisite capital to pay the rent ahead of time and access to credit was limited (for reasons to be explained below). He could work as wage labor, but then the landlord would have to monitor him, to ensure that he worked. Sharecropping represented a compromise between balancing concerns about risk sharing and incentives. The underlying information problem was that the input of the worker could not he observed, but only his output, which was not perfectly correlated with his input. The sharecropping contract could be thought of as a combination of a rental contract *plus* an insurance contract, in which the landlord "rebates" part of the rent if crops turn out badly. There is not full insurance (which would be equivalent to a wage contract) because such insurance would attenuate all incentives. The adverse effect of insurance on incentives to avoid the insured-against contingency is referred to as *moral hazard*.[10]

In Stiglitz (1974b) I analyzed the equilibrium sharecropping contract. In that paper, I recognized the similarity of the incentive problems I explored to those facing modern corporations, e.g., in providing incentives to their managers – a type of problem later to be called the *principal-agent problem* (Stephen A. Ross, 1973). There followed a large literature on optimal and equilibrium incentive schemes, in labor, capital, and insurance markets.[11] An important principle was that contracts had to be based on *observables*, whether they be inputs, processes, or outcomes. Many of the results obtained earlier in the work on adverse selection had their parallel in this area of "adverse incentives." For instance, Arnott and I (1988a, 1990) analyzed equilibria which entail partial insurance as a way of mitigating the adverse incentive effects (just as partial insurance characterized equilibrium with adverse selection).

Equilibrium wage and price distributions

The fourth strand of my research looked at the issue of wage differentials from a different perspective. My earlier work had suggested that firms that faced higher turnover might pay higher wages to mitigate the problem. But one of the reasons that individuals quit is to obtain a higher-paying job, so the turnover rate in turn depends on the wage distribution. The challenge was to formulate an *equilibrium* model that incorporated both of these observations, that is, where the wage distribution *itself* which motivated the search was *explained* as part of the equilibrium.

More generally, efficiency wage theory said that firms might pay a higher wage than necessary to obtain workers; but the level of the efficiency wage might vary across firms. For example, firms with higher turnover costs, or for which worker inefficiency could lead to large losses of capital, or for which monitoring was more difficult, might find it desirable to pay higher wages. The implication was that similar labor might receive quite different compensation in different jobs. The distribution of wages might not, in general, be explicable solely in terms of differences in abilities.

I was to return to these four themes repeatedly in my research over the following three decades.

From the competitive paradigm to the information paradigm

In the previous section, I described how the disparities between the models economists used and the world that I saw, especially in Kenya, had motivated a search for an alternative paradigm. But there was another motivation, driven more by the internal logic and structure of the competitive model itself.

The competitive model virtually made economics a branch of engineering (no aspersions on that noble profession intended), and the participants in the economy better or worse engineers. Each was solving a maximization problem, with full information: households maximizing utility subject to budget constraints, firms maximizing profits (market value), and the two interacting in competitive product, labor, and capital markets. One of the peculiar implications was that there never were disagreements about what the firm should do. Alternative management teams would presumably come up with the same solution to the maximization problems. Another peculiar implication was for the meaning of risk: When a firm said that a project was risky, that (should have) meant that it was highly correlated with the business cycle, not that it had a high chance of failure (Stiglitz, 1989g). I have already described some of the other peculiar implications of the model: the fact that there was no unemployment or credit rationing, that it focused on only a limited subset of the information problems facing society, that it seemed not to address issues such as incentives and motivation.

But much of the research in the profession was directed not at these big gaps, but at seemingly more technical issues – at the mathematical structures. The underlying *mathematics* required assumptions of convexity and continuity, and with these assumptions one could prove the existence of equilibrium and its (Pareto) efficiency (see Gerard Debreu, 1959; Arrow, 1964). The standard proofs of these fundamental theorems of welfare economics did not even list in their enumerated assumptions those concerning information: the perfect information assumption was so ingrained it did not have to be explicitly stated. The *economic* assumptions to which the proofs of efficiency called attention concerned the absence of externalities and public goods. The market failures approach to the economics of the public sector (Francis M. Bator, 1958) discussed alternative approaches by which these market failures could be corrected, but these market failures were highly circumscribed by assumption.

There was, moreover, a curious disjunction between the language economists used to explain markets and the models they constructed. They talked about the information efficiency of the market economy, though they focused on a single information problem, that of scarcity. But there are a myriad of other information problems faced by consumers and firms every day, concerning, for instance, the prices and qualities of the various objects that are for sale in the market, the quality and efforts of the workers they hire, or the potential returns to investment projects. In the standard paradigm, the competitive general-equilibrium model (for which Kenneth J. Arrow and Gerard Debreu received Nobel Prizes in 1972 and 1983, respectively), there were no shocks, no unanticipated events: At the beginning of time, the full equilibrium was solved, and everything from then on was an unfolding over time of what had been planned in each of the contingencies. In the real world, the critical question was: how, and how well, do markets handle fundamental problems of information?

There were other aspects of the standard paradigm that seemed hard to accept. It argued that institutions did not matter – markets could see through them, and equilibrium was simply determined by the laws of supply and demand. It said that the distribution of wealth did not matter, so long as there were well-defined property rights (Ronald H. Coase [1960], who won the Nobel Prize in 1991). And it said that (by and large) history did not matter – knowing preferences and technology and initial endowments, one could describe the time path of the economy.

Work on the economics of information began by questioning each of these underlying premises. Consider, to begin with, the convexity assumptions which corresponded to long-standing principles of diminishing returns. With imperfect information (and the costs of acquiring it) these assumptions were no longer plausible. It was not just that the cost of acquiring information could be viewed as fixed costs.[12] My work with Roy Radner (Radner and Stiglitz, 1984) showed that there was a *fundamental nonconcavity in the value of information*, that is, under quite general conditions, it never paid to buy just a little bit of information. Arnott and Stiglitz (1988a) showed that such problems were pervasive in even the simplest of moral hazard problems (where individuals had a choice of alternative actions, e.g. the amount of risk to undertake). While we had not repealed the law of diminishing returns, we had shown its domain to be more limited than had previously been realized.

Michael Rothschild and I (1976) showed that under natural formulations of what might be meant by a competitive market with imperfect information, equilibrium often did not exist[13] – even when there was an arbitrarily small amount of information imperfection.[14] While subsequent research has looked for alternative definitions of equilibrium (e.g., Riley, 1979), we remain unconvinced; most of these alternatives violate the natural meaning of "competition," that each participant in the market is so small that he believes that he will have no effect on the behavior of others (Rothschild and Stiglitz, 1997).

The new information paradigm went further in undermining the foundations of competitive equilibrium analysis, the basic "laws" of economics. For example, we have shown how, when prices affect "quality" – either because of incentive or selection effects – equilibrium may be characterized by demand not equaling supply; firms will not pay lower wages to workers, even when they can obtain such workers, because doing so will raise their labor costs. Contrary to the law of one price, we have shown that the market will be characterized by wage and price distributions, even when there is no exogenous source of "noise" in the economy, and even when all firms and workers are (otherwise) identical. Contrary to standard competitive results, we have shown that in equilibrium, firms may charge a price in excess of the marginal costs, or workers may be paid a wage in excess of their reservation wage, so that the incentive to maintain a reputation is maintained (see also Benjamin Klein and Keith B. Leffler, 1981; Shapiro, 1983). Contrary to the efficient markets hypothesis (Eugene F. Fama, 1970), which holds that stock prices convey all the relevant information from the informed to the uninformed, Sanford J. Grossman and I (1976, 1980a) showed that, when information is costly to collect, stock prices necessarily aggregate information imperfectly (to induce people to gather information, there must be an "equilibrium amount of disequilibrium"). Each of these cornerstones of the competitive paradigm was rejected, or was shown to hold only under much more restrictive conditions.

The most fundamental reason that markets with imperfect information differ from those in which information is complete is that, with imperfect information, market actions or choices convey information. Market participants know this and respond accordingly. For example, firms provide guarantees not only because they are better able to absorb the risk of product failure but to convey information about their confidence in their products. A person takes an insurance policy with a large deductible to convey to the insurer his belief that the likelihood of his having an accident is low. Information may also be concealed: A firm may not assign an employee to a highly visible job, because it knows that the assignment will be interpreted as an indication that the employee is good, making it more likely that a rival will try to hire the person away.

One of the early insights (Akerlof, 1970) was that, with imperfect information, markets may be thin or absent. The absence of particular markets, e.g., for risk, has profound implications for how *other* markets function. The fact that workers and firms cannot buy insurance against many of the risks which they face affects labor and capital markets; it leads, for instance, to labor contracts in which the employer provides *some* insurance. But the design of these more complicated, but still imperfect and incomplete, contracts affects the efficiency, and overall performance, of the economy.

Perhaps most importantly, under the standard paradigm, markets are Pareto efficient, except when one of a limited number of market failures occurs. Under the imperfect information paradigm, markets are almost never Pareto efficient.

While information economics thus undermined these long-standing principles of economics, it also provided explanations for many phenomena that had long been unexplained. Before turning to these applications, I want to present a somewhat a more systematic account of the *principles* of the economics of information.

Some problems in constructing an alternative paradigm

The fact that information is imperfect was, of course, well recognized by all economists. The reason that models with imperfect information were not developed earlier was that it was not obvious how to do so: While there is a single way in which information is perfect, there are an infinite number of ways in which information can be imperfect. One of the keys to success was formulating simple models in which the set of relevant information could be fully specified – and so the precise ways in which information was imperfect could also be fully specified. But there was a danger in this methodology, as useful as it was: In these overly simplistic models, full revelation of information was sometimes possible. In the real world, of course, this never happens, which is why in some of the later work (e.g., Grossman and Stiglitz, 1976, 1980a), we worked with models with an infinite number of states. Similarly there may well be ways of fully resolving incentive problems in simple models, which collapse when models are made more realistic, for example by combining selection and incentive problems (Stiglitz and Weiss, 1986).

Perhaps the hardest problem in building the new paradigm was modeling equilibrium. It was important to think about both sides of the market – employers and employees, insurance company and the insured, lender and borrower. Each had to be modeled as "rational," in some sense, making inferences on the basis of available information and behaving accordingly. I wanted to model *competitive* behavior, where each actor in the economy was small, and believed he was small – and so his actions could not or would not affect the equilibrium (though others' inferences about himself might be affected). Finally, one had to think carefully about what was the feasible set of actions: what might each side do to extract or convey information to others.

As we shall see, the variety of results obtained (and much of the confusion in the early literature) arose partly from a failure to be as clear as one might have been about the assumptions. For instance, the standard adverse selection model had the quality of the good offered in the market (say of used cars, or riskiness of the insured) depending on price. The car buyer (the seller of insurance) knows the *statistical* relationship between price and quality, and this affects his demand. The market equilibrium is the price at which demand equals supply. But that is an equilibrium if and only if there is no way by which the seller of a good car can convey that information to the buyer – so that he can earn a quality premium – and if there is no way by which the buyer can sort out good cars from bad cars. Typically, there are such ways, and it is the attempt to elicit that information which has profound effects on how markets function. To develop a new paradigm, we had to break out from long-established premises, to ask what should be taken as assumptions and what should be derived from the analysis. Market clearing could not be taken as an assumption; neither could the premise that a firm sells a good at a particular price to all comers. One could not *begin* the analysis even by assuming that in competitive equilibrium there would be zero profits. In the standard theory, if there were positive profits, a firm might enter, bidding away existing customers. In the new theory, the attempt to bid away new customers by slightly lowering prices might lead to marked changes in their behavior or in the mix of customers, in such a way that the profits of the new entrant actually became negative. One had to rethink all the conclusions from first premises.

We made progress in our analyses because we began with highly simplified models of particular markets, that allowed us to think through carefully each of the assumptions and conclusions. From the analysis of particular markets (whether the insurance market, the education market, the labor market, or the land tenancy/sharecropping market), we attempted to identify general principles, to explore how these principles operated in each of the other markets. In doing so, we identified particular features, particular informational assumptions, which seemed to be more relevant in one market or another. The nature of competition in the labor market is different from that in the insurance market or the capital market, though these markets have much in common. This interplay, between looking at the ways in which such markets are similar and dissimilar, proved to be a fruitful research strategy.[15]

Sources of information asymmetries

Information imperfections are pervasive in the economy: indeed, it is hard to imagine what a world with perfect information would be like. Much of the research I describe here focuses on *asymmetries* of information, the fact that different people know different things. Workers know more about their own abilities than the firm does; the person buying insurance knows more about his health, e.g., whether he smokes and drinks immoderately, than the insurance firm. Similarly, the owner of a car knows more about the car than potential buyers; the owner of a firm knows more about the firm than a potential investor; the borrower knows more about the riskiness of his project than the lender does; and so on.

An essential feature of a decentralized market economy is that different people know different things, and in some sense, economists had long been thinking of markets with information asymmetries. But the earlier literature had neither thought about how these were created, or what their consequences might be. While such information asymmetries inevitably arise, the extent to which they do so and their consequences depend on how the market is structured, and the recognition that they will arise affects market behavior. For instance, even if an individual has no more information about his ability than potential employers, the moment he goes to work for a specific employer, an information asymmetry has been created – the employer may now know more about the individual's ability than others do. A consequence is that the "used labor" market may not work well. Other employers will be reserved in bidding for the worker's services, knowing that they will succeed in luring him away from his current employer only if they bid too much. This impediment to labor mobility gives market power to the first employer, which he will be tempted to exercise. But then, because a worker knows he will tend to be locked into a job, he will be more risk averse in accepting an offer. The terms of the initial contract thus have to be designed to reflect the diminution of the worker's bargaining power that occurs the moment he accepts a job.

To take another example, it is natural that in the process or oil exploration, a company may obtain information relevant to the likelihood that there will be oil in a neighboring tract – an informational externality (see Stiglitz, 1975d; Jeffrey J. Leitzinger and Stiglitz, 1984). The existence of this asymmetric information affects the nature of the bidding for oil rights on the neighboring tract. Bidding when there is known to be asymmetries of information will be markedly different from that where such asymmetries do not exist (Robert B. Wilson, 1977). Those who are uninformed will presume that they will win only if they bid too much – information asymmetries exacerbate the problem of the "winner's curse" (Wilson, 1969; Edward Capen *et al.*1971). The government (or other owners of large tracts to be developed) should take this into account in its leasing strategy. And the bidders in the initial leases too will take this into account: part of the value of winning in the initial auction is the information rent that will accrue in later rounds.

While early work in the economics of information dealt with how markets overcame problems of information asymmetries, later work turned to how actors in markets *create* information problems, for example in an attempt to exploit market power. An example is managers of firms who attempt to entrench themselves, and reduce competition in the market for managers, by taking actions to increase information asymmetry (Andrei Shleifer and Robert W. Vishny, 1989; Aaron S. Edlin and Stiglitz, 1995). This is an example of the general problem of corporate governance, to which I will return later. Similarly, the presence of information imperfections give rise to market power in product markets. Firms can exploit this market power through "sales" and other ways of differentiating among individuals who have different search costs (Salop, 1977; Salop and Stiglitz, 1977, 1982; Stiglitz, 1979a). The price dispersions which exist in the market are *created* by the market – they are not just the failure of markets to arbitrage fully price differences caused by shocks that affect different markets differently.

Overcoming information asymmetries

I now want to discuss briefly the ways by which information asymmetries are dealt with, how they can be (partially) overcome.

Incentives for gathering and disclosing information

There are two key issues: what are the *incentives* for obtaining information, and what are the *mechanisms*. My brief discussion of the analysis of education as a screening device suggested the fundamental incentive: More able individuals (lower risk individuals, firms with better products) will receive a higher wage (will have to pay a lower premium, will receive a higher price for their products) if they can establish that they are more productive (lower risk, higher quality).

We noted earlier that while some individuals have an incentive to disclose information, some have an incentive not to have the information disclosed. Was it possible that in market equilibrium, only *some* of the information would be revealed? One of the early important results was that, if the more able can costlessly establish that they are more able, then the market will be fully revealing, even though those who are below average would prefer that no information be revealed. In the simplest models, I described a process of unraveling: If the most able could establish his ability, he would; but then all but the most able would be grouped together, receiving the mean marginal product of that group; and the most able of that group would have an incentive to reveal his ability. And so on down the line, until there was full revelation. (I jokingly referred to this as "Walras' Law of Sorting" – if all but one group sorts itself out from the others, then the last group is also identified.)

What happens if those who are more able cannot credibly convince potential employers of their ability? The other side of the market has an incentive too to gather information. An employer that can find a worker that is better than is recognized by others will have found a bargain, because the worker's wage will be determined by what others think of him. The problem, as we noted, is that if what the employer knows becomes known to others, the worker's wage will be bid up, and the employer will be unable to appropriate the returns on his investment in information acquisition.

The fact that competition makes it difficult for the screener to appropriate the returns from screening has an important implication: In markets where, for one reason or another, the more able cannot fully convey their attributes, investment in screening requires *imperfect competition in screening*. The economy, in effect, has to choose between two different imperfections: imperfections of information or imperfections of competition. Of course, in the end, there will be both forms of imperfection, and no particular reason that these imperfections will be "balanced" optimally (Stiglitz, 1975b; Dwight Jaffee and Stiglitz, 1990). This is but one of many examples of the *interplay* between market imperfections. Earlier, for instance, we discussed the incentive problems associated with sharecropping, which arise when workers do not own the land that they till. This problem could be overcome if individuals could borrow to buy their land. But capital market imperfections – limitations on the ability to borrow, which themselves arise from information imperfections – explain why this "solution" does not work.

There is another important consequence: if markets were fully informationally efficient – that is, if information disseminated instantaneously and perfectly throughout the economy – then no one would have any incentive to gather information, so long as there was any cost of doing so. Hence markets cannot be fully informationally efficient (Grossman and Stiglitz, 1976, 1980a).

Mechanisms for elimination of reducing information asymmetries

In simple models where (for example) individuals know their own abilities there might seem an easy way to resolve the problem of information asymmetry: Let each person tell his true characteristic. Unfortunately, individuals do not necessarily have the incentive to tell the truth. Talk is cheap. Other methods must be used to convey information credibly.

The simplest way by which that could be done was an exam. Models of competitive equilibrium (Arrow, 1973; Stiglitz, 1974a) with exams make two general points. First, in equilibrium *the gains of the more able were largely at the expense of the less able*. Establishing that an individual is of higher ability provides that person with higher wages, but simultaneously establishes that others are of lower ability. Hence the private returns to expenditures on educational screening exceed the social returns. It was clear that there were important *externalities* associated with information, a theme which was to recur in later work. Second, and a more striking result, there could exist multiple equilibria – one in which information was fully revealed (the market identified the high and low ability people) and another in which it was not (called a pooling equilibrium). The pooling equilibrium Pareto-dominated the equilibrium with full revelation. This work, done some 30 years ago, established two results of great policy import, which remarkably have not been fully absorbed into policy discussions even today. First, markets do not provide appropriate incentives for information disclosure. There is, in principle, a role for government. And second, expenditures on information may be too great (see also Hirshleifer, 1971).

Conveying information through actions

But much of the information firms glean about their employees, banks about their borrowers, or insurance companies about their insured, comes not from examinations but from making inferences based on their *behavior*. This is a commonplace in life – but it was not in our economic models. As I have already noted, the early discussions of adverse selection in insurance markets recognized that as an insurance company raised its premiums, those who were least likely to have an accident might decide not to purchase the insurance; the willingness to purchase insurance at a particular price conveyed information to the insurance company. George Akerlof recognized that this phenomenon is far more general: the owner's willingness to sell a used car, for instance, conveyed information about the car's quality.

Bruce C. Greenwald (1979, 1986) took these ideas one important step further, showing how adverse selection applied to labor and capital markets (see also Greenwald et al., 1984; Stewart C. Myers and Nicholas S. Majluf, 1984). For example, the willingness of insiders in a firm to sell stock at a particular price conveys information about their view of what the stock is really worth. Akerlof's insight that the result of these information asymmetries was that markets would be thin or absent helped explain why labor and capital markets often did not function well. It provided part of the explanation for why firms raised so little of their funds through equity (Mayer, 1990). Stigler was wrong: imperfect information was not just like a transactions cost.

There is a much richer set of actions which convey information beyond those on which traditional adverse selection models have focused. An insurance company wants to attract healthy applicants. It might realize that by locating itself on the fifth floor of a walk-up building, only those with a strong heart would apply. The willingness or ability to walk up five floors conveys information. More subtly, it might recognize that how far up it needs to locate itself, if it only wants to get healthy applicants, depends on other elements of its strategy, such as the premium charged. Or the company may decide to throw in a membership in a health club, but charge a higher premium. Those who value a health club – because they will use it – willingly pay the higher premium. But these individuals are likely to be healthier.

There are a host of other actions which convey information. The quality of the guarantee offered by a firm can convey information about the quality of the product; only firms that believe that their product is reliable will be willing to offer a good guarantee. The guarantee is desirable not just because it reduces risk, but because it conveys information. The number of years of schooling may convey information about the ability of an individual. More able individuals may go to school longer, in which case the increase in wages associated with an increase in schooling may not be a consequence of the human capital that has been added, but rather simply be a result of the sorting that occurs. The size of the deductible that an individual chooses in an insurance policy may convey information about his view about the likelihood of an accident or the size of the accidents he anticipates – on *average*, those who are less likely to have an accident may be more willing to accept high deductibles. The willingness of an entrepreneur to hold large fractions of his wealth in a firm (or to retain large fractions of the shares of the firm) conveys information about his beliefs in the firm's future performance. If a firm promotes an individual to a particular job, it may convey information about the firm's assessment of his ability.

The fact that these actions may convey information affects behavior. In some cases, the action will be designed to obfuscate, to limit information disclosure. The firm that knows that others are looking at who it promotes, and will compete more vigorously for those workers, may affect the willingness of the firm to promote some individuals or assign them to particular jobs (Michael Waldman, 1984). In others, the action will be designed to convey information in a credible way to alter beliefs. The fact that customers will treat a firm that issues a better guarantee as if its product is better – and therefore be willing to pay a higher price – may affect the guarantee that the firm is willing to issue. Knowing that selling his shares will convey a negative signal concerning his views of the future prospects of his firm, an entrepreneur may retain more of the shares of the firm; he will be less diversified than he otherwise would have been (and accordingly, he may act in a more risk-averse manner).

A simple lesson emerges: Some individuals wish to convey information; some individuals wish not to have information conveyed (either because such information might lead others to think less well of them, or because conveying information may interfere with their ability to appropriate rents). In either case, the fact that actions convey information leads people to alter their behavior, and changes how markets function. This is why information imperfections have such profound effects.

Once one recognizes that actions convey information, two results follow. First, in making decisions about what to do, individuals will not only think about what they like (as in traditional economics) but how it will affect others' beliefs about them. If I choose to go to school longer, it may lead others to believe that I am more able. I may therefore decide to stay in school longer, not because I value what is being taught, but because I value how it changes others' beliefs concerning my ability. This means, of course, that we have to rethink completely firm and household decision-making.

Secondly, we noted earlier that individuals have an incentive to "lie" – the less able to say that they are more able. Similarly, if it becomes recognized that those who walk up to the fifth floor to apply for insurance are more healthy, then I might he willing to do so even if I am not so healthy, simply to fool the insurance company. Recognizing this, one needs to look for ways by which information is conveyed *in equilibrium*. The critical insight, in how that could occur was provided in a paper I wrote with Michael Rothschild (1976). If those who were more able, less risk prone, or more creditworthy *acted* in some observable way (had different preferences) than those who were less able, less risk prone, or less creditworthy, then it might be possible to design a set of *choices*, which would result in those with different characteristics in effect *identifying* themselves through their *self-selection*. The particular mechanism which we explored in our insurance model illustrates how self-selection mechanisms work. People who know they are less likely to have an accident will be more willing to accept an insurance policy with a high deductible, so that an insurance company that offered two policies, one at a high premium and no deductible, one with a low premium and high deductible, would be able to sort out who were high risk and who low. It is an easy matter to construct choices which thus *separate* people into classes.

It was clear that information was conveyed because the actions were costly, and more costly for some than others. The attempt to convey information had to *distort* behavior. Our analysis also made it clear that it was not just information asymmetries, but information imperfections more generally, that were relevant. Even if those buying insurance did not know their accident probabilities (or know them with greater accuracy than the insurance company), so long as those with higher accident probabilities *on average* differed in some way reflected in their preferences and actions, self-selection mechanisms could and would be employed to sort.

Yet another set of issues arise from the fact that actions may not be costlessly observable. The employer would like to know how hard his worker is working; the lender would like to know the actions which borrower will undertake. These asymmetries of information about *actions* are as important as the earlier discussed asymmetries. Just as in the adverse selection model, the seller of insurance may try to overcome the problems posed by information asymmetries by *examination*, so too in the moral hazard or adverse incentive model, he may try to *monitor* the actions of the insured. But examinations and monitoring are costly, and while they yield some information, typically there remains a high level of residual information imperfection. One responses to this problem is to try to induce desired behavior through the setting of contract terms. For example, borrowers' risk-taking behavior may be affected by the interest rate charged by the lender (Stiglitz and Weiss, 1981).

Consequences for market equilibrium

The law of supply and demand had long been treated as a fundamental principle of economics. But there is in fact no law that requires the insurance firm to sell to all who apply at the announced premium, or the lender to lend to all who apply at the announced interest rate, or the employer to employ all those who apply at the posted wage. With perfect information and perfect competition, any firm that charged a price higher than the others would lose all of its customers; and at the going price, one faced a perfectly elastic supply of customers. In adverse selection and incentive models, what mattered was not just the supply of customers or employees or borrowers, but their "quality" – the riskiness of the insured or the borrower, the returns on the investment, the productivity of the worker.

Since "quality" may increase with price, it may be profitable (for example) to pay a higher wage than the "market-clearing" wage, whether the dependence on quality arises from adverse selection or adverse incentive effects (or, in the labor market, because of morale or nutritional effects). The consequence, as we have noted, is that market equilibrium may be characterized by demand not equaling supply in the traditional sense. In credit market equilibrium, the supply of loans may be rationed (William R. Keeton, 1979; Jonathan Eaton and Mark Gersovitz, 1981; Stiglitz and Weiss, 1981). Or, in the labor market, the wage rate may be higher than that at which the demand for labor equals the supply (an efficiency wage), leading to unemployment.[16]

Analyzing the choices which arise in *full* equilibrium, taking into account fully not only the knowledge that the firms have, say, about their customers but also the knowledge that customers have about how firms will make inferences about them from their behavior, and taking into account the fact that the inferences that a firm might make depends not only on what that firm does, but also on what other firms do, turned out, however, to be a difficult task. The easiest situation to analyze was that of a monopolist (Stiglitz, 1977). The monopolist could construct a set of choices that would *differentiate* among different types of individuals, and analyze whether it was profit maximizing for him to do so fully, or to (partially) "pool" – that is, offer a set of contracts such that several types might choose the same one. This work laid the foundations of a *general theory of price discrimination*. Under standard theories of monopoly, with perfect information, firms would have an incentive to price discriminate perfectly (extracting the full consumer surplus from each). If they did this, then monopoly would in fact be nondistortionary. Yet most models assumed no price discrimination (that is, the monopolist offered the same price to all customers), without explaining why they did not do so. The new work showed how, given limited information, firms could price discriminate, but could do so only imperfectly. Subsequent work by a variety of authors (such as William J. Adams and Yellen, 1976; Salop, 1977) explored ways by which a monopolist might find out relevant characteristics of his customers. Information economics thus provided the first coherent theory of monopoly.

The reason that analyzing monopoly was easy is that the monopolist could structure the entire choice set facing his customers. The hard question is to describe the full competitive equilibrium, e.g., a set of insurance contracts such that no one can offer an alternative set that would be profitable. Each firm could control the choices that it offered, but not the choices offered by others; and the decisions made by customers depended on the entire set of choices available. In our 1976 paper, Rothschild and I succeeded in analyzing this case.

Three striking results emerged from this analysis. The first I have already mentioned: Under plausible conditions, given the natural definition of equilibrium, equilibrium might not exist. There were two possible forms of equilibria: *pooling equilibria*, in which the market is not able to distinguish among the types, and *separating equilibria*, in which it is. The different groups "separate out" by taking different actions. We showed in our context that there never could be a pooling equilibrium – if there were a single contract that everyone bought, there was another contract that another firm could offer which would "break" the pooling equilibrium. On the other hand, there might not exist a separating equilibrium either, if the cost of separation was too great. Any putative separating equilibrium could be broken by a profitable pooling contract, a contract which would be bought by both low risk and high risk types.[17]

Second, even small amounts of imperfections of information can change the standard results concerning the existence and characterization of equilibrium. Equilibrium, for instance, never exists when the two types are very near each other. As we have seen, the competitive equilibrium model is simply not robust.

Third, we now can see how the fact that actions convey information affects equilibrium. In perfect information models, individuals would fully divest themselves of the risks which they face, and accordingly would act in a risk neutral manner. We explained why insurance markets would not work well – why most risk-averse individuals would buy only partial insurance. The result was important not only for the insights it provided into the workings of insurance markets, but because there are important elements of insurance in many trans-actions and markets. The relationship between the landlord and his tenant, or the employer and his employee, contains an insurance component.

In short, the general principle that actions convey information applies in many contexts. Further, limitations on the ability to divest oneself of risk are important in explaining a host of contractual relationships.

Sorting, screening, and signaling

In equilibrium, both buyers and sellers, employers and employees, insurance company and insured, and lender and creditor are aware of the informational consequences of their actions. In the case where, say, the insurance company or employer takes the initiative in sorting out applicants, self-selection is an alternative to examinations as a sorting device. In the case where the insured, or the employee, takes the initiative to identify himself as a more attrac-tive contractual partner, then it is conventional to say he is *signaling* (Spence, 1973). But of course, in equilibrium both sides are aware of the consequences of alternative actions, and the differences between signaling and self-selection screening models lie in the technical-ities of game theory, and in particular whether the informed or uninformed player moves first.[18]

Still, some of the seeming differences between signaling and screening models arise because of a failure to specify a *full* equilibrium. We noted earlier that there might be many separating contracts, but a unique separating equilibrium. We argued that if one considered any other separating set of contracts, then (say, in the insurance market) a firm could come in and offer an alternative set of contracts and make a profit. Then the original set of sepa-rating contracts could not have been an equilibrium. The same is true in, say, the education signaling model. There are many educational systems which "separate" – that is, the more able choose to go to school longer, and the wages at each level of education correspond to the productivity of those who go to school for that length of time. But all except one are not *full equilibria*. Assume, for instance, there were two types of individuals, of low ability and of high ability. Then if the low-ability person has 12 years of schooling, then any education system in which the high-ability person went to school sufficiently long – say, more than 14 years – might separate. But the low-ability types would recognize that if they went to school for 11 years, they would still be treated as having low ability. The unique equilib-rium level of education for the low-ability person is that which maximizes his net income (taking into account the productivity gains and costs of education). The unique equilibrium level of education for the high-ability type is the lowest level of education such that the low-ability type does not have the incentive to mimic the high-ability person's educational attainment.

The education system, of course, was particularly infelicitous for studying *market* equilib-rium. The structure of the education system is largely a matter of public choice, not of market processes. Different countries have chosen markedly different systems. The minimum lever of education is typically not a matter of choice, but set by the government. Within educational systems, examinations play as important a role as self-selection or signaling, though *given* a certain standard of testing, there is a process of self-selection involved in deciding whether to stay in school, or to try to pass the examination. For the same reason, the problems of existence which arise in the insurance market are not relevant in the education market – the "competitive" supply side of the market is simply absent. But when the signaling concepts are translated into contexts in which there is a robust competitive market, the problems of existence cannot be so easily ignored. In particular, when there is a continuum of types, as in the Spence (1973) model, there never exists a screening equilibrium.

Equilibrium contracts

The work with Rothschild was related to earlier work that I had done on incentives (such as the work on sharecropping) in that both lines of work entailed an "equilibrium in contracts." The contracts that had characterized economic relations in the standard competitive model were extraordinarily simple: I will pay you a certain amount if you do such and such. If you did not perform as promised, the pay was not given. But with perfect information, individuals simply would not sign contracts that they did not intend to fulfill. Insurance contracts were similarly simple: A payment occurred if and only if particular specified events occurred.

The work on sharecropping and on equilibrium with competitive insurance markets showed that with imperfect information, a far richer set of contracts would be employed and thus began a large literature on the theory of contracting. In the simple sharecropping contracts of Stiglitz (1974b), the contracts involved shares, fixed payments, and plot sizes. More generally, optimal payment structures related payments to *observables*, such as inputs, processes, or outputs.[19] Further, because what goes on in one market affects other parts of the economy, the credit, labor, and land markets are *interlinked*; one could not decentralize in the way hypothesized by the standard perfect information model. (Avishay Braverman and Stiglitz, 1982, 1986a, b, 1989).

These basic principles were subsequently applied in a variety of other market contexts. The most obvious was the design of labor contracts (Stiglitz, 1975a). Payments to workers can depend not only on output, but on *relative* performance, which may convey more relevant information than absolute performance. For example, the fact that a particular company's stock goes up when all other companies' stock goes up may say very little about the performance of the manager. Nalebuff and Stiglitz (1983a, b) analyzed the design of these relative performance compensation schemes (contests).

Credit markets too are characterized by complicated equilibrium contracts. Lenders may specify not only an interest rate, but also impose other conditions (collateral requirements, equity requirements) which would have both incentive and selection effects.[20] Indeed, the simultaneous presence of both selection and incentive effects is important in credit markets. In the absence of the former, it might be possible to increase the collateral requirement *and* raise interest rates, still ensuring that the borrower undertook the safe project.

As another application, "contracting" – including provisions that help information be conveyed and risks be shared – have been shown to play an important role in explaining macroeconomic rigidities. See, for instance, Costas Azariadis and Stiglitz (1983), the papers of the symposium in the 1983 *Quarterly Journal of Economics*, the survey article by Sherwin Rosen (1985), Arnott et al. (1988), and Lars Werin and Hans Wijkander (1992). Moreover, problems of asymmetries of information can help explain the perpetuation of seemingly inefficient contracts (Stiglitz, 1992b).

Equilibrium wage and price distributions

One of the most obvious differences between the predictions of the model with perfect information and what we see in everyday life is the conclusion that the same good sells for the same price everywhere. In reality, we all spend a considerable amount of time shopping for good buys. The differences in prices represent more than just differences in quality or service. There are *real* price differences. Since Stigler's classic paper (1961), there has been a large literature exploring optimal search behavior. However Stigler, and most of the search literature, took the price or wage distribution as given. They did not ask how the distribution might arise and whether, given the search costs, it could be sustained.

As I began to analyze these models, I found that there could he a nondegenerate equilibrium wage or price distribution even if all agents were identical, e.g., faced the same search costs. Early on, it had become clear that even small search costs could make a large difference to the behavior of product and labor markets. Peter A. Diamond (1971) had independently made this point in a highly influential paper, which serves to illustrate powerfully the lack of robustness of the competitive equilibrium theory. Assume for example, as in the standard theory, that all firms were charging the competitive price, but there is an epsilon cost of searching, of going to another store. Then any firm which charged half an epsilon more would lose no customers and thus would choose to increase its price. Similarly, it would pay all other firms to increase their prices. But at the higher price, it would again pay each to increase price, and so on until the price charged at every firm is the monopoly price, even though search costs are small. This showed convincingly that the competitive price was not the equilibrium. But in some cases, not even the monopoly price was an equilibrium. In general, Salop and Stiglitz (1977, 1982, 1987) and Stiglitz (1979b, 1985c, 1987b, 1989c) showed that in situations where there were even small search costs, markets might be characterized by a price distribution. The standard wisdom that said that not everyone had to be informed tc ensure that the market acted perfectly competitive was simply not, in general, true (see Stiglitz, 1989c, for a survey).

Efficiency of the market equilibrium and the role of the state

The fundamental theorems of neoclassical welfare economics state that competitive economies will lead, as if by an invisible hand, to a (Pareto-) efficient allocation of resources, and that every Pareto-efficient resource allocation can be achieved through a competitive mechanism, provided only that the appropriate lump-sum redistributions are undertaken. These theorems provide both the rationale for the reliance on free markets, and for the belief that issues of distribution can be separated from issues of efficiency, allowing the economist the freedom to push for reforms which increase efficiency, regardless of their seeming impact on distribution. (If society does not like the distributional consequences of a policy, it should simply redistribute income.)

The economics of information showed that neither of these theorems was particularly relevant to real economies. To be sure, economists over the preceding three decades had identified important market failures – such as the externalities associated with pollution – which required government intervention. But the scope for market failures was limited, and thus the arenas in which government intervention was required were correspondingly limited.

Early work, already referred to, had laid the foundations for the idea that economies with information imperfections would not be Pareto efficient, *even taking into account the costs of obtaining information*. There were interventions in the market that could make all parties better off. We had shown, for instance, that incentives for the disclosure and acquisition of information were far from perfect. On the one hand, imperfect appropriability meant that there might be insufficient incentives to gather information; but on the other, the fact that much of the gains were "rents," gains by some at the expense of others, suggested that there might be excessive expenditures on information. A traditional argument for unfettered capital markets was that there are strong incentives to gather information; discovering that some stock was more valuable than others thought would be rewarded by a capital gain. This price discovery function of capital markets was often advertised as one of its strengths. But while the individual who discovered the information a nanosecond before anyone else might be better off, was society as a whole better off? If having the information a nanosecond earlier did not lead to a change in real decisions (e.g., concerning investment), then it was largely redistributive, with the gains of those obtaining the information occurring at the expense of others (Stiglitz, 1989c).

There are potentially other inefficiencies associated with information acquisition. Information can have adverse effects on volatility (Stiglitz, 1989i). And information can lead to the destruction of markets, in ways which lead to adverse effects on welfare. For example, individuals may sometimes have incentives to create information asymmetries in insurance markets, which leads to the destruction of those markets and a lowering of overall welfare. Welfare might be increased if the acquisition of this kind of information could be proscribed. Recently, such issues have become sources of real policy concern in the arena of genetic testing. Even when information is available, there are issues concerning its use, with the use of certain kinds of information having either a discriminatory intent or effect, in circumstances in which such direct discrimination itself would be prohibited.[21]

While it was perhaps not surprising that markets might not provide appropriate incentives for the acquisition and dissemination of information, the market failures associated with imperfect information may be far more profound. The intuition can be seen most simply in the case of models with moral hazard. There, the premium charged is associated with the *average* risk and, therefore, the average care, taken by seemingly similar individuals. The moral hazard problem arises because the level of care cannot be observed. Each individual ignores the effect of his actions on the premium; but when they all take less care, the premium increases. The lack of care by each exerts a negative externality on others. The essential insight of Greenwald and Stiglitz (1986)[22] was to recognize that such externality-like effects are pervasive whenever information is imperfect or markets incomplete – that is always – and as a result, markets are essentially never constrained Pareto efficient. In short, market failures are pervasive. Arnott *et al.*(1994) provide a simple exposition of this point using the standard self-selection and incentive compatibility constraints.

An important implication is that efficient allocations cannot in general be decentralized via competitive markets. The notion that one could decentralize decision-making to obtain (Pareto-) efficient resource allocation is one of the fundamental ideas in economics. Greenwald and Stiglitz (1986) showed that that was not possible in general. A simple example illustrates what is at issue. An insurance company cannot monitor the extent of smoking, which has an adverse effect on health. The government cannot monitor smoking any better than the insurance company, but it can impose taxes, not only on cigarettes, but also on other commodities which are complements to smoking (and subsidies on substitutes which have less adverse effects). See Arnott and Stiglitz (1991a) and Stiglitz (1989a, 1998b).

A related result from the new information economics is that issues of efficiency and equity cannot easily be delinked. For example, with imperfect information, a key source of market failure is *agency problems*, such as those which arise when the owner of land is different from the person working the land. The extent of agency problems depends on the distribution of wealth, as we noted earlier in our discussion of sharecropping. Moreover, the notion that one could separate out issues of equity and efficiency also rested on the ability to engage in lump sum redistributions. But as Mirrlees (1971) had pointed out, with imperfect information, this was not possible; all redistributive taxation must be distortionary. But this fact implies that interventions in the market which change the before-tax distribution of income could be desirable, because they lessened the burden on redistributive taxation (Stiglitz, 1998a). Again, the conclusion: The second welfare theorem, effectively asserting the ability to separate issues of distribution and efficiency, was not true.

In effect, the Arrow-Debreu model had identified the *single set* of assumptions under which markets were efficient. There had to be perfect information; more accurately, information could not be *endogenous*, it could not change either as a result of the actions of any individual or firm or through investments in information. But in the world we live in, a model which assumes that information is *fixed* seems irrelevant.

As the theoretical case that markets in which information is imperfect were not efficient became increasingly clear, several new arguments were put forward against government intervention. One we have already dealt with: that the government too faces informational imperfections. Our analysis had shown that the incentives and constraints facing government differed from those facing the private sector, so that even when government faced exactly the same *informational* constraints, welfare could be improved (Stiglitz, 1989a).

There was another rear-guard argument, which ultimately holds up no better. It is that market failures – absent or imperfect markets – give rise to nonmarket institutions. For example, the absence of death insurance gave rise to burial societies. Families provide insurance to their members against a host of risks for which they either cannot buy insurance, or for which the insurance premium is viewed as too high. But in what I call the *functionalist fallacy*, it is easy to go from the observation that an institution arises to fulfill a function to the conclusion that actually, *in equilibrium*, it serves that function. Those who succumbed to this fallacy seemed to argue that there was no need for government intervention because these nonmarket institutions would "solve" the market failure, or at least do as well as any government. Richard Arnott and I (1991a) showed that, to the contrary, nonmarket institutions could actually make matters worse. Insurance provided by the family could crowd out market insurance, for example. Insurance companies would recognize that the insured would take less risk because they had obtained insurance from others, and accordingly cut back on the amount of insurance that they offered. But since the non-market (family) institutions did a poor job of divesting risk, welfare could be decreased.

The Arnott-Stiglitz analysis reemphasized the basic point made at the end of the last subsection: it was only under very special circumstances that markets could be shown to be efficient. Why then should we expect an equilibrium involving nonmarket institutions and markets to be efficient?

Further applications of the new paradigm

Of all the market failures, the extended periods of underutilization of resources – especially human resources – is of the greatest moment. The consequences of unemployment are exacerbated in turn by capital market imperfections, which imply that even if the future prospects of an unemployed individual are good, he cannot borrow enough to sustain his standard of living.

We referred earlier to the dissatisfaction with traditional Keynesian explanations, in particular, the lack of microfoundations. This dissatisfaction gave rise to two schools of thought.

One sought to use the old perfect market paradigm, relying heavily on representative agent models. While information was not perfect, expectations were rational. But the representative agent model, by construction, ruled out the information asymmetries which are at the heart of macroeconomic problems. If one begins with a model that *assumes* that markets clear, it is hard to see how one can get much insight into unemployment (the failure of the labor market to clear).

The construction of a macroeconomic model which embraces the consequences of imperfections of information in labor, product, and capital markets has become one of my major preoccupations over the past 15 years. Given the complexity of *each* of these markets, creating a general-equilibrium model – simple enough to be taught to graduate students or used by policy makers – has not proven to be an easy task. At the heart of that model lies a new theory of the firm, for which the theory of asymmetric information provides the foundations. The modern theory of the firm in turn rests on three pillars, the theory of corporate finance, the theory of corporate governance, and the theory of organizational design.

Theory of the firm

Under the older, perfect information theory (Franco Modigliani and Merlon H. Miller, 1958, 1961; see also Stiglitz, 1969a, 1974c, 1988d), it made no difference whether firms raised capital by debt or equity, in the absence of tax distortions. But information is at the cone of finance. The information required to implement equity contracts is greater than for debt contracts (Robert J. Townsend, 1979; Greenwald and Stiglitz, 1992). Most importantly, the willingness to hold (or to sell) shares conveys information (Hayne E. Leland and David H. Pyle, 1977; Ross, 1977; Stiglitz, 1982c; Greenwald et al., 1984; Myers and Majluf, 1984; Thomas F. Hellman and Stiglitz, 2000; for empirical verification see, e.g., Paul Asquith and David W. Mullins, Jr., 1986), so that how firms raise capital does make a difference. In practice, firms rely heavily on debt (as opposed to equity) finance (Mayer, 1990), and bankruptcy, resulting from the failure to meet debt obligations, matters. Both because of the cost of bankruptcies and limitations in the design of managerial incentive schemes, firms act in a risk-averse manner – with risk being more than just correlation with the business cycle (Greenwald and Stiglitz, 1990a; Stiglitz, 1989g). Moreover, because of the potential for credit rationing, not only does the firm's net worth matter, but so does its asset structure, including its liquidity.[23]

While there are many implications of the theory of the risk-averse firm facing credit rationing, some of which are elaborated upon in the next section, one example should suffice to highlight the importance of these ideas. In traditional neoclassical investment theory, investment depends on the real interest rate and the firm's perception of expected returns. The firm's cash flow or its net worth should make no difference. The earliest econometric studies of investment, by Edwin Kuh and John R. Meyer (1957), suggested however that this was not the case. Nevertheless these variables were excluded from econometric analyses of investment for two decades following the work of Robert E. Hall and Dale W. Jorgenson (1967). It was not until work on asymmetric information had restored theoretical respectability that it became acceptable to introduce financial variables Into investment regressions. When that was done, it was shown that – especially for small and medium-sized enterprises – these variables are crucial. (For a survey of the vast empirical literature see R. Glenn Hubbard, 1998).

In the traditional theory, firms simply maximized the expected present discounted value of profits (which equaled market value); with perfect information, how that was to be done was simply an engineering problem. Disagreements about what the firm should do were of little moment. In that context, *corporate governance* – how firm decisions were made – mattered little as well. But again, in reality, corporate governance matters a great deal. There *are* disagreements about what the firm should do – partly motivated by differences in judgments, partly motivated by differences in objectives (Stiglitz, 1972b; Grossman and Stiglitz, 1977, 1980b). Managers can take actions which advance their interests at the expense of that of shareholders, and majority shareholders can advance their interests at the expense of minority shareholders. The owners not only could not monitor their workers and managers, because of asymmetries of information, they typically did not even know what these people who were supposed to be acting on their behalf *should* do. That there were important consequences for the theory of the firm of the separation of ownership and control had earlier been noted by Adolph A. Berle and Gardiner C. Means (1932), but it was not until information economics that we had a coherent way of thinking about the implications (Jensen and William H. Meckling, 1976; Stiglitz, 1985a).

Some who still held to the view that firms would maximize their market value argued that (the threat of) takeovers would ensure competition in the market for managers and hence promote stock market value maximization. If the firm were not maximizing its stock market value, then it would pay someone to buy the firm, and change its actions so that its value would increase. Early on in this debate, I raised questions on theoretical grounds about the efficacy of the takeover mechanism (Stiglitz, 1972b). The most forceful set of arguments were subsequently put forward by Grossman and Hart (1980), who observed that any small shareholder who believed that the takeover would subsequently increase market value would not be willing to sell his shares. The subsequent work by Shleifer and Vishny (1989) and Edlin and Stiglitz (1995), referred to earlier, showed how existing managers could take actions to reduce the effectiveness of competition for management, i.e., the threat of takeovers, by increasing asymmetries of information.

So far, we have discussed two of the three pillars of the modern theory of the firm: corporate finance and corporate governance. The third is *organizational design*. In a world with perfect information, organizational design too is of little moment. In practice, it is of central concern to businesses. For example, as we have already discussed, an organizational design that has alternative units performing comparable tasks can enable a firm to glean information on the basis of which better incentive systems can be based. (Nalebuff and Stiglitz, 1983a, b). But there is another important aspect of organization design. Even if individuals are well intentioned, with limited information, mistakes get made. To err is human. Raaj K. Sah and I, in a series of papers (1985, 1986, 1988a, b, 1991) explored the consequences of alternative organizational design and decision-making structures for organizational mistakes: for instance, whether good projects get rejected or bad projects get accepted. We suggested that, in a variety of circumstances, decentralized polyarchical organizational structures have distinct advantages (see also Sah, 1991; Stiglitz, 1989d). These papers are just beginning to spawn a body of research; see, for example, Bauke Visser (1998), Amar Bhide (2001), and Michael Christensen and Thorbjorn Knudsen (2002).

Macroeconomics

With these points made, we can return to the important area of *macroeconomics*. The central macroeconomic issue is unemployment. The models I described earlier explained why unemployment could exist *in equilibrium*. But much of macroeconomics is concerned with *dynamics*, with explaining why sometimes the economy seems to amplify rather than absorb shocks, and why the effects of shocks may long persist. In joint work with Bruce Greenwald and Andy Weiss, I have shown how theories of asymmetric information can help provide explanations of these phenomena. (For an early survey, see Greenwald and Stiglitz [1987a, 1988b, 1993b] and Stiglitz [1988b, 1992a].) The imperfections of capital markets – the phenomena of credit and equity rationing which arise because of information asymmetries – are key. They lead to risk-averse behavior of firms and to households and firms being affected by cash flow constraints.

Standard interpretations of Keynesian economics emphasized the importance of wage and price rigidities, but without a convincing explanation of how those rigidities arise. For instance, some theories had shown the importance of costs of adjustment of prices (Akerlof and Yellen, 1985; N. Gregory Mankiw, 1985). Still at issue, though, is why firms tend to adjust quantities rather than prices, even though the costs of adjusting quantities seem greater than those of prices. The Greenwald Stiglitz theory of adjustment (1989) provided an explanation based on capital market imperfections arising from information imperfections. In brief, it argued that the risks created by informational imperfections are generally greater for price and wage adjustments than from quantity adjustments. Risk-averse firms would make smaller adjustments to those variables for which the consequences of adjustment were more uncertain.

But even though wages and prices were not perfectly flexible, neither were they perfectly rigid, and indeed in the Great Depression, they fell by a considerable amount. There had been large fluctuations in earlier periods, and in other countries, in which there had been a high degree of wage and price flexibility. Greenwald and I (1987a, b, 1988b, c, d, 1989, 1990b, 1993a, b, 1995) argued that other market failures, in particular, the imperfections of capital markets and incompleteness in contracting, were needed to explain key observed macroeconomic phenomena. In debt contracts, which are typically not indexed for changes in prices, whenever prices fell below the level expected (or in variable interest rate contracts, whenever real interest rates rose above the level expected) there were transfers from debtors to creditors. In these circumstances, excessive downward price flexibility (not just price rigidities) could give rise to problems; Irving Fisher (1933) and Stiglitz (1999d) emphasize the consequences of differences in the speed of adjustment of different prices. These (and other) redistributive changes had large real effects, and could not be insured against because of imperfections in capital markets. Large shocks could lead to bankruptcy, and with bankruptcy (especially when it results in firm liquidation) there was a loss of organizational and informational capital.[24] Even if such large changes could be forestalled, until there was a resolution, the firm's access to credit would be impaired, and for good reason. Moreover, without "clear owners" those in control would in general not have incentives to maximize the firm's value.

Even when the shocks were not large enough to lead to bankruptcy, they had impacts on firms' ability and willingness to take risks. Since all production is risky, shocks affect aggregate supply, as well as the demand for investment. Because firm net worth would only he restored over time, the effects of a shock persisted. By the same token, there were hysteresis effects associated with policy: An increase in interest rates which depleted firm net worth had impacts even after the interest rates were reduced. Firms that were bankrupted with high interest rates remain so. If firms were credit rationed, then reductions in liquidity could have particularly marked effects (Stiglitz and Weiss, 1992). Every aspect of macroeconomic behavior is affected: The theories helped explain, for instance, the seemingly anomalous cyclical behavior of inventories (the procyclical movements in inventories, counter to the idea of production smoothing, result from cash constraints and the resulting high shadow price of money in recessions); or of pricing (in recessions, when the "shadow price" of capital is high, firms do not find it profitable to invest in acquiring new customers by cutting prices). In short, our analysis emphasized the supply-side effects of shocks, the interrelationships between supply and demand side effects, and the importance of *finance* in propagating fluctuations.

Earlier, I described how the information paradigm explained credit rationing. A second important strand in our macroeconomic research explored the link between credit rationing and macroeconomic activity (Alan S. Blinder and Stiglitz, 1983), explained the role of banks as risk-averse firms, as information institutions involved in screening and monitoring, in determining the supply of credit (Greenwald and Stiglitz, 1990b, 1991, 2002; Stiglitz and Weiss, 1990), described the macroeconomic impacts of changes in financial regulations, and analyzed the implications for monetary policy under a variety of regimes, including dollarization (Stiglitz, 2001d). These differed in many respects from the traditional theories, such as those based on the transactions demand for money, the microfoundations of which were increasingly being discredited as money became increasingly interest bearing (the interest rate was not the opportunity cost of holding money) and as credit, not money, was increasingly being used for transactions. We also explained the importance of credit linkages (e.g., not only between banks and firms but among firms themselves) and their role in transmitting shocks throughout the economy. A large body of empirical work has subsequently verified the importance of credit constraints for macroeconomic activity, especially investment (see Kuh and Meyer (1957), Charles W. Calomiris and Hubbard (1990), and Hubbard (1990)).

Growth and development[25]

While most of the macroeconomic analysis focused on exploring the implications of imperfections of credit markets for cyclical fluctuations, another strand of our research program focused on growth. The importance of capital markets for growth had long been recognized; without capital markets firms have to rely on retained earnings. But how firms raise capital is important for their growth. In particular, "equity rationing" – especially important in developing countries, where informational problems are even greater – impedes firms' willingness to invest and undertake risks, and thus slows growth. Changes in economic policy which enable firms to bear more risk (e.g., by reducing the size of macroeconomic fluctuations, or which enhance firms' equity base, by suppressing interest rates, which result in firms having larger profits) enhance economic growth. Conversely, policies, such as those associated with IMF interventions, in which interest rates are raised to very high levels, discourage the use of debt, forcing firms to rely more heavily on retained earnings.

The most challenging problems for growth lie in economic development. Typically, market failures are more prevalent in less developed countries, and these market failures are often associated with information problems – the very problems that inspired much of the research described in this paper (see Stiglitz, 1985b, 1986a, 1988a, 1989e, h, 1991a, 1997a; Braverman et al., 1993). While these perspectives help explain the failures of policies based on *assuming* perfect or well-functioning markets, they also direct attention to policies which might remedy or reduce the consequences of informational imperfections (World Bank, 1999).

One of the most important determinants of the pace of growth is the acquisition of knowledge. For developed countries, this requires investment in research; for less developed countries, efforts at closing the knowledge gap between themselves and more developed countries. Knowledge is, of course, a particular *form* of information, and many of the issues that are central to the economics of information are also key to understanding research – such as the problems of appropriability, the fixed costs associated with investments in research (which give rise to imperfections in competition), and the public good nature of information. It was thus natural that I turned to explore the implications in a series of papers that looked at both equilibrium in the research industry and the consequences for economic growth.[26] While it is not possible to summarize briefly the results, one conclusion does stand out: Market economies in which research and innovation play an important role are not well described by the standard competitive model, and the market equilibrium, without government intervention, is not in general efficient.

Theory of taxation[27]

One of the functions of government is to redistribute income. Even if it did not actively wish to redistribute, the government has to raise revenues to finance public goods, and there is a concern that the revenue be raised in an equitable manner, e.g., that those who are more able to contribute do so. But government has a problem of identifying these individuals, just as (for example) a monopolist may find it difficult to identify those who are willing to pay more for its product. Importantly, the self-selection mechanisms for information revelation that Rothschild and I had explored in our competitive insurance model or that I had explored in my paper on discriminating monopoly can be applied here. (The problem of the government, maximizing social "profit," i.e., welfare, subject to the information constraints, is closely analogous to that of the monopolist, maximizing private profit subject to information constraints. For this reason, Mirrlees' (1971) paper on optimal taxation, though not couched in information theoretic terms, was an important precursor to the work described here.)

The critical question for the design of a tax system thus becomes *what is observable*. In older theories, in which information was perfect, lump-sum taxes and redistributions made sense. If ability is not directly observable, the government had to rely on other observables – like income – to make inferences; but, as in all such models, market participants, as they recognize that inferences are being made, alter their behavior. In Mirrlees (1971) only income was assumed observable. But in different circumstances, either more or less information might be available. It might be possible to observe hours worked, in which case wages would be observable. It might be possible to observe the quantity of each good purchased by any particular individual or it might be possible to observe only the aggregate quantity of goods produced.

For each information structure, there is a *Pareto-efficient tax structure*, that is, a tax structure such that no group can be made better off without making some other group worse off. The choice among such tax structures depends on the social welfare function, including attitudes towards inequality.[28] While this is not the occasion to provide a complete description of the results, two are worth noting: What had been thought of as optimal commodity tax structures (Frank P. Ramsey, 1927) were shown to be part of a Pareto-efficient tax system only under highly restricted conditions, e.g., that there was no income tax (see Atkinson and Stiglitz, 1976; Sah and Stiglitz, 1992; Stiglitz, 1998a). On the other hand, it was shown that in a central benchmark case, it was not optimal to tax interest income.

Theory of regulation and privatization

The government faces the problems posed by information asymmetries in regulation as well as in taxation. Over the past quarter century, a huge literature has developed making use of self-selection mechanisms (see, for example, David E. M. Sappington and Stiglitz [1987a];

Jean-Jacques Laffont and Tirole [1993]), allowing far better and more effective systems of regulation than had existed in the past. An example of a sector in which government regulation is of particular importance is banking; we noted earlier that information problems are at the heart of credit markets, and it is thus not surprising that market failures be more pervasive, and the role of the government more important in those markets (Stiglitz, 1994d). Regulatory design needs to take into account explicitly the limitations in information (see, e.g., Hellman et al., 2000; Patrick Honahan and Stiglitz, 2001; Stiglitz, 2001c; Greenwald and Stiglitz, 2002).

The 1980s saw a strong movement towards privatizing state enterprises, even in areas in which there was a natural monopoly, in which case government ownership would be replaced with government regulation. While it was apparent that there were frequently problems with government ownership, the theories of imperfect information also made it clear that even the best designed regulatory systems would work imperfectly. This naturally raised the question of under what circumstances we could be sure that privatization would enhance economic welfare. As Herbert A. Simon (1991), winner of the 1978 Nobel Prize, had emphasized, both public and private sectors face information and incentive problems; there was no compelling theoretical argument for why large private organizations would solve these incentive problems better than public organizations. In work with Sappington (1987b), I showed that the conditions under which privatization would necessarily be welfare enhancing were extremely restrictive, closely akin to those under which competitive markets would yield Pareto efficient outcomes (see Stiglitz [1991b, 1994c] for an elaboration and applications).

Some policy debates

The perspectives provided by the new information paradigm not only shaped theoretical approaches to policy, but in innumerable concrete issues also led to markedly different policy stances from those wedded to the old paradigm.

Perhaps most noted were the controversies concerning development strategies, where the *Washington consensus* policies, based on market fundamentalism – the simplistic view of competitive markets with perfect information, inappropriate even for developed countries, but particularly inappropriate for developing countries – had prevailed since the early 1980's within the international economic institutions. Elsewhere, I have documented the failures of these policies in development (Stiglitz, 1999c), as well as in managing the transition from communism to a market economy (see, for instance, Athar Hussein et al., 2000; Stiglitz, 2000a, 2001e) and in crisis management and prevention (Stiglitz, 2000b). Ideas matter, and it is not surprising that policies based on models that depart as far from reality as those underlying the Washington consensus so often led to failure.

This point was brought home perhaps most forcefully by the management of the East Asia crisis which began in Thailand on July 2, 1997. While I have written extensively on the many dimensions of the failed responses (Jason Furman and Stiglitz, 1998; Stiglitz, 1999e), here I want to note the close link between these failures and the theories put forward here. Our work had emphasized the importance of maintaining the credit supply and the risks of (especially poorly managed) bankruptcy. Poorly designed policies could lead to an unnecessarily large reduction in credit availability and unnecessary large increases in bankruptcy, both leading to large adverse effects on aggregate supply, exacerbating the economic downturn. But this is precisely what the IMF did: by raising interest rates to extremely high levels in countries where firms were already highly leveraged, it forced massive bankruptcy, and the economies were thus plunged into deep recession. Capital was not attracted to the country, but rather fled. Thus, the policies even failed in their stated purpose, which was to stabilize the exchange rate. There were strong hysteresis effects associated with these policies: when the interest rates were subsequently lowered, firms that had been forced into bankruptcy did not become "unbankrupt," and the firms that had seen their net worth depleted did not see an immediate restoration. There were alternative policies available, debt standstills followed by corporate financial restructurings, for example; while these might not have avoided a downturn, they would have made it shorter and more shallow. Malaysia, whose economic policies conformed much more closely to those than our theories would have suggested, not only recovered more quickly, but was left with less of a legacy of debt to impair its future growth, than did neighboring Thailand, which conformed more closely to the IMF's recommandation. (For discussions of bankruptcy reform motivated by these experiences see Marcus Miller and Stiglitz, 1999; Stiglitz, 2000e.)

On another front, the *transition from communism to a market economy* represents one of the most important economic experiments of all time, and the failure (so far) in Russia, and the successes in China, shed considerable light on many of the issues which I have been discussing. The full dimension of Russia's failure is hard to fathom. Communism, with its central planning (requiring more information gathering, processing, and dissemination capacity than could be managed with *any* technology), its lack of incentives, and its system rife with distortions, was viewed as highly inefficient. The movement to a market, it was assumed, would bring enormous increases in incomes. Instead, incomes plummeted, a decline confirmed not only by GDP statistics and household surveys, but also by social indicators. The numbers in poverty soared, from 2 percent to upwards of 40 percent, depending on the measure used. While there were many dimensions to these failures, one stands out: the privatization strategy, which paid little attention to the issues of corporate governance which we stressed earlier. Empirical work (Stiglitz, 2001e) confirms that countries that privatized rapidly but lacked "good" corporate governance did not grow more rapidly. Rather than providing a basis for wealth creation, privatization led to asset stripping and wealth destruction (Hussein *et al.*, 2000; Stiglitz, 2000a).

Beyond information economics

We have seen how the competitive paradigm that dominated economic thinking for two centuries was not robust, did not explain key economic phenomena, and led to misguided policy prescriptions. The research over the past 30 years on information economics that I have just described has focused, however, on only one aspect of my dissatisfaction with that paradigm. It is not easy to change views of the world, and it seemed to me the most effective way of attacking the paradigm was to keep within the standard framework as much as possible. I only varied one assumption – the assumption concerning perfect information – and in ways which seemed to me highly plausible.

There were other deficiencies in the theory, some of which were closely connected. The standard theory assumed that technology and preferences were fixed. But changes in technology, R & D, are at the heart of capitalism. The new information economics – extended to incorporate changes in knowledge – at last began to address systematically these foundations of a market economy.

As I thought about the problems of development, I similarly became increasingly convinced of the inappropriateness of the assumption of fixed preferences, and of the importance of embedding economic analysis in a broader social and political context. I have criticized the Washington consensus development strategies partly on the grounds that they perceived of development as nothing more than increasing the stock of capital and reducing economic distortions. But development represents a far more fundamental transformation of society, including a change in "preferences" and attitudes, an acceptance of change, and an abandonment of many traditional ways of thinking (Stiglitz, 1995, 1999c). This perspective has strong policy implications. For instance, some policies are more conducive to effecting a development transformation. Many of the policies of the IMF – including the manner in which it interacted with governments, basing loans on conditionality – were counterproductive. A fundamental change in development strategy occurred at the World Bank in the years I was there, one which embraced this more comprehensive approach to development. By contrast, policies which have ignored social consequences have frequently been disastrous. The IMF policies in Indonesia, including the elimination of food and fuel subsidies for the very poor as the country was plunging into depression, predictably led to riots. The economic consequences are still being felt.

In some ways, as I developed these perspectives, I was returning to a theme I had raised 30 years ago, during my work on the efficiency wage theory in Kenya. In that work I had suggested psychological factors – morale, reflecting a sense that one is receiving a fair wage – could affect efforts, an alternative, and in some cases more persuasive reason for the efficiency wage theory. It is curious how economists have almost studiously ignored factors, which are not only the center of day-to-day life, but even of business school education. Surely, if markets were efficient, such attention would not be given to such matters, to issues of corporate culture and intrinsic rewards, unless they were of some considerable importance. And if such issues are of importance within a firm, they are equally important within a society.

Finally, I have become convinced that the dynamics of change may not be well described by equilibrium models that have long been at the center of economic analysis. Information economics has alerted us to the fact that history matters; there are important hysteresis effects. Random events – the Black Plague, to take an extreme example – have consequences that are irreversible. Dynamics may be better described by evolutionary processes and models, than by equilibrium processes. And while it may be difficult to describe fully these evolutionary processes, this much is already clear: there is no reason to believe that they are, in any general sense, "optimal." (I discussed these issues briefly in Stiglitz [1975b, 1992e, 1994c] and Sah and Stiglitz [1991]; some of the problems are associated with capital market imperfections.)

Many of the same themes that emerged from our simpler work in information economics applied here. For instance, in the information-theoretic models discussed above we showed that multiple equilibria (some of which Pareto-dominated others) could easily arise. So, too, here (Stiglitz, 1995). This in turn has several important consequences, beyond the observation already made that history matters. First, it means that one cannot simply predict where the economy will be by knowing preferences, technology, and initial endowments. There can a high level of indeterminacy (see, e.g., Stiglitz, 1973c) Second, as in Darwinian ecological models, the major determinant of one's environment is the behavior of others, and their behavior may in turn depend on their beliefs about others' behavior (Hoff and Stiglitz, 2001). Third, government intervention can sometimes move the economy from one equilibrium to another; and having done that, continued intervention might not be required.

The political economy of information

Information affects political processes as well as economic ones. First, we have already noted the distributive consequences of information disclosures. Not surprisingly, then, the "information rules of the game," both for the economy and for political processes, can become a subject of intense political debate. The United States and the IMF argued strongly that lack of transparency was at the root of the 1997 financial crisis, and said that the East Asian countries had to become more transparent. The attention to quantitative data on capital flows and loans by the IMF and the U.S. Treasury could be taken as conceding the inappropriateness of the competitive paradigm (in which *prices* convey all the relevant information); but the more appropriate way of viewing the debate was *political*, a point which became clear when it was noted that partial disclosures could be of only limited value. Indeed, they could possibly be counterproductive, as capital would be induced to move through channels involving less disclosure, channels like off-shore banking centers, which were also less well regulated. When demands for transparency went beyond East Asia to Western hedge funds and offshore banking centers, suddenly the advocates of more transparency became less enthralled, and began praising the advantages of partial secrecy in enhancing incentives to gather information. The United States and the Treasury then opposed the OECD initiative to combat money laundering through greater transparency of offshore banking centers – these institutions served particular *political and economic interests* – until it became clear that terrorists might be using them to help finance their operations. At that point, the balance of American interests changed, and the Treasury changed its position.

Political processes inevitably entail asymmetries of information (for a more extensive discussion, see Patrick D. Moynihan, 1998; Stiglitz, 2002b): our political leaders are *supposed* to know more about threats to defense, about our economic situation, etc., than ordinary citizens. There has been a delegation of responsibility for day-to-day decision-making, just as there is within a firm. The problem is to provide incentives for those so entrusted to act on behalf of those who they are supposed to be serving – the standard principal-agent problem. Democracy – contestability in political processes – provides a check on abuses of the powers that come from delegation just as it does in economic processes; but just as we recognize that the takeover mechanism provides an imperfect check on management, so too we should recognize that the electoral process provides an imperfect check on politicians. As in the theory of the firm where the current management has an incentive to *increase* asymmetries of information in order to enhance market power, so too in public life. And as disclosure requirements – greater transparency – can affect the effectiveness of the takeover mechanism and the overall quality of corporate governance, so too these factors can affect political contestability and the quality of public governance.

In the context of political processes, where "exit" options are limited, one needs to be particularly concerned about abuses. If a firm is mismanaged – if the managers attempt to enrich themselves at the expense of shareholders and customers and entrench themselves against competition, the damage is limited – customers, at least, can switch. But in political processes, switching is not so easy. If all individuals were as selfish as economists have traditionally modeled them, matters would indeed be bleak, for – as I have put it elsewhere – ensuring the public good is itself a public good. But there is a wealth of evidence that the economists' traditional model of the individual is too narrow – and that indeed intrinsic rewards, e.g., of public service, can be even more effective than extrinsic rewards, e.g., monetary compensation (which is not to say that compensation is not of some importance). This public spiritedness (even if blended with a modicum of self-interest) is manifested in a variety of civil society organizations, through which individuals voluntarily work together to advance their perception of the collective interests.

There are strong incentives on the part of those in government to reduce transparency. More transparency reduces their scope for action – it not only exposes mistakes, but also corruption (as the expression goes, "sunshine is the strongest antiseptic"). Government officials may try to enhance their power by trying to advance specious arguments for secrecy, and then saying, in effect, to justify their otherwise inexplicable or self-serving behavior, "trust me ... if you only knew what I knew."

There is a further rationale for secrecy, from the point of view of politicians: Secrecy is an artificially created scarcity of information, and like most artificially created scarcities, it gives rise to rents, rents which in some countries are appropriated through outright corruption (selling information). In other contexts these rents become part of a "gift exchange," as when reporters trade "puff pieces" and distorted coverage in exchange for privileged access to information. I was in the unfortunate position of watching this process work, and work quite effectively. Without unbiased information, the effectiveness of the check that can be provided by the citizenry is limited; without good information, the contestability of the political processes can be undermined.

One of the lessons of the economics of information is that these problems cannot be fully resolved, but that laws and institutions can decidedly improve matters. Right-to-know laws, for example, which require increased transparency, have been part of governance in Sweden for 200 years; they have become an important if imperfect check on government abuses in the United States over the past quarter century. In the past five years, there has become a growing international acceptance of such laws; Thailand has gone so far as to include such laws in its new constitution. Regrettably, these principles of transparency have yet to be endorsed by the international economic institutions.

Concluding remarks

In this article I have traced the replacement of one paradigm with another. The deficiencies of the neoclassical paradigm – the failed predictions, the phenomena that were left unexplained – made it inevitable that it would be challenged. One might ask, though, how can we explain the persistence of this paradigm for so long? Despite its deficiencies, the competitive paradigm did provide insights into many economic phenomena. There are some markets in which the issues which we have discussed are not important – the market for wheat or corn – though even there, pervasive government interventions make the reigning competitive paradigm of limited relevance. The underlying forces of demand and supply are still important, though in the new paradigm, they become only part of the analysis; they are not the whole analysis. But one cannot ignore the possibility that the survival of the paradigm was partly because the belief in that paradigm, and the policy prescriptions that were derived from it, has served certain interests.

As a social scientist, I have tried to follow the analysis, wherever it might lead. My colleagues and I know that our ideas can be used or abused – or ignored. Understanding the complex forces that shape our economy is of value in its own right; there is an innate curiosity about how this system works. But, as Shakespeare said, "All the world's a stage, and all the men and women merely players." Each of us in our own way, if only as a voter, is an actor in this grand drama. And what we do is affected by our perceptions of how this complex system works.

I entered economics with the hope that it might enable me to do something about unemployment, poverty, and discrimination. As an economic researcher, I have been lucky enough to hit upon some ideas that I think do enhance our understanding of these phenomena. As an educator, I have had the opportunity to reduce some of the asymmetries of information, especially concerning what the new information paradigm and other developments in modern economic science have to say about these phenomena, and to have had some first-rate students who, themselves, have pushed the research agenda forward.

As an individual, I have however not been content just to let others translate these ideas into practice. I have had the good fortune to be able to do so myself, as a public servant both in the American government and at the World Bank. We have the good fortune to live in democracies, in which individuals can fight for their perception of what a better world might be like. We as academics have the good fortune to be further protected by our academic freedom. With freedom comes responsibility: the responsibility to use that freedom to do what we can to ensure that the world of the future be one in which there is not only greater economic prosperity, but also more social justice.

Acknowledgments

This article is a revised version of the lecture Joseph E. Stiglitz delivered in Stockholm, Sweden on December 8, 2001, when he received the Bank of Sweden Prize in Economic Sciences in Memory of Alfred Nobel. The article is copyright© The Nobel Foundation 2001 and is published here with the permission of the Nobel Foundation.

Notes

1 See John Williamson (1990) for a description and Stiglitz (1999c) for a critique.
2 Review articles include Stiglitz (1975b, 1985d, 1987a, 1988b, 1992a, 2000d) and John G. Riley (2001). Book-length references include, among others, Drew Fudenberg and Jean Tirole (1991), Jack Hirshleifer and Riley (1992), and Oliver D. Hart (1995).
3 "If the legal rate ... was fixed so high ... the greater part of the money which was to be lent, would be lent to prodigals and profectors, who alone would be willing to give this higher interest. Sober people, who will give for the use of money no more than a part of what they are likely to make by the use of it, would not venture into the competition" (Smith, 1776). See also Jean-Charles-Leonard Simonde de Sismondi (1815), John S. Mill (1848), and Alfred Marshall (1890), as cited in Stiglitz (1987a).
4 There was so many of these that the *Journal of Economic Perspectives* ran a regular column with each issue highlighting these paradoxes. For a discussion of other paradoxes, see Stiglitz (1973b, 1982d, 1989g).
5 Robert E. Lucas, Jr., (1987), who won the Nobel Prize in 1995, uses the perfect markets model with a representative agent to try to argue that these cyclical fluctuations in fact have a relatively small welfare costs.
6 See, e.g., Theodore W. Schultz (1960), who won the Nobel Prize in 1979, and Jacob Mincer (1974). At the time, there was other ongoing work criticizing the human-capital formulation, which focused on the role of education in socialization and providing credentials; see, for example, Samuel Bowles and Herbert Gintis (1976).
7 See Michael P. Todaro (1969) and John R. Harris and Todaro (1970). I developed these ideas further in Stiglitz (1969b).
8 Others were independently coming to the same insight, in particular, Edmund S. Phelps (1968). Phelps and Sidney G. Winter (1970) also realized that the same issues applied to product markets, in their theory of customer markets.
9 In Nairobi, in 1969, I wrote a long, comprehensive analysis of efficiency wages, entitled "Alternative Theories of Wage Determination and Unemployment in LDC's." Given the custom of writing relatively short papers, focusing on one issue at a time, rather than publishing the paper as a whole, I had to break the paper down into several parts. Each of these had a long gestation period. The labor turnover paper was published as Stiglitz (1974a); the adverse selection model as Stiglitz (1982a, 1992d [a revision of a 1976 unpublished paper]). I elaborated on the nutritional efficiency wage theory in Stiglitz (1976). Various versions of these ideas have subsequently been elaborated on in a large number of papers, including Andrew W. Weiss (1980), Stiglitz (1982f, 1986b, 1987a, 1987g),

Akerlof and Yellen (1986), Andres Rodriguez and Stiglitz (1991a, b), Raaj K. Sah and Stiglitz (1992), Barry J. Nalebuff et al. (1993), and Patrick Rey and Stiglitz (1996).

10 This term, like adverse selection, originates in the insurance literature. Insurance firms recognized that the greater the insurance coverage, the less incentive there was for the insured to take care; if a property was insured for more than 100 percent of its value, there was even an incentive to have an accident (a fire). Not taking appropriate care was thought to be "immoral"; hence the name. Arrow's work in moral hazard (Arrow, 1963, 1965) was among the most important precursors, as it was in the economics of adverse selection.

11 For a classic reference see Hart and Bengt Holmström (1987). In addition, see Stiglitz (1975a, 1982c), Kevin J. Murphy (1985), Michael C. Jensen and Murphy (1990), Joseph G. Haubrich (1994), and Brian J. Hall and Jeffrey B. Liebman (1998).

12 In the natural "spaces," indifference curves and isoprofit curves were ill behaved. The non-convexities which naturally arose implied, in turn, that equilibrium might be characterized by randomization (Stiglitz, 1975b), or that Pareto-efficient tax and optimal tax policies might be characterized by randomization (see Stiglitz [1982g], Amott and Stiglitz [1988a], and Dagobert L. Brito *et al.*[1995]). Even small fixed costs (of search, of finding out about characteristics of different investments, of obtaining information about relevant technology) imply that markets will not be *perfectly* competitive; they will be better described by models of *monopolistic competition* (see Avinash K. Dixit and Stiglitz [1977], Steven Salop [1977], and Stiglitz [1979a, b, 1989f]), though the basis of imperfect competition was markedly different from that originally envisioned by Edward H. Chamberlin (1933).

13 Nonconvexities naturally give rise to discontinuities, and discontinuities to problems of existence, but the non-existence problem that Rothschild and I had uncovered was of a different, and more fundamental nature. The problem was in part that a single action of an individual – a choice of one insurance policy over another – discretely changed beliefs, e.g., about his type; and that a slight change in the actions of, say an insurance firm – making available a new insurance policy – could lead to discrete changes in actions, and thereby beliefs. Partha Dasgupta and Eric Maskin (1986) have explored mixed strategy equilibria in game-theoretic formulations, but these seem less convincing than the imperfect competition resolutions of the existence problems described below. I explored other problems of non-existence in the context of moral hazard problems in work with Richard Amott (1987, 1991b).

14 This had a particularly inconvenient implication: when there was a continuum of types, such as in the A. Michael Spence (1973. 1974) models, a full equilibrium never existed.

15 Some earlier work, especially in general-equilibrium theory, by Leonid Hurwicz (1960, 1972), Jacob Marschak and Radner (1972), and Radner (1972), among others, had recognized the importance of problems of information, and had even identified some of the ways that limited information affected the nature of the market equilibrium (e.g., one could only have contracts that were contingent on states of nature that were observable by both sides to the contract). But the attempt to modify the abstract theory of general equilibrium to incorporate problems of information imperfects proved, in the end, less fruitful than the alternative approach of beginning with highly simplified, quite concrete models. Arrow (1963, 1965, 1973, 1974, 1978), while a key figure within the general-equilibrium approach, was one of the first to identify the importance of adverse selection and moral hazard effects.

16 Constructing *equilibrium models* with these effects is more difficult than might seem to be the case at first, since each agent's behavior depends on opportunities elsewhere, i.e., the behavior of others. For example, the workers that a firm attracts at a particular wage depend on the wage offers of other firms. Shapiro and Stiglitz (1984), Rodríguez and Stiglitz (1991a, b), and Rey and Stiglitz (1996), represent attempts to come to terms with these general-equilibrium problems.

17 Of course, insurance markets do exist in the real world. I suspect that a major limitation of the applicability of Rothschild-Stiglitz (1976) is the assumption of perfect competition. Factors such as search costs and uncertainty about how easy it is to get a company to pay a claim make the assumption of perfect competition less plausible. Self-selection is still relevant, but some version of monopolistic competition, may be more relevant than the model of perfect competition.

18 See, in particular, Stiglitz and Weiss (1983a, 1994) and Shiro Yabushita (1983). As we point out, in the real world, who moves first ought to be viewed as an endogenous variable. In such a context, it appears that the screening equilibria are more robust than the signaling equilibrium. Assume, for instance, that there were some signaling equilibrium that differed from the screening equilibrium,

e.g., there were a pooling equilibrium, sustained because of the out-of-equilibrium beliefs of firms. Then such an equilibrium could be broken by a prior or later move of firms.

19 In Stiglitz (1974b) the contracts were highly linear. In principle, generalizing payment structures to nonlinear functions was simple. Though even here, there were subtleties, e.g., whether individuals exerted their efforts before they knew the realization of the state of nature, and whether there were bounds on the penalties that could be imposed, in the event of bad outcomes (James A. Mirrlees [1975b]; Stiglitz [1975a]; Mirrlees [1976]). The literature has not fully resolved the reason that contracts are often much simpler than the theory would have predicted (e.g., payments are linear functions of output), and do not adjust to changes in circumstances (see, e.g., Franklin Allen, 1985; Douglas Gale, 1991).

20 See, for instance, Stiglitz and Weiss (1983b, 1986, 1987). Even with these additional instruments there could still be nonmarket-clearing equilibria.

21 See, e.g., Rothschild and Stiglitz (1982, 1997). For models of statistical discrimination and some of their implications, see Arrow (1972), Phelps (1972), and Stiglitz (1973a, 1974d). See also Stiglitz (1984a).

22 Greenwald and Stiglitz (1986) focus on models with adverse selection and incentive problems. Greenwald and Stiglitz (1988a) showed that similar results hold in the context of search and other models with imperfect information. Earlier work, with Shapiro (1983) had shown, in the context of a specific model, that equilibria in an economy with an agency or principal-agent problem were not (constrained) Pareto efficient. Later work, with Arnott (1990), explored in more detail the market failures that arise with moral hazard. Earlier work had shown that with imperfect risk markets, themselves explicable by imperfections of information, market equilibrium was Pareto inefficient. See David M. G. Newbery and Stiglitz (1982, 1984) and Stiglitz (1972a, 1981, 1982b).

23 The very concept of liquidity – and the distinction between lack of liquidity and insolvency – rests on information asymmetries. If there were perfect information, any firm that was liquid would be able to obtain finance, and thus would not face a liquidity problem.

24 In traditional economic theories bankruptcy played little role, partly because control (who made decisions) did not matter, and so the change in control that was consequent to bankruptcy was of little moment, partly because with perfect information, there would be little reason for lenders to lend to someone, rather than extending funds through equity (especially if there were significant probabilities of, and costs to, bankruptcy). For an insightful discussion about control rights see Hart (1995).

25 For discussions of growth, see Greenwald et al.(1990) and Stiglitz (1990, 1992c, 1994a, b). The somewhat separate topic of development is analyzed in Stiglitz (1985b, 1986a, 1988a, 1989b, e, h, 1991a, 1993, 1995, 1996, 1997a, b, 1998b, 1999b, c, 2000c, 2001a, b), Sah and Stiglitz (1989a, b), Karla Hoff and Stiglitz (1990, 1998, 2001), Nicholas Stern and Stiglitz (1997), and Stiglitz and Shahid Yusuf (2000).

26 There were, of course, several precursors to what has come to be called endogenous growth theory. See in particular, the collection of essays in Karl Shell (1967) and Anthony B. Atkinson and Stiglitz (1969). For later work, see, in particular, Dasgupta and Stiglitz (1980a, b, 1981, 1988), Dasgupta et al. (1982), and Stiglitz (1987c, d, 1990).

27 The discussion of this section draws upon Mirrlees (1971, 1975a), Atkinson and Stiglitz (1976), Stiglitz (1982e, 1987f), Arnott and Stiglitz (1986), and Brito et al.(1990, 1991, 1995).

28 In that sense, Mirrlees' work confounded the two stages of the analysis. He described the point along the Pareto frontier that would be chosen by a government with a utilitarian social welfare function. Some of the critical properties, e.g., the zero marginal tax rate at the top, were, however, characteristics of *any* Pareto-efficient tax structure, though that particular property was not *robust – that is*, it depended strongly on his assumption that relative wages between individuals of different abilities were fixed (see Stiglitz, 2002a).

References

Adams, William J. and Yellen, Janet L. "Commodity Bundling and the Burden of Monopoly." *Quarterly Journal of Economics*, August 1976, *90*(3), pp. 475–98.

Akerlof, George A. "The Market for 'Lemons': Quality Uncertainty and the Market Mechanism." *Quarterly Journal of Economics*, August 1970, *84*(3), pp. 488–500.

Akerlof, George A. and Yellen, Janet L. "A Near-Rational Model of the Business Cycle with Wage and Price Inertia." *Quarterly Journal of Economics*, 1985, Supp., *100*(5), pp. 823–38.

Akerlof, George A. and Yellen, Janet L., eds., *Efficiency wages model of the labor market*. New York: Cambridge University Press, 1986.

Akerlof, George A. and Yellen, Janet, L. "The Fair Wage-Effort Hypothesis and Unemployment." *Quarterly Journal of Economics*, May 1990, *105*(2), pp. 255–83.

Allen, Franklin. "On the Fixed Nature of Share cropping Contracts." *Economic Journal*, March 1985, *95*(377), pp. 30–48.

Arnott, Richard J., Greenwald, Bruce C. and Stiglitz, Joseph E. "Information and Economic Efficiency." *Information Economics and Policy*, March 1994, *6*(1), pp. 77–88.

Arnott, Richard J., Hosios, Arthur J. and Stiglitz, Joseph E. "Implicit Contracts, Labor Mobility, and Unemployment." *American Economic Review*, December 1988, *78*(5), pp. 1046–66.

Arnott, Richard J. and Stiglitz, Joseph E. "Labor Turnover, Wage Structures, and Moral Hazard: The Inefficiency of Competitive Markets." *Journal of Labor Economics*, October 1985, *3*(4), pp. 434–62.

——, "Moral Hazard and Optimal Commodity Taxation." *Journal of Public Economics*, February 1986, *29*(1), pp. 1–24.

——, "Equilibrium in Competitive Insurance Markets with Moral Hazard." Princeton University Discussion Paper No. 4, October 1987.

—— "Randomization with Asymmetric Information." *RAND Journal of Economics*, Autumn 1988a, *19*(3), pp. 344–62.

——, "The Basic Analytics of Moral Hazard." *Scandinavian Journal of Economics*, September 1988b, *90*(3), pp. 383–413.

——, "The Welfare Economics of Moral Hazard," in H. Louberge, ed., *Risk information and insurance: Essays in the memory of Karl H. Borch*. Norwell, MA: Kluwer, 1990, pp. 91–122.

—— "Moral Hazard and Nonmarket Institutions: Dysfunctional Crowding Out or Peer Monitoring?" *American Economic Review*, March 1991a, *81*(1), pp. 179–90.

——, "Price Equilibrium, Efficiency, and Decentralizability in Insurance Markets." National Bureau of Economic Research (Cambridge, MA) Working Paper No. 3642, March 1991b.

Arrow, Kenneth J., "Uncertainty and the Welfare Economics of Medical Care." *American Economic Review*, December 1963, *53*(5), pp. 941–73.

——, "The Role of Securities in the Optimal Allocation of Risk-bearing." *Review of Economic Studies*, April 1964, *31*(2), pp. 91–96.

——, *Aspects of the theory of risk-bearing (Yrjo Jahnsson lectures)*. Helsinki, Finland: Yrjo Jahnssonin Saatio, 1965.

——, "Some Mathematical Models of Race in the Labor Market," in A. H. Pascal, ed., *Racial discrimination in economic life*. Lanham, MD: Lexington Books, 1972, pp. 187–204.

——, "Higher Education as a Filter." *Journal of Public Economics*, July 1973, *3*(2), pp. 193–216.

——, "Limited Knowledge and Economic Analysis." *American Economic Review*, March 1974, *64*(1), pp. 1–10.

——, "Risk Allocation and Information: Some Theoretical Development." *Geneva Papers on Risk and Insurance*, June 1978, 8.

Asquith, Paul and Mullins, David W., Jr., "Equity Issues and Offering Dilution." *Journal of Financial Economics*, January–February 1986, *15*(1–2), pp. 61–89.

Atkinson, Anthony B. and Stiglitz, Joseph E., "A New View of Technological Change." *Economic Journal*, September 1969, *79*(315), pp. 573–78.

——, "The Design of Tax Structure: Direct Versus Indirect Taxation." *Journal of Public Economics*, July–August 1976, *6*(1–2), pp. 55–75.

Azariadis, Costas and Stiglitz, Joseph E., "Implicit Contracts and Fixed Price Equilibria." *Quarterly Journal of Economics*, 1983, Supp., *98*(3), pp. 1–22.

Bator, Francis M., "The Anatomy of Market Failure." *Quarterly Journal of Economics*, August 1958, *72*(3), pp. 351–79.

Becker, Gary, *The economics of discrimination*, 2nd Ed. Chicago: University of Chicago Press, 1971.

Berle, Adolph A. and Means, Gardiner C. *The modern corporation and private property*. New York: Harcourt Brace and World, 1932.

Bhide, Amar, "Taking Care: Ambiguity, Pooling and Error Control." Working paper, Columbia Business School, November 2001.

Blinder, Alan S. and Stiglitz, Joseph E., "Money, Credit Constraints, and Economic Activity." *American Economic Review*, May 1983 *(Papers and Proceedings)*, *73*(2), pp. 297–302.

Bowles, Samuel and Gintis, Herbert, *Schooling in capitalist America*. New York: Basic Books, 1976.

Braverman, Avishay and Stiglitz, Joseph E., "Sharecropping and the Interlinking of Agrarian Markets." *American Economic Review*, September 1982, *72*(4), pp. 695–715.

——, "Cost-Sharing Arrangements under Sharecropping: Moral Hazard, Incentive Flexibility, and Risk." *Journal of Agricultural Economics*, August 1986a, *68*(3), pp. 642–52.

——, "Landlords, Tenants and Technological Innovations." *Journal of Development Economics*, October 1986b, *23*(2), pp. 313–32.

——, "Credit Rationing, Tenancy, Productivity, and the Dynamics of Inequality," in P. Bardhan, ed., *The economic theory of agrarian institutions*. Oxford University Press, 1989, pp. 185–202.

Brito, Dagobert L.; Hamilton, Jonathan H.; Slutsky, Steven M. and Stiglitz, Joseph E. "Pareto Efficient Tax Structures." *Oxford Economic Papers*, January 1990, *42*(1), pp. 61–77.

——, "Dynamic Optimal Income Taxation With Government Commitment." *Journal of Public Economics*, February 1991. *44*(1), pp. 15–35.

——, "Randomization in Optimal Income Tax Schedules." *Journal of Public Economics*, February 1995, *56*(2), pp. 189–223.

Braverman, Avishay, Hoff, Karla and Stiglitz, Joseph E., eds. *The economics of rural organization: Theory, practice, and policy*. New York: Oxford University Press, 1993.

Calomiris, Charles W. and Hubbard, R. Glenn, "Firm Heterogeneity. Internal Finance, and Credit Rationing." *Economic Journal*, March 1990, *100*(399), pp. 90–104.

Capen, Edward, Clapp, Robert and Campbell, William, "Competitive Bidding in High Risk Situations." *Journal of Petroleum Technology*, June 1971, *23*(1), pp. 641–53.

Chamberlin, Edward H., *The theory of monopolistic competition*. Cambridge, MA: Harvard University Press, 1933.

Christensen, Michael and Knudsen, Thorbjorn, "The Architecture of Economic Organization: Toward a General Framework." University of Southern Denmark Working Paper No. 02–7. January 2002.

Coase, Ronald H., "The Problem of Social Cost." *Journal of Law and Economics*, October 1960, 3, pp. 1–44.

Dasgupta, Partha, Gilbert, Richard J. and Stiglitz, Joseph E., "Invention and Innovation under Alternative Market Structures: The Case of Natural Resources." *Review of Economic Studies*, October 1982, *49*(4), pp. 567–82.

Dasgupta, Partha and Maskin, Eric, "The Existence of Equilibrium in Discontinuous Economic Games, I: Theory." *Review of Economic Studies*, January 1986, *53*(1), pp. 1–26.

Dasgupta, Partha and Stiglitz, Joseph E. "Industrial Structure and the Nature of Innovative Activity." *Economic Journal*, June 1980a, *90*(358), pp. 266–93.

——, "Uncertainty, Market Structure and the Speed of R&D." *Bell Journal of Economics*, Spring 1980b, *11*(1), pp. 1–28.

——, "Entry, Innovation, Exit: Toward a Dynamic Theory of Oligopolistic Industrial Structure." *European Economic Review*, February 1981, *15*(2), pp. 137–58.

——, "Learning by Doing, Market Structure, and Industrial and Trade Policies." *Oxford Economic Papers*, 1988, *40*(2), pp. 246–68.

Debreu, Gerard, *The theory of value*. New Haven, CT: Yale University Press, 1959.

Diamond, Peter A., "A Model of Price Adjustment." *Journal of Economic Theory*, June 1971, *3*(2), pp. 156–68.

Dixit, Avinash K. and Stiglitz, Joseph E., "Monopolistic Competition and Optimal Product Diversity." *American Economic Review*, June 1977, *67*(3), pp. 297–308.

Eaton, Jonathan and Gersovitz, Mark, "Debt with Potential Repudiation: Theoretical and Empirical Analysis." *Review of Economic Studies*, April 1981, *48*(2), pp. 289–309.

Edlin, Aaron S. and Stiglitz, Joseph E., "Discouraging Rivals: Managerial Rent-Seeking and Economic Inefficiencies." *American Economic Review*, December 1995, *85*(5), pp. 1301–12.

Fama, Eugene F., "Efficient Capital Markets: a Review and Empirical Work." *Journal of Finance*, May 1970, *25*(2), pp. 383–417.

Fields, Gary S., "Private and Social Returns to Education to Labor Surplus Economies." *Eastern Africa Economic Review*, June 1972, *4*(1), pp. 41–62.

Fisher, Irving, "The Debt Deflation Theory of Great Depressions." *Econometrica*, October 1933, *1*(4), pp. 337–57.

Fudenberg, Drew and Tirole, Jean, *Game theory*. Cambridge, MA: MIT Press, 1991.

Furman, Jason and Stiglitz, Joseph E., "Economic Crises: Evidence and Insights from East Asia." *Brookings Papers on Economic Activity*, 1998, (2), pp. 1–114.

Gale, Douglas., "Optimal Risk Sharing through Renegotiation of Simple Contracts." *Journal of Financial Intermediation*, December 1991, *1*(4), pp. 283–306.

Greenwald, Bruce C., *Adverse selection in the labor market.* New York: Garland Press, 1979.

——, "Adverse Selection in the Labor Market." *Review of Economic Studies*, July 1986, *53*(3), pp. 325–47.

Greenwald, Bruce C., Kohn, Meir and Stiglitz, Joseph E., "Financial Market Imperfections and Productivity Growth." *Journal of Economic Behavior and Organization*, June 1990, *13*(3), pp. 321–45.

Greenwald, Bruce C. and Stiglitz, Joseph E., "Externalities in Economies with Imperfect Information and Incomplete Markets." *Quarterly Journal of Economics*, May 1986, *101*(2), pp. 229–64.

——, "Keynesian, New Keynesian and New Classical Economics." *Oxford Economic Papers*, March 1987a, *39*(1), pp. 119–33.

——, "Imperfect Information, Credit Markets and Unemployment." *European Economic Review*, 1987b, *31*(1–2), pp. 444–56.

——, "Pareto Inefficiency of Market Economies: Search and Efficiency Wage Models." *American Economic Review*, May 1988a (Papers and Proceedings), *78*(2), pp. 351–55.

——, "Examining Alternative Macroeconomic Theories." *Brookings Papers on Economic Activity*, 1988b, (1), pp. 207–60.

——, "Imperfect Information, Finance Constraints and Business Fluctuations," in M. Kohn and S. C. Tsiang, eds., *Finance constraints, expectations, and macroeconomics.* Oxford: Oxford University Press, 1988c, pp. 103–40.

——, "Money, Imperfect Information and Economic Fluctuations," in M. Kohn and S. C. Tsiang, eds., *Finance constraints, expectations and macroeconomics.* Oxford: Oxford University Press, 1988d, pp. 141–65.

——, "Toward a Theory of Rigidities." *American Economic Review*, May 1989 (Papers and Proceedings), *79*(2), pp. 364–69.

——, "Asymmetric Information and the New Theory of the Firm: Financial Constraints and Risk Behavior." *American Economic Review*, May 1990a (Papers and Proceedings), *80*(2), pp. 160–65.

——, "Macroeconomic Models with Equity and Credit Rationing," in R. Glenn Hubbard, ed., *Asymmetric information, corporate finance, and investment.* Chicago: University of Chicago Press, 1990b, pp. 15–42.

——, "Toward a Reformulation of Monetary Theory: Competitive Banking." *Economic and Social Review*, October 1991, *23*(1), pp. 1–34.

——, "Information, Finance and Markets: The Architecture of Allocative Mechanisms." Industrial and Corporate Change, 1992, *1*(1), pp. 37–68.

——, "Financial Market Imperfections and Business Cycles." *Quarterly Journal of Economics*, February 1993a, *108*(1), pp. 77–114.

——, "New and Old Keynesians." *Journal of Economic Perspectives*, Winter 1993b, *7*(1), pp. 23–44.

——, "Labor Market Adjustments and the Persistence of Unemployment." *American Economic Review*, May 1995 (Papers and Proceedings), *85*(2), pp. 219–25.

——, Towards a new paradigm for monetary economics. London: Cambridge University Press, 2003.

Greenwald, Bruce C.; Stiglitz, Joseph E. and Weiss, Andrew W., "Informational Imperfections in the Capital Markets and Macroeconomic Fluctuations." *American Economic Review*, May 1984 *(Papers and Proceedings)*, *74*(2), pp. 194–99.

Grossman, Sanford J. and Hart, Oliver D., "Take-over Bids, the Free-Rider Problem, and the Theory of the Corporation." *Bell Journal of Economics*, Spring 1980, *11*(1), pp. 42–64.

Grossman, Sanford J. and Stiglitz, Joseph E., "Information and Competitive Price Systems." *American Economic Review*, May 1976 *(Papers and Proceedings)*, *66*(2), pp. 246–53.

——, "On Value Maximization and Alternative Objectives of the Firm." *Journal of Finance*, May 1977, *32*(2), pp. 389–402.

——, "On the Impossibility of Informationally Efficient Markets." *American Economic Review*, June 1980a, *70*(3), pp. 393–408.

——, "Stockholder Unanimity in the Making of Production and Financial Decisions." *Quarterly Journal of Economics*, May 1980b, *94*(3), pp. 543–66.

Hall, Brian J. and Liebman, Jeffrey B. "Are CEO's Really Paid Like Bureaucrats?" *Quarterly Journal of Economics*, August 1998, *113*(3), pp. 653–91.

Hall, Robert E. and Jorgenson, Dale W., "Tax Policy and Investment Behavior." *American Economic Review*, June 1967, *57*(3), pp. 391–414.

Harris, John R. and Todaro, Michael P., "Migration, Unemployment and Development: A Two-Sector Analysis." *American Economic Review*, March 1970, *60*(1), pp. 126–42.

Hart, Oliver D., *Firms, contracts, and financial structure*. Oxford: Oxford University Press, 1995.

Hart, Oliver D. and Holmstrom, Bengt, "The Theory of Contracts," in T. Bewley, ed., *Advances of economic theory: Fifth World Congress*. Cambridge: Cambridge University Press, 1987, pp. 71–155.

Haubrich, Joseph G., "Risk Aversion, Performance Pay, and the Principal-Agent Problem." *Journal of Political Economy*, April 1994, *102*(2), pp. 258–76.

Hellman, Thomas F. and Stiglitz, Joseph E., "Credit and Equity Rationing in Markets with Adverse Selection." *European Economic Review*, February 2000, *44*(2), pp. 281–304.

Hellman, Thomas F., Murdock, Kevin C. and Stiglitz, Joseph E., "Liberalization, Moral Hazard in Banking and Prudential Regulation: Are Capital Requirements Enough?" *American Economic Review*, March 2000, *90*(1), pp. 147–65.

Hirshleifer, Jack. "The Private and Social Value of Information and the Reward to Inventive Activity." *American Economic Review*, September 1971, *61*(4), pp. 561–74.

Hirshleifer, Jack and Riley, John G., *The analytics of uncertainty and information*. Cambridge: Cambridge University Press, 1992.

Hoff, Karla and Stiglitz, Joseph E., "Imperfect Information and Rural Credit Markets: Puzzles and Policy Perspectives." *World Bank Economic Review*, September 1990, *4*(3), pp. 235–50.

——, "Moneylenders and Bankers: Price-Increasing Subsidies in a Monopolistically Competitive Market." *Journal of Development Economics*, April 1998, *55*(2), pp. 485–518.

——, "Modern Economic Theory and Development," in G. Meier and J. E. Stiglitz, eds., *Frontiers of development economics: The future in perspective*. New York: Oxford University Press, March 2001, pp. 389–485.

Honahan, Patrick and Stiglitz, Joseph E., "Robust Financial Restraint," in G. Caprio, P. Honohan, and J. E. Stiglitz, eds., *Financial liberalization: How far, how fast?* New York: Cambridge University Press, October 2001, pp. 31–62.

Hubbard, R. Glenn, ed., *Asymmetric information, corporate finance, and investment*. Chicago: University of Chicago Press, 1990.

——, "Capital-Market Imperfections and Investment." *Journal of Economic Literature*, March 1998, *36*(1), pp. 193–225.

Hurwicz, Leonid., "Optimality and Informational Efficiency in Resource Allocation Processes," in K. J. Arrow, S. Karlin, and P. Suppes, eds., *Mathematical Methods in the Social Sciences*. Stanford, CA: Stanford University Press, 1960, pp. 27–46.

——, "On Informationally Decentralized Systems," in C. B. McGuire and R. Radner, eds., *Decision and organization*. Amsterdam: North-Holland, 1972, pp. 297–336.

Hussein, Athar, Stern, Nicholas and Stiglitz, Joseph E., "Chinese Reforms from a Comparative Perspective," in P. J. Hammond and G. D. Myles, eds., *Incentives, organization, and public economics: Papers in honour of Sir James Mirrlees*. Oxford: Oxford University Press, 2000, pp. 243–77.

Jaffee, Dwight and Stiglitz, Joseph E., "Credit Rationing," in B. Friedman and F. Hahn, eds., *Handbook of monetary economics*, Vol. 2. Amsterdam: North-Holland, 1990, pp. 837–88.

Jensen, Michael C. and Meckling, William H. "Theory of the Firm: Managerial Behavior, Agency Costs and Ownership Structure." *Journal of Financial Economics*, October 1976, *3*(4), pp. 305–60.

Jensen, Michael C. and Murphy, Kevin J., "Performance Pay and Top-Management Incentives." *Journal of Political Economy*, April 1990, *98*(2), pp. 225–64.

Keeton, William R., *Equilibrium credit rationing*. New York: Garland Press, 1979.

Keynes, John Maynard, *The general theory of employment, interest and money*. New York: Harcourt Brace, 1936.

Klein, Benjamin and Leffler, Keith B. "The Role of Market Forces in Assuring Contractual Performance." *Journal of Political Economy*, August 1981, *89*(4), pp. 615–41.

Kuh, Edwin and Meyer, John R., *The investment decision: An empirical study*. Cambridge, MA: Harvard University Press, 1957.

Laffont, Jean-Jacques and Tirole, Jean, *A theory of incentives in procurement and regulation*. Cambridge, MA: MIT Press, 1993.

Leibenstein, Harvey. "The Theory of Underemployment in Backward Economies." *Journal of Political Economy*, April 1957, *65*(2), pp. 91–103.

Leitzinger, Jeffrey J. and Stiglitz, Joseph E., "Information Externalities in Oil and Gas Leasing." *Contemporary Policy Issues*, March 1984, (5), pp. 44–57.

Leland, Hayne E. and Pyle, David H., "Informational Asymmetries, Financial Structure, and Financial Intermediation." *Journal of Finance*, May 1977, *32*(2), pp. 371–87.

Lucas, Robert E., Jr., *Models of business cycles*. New York: Blackwell, 1987.

Mankiw, N. Gregory. "Small Menu Costs and Large Business Cycles: A Macroeconomic Model of Monopoly." *Quarterly Journal of Economics*, May 1985, *10*(2), pp. 529–37.

Marschak, Jacob and Radner, Roy, *Economic theory of teams*. New Haven, CT: Yale University Press, 1972.

Marshall, Alfred, *Principles of economics*. London: Macmillan, 1890.

Mayer, Colin, "Financial Systems, Corporate Finance, and Economic Development," in R. G. Hubbard, ed., *Asymmetric information, corporate finance and investment*. Chicago: University of Chicago Press, 1990, pp. 307–32.

Mill, John S., *Principles of political economy with some of their applications to social philosophy*. London: John W. Parker, 1848.

Miller, Marcus and Stiglitz, Joseph E., "Bankruptcy Protection Against Macroeconomic Shocks: The Case for a 'Super Chapter 11'." Unpublished manuscript presented at the World Bank Conference on Capital Flows, Financial Crises, and Policies, April 1999.

Mincer, Jacob, *Schooling, experience and earnings*. New York: Columbia University Press, 1974.

Mirrlees, James A., "An Exploration in the Theory of Optimum Income Taxation." *Review of Economic Studies*, April 1971, *38*(2), pp. 175–208.

——, "Optimal Commodity Taxation in a Two-Class Economy." *Journal of Public Economics*, February 1975a, *4*(1), pp. 27–33.

——, "The Theory of Moral Hazard and Unobservable Behaviour I." Mimeo, Nuffield College, 1975b.

——, "The Optimal Structure of Incentives and Authority within an Organization." *Bell Journal of Economics*, Spring 1976, *7*(1), pp. 105–31.

Modigliani, Franco and Miller, Merton H., "The Cost of Capital, Corporation Finance, and the Theory of Investment." *American Economic Review*, June 1958, *48*(3), pp. 261–97.

——, "Dividend Policy, Growth, and the Valuation of Shares." *Journal of Business*, October 1961, *34*(4), pp. 411–33.

Moynihan, Patrick D., *Secrecy: The American experience*. New Haven, CT: Yale University Press, 1998.

Murphy, Kevin J., "Corporate Performance and Managerial Remuneration: An Empirical Analysis." *Journal of Accounting and Economics*, 1985, *7*(1–3), pp. 11–42.

Myers, Stewart C. and Majluf, Nicholas S., "Corporate Financing and Investment Decisions When Firms Have Information That Investors Do Not Have." *Journal of Financial Economics*, June 1984, *13*(2), pp. 187–221.

Nalebuff, Barry J., Rodriguez, Andres and Stiglitz, Joseph E., "Equilibrium Unemployment as a Worker Screening Device." National Bureau of Economic Research (Cambridge, MA) Working Paper No. 4357, May 1993.

Nalebuff, Barry J. and Stiglitz, Joseph E., "Information, Competition and Markets." *American Economic Review*, May 1983a *(Papers and Proceedings)*, *73*(2), pp. 278–83.

——, "Prizes and Incentives: Toward a General Theory of Compensation and Competition." *Bell Journal of Economics*, Spring 1983b, *14*(1), pp. 21–43.

Newbery, David M. G. and Stiglitz, Joseph E., "The Choice of Techniques and the Optimality of Market Equilibrium with Rational Expectations." *Journal of Political Economy*, April 1982, *90*(2), pp. 223–46.

——, "Pareto Inferior Trade." *Review of Economic Studies*, January 1984, *51*(1), pp. 1–12.

Phelps, Edmund S., "Money-Wage Dynamics and Labor-Market Equilibrium." *Journal of Political Economy*, July–August 1968, Pt. 2, *76*(4), pp. 678–711.

——, "The Statistical Theory of Racism and Sexism." *American Economic Review*, September 1972, *62*(4), pp. 659–61.

Phelps, Edmund S. and Winter, Sidney G., "Optimal Price Policy under Atomistic Competition," in E. Phelps, *et al.*, eds., *Microeconomic foundations of employment and inflation theory*. New York: Norton, 1970, pp. 309–37.

Radner, Roy, "Existence of Equilibrium of Plans, Prices, and Price Expectations in a Sequence of Markets." *Econometrica*, March 1972, *40*(2), pp. 289–303.

Radner, Roy and Stiglitz, Joseph E., "A Nonconcavity in the Value of Information," in M. Boyer and R. Khilstrom, eds., *Bayesian models in economic theory.* New York: Elsevier, 1984, pp. 33–52.

Ramsey, Frank P., "A Contribution to the Theory of Taxation." *Economic Journal,* March 1927, *37*(145), pp. 47–61.

Rey, Patrick and Stiglitz, Joseph E., "Moral Hazard and Unemployment in Competitive Equilibrium." Unpublished manuscript, University of Toulouse, July 1996.

Riley, John G., "Informational Equilibrium." *Econometrica,* March 1979, *47*(2), pp. 331–60.

——, "Silver Signals: Twenty-Five Years of Screening and Signaling." *Journal of Economic Literature,* June 2001, *39*(2), pp. 432–78.

Rodríguez, Andrés and Stiglitz, Joseph E., "Equilibrium Unemployment, Testing, and the Pure Theory of Selection." Unpublished manuscript presented at the NBER/CEPR Conference on Unemployment and Wage Determination, Boston, October 1991a.

——, "Unemployment and Efficiency Wages: The Adverse Selection Model." Unpublished manuscript presented at NBER/CEPR Conference on Unemployment and Wage Determination, Boston, October 1991b.

Rosen, Sherwin. "Implicit Contracts: A Survey." *Journal of Economic Literature,* September 1985, *23*(3), pp. 1144–75.

Ross, Stephen A., "The Economic Theory of Agency: The Principals Problem." *American Economic Review,* May 1973 *(Papers and Proceedings),* *63*(2), pp. 134–39.

——, "The Determination of Financial Structure: The Incentive-Signalling Approach." *Bell Journal of Economics,* Spring 1977, *8*(1), pp. 23–40.

Rothschild, Michael and Stiglitz, Joseph E., "Equilibrium in Competitive Insurance Markets: An Essay on the Economics of Imperfect Information." *Quarterly Journal of Economics,* November 1976, *90*(4), pp. 629–49.

——, "A Model of Employment Outcomes Illustrating the Effect of the Structure of Information on the Level and Distribution of Income." *Economic Letters,* 1982, *10*(3–4), pp. 231–36.

——, "Competition and Insurance Twenty Years Later." *Geneva Papers on Risk and Insurance Theory,* December 1997, *22*(2), pp. 73–79.

Sah, Raaj K., "Fallibility in Human Organizations and Political Systems." *Journal of Economic Perspectives,* Spring 1991, *5*(2), pp. 67–88.

Sah, Raaj K. and Stiglitz, Joseph E., "Human Fallibility and Economic Organization." *American Economic Review,* May 1985 *(Papers and Proceedings),* *75*(2), pp. 292–96.

——, The Architecture of Economic Systems: Hierarchies and Polyarchies." *American Economic Review,* September 1986, *76*(4), pp. 716–27.

——, "Committees, Hierarchies and Polyarchies." *Economic Journal,* June 1988a, *98*(391), pp. 451–70.

——, "Qualitative Properties of Profit-Maximizing K-out-of-N Systems Subject to Two Kinds of Failure." *IEEE Transactions on Reliability,* December 1988b, *37*(5), pp. 515–20.

——, "Sources of Technological Divergence between Developed and Less Developed Economies," in G. Calvo, R. Findlay, P. Kouri, and J. Braga de Macedo, eds., *Debt, stabilizations and development: Essays in memory of Carlos Diaz-Alejandro.* Cambridge, MA: Blackwell (for WIDER of the United Nations University), 1989a, pp. 423–46.

——, "Technological Learning, Social Learning and Technological Change," in S. Chakravarty, ed., *The balance between industry and agriculture in economic development: Proceedings of the Eighth World Congress of the International Economic Association, Delhi, India, volume 3, Manpower and transfers.* New York: St. Martin's, 1989b, pp. 285–98.

——, "The Quality of Managers in Centralized Versus Decentralized Organizations." *Quarterly Journal of Economics,* February 1991, *106*(1), pp. 289–95.

——, *Peasants versus city-dwellers: Taxation and the burden of economic development.* Oxford: Clarendon Press, 1992.

Salop, Steven, "The Noisy Monopolist: Information, Price Dispersion and Price Discrimination." *Review of Economic Studies,* October 1977, *44*(3), pp. 393–406.

——, "Monopolistic Competition with Outside Goods." *Bell Journal of Economics,* Spring 1979, *10*(1), pp. 141–56.

Salop, Steven and Stiglitz, Joseph E., "Bargains and Ripoffs: A Model of Monopolistically Competitive Price Dispersions." *Review of Economic Studies,* October 1977, *44*(3), pp. 493–510; reprinted in

S. A. Lippman and D. K. Levine, eds., *The economics of information*. Aldershot, U.K.: Elgar, 1995, pp. 198–215.

———, "The Theory of Sales: A Simple Model of Equilibrium Price Dispersion with Identical Agents." *American Economic Review*, December 1982, *72*(5), pp. 1121–30.

———, "Information, Welfare and Product Diversity," in G. Feiwel, ed., *Arrow and the foundations of the theory of economic policy*. New York: New York University Press, 1987, pp. 328–40.

Samuelson, Paul A., *Foundations of economic analysis*. Cambridge, MA: Harvard University Press, 1947.

Sappington, David E. M. and Stiglitz, Joseph E., "Information and Regulation," in E. Bailey, ed., *Public regulation*. London: MIT Press, 1987a, pp. 3–43.

———, "Privatization, Information and Incentives." *Journal of Policy Analysis and Management*, 1987b, *6*(4), pp. 567–82.

Schultz, Theodore W., "Capital Formation by Education." *Journal of Political Economy*, December 1960, *68*(6), pp. 571–83.

Shapiro, Carl. "Premiums for High Quality Products as Returns to Reputations." *Quarterly Journal of Economics*, November 1983, *98*(4), pp. 659–80.

Shapiro, Carl and Stiglitz, Joseph E., "Equilibrium Unemployment as a Worker Discipline Device." *American Economic Review*, June 1984, *74*(3), pp. 433–44.

Shell, Karl, ed. *Essays on the theory of optimal economic growth*. Cambridge, MA: MIT Press, 1967.

Shiller, Robert J., *Irrational exuberance*. Princeton, NJ: Princeton University Press, 2000.

Shleifer, Andrei and Vishny, Robert W., "Management Entrenchment: The Case of Manager-Specific Assets." *Journal of Financial Economics*, November 1989, *25*(1), pp. 123–39.

Simon, Herbert A., "Organizations and Markets." *Journal of Economic Perspectives*, Spring 1991, *5*(2), pp. 25–44.

Simonde de Sismondi, Jean-Charles-Leonard. *Political economy*. New York: Kelley, 1966 (first published in 1815).

Smith, Adam., *An inquiry into the nature and causes of the wealth of nations*. Chicago: University of Chicago Press, 1977 (first published in 1776).

Spence, A. Michael., "Job Market Signaling." *Quarterly Journal of Economics*, August 1973, *87*(3), pp. 355–74.

———, *Market signaling: Information transfer in hiring and related processes*. Cambridge, MA: Harvard University Press, 1974.

Stern, Nicholas and Stiglitz, Joseph E., "A Framework for a Development Strategy in a Market Economy," in E. Malinvaud and A. K. Sen, eds., *Development strategy and the management of the market economy*. Oxford: Clarendon Press, 1997, pp. 253–95.

Stigler, George J., "The Economics of Information." *Journal of Political Economy*, June 1961, *69*(3), pp. 213–25.

———, "Imperfections in the Capital Market." *Journal of Political Economy*, May/June 1967, *75*(3), pp. 287–92.

Stiglitz, Joseph E., "A Re-Examination of the Modigliani-Miller Theorem." *American Economic Review*, December 1969a, *59*(5), pp. 784–93.

———, "Rural-Urban Migration, Surplus Labour, and the Relationship between Urban and Rural Wages." *East African Economic Review*, December 1969b, *1*(2), pp. 1–27.

———, "On the Optimality of the Stock Market Allocation of Investment." *Quarterly Journal of Economics*, February 1972a, *86*(1), pp. 25–60.

———, "Some Aspects of the Pure Theory of Corporate Finance: Bankruptcies and Take-Overs." *Bell Journal of Economics*, Autumn 1972b, *3*(2), pp. 458–82.

———, "Approaches to the Economics of Discrimination." *American Economic Review*, May 1973a (*Papers and Proceedings*), *62*(2), pp. 287–95; reprinted in W. Darity and C. Boshamer, eds., *Economics and discrimination*. Aldershot, U.K.: Elgar, 1993, pp. 325–33.

———, "Taxation, Corporate Financial Policy and the Cost of Capital." *Journal of Public Economics*, February 1973b, *2*(1), pp. 1–34.

———, "The Badly Behaved Economy with the Well Behaved Production Function," in J. A. Mirrlees and N. H. Stern, eds., *Models of economic growth*. London: MacMillan, 1973c, pp. 118–37.

———, "Alternative Theories of Wage Determination and Unemployment in L.D.C.'s: The Labor Turnover Model." *Quarterly Journal of Economics*, May 1974a, *88*(2), pp. 194–227.

——, "Incentives and Risk Sharing in Sharecropping." *Review of Economic Studies*, April 1974b, *41*(2), pp. 219–55.

——, "On the Irrelevance of Corporate Financial Policy." *American Economic Review*, December 1974c, *64*(6), pp. 851–66.

——, "Theories of Discrimination and Economic Policy," in G. von Furstenberg, B. Harrison, and A. R. Horowitz, eds., *Patterns of racial discrimination*. Lanham, MD: Lexington Books, 1974d, pp. 5–26.

——, "Incentives, Risk and Information: Notes Toward a Theory of Hierarchy." *Bell Journal of Economics*, Autumn 1975a, *6*(2), pp. 552–79.

——, "Information and Economic Analysis," in J. M. Parkin and A. R. Nobay, eds., *Current economic problems*. Cambridge: Cambridge University Press, 1975b, pp. 27–52.

——, "The Theory of Screening, Education and the Distribution of Income." *American Economic Review*, June 1975c, *65*(3), pp. 283–300.

——, "The Efficiency of Market Prices in Long Run Allocations in the Oil Industry," in G. M. Brannon, ed., *Studies in energy tax policy*. Cambridge, MA: Ballinger, 1975d, pp. 55–99.

——, "The Efficiency Wage Hypothesis, Surplus Labour, and the Distribution of Income in L.D.C.s." *Oxford Economic Papers*, July 1976, *28*(2), pp. 185–207.

——, "Monopoly, Non-linear Pricing and Imperfect Information: The Insurance Market." *Review of Economic Studies*, October 1977, *44*(3), pp. 407–30.

——, "Equilibrium in Product Markets with Imperfect Information." *American Economic Review*, May 1979a (*Papers and Proceedings*), *69*(2), pp. 339–45.

——, "On Search and Equilibrium Price Distributions," in M. Boskin, ed., *Economics and human welfare: Essays in honor of Tibor Scitovsky*. New York: Academic Press, 1979b, pp. 203–36.

——, "Pareto Optimality and Competition." *Journal of Finance*, May 1981, *36*(2), pp. 235–51.

——, "Alternative Theories of Wage Determination and Unemployment: The Efficiency Wage Model," in M. Gersovitz, C. F. Diaz Alejandro, G. Ranis, and M. R. Rosenzweig, eds., *The theory and experience of economic development: Essays in honor of Sir Arthur W. Lewis*. London: Allen and Unwin, 1982a, pp. 78–106.

——, "The Inefficiency of the Stock Market Equilibrium." *Review of Economic Studies*, April 1982b, *49*(2), pp. 241–61.

——, "Information and Capital Markets," in W. F. Sharpe and C. Cootner, eds., *Financial economics: Essays in honor of Paul Cootner*. Upper Saddle River, NJ: Prentice Hall, 1982c, pp. 118–58.

——, "Ownership, Control and Efficient Markets: Some Paradoxes in the Theory of Capital Markets," in K. D. Boyer and W. G. Shepherd, eds., *Economic regulation: essays in honor of James R. Nelson*. East Lansing, MI: Michigan State University Press, 1982d, pp. 311–41.

——, "Self-Selection and Pareto Efficient Taxation." *Journal of Public Economics*, March 1982e, *17*(2), pp. 213–40.

——, "The Structure of Labor Markets and Shadow Prices in L.D.C.'s," in R. Sabot, ed., *Migration and the labor market in developing countries*. Boulder, CO: Westview, 1982f, pp. 13–64.

——, "Utilitarianism and Horizontal Equity: The Case for Random Taxation." *Journal of Public Economics*, June 1982g, *18*(1), pp. 1–33.

——, "Information, Screening and Welfare," in M. Boyer and R. Khilstrom, eds., *Bayesian models in economic theory*. New York: Elsevier, 1984a, pp. 209–39.

——, "Price Rigidities and Market Structure." *American Economic Review*, May 1984b (*Papers and Proceedings*), *74*(2), pp. 350–56.

——, "Credit Markets and the Control of Capital." *Journal of Money, Credit, and Banking*, May 1985a, *17*(2), pp. 133–52.

——, "Economics of Information and the Theory of Economic Development." *Revista de Econometria*, April 1985b, *5*(1), pp. 5–32.

——, "Equilibrium Wage Distribution." *Economic Journal*, September 1985c, *95*(379), pp. 595–618.

——, "Information and Economic Analysis: A Perspective." *Economic Journal*, 1985d, Supp., 95, pp. 21–41.

——, "The New Development Economics." *World Development*, 1986a, *14*(2), pp. 257–65.

——, "Theories of Wage Rigidities," in J. L. Butkiewicz, K. J. Koford, and J. B. Miller, eds., *Keynes' economic legacy: Contemporary economic theories*. New York: Praeger, 1986b, pp. 153–206.

——, "The Causes and Consequences of the Dependence of Quality on Prices." *Journal of Economic Literature*, March 1987a, *25*(1), pp. 1–48.

——, "Competition and the Number of Firms in a Market: Are Duopolies More Competitive Than Atomistic Markets?" *Journal of Political Economy*, 1987b, *95*(5), pp. 1041–61.

——, "Design of Labor Contracts: Economics of Incentives and Risk-Sharing," in H. Nalbantian, ed., *Incentives, cooperation and risk sharing*. Totowa, NJ: Rowman and Littlefield, 1987c, pp. 47–68.

——, "Learning to Learn, Localized Learning and Technological Progress," in P. Dasgupta and P. Stoneman, eds., *Economic policy and technological performance*. Cambridge: Cambridge University Press, 1987d, pp. 125–53.

——, "On the Microeconomics of Technical Progress," in J. M. Katz, ed., *Technology generation in Latin American manufacturing industries*. New York: St. Martin's Press, 1987e, pp. 56–77.

——, "Efficient and Optimal Taxation and the New New Welfare Economics," in A. Auerbach and M. Feldstein, eds., *Handbook of public economics*. New York: Elsevier, 1987f, pp. 991–1042.

——, "The Wage-Productivity Hypothesis: Its Economic Consequences and Policy Implications," in M. J. Boskin, ed., *Modern developments in public finance*. Oxford: Blackwell, 1987g, pp. 130–65.

——, "Economic Organization, Information, and Development," in H. Chenery and T. N. Srinivasan, eds., *Handbook of development economics*. New York: Elsevier, 1988a, pp. 185–201.

——, "Money, Credit, and Business Fluctuations." *Economic Record*, December 1988b, *64*(187), pp. 62–72.

——, "On the Relevance or Irrelevance of Public Financial Policy," in K. J. Arrow and M. J. Boskin, ed., *The economics of public debt: Proceedings of a conference held by the International Economic Association*. New York: St. Martin's, 1988c, pp. 41–76.

——, "Why Financial Structure Matters." *Journal of Economic Perspectives*, Autumn 1988d, *2*(4), pp. 121–26.

——, "On the Economic Role of the State," in A. Heertje, ed., *The economic role of the state*. Oxford, U.K.: Blackwell, 1989a, pp. 9–85.

——, "Financial Markets and Development." *Oxford Review of Economic Policy*, Winter 1989b, *5*(4), pp. 55–68.

——, "Imperfect Information in the Product Market," in R. Schmalensee and R. D. Willig, eds., *Handbook of industrial organization*, Vol. 1. New York: Elsevier, 1989c, pp. 769–847.

——, "Incentives, Information and Organizational Design." *Empirica*, January 1989d, *16*(1), pp. 3–29.

——, "Markets, Market Failures and Development." *American Economic Review*, May 1989e (*Papers and Proceedings*), *79*(2), pp. 197–203.

——, "Monopolistic Competition and the Capital Market," in G. Feiwel, ed., *The economics of imperfect competition and employment – Joan Robinson and beyond*. New York: New York University Press, 1989f, pp. 485–507.

——, "Mutual Funds, Capital Structure, and Economic Efficiency," in S. Bhattacharya and G. Constantinides, eds., *Theory of valuation – frontiers of modern financial theory*, Vol. 1. Totowa, NJ: Rowman and Little field, 1989g, pp. 342–56.

——, "Rational Peasants, Efficient Institutions and the Theory of Rural Organization," in P. Bardhan, ed., *The economic theory of agrarian institutions*. Oxford: Clarendon Press, 1989h, pp. 18–29.

——, "Using Tax Policy to Curb Speculative Short-Term Trading." *Journal of Financial Services Research*, December 1989i, *3*(2–3), pp. 101–15.

——, "Growth Theory: Comments: Some Retrospective Views on Growth Theory," in P. Diamond, ed., *Growth/productivity/unemployment: Essays to celebrate Bob Solow's birthday*. Cambridge, MA: MIT Press, 1990, pp. 50–68.

——, "Development Strategies: The Roles of the State and Private Sector," in S. Fischer, D. de Tray, and S. Shekhar, eds., *Proceedings of the World Bank annual conference on development economics 1990*. Washington, DC: World Bank, 1991a, pp. 430–33.

——, "Some Theoretical Aspects of the Privatization: Applications to Eastern Europe," in *Rivista di Politica Economica*, December 1991b, *81*(158), pp. 199–224; reprinted in M. Baldassarri, L. Paganetto, and E. S. Phelps, eds., *Privatization processes in Eastern Europe*. Rome: St. Martin's, 1993, pp. 179–204.

——, "Capital Markets and Economic Fluctuations in Capitalist Economies." *European Economic Review*, April 1992a, *36*(2–3), pp. 269–306.

——, "Contract Theory and Macroeconomic Fluctuations," in L. Werin and H. Wijkander, eds., *Contract economics*. Cambridge, MA: Blackwell, 1992b, pp. 292–322.

——, "Explaining Growth: Competition and Finance." *Rivista di Politica Economica*, November 1992c, *82*(169), pp. 277–43.

——, "Prices and Queues as Screening Devices in Competitive Markets," in D. Gale and O. Hart, eds., *Economic analysis of markets and games: Essays in honor of Frank Hahn*. Cambridge, MA: MIT Press, 1992d, pp. 128–66.

——, "Notes on Evolutionary Economics: Imperfect Capital Markets, Organizational Design, Long-run Efficiency." Unpublished manuscript presented at a Conference at Osaka University, 1992e.

——, "Consequences of Limited Risk Markets and Imperfect Information for the Design of Taxes and Transfers: An Overview," in K. Hoff, A. Braverman, and J. Stiglitz, eds., *The economics of rural organization: Theory, practice, and policy*. New York: Oxford University Press, 1993.

——, "Economic Growth Revisited." Industrial and Corporate Change, 1994a, *3*(1), pp. 65–110.

——, "Endogenous Growth and Cycles," in Y. Shionoya and M. Perlman, eds., *Innovation in technology, industries, and institutions: Studies in Schumpeterian perspectives*. Ann Arbor, MI: University of Michigan Press, 1994b, pp. 121–56.

——, *Whither socialism?* Cambridge, MA: MIT Press, 1994c.

——, "The Role of the State in Financial Markets," in M. Bruno and B. Pleskovic, eds., *Proceedings of the World Bank conference on development economics*, 1993. Washington, DC: World Bank, 1994d, pp. 41–46.

——, "Social Absorption Capability and Innovation," in Bon Ho Koo and D. H. Perkins, eds., *Social capability and long-term economic growth*. New York: St. Martin's, 1995, pp. 48–81.

——, "Some Lessons from the East Asian Miracle." *World Bank Research Observer*, August 1996, *11*(2), pp. 151–77.

——, "The Role of Government in Economic Development," in M. Bruno and B. Pleskovic, eds., *Annual World Bank conference on development economics*, 1996. Washington, DC: World Bank, 1997a, pp. 11–23.

——, "The Role of Government in the Economies of Developing Countries," in E. Malinvaud and A. K. Sen, eds., *Development strategy and the management of the market economy*. Oxford: Clarendon, 1997b, pp. 61–109.

——, "Pareto Efficient Taxation and Expenditure Policies, With Applications to the Taxation of Capital, Public Investment, and Externalities." Unpublished manuscript, presented at conference in honor of Agnar Sandmo, January 1998a.

——, "Towards a New Paradigm for Development: Strategies, Policies and Processes." Unpublished manuscript, 9th Raul Prebisch Lecture delivered at the Palais des Nations, Geneva, UNCTAD, October 1998b.

——, "Interest Rates, Risk, and Imperfect Markets: Puzzles and Policies." *Oxford Review of Economic Policy*, 1999a, *15*(2), pp. 59–76.

——, "Knowledge for Development: Economic Science, Economic Policy, and Economic Advice," in B. Pleskovic and J. E. Stiglitz, eds., *Proceedings from the annual bank conference on development economics, 1998*. Washington DC: World Bank, 1999b, pp. 9–58.

——, "More Instruments and Broader Goals: Moving Toward the Post-Washington Consensus." *Revista de Economia Politica*, January–March 1999c, *19*(1), pp. 94–120; reprinted in Ha-Joon Chang, ed., *The rebel within: Joseph Stiglitz at the World Bank*. London: Anthem, 2001, pp. 19–56.

——, "Toward a General Theory of Wage and Price Rigidities and Economic Fluctuations." *American Economic Review*, May 1999d (*Papers and Proceedings*), *89*(2), pp. 75–80.

——, "Responding to Economic Crises: Policy Alternatives for Equitable Recovery and Development." *Manchester School*, 1999e, Spec. Iss., *67*(5), pp. 409–27.

——, "Whither Reform? Ten Years of the Transition," in B. Pleskovic and J. E. Stiglitz, eds., *Proceedings of the annual bank conference on development economics, 1999*. Washington, DC: World Bank, 2000a, pp. 27–56.

——, "Capital Market Liberalization, Economic Growth, and Instability." *World Development, June* 2000b, *28*(6), pp. 1075–86.

——, "Formal and Informal Institutions," in P. Dasgupta and I. Serageldin, eds., *Social capital: A multifaceted perspective*. Washington, DC: World Bank, 2000c, pp. 59–68.

——, "The Contributions of the Economics of Information to Twentieth Century Economics." *Quarterly Journal of Economics*, November 2000d, *115*(4), pp. 1441–78.

——, "Some Elementary Principles of Bankruptcy," in *Governance, equity and global markets (proceedings of annual bank conference for development economics in Europe, June 1999)*. Paris: La Documentation Francaise, 2000e.

——, "Challenges in the Analysis of the Role of Institutions in Economic Development," in G. Kochendorfer-Lucius and B. Pleskovic, eds., *The institutional foundations of a market economy*, Villa Borsig Workshop Series 2000. Berlin: German Foundation for International Development (DSE), 2001a, pp. 15–28.

——, "From Miracle to Recovery: Lessons from Four Decades of East Asian Experience," in Shahid Yusuf, ed., *Rethinking the East Asian miracle*. Washington, DC: World Bank, 2001b.

——, "Principles of Financial Regulation: A Dynamic Approach." *World Bank Observer*, Spring 2001c, *16*(1), pp. 1–18.

——, "Crisis y Restructuración Financiera: el Papel de la Banca Central." *Cuestiones Económicas*, 2001d, *17*(2), pp. 3–24.

——, "Quis Custodiet Ipsos Custodes? Corporate Governance Failures in the Transition," in J. E. Stiglitz and P.-A. Muet, eds., *Governance, equity, and global markets: the annual bank conference on development economics in Europe*. New York: Oxford University Press, 2001e, pp. 22–54.

——, "New Perspectives on Public Finance: Recent Achievements and Future Challenges." *Journal of Public Economics*, December 2002a, *86*(3), pp. 341–360.

——, "On Liberty, the Right to Know and Public Discourse: The Role of Transparency in Public Life," in M. Gibney, ed., *Globalizing rights*. Oxford, U.K.: Oxford University Press, 2002b.

Stiglitz, Joseph E. and Weiss, Andrew W. "Credit Rationing in Markets with Imperfect Information." *American Economic Review*, June 1981, *71*(3), pp. 393–410.

——, "Alternative Approaches to the Analysis of Markets with Asymmetric Information." *American Economic Review*, March 1983a, *73*(1), pp. 246–49.

——, "Incentive Effects of Termination: Applications to the Credit and Labor Markets." *American Economic Review*, December 1983b, *73*(5), pp. 912–27.

——, "Credit Rationing and Collateral," in J. Edwards, J. Franks, C. Mayer, and S. Schaefer, eds., *Recent developments in corporate finance*. New York: Cambridge University Press, 1986, pp. 101–35.

——, "Credit Rationing: Reply." *American Economic Review*, March 1987, *77*(1), pp. 228–31.

——, "Banks as Social Accountants and Screening Devices for the Allocation of Credit." *Greek Economic Review*, Autumn 1990, Supp., 12, pp. 85–118.

——, "Asymmetric Information in Credit Markets and Its Implications for Macroeconomics." *Oxford Economic Papers*, October 1992, *44*(4), pp. 694–724.

——, "Sorting Out the Differences Between Screening and Signaling Models," in M. O. L. Bacharach, M. A.H. Dempster, and J. L. Enos, eds., *Mathematical models in economics*. Oxford: Oxford University Press, 1994.

Stiglitz, Joseph E. and Yusuf, Shahid., "Development Issues: Settled and Open," in G. M. Meier and J. E. Stiglitz, eds., *Frontiers of development economic: The future in perspective*. Oxford: Oxford University Press, May 2000, pp. 227–68.

Todaro, Michael P. "A Model of Labor Migration and Urban Unemployment in Less Developed Countries." *American Economic Review*, March 1969, *59*(1), pp. 138–48.

Townsend, Robert J., "Optimal Contracts and Competitive Markets with Costly State Verifications." *Journal of Economic Theory*, October 1979, *21*(2), pp. 265–93.

Visser, Bauke. "Binary Decision Structures and the Required Detail of Information." European University Institute Working Paper No. 89/1, February 1998.

Waldman, Michael. "Job Assignments, Signaling and Efficiency." *RAND Journal of Economics*, Summer 1984, *15*(2), pp. 255–67.

Weiss, Andrew W. "Job Queues and Layoffs in Labor Markets with Flexible Wages." *Journal of Political Economy*, June 1980, *88*(3), pp. 526–38.

Werin, Lars and Wijkander, Hans, eds., *Contract economics*. Cambridge, MA and Oxford, U.K.: Blackwell, 1992. [*Proceedings of Contract: Determinants, Properties and Implications*, 1990 Nobel Symposium 77, Saltsjöbaden, Sweden.]

Williamson, John. "What Washington Means by Policy Reform," in J. Williamson, ed., *Latin American adjustment: How much has happened?* Washington, DC: Institute of International Economics, April 1990, pp. 5–20.

Wilson, Robert B. "Competitive Bidding with Disparate Information." *Management Science*, March 1969, *15*(7), pp. 446–48.

——, "A Bidding Model of Perfect Competition." *Review of Economic Studies*, 1977, *44*(3), pp. 511–18.

World Bank, ed. *Knowledge for development*: 1998/99 world development report. Washington, DC: World Bank, 1999.

Yabushita, Shiro, "Theory of Screening and the Behavior of the Firm." *American Economic Review*, March 1983, *73*(1), pp. 242–45.

17 Duopoly models with consistent conjectures

Timothy F. Bresnahan

The theory of oligopoly price is very sensitive to behavioral assumptions. Even given identical assumptions about costs and demand, different models can predict every price between marginal cost and monopoly. This paper selects a single oligopoly model, and thus predicts a single oligopoly price. The selection criterion is consistency of conjectures; each firm's conjectures about the way other firms react to it will be correct.

The two classical oligopoly theories, Bertrand and Cournot, make identical assumptions about costs and demand, but different assumptions about firm behavior. In Cournot equilibrium, each firm maximizes profit given the *quantity* of output other firms produce. In Bertrand equilibrium, each firm maximizes given the *prices* other firms charge. This difference in behavioral assumptions leads to a large divergence in predicted prices. Cournot predicts positive markups that decline as the number of firms increases, while Bertrand predicts marginal cost pricing even in duopoly. Clearly both models cannot be correct. Is their truth an empirical question, as recent work suggests?[1] This paper attempts to decide on theoretical grounds.

No attempt to decide among Bertrand, Cournot, and their more modern competitors can be based on mathematical correctness. Economic criteria must guide the decision. Oligopoly models are examples of what game theorists call Nash equilibrium. In them, every firm maximizes profits given the actions of all other firms. The mathematics does not care whether "actions" are defined to be prices (Bertrand), quantities (Cournot), or any other variables. Yet these distinctions are crucial to the economics of the situation. The notion of Nash equilibrium already entails one economic condition – individual rationality. This paper will determine the correct definition of actions by imposing a further economic condition – consistency of conjectures.[2]

The precise sense in which conjectures are to be consistent is this; the *conjectural variation* and the *reaction function* will be equated. The conjectural variation is the firm's conjecture about other firms' behavior. In Cournot, for example, each firm conjectures that all other firms' quantities are constant. The reaction function is the firm's actual behavior. It is the solution to the profit-maximizing problem, and tells what the firm will do as a function of all other firms' actions. Clearly, what the firm conjectures affects how it reacts. This paper will search for cases where conjectures and reactions are the same – where each firm's conjectures about other firms' reactions are perfectly correct, locally.[3]

Every notion of Nash equilibrium has the feature that, in equilibrium, each firm's beliefs about the *level* of all other firms' actions are confirmed. For example, in Cournot duopoly, each firm's equilibrium quantity is that one which induces the other firm to produce its equilibrium quantity. The firms are right in their beliefs, in Fellner's famous remark, but right for the wrong reason. That is, it is not actually true, as conjectured by the firm, that the other firm's quantity is a constant. The other firm's quantity depends nontrivially on ours – the reaction function does not have zero slope, although the conjecture does. This paper will find Nash equilibrium notions in which firms are right for the right reason. In equilibrium, they will be correct not only about the *levels* of one anothers' actions but also about the *functions* according to which they are reacting.[4] One might view this as a kind of rational expectations oligopoly theory. Consistency of conjectures makes the way firms react to one another endogenous by requiring that it be correct.

In the next section, a consistent conjectures equilibrium *(CCE)* is defined. A series of examples show what *CCE* price is under different assumptions about cost and demand. For example, with constant marginal costs the Bertrand conjectures (which imply marginal cost pricing) are consistent. A second section gives the central theorem of the paper: Under certain assumptions about cost and demand, the *CCE* exists and is unique. Uniqueness is a very important property – when the *CCE* is unique, consistency of conjectures solves the problem of too many oligopoly solution concepts by determining a single equilibrium price and quantity. Section III points out two ways in which increasing returns to scale could cause nonexistence of the *CCE*. Section IV investigates the role of the *CCE* when the conditions of the duopoly are set by firm's investments in capacity. It concludes that, with constant returns, capacity cannot serve as a barrier to entry. Defense of the *CCE* as a sensible way to solve the oligopoly problem is postponed until Section V.

I

This section establishes notation and defines a consistent conjectures equilibrium. In the classical case studied by Bertrand and Cournot (constant marginal cost) it is shown that the Cournot equilibrium is not a *CCE*. It is further shown that the Bertrand equilibrium is a *CCE* in this case. The section concludes by examining two examples in which the *CCE* lies between Bertrand and Cournot, depending on the cost and demand functions.

The quantity produced by firm i $(i = 1, 2)$ is labelled q_i. The vector of both firms' outputs is called q:

$$q \equiv (q_1, q_2). \tag{17.1}$$

If the products are perfect substitutes, it will be convenient to define the industry quantity, Q:

$$q \equiv q_1 + q_2. \tag{17.2}$$

Let us assume that the inverse demand functions are all defined. The notation for demand is

$$P_i = P_i(q_1, q_2). \tag{17.3}$$

When the products are perfect substitutes, (17.3) takes the form

$$P_i = P = P(Q). \tag{17.4}$$

The costs to firm i are given by the cost function $c_i(q_i)$.

Let us use the notational convention of Lester Telser and write all oligopoly solution concepts as if they had quantities as strategic variables. To do this, we adopt the idea of conjectural variation, r. Firm i acts as if it believes

$$\partial q_j / \partial q_i = r_{ij}(q_i) \quad \text{for } j = 1, 2; \ j \neq i. \tag{17.5}$$

Throughout, it shall be maintained the convention that firm j is the other firm when speaking about firm i. The observable implication of (17.5) is that firm i acts as if it believes that it faces a demand curve with slope

$$\frac{dP_i}{dq_i} = \frac{\partial P_i}{\partial q_i} + \frac{\partial P_i}{\partial q_j} r_{ij}(q_i). \tag{17.6}$$

Some examples may clear up the notion of conjectural variation. Let the two products be perfect substitutes. Then firm 1 acts as if it faces a demand curve with slope

$$\frac{dP}{dq_1} = P'(Q)(1 + r_{12}(q_1)). \tag{17.7}$$

Thus, if $r_{12} = 0$, firm 1 is a Cournot player. If $r_{12} = -1$, firm 1 is a Bertrand player, since in this case total quantity, and therefore price, is conjectured to be a constant. If $r_{12} = 1$, firm 1 acts like a colluder. In this case, the firm acts as if it can affect total output, but not its own market share. If $r_{21} = r_{12}$ in any of the above cases, then the reaction functions yield the named equilibrium concepts – Cournot, Bertrand, or Collusion. Of course, $r_{ij}(q_i)$ could be a more complicated function, and r_{12} need not equal r_{21}. What is important here is that assumptions about r are assumptions about the equilibrium concept.

We now examine the impact of the solution concept, that is, the r, on firm behavior. The profit function for firm i is

$$\Pi_i = P_i(q)q_i - c_i(q_i). \tag{17.8}$$

The corresponding first-order condition for a profit maximum is

$$0 = q_i \left(\frac{\partial P_i(q_1, q_2)}{\partial q_i} + \frac{\partial P_i(q_1, q_2)}{\partial q_j} r_{ij}(q_i) \right) + P_i(q_1, q_2) - \frac{\partial c_i(q_i)}{\partial q_i}. \tag{17.9}$$

which implicitly defines q_i in terms of the quantity produced by the other firm, q_j. The reaction function ρ is defined by

$$q_i = \rho_i(q_j) \quad \text{solves (17.9)} \tag{17.10}$$

What function ρ is depends on r_{ij}, as well as on the cost and demand functions. Note that in (17.9), the actual q_j enters even though firm i supposedly has conjectures about what q_j will be. These conjectures, therefore, are unlike those of a Stackelberg leader. In the present model, each firm does in fact react to the other, in a way that depends on conjectures. For any given conjectures, we could define an oligopoly equilibrium point, q^*, in the usual way:

$$\text{if } q_1^* = \rho_1(q_2^*) \quad \text{and} \quad q_2^* = \rho_2(q_1^*) \tag{17.11}$$

then q^* is an equilibrium. I now extend this definition so that the conjectures are correct as well.

DEFINITION: A consistent conjectures equilibrium is a pair of quantities q^*, and of conjectures $(r_{12}(q_1), r_{21}(q_2))$, such that

$$q_1^* = \rho_1(q_2^*), \quad q_2^* = \rho_2(q_1^*) \tag{17.12}$$

and there is some $\varepsilon > 0$, such that

$$r_{12}(q_1) = \frac{\partial p_2(q_1)}{\partial q_1} \quad \text{for all } q_1^* - \varepsilon < q_1 < q_1^* + \varepsilon; \tag{17.13}$$

$$r_{21}(q_2) = \frac{\partial p_1(q_2)}{\partial q_2} \quad \text{for all } q_2^* - \varepsilon < q_2 < q_2^* + \varepsilon. \tag{17.14}$$

The way to read (17.13) is: r_{12} is one's conjecture about two, p_2 two's actual behavior. In this definition (17.12) assures that both firms are correct about the *level* of one another's reaction functions. This is merely the usual Nash equilibrium condition. What (17.13) and (17.14) assure is that the firms are correct about the higher order derivatives as well. Perhaps the definition can be clarified by the familiar observation that the Cournot conjectures and reaction functions are not the same.

Example 1

Cournot equilibrium is not a *CCE* when marginal costs are constant, demand is linear, and products are perfect substitutes. Recall that the Cournot solution concept is defined by $r_{12} = r_{21} = 0$. With constant marginal cost $\partial c / \partial q_i$, firm 1's profit is given by

$$\Pi_1 = [P(Q) - \partial_c / \partial q_i] q_1 \tag{17.15}$$

and the analog of (17.9) is

$$q_1 P'(Q) + p(Q) - \partial_c / \partial q_i = 0 \tag{17.16}$$

An implicit differentiation gives the slope of 1's reaction function:

$$\partial p_1 / \partial q_2 = -P'(Q)/2P'(Q) = -1/2 \tag{17.17}$$

Exactly the same analysis could be carried out for firm 2, yielding

$$\partial p_2 / \partial q_1 = -P'(Q)/2P'(Q) = -1/2 \tag{17.18}$$

If the Cournot conjectures are to be consistent, (17.17) and (17.18) must be zero. Since they are equal to $-1/2$ everywhere, the Cournot conjectures are inconsistent, as is well known. Each firm assumes that the other firm's quantity is constant. Yet each firm, because of that assumption, has a reaction function which is not a constant. The firms optimal behavior differs from their assumption about one another's behavior.

The Cournot example makes clear that Cournot firms are not very sophisticated. I will not proceed by giving firms more sophisticated behavior: quite the reverse. We will look for those conjectures which are held by the firm to be certainly true, and which just happen to turn out to be correct. The spirit of this enterprise is therefore not one of giving firms discretion, but of removing their discretion by imposing correctness. Let us now search for the *CCE* under the same constant marginal cost assumption.

Example 2

Under the constant *mc* assumption, the Bertrand equilibrium is a *CCE* for any demand function $P(Q)$. Let the firms have identical linear conjectures with slope r. That is, $r_{12} = r_{21} = r$. Then the first-order condition for firm 1 is

$$(1+r)q_1 P'(Q) + P(Q) - \partial c/\partial q_i = 0 \tag{17.19}$$

and the slope of the reaction function is

$$\frac{\partial p_1}{\partial q_2} = -\frac{P'(Q) + (1+r)q_1 P''(Q)}{(2+r)P'(Q) + (1+r)q_1 P''(Q)} \tag{17.20}$$

Note that if $r = -1$ (Bertrand), then the reaction function has slope -1 as well. Since the situation is symmetric, firm 2's reaction function has the same slope. Therefore the Bertrand equilibrium is a *CCE* for this case.

The economic intuition of this example is straightforward. Recall that the Bertrand equilibrium has price equal to marginal cost. Suppose that one duopolist's behavior is: charge marginal cost and meet all demand. The only possible action for the other firm is marginal cost pricing. No action that attempts to reduce industry quantity can work, since the first firm will meet demand at marginal cost.

The conclusion that the Bertrand equilibrium is the *CCE* depends in a critical way on the cost and demand assumptions of the classical models. Let us now consider two examples in which those assumptions are relaxed. In the first of these, the constant marginal cost assumption is relaxed, and the marginal cost function is allowed to slope up. As the slope moves from horizontal to vertical, the *CCE* moves from Bertrand to Cournot.

Example 3

Let the total cost function be quadratic:

$$c(q_i) = c_0 + c_1 q_i + c_2 (q_i)^2/2 \tag{17.21}$$

with c_0, c_1, c_2 all nonnegative. Further, let $P(Q)$ be linear with slope d. With a linear conjecture with slope r_{12}, firm 1's first-order condition is

$$P(Q) + d(1+r_{12})q_1 - (\partial c(q_i)/\partial q_1) = 0 \tag{17.22}$$

The derivative of 1's reaction function is then

$$\partial p_1/\partial p_2 = -d/[(2+r_{12})d - c_2] \tag{17.23}$$

A straightforward calculation (shown in the Appendix) yields the slopes at the *CCE*. These equate the *r*s to the *ρ*s.

$$r_{12} = r_{21} = -1 + c_2[1 - (1 - 4d/c_2)^{1/2}]/2d \tag{17.24}$$

As can be seen by inspection, the slopes of the consistent conjectures in this case lie between 0 (Cournot) and -1 (Bertrand). The *CCE* is determined by the ratio of the slopes of the marginal cost and demand functions. When that ratio is zero (constant marginal cost) the *CCE* is Bertrand equilibrium. As the ratio approaches infinity (vertical *mc*) the *CCE* approaches Cournot equilibrium. The latter polar case clarifies the intuition; if marginal cost curves are vertical, there are no sensible strategic variables except quantities.

In the next example, the *CCE* departs from Bertrand because the duopolists' products are not perfect substitutes. Again the intuition is clear. One would expect that the closer substitutes products are, the more competitive firm interactions are.

Example 4

Let the inverse demand function be linear and exhibit some product differentiation.

$$\partial P_i / \partial q_k = d_{ik}; \quad i, k = 1, 2 \tag{17.25}$$

Marginal costs are constant at a $\partial c / \partial q_i$. In this context, the Cournot conjectures continue to have slope zero. But the slope of the Bertrand conjectures is

$$r_{ij} = -d_{jj} / d_{ji} \tag{17.26}$$

which is -1 only if the products are perfect substitutes. In the case of imperfect substitutes, therefore, the Bertrand equilibrium prices are above marginal cost. The *CCE* prices are yet higher. To see this, first calculate the first-order maximum condition for firm i:

$$0 = P_i(q) - \partial c / \partial q_i + q_i (d_{ii} + d_{ij} r_{ij}) \tag{17.27}$$

The reaction function has slope:

$$\partial p_i / \partial q_j = -d_{ij} / (2 d_{ii} + d_{ij} r_{ij}) \tag{17.28}$$

An easy calculation (see the Appendix) gives the *CCE* conjectures' slopes:

$$r_{ij} = [-d_{ii} d_{jj} + [(d_{ii} d_{ij})(d_{ii} + d_{jj} - d_{ij} + d_{ji})]^{1/2} / d_{ij} d_{jj}] \tag{17.29}$$

Note that the *CCE* conjectures do not involve square roots of negative numbers as long as both demand functions slope down in own price and the products are no more than perfect substitutes. Equation (17.29) has two interesting polar cases. First, if either d_{12} or d_{21} is zero, the consistent conjectures are those of Cournot. (And of Bertrand – without demand-side interaction, all oligopoly solution concepts are identical.) Second, if the determinant under the second radical is zero, that is, if the products are perfect substitutes, the *CCE* is Bertrand. In general, the *CCE* lies between Bertrand and Cournot, with the Jacobian determinant of the demand function determining exactly where.

II

This section investigates the (local) sense in which a general linear duopoly has a unique *CCE*. Uniqueness is important, because it shows that the *CCE* does determine a single duopoly equilibrium. Before stating the uniqueness theorem, let us look at one more example, which shows that the conjectures must be completely correct for the *CCE* to be unique.

Example 5

Suppose that firms have nonlinear conjectures ($r_{ij}(q_i)$ not a constant) but that we only require that their conjectures be linearly correct. This partial consistency imposes no restriction on the equilibrium prices and quantities. The example again uses the constant marginal cost case with perfect substitutes. Demand has slope d and cost c'. But now the conjectural variations are quadratic, with slopes:

$$r_{ij}(q_i) = r_1 + r_2 \cdot (q_i - \theta) \tag{17.30}$$

where r_1, r_2, and 0 are parameters. Then the slope of firm i's reaction function is

$$\partial \rho_i(q_j)/\partial q_j = -1/(2 + r_{ij}(q_i) + r_2 q_i) \tag{17.31}$$

The limited notion of consistency is this: at the equilibrium quantities, the slopes of the actual reaction functions are equal to the conjectured slopes. The second derivatives are left arbitrary.

With that notion, we can get limited consistency of any reaction slope between 0 and -1. First, set r_1 equal to the desired reaction slope. Set θ equal to the equilibrium quantity at that slope. That leaves this equation for the reaction slopes at those equilibrium quantities:

$$\partial \rho_i(\theta)/\partial q_j = -1/(2 + r_1 + r_2 \theta) \tag{17.32}$$

and then r_2 can be picked at will to make the reaction function have slope r_1.

The example clearly generalizes as far as desired. The firms could be incorrect about the forty-second derivative of the reaction function, rather than the second. Prices would still be arbitrary. The sense in which consistent conjectures are correct is therefore quite strong. The reaction functions are exactly the same functions as the conjectures, at least at the equilibrium point.

The assumptions needed for the uniqueness theorem should be familiar from remarks surrounding the examples:

ASSUMPTION 1 *The inverse demand functions are linear in the positive orthant and are truncated at the axes. In the interior of the positive orthant, the Jacobian of the demand system is negative semidefinite. It is negative definite unless the products are perfect substitutes.*

ASSUMPTION 2 *The total cost function is quadratic, positive-valued, increasing, and convex over positive quantities. That is, both total and marginal cost functions slope up.*

These assumptions combine the elements of departure from the classical case of examples 3 and 4.

ASSUMPTION 3 *Fixed costs are not so large as to swamp variable profits, nor are the firms' cost functions so different that one is dominated out of the market. (This assumption will be made precise in the course of the proof. Without it, uniqueness would not be called into question, but existence would.)*

THEOREM 1 *Under Assumptions 1–3, there is a CCE with linear conjectures. The CCE is unique in the class of polynomial conjectures. (Proof is shown in the Appendix.)*

Uniqueness in the class of polynomial conjectures is about as strong a result as can be gotten here. The reason for this is that conjectures about behavior far from the equilibrium point are irrelevant. If, say, doubling output were conjectured to cut profit by one-third instead of one-half, there would be no effect on behavior. Precisely the sense in which the *CCE* can be unique is local. The conjectures and the reaction function have the same Taylor series at the equilibrium point. Since the polynomials in the theorem are of arbitrarily large degree, this is what has been proven. For example, it has been shown that the equilibrium notion of Bertrand is the uniquely correct one in the classical case of constant marginal cost.

III

This section presents two examples of nonexistence of the *CCE* under increasing returns to scale. The first of these posits perfect substitutes, constant marginal costs, and nonzero fixed costs. The second example is constructed with a linear, downward-sloping marginal cost function.

When *mc* is constant and products are perfect substitutes, the *CCE* equilibrium concept will be Bertrand. Then equilibrium prices will be equal to *mc* – an unfortunate outcome for firms with fixed costs. Since revenue just covers variable cost, profits will be negative. Exit should follow. This *CCE*, which was an equilibrium given only local information, is not an equilibrium when the total conditions are taken into account. Thus, in this case, there will be no *CCE*.

Example 6

The cost function is the quadratic one of example 3, above. But here $c_o = 0$, $c_l > 0$, $c_2 < 0$, so that *mc* slopes down. $P(Q)$ is linear with slope d. The inverse demand function cuts the *mc* curve from above in the positive orthant. I begin by looking for a *CCE* with linear conjectures. The derivatives of the reaction functions are exactly as in example 3, above:

$$\partial p_1/\partial q_2 = -d/(d(2+r_{12}) - c_2) \tag{17.33}$$

$$\partial p_2/\partial q_1 = -d/(d(2+r_{21}) - c_2) \tag{17.34}$$

Imposing the conditions of the *CCE* and substituting (17.33) into (17.34) yields

$$r_{12}\left[2 - \frac{1}{2+r_{12}-c_2/d} - \frac{c_2}{d}\right] = -1 \tag{17.35}$$

The quadratic equation implied has determinant

$$(2 - c_2/d)^2 - 4 < 0, \quad \text{if } c_2 < 0 \tag{17.36}$$

Thus no linear *CCE* exists for $c_2 < 0$.[5] Since Lemma 2 (see the Appendix) shows that linear duopolies like this one have linear *CCE's* if they have any polynomial ones, no polynomial *CCE* exists for this technology.

It is easy to understand the nature of this nonexistence proof, and of the comparable result when the technology has fixed costs and constant marginal costs. In these instances, global increasing returns reign. Any duopoly equilibrium is dominated in cost terms by some single firm outcome. Hence it is the theory of entry, not of duopoly, which determines price.

Monopoly equilibria do exist. Thus only equilibria with the cost minimizing number of firms in operation exist.

IV

This section presents an example of capacity investment oligopoly. In it, firms invest in fixed capital in advance of the market period. Then it is the *SR* cost function which is relevant to the market equilibrium. Since the market equilibrium is a *CCE*, there is no intertemporal inconsistency in firms' beliefs about one anothers' behavior. The example explores the nature of capacity as a barrier to entry (see Michael Spence) under the assumption that the post-entry duopoly solution concept is a *CCE*. It clearly shows that capacity alone is not a sufficient barrier with a constant returns Leontief technology.

Example 7

Producers must invest in fixed capital in advance of the market period, and cannot alter their capacity during the market period. The overall production technology is Leontief:

$$q_i = \min[L_i/\lambda, K_i/\kappa] \tag{17.37}$$

where L_i is labour, K_i capital in place, and λ and κ are constants. Label firm i's capacity by $k_i = K_i/\kappa$. Then the short-run (fixed K_i) marginal cost is

$$srmc_i = \begin{cases} c & 0 \le q_i < k_i \\ \infty & q_i \ge k_i \end{cases} \tag{17.38}$$

where c is λ times the wage rate. Long-run total costs include a charge for capital, of course. Let f be κ times the interest rate. Then,

$$lrmc_i = c + f \tag{17.39}$$

As before, demand is linear: $P = A + d(q_i + q_2)$

The equilibrium concept has two stages, capacity and market. By imposing *CCE* on the market equilibrium, we insure that perfect foresight at the capacity investment stage involves no inconsistency. As a first step, let us calculate the market *CCE* as a function of capacities. The capacity constraint changes the firms' maximization problems, since profit maxima can come either at an interior solution or at the capacity constraint. The Kuhn-Tucker conditions for a profit maximum are

$$q_i d(1 + r_{ij}) + P(Q) - c - \ge 0, \tag{17.40}$$

$$[q_i d(l + r_{ij}) + P(Q) - c][k_i - q_i] = 0$$

In working toward calculation of the *CCE*, it will be useful to have a few points on the mapping from conjectures to reaction slopes on hand, as in Table 17.1. The table shows what kind of *CCEs* are possible. Both firms could be unconstrained; in this case they will be Bertrand players, as example (2) showed. This occurs only if industry capacity is sufficient to set demand price to c. Alternatively, both firms could be constrained; this occurs when their

Table 17.1

Constrained?	Conjecture	Reaction
yes	any	0
no	0	−1/2
no	−1	−1

capacities are both so small that the constraint binds with the (correct) conjecture of zero. Lastly, one firm could be constrained (with conjecture −1/2) and the other unconstrained (with conjecture 0).

Manipulation of the first-order conditions reveals the regions in capacity space in which each of these equilibria can obtain. In Figure 17.1, region I has both firms constrained, region II, neither, while in regions III and IV firms one and two only are constrained, respectively. In region V there are two equilibria. Either firm 1 or firm 2 can be constrained but not both.

The nonuniqueness of equilibrium in region V is not disturbing in the context of the two-stage game. Any notion of individual rationality suggests that no firm will invest in capacity and then become unconstrained. Therefore the interior of regions III, IV, and V can be ruled out. On the border, of course, the profits are the same whether the firm is viewed as just constrained or just not. A problem might arise if each firm took the (optimistic) view that it was going to be the constrained firm, even if it had the larger capacity. These mutually inconsistent expectations could lead to inconsistent two-stage equilibria.

More interesting is the light in which this example places the use of capacity as a barrier to entry. How does an incumbent firm's excess capacity serve as a signal of willingness to compete *ex post* entry? If the post-entry solution concept is the *CCE*, capacity does not have the desired effect. With constant returns to scale, the incumbent cannot find a capacity which induces the potential entrant to stay out. This is true even if we assume that the incumbent is a Stackelberg leader in the capacity game. The key to the proof is the nature of the *CCE* when either firm's capacity is small.

To see that capacity cannot be a barrier, assume that firm 1 is the incumbent. Divide the problem of the entrant, firm 2, into two cases depending on firm 1's capacity.

Case I: $k_1 < -(A - c)/2d$. In this case, if firm 2 enters at small enough capacity, the *CCE* will be in region I, both firms constrained. Therefore, if firm 1 was making positive profits, firm 2 can find a small enough capacity to make positive profits as well.

Case II: $k_i \geq -(A - c)/2d$. In this case, firm 1 will have excess capacity even after entry at small k_2. In region IV, where firm 2 is capacity constrained, firm 1 is not. In that region, firm 1 (correctly) conjectures that firm 2's output is constant, while firm 2 knows r_{21}, to be −1/2. Then the equilibrium market values will be

$$q_2 = k_2, q_1 = -(A - c)/2d - k_2/2 \tag{17.41}$$

$$P = A - (A - c)/2 + dk_2/2 \tag{17.42}$$

$$\Pi_2 = [(A - c)/2 + dk_2/2 - f]k_2 \tag{17.43}$$

Equation (17.43) says that the condition for firm 2 to be unable to find a capacity investment which yields positive profit is

$$f > (A - c)/2 \tag{17.44}$$

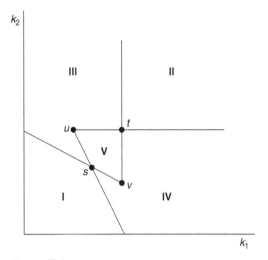

Figure 17.1

Note: $s = \left[\dfrac{A-c}{-3d}, \dfrac{A-c}{-3d}\right]$; $t = \left[\dfrac{A-c}{-2d}, \dfrac{A-c}{-2d}\right]$; $u = \left[\dfrac{A-c}{-4d}, \dfrac{A-c}{-2d}\right]$; $v = \left[\dfrac{A-c}{-2d}, \dfrac{A-c}{-4d}\right]$.

But this is exactly the condition that firm 1's monopoly price not cover capital charges should entry be deterred. Thus deterring entry cannot be profitable.

This example shows that excess capacity alone is not a barrier to entry when all players correctly anticipate the post entry equilibrium. This is true even though the incumbent firm can alter the "rules of the game" as well as its "initial conditions" in Avinash Dixit's useful distinction. It is clear from the proof that this result leans heavily on the assumption of constant returns down to arbitrarily small scale.

V

This section defends consistency of conjectures as a reasonable restriction on the oligopoly solution concept. The defense, suprisingly enough, has nothing to do with dynamics. Indeed, the problem of constructing an informationally consistent oligopoly is a formidable one, as yet unsolved. The first half of this section treats dynamic arguments; the results are quite negative. The second half treats the comparative statics of equilibrium; they lead naturally to the *CCE*.

One argument against some oligopoly solution concepts is that they have "inconsistent dynamics." Although I will not use the dynamic inconsistency argument, it is instructive to step through it for Cournot equilibrium. Begin with an arbitrary quantity for firm one, say q_1. Let firm two take q_1 as given and move to its profit-maximizing output, $q_2 = p_2(q_1)$. Now firm one will move to $q_1 = p_1(q_2)$.... Continue until convergence at the equilibrium quantities. At every step, each firm has maximized profit, taking the quantity of the other firm as given. Yet the other firm's quantity has in fact changed; the firm should notice this and take advantage of the information. A possible argument for the *CCE* arises from this dynamic inconsistency. If firms' conjectures are everywhere correct, they will be confirmed by these dynamics.

The inconsistent dynamics argument is unsatisfactory because it confuses statics and dynamics. Is it an argument against Cournot equilibrium or against the particular dynamic used to reach it? Economists routinely object to similar cobweb dynamics for perfect competition on rational expectations grounds. Perhaps here, as there, the fault could lie in the dynamic rather than in the equilibrium notion. It would be desirable[6] to construct a better argument, a rational expectations oligopoly, in which dynamic considerations affect the static equilibrium concept. But it is not necessary.

Fortunately, it is not necessary to work out the disequilibrium dynamics of oligopoly to defend the *CCE*. The comparative statics of equilibrium give firms enough information to recover one anothers' behavior. Suppose that some variable exogenous to the oligopoly (say, costs, the location of the demand curve) is changed. Equilibrium prices and quantities will change whatever the nature of the equilibrium concept. Suppose that firms learn nothing about one anothers' behavior from the dynamic process by which the new equilibrium is obtained. They can still learn one anothers' reactions from the location of the new equilibrium. A Cournot firm, knowing the costs, the demands, and that it has reaction slope $-1/2$ can easily learn from the movement of market price the one thing it does not know – the slope of the other firm's reaction. The natural experiment, the movement of exogenous variables, can reveal to firms that their conjectures are inconsistent. This argument does not depend in any critical way on the belief that the equilibrium comparative statics "actually happen." Consider a two-stage oligopoly like the one in the last section. Firms must first pick capacity, and then, with capacity fixed, price or output. At the first stage the only reasonable expectations to give firms are the correct ones. They should be able to calculate their eventual profits as a function of their capacities. Performing that calculation requires knowledge of the second-stage equilibrium concept. Are we to assume, then, that at the second stage they forget their knowledge of one anothers' behavior? There will be no intertemporal inconsistency in their knowledge if the market equilibrium notion is the *CCE*.

The sense of the *CCE* is then this. If firms have inconsistent conjectures and it is possible for them to learn how their industry reacts to exogenous shocks, they will learn that their conjectures are wrong. If they have consistent conjectures, nothing in the comparative statics of equilibrium will reveal those conjectures to be wrong. By what dynamic process the conjectures will come to be consistent is an unsolved problem, as is the possibility of an informationally consistent, stable dynamic for oligopoly prices and quantities.

Conclusion

This paper has solved, in one sense, "the oligopoly problem." The indeterminacy of duopoly price due to a multiplicity of solution concepts has been removed. The cost of a determinate price is the denial of all discretion in firm behavior.[7] Whether this cost is justified depends on the reasonableness of the conditions imposed.

The reasonableness of the *CCE* as such a condition was discussed in the last section. A second defense can be constructed from the solution yielded by the *CCE*. When products are perfect substitutes and marginal costs are constant, pricing will be competitive. When the marginal cost function slopes up or when products are less perfect substitutes, pricing becomes less competitive. This, I think, is a quite intuitive theory of competition. Competition comes about when increases in quantity have no adverse affects on costs and when products are close substitutes.

Related results hint at but do not resolve a connection between increasing returns to scale and entry. First, in two cases of increasing returns, there is no duopoly *CCE*. Second, capacity cannot serve as a barrier to entry when returns are constant down to arbitrarily small scale.[8]

These results seem to point at a theory in which entry is determined by cost-minimizing market structure. More work on this appears warranted.

APPENDIX: PROOF OF THEOREM 1

Theorem 17.1 can be proved in two lemmas. The first shows that there is exactly one *CCE* under the assumption that conjectures are linear. The second shows that, when the cost and demand systems are linear, any polynomial conjecture must be linear to be correct.
   Recall some notation:

$$d_{ij} \equiv \partial P_i / \partial q_j \tag{17.A1}$$

$$c_i(q_i) = c_{i0} + c_{i1}q_i + c_{i2}(q_i)^2/2$$

$$\rho_i(q_j) \quad \text{is firm } i \text{ reacting to } j \tag{17.A2}$$

$$r_{ij}(q_i) \quad \text{is } i\text{'s conjecture about } j \tag{17.A3}$$

LEMMA 1 *Under the assumptions of Theorem 1, there is exactly one CCE with linear conjectures.*

PROOF: The first-order conditions are

$$0 = P_i - \partial c_i(q_i)/\partial q_i + (d_{ii} + d_{ij}r_{ij})q_i; \quad i = 1, 2 \tag{17.A4}$$

The slopes of the reaction functions are

$$\frac{\partial \rho_i(q_j)}{\partial q_j} = \frac{-d_{ij}}{2d_{ii} - c_{i2} + d_{ij}r_{ij}} \quad i = 1, 2 \; j \neq i \tag{17.A5}$$

Note that the linear economic structure implies that the ρ_{ij} are constant if the r_{ji}, are. The *CCE* is defined by setting $\rho_{21} = r_{12}$, $\rho_{12} = r_{21}$. This leaves a quadratic equation in r_{12} and r_{21}. The roots are

$$r_{ij} = -\alpha \pm [(\alpha)(\alpha - 4d_{12}d_{21})]^{1/2}/[2d_{ij}(2d_{jj} - c_{j2})] \tag{17.A6}$$

where

$$\alpha \equiv (2d_{11} - c_{12})(2d_{22} - c_{22}) \tag{17.A7}$$

The numbers under the radicals are always nonnegative. $\alpha > 0$ since $d_{ii} < 0$, $c_{i2} \geq 0$. $\alpha > 4d_{12}d_{21}$ since the products are assumed to be no more than perfect substitutes.
   Equation (17.A6) seems to imply that there are two *CCEs*. (Not four, since taking the positive radical in r_{12} implies taking it in r_{21}, as well.) One of these is economically meaningless, since it occurs at negative quantities. The true *CCE* is found by taking the positive radical. To see this, substitute (17.A6) back into the first-order condition (17.A4):

$$0 = P_i - \partial c_i(q_i)/\partial q_i \tag{17.A8}$$
$$+ [d_{ii} + \{-\alpha \pm [(\alpha)(\alpha - 4d_{12}d_{21})]^{1/2}\}/[2(2d_{jj} - c_{j2})]]q_i$$

Since the markup $P_i - \partial c_i(q_i)/\partial q_i$ is always positive, the sign of q_i depends only on the bracketed term. Expanding the bracket yields

$$d_{ii} - \frac{2d_{ii} - c_{i2}}{2} \tag{17.A9}$$

$$\pm \frac{2d_{ii} - c_{i2}}{2}\left(\frac{\alpha - 4d_{12}d_{21}}{\alpha}\right)^{1/2}$$

Since $d_{ii} < 0$, $c_{i2} \geq 0$, (17.A6) is negative if and only if the positive radical is taken. Hence $q_i > 0$ only if the positive radical is taken.

It should be mentioned at this point that, in the definition of the *CCE*, we have not allowed firms to shut down. Using only local information, we have no way of telling whether price is over average cost. There are two ways for the total condition to fail. One is if the fixed costs are so high that they overwhelm operating profits. This can clearly be dealt with only by calculating operating profits and assuming fixed costs smaller. The other difficulty arises when the firms are close substitutes and one of them has a cost advantage. For example, when mc is constant, and the products perfect substitutes, both firms must have the same mc or there is no equilibrium. This, too, is dealt with by direct ruling out under Assumption 3.

The exact assumptions on technology and demand made in Assumption 3 can now be spelled out explicitly. First, let the reaction slopes take on their *CCE* values:

$$r_{ij} = -\alpha + [(\alpha)(\alpha - 4d_{12}d_{21})]^{1/2}/[2d_{ij}(2d_{ji} - c_{j2})] \tag{17.A10}$$

Then write out the equations defining the equilibrium quantities:

$$(2d_{11} + d_{12}r_{12} - c_{12})q_1 + d_{12}q_2 = c_{11} - d_{10} \tag{17.A11}$$

$$d_{21}q_1 + (2d_{22} + d_{21}r_{12} - c_{22})q_2 = c_{21} - d_{20}$$

the condition for q_i to be positive is then

$$[2d_{jj} + d_{ji}r_{ji} - c_{j2}](c_{i1} - d_{i0}) - d_{ij}(c_{j1} - d_{j0}) < 0 \tag{17.A12}$$

This condition will be satisfied whenever i's zero-quantity markup is not too much less than j's, or when i's demand is suitably independent of j's (in the sense that d_{ij} is small). The other half of Assumption 3 is that no shutdown occur. Using (17.A4), the condition that firm i's price exceed average cost is

$$mc - ac > q_i[d_{ii} + d_{ij}r_{ij}] \tag{17.A13}$$

Since the bracketed term is negative, the right-hand side is as well. Thus price can fall below average cost only when average cost exceeds marginal in equilibrium. Since average cost is not falling under Assumption 2, this is only the assumption that the fixed costs are not too large.

LEMMA 2 *In the linear situation of theorem 1, any CCE with polynomial conjectures has linear conjectures. This is a straightforward proof by contradiction. Assume that $r_{12}(q_1)$*

and $r_{21}(q_2)$ are polynomials of arbitrarily large order, say of order k. I reproduce the first-order condition:

$$0 = P_i - c_i'(q_i) + q_i(d_{ii} + d_{ij}r_{ij}(q_i)) \quad i = 1, 2, \ j \neq i \tag{17.A14}$$

The reaction function is defined by solving (17.A9) for q_i in terms of q_j. The slope of the reaction function is

$$\partial\rho_i(q_j)/\partial q_j = -d_{ij}/(2d_{ii} - c_{i2} + d_{ij}r_{ij}(q_i) + d_{ij}q_i\partial r_{ij}(q_i)/\partial q_i) \tag{17.A15}$$

The denominator of the right-hand side (17.A14) is a kth order polynomial in q_i. Firm i's reaction function has been assumed to be a polynomial in q_j. Therefore the left-hand side of (17.A14) is a $k - 1$th order polynomial in q_j. Clearly there is no ε neighborhood on which these two assumptions are consistent unless $k = 0$, the conjectures are linear.

Acknowledgements

Comments from H. Sonnenschein, E. Green, William Novshek, S. Freeman, R. Porter, R. Willig, the managing editor, and a referee have been very helpful. Responsibility for any remaining errors lies with me.

Notes

1 Two recent papers treating the oligopoly equilibrium notion as an empirical question are Elie Appelbaum and my own.
2 A review of oligopoly models, of the idea that they can predict any prices, and of the notion of "conjecture" can be found in William Fellner or James Friedman.
3 Similar notions of consistency have been taken up independently by other researchers. See John Laitner, David Ulph, and Morton Kamien and Nancy Schwartz.
4 The phrase "consistency of conjectures" or similar ones have sometimes been used to indicate correctness about the levels of strategic variables. This paper adapts the more common usage and calls correctness about levels "being in equilibrium."
5 Note that the determinant is positive if $2d < c_2 < 0$. But then the inverse demand function cuts mc from below and the second-order conditions cannot hold.
6 It is quite difficult. The discussions of oligopoly by Takashi Negishi and by D. W. Bushaw and Robert W. Clower (ch. 7) as well as the "conjectural equilibria" of Frank Hahn and Jose Trujillo will be useful in attacking the out-of-equilibrium dynamics. The theory will have to treat several thorny issues. One is a kind of higher-order inconsistency. Suppose constant marginal cost duopolists begin with Cournot ($r = 0$) conjectures. Each then observes that the other has a reaction with slope $-1/2$, and updates its conjecture to have this slope. This gives them (optimally: see (17.23), above) reactions with slope $-2/3$. And this process will continue until they converge to the consistent Bertrand conjectures. Note that the same dynamic inconsistency argument raised against Cournot dynamics can be raised here. The firms are acting as if one anothers' *reactions* are fixed. Why do they not notice that they are changing? In light of this line of argument, I am not sanguine about the possibilities of a fully consistent oligopoly dynamic.
7 A discussion of the role of discretion in the theory of the firm in general and in industrial organization in particular can be found in Donald Hay and Derek Morris.
8 Some earlier readers of this paper feel that this suggests that the *CCE* is a "perfectness" notion, alluding to the work of Thomas Marschak and R. Selten. I can see no more than analogy in this, although the suggestion is intriguing.

References

E. Appelbaum, "Estimating the Degree of Oligopoly Power," Unpublished Paper, Queens Univ. 1979.

T. Bresnahan, "Competition and Collusion in the American Automobile Industry, The 1955 Price War," Unpublished Paper, Stanford Univ. 1980.

D. W. Bushaw and Robert W. Clower, *Introduction to Mathematical Economics*, Homewood: Richard D. Irwin, 1957.

A. Dixit, "The Role of Investment in Entry-Deterrence," *Econ. J.,* Mar. 1980, Vol. *90*, pp. 95–100.

William Fellner, *Competition Among the Few*, New York: Knopf, 1949.

J. F. Friedman, *Oligopoly and the Theory of Games*, Amsterdam: North-Holland, 1977.

F. Hahn, "On Non-Walrasian Equilibria," *Rev. Econ. Stud.,* Feb. 1978, *45*, pp. 1–18.

D. A. Hay and D. J. Morris, *Industrial Economics, Theory and Evidence*, Oxford: Oxford University Press, 1979.

M. I. Kamien and N. L. Schwartz, "Conjectural Variations," Unpublished Paper, Northwestern Univ. 1980.

J. Laitner, "'Rational' Duopoly Equilibria," Unpublished Paper, Univ. Michigan 1979.

T. Marschak and R. Selten, "Restabilizing Responses, Inertia Supergames, and Oligopolistic Equilibria," *Quart. J. Econ.,* Feb. 1978, *42*, 71–94.

T. Negishi, "Monopolistic Competition and General Equilibrium," *Rev. Econ. Stud.,* June 1961, *28*, 196–201.

A. M. Spence, "Entry, Capacity, Investment and Oligopolistic Pricing," *Bell J. Econ.* Autumn 1977, *8*, 534–44.

L. G. Telser, *Competition, Collusion and Game Theory*, Chicago: Aldine-Atherton 1972.

J. Trujillo, "An Alternative Concept of Rationality for Conjectural Equilibria," Unpublished doctoral dissertation, Univ. Minnesota 1980.

D. Ulph, "Rational Conjectures in the Theory of Oligopoly," Unpublished Paper, University College, London, 1979.

18 Games economists play

A noncooperative view

Franklin M. Fisher

Introduction

For some thirty years following World War II, most bright young economists did not go into industrial organization. It was not hard to see why this was so. The quick, big payoffs in economics tend to go to theorists, and industrial organization was a subject in which theory was not only unsatisfactory, but moribund. The promise of the Chamberlin-Robinson revolution of the early 1930s had not been fulfilled, and, while institutional and verbal-theoretic writings on the subject were sometimes illuminating, there was no hard analytic theory formalizing the structure-conduct-performance paradigm. Oligopoly, in particular, showed no signs of analytic tractability.

Today, the atmosphere is altogether different. The profession is full of young theorists whose principal occupation is industrial organization. Indeed, industrial organization has become *the* hot topic for microtheorists. Journals, meetings, and seminars abound in research on oligopoly, and, judging by the market, this is a booming industry.

Of course, the principal reason for the change is the rise of game theory and its applications in these areas. Von Neumann and Morgenstern's great work was published in 1944 and hailed immediately by theorists (von Neumann and Morgenstern, 1944). Jacob Marschak, indeed, stated in reviewing it (Marschak, 1946, p. 115): "Ten more such books and the progress of economics is assured." Nevertheless, it was not until the last decade that game theory came to the ascendant as the premier fashionable tool of microtheorists.

That ascendancy appears fairly complete. Bright young theorists today tend to think of every problem in game-theoretic terms, including problems that are easier to deal with in other forms. Every department feels it needs at least one game theorist or at least one theorist who thinks in game-theoretic terms. Oligopoly theory in particular is totally dominated by the game-theoretic approach. The field appears to be in an exciting stage of ferment.

To understand why I believe that such excitement is not warranted, it is necessary to step back, briefly review the history of oligopoly theory before the game-theory revolution, and consider what it is that one wants theory to deliver.

Oligopoly theory before game theory[1]

As we all know, oligopoly theory began with Cournot and his two bottlers of mineral spring water. Cournot assumed that each seller takes the other's output as constant and derived an equilibrium as the point at which each seller's output is optimal, given the other.

There are two well-known apparent problems with the Cournot solution in its original form. One is that there appears to be no reason to limit the activities of the sellers to setting outputs. This led Bertrand and Edgeworth to consider similar assumptions as to price setting, and, indeed, capacities, research and development expenditures, advertising, and other variables can also be objects of strategic choice. The solution is quite dependent on just what it is that one takes the oligopolists to be setting.

The second apparent problem with the Cournot assumption is that the participants in the model are very stupid. Each of them takes the other's output as given, but the very process of adjustment shows them not only that this is mistaken, but that, in fact, the rival's output reacts to that of the given seller. This led von Stackelberg to inquire as to what would happen if one of the sellers woke up and then to generalize (or try to) as to what might happen if they both did. This line of development led to a messy collection of cases, which can best be summarized by saying that the results depend very heavily on just what each oligopolist is assumed to be conjecturing about its rivals.

What *should* such conjectures be? It is fair to say that, at this stage of the theory, there was *and probably could not be* a good answer to this question if one considers the agents involved to be perfectly sensible. This is so since *any* conjecture as to rival's behavior appears to lead to a change in that behavior if the rival realizes that one is making it. So long as one remains within a static, one-shot context, there is no really satisfactory way of treating this. (One of the positive things one can say about game-theoretic developments is that they clarified what is involved here. See Tirole (1988, Chaps. 6 and 8).)

In any event, the major change in the way the profession thought about such subjects was brought about by Edward Chamberlin, in work incorporated in his *Theory of Monopolistic Competition* (1933).[2] Chamberlin pointed out that the oligopolists being studied could figure out their problem quite as well as economists could. He suggested that they would reach the cooperative solution – called the "joint-maximization" solution – at which total profits are maximized. While that solution is not what we would now call a "Nash equilibrium," and any of the rivals can improve itself by deviating, Chamberlin argued that such deviations will not happen because they are foreseen to be ultimately self-defeating.

Of course, as was quickly recognized, the joint-maximization solution is not a fully compelling answer. For one thing, the temptation to cheat is very strong. Put in modern terms, the oligopolists are in a prisoners' dilemma, and it will not be easy to be sure that the cooperative solution holds up unless explicit communication is permitted. Indeed, in a changing world oligopolists may not be sure where the joint-maximization solution is and may misinterpret moves toward a changed joint-maximization position as attempts to cheat on the tacit agreement.

Second, save in the convenient but unrealistic case of pure symmetry, if side payments are not allowed, some oligopolists may not like the joint-maximization solution very much.

(For example, that solution may require high-cost firms to shut down.) If they like it less than they would a noncooperative outcome, Chamberlin's reasoning will break down.

Despite these defects (or perhaps because of them), it is fair to say that Chamberlin's suggestion changed the way in which we think about oligopoly in practice. The study of any real oligopoly has largely become the study of how the joint-maximization solution is or is not achieved and of the reasons why. One need search no further for an example than the story of OPEC.

One also need not search very far to conclude that there is not much hard theory in all this. As early as William Fellner's classic *Competition among the Few* (1949), one finds a complete description of the issues involved in deviation from joint maximization. That description would hardly be different today, but while the issues are well described in Fellner, they are not formalized in any very adequate way.

To sum up, as of the early 1950s, the state of oligopoly theory could reasonably be described as follows: A great many outcomes were known to be possible. The context in which the theory was set was important, with outcomes depending on what variables the oligopolists used and how they formed conjectures about each other. A leading class of cases concerned the joint-maximization solution and when it would or would not be achieved. The answer to the latter question was also known to be very dependent on the context and experience of the oligopolists. Plainly, the theory was in a messy and unsatisfactory state.

The application of game theory to oligopoly

I want now to consider what it is that we know about oligopoly after some years of intensive application of game theory. I begin by going back to Cournot's duopolists bottling water from a mineral spring. Here we know the following: If the two duopolists each choose only output, and if the game they are playing is played only once, then the Cournot solution is the (usually unique) Nash equilibrium of the game. In other words, the Cournot solution gives the only pair of outputs at which each duopolist is playing its best response, given the output of the other one.

This hardly seems much of an advance. Cournot knew that his solution had this property, even if he did not phrase it in such terms. Yet the fact that the Cournot solution is a Nash equilibrium has caused a rash of revitalized interest in it. Indeed, so fascinated are some economists by this fact that I know of two cases of quite distinguished academics who either proposed to testify or did testify in antitrust cases that one should analyze real markets by using the Cournot solution. One, indeed, proposed to testify that in deciding whether to allow a merger in the petroleum industry, one should predict the effects on output and prices in terms of the change in the Cournot solution.

That, I think, is theory run riot. The petroleum industry does not consist of firms playing the one-shot Cournot output-choosing game. Neither does any other real-life industry. That makes the one-shot game totally uninteresting. Further, even on its own terms, the fact that the Cournot solution is a Nash equilibrium is only a complex way of translating what Cournot already knew. It has the merit of avoiding the rather silly Cournot dynamic story of adjustment in which the Cournot conjecture is repeatedly proved false. So far as I can see, however, that is its only merit.[3]

Indeed, once one has more than two oligopolists, even the fact that the Cournot solution is a Nash equilibrium loses its appeal. This is so since the Nash equilibrium concept itself is not the only appealing one. As B. Douglas Bernheim (1984) and David Pearce (1984) have independently pointed out, the arguments that make Nash a sensible concept also apply to what they call "rationalizable equilibrium." A Nash equilibrium is appealing because so long as you play your Nash strategy, it pays me to play mine, and *vice versa*. But suppose I think that you think that I will not play Nash. Then it may pay me not to play Nash, and that may validate your conjecture. Rationalizable equilibria (of which Nash equilibria are a subset) are points at which the strategies played are justified by a consistent (if possibly incorrect) system of conjectures as to what *A* thinks *B* thinks *A* thinks *B* thinks *A* will play, and so forth. Bernheim has shown that, with three or more oligopolists, there is a whole continuum of rationalizable equilibria in the one-shot Cournot output-choosing game.

Put this aside for the moment, however, and concentrate on the popular Nash equilibrium concept. Much of the game-theoretic study of oligopoly consists of analyzing one-shot games in contexts richer than that of quantity-setting. When one does so, one gets richer results. A great many interesting stories have been told in this way. In terms of general propositions, however, about all that one can say is that the results depend heavily on the context – on the particular setting in which the oligopoly game is supposed to be played.

As already remarked, however, real industries are not involved in one-shot games. The whole literature at least from Chamberlin's insight on through the limitations of joint max-imization revolves around the fact that repeated experience matters. To put it another way, Chamberlin's view that symmetric oligopolists will certainly not be stupid enough to fight rests on the notion that they must go on living with each other. It is perfectly true that if the game is played only once, the joint-maximization solution cannot be the outcome of the prisoners' dilemma. Tacit collusion is only made possible by the fact that the game, or games like it, will be played again or that the prisoners will have to deal with each other in later contexts.

What, then, does game theory have to say about repeated games? Alas, nothing remarkably helpful to the general analysis of oligopoly. The best known result here is the so-called "folk theorem," which states that, in an infinitely repeated game with low enough discount rates, any outcome that is individually rational can turn out to be a Nash equilibrium (Fudenberg and Maskin, 1986). Crudely put: anything that one might imagine as sensible can turn out to be the answer. While the folk theorem itself requires a number of assumptions, the existence of an embarrassingly large number of equilibria appears to be a fairly general phenomenon. This is a case in which theory is poverty-stricken by an embarrassment of riches.

Faced with this problem, there are two ways in which one might go. The first of these is to try to cure it by refining the notion of equilibrium used. This is a sensible thing to do, and there have been some advances here. (See Fudenberg and Tirole, 1989, for an excellent summary.) Unfortunately, those advances do not cure the problem of the existence of a vast multiplicity of equilibria.

Nor can one much improve matters by tacking on considerations of Pareto optimality. This is often done by authors simply asserting (rather uncomfortably) that the players will naturally not choose Nash equilibria that are Pareto dominated. The problem here is that this tacks on to the pure concept of Nash equilibrium the view that certain equilibria stand out from others. That may very well be true, and, if it is, it may be an important insight, but in that case the question of *why* certain equilibria stand out becomes the central question. Further, Pareto efficiency often does not reduce the equilibrium set to a happily small size.

To return to the oligopoly context, at least with low enough discount rates and an infinite horizon, one of the Nash equilibria in any repeated game will be the old joint-maximization solution, and this is likely also to be the case with less extreme assumptions.[4] By definition that solution is Pareto efficient (for the oligopolists). To observe that Pareto-efficient solu-tions may have special properties is, in part, to repeat Chamberlin's insight that oligopolists are likely to choose the joint-maximization solution. The question of when this will or will not happen then becomes one of paramount importance. But we have been here before.

I shall have some more favorable things than this to say about the game-theoretic approach to oligopoly, but the following summarizes my general view of where things stand: A great many outcomes are known to be possible. The context in which the theory is set is important, with outcomes depending on what variables the oligopolists use and how they form conjec-tures about each other. A leading class of cases concerns the joint-maximization solution and when it will or will not be achieved. The answer to the latter question is also known to be very dependent on the context and experience of the oligopolists.

Of course, these are the very words I used in describing the pre-game-theory state of oligopoly theory. I must add, however, that, in a way, I have been overly generous to the results of game theory here. I stated that "a leading class of cases concerns the joint-maximization solution and when it will or will not be achieved." In fact, while I strongly believe that this ought to be a central question of oligopoly theory, game theory, with its concentration on equilibria, has partially succeeded in obscuring its importance.[5]

Generalizing theory and exemplifying theory

To say in such sweeping terms that game theory has still left oligopoly theory with a large variety of outcomes and with the same problems as before is not necessarily to say that game theory has failed or has produced no useful results. To go deeper into the matter requires a consideration of what it is that one should ask a theory to do.

In fairly broad terms, there are two styles of theory in economics. I shall refer to these as "generalizing theory" and "exemplifying theory," respectively. They both have very important uses.

Generalizing theory proceeds from wide assumptions to inevitable consequences. It speaks in terms of what must happen, given the background circumstances. Good examples here involve general equilibrium. In that area, existence theory or, perhaps even better, the two welfare theorems give broadly (but, of course, not universally) applicable results. One need not look on so grand a stage for examples of generalizing theory, however. At the level of the individual consumer, Slutsky's equation and the other properties of the substitution terms are propositions that apply under very wide circumstances. They provide general propositions describing what must happen, given fairly general assumptions.

Of course, there is no reason that generalizing (or any other) theory must be purely qualitative. I most certainly do not mean to exclude from generalizing theory the kind of proposition that states that certain effects depend on the values of various variables, with the parameters left to be estimated by econometric means. In the world of empirical economics, such propositions are central, with the role of theory being to specify the important variables and, if we are lucky, to tell us something about admissible functional forms. Generalizing theory can be, and usually is, parameter-dependent.

Whether qualitative or quantitative, however, the grand propositions of generalizing theory are not always available. Further, in finding them it may be useful to work inductively, building up general propositions from simpler cases. This leads to the use of exemplifying theory – also sometimes termed "MIT-style theory" – which is very widespread in the profession.

Exemplifying theory does not tell us what *must* happen. Rather it tells us what *can* happen. In a good exemplifying-theory paper, the model is stripped bare, with specializing assumptions made so that one can concentrate on the phenomena at issue. (For example, rather than trying to deal with a hard problem in full generality, it may be useful and illuminating to assume that all consumers have the same constant-relative-risk-aversion utility function.) When well handled, exemplifying theory can be very illuminating indeed, suggestively revealing the possibility of certain phenomena. What such theory lacks, of course, is generality. The very stripping-down of the model that makes it easy (or even possible) to see what is going on also prevents us from knowing how the results will stand up in more general settings.

Returning to my main subject, it should be plain that (with or without game theory) the status of the theory of oligopoly is that of exemplifying theory. We know that a lot of different things *can* happen. We do not have a full, coherent, formal theory of what *must* happen or a theory that tells us how what happens depends on well-defined, measurable variables.[6]

It is true, of course (as a reader of this paper has pointed out), that the folk theorem is itself an example of generalizing theory, although a negative one. It tells us that we cannot hope for a general oligopoly theory based only on cost and demand functions and free of the context in which oligopolists operate. But that result (which is not exactly a great surprise) is precisely the point. We need a generalizing theory as to how that context influences the outcome.

Such a theory is presently lacking. At present, oligopoly theory consists of a large number of stories, each one an anecdote describing what might happen in some particular situation. Such stories can be very interesting indeed. Elie Wiesel (1966, preceding numbered pages) has said that "God made man because He loves stories," and economists (not merely game theorists) are plainly made in the divine image in this respect.

The following is a case of exemplifying theory at its best.[7] In the IBM antitrust case, one of the claims was that IBM had engaged in something called "premature announcement."[8] While it is not clear exactly what the U.S. government had in mind, "premature announcement" must mean that in some sense IBM announced products sooner than it should have. Now, in the computer industry, it was (and to some extent still is) common practice to announce products before they are ready to be shipped. Such an announcement was a rather formal matter, marking the beginning of the taking of orders. Since computers tended to be built to order rather than to stock and since customers needed time to prepare for the installation of a new computer, there were good reasons for announcing in advance of shipment, and every manufacturer did so. The question then arises of what "premature" announcement can mean. In my testimony and my book on the IBM case (Fisher, McGowan, and Greenwood, 1983), I argued that unless an announcement was made in bad faith (in which case, with rational customers, it was unlikely to represent a practice that could be successfully repeated), it could not be "premature" in the sense of being anticompetitive. While I still believe that to be usually true (and certainly to have been true given the facts of the IBM case), Joseph Farrell and Garth Saloner (1986) have produced a counterexample, showing that there are circumstances in which early truthful announcements can be anticompetitive. This occurs because of network externalities not taken into account by customers opting for a given technology. On the other hand, there is a danger to such stories. Economists are so fond of theoretically consistent tales that they sometimes overlook the fact that exemplifying theory does not provide an inevitable description. The case of the economists who proposed to apply Cournot to the petroleum industry is one example. Another is occasionally provided by articles having to do with network externalities. In that area the authors, having constructed an interesting and plausible story as to how a firm might unfairly limit the ability of competitors to hook-up their machines, tend to assume without close examination that the story must fit the facts of the IBM or other antitrust cases.

Such lapses may be considered the understandable excesses of youthful zeal, and they do not limit the usefulness of exemplifying theory, properly understood. That usefulness, however, is naturally limited. Exemplifying theory must always remain a collection of stories unless those stories point the way to some unifying principle – to a generalizing theory.

Towards a general theory of oligopoly

In the case of oligopoly, what would such a generalizing theory be? What questions would it answer? This is fairly easy to say, although very hard to accomplish.

As we have seen, oligopoly theory is a collection of stories. We have a large and increasing number of formal anecdotes in which the outcome appears to depend heavily on the context.

The role of a true generalizing theory of oligopoly is to tell us the nature of that dependence, in older terms, to tell us how conduct and performance depend upon structure.

I can put this rather pointedly in terms of an example. Everything we know about oligopoly, both with and without game theory, tells us that the characteristics of particular oligopoly environments can substantially influence the outcome. As a teacher of mine (probably Carl Kaysen) once remarked some thirty years ago, it may very well be the case that one cannot understand the history of the American rubber tire industry without knowing that Harvey Firestone was an aggressive guy who believed in cutting prices. Maybe so. But then, as someone else (probably Mordecai Kurz or Kenneth Arrow) remarked to me a few years ago, the job of theory is to discover what characteristics of the rubber tire industry made such aggressive behavior a likely successful strategy. Absolutely right. That question would be answered if we had a generalizing theory of oligopoly. As it stands, we are a long way from an answer.

To see what I have in mind in a more general context, consider the question of policy towards horizontal mergers. In the United States such a policy forms an important, and sometimes controversial, part of our antitrust policy. As part of that policy, the Department of Justice has issued *Merger Guidelines* that state when a merger is or is not likely to be opposed. While the standards set forth in the *Guidelines* do not have the force of law, they play a very powerful role in influencing what mergers do or do not take place, and there is a lamentable tendency for the authorities to take them as carved in stone instead of as tests to see whether further investigation is warranted.[9]

A principal feature of the *Guidelines* is the stress they put on the Herfindahl-Hirschman index of concentration (the "HHI"). That index is defined as the sum of squares of the shares of the firms in the market multiplied by 10,000, for ease of scaling. To get an idea of the orders of magnitude involved, observe that a market with n equally-sized firms will have an HHI of $10,000/n$, so that five equal firms mean an HHI of 2,000, while 10 equal firms mean an HHI of 1,000. The HHI has a number of fairly natural arithmetic properties.

The problem is that we have little idea as to whether the HHI has any *economic* properties. Thus, when the *Guidelines* speak of opposing a merger which increases an HHI already over 1,800 by at least 100 points, it is impossible to say with any precision whether a sensible policy is being described.

This difficulty arises for more than one reason. First, while it seems sensible that the practice of tacit collusion – the tendency towards the cooperative, joint-maximization solution – is more likely, the more concentrated the industry, other things equal, oligopoly theory is remarkably silent on the question of what concentration levels are dangerous. Indeed, there is little theory showing that the aesthetically appealing HHI is the correct measure. Second, while it seems likely that increased concentration matters, other things equal, we are very far from having a decent specification of just what those other things are and how to measure them. A policy that uses concentration levels in different industries should be based on a theory that takes account of the many other phenomena that make industries differ in terms of the likelihood of tacit collusion. We have no such theory. We do not even know what the crucial phenomena are, save in a very general way. Most of what we know, we knew forty years ago.

There have, of course, been repeated attempts to solve this problem by empirical studies using cross-sectional regressions across industries. These attempts have not been successful. Not surprisingly, what repeatedly shows up in such studies is the lack of a generalizing theory to inform the empirical efforts. We do not even know what dependent variable to use, and the studies in question commonly use dependent variables, such as the accounting rate of return or the profits-sales ratio, that exemplifying theory shows to be fatally flawed (Fisher and McGowan, 1983; Fisher, 1987b). The specification of the right-hand side of the regressions or of the direction of causation is not in much better shape (Demsetz, 1973).[10]

The authors of such studies may not always be good theorists, but good theorists are not helping them much. A primary aim of oligopoly theory should be the synthesizing of the individual stories of exemplifying theory to the point where such empirical studies can be done sensibly. We are not near such a point, and, worse, theorists working in the area do not seem to have that end in view.

Has game theory helped?

Despite the fact that we do not seem close to a generalizing theory of oligopoly or, more generally, of the structure-conduct-performance relationship, it may not be fair to say that little progress has been made. After all, to a very large extent, the problem lies in the underlying phenomena themselves rather than in the methods used to investigate them. It appears plain that oligopoly is a very rich subject with many different kinds of outcomes possible. Hence, before a generalizing theory becomes available, it is crucial to develop a rich set of cases from which to generalize. The development of such a set is the job of exemplifying theory.

In this regard it may be argued that the game-theory revolution has been particularly important. By systematizing the way we think about particular examples, game theory may be paving the way for the generalizing theory that we need. On this view, even if game theory merely retells informal anecdotes in a formal manner, it is performing an important service by systematizing our thought and helping us to understand what the crucial features of those anecdotes are.

As my discussion of the example of "premature announcement" shows, I certainly agree that formal argument and exemplifying theory are important. Nevertheless, I do not believe that game theory is in fact preparing the way for generalizing theory.[11] This is so for two reasons. First, game theory in normal form is an inconvenient language with which to prepare the way for the generalizing theory of oligopoly. Second, while game theory in its extensive form may very well be a highly useful language in this regard, most of the existing literature has concentrated on one-shot games, and these are not the interesting ones. I now consider these two points in greater detail.

Game theory can be utilized by considering games in either their normal or their extensive forms. In normal form a game is reduced to a vector-valued function that maps the strategies chosen by the different players into the payoffs. (In the case of discrete, two-person games, this is simply a matrix.) This form is convenient for proving theorems.

Unfortunately, the normal form is not a convenient one for the study of oligopoly or, more generally, of the effects of market structure on conduct and performance. Those effects appear to depend very much on the context. In particular, the ease with which tacit collusion (joint maximization) does or does not take place has much to do with the particulars of the situation in which the oligopolists find themselves. How uniform is the product? How is cheating detected? How are prices quoted, and do most transactions take place at list prices? And so forth. These are all questions of context, and they are suppressed when one represents that context only in terms of strategies describing the actions that will be taken under every conceivable contingency.

I want to be very clear about this. I am not saying that rich contexts cannot be modelled in normal-form game theory. Of course they can. What I am saying is that normal-form game theory is not a convenient way to do it – not a convenient language, as it were. Because it suppresses rich contextual detail, normal-form theorizing about oligopoly makes it awkward at best to come to grips with the central generalizing problem: How do the different aspects of the context interact to produce conduct and performance? Looking at Nash equilibria in normal-form games is not likely to lead to a high payoff here.

The same objection, however, certainly does not apply to game theory in its extensive form, an area that has recently been more and more developed. Here I quote my colleagues, Drew Fudenberg and Jean Tirole (1987, p. 176). I do so at some length, because this passage seems to me to be an excellent statement of the uses of game theory in industrial organization, by two thoughtful, first-class practitioners. It is a statement with which I agree, despite my generally skeptical tone.

> Game theory has had a deep impact on the theory of industrial organization. . . . The reason it has been embraced by a majority of researchers in the field is that it imposes some discipline on theoretical thinking. It forces economists to clearly specify the strategic variables, their timing, and the information structure faced by firms. As is often the case in economics, the researcher learns as much from constructing the model (the "extensive form") as from solving it because in constructing the model one is led to examine its realism. (Is the timing of entry plausible? Which variables are costly to change in the short run? Can firms observe their rivals' prices, capacities, or technologies in the industry under consideration? Etc.)
>
> A drawback of [*sic*] the use of game theory is the freedom left to the modeller when choosing the extensive form. Therefore, economists have long been tempted to use so-called reduced forms, which try to summarize the more complicated real world game, as for example, in the literature on conjectural variations, including the kinked demand curve story. This approach is attractive, but has several problems. The obvious one is that the modeller can only be sure that the reduced form yields the solution of a full-fledged model if he has explicitly solved the model. Also, reduced forms are most natural for the description of steady states, and are thus ill-suited to describe battles for market shares (like price wars, predation, entry and exit), or to study the adjustment paths to outside shocks or government intervention. (Reduced forms are not robust to structural changes.) While the reduced-form approach is simpler, and so more amenable to applications, we believe that the focus on "primitives" implied by the extensive-form approach allows a clearer assessment of the model. Furthermore, the diversity of "reasonable" extensive forms may to some extent reflect the wealth of strategic situations in industries.

This seems to me to recognize quite correctly the importance of context, and hence the importance of doing exemplifying theory by using extensive forms. Unfortunately, generalizing theory is more easily done in normal form, but I strongly believe that extensive-form game theory is the way to systematize our thinking about examples.

Alas, the examples that we are accumulating in this fashion are not the important ones for generalizing theory because of the one-shot/repeated-game distinction discussed earlier. Most of extensive-form oligopoly game theory is an accumulation of examples showing what can happen in one-shot games in different contexts. But the crucial question for oligopoly theory is not that of the outcome of one-shot games. Rather it concerns the factors and circumstances leading to cooperative, joint-maximizing outcomes in repeated games. There, as already mentioned, little is known, and the folk theorem strongly suggests that simply analyzing Nash equilibria (still less more general concepts of equilibrium) cannot tell us what we want to know.

Let me give an example here. Douglas Bernheim and Michael Whinston (1987) have circulated an excellent discussion paper on the effect of multimarket contact on collusive behavior. In it they attempt to formalize the notion that firms that face each other in many markets are more likely to collude than firms facing each other in only one. They show that in fairly general circumstances multimarket contact raises the incentive for collusion – changing the relative costs and benefits of cooperating versus cheating to make cooperation relatively more attractive. This is an example of the game-theoretic analysis of oligopoly at its best. It comes fairly close to doing what I am asking for – formally explaining how changes in the context can influence the likelihood of collusion.

Nevertheless, the paper falls short of that goal. It only shows (indeed, it only *can* show) that multimarket contact makes collusion more attractive. But collusion is always attractive if it can be sustained and will often be a Nash equilibrium in the repeated game. The question that Bernheim and Whinston do not (and probably cannot) fully address is that of how (or whether) multimarket contact assists oligopolists in achieving the collusive equilibrium; they only show that increasing such contact increases the oligopolists' *desire* to achieve collusion.

The point is that one suspects that – unlike Shakespeare's dictum on drink and lechery (*Macbeth*, Act II, Scene 3) – multimarket contact does both provoke the desire *and* assist the performance. In this case the "performance" has to do with the mechanism of coordination, with the way in which the oligopolists grope their way to the collusive outcome instead of to some other equilibrium. Here, multimarket contact is likely to assist because it provides the oligopolists with increased experience in dealing with and signalling to each other. It is true that the "desire" will also assist by changing priors so that a given ambiguous move is less likely to be interpreted as cheating than were collusion relatively less attractive. But the full, rich, contextual story of how multimarket contact affects the ability to get to joint maximization cannot be told by concentrating on Nash equilibria.

In short, I think game-theoretic oligopoly theorists are studying the wrong thing. They are accumulating a wealth of anecdotal material about one-shot oligopoly games when what one wants to know concerns the factors that lead the collusive equilibrium to be chosen in repeated games. So far as I can see, modern oligopoly theory has made little progress on that centrally important question.

I close by briefly commenting on another example, this time a very well-known one that in a general (although not a specific) sense exemplifies my problems with this literature. I refer to the famous articles on Selten's (1978) chain-store paradox (Kreps and Wilson, 1982; Milgrom and Roberts, 1982). These authors consider the following question. Suppose that there is a monopolist faced with a succession of possible entrants (either a chain store with possible entrants in a variety of local markets or, more conveniently for my purposes, a firm with potential entrants arising over time). As each potential entrant appears, the incumbent firm can either fight or allow entry. It is assumed that fighting can keep a particular entrant out but that the relative costs and benefits are such that, were there only one entrant, it would be preferable for the incumbent to allow entry and accept a reduction from monopoly to duopoly profits than it would be to fight successfully. Further, assume that this is common knowledge.

In this situation the incumbent firm will certainly not fight a single entrant. One might suppose, however, that with multiple entrants the incumbent will fight early entrants to establish a reputation for toughness. Not so. Since the incumbent will certainly not fight the last entrant and the last entrant will know this, there is no point in fighting the next-to-last entrant. Since everyone can figure this out, the incumbent cannot gain by fighting the second-to-last entrant or, by extension, by fighting anybody. Hence, there is no reputation for toughness to be gained.

Of course, this result seems somehow wrong when there are enough potential entrants, and the articles under discussion do a quite interesting job of altering things slightly to come up with a different answer. The authors show that so long as entrants believe that there is a slight probability that the incumbent is irrational, it may pay the incumbent to fight.

This is a first-rate piece of analysis and an early example of the utility of employing the extensive form. It has also led to further work on reputation effects (see, for example, Kreps, Milgrom, Roberts, and Wilson (1982); Fudenberg and Levine (1989)). Nevertheless, in my view the point of the original analysis is open to question.

The reason the "paradox" arises in the first place is that it is assumed that there is a last potential entrant. Without that, the story does not unravel, and it is easy to see that engaging in predatory behavior for the sake of reputation will make sense.[12] But real-life incumbents do not face a well-defined finite set of potential entrants. Corporations in most contexts are assumed to have an infinite time horizon and surely cannot believe that any particular fight will be the last. One need go no farther to find a possible reason for predation in such contexts.

This being so, why go to such admittedly elegant lengths to study the question with finite entry? The reply given me some years ago by one of the authors is that the answer of infinite entry is uninteresting.

In one sense that reply is absolutely right. The infinite-entry answer does not compare in elegance and sophistication with the one given by the four authors. But in another sense, the reply exemplifies what is wrong with modern game theory as applied to industrial organization and especially to oligopoly. There is a strong tendency for even the best practitioners to concentrate on the analytically interesting questions rather than on the ones that really matter for the study of real-life industries. The result is often a perfectly fascinating piece of analysis. But so long as that tendency continues, those analyses will remain merely games economists play.

Acknowledgment

An earlier version of this article was presented as an invited lecture at the Australasian meetings of the Econometric Society, Christchurch, New Zealand, August, 1987. I am grateful to the organizers of those meetings for the opportunity and to Drew Fudenberg, John Riley, Jean Tirole, and Michael Whinston for comments and criticism but absolve them of responsibility for errors or for the views expressed. In view of what I have to say about "new developments on the oligopoly front" in the last thirty years, I wish to dedicate this paper to my friend and colleague, Franco Modigliani, on the occasion of his becoming Institute Professor Emeritus.

Notes

1 For a summary of the early literature and full references, see Fellner (1949).

2 It is interesting to note that Joan Robinson, in her *The Economics of Imperfect Competition* (1933) which is often paired with Chamberlin's book, simply failed to understand the oligopoly problem altogether. She assumed (p. 21) that the behavior of each oligopolist can be modelled by creating a demand curve *taking the optimal reactions of rivals into account* and then having the oligopolist set marginal revenue equal to marginal cost. This totally begs the question of what those optimal reactions are – and the fact that one cannot know the answer to that before creating the theory is the central core of the oligopoly problem. Chamberlin put in considerable effort during his lifetime to differentiate his product from that of Joan Robinson. In the oligopoly dimension, at least, he was right.

342   *Franklin M. Fisher*

3 The fact that the static Cournot outcome can be an equilibirium in a dynamic game is more interesting, however, (see Maskin and Triole, 1987).

4 If it were true that joint maximization is an equlibirium only under well-defined special circumstances, we would have a very useful, strong result. I do not beleive this to be the case, however.

5 This is not to say that it is uninteresting to know when joint maximization is or is not an equilibrium and what the properties of collusive equilibria are. (See Fudenberg, Levine, and Maskin (1989) and Green and Porter (1984).)

6 A reader of this article objects, stating that we surely know that detection lags or secrecy hurt collusion. That is quite true, but we have known it for a long time. Formal theory has not added much to our knowledge here nor provided us with a way of assessing the importance of such effects against others.

7 Carl Shapiro's accompanying article (Shapiro, 1989) largely consists of a survey of the accomplishments of game-theoretic analysis in producing exemplifying theory in industrial organization. I do not quarrel with the proposition that such accomplishments exist; indeed, every article I discuss here is one that I regard favorably. That only reinforces my pessimistic view as to the nature of the progress being made towards generalizing theory.

8 *United States v. International Business Machines Corporation*, Docket Number 69, Civ. (DNE) Southern District of New York (Dismissed 1982). For a detailed discussion of the "premature announcement" issues, see Fisher, McGowan, and Greenwood (1983, pp. 289–99).

9 For a fuller discussion of merger policy and the *Guidelines,* see Fisher (1987a).

10 In his accompanying article (Shapiro, 1989), Carl Shapiro points to the empirical literature as generally supporting a smooth relationship between market structure and performance in the form of price-cost margins. For the reasons given, I regard that evidence as a very weak reed on which to lean.

11 The proposition that game theory systematizes thought and thus leads to generalizing theory is reminiscent of the argument that used to be given for the teaching of Latin. It was said that Latin might or might not be interesting for its own sake but that studying it helps to systematize the way one thinks about language. Speaking as one who studied Latin for four years, I believe that argument to have been correct. I do not believe the parallel proposition about game theory.

12 Indeed, with an unbounded set of entrants, the entire problem reduces to Pascal's wager: The rational person preys when faced with the infinite! See Milgrom and Roberts (1982, pp. 305–06) for a formal demonstration.

References

Bernheim, B.D. "Rationalizable Strategic Behavior." *Econometrica*, Vol. 52 (1984), pp. 1007–28.
—— and Whinston, M. "Multimarket Contact and Collusion." Harvard Institute of Economic Research Discussion Paper No. 1317 (1987).
Chamberlin, E. *The Theory of Monopolistic Competition.* Cambridge: Harvard University Press, 1933.
Demsetz, H. "Industry Structure, Market Rivalry, and Public Policy." *Journal of Law and Economics*, Vol. 16 (1973), pp. 1–10.
Farrell, J. and Saloner, G. "Installed Base and Compatibility: Innovation, Product Preannouncements, and Predation." *American Economic Review*, Vol. 76 (1986), pp. 940–55.
Fellner, W. *Competition among the Few.* New York: Alfred A. Knopf, (1949).
Fisher, F.M. "Horizontal Mergers: Triage and Treatment." *Journal of Economic Perspectives*, Vol. 1 (1987a), pp. 23–40.
—— "On the Misuse of the Profits-Sales Ratio to Infer Monopoly Power." *RAND Journal of Economics*, Vol. 18 (1987b), pp. 384–96.
—— and Mcgowan, J.J., "On the Misuse of Accounting Rates of Return to Infer Monopoly Profits." *American Economic Review*, Vol. 73 (1983), pp. 82–97.
——, ——, and Greenwood, J.E., *Folded, Spindled, and Mutilated: Economic Analysis and U.S. v. IBM.* Cambridge: MIT Press, 1983.
Fudenberg, D. and Levine, D.K. "Reputation and Equilibrium Selection in Games with a Patient Player." *Econometrica*, Vol. 57 (1989), pp. 759–78.
—— and Maskin, E., "The Folk Theorem in Repeated Games with Discounting and with Incomplete Information." *Econometrica*, Vol. 54 (1986), pp. 533–54.

—— and Tirole, J., "Understanding Rent Dissipation: On the Use of Game Theory in Industrial Organization." *American Economic Review: Proceedings*, Vol. 77 (1987), pp. 176–83.

—— and ——, "Noncooperative Game Theory for Industrial Organization: An Introduction and Overview" in R. Schmalensee and R. Willig, eds., *Handbook of Industrial Organization*, Amsterdam: North Holland, (1989).

——, Levine, D., and Maskin, E., "The Folk Theorem in Repeated Games with Imperfect Public Information." Mimeo, 1989.

Green, E.J. and Porter, R.H. "Noncooperative Collusion under Imperfect Price Information." *Econometrica*, Vol. 52 (1984), pp. 87–100.

Kreps, D.M. and Wilson, R. "Reputation and Imperfect Information." *Journal of Economic Theory*, Vol. 27 (1982), pp. 253–79.

——, Milgrom, P., Roberts, D.J., and Wilson, R. "Rational Cooperation in the Finitely Repeated Prisoner's Dilemma." *Journal of Economic Theory*, Vol. 27 (1982), pp. 245–52.

Marschak, J., "Neumann and Morgenstern's New Approach to Static Economics." *Journal of Political Economy*, Vol. 54 (1946), pp. 97–115.

Maskin, E. and Tirole, J. "A Theory of Dynamic Oligopoly, III." *European Economic Review*, Vol. 31 (1987), pp. 947–68.

Milgrom, P. and Roberts, D.J., "Predation, Reputation, and Entry Deterrence." *Journal of Economic Theory*, Vol. 27 (1982), pp. 280–312.

Pearce, D.G. "Rationalizable Strategic Behavior and the Problem of Perfection." *Econometrics*, Vol. 52 (1984), pp. 1029–50.

Robinson, J., *The Economics of Imperfect Competition*. London: MacMillan, 1933.

Selten, R. "The Chain-Store Paradox." *Theory and Decision*, Vol. 9 (1978), pp. 127–59.

Shapiro, C. "The Theory of Business Strategy." *RAND Journal of Economics*, Vol. 20 (1989), pp. 125–37.

Tirole, J., *The Theory of Industrial Organization*. Cambridge: MIT Press, 1988.

Von Neumann, J., and Morgenstern, O. *Theory of Games and Economic Behavior*. Princeton: Princeton University Press, 1944.

Wiesel, E. *The Gates of the Forest*. New York: Holt, Rinehart & Winston of Canada: 1966.

19 The approach of institutional economics

Geoffrey M. Hodgson

> *By means of the old, we come to know the new.*
> Confucius

I Introduction

Today, the term "new institutional economics" is in widespread use and is associated with a vast literature. Clearly, the temporal adjective in the adopted title of this broad set of postwar theories and approaches has been intended to demarcate the "new institutional economics" from the "old" institutional economics of Thorstein Veblen, John Commons, and Wesley Mitchell. This earlier institutionalism had actually been dominant in economics departments in American universities just after the First World War.[1]

Despite this, little detailed reference has been made by leading exponents of the "new" institutional economics to this predecessor. Two factors may help to explain this oversight. The first is that the history of economic thought is currently a much neglected subdiscipline, and there is now widespread unfamiliarity with the "old" American institutionalism, despite its favored geographic location and accessible language. The second reason is that since its decline in America after 1930 the "old" institutionalism has been repeatedly written off, and is dismissed for failing to provide a systematic and viable approach to economic theory. It is also widely – and wrongly – believed that institutionalism was essentially anti-theoretical and descriptive.

However, characterizations of the "old" institutionalism as purely descriptive or anti-theoretical do not bear up to close scrutiny. Particularly in the writings of Veblen and Commons, there is a strong emphasis on the importance and priority of the tasks of theoretical explanation and theoretical development. Whatever their limitations, the early institutionalists addressed crucial theoretical issues.

For example, Veblen (1899, 1919) was the first social scientist to attempt to develop a theory of economic and institutional evolution along essentially Darwinian lines (Hodgson 1993). Veblen's work shares common features with the much later attempts by economists to use evolutionary metaphors from biology by Armen Alchian (1950), Friedrich Hayek (1988), Kenneth Boulding (1981), and Nelson and Sidney Winter (1982). In addition, Commons (1924, 1934) has been acknowledged as a major influence on, for example, the behavioral economics of Herbert Simon (1979) and even the "new" institutionalism of Oliver Williamson (1975). Institutionalists also developed a number of theories of pricing behavior in imperfectly competitive markets (Marc Tool 1991). Traces of the surviving influence of "old" institutionalist ideas are found in many other areas of theoretical and applied economics. Indeed, the influence of institutionalism persisted for some time after the Second World War.[2]

Nevertheless, there is a shred of justification for the dismissive statements. Ever since Veblen there has been a failure of the "old" institutionalists to agree upon, let alone develop, a systematic theoretical core. American institutionalism has bequeathed no integrated theoretical system of the stature or scope of that of Karl Marx, Alfred Marshall, Leon Walras, or Vilfredo Pareto. The reasons for this failure cannot be discussed here, save to note that it was not because of a naive and unsustainable belief that economics can proceed with data alone, and without any theory. Although several institutionalists put their faith in data, they all retained some degree of belief in the importance of a theoretical project.

The primary reasons for the failure of institutionalism lie elsewhere. In particular, the old institutionalism was partially disabled by a combined result of the profound shifts in social science in the 1910–1940 period and of the rise of a mathematical style of neo-classical economics in the depression-stricken 1930s. Behaviorist psychology and positivist philosophy displaced the instinct psychology and pragmatist philosophy upon which the early institutionalism had been built. With their use of formal techniques, mathematical economists caught the imagination of both theorists and policy makers. In comparison, institutionalism was regarded as technically less rigorous, and thereby inferior.

An adequate history of American institutionalism remains to be written. The purpose of the present essay is quite different. The main aims are: to outline the institutionalist approach in broad terms, and to address and evaluate a few "hard core" propositions that were prominent in early institutionalism. A key argument in this paper is that the "old" institutionalism offers a radically different perspective on the nature of human agency, based on the concept of habit. Habits and rules are seen as necessary for human action. A habit-dominated conception of human behavior not only has significant support from psychology, it is also worthy of development and further elaboration by economists.

In an institutionalist view, the concept of habit connects crucially with the analysis of institutions. This issue has important implications for both microeconomic and macroeconomic analysis. Some illustrative applications of this general approach are considered in both these domains, with arguments why it is important to take account of habit in human behavior. These approaches do not rely on the standard assumptions of individual rationality. However, while outlining the essentials of a broadly institutionalist approach, it is conceded that institutionalism itself requires much more theoretical and methodological development.

The structure of this paper is as follows. Section II sketches how institutional economists proceed in practice. It is noted that institutionalism does not attempt to build an all-embracing, general theory. Instead, complex phenomena are approached with a limited number of common concepts and specific theoretical tools. Section III of this paper defines and elaborates the core concepts of habits and institutions, as rooted in the early institutionalist theory of Veblen and Commons. Section IV shows how much work in the "new" institutionalist vein, including the problem of "institutional infinite regress," points to a required reformulation of the "new" institutionalist project and a possible convergence with the thinking of the "old" institutionalists. Section V considers the circumstances in which it is necessary or convenient for an agent to rely on habits and rules. Not only are habits and rules ubiquitous, but we are typically required to rely on them whether or not (bounded) optimization is possible. Section VI concludes the essay.[3]

II Institutionalist approaches to economic analysis

The core ideas of institutionalism concern institutions, habits, rules, and their evolution. However, institutionalists do not attempt to build a single, general model on the basis of those ideas. Instead, these ideas facilitate a strong impetus toward specific and historically located approaches to analysis. In this respect there is an affinity between institutionalism and biology. Evolutionary biology has a few laws or general principles by which origin and development can be explained. Analysis of the evolution of a specific organism requires detailed data concerning the organism and its environment, and also specific explanations relevant to the species under consideration. Evolutionary biology requires both specific and general theories. In contrast, in physics there are repeated attempts to formulate the general theory of all material phenomena – the so-called "theory of everything" (Jack Cohen and Ian Stewart 1994). In its relatively greater emphasis upon specificities, institutional economics resembles biology rather than physics.

The institutionalist approach moves from general ideas concerning human agency, institutions, and the evolutionary nature of economic processes to specific ideas and theories, related to specific economic institutions or types of economy. Accordingly, there are multiple levels, and types, of analysis. Nevertheless, the different levels must be linked together. A crucial point here is that the concepts of habit and of an institution (both defined in Section III) help to provide the link between the specific and the general.

In contrast, neoclassical economics moves from a universal theoretical framework concerning rational choice and behavior, and moves directly to theories of price, economic welfare, and so on.[4] However, institutional economics does not presume that its habit-based conception of human agency itself provides enough to move toward operational theory or analysis. Additional elements are required. In particular, an institutionalist would stress the need to show how specific groups of common habits are embedded in, and reinforced by, specific social institutions. In this manner, institutionalism moves from the abstract to the concrete. Instead of standard theoretical models of given, rational individuals, institutionalism builds upon psychological, anthropological, sociological, and other research into how people behave. Indeed, if institutionalism had a general theory, it would be a general theory indicating how to develop specific and varied analyses of specific phenomena.

An illustration: theories of pricing

As an illustration, consider the theory of price formation. Subsequent to Veblen's iconoclastic attacks on rational economic man, institutionalists were themselves divided on whether Marshallian or other neoclassical price theories were acceptable and compatible with institutionalism. While institutionalists generally rejected rational economic man, this did not necessarily mean the abandonment of all the apparatus of Marshallian price theory.[5] Unlike the stationary outcomes of general equilibrium theory, partial equilibrium models could seemingly be placed in an ongoing, evolutionary context. Where institutionalists did agree, however, was that it was necessary to develop specific theories of pricing that reflected the institutional and market structures of the modern economy. Furthermore, any attainable general theory of prices would necessarily be highly limited in its explanatory properties, because of the variety of institutional processes of price formation in the real world.

The basis of price theory in institutionalism is thus quite different from that in other schools of economics. Neoclassical economics relies on the universal concepts of supply, demand, and marginal utility. Adam Smith, David Ricardo, and Marx relied on the labor theory of value. By contrast, in institutionalism prices are social conventions, reinforced by habits and embedded in specific institutions. Such conventions are varied and reflect the different types of commodity, institution, mode of calculation, and pricing process.

If prices are conventions then they depend in part on ideas and habits. A theory of price must in part be a theory of ideas, expectations, habits, and institutions, involving routines and processes of valuation. Without such a theory, there is no adequate explanation of how individuals calculate or form expectations of the future.

It was in this vein that a great deal of empirical and theoretical work on the pricing process was carried out by institutionalists and others in the first half of the twentieth century. Instead of a general theory of price, attempts were made to develop specific theories of pricing, each related to real-world market structures and types of corporate organization. It was in this context that much of the early work on oligopoly pricing was pioneered, including several theories of "mark-up," "administered," or "full cost" pricing (Tool 1991). No less than other economists, institutionalists want to develop theoretical explanations of such crucial real world phenomena as price. Where they differ, however, is in stressing the practical and explanatory limitations of any possible *general* theory of all prices.

An institutionalist approach to the theory of pricing proceeds by first examining the institutions in which the prices are being formed. All aspects of the institutions that are closely bound up with the process of price formation are relevant. What are the costs and how are they evaluated? What routines govern the calculation of prices? What information is available and what is unknown? By what routines is information obtained and used? What routines are used to revise prices in line with the experience on the market? What is the strategy concerning competitive pricing? How does this relate to market structure?

Obviously, a process of abstraction and simplification is required to deal with all this complexity. As a result of detailed investigations, it may be possible to abstract some key processes governing the formation of prices. One of the best examples of this approach is the work on "administered pricing" by Gardiner Means and his collaborators (Caroline Ware and Means 1936). There is also a close institutionalist affinity with the behavioral theory of the firm (Richard Cyert and James March 1964) and with the theory of information clustering and networking in financial markets (Wayne Baker 1984). None of these studies assumes perfect information or perfect competition. The starting point is an investigation of how prices are actually formed in specific institutional contexts, followed by the formulation of a pricing theory that is specific to the type of institution being investigated.

Institutionalism has no general theory of price but a set of guideline approaches to specific problems. These lead to historically and institutionally specific studies which are arguably of more operational value than any all-embracing general theory. Regrettably, specific studies of market institutions and pricing processes have received far less research resources and prestige than general equilibrium and other highly abstract approaches.

Starting from habit: some macroeconomic illustrations

Much empirical data in economics are consistent with the prevalence of habitual activity, even at the macroeconomic level. Consider, for example, the now neglected theory of the consumption function developed by James Duesenberry (1949). This theory was heavily influenced by Veblen and stressed the role of habit in consumer behavior. Duesenberry's theory did not fall out of favor because it did badly on empirical tests. In fact it predicted rather well. Instead, the theory was discarded primarily because it was not seen to conform with the presumptions of rational choice theory (Francis Green 1979). Duesenberry's theory proceeded on the assumption that an established level of income, plus prevailing cultural norms, would lead to a habitual pattern of consumer behavior. The consumer acts imitatively and adaptively, and also on the basis of ingrained habits. Similarly, the major subsequent study of aggregate consumer demand in the USA, by Hendricks Houthakker and Lester Taylor (1966), also found that a major part of consumer spending is subject to inertia, that is, primarily dependent on preceding consumption.

It is beside the point to suggest that all such phenomena can be recast into a more complex model where habit is formulated as a convoluted result of utility maximizing behavior. In principle, the possibility of such a recasting cannot be denied. The point is that the evidence alone does not bestow theoretical primacy to rational choice modeling. (Theoretical arguments against the primacy of the rationality assumptions are raised later in this essay.) Furthermore, the standard principle of parsimony can be used to support a fundamental assumption of human inertia or habit, no less that the standard axioms of rationality.

In general, institutional economists approach the analysis of macroeconomic systems by examining patterns and regularities of human behavior, expecting to find a great deal of imitation, inertia, lock-in and "cumulative causation."[6] Importantly, regularities or stability at the systemic level may arise not despite, but because of variations at the micro-level. In complex systems, macro-stability may *depend on* micro-chaos (Francesca Chiaromonte and Giovanni Dosi 1993; Cohen and Stewart 1994). Or systemic constraints may prevail over micro-variations (Gary Becker 1962; Dhananjay Gode and Shyam Sunder 1993).

The prominent view that it is necessary to build microeconomics on "sound microfoundations" – to derive macro-regularities from micro-stabilities – is quite different. In contrast, institutional economics sees regularities at the systemic level as being reinforced through positive feedbacks that act, in part, upon the microeconomic elements. Hence the latter are not taken as given. The institutional*izing* function of institutions means that macroeconomic order and relative stability is reinforced alongside variety and diversity at the microeconomic level. Ironically, by assuming *given* individuals, the microfoundations project in orthodox economics had typically to assume furthermore that each and every individual was *identical* in order to attempt to make the analysis tractable. In contrast, institutionalism points not to a spurious supra-individual objectivity, nor to the uniformity of individual agents, but to the concept of socio-economic order, arising upon variety at the micro-level.

Individual habits both reinforce, and are reinforced by, institutions. Through this circle of mutual engagement, institutions are endowed with a stable and inert quality. Further, institutions play an essential role in providing a cognitive framework for interpreting sense-data arid in providing intellectual habits or routines for transforming information into useful knowledge. The strong influence of institutions upon individual cognition provides some significant stability in socioeconomic systems, partly by buffering and constraining the diverse and variable actions of many agents.

With this line of argument the relative autonomy of macroeconomics and the idea of the workability of aggregates is reinstated. This contrasts with reductionist modes of theoretical analysis that see macroeconomic phenomena as necessarily explained by the micro-economic. Here the institutionalists made a significant contribution. Mitchell and his colleagues in the National Bureau for Economic Research in the 1920s and 1930s played a vital role in the development of national income accounting and suggested that aggregate, macroeconomic phenomena have an ontological and empirical legitimacy. This important incursion against reductionism created space for the Keynesian revolution. Through the development of national income accounting, the work of Mitchell and his colleagues influenced and inspired the macroeconomics of John Maynard Keynes. Partly for this reason, there is a close and explicit affinity between institutionalism and what is often described as "Post Keynesian" macroeconomics.

The fact that institutions typically portray a degree of invariance over long periods of time, and may outlast individuals, provides a reason for choosing institutions rather than individuals as a basic unit. Most institutions are temporally prior to the individuals that relate to them. We are all born into and socialized within a world of institutions. Recognizing this, institutionalists focus on the specific features of specific institutions, rather than building a general and ahistorical model of the individual agent.

However, the proposed alternative is not a methodological collectivism where individual behavior is entirely explained by the institutional or cultural environment. Complete explanations of parts in terms of wholes are beset with problems of equivalent stature to those of the inverse procedure. Just as structures cannot be adequately explained in terms of individuals, individuals cannot adequately be explained in terms of structures.

The failure of the mainstream microfoundations project confirms the difficulty of modeling the whole in terms of the individual parts (S. Abu Turab Rizvi 1994). Furthermore, institutionalists reject the idea of the primary ontological unit of the given, institution-free individual, upon which the microfoundations project rested. (This issue is explored in more detail below.) Arguably, the failure of the mainstream microfoundations project points to the need to develop a quite different overall approach In this there are both microeconomic and macroeconomic levels of analysis, each with a degree of relative theoretical autonomy, but at the same time both levels are connected by conceptual links and spanning explanations.

The abandonment of a standard microfoundations approach does not mean that institutionalists are necessarily deprived of the capacity to build models or make predictions. On the contrary, repeated studies – including those cited above – have shown that models with strong elements of inertia, explained in terms of habit persistence, are good predictors in the macroeconomic sphere. It is also well-known econometric folklore that naive prediction models, based on simple extrapolations from the recent past into the future, are often much better predictors of macroeconomic performance than much more sophisticated economic models. Institutionalists regard such results as confirmation of the phenomena of habit persistence, and of institutional lock-in and self-reinforcement.

Institutionalism works from the "stylized facts" of the macroeconomic system and attempts to uncover the underlying structural features of the system that help explain these outcomes. This requires analyses that are both quantitative and qualitative. Consider an example, starting from the stylized fact that productivity growth in the United States economy has been lower in the last 40 years or so than in many East Asian and other competing countries. Data may also reveal the stylized fact that the proportion of GNP devoted to investment in the United States has been relatively low. But, for the institutionalist, the analysis does not stop with mere statistical correlation. The task is to explain the institutional constraints and causal processes giving rise to both low investment and low productivity growth.

Consider a tentative hypothesis. The functional and cultural separation of financial from industrial institutions may have encouraged a short-term orientation toward investment returns. The sparse institutional connections between finance and industry, and the relative lack of shared personnel and shared vested interests, may allow the financial sector to concentrate on maximizing its returns to short-, rather than long-term, investment. Furthermore, the relatively low degree of cross ownership between industrial corporations may further encourage a primary orientation of the corporation toward short-term financial markets and short-term investment decisions. A first step in appraising this hypothesis would be to validate its key assumptions, for example by looking at the U.S. data on the distribution of share ownership, including cross share ownership between financial and industrial corporations.

An important next step would be to carry out similar and comparative investigations in relevant economies with higher rates of productivity growth, such as Japan. The existence elsewhere of higher degrees of corporate cross ownership of stocks and shares would provide a basis for attempting to evaluate the hypothesis still further. Econometric evidence of a significant statistical correlation between the relevant variables would be important, but far from enough. Institutionalists stress the need to outline the real causal linkages involved, rather than mere correlation between variables. Hence it is important to explain the causal mechanisms linking share ownership structures with low investment, and, in turn, with lower growth rates of productivity. Such causal explanations could involve many factors, including national cultures, political systems, and so on. Institutionalists are not wedded to any one hypothesis or any one theory on this issue, but in general the institutional approach stresses the importance of comparative institutional analysis, and the examination of a broad set of factors, in searching for an adequate causal explanation.

The institutionalist approach: some general remarks

For some, the general approach outlined above may seem fairly obvious, adding nothing new. Several points can be made in response to such a remark. First, there is a degree of emphasis on institutional and cultural factors that is not found in mainstream economic theory. Second, the analysis is openly inter-disciplinary, in recognizing insights from politics, sociology, psychology, and other sciences. Third, there is no recourse to the model of the rational, utility-maximizing agent. Inasmuch as a conception of the individual agent is involved, it is one which emphasizes both the prevalence of habit and the possibility of capricious novelty. Fourth, mathematical and statistical techniques are recognized as the servants of, rather than the essence of, economic theory. Fifth, the analysis does not start by building mathematical models: it starts from stylized facts and theoretical conjectures concerning causal mechanisms. Sixth, extensive use is made of historical and comparative empirical material concerning socio-economic institutions. In several of these respects, institutional economics is at variance with much of modern mainstream economic theory.

This should not and does not mean, however, that institutionalists become mere data-gatherers. No understanding nor explanation is possible without theory. Veblen and Commons, as founders of the "old" institutionalism, knew that theory does not arise by induction from data. All empirical analyses presuppose a set of concepts and an implicit or explicit theory. For this reason, to start from stylized facts must itself require a prior conceptual framework. Institutionalism attempts to provide this broad framework in terms of a set of meta-theoretic and methodological guidelines. There is no single, agreed set of definitive guidelines among institutionalists, but a number of common themes emerge.

For example, a central problem is the identification of what may be termed "ideal types." These are abstract descriptions of situations, phenomena, or persons that indicate the general features on which a theorist will focus as crucial for purposes of explanation. It is impossible to include all details and all features in such a venture because socio-economic systems are too complex and are open in the sense in which they interact with their outside environment. A process of abstraction must occur where the essential structures and features of the system are identified. The crucial question, of course, is which ideal type is to be selected in the analysis of a given phenomenon. To answer this question requires a methodology to distinguish between the general and the specific aspects of any given phenomenon. By making this distinction, and perhaps by using comparative material from other socio-economic systems, it is possible to construct and develop hypotheses concerning the key causal linkages behind the observed phenomena.

This is an all-too-sketchy account of the methodological and meta-theoretical foundations of the institutionalist approach. Constraints of space prevent further elaboration. What is clear, however, is that such methodological issues have become lively topics of debate in the 1980s and 1990s, with a veritable explosion of literature in the area of economic methodology. Institutionalists have made significant contributions to this literature and are thus playing a part in the development of appropriate approaches to economic analysis.

Some contemporary issues in institutionalist theory

It has already been admitted that institutionalism lacks a systematic core theory. Institutionalism does not seek a general theory of everything but it does require a coherent framework of analysis and a workable methodology.

In particular, there remains important scope for the development of an institutionalist microeconomics. Although past institutionalists made significant progress in the development of theories of pricing in imperfectly competitive markets, there is still a great of work that can be done. In economics since the Second World War such alternative approaches have received negligible research resources. However, alternative theories of consumer behavior have flowered in other disciplines, such as marketing (Roger Mason 1995). Some of this research has a strong institutionalist flavor, in part because it brings together insights from psychology and other social sciences. In developing theories of individual economic behavior, as well as elsewhere, institutionalists look forward to the possibility of a much more extensive and fruitful dialogue across disciplinary barriers.

The institutionalist emphasis on habit and routine also fits in well with the evolutionary models developed by Nelson and Winter (1982) and their followers. As Veblen (1899) himself suggested, the evolutionary paradigm provides a basis for encapsulating both continuity and change, both inertia and novelty. Habits or routines may adapt slowly or "mutate" as agents attempt purposeful improvements. In addition, there is some selection process by which some habits and routines are retained and imitated, and others fall out of use. Institutionalism is congenitally an "evolutionary economics." Like all work in this vein, it is biased toward dynamic rather than equilibrium-oriented modes of theorizing.

Problems of cognition and learning have been thematic to institutionalism since its inception. Instead of the presumed bedrock of given individuals, there is the idea of interactive and partially malleable agents, mutually entwined in a web of partially durable and self-reinforcing institutions. Institutionalist theory is admittedly underdeveloped in this area but institutionalists may potentially be in a relatively strong theoretical position. Although mainstream economics has addressed the concept of learning in recent years, at root there are severe problems in the approach based on the assumption of a rational actor. The key question is what is meant by "rational learning." How can agents be said to be rational at any given moment when they are in the process of learning? The very act of learning means that not all information is possessed and global rationality is compromised or ruled out. Furthermore, much more than inputting data or estimating probabilities is involved. Learning is more than the acquisition of information; it is the development of new means and modes of cognition, calculation, and assessment. This means that agents are building up new representations of the environment in which they operate, in place of former conceptions and habits of thought. In particular, if the methods and criteria of "optimization" are themselves being learned how can learning itself be optimal?

Institutionalists bring a different perspective to the analysis of learning by seeing it, in part, as a transformative and reconstitutive process, involving the creation of new habits, propensities, and conceptual frameworks (Veblen 1919; James Murphy 1994; Henry Plotkin 1994). Institutionalists need to capitalize on their prima facie conceptual and methodological advantage in this area and develop theories of learning that are appropriate for a knowledge-intensive and rapidly changing world.

The remainder of this essay explores further some of the methodological and theoretical issues that have been raised. The following section outlines some of the core theoretical characteristics of institutionalism. Subsequent sections address the problem of reductionism in economic theory, and show that mainstream explanations of economic and institutional phenomena in terms of given, rational individuals are not as robust as is often supposed. These arguments give further credence to the institutionalist approach.

III Some core characteristics of institutionalist theory

The "new" and the "old" institutionalism compared

What is the essential difference between the "old" and the "new" institutionalism? Answering this question is made more difficult because there is no unanimity, even among its adherents, as to what is precisely to be included in the "new" variety. Nevertheless, an answer is possible if we focus on the common theoretical core of some of the most prominent and influential "new" institutionalist writings, such as by North (1981), Richard Posner (1973), Andrew Schotter (1981), and Williamson (1975). Despite their analytical and policy differences, there are some common presumptions behind all these works.

The characteristic "new" institutionalist project is the attempt to explain the emergence of institutions, such as the firm or the state, by reference to a model of rational individual behavior, tracing out the unintended consequences in terms of human interactions. An initial institution-free "state of nature" is assumed. The explanatory movement is from individuals to institutions, taking individuals as given. This approach is often described as "methodological individualism."[7]

Along these lines, Carl Menger (1892) long ago saw the institution of money as emanating in an undesigned manner from the communications and interactions of individual agents. Once convenient regularities become prominent, a circular process of institutional self-reinforcement takes place. Emerging to overcome the difficulties of barter, money is chosen because it is convenient, and it is convenient because it is chosen. Other similar examples in the "new" institutionalist literature include traffic conventions (Schotter 1981; Robert Sugden 1986). For example, once a majority of car drivers stick to the right-hand side of the road, it is clearly rational for all drivers to follow the same rule. Accordingly, the emergent convention is reinforced and institutionalized by imitation, and by efficient use of *"all* relevant information" (Schotter 1981, p. 160). We may stylize a core idea involved here in terms of an action–information loop, as shown in Figure 19.1.

As well as in Menger's writings, this important core theme of an action–information loop is clearly evident, for example, in North's (1981) theory of the development of capitalism, Williamson's (1975) transaction cost analysis of the firm, and Schotter's (1981) game-theoretic analysis of institutions. The value of this core idea should not be denied.

However, despite the temporal adjective, the "new" institutionalism is built upon some antiquated assumptions concerning the human agent, derived from the individualism of the Enlightenment. In this 300-year tradition, a key idea is the notion that the individual can, in a

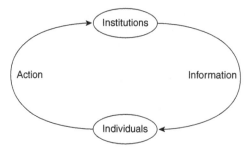

Figure 19.1 The institutionalist action–information loop

sense, be "taken for granted." Accordingly, the individual is taken as the elemental building block in economic theory. Strictly, it is not a question of whether or not a theorist is found to admit that individuals – or their wants and preferences – are changed by circumstances. Indeed, many economists admit that individuals might so be changed. What is crucial is the individualistic economist assumes, *for the purposes of economic enquiry*, that individuals and their preference functions should be taken as given. Thus the demarcating criterion is not the matter of individual malleability per se, but the willingness, or otherwise, to consider this issue as an important or legitimate matter for economic analysis. The commonplace statement by mainstream economists that tastes and preferences are not the explananda of economics thus derives directly from the individualist tradition. Likewise, the conception of economics as "the science of choice" takes the choosing individual and her preference functions as given. Unlike the "old" institutionalism, the "new" institutionalism has also taken such individualistic presuppositions on board.

A common thread in the literature of "old" institutionalism, from Veblen through Commons and Mitchell, to Myrdal and Galbraith, is the idea that in economic analysis the individual should not always be taken as given. The general use of given preference functions to model individuals is rejected by institutionalists. Individuals interact to form institutions, while individual purposes or preferences also are molded by socio-economic conditions. The individual is both a producer and a product of her circumstances.[8]

It is possible to distinguish the new institutionalism from the "old" by means of the above criterion. This distinction holds despite important theoretical and policy differences within both the new and the old institutionalist camps.[9] However, there are conceptual difficulties with the "new" institutionalist approach. It is argued below that to proceed from the assumption of given individuals in an institution-free "state of nature" is theoretically misconceived. Accordingly, developments in the "new" institutionalism show some sign of yielding some ground to the "old," or at least creating the possibility of a fruitful dialog between the two approaches.

Notably, some leading mainstream economists seem to be moving toward the view that the individual thould not be taken as given. Joseph Stiglitz (1994, pp. 272–73) has accepted that "certain aspects of human nature are endogenous to the system ... traditional economic theory was clearly wrong in treating individuals as immutable." A foremost agenda item for institutional economics is to incorporate a richer, context-dependent conception of human agency within a systematic and rigorous theory.

Agency and habit

Rejecting the mainstream approach to economic theory, with its conception of the utility-maximizing individual, the founders of the "old" institutionalism promoted an alternative conception of human agency. Such an alternative was well developed by the early twentieth century, in the influential writings of instinct psychologists such as William James and William McDougall, and pragmatist philosophers such as Charles Sanders Peirce. For all these writers the influence of Darwinian biology was crucial. Although instinct psychology was subsequently eclipsed by behaviorism (Carl Degler 1991) it enjoys a rehabilitation today (Leda Cosmides and John Tooby 1994a, 1994b; Plotkin 1994; Arthur Reber 1993).

Following these leading psychologists and philosophers of their time, the early institutionalists saw habit as the basis of human action and belief. Habit can be defined as a largely non-deliberative and self-actuating propensity to engage in a previously adopted pattern of behavior. A habit is a form of self-sustaining, nonreflective behavior that arises in repetitive situations.

Many modern economists have addressed habit. However, mainstream economists typically regard habit as an evocation or appendage of rational choice, and thereby explicable in its terms. Habits are seen as the result of an earlier choice, or as a deliberate means of avoiding endless deliberation. Rationality thus retains explanatory primacy (Becker 1992; Robert Pollak 1970).

The treatment of habit by the philosophers and psychologists who influenced the early institutionalists was quite different. The explanatory arrow ran in the opposite direction: instead of habits being explained in terms of rational choice, rational choice was explained in terms of habits. Further, habit was linked with knowledge and belief, seeing the essence of belief as the establishment of habit. All ideas, including beliefs, preferences, and rational modes of calculation, were regarded as evolutionary adaptations to circumstances, established through the acquisition of habitual propensities.

At first sight, both approaches seem feasible: habit can be regarded as the basis of rational choice, or rational choice can be seen as the procreator of habits. The fact that economists display an habitual inclination to assert the latter should not obscure the possibility of a reverse ordering. (If the allegation of the priority of rationality over habit is itself simply a matter of habit then it is by that fact undermined.) The problem of adjudication between these two paradigms is not as straightforward as is often assumed.

It is as if institutionalists and rational choice theorists have been engaged in a century-long game of Go. Each has been trying to place the pieces of an argument in an intricate attempt to encircle the postulates of the other. Notably, however, leading advocates of the rational choice paradigm, such as Becker (1962) have demonstrated that an "irrational" mode of behavior, in which agents are ruled by habit and inertia, is just as capable of predicting the standard downward-sloping demand curve and the profit-seeking activity of firms. Becker showed how the negatively inclined market demand curve can result from habitual behavior. Actors "can be said to behave not only 'as if' they were rational but also 'as if' they were irrational: the major piece of empirical evidence justifying the first statement can equally well justify the second" (Becker 1962, p. 4).

Kenneth Arrow has also accepted the possibility of an alternative approach based on habit. After outlining a possible "non rational" and habit-based model of human behavior, Arrow (1986, p. S386) remarked: "Without belaboring the point, I simply observe that this theory is not only a logically complete explanation of behavior but one that is more powerful than standard theory and at least as capable of being tested."

Accordingly, the "accuracy of the predictions" or other familiar criteria for theory selection do not give outright victory to rational choice. Common arguments for regarding rational choice as pre-eminent do not carry as much weight as has been supposed. This question of the explanatory primacy of habit versus that of rational choice will be explored again later in this essay. For now, there is at least a prima facie case for examining the distinctive treatment of habit in the work of the "old" institutionalists.

To many mainstream economists, such a habit-driven characterization of the agent is excessively deterministic, seemingly denying free will and choice.[10] However, it can be argued that the conception of the agent as an utility-maximizer based on fixed preference functions itself denies free will and choice. An individual ruled by her preferences is made a prisoner, not simply of her social environment, but also of her utility function. It is as if she is a robot, programmed by her preferences. Within such a deterministic machinery, critics find it difficult to find any place for real choice. As James Buchanan (1969, p. 47) once remarked: "Choice, by its nature, cannot be predetermined and remain choice."

In trying to gain a deeper understanding of the nature of human agency we are addressing an age-old, highly complex, and inadequately resolved philosophical and psychological problem. In some of the best writings in the area we find attempts to reconcile habitual behavior, on the one hand, and purposefulness, choice, novelty, and creativity, on the other (Michael Polanyi 1967; Murphy 1994; Plotkin 1994). Common to these approaches is the idea of habits being the foundation of learned behavior. Accordingly, examining the ways in which new habits are acquired is as important as a recognition of their durability. This dual stress is thematic to the institutionalism of Veblen and others, and retains its theoretical relevance today.

From habits to institutions

One of the most useful definitions of an institution was provided by the institutional economist Walton Hamilton (1932, p. 84). He saw an institution as "a way of thought or action of some prevalence and permanence, which is embedded in the habits of a group or the customs of a people." This elaborates Veblen's (1919, p. 239) earlier definition of an institution as "settled habits of thought common to the generality of men." Notably, in the "old" institutionalism, the concept of habit plays a central role both in its definition of an institution, as in its picture of human agency.

Although, by contrast, definitions of an institution in the "new" institutionalism do not typically include the notion of habit, they often share with the older institutionalism a broad, rather than a narrow, conception of an institution. Institutions, are regarded as general regularities in social behavior (Schotter 1981, p. 11) or "the rules of the game in society or . . . the humanly devised constraints that shape human interaction" (North 1990, p. 3).

All these definitions, "new" and "old" institutionalist alike, involve a relatively broad concept. They encompass not simply organizations – such as corporations, banks, and universities – but also integrated and systematic social entities such as money, language, and law. The case for such a broad definition of institutions is that all such entities involve common characteristics:

- All institutions involve the interaction of agents, with crucial information feedbacks.
- All institutions have a number of characteristic and common conceptions and routines.
- Institutions sustain, and are sustained by, shared conceptions and expectations.
- Although they are neither immutable nor immortal, institutions have relatively durable, self-reinforcing, and persistent qualities.
- Institutions incorporate values, and processes of normative evaluation. In particular, institutions reinforce their own moral legitimation: that which endures is often – rightly or wrongly – seen as morally just.

A broad definition of an institution is consistent with long-standing practice in the social sciences. More narrowly, organizations may be defined as a special subset of institutions, involving deliberate coordination (Viktor Vanberg 1994), and recognized principles of sovereignty and command. Language is an example of an institution that is not an organization. A business corporation is an institution and also an organization. All institutions and organizations exhibit the five characteristics above.

However, a key difference between the "old" and the "new" institutionalism here is that in the former the concept of habit is central. For the "old" institutionalists, habit is regarded as crucial to the formation and sustenance of institutions. Habits form part of our cognitive abilities. Cognitive frameworks are learned and emulated within institutional structures. The individual relies on the acquisition of such cognitive habits, before reason, communication, choice, or action are possible.

Learned skills become partially embedded in habits. When habits become a common part of a group or a social culture they grow into routines or customs (Commons 1934, p. 45). Institutions are formed as durable and integrated complexes of customs and routines. Habits and routines thus preserve knowledge, particularly tacit knowledge in relation to skills, and institutions act through time as their transmission belt.

Institutions are regarded as imposing form and social coherence upon human activity partly through the continuing production and reproduction of habits of thought and action. This involves the creation and promulgation of conceptual schemata and learned signs and meanings. Institutions are seen as a crucial part of the cognitive processes through which sense-data are perceived and made meaningful by agents. Indeed, as discussed below, rationality itself is regarded as reliant upon institutional props.

The availability of common cognitive tools, as well as congenital or learned dispositions for individuals to conform with other members of the same group, work together to mold individuals' goals and preferences. Accordingly, individuals are not taken as given. In mainstream economics, widespread lip-service to notions of individuality and choice may have helped to obscure the degree in reality to which conformism or emulation actually occur, even in modern competitive economies. For an "old" institutionalist, such outcomes are an important part of the institutional self-reinforcing process.

From an "old" institutionalist perspective, the institutional action–information loop in Figure 19.1 stands out in higher relief. The imitation and emulation of behavior leads to the spread of habits, and to the emergence or reinforcement of institutions. In turn, institutions foster and underline particular behaviors and habits, and help transmit them to new members of the group. The additional emphasis here concerns the role of habit both in sustaining individual behavior, and in providing the individual with cognitive means by which incoming information can be interpreted and understood. Our understanding of the durable and self-reinforcing qualities of institutions is enhanced.

The thrust of the "old" institutionalist approach is to see behavioral habit and institutional structure as mutually entwined and mutually reinforcing: both aspects are relevant to the full picture (Commons 1934, p. 69). Choosing institutions as units of analysis does not necessarily imply that the role of the individual is surrendered to the dominance of institutions. A dual stress on both agency and structure is required, redolent of similar arguments in sociology and philosophy (Roy Bhaskar 1979; Anthony Giddens 1984; Harrison White 1992). Both individuals and institutions are mutually constitutive of each other. Institutions mold, and are molded by, human action.

Institutions are both "subjective" ideas in the heads of agents and "objective" structures faced by them. The twin concepts of habit and institution may thus help to overcome the philosophical dilemma between realism and subjectivism in social science. Actor and structure, although distinct, are thus connected in a circle of mutual interaction and interdependence.

Summarizing the argument so far, it has been shown in this section that the wider recognition of the importance of institutions and rules in human society is endorsed by institutional economics in the Veblen-Commons tradition, but with an additional and crucial stress on the role of habit. A circle of interaction between actor and structure is based on the linked concepts of habit and institution. Section IV below adds further credence to this argument by considering some difficulties that are raised when the explanatory circle is broken and the individual is given unwarranted ontological and explanatory priority.

IV Explaining institutions: the problem of institutional infinite regress

In this section it is argued that attempts to explain the origin and sustenance of institutions on the basis of the assumption of given individuals have internal flaws and inconsistencies. Accordingly, attempts to explain institutions in this way may have to be abandoned. The door is opened to a more open-ended and evolutionary approach, redolent of the earlier institutionalists.

Two opposite types of error are possible. The "cultural determinists" place too much stress on the molding of individuals by institutions.[11] Such "oversocialized" views of human behavior have been widely criticized (Mark Granovetter 1985). At the opposite end of the spectrum, the "new institutional economics" gives no more than weak stress to the processes of institutional conditioning, and focuses primarily on the emergence of institutions out of the interactions of given individuals. This section explores the problems that may arise if exclusive stress is put on the latter direction of causality.

The distinctive "new" institutionalist project has been identified as the attempt to explain the existence of institutions by reference to a given model of individual behavior, and on the basis of an initial institution-free "state of nature." The procedure is to start with given individuals and to move on to explain institutions.

Admittedly, substantial heuristic insights about the development of institutions and conventions have been gained on the basis of the assumption of given, rational individuals. The main problem addressed here is the incompleteness of the research program in its attempt to provide a general theory of the emergence and evolution of institutions. Some tentative and "evolutionary" approaches to solving this problem are addressed at the end of this section.

Internal problems in explanations based on given individuals

Alexander Field (1979, 1984) has advanced a key problem in the new institutionalist project to attempt to explain institutions solely in terms of given, rational individuals. In trying to explain the origin of social institutions from given individuals, the new institutional economics has to presume a social framework governing their interaction. In any original, hypothetical, "state of nature" from which institutions are seen to have emerged, a number of rules, and cultural and social norms are already presumed. No "thought experiment" involving an institution-free "state of nature" has yet been postulated without them.

For example, game theorists such as Schotter (1981) take the individual "for granted," as an agent unambiguously maximizing her expected payoff. Yet, in attempting to explain the origin of institutions through game theory, Field (1984) points out that certain norms and rules must inevitably be presumed at the start. There can be no games without prior rules, and thus game theory can never explain the elemental rules themselves. Even in a sequence of repeated games, or of games about other (nested) games, at least one game or meta-game, with a structure and payoffs, must be assumed at the outset. Any such attempt to deal with history in terms of sequential or nested games is thus involved in a problem of infinite regress: even with games about games about games to the nth degree there is still at least one preceding game left to be explained.

As another example, Williamson's transaction cost theory of the firm takes its original state of nature as the market. In a famous passage he writes that "in the beginning there were markets" (Williamson 1975, p. 20); this starting point is characteristic of his approach. From this original context, some individuals go on to create firms and hierarchies. These endure if they involve lower transaction costs.

However, the market itself is an institution. The market involves social norms, customs, instituted exchange relations, and – sometimes consciously organized – information networks that themselves have to be explained (Dosi 1988; Hodgson 1988). Market and exchange relations themselves involve complex rules. In particular, the institution of private property itself requires explanation. Markets are not an institution-free beginning. As if in search of the original, institution-free, state of nature prior to property and markets, Williamson (1983) argues that private property can emerge through "private ordering," that is, individual-to-individual transactions, without state legislation or interference.

The question of the possibility of property and contract without any role for the state is debated in legal theory. However, there is another fundamental objection to the idea of attempting to ground explanations of property or institutions on individuals alone. Even if the state is absent, individuals rely on customs, norms, and, most emphatically, the institution of language, in order to interact. Interpersonal communication, which is essential to all stories of institutional emergence, itself depends on linguistic and other rules and norms. The shared concept of individual property requires some means of communication using common concepts and norms, both before and after explicit or tacit recognition of property rights can be established. Even if the state can be absent from these processes, some prior institutions are still required.[12] Before an individual may choose, he or she requires a conceptual framework to make sense of the world.[13] More generally, considering the action–information loop in Figure 19.1 above, the reception of "information" in the new institutionalist story requires a paradigm or cognitive frame to process and make sense of that information. Further, our interaction with others requires the use of the institution of language. We cannot understand the world without concepts and we cannot communicate without some form of language. Without the prior institutionalization of individuals, the action–information loop cannot be completed. As the "old" institutionalists argue, the transmission of information from institution to individual is impossible without a coextensive process of enculturation, in which the individual learns the meaning and value of the sense-data that is communicated. The "information" arrow on the right hand side the figure *always and necessarily* involves such a process of enculturation. Information cannot be received unless the individual has to some degree been enculturated through prior engagement with institutions.[14] Communication requires an institutionalized individual.

In the "old" institutional economics, cognition and habit have a central place. Knowledge and learning are stressed. There is also an insistence that the perception of information is not possible without prior habits of thought to endow it with meaning. Without such habits, agents cannot perceive or make use of the data received by their senses. Habits thus have a crucial cognitive role: "All facts of observation are necessarily seen in the light of the observer's habits of thought" (Veblen 1914, p. 53). Such habits are acquired through involvement in institutions.

The central "new" institutionalist project of explaining institutions from individuals alone is thus misconceived. The problem of infinite regress identified here undermines any "new institutionalist" claim that the explanation of the emergence of institutions can start from some kind of original, institution-free ensemble of (rational) individuals, in which there is supposedly no rule or institution to be explained. At the very minimum, "new" institutionalist stories of the development of institutions depend upon interpersonal communication of information. And the communication of information itself requires shared concepts, conventions, rules, routines, and norms. These, in turn, have to be explained.

Which came first: the chicken or the egg?

What is being contested here is the possibility of using given individuals as the institution-free starting point in the explanation. It is not possible to understand how institutions are constructed without seeing individuals as embedded in a culture made up of many interacting institutions. Institutions not only constrain but also influence individuals. Accordingly, if there are institutional influences on individuals and their goals, then these are worthy of explanation. In turn, the explanation of those may be in terms of other purposeful individuals. But where should the analysis stop? The purposes of an individual could be partly explained by relevant institutions, culture, and so on. These, in their turn, would be partly explained in terms of other individuals. But these individual purposes and actions could then be partly explained by cultural and institutional factors, and so on, indefinitely.

We are involved in an apparently infinite regress, similar to the puzzle "which came first, the chicken or the egg?" Such an analysis never reaches an end point. It is simply arbitrary to stop at one particular stage in the explanation and say "it is all reducible to individuals" just as much as to say it is "all social and institutional." The key point is that in this infinite regress, neither individual nor institutional factors have complete explanatory primacy. The idea that all explanations have ultimately to be in terms of individuals (or institutions) alone is thus unfounded.

There is thus an unbreakable circle of determination. This does not mean, however, that institutions and individuals have equivalent ontological and explanatory status. Clearly, they have different characteristics. Their mechanisms of reproduction and procreation are very different. Individuals are purposeful, whereas institutions are not, at least in the same sense. Institutions have different life spans from individuals, sometimes enduring the passing of the individuals they contain. Crucially, each individual is born into, and molded by, a world of pre-existing institutions: even if these institutions were made by others and can be changed.

We have seen that the new institutionalist project to explain the emergence of institutions on the basis of given individuals runs into difficulties, particularly with regard to the conceptualization of the initial state from which institutions are supposed to emerge. This does not mean that all "new" institutionalist research is without value, but it indicates that the starting point of explanations cannot be institution-free: the main project has to be reformulated as just a part of a wider theoretical analysis of institutions. The reformulated project would stress the evolution of institutions, in part from other institutions, rather than from a hypothetical, institution-free "state of nature." What is required is a theory of process, evolution, and learning, rather than a theory that proceeds from an original, institution-free, "state of nature" that is both artificial and untenable.

Toward evolutionary explanations of institutional change

In some cases the "comparative statics" character of such "new" institutionalist explanations is obvious. However, one of the reasons for the rise of "evolutionary" thinking in economics since the early 1980s has been an attempt to break the constraints of this mode of explanation with its two fixed end-points. Because there is no answer to the chicken-or-egg question, the question itself has to be changed. The question should no longer be "which came first?" but "what processes explain the development of both of them?" This implies a movement away from comparative statics and toward a more evolutionary and open-ended framework of analysis. Some moves in this direction by two prominent "new" institutionalists have already led to a degree of convergence with the evolutionary and open-ended ideas of the "old" institutionalists. This is apparent in the later works of Hayek (1988) and the recent writings of North (1990).

Such evolutionary explanations involve the search for "a theory of the process of consecutive change, realized to be self-continuing or self-propagating and to have no final term" (Veblen 1919, p. 37). Emphatically, abandoning the attempt to explain all institutions in terms of given individuals does not mean the abandonment of theoretical explanation. Instead, the origins and development of organizations and institutions are seen as an evolutionary process. Today, there is a substantial amount of work going on in this area, with extensive use being made of evolutionary metaphors taken from biology.

V The necessity of habits and rules

This section extends the argument further by showing how rational individuals depend on habits and rules. The prominent idea of the utility-maximizing individual has permitted economists to ignore the procedures and rules that are knowingly or unwittingly employed by agents. Most explanations of behavior, including the role-driven and the habitual, can seemingly be encompassed within the framework of utility-maximization. Accordingly, the underlying psychological and other explanatory issues have been largely ignored. The encompassing assumption of the "rational" agent is deemed to be sufficient.

The contention here, however, concerns the explanatory primacy of habit over such all-encompassing conception of rational behavior. We start by posing a question: under what circumstances is it necessary or convenient for an agent to rely on habits or rules?[15] The question of how habits and rules are replicated and transmitted in society is sidestepped here to focus on a decision situation giving rise to their use. It is argued that even optimization requires the deployment of rules, and for this reason mainstream economics cannot legitimately ignore these questions. This suggests that a detailed analysis of the evolution of specific habits and rules – including the pecuniary rationality of agents in a market economy – should be installed at the core of economics and social theory.

Rules are conditional or unconditional patterns of thought or behavior which can be adopted either consciously or unconsciously by agents. Generally rules have the form: in circumstances X, do Y. Habits may have a different quality: rule-following may be conscious and deliberative whereas habitual action is characteristically unexamined. Rules do not necessarily have a self-actuating or autonomic quality but clearly, by repeated application, a rule can become a habit. Often it is easier to break a rule than to change a habit, because our awareness of our own habits is often incomplete; they have a self-actuating character, being established in subliminal areas of our nervous system. However, habits still have the same general form: in circumstances X, action Y follows.

A familiar question of enduring controversy is the extent to which optimizing techniques are applicable to decision situations in the real world. Much of modern economics is founded on the assumption that they are. If assumptions of perfect information are dropped, it is typically assumed that uncertain or complex decision problems can still be accommodated using probabilities. Against this, a number of critics have argued that a significant proportion of decision problems are not amenable to probabilistic or other optimization techniques (e.g., Veblen 1919; Keynes 1937; Simon 1957, 1979).

Optimization and rules

However, we shall sidestep this well-known controversy here, to focus on a (large or small) class of decision situations in which (bounded) optimization may be possible. Consider mathematical optimization problems and their solutions. The procedures of linear programming and differential calculus, for example, sustain methods of optimization with strict rules. Optimizing procedures always involve rules: namely the rules of computation and optimization.[16]

Conventional accounts sometimes neglect the universal need for rules of calculation to reach optima. One reason for this is that optimization processes are often confused with optimal outcomes. However, statements of equilibrium conditions are not the same thing as the specification of algorithmic or other procedures required to attain equilibria: outcome is not the same as process. Another reason for the neglect is the widespread belief that optimization involves choice and rule-following denies it. On the contrary, as argued above, mechanical optimization excludes genuine choice.

All explicit optimization procedures must involve rules. This raises the secondary but important question of their origin. Notably, optimization itself cannot provide a complete explanation of either the origin of rules or the adoption of rule-driven behavior. As all optimization involves intrinsic rules, the idea of explaining all rules on the basis of the optimizing behaviors of agents involves circular reasoning and is thus misconceived. Hence the question of "where do the original rules come from?" remains, *and it cannot be answered completely in terms of optimization itself*. It is necessary to consider additional explanations of their genesis, at least to supplement the optimization story. In search of this "first cause" we are forced to consider explanations other than optimization for the reliance of the individual upon rules.

There is also the case of the intuitive optimizer, with tacit skills. Although the skills may not be codifiable, they are embedded in habits of the same general form: in circumstances X, do Y. Likewise, the formation of these habits cannot be explained by optimization alone, without addressing the other rules, habits, or instincts that led to their origin.

This primary reliance on habits or rules limits the scope of rational optimization. Rationality always depends on prior habits or rules as props (Hodgson 1988). Hence rational optimization alone can never supply the complete explanation of human behavior and institutions that some theorists seem to be striving for. Given that explanation in social science requires more than this powerful idea at its core, arguably we must rely on more complex, contingent, and multifaceted behavioral specifications.

As a result, neoclassical economics could be regarded as a special and (highly) restricted case of the "old" institutional economics, which accepted the ubiquity of habits and rules. In contrast to their image as myopic and anti-theoretical data-gatherers, institutionalists have the potential to achieve a higher level of theoretical generality. Winter (1971) has argued that neoclassical economics is a special case of behavioral economics. We may conclude, further, that both behavioral economics and neoclassical economics are special cases of institutional economics. At its foundations, institutional economics has greater generality and encompasses neoclassical economics as a special case.

The ubiquity of habits and rules

The importance of habits and rules is underlined by consideration of types of decision situation or procedure other than optimization, such as decision making in the context of complexity or uncertainty. In particular, Ronald Heiner (1983) has shown that individuals are obliged to rely on relatively simple procedures and decision-rules in such situations. There are long and established arguments that individuals must rely on "conventions" or "rules of thumb" in situations of radical uncertainty (Keynes 1937; Simon 1957).

Skilled deployment of rules must also involve acquired habits. Habits are used even by firms or individuals attempting to optimize in some way. As the "old" institutional economist John Maurice Clark (1918, p. 26) noted, "it is only by the aid of habit that the marginal utility principle is approximated in real life." It is an institutionalist tenet that habit has ontological and explanatory primacy over rational choice. Again this implies a greater level of generality for the core institutionalist approach.[17]

In practice, the human agent cannot be a "lightning calculator" (Veblen 1919, p. 73), quickly, effortlessly, and inexplicably finding the optimum just as we can readily locate the lowest point of a U-curve in a simple textbook diagram. Even with given and unambiguous information, complex optimization problems typically involve difficulties not only of specification but of computability. Artificially intelligent systems even in moderately complex environments require "inherited" framing procedures to structure the incoming information (Zenon Pylyshyn 1986).

Evolution and the limits to rationality

Strikingly, recent developments in evolutionary psychology (Cosmides and Tooby 1994a, 1994b; Plotkin 1994; Reber 1993) give strong support to the "old" institutionalist idea of the primacy of habits. The key argument in this literature is that postulates concerning the rational capacities of the human brain must give an explanation of their evolution according to established principles of evolutionary biology.

What may be termed the Principle of Evolutionary Explanation demands that any behavioral assumption in the social sciences must itself be capable of explanation along (Darwinian) evolutionary lines.[18] However, the empirical and theoretical work of modern evolutionary psychologists suggests that, even in highly intelligent organisms, global rationality is very unlikely to emerge through evolution. In other words, the standard assumption of the rational actor fails to satisfy the Principle of Evolutionary Explanation.

In an evolutionary view of intelligence it is recognized that tacit knowledge and implicit learning of a habitual character are ubiquitous even in higher animals, including humans. This is because higher levels of deliberation and consciousness are recent arrivals on the evolutionary scene, and certainly came after the development of more basic mechanisms of cognition and learning in organisms. That being the case, many of our evolved cognitive processes must be able to proceed below the level of full deliberation and awareness.

Cosmides and Tooby (1994a) postulate that the mind is riddled with functionally specific circuits. This contrasts with what they describe as the "Standard Social Science Model," where the mind harbors general cognitive processes – such as "reasoning," "induction," and "learning" – that are "context-independent," "domain-general," or "context-free." They show that this abstract and generalist view of the mind is difficult to reconcile with modern evolutionary biology, giving experimental evidence to support their argument.

A key argument is that all-purpose optimizing techniques are difficult to construct and utilize. First, what counts as adaptive or (near) optimal behavior differs markedly from situation to situation. Second: "Combinatorial explosion paralyzes even moderately domain-general systems when encountering real-world complexity. As generality is increased by adding new dimensions to a problem space or new branch points to a decision tree, the computational load increases with catastrophic rapidity" (Cosmides and Tooby 1994a, p. 56). Third, the generality of all-purpose mechanisms undermines their performance: "when the environment is clueless, the mechanism will be too. Domain-specific mechanisms are not limited in this way. They can be constructed to fill in the blanks when perceptual evidence is lacking or difficult to obtain" (p. 57). As a result: "The mind is probably more like a Swiss army knife than an all-purpose blade" (p. 60).

In evolutionary terms, time does not "hammer logic into men." Cosmides and Tooby produced evidence that humans are generally poor at solving general, logical problems. However, when these problems are reformulated in terms of social interactions, our ability to solve them increases markedly, despite the fact that the logical structure of the problem has not changed. This is clear evidence of special design in brain, rather than ability to solve general logical problems.[19]

Theories of human behavior must be consistent with our understanding of evolutionary origins: "The human brain did not fall out of the sky, an inscrutable artefact of unknown origin, and there is no longer any sensible reason for studying it in ignorance of the causal processes that constructed it" (Cosmides and Tooby 1994a, p. 68). Applied to economics itself, this principle establishes the untenability of the prominent assumption "that rational behavior is the state of nature, requiring no explanation" (Cosmides and Tooby 1994b, p. 327). If rational behavior is to be assumed, then its evolution has to be explained.

The reintroduction of the concepts of habit and instinct into a theory of human behavior helps to provide a foundation upon which a theory of institutions can be built. We have shown that the grounding of such a theory on the idea of the given, rational individual is both unsuccessful, and untenable in ongoing, evolutionary terms. The introduction of habit and instinct provides a consistency between the socio-economic and biotic levels of analysis, and establishes an important link between the socio-economic and the natural world. The institutional action–information loop no longer hangs in empty space: it has a biotic grounding.

This does not mean that explanations of socio-economic phenomena have to be in biological terms. Socio-economic reality has emergent properties that defy such a reduction. They are different levels of analysis, but, ultimately, propositions at one level do have to be consistent with those at another. This is a key reason why economics has to take account of evolutionary biology (Hodgson 1993).

VI Conclusion

By institutions, individuals are not merely constrained and influenced. Jointly with our natural environment and our biotic inheritance, as social beings we are *constituted* by institutions. They are given by history and constitute our socio-economic flesh and blood. This proposition must cohabit with the more widely accepted – and equally valid – notion that institutions, knowingly or unknowingly, are formed and changed by individuals.

It has been suggested above that the breakdown of the microfoundations project provides institutionalism with a significant entrée. Its focus on institutions as durable and typically self-reinforcing entities provides a convenient micro–macro link. To see the role of the individual in relation to institutions is to focus on the micro aspect. To take the institution as a socially constructed invariant – or emergent property – is a basis for consideration of macroeconomic dynamics and behavior. Accordingly, "old" institutionalists and mainstream economists have a great deal to learn from each other.

However, some would dismiss those scholars that reject the rational actor paradigm as being outside "economics," and consign them to "sociology." In response, these vigilantes of "economic correctness" have to face two severe problems. First, leading economists such as Smith, Ricardo, Marx, Keynes, Hayek, Simon, and Coase, all failed to incorporate the standard picture of "rational economic man" in their writings or expressed profound misgivings about his behavior. Second, the problem also has to be faced that much of "sociology" has now embraced rational choice (for example, James Coleman 1990).

Among twentieth century economists the prevailing practice has been to regard the subject as being defined not as a study of a real object – the economy – but in terms of a single approach and set of core assumptions. If the subject is defined in this way then not much theoretical pluralism within economics is possible; we are stuck with a single type of theory or approach. Elsewhere, however, a science is normally defined as the study of a particular aspect of objective reality: physics is about the nature and properties of matter and energy, biology about living things, psychology about the psyche, and so on. It is on the basis of their wish to study and understand real world *economies* that the "old" institutionalists can retain claim to the title of being *economists*.

In fact, the boundary between economics and sociology that has endured by the prevailing consensus for the last 60 years or so is now being violated on both sides. The line of demarcation defined by "the science of rational choice" is thus losing its legitimacy, and the most reasonable alternative is to attempt once again to redefine economics as the intellectual discipline concerned with the study of economic systems. In other words, it should be defined, as in other sciences, in terms of its object of analysis, rather than by any set of prior tenets.

It may be conjectured that the loss of the reigning twentieth-century boundaries between the social sciences foreshadows a great centennial climacteric in these intellectual disciplines. For long the butt of the critic from the heterodox fringes, rational economic man has increasingly come under challenge from the mainstream in recent years, partly because of developments in game theory. It has been suggested by leading economists such as Frank Hahn (1991) that one of the central responses to the developing crisis will be the deconstruction of the rational actor that has long ruled economics. Optimizing activity will be recognized as no more than a special case of a larger set of possible modes of behavior, with all of them being required to render viable explanations of their origin and evolution.

Biology is widely seen as the science of the twenty-first century. Following this lead – and to conjecture further – in the renewed social sciences the uniting and fundamental precepts will be the principles of evolution themselves, still taking strong inspiration from the methodology and approach of Darwin. We shall thereby take a huge step back in time and visit the evolutionary controversies of the 1890s and early 1900s – and the intellectual world of Peirce, James, Veblen, and Commons – and discover that much of what we want to say has already been said before. Only then will we be able to read the works of the "old" institutionalists and fully appreciate their achievement.

Acknowledgment

The author is particularly grateful to Peter Corning, Masashi Morioka, Richard Nelson, John Nightingale, Douglass North, Paul Twomey, and three anonymous referees for discussions, critical comments, or other assistance. The Japan Society for the Promotion of Science, and the European Commission Phare-ACE program are thanked for their financial assistance with this research.

Notes

1 Throughout this article, the terms "institutionalism" and "institutional economics," when without a temporal adjective, will be taken to refer to the institutionalism in the tradition of Veblen, Commons, and Mitchell.

2 Notably, several institutionalists or their fellow travelers have been elected as Presidents of the American Economic Association since 1945: John Kenneth Galbraith, Edwin Witte, Morris Copeland, George Stocking, and Boulding. In addition, the "old" institutionalists Simon Kuznets and Gunnar Myrdal received Nobel Prizes in 1971 and 1974 respectively. Other schools of thought resemble institutionalism. For example, much of post-Keynes "Cambridge" economics had a strong institutionalist flavor, particularly the work of Nicholas Kaldor and Joan Robinson. The more recent work of Robert Boyer, Michel Aglietta, and other members of the French *regulation* school also has strong institutionalist affinities.

3 Restrictions of space prevent extensive references to the literature. The reader is referred to Hodgson et al. (1994) for an encyclopedic treatment of some of the topics discussed here, for wider references, and for discussions of many other issues pertinent to institutionalism.

4 Neoclassical economics (a term originally coined by Veblen) may be conveniently defined as an approach which (1) assumes rational, maximizing behavior by agents with given and stable preference functions, (2) focuses on attained, or movements toward, equilibrium states, and (3) excludes chronic information problems (such as uncertainty of the type explored by Frank Knight and John Maynard Keynes). Notably, some recent developments in modern economic theory – such as in game theory – reach to or even lie outside the boundaries of this definition.

5 Note that "new" institutionalist Ronald Coase has also rejected the standard rationality assumptions while working within a broadly Marshallian framework.

6 Veblen was one of the first to develop the concept of cumulative causation that directly or indirectly influenced Allyn Young, Myrdal, Kaldor, and others. See Veblen (1919, pp. 70–77, 173–77, 240–43, 370, 436) and Hodgson (1993, ch. 9).

7 The enormous and controversial literature on this topic is too large to address here. See Hodgson (1988) for a survey and discussion.

8 The recent work of Becker (1996) might at first sight appear to "take account of tastes" by building a model with "endogenous preferences" – in which individual utility functions contain arguments such as "culture." This is not the case because an immanently conceived (meta)preference function for each individual is still assumed at the outset; it is an unexplored "black box" that still remains to be explained.

9 Notably, and in contrast to the accounts in Richard Langlois (1986) and Malcolm Rutherford (1994), this criterion places the work of Nelson and Winter (1982) squarely in the "old" institutionalist category. This affinity with the "old" institutionalism is now recognized by Nelson and Winter themselves. In addition, some of the later writings of Hayek (1988) come closer to the old institutionalism, as do recent works by North (1990).

10 Note that, contrary to a widespread misconception, Veblen (1899, p. 15; 1914, pp. 31–32; 1919, p. 75; 1934, pp. 80, 175) repeatedly asserted that human behavior was purposeful.

11 Rutherford (1994, pp. 40–41) notes how American institutionalism itself moved toward cultural determinism and methodological collectivism in the post-1940 period. Such a one-sided emphasis was not found in the earlier institutionalism of Veblen and Commons.

12 Whether common agreement to and practical enforcement of property can arise without the existence of a state is a matter of continuing debate. The classic "old" institutionalist argument that the state was required historically in order to establish labor, land, and money markets is in Karl Polanyi (1944). Despite his celebrated argument concerning the undesigned evolution of money

from individual interactions, even Menger (1936) recognized that the state may be necessary to maintain the integrity of the monetary unit.

13 This raises a problem in Young-Back Choi's (1993) innovative work. While developing a theory of conventions and institutions he takes the individual as "the basic unit of analysis" (p. 5). Choi (pp. 32–9) is thus impelled to have this individual somehow *choosing* the conceptual "paradigm" by which she makes sense of the uncertain world in which she is situated. The unanswered question is on what basis has such an individual "elected to adopt" (p. 39) one paradigm rather than another? Surely this choice itself requires a conceptual framework or paradigm, and norms and criteria of judgement, to make some sense of the situation in which the choice is made. The choice of paradigm itself requires a paradigm. Again we have a problem of infinite regress.

14 This raises the question of how a newborn infant may acquire information. Our incapacity to learn without prior conceptual frameworks means – as James argued long, ago and Plotkin (1994) and others elaborate – that much of our initial capacity to learn must be genetically inherited and instinctive. In the eyes of modern psychology, Veblen's adherence to the concept of instinct is not as old-fashioned as it used to seem.

15 For a treatment of this issue in greater depth see Hodgson (1997).

16 Notably, Vanberg (1994) has suggested that rational choice and rule-following behavior are incompatible. He argues that it is inherently inconsistent to speak of a "rational choice to follow rules" or a "rational choice among rules." To Vanberg, the essence of following a rule is to be partially unresponsive to the changing particularities of each choice situation. This is contrasted with the concept of choice, where an individual is deemed free of such "*pre-programmed* behavior." However, first, the quality of being unresponsive to changing particularities is not a universal feature of rule-following behavior. There are conditional rules that discriminate between different environmental conditions and point to different outcomes in different circumstances. Second, the very idea of rational *calculation*, as shown below, must itself depend on computational rules. Vanberg has also failed to recognize that strict optimization must necessarily exclude choice. As noted above, a utility-maximizer is essentially a taste-satisfying machine. If choice means the possibility of acting otherwise then it cannot be predetermined by either preference functions or rules.

17 Clark (1918, p. 25) also wrote: "a good hedonist would stop calculating when it seemed likely to involve more trouble than it was worth." Hence Simon's concept of satisficing behavior finds a clear precedent in the work of an "old" institutional economist.

18 Without giving it a name, Veblen (1934, pp. 79–80) clearly made use of this principle, in his discussions of the origins of habits, purposeful behavior, and so on.

19 Significantly, Plotkin has distanced evolutionary psychology from genetic reductionism. He argues that intelligent behavior "cannot be reductively explained by genetics or genetics and development" (Plotkin 1994, p. 176).

References

Alchian, Armen A. "Uncertainty, Evolution and Economic Theory," *J. Polit. Econ.*, June 1950, *58*(2), pp. 211–21.

Arrow, Kenneth J. "Rationality of Self and Others in an Economic System," *J. Bus.*, *59*(4), Oct. 1986, pp. S385–99; reprinted in Robin M. Hogarth and Melvin W. Reder, eds. *Rational choice: The contrast between economics and psychology.* Chicago and London: U. of Chicago Press,. 1986, pp. 201–15.

Baker, Wayne E. "The Social Structure of a National Securities Market," *Amer. J. Sociology*, Jan. 1984, *89*(4), pp. 775–811.

Becker, Gary S. "Irrational Behavior and Economic Theory," *J. Polit. Econ. 70*(1), Feb. 1962, pp. 1–13.

——. "Habits, Addictions, and Traditions," *Kyklos*, 1992, *45*(3), pp. 327–45.

——.*Accounting for tastes.* Cambridge, MA: Harvard U. Press, 1996.

Bhaskar, Roy. *The possibility of naturalism: A philosophical critique of the contemporary human sciences.* Brighton: Harvester, 1979.

Boulding, Kenneth E. *Evolutionary economics.* Beverly Hills, CA: Sage Publications, 1981.

Buchanan, James M. "Is Economics the Science of Choice?" in *Roads to freedom: Essays in honor of Friedrich A. von Hayek.* Eds.: Erich Streissler et al. London: Routledge and Kegan Paul, 1969, pp. 47–64.

Chiaromonte, Francesca and Dosi, Giovanni. "Heterogeneity, Competition, and Macroeconomic Dynamics," *Structural Change and Economic Dynamics*, June 1993, *4*(1), pp. 39–63.

Choi, Young Back. *Paradigms and conventions: Uncertainty, decision making, and entrepreneurship.* Ann Arbor: U. of Michigan Press, 1993.

Clark, John Maurice. "Economics and Modern Psychology" Parts I and II, *J. Polit. Econ.*, Jan.–Feb. 1918, 26(1–2), pp. 1–30, 136–66; reprinted in John Maurice Clark. *Preface to social economics.* New York: Augustus Kelley, 1967, pp. 92–169.

Cohen, Jack and Stewart, Ian. *The collapse of chaos: Discovering simplicity in a complex world.* London and New York: Viking, 1994.

Coleman, James S. *Foundations of social theory.* Cambridge, MA: Harvard U. Press, 1990.

Commons, John R. *The legal foundations of capitalism.* New York: Macmillan, 1924.

——.*Institutional economics: Its place in political economy.* New York: Macmillan, 1934.

Cosmides, Leda and Tooby, John. "Beyond Intuition and Instinct Blindness: Toward an Evolutionarily Rigorous Cognitive Science," *Cognition,* Apr.–June 1994a, 50(1–3), pp. 41–77.

——."Better than Rational: Evolutionary Psychology and the Invisible Hand," *Amer. Econ. Rev.*, May 1994b, 84(2), pp. 377–32.

Cyert, Richard M. and March, James G. *A behavioral theory of the firm.* Engelwood Cliffs, NJ: Prentice-Hall, 1963.

Degler, Carl N. *In search of human nature: The decline and revival of Darwinism in American social thought.* Oxford and New York: Oxford U. Press, 1991.

Dosi, Giovanni. "Institutions and Markets in a Dynamic World," *Manchester School of Economics and Social Studies,* June 1988, 56(2), pp. 119–46.

Duesenberry, James S. *Income, saving and the theory of consumer behavior.* Cambridge MA: Harvard U. Press, 1949.

Field, Alexander J. "On the Explanation of Rules Using Rational Choice Models," *J. Econ. Issues,* Mar. 1979, 13(1), pp. 49–72.

——."Microeconomics, Norms, and Rationality," *Econ. Devel. Cult. Change,* July 1984, 32(4), pp. 683–711.

Giddens, Anthony. *The constitution of society: Outline of the theory of structuration.* Cambridge: Polity Press, 1984.

Gode, Dhananjay K. and Sunder, Shyam. "Allocative Efficiency of Markets with Zero-Intelligence Traders: Market as a Partial Substitute for Individual Rationality," *J. Polit. Econ.*, Feb. 1993, 101(1), pp. 119–37.

Granovetter, Mark. "Economic Action and Social Structure: The Problem of Embeddedness," *Amer. J. Sociology,* Nov. 1985, 91(3), pp. 481–510.

Green, Francis. "The Consumption Function: A Study of a Failure in Positive Economics," in *Issues in political economy: A critical approach.* Eds.: Francis Green and Petter Nore. London: Macmillan, 1979, pp. 33–60.

Hahn, Frank H. "The Next Hundred Years," *Econ. J.*, Jan. 1991, 101(404), pp. 47–50.

Hamilton, Walton H. "Institution," in *Encyclopaedia of the social sciences.* Eds.: Edwin R. A. Seligman and Alvin Johnson. New York: Macmillan, 1932, Vol. 8, pp. 84–89.

Hayek, Friedrich A. von *The fatal conceit: The errors of socialism. The collected works of Friedrich August Hayek.* Vol. I. Ed.: W. W. Bartley III. London: Routledge, 1988.

Heiner, Ronald A. "The Origin of Predictable Behavior," *Amer. Econ. Rev.*, Dec. 1983, 73(4), pp. 560–95.

Hodgson, Geoffrey M. *Economics and institutions: A manifesto for a modern institutional economics.* Cambridge: Polity Press; Philadelphia: U. of Pennsylvania Press, 1988.

——.*Economics and evolution: Bringing life back into economics.* Cambridge: Polity Press; Ann Arbor, MI: U. of Michigan Press, 1993.

——."The Ubiquity of Habits and Rules," *Cambridge J. Econ.*, Nov. 1997, 21(6), pp. 663–84.

Hodgson, Geoffrey M.; Samuels, Warren J. and Tool, Marc R., eds. *The Elgar companion to institutional and evolutionary economics.* Aldershot: Edward Elgar, 1994.

Houthakker, Hendricks S. and Taylor, Lester D. *Consumer demand in the United States, 1929–1970: Analyses and projections.* Cambridge, MA: Harvard U. Press, 1966.

Keynes, John Maynard. "The General Theory of Employment," *Quart. J. Econ.*, Feb. 1937, 51(1), pp. 209–23; reprinted in Keynes, John Maynard. *The collected writings of John Maynard Keynes.* Vol. XIV. *The General Theory and after: Part II: Defence and development.* London: Macmillan, 1973, pp. 109–23.

Langlois, Richard N., ed. *Economics as a process: Essays in the new institutional economics.* Cambridge and New York: Cambridge U. Press, 1986.

Mason, Roger. "Interpersonal Effects on Consumer Demand in Economic Theory and Marketing Thought, 1890–1950," *J. Econ. Issues*, Sept. 1995, *29*(3), pp. 871–81.

Menger, Carl. "On the Origins of Money," *Econ. J.*, June 1892, *2*(2), pp. 239–55.

——."Geld," in *The collected works of Carl Menger.* Vol. IV. *Schriften über Geldtheorie und Währungspolitik.* London: London School of Economics, 1936, pp. 1–116.

Murphy, James B. "The Kinds of Order in Society," in *Natural images in economic thought: Markets read in tooth and claw.* Ed.: Philip Mirowski. Cambridge and New York: Cambridge U. Press, 1994, pp. 536–82.

Nelson, Richard R. and Winter, Sidney G. *An evolutionary theory of economic change.* Cambridge, MA: Harvard U. Press, 1982.

North, Douglass C. *Structure and change in economic history.* New York: Norton, 1981.

——.*Institutions, institutional change, and economic performance.* Cambridge: Cambridge U. Press, 1990.

Plotkin, Henry C. *Darwin machines and the nature of knowledge: Concerning adaptations, instinct, and the evolution of intelligence.* Harmondsworth: Penguin, 1994.

Polanyi, Karl. *The great transformation.* New York: Rinehart, 1944.

Polanyi, Michael *The tacit dimension.* London: Routledge and Kegan Paul, 1966.

Pollak, Robert A. "Habit Formation and Dynamic Demand Functions," *J. Polit. Econ.*, July–Aug. 1970, *78*(4), pp. 745–63.

Pylyshyn, Zenon W., ed. *The Robot's dilemma: The frame problem in artificial intelligence.* Norwood, NJ: Ablex, 1986.

Posner, Richard A. *Economic analysis of law.* Boston: Little, Brown, 1973.

Reber, Arthur S. *Implicit learning and tacit knowledge: An essay on the cognitive unconscious.* Oxford: Oxford U. Press, 1993.

Rizvi, S. Abu Turab. "The Microfoundations Project in General Equilibrium Theory," *Cambridge J. Econ.*, Aug. 1994, *18*(4), pp. 357–77.

Rutherford, Malcolm C. *Institutions in economics: The old and the new institutionalism.* Cambridge and New York: Cambridge U. Press, 1994.

Schotter, Andrew. *The economic theory of social institutions.* Cambridge and New York: Cambridge U. Press, 1981.

Simon, Herbert A. *Models of man: social and rational; Mathematical essays on rational human behavior in a social setting.* New York: Wiley, 1957.

——."Rational Decision Making in Business Organizations," *Amer. Econ. Rev.*, Sept. 1979, pp. *69*(4), 493–513.

Stiglitz, Joseph E. *Whither socialism?* Cambridge, MA: MIT Press, 1994.

Sugden, Robert. *The economics of rights, cooperation, and welfare.* Oxford: Blackwell, 1986.

Tool, Marc R. "Contributions to an Institutional Theory of Price Determination," in *Rethinking economics: Markets, technology and economic evolution.* Eds.: Geoffrey M. Hodgson and Ernesto Screpanti. Aldershot: Edward Elgar, 1991, pp. 19–39.

Vanberg, Viktor J. *Rules and choice in economics.* London: Routledge, 1994.

Veblen, Thorstein B. *The theory of the leisure class: An economic study in the evolution of institutions.* New York: Macmillan, 1899.

——.*The instinct of workmanship, and the state of the industrial arts.* New York: Augustus Kelley, 1914.

——.*The place of science in modern civilisation and other essays.* New York: Huebsch, 1919.

——.*Essays on our changing order.* Ed.: Leon Ardzrooni. New York: The Viking Press, 1934.

Ware, Caroline F. and Means, Gardiner C. *The modern economy in action.* New York: Harcourt Brace, 1936.

White, Harrison C. *Identity and control: A structural theory of social action.* Princeton: Princeton U. Press, 1992.

Williamson, Oliver E. *Markets and hierarchies, analysis and anti-trust implications: A study in the economics of internal organization.* New York: Free Press, 1975.

——."Credible Commitments: Using Hostages to Support Exchange," *Amer. Econ. Rev.*, Sept. 1983, *74*(3), pp. 519–40.

Winter, Sidney G., Jr. "Satisficing, Selection, and the Innovating Remnant," *Quart. J. Econ.*, May 1971, *85*(2), pp. 237–61.

Part IV

Pricing theory

Introduction

Pricing is arguably the subject that has benefited most from the increasing familiarity of economists with business practices and, inversely, from the reliance of business on sophisticated economic analyses.

Beyond the basic case of uniform pricing (where the unit prices are the same for any quantity bought, to every customer), first-, second-, and third-degree price discriminations[1] have long been a staple of principles textbooks. These are now subsumed under the moniker "non-uniform pricing." In other words, any pricing scheme that does not consist of a single price for all customers at any moment could be considered non-uniform. Non-uniform pricing can be either "value-based" or "cost-based." In the former, variations in unit prices are based on the non-uniformity in consumers' willingness to pay; in the latter, they reflect the heterogeneity of unit costs.

Most non-uniform pricing schemes aim at taking advantage of, or simply mitigating, four problems: (1) Preference heterogeneity, (2) the effect of time, (3) consumption interdependence, and (4) information imperfections.

(1) The fact that individuals' preferences are diverse poses a special challenge for firms who wish to increase their profits above what could be achieved with uniform pricing. Among the most influential works in this area is Oi's (1971) two-part tariff (subsequently generalized into multi-part tariffs) which shows that profits could be improved by charging a constant "entry fee" coupled with a variable user fee.

(2) Another line of research is built on the recognition that a product usually lasts more than one period. This raises two major issues: (a) The optimal durability[2] of a product and (b) the competition between new goods and used goods, i.e., the firm is in effect competing with itself. This problem was tackled first, again, by Coase (1972). Another variation on the theme of time-dependency is peak-load pricing[3] which combines the time dimension and price discrimination, with the added twist that output quantities in different periods come from the same installed capacity. Pricing of experience goods – goods that must be used for some time before their values can be fully appreciated – also falls into this category. Other time-sensitive pricing schemes take advantage of non-negligible switching costs, and therefore lock-ins – difficulties in learning to use a similar but different product, for example, as in moving from one word-processing program to another.

(3) Some products are related to other products, either in production or especially in consumption. The two major pricing methods to exploit possible "togetherness"

are: (a) bundling, and (b) network externalities. By selling the products as a bundle, and/or offering them separately at different prices, the firm could actually practice a kind of discrimination.[4]

Product interdependence could also be the reason why, in some cases, having many people use the same product would reduce costs and create additional benefits not reflected in the price of that product. In other words, the value of a product or service increases with the number of users; for instance the value of a telephone increases with the number of people who have telephones. This phenomenon is known as network economies and externalities. For a positive network externality to exist,[5] however, all products in the network must share some common standards so that they would work together. Since the product that sets the standard thus has a marketing edge, this gives rise to competition within and between standards. Standards, in other words, might be used as a strategic tool.

(4) In the pricing schemes mentioned above, the imperfection of information is either intrinsic, or added later to the model for realism. But information imperfections could be the driving force behind an analysis. The firm might, for instance, take advantage of its competitor's and/or buyer's inadequate information to send them a signal designed to make them act in a way that would improve its profits. The firm might also design a screening method to filter out undesirable buyers or, inversely, to attract desirable buyers.[6] Auction is a time-honored way to deal with asymmetric information: the auctioneer does not know how high the highest bidder will bid, and the bidder does not know how high other bidders would be willing to go. By auctioning its product, a monopoly that faces very few buyers could force the buyer with the highest willingness to pay to reveal himself.[7]

Part IV has seven articles. Dixit and Stiglitz (1977) is quite useful in that it sets up a very tractable model for the difficult and important phenomenon of product diversity, and how it impacts preferences. Its technique of using a CES utility function to parametrize preferences for product diversity has been imitated in many models in international trade and industrial organization. Oi (1971) is the path-breaking analysis of two-part tariff. Although there are many articles on multipart-pricing that come later, it remains a pleasure to read this grand-daddy of them all. Adams and Yellen (1976) is a classic article on bundling. Steiner (1957) introduces peak-load pricing to the literature. Nalebuff (2004) shows that bundling could also deter entry. Klemperer (2002) discusses some of the basic issues about auction. Liebowitz and Margolis (1998) introduces us to network effects.

Notes

1 A classification originated with Joan Robinson (1933).
2 Durability being one dimension of product quality.
3 Also known as time-of-use pricing.
4 The first economist who noticed this problem was perhaps Stigler (1968), but the truly path-breaking analysis was Adams and Yellen (1976), followed by Schmalensee (1982, 1984), McAfee, McMillan, and Whinston (1989), Bakos and Brynjolfsson (2000) and many others.
5 Obviously, network externalities could be negative, too, as in congestion.
6 For example, insurance companies pitching their product to those who identify themselves as either low-risk or not needing it.
7 McAfee and McMillan (1987) is a convenient gateway to the literature on auction and bidding.

References

Adams, W. J. and Yellen, J. L. (1976) "Commodity Bundling and the Burden of Monopoly," *Quarterly Journal of Economics* 90, pp. 475–98.

Bakos, Y. and Brynjolfsson, E. (2000) "Bundling and Competition on the Internet: Aggregation, Strategies for Information Goods," *Marketing Science* 19, pp. 63–82.

Coase, R. (1972) "Durability and Monopoly," *Journal of Law and Economics* 15, 143–49.

DeSalvo, J. and Huq, M. (2002) "Introducing Non Linear Pricing into Consumer Choice Theory," *Journal of Economic Education*, 33(2), pp. 166–79.

Dixit, A. and Stiglitz, J. (1977) "Monopolistic Competition and Optimal Product Diversity," *The American Economic Review*, 67: 297–308.

Klemperer, P. (2002) "What Really Matters in Auction Design," *The Journal of Economic Perspectives*, 16: 169–89.

Liebowitz, S. and Margolis, S. (1998) "Network Externalities (Effects)," in *The New Palgrave Dictionary of Economics and the Law*, pp. 76–93, edited by P. Newman, London: Macmillan.

McAfee, R. P. and McMillan, J. (1987) "Auctions and Bidding," *Journal of Economic Literature*, XXV, 699–738.

McAfee, R. P., McMillan, J. and Whinston, M. D. (1989) "Multiproduct Monopoly, Commodity Bundling and Correlation of Values," *Quarterly Journal of Economics* 104, pp. 371–84.

Nalebuff, B. (2004) "Bundling as an Entry Barrier," *The Quarterly Journal of Economics* 119(1): 159–87.

Oi, W. (1971) "A Disneyland Dilemma: Two-part Tariffs for a Mickey Mouse monopoly," *Quarterly Journal of Economics*, 85(1): 77–96.

Robinson, J. (1933) *The Economics of Imperfect Competition*, London: Macmillan.

Schmalensee, R. (1982) "Commodity Bundling by Single-Product Monopolies," *Journal of Law and Economics* XXV, 67–71.

Schmalensee, R. (1984) "Gaussian Demand and Commodity Bundling," *Journal of Business* 57(1), pp. 5211–5230.

Steiner, P. (1957) "Peak Loads and Efficient Pricing," *Quarterly Journal of Economics*, 71(4): 585–610.

Stigler, G. J. (1968) *The Organization of Industry*, Chicago: University of Chicago Press.

20 Monopolistic competition and optimum product diversity

Avinash K. Dixit and Joseph E. Stiglitz

The basic issue concerning production in welfare economics is whether a market solution will yield the socially optimum kinds and quantities of commodities. It is well known that problems can arise for three broad reasons: distributive justice; external effects; and scale economies. This paper is concerned with the last of these.

The basic principle is easily stated.[1] A commodity should be produced if the costs can be covered by the sum of revenues and a properly defined measure of consumer's surplus. The optimum amount is then found by equating the demand price and the marginal cost. Such an optimum can be realized in a market if perfectly discriminatory pricing is possible. Otherwise we face conflicting problems. A competitive market fulfilling the marginal condition would be unsustainable because total profits would be negative. An element of monopoly would allow positive profits, but would violate the marginal condition.[2] Thus we expect a market solution to be suboptimal. However, a much more precise structure must be put on the problem if we are to understand the nature of the bias involved.

It is useful to think of the question as one of quantity versus diversity. With scale economies, resources can be saved by producing fewer goods and larger quantities of each. However, this leaves less variety, which entails some welfare loss. It is easy and probably not too unrealistic to model scale economies by supposing that each potential commodity involves some fixed set-up cost and has a constant marginal cost. Modeling the desirability of variety has been thought to be difficult, and several indirect approaches have been adopted. The Hotelling spatial model, Lancaster's product characteristics approach, and the mean-variance portfolio selection model have all been put to use. These lead to results involving transport costs or correlations among commodities or securities, and are hard to interpret in general terms. We therefore take a direct route, noting that the convexity of indifference surfaces of a conventional utility function defined over the quantities of all potential commodities already embodies the desirability of variety. Thus, a consumer who is indifferent between the quantities (1,0) and (0,1) of two commodities prefers the mix (1/2, 1/2) to either extreme. The advantage of this view is that the results involve the familiar own-and cross-elasticities of demand functions, and are therefore easier to comprehend.

There is one case of particular interest on which we concentrate. This is where potential commodities in a group or sector or industry are good substitutes among themselves, but poor substitutes for the other commodities in the economy. Then we are led to examining the market solution in relation to an optimum, both as regards biases within the group, and between the group and the rest of the economy. We expect the answer to depend on the intra- and intersector elasticities of substitution. To demonstrate the point as simply as possible, we shall aggregate the rest of the economy into one good labeled 0, chosen as the numeraire.

The economy's endowment of it is normalized at unity; it can be thought of as the time at the disposal of the consumers.

The potential range of related products is labeled $1, 2, 3, \ldots$ Writing the amounts of the various commodities as x_0 and $x = (x_1, x_2, x_3 \ldots)$, we assume a separable utility function with convex indifference surfaces:

$$u = U(x_0, V(x_1, x_2, x_3 \ldots))$$ (20.1)

In Sections I and II we simplify further by assuming that V is a symmetric function, and that all commodities in the group have equal fixed and marginal costs. Then the actual labels given to commodities are immaterial, even though the total number n being produced is relevant. We can thus label these commodities $1, 2, \ldots, n$, where the potential products $(n + 1), (n + 2), \ldots$ are not being produced. This is a restrictive assumption, for in such problems we often have a natural asymmetry owing to graduated physical differences in commodities, with a pair close together being better mutual substitutes than a pair farther apart. However, even the symmetric case yields some interesting results. In Section III, we consider some aspects of asymmetry.

We also assume that all commodities have unit income elasticities. This differs from a similar recent formulation by Michael Spence, who assumes U linear in x_0, so that the industry is amenable to partial equilibrium analysis. Our approach allows a better treatment of the intersectoral substitution, but the other results are very similar to those of Spence.

We consider two special cases of (20.1). In Section I, V is given a *CES* form, but U is allowed to be arbitrary. In Section II, U is taken to be Cobb-Douglas, but V has a more general additive form. Thus the former allows more general intersector relations, and the latter more general intrasector substitution, highlighting different results.

Income distribution problems are neglected. Thus U can be regarded as representing Samuelsonian social indifference curves, or (assuming the appropriate aggregation conditions to be fulfilled) as a multiple of a representative consumer's utility. Product diversity can then be interpreted either as different consumers using different varieties, or as diversification on the part of each consumer.

I Constant-elasticity case

Demand functions

The utility function in this section is

$$u = U\left(x_0, \left\{\sum_i x_i^\rho\right\}^{1/\rho}\right)$$ (20.2)

For concavity, we need $\rho < 1$. Further, since we want to allow a situation where several of the x_i are zero, we need $\rho > 0$. We also assume U homothetic in its arguments.

The budget constraint is

$$x_0 + \sum_{i=1}^{n} p_i x_i = I$$ (20.3)

where p_i are prices of the goods being produced, and I is income in terms of the numeraire, i.e., the endowment which has been set at 1 plus the profits of the firms distributed to the consumers, or minus the lump sum deductions to cover the losses, as the case may be.

In this case, a two-stage budgeting procedure is valid.[3] Thus we define dual quantity and price indices

$$y = \left\{ \sum_{i=1}^{n} x_i^{\rho} \right\}^{1/\rho} \qquad q = \left\{ \sum_{i=1}^{n} p_i^{-1/\beta} \right\}^{-\beta} \tag{20.4}$$

where $\beta = (1 - \rho)/\rho$, which is positive since $0 < p < 1$. Then it can be shown[4] that in the first stage,

$$y = I \frac{s(q)}{q} \qquad x_0 = I(1 - s(q)) \tag{20.5}$$

for a function s which depends on the form of U. Writing $\sigma(q)$ for the elasticity of substitution between x_0 and y, we define $\theta(q)$ as the elasticity of the function s, i.e., $q s'(q)/s(q)$. Then we find

$$\theta(q) = \{1 - \sigma(q)\}\{1 - s(q)\} < 1 \tag{20.6}$$

but $\theta(q)$ can be negative as $\sigma(q)$ can exceed 1.

Turning to the second stage of the problem, it is easy to show that for each i,

$$x_i = y \left[\frac{q}{p_i} \right]^{1/(1-\rho)} \tag{20.7}$$

where y is defined by (20.4). Consider the effect of a change in p_i, alone. This affects x_i, directly, and also through q; thence through y as well. Now from (20.4) we have the elasticity

$$\frac{\partial \log q}{\partial \log p_i} = \left(\frac{q}{p_i} \right)^{1/\beta} \tag{20.8}$$

So long as the prices of the products in the group are not of different orders of magnitude, this is of the order $(1/n)$. We shall assume that n is reasonably large, and accordingly neglect the effect of each p_i, on q; thus the indirect effects on x_i. This leaves us with the elasticity

$$\frac{\partial \log x_i}{\partial \log p_i} = \frac{-1}{(1-\rho)} = \frac{-(1+\beta)}{\beta} \tag{20.9}$$

In the Chamberlinian terminology, this is the elasticity of the *dd* curve, i.e., the curve relating the demand for each product type to its own price with all other prices held constant.

In our large group case, we also see that for $i \neq j$, the cross elasticity $\partial \log x_i/\partial \log p_j$ is negligible. However, if all prices in the group move together, the individually small effects add to a significant amount. This corresponds to the Chamberlinian *DD* curve. Consider a symmetric situation where $x_i = x$ and $p_i = p$ for all i from 1 to n. We have

$$y = xn^{1/\rho} = xn^{1+\beta}$$
$$q = pn^{-\beta} = pn^{-(1-\rho)/\rho} \tag{20.10}$$

and then from (20.5) and (20.7),

$$x = \frac{Is(q)}{pn} \tag{20.11}$$

The elasticity of this is easy to calculate; we find

$$\frac{\partial \log x}{\partial \log p} = -[1 - \theta(q)] \tag{20.12}$$

Then (20.6) shows that the *DD* curve slopes downward. The conventional condition that the *dd* curve be more elastic is seen from (20.9) and (20.12) to be

$$\frac{1}{\beta} + \theta(q) > 0 \tag{20.13}$$

Finally, we observe that for $i \neq j$,

$$\frac{x_i}{x_j} = \left[\frac{p_j}{p_i}\right]^{1/(1-\rho)} \tag{20.14}$$

Thus $1/(1-\rho)$ is the elasticity of substitution between any two products within the group.

Market equilibrium

It can be shown that each commodity is produced by one firm. Each firm attempts to maximize its profit, and entry occurs until the marginal firm can only just break even. Thus our market equilibrium is the familiar case of Chamberlinian monopolistic competition, where the question of quantity versus diversity has often been raised.[5] Previous analyses have failed to consider the desirability of variety in an explicit form, and have neglected various intra- and intersector interactions in demand. As a result, much vague presumption that such an equilibrium involves excessive diversity has built up at the back of the minds of many economists. Our analysis will challenge several of these ideas.

The profit-maximization condition for each firm acting on its own is the familiar equality of marginal revenue and marginal cost. Writing c for the common marginal cost, and noting that the elasticity of demand for each firm is $(1+\beta)/\beta$, we have for each active firm:

$$p_i\left(1 - \frac{\beta}{1+\beta}\right) = c$$

Writing p_e for the common equilibrium price for each variety being produced, we have

$$p_e = c(1+\beta) = \frac{c}{\rho} \tag{20.15}$$

The second condition for equilibrium is that firms enter until the next potential entrant would make a loss. If n is large enough so that 1 is a small increment, we can assume that the marginal firm is exactly breaking even, i.e., $(p_n - c)x_n = a$, where x_n is obtained from the demand function and a is the fixed cost. With symmetry, this implies zero profit for all intramarginal firms as well. Then $I = 1$, and using (20.11) and (20.15) we can write the condition so as to yield the number n_e of active firms:

$$\frac{s(p_e n_e^{-\beta})}{p_e n_e} = \frac{q}{\beta c} \qquad (20.16)$$

Equilibrium is unique provided $s(p_e n^{-\beta})/p_e n$ is a monotonic function of n. This relates to our earlier discussion about the two demand curves. From (20.11) we see that the behavior of $s(pn^{-\beta})/pn$ as n increases tells us how the demand curve DD for each firm shifts as the number of firms increases. It is natural to assume that it shifts to the left, i.e., the function above decreases as n increases for each fixed p. The condition for this in elasticity form is easily seen to be

$$1 + \beta \theta(q) > 0 \qquad (20.17)$$

This is exactly the same as (20.13), the condition for the dd curve to be more elastic than the DD curve, and we shall assume that it holds.

The condition can be violated if $\sigma(q)$ is sufficiently higher than one. In this case, an increase in n lowers q, and shifts demand towards the monopolistic sector to such an extent that the demand curve for each firm shifts to the right. However, this is rather implausible.

Conventional Chamberlinian analysis assumes a fixed demand curve for the group as a whole. This amounts to assuming that $n \cdot x$ is independent of n, i.e., that $s(pn^{-\beta})$ is independent of n. This will be so if $\beta = 0$, or if $\sigma(q) = 1$ for all q. The former is equivalent to assuming that $p = 1$, when all products in the group are perfect substitutes, i.e., diversity is not valued at all. That would be contrary to the intent of the whole analysis. Thus, implicitly, conventional analysis assumes $\sigma(q) = 1$. This gives a constant budget share for the monopolistically competitive sector. Note that in our parametric formulation, this implies a unit-elastic DD curve, (20.17) holds, and so equilibrium is unique.

Finally, using (20.7), (20.11), and (20.16), we can calculate the equilibrium output for each active firm:

$$x_e = \frac{a}{\beta c} \qquad (20.18)$$

We can also write an expression for the budget share of the group as a whole:

$$s_e = s(q_e) \qquad (20.19)$$

where $\quad q_e = p_e n_e^{-\beta}$

These will be useful for subsequent comparisons.

Constrained optimum

The next task is to compare the equilibrium with a social optimum. With economies of scale, the first best or unconstrained (really constrained only by technology and resource availability) optimum requires pricing below average cost, and therefore lump sum transfers to firms to cover losses. The conceptual and practical difficulties of doing so are clearly formidable. It would therefore appear that a more appropriate notion of optimality is a constrained one, where each firm must have nonnegative profits. This may be achieved by regulation, or by excise or franchise taxes or subsidies. The important restriction is that lump sum subsidies are not available.

We begin with such a constrained optimum. The aim is to choose n, p_i, and x_i, so as to maximize utility, satisfying the demand functions and keeping the profit for each firm nonnegative. The problem is somewhat simplified by the result that all active firms should have the same output levels and prices, and should make exactly zero profit. We omit the proof. Then we can set $I = 1$, and use (20.5) to express utility as a function of q alone. This is of course a decreasing function, Thus the problem of maximizing u becomes that of minimizing q, i.e.,

$$\min_{n, p} pn^{-\beta}$$

subject to

$$(p - c)\frac{s(pn^{-\beta})}{pn} = a \tag{20.20}$$

To solve this, we calculate the logarithmic marginal rate of substitution along a level curve of the objective, the similar rate of transformation along the constraint, and equate the two. This yields the condition

$$\frac{\frac{c}{p-c} + \theta(q)}{1 + \beta\theta(q)} = \frac{1}{\beta} \tag{20.21}$$

The second-order condition can be shown to hold, and (20.21) simplifies to yield the price for each commodity produced in the constrained optimum, p_c, as

$$p_c = c(1 + \beta) \tag{20.22}$$

Comparing (20.15) and (20.22), we see that the two solutions have the same price. Since they face the same break-even constraint, they have the same number of firms as well, and the values for all other variables can be calculated from these two. Thus we have a rather surprising case where the monopolistic competition equilibrium is identical with the optimum constrained by the lack of lump sum subsidies. Chamberlin once suggested that such an equilibrium was "a sort of ideal"; our analysis shows when and in what sense this can be true.

Unconstrained optimum

These solutions can in turn be compared to the unconstrained or first best optimum. Considerations of convexity again establish that all active firms should produce the same output. Thus we are to choose n firms each producing output x in order to maximize

$$u = U(1 - n(a + cx), xn^{1+\beta}) \tag{20.23}$$

where we have used the economy's resource balance condition and (20.10). The first-order conditions are

$$-ncU_0 + n^{1+\beta}U_y = 0 \tag{20.24}$$

$$-(a+cx)U_0 + (1+\beta)xn^\beta U_y = 0 \tag{20.25}$$

From the first stage of the budgeting problem, we know that $q = U_y/U_0$. Using (20.24) and (20.10), we find the price charged by each active firm in the unconstrained optimum, p_u, equal to marginal cost

$$p_u = c \tag{20.26}$$

This, of course, is no surprise. Also from the first-order conditions, we have

$$x_u = \frac{a}{c\beta} \tag{20.27}$$

Finally, with (20.26), each active firm covers its variable cost exactly. The lump sum transfers to firms then equal an, and therefore $l = 1 - an$, and

$$x = (1 - an)\frac{s(pn^{-\beta})}{pn}$$

The number of firms n_u is then defined by

$$\frac{s(cn_u^{-\beta})}{n_u} = \frac{a/\beta}{1 - an_u} \tag{20.28}$$

We can now compare these magnitudes with the corresponding ones in the equilibrium or the constrained optimum. The most remarkable result is that the output of each active firm is the same in the two situations. The fact that in a Chamberlinian equilibrium each firm operates to the left of the point of minimum average cost has been conventionally described by saying that there is excess capacity. However, when variety is desirable, i.e., when the different products are not perfect substitutes, it is not in general optimum to push the output of each firm to the point where all economies of scale are exhausted.[6] We have shown in one case that is not an extreme one, that the first best optimum does not exploit economies of scale beyond the extent achieved in the equilibrium. We can then easily conceive of cases where the equilibrium exploits economies of scale too far from the point of view of social optimality. Thus our results undermine the validity of the folklore of excess capacity, from the point of view of the unconstrained optimum as well as the constrained one.

A direct comparison of the numbers of firms from (20.16) and (20.28) would be difficult, but an indirect argument turns out to be simple. It is clear that the unconstrained optimum has higher utility than the constrained optimum. Also, the level of lump sum income in it is less than that in the latter. It must therefore be the case that

$$q_u < q_c = q_e \tag{20.29}$$

Further, the difference must be large enough that the budget constraint for x_0 and the quantity index y in the unconstrained case must lie outside that in the constrained case in the relevant region, as shown in Figure 20.1. Let C be the constrained optimum, A the unconstrained optimum, and let B be the point where the line joining the origin to C meets the indifference curve in the unconstrained case. By homotheticity the indifference curve at B is parallel to that at C, so each of the moves from C to B and from B to A increases the value of y. Since the value of x is the same in the two optima, we must have

$$n_u > n_c = n_e \tag{20.30}$$

Thus the unconstrained optimum actually allows more variety than the constrained optimum and the equilibrium; this is another point contradicting the folklore on excessive diversity.

Using (20.29) we can easily compare the budget shares. In the notation we have been using, we find $s_u \gtrless s_C$ as $\theta(q) \gtrless 0$, i.e., as $\sigma(q) \gtrless 1$ providing these hold over the entire relevant range of q.

It is not possible to have a general result concerning the relative magnitudes of x_0 in the two situations; an inspection of Figure 20.1 shows this. However, we have a sufficient condition:

$$x_{0u} = (1 - an_u)(1 - s_u) < 1 - s_u \leq 1 - s_c$$
$$= x_{0c} \text{ if } \sigma(q) \geq 1$$

In this case the equilibrium or the constrained optimum use more of the numeraire resource than the unconstrained optimum. On the other hand, if $\sigma(q) = 0$ we have L-shaped isoquants, and in Figure 20.1, points A and B coincide giving the opposite conclusion.

In this section we have seen that with a constant intrasector elasticity of substitution, the market equilibrium coincides with the constrained optimum. We have also shown that the unconstrained optimum has a greater number of firms, each of the same size. Finally, the resource allocation between the sectors is shown to depend on the intersector elasticity of substitution. This elasticity also governs conditions for uniqueness of equilibrium and the second-order conditions for an optimum.

Henceforth we will achieve some analytic simplicity by making a particular assumption about intersector substitution. In return, we will allow a more general form of intrasector substitution.

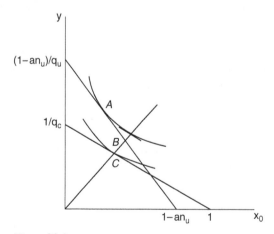

Figure 20.1

II Variable elasticity case

The utility function is now

$$u = x_0^{1-\gamma} \left\{ \sum_i v(x_i) \right\} \gamma \qquad (20.31)$$

with v increasing and concave, $0 < \gamma < 1$. This is somewhat like assuming a unit inter-sector elasticity of substitution. However, this is not rigorous since the group utility $V(x) = \sum_i v(x_i)$ is not homothetic and therefore two-stage budgeting is not applicable.

It can be shown that the elasticity of the *dd* curve in the large group case is

$$-\frac{\partial \log x_i}{\partial \log p_i} = -\frac{v'(x_i)}{x_i v''(x_i)} \quad \text{for any } i \qquad (20.32)$$

This differs from the case of Section I in being a function of x_i. To highlight the similarities and the differences, we define $\beta(x)$ by

$$\frac{1+\beta(x)}{\beta(x)} = -\frac{v'(x)}{x v''(x)} \qquad (20.33)$$

Next, setting $x_i = x$ and $p_i = p$ for $i = 1, 2, \ldots, n$, we can write the *DD* curve and the demand for the numeraire as

$$x = \frac{I}{np} w(x), \qquad x_0 = I[1 - w(x)] \qquad (20.34)$$

where

$$w(x) = \frac{\gamma \rho(x)}{[\gamma \rho(x) + (1-\gamma)]}$$

$$\rho(x) = \frac{x v'(x)}{v(x)} \qquad (20.35)$$

We assume that $0 < \rho(x) < 1$, and therefore have $0 < w(x) < 1$.

Now consider the Chamberlinian equilibrium. The profit-maximization condition for each active firm yields the common equilibrium price p_e in terms of the common equilibrium output x_e as

$$p_e = c[1 + \beta(x_e)] \qquad (20.36)$$

Note the analogy with (20.15). Substituting (20.36) in the zero pure profit condition, we have x_e defined by

$$\frac{c x_e}{a + c x_e} = \frac{1}{1 + \beta(x_e)} \qquad (20.37)$$

Finally, the number of firms can be calculated using the *DD* curve and the break-even condition, as

$$n_e = \frac{\omega(x_e)}{a + cx_e} \tag{20.38}$$

For uniqueness of equilibrium we once again use the conditions that the *dd* curve is more elastic than the *DD* curve, and that entry shifts the *DD* curve to the left. However, these conditions are rather involved and opaque, so we omit them.

Let us turn to the constrained optimum. We wish to choose n and x to maximize u, subject to (20.34) and the break-even condition $px = a + cx$. Substituting, we can express u as a function of x alone:

$$u = \gamma^\gamma (1 - \gamma)^{(1-\gamma)} \frac{\left[\dfrac{\rho(x)v(x)}{a + cx}\right]^\gamma}{\gamma\rho(x) + (1 - \gamma)} \tag{20.39}$$

The first-order condition defines x_c:

$$\frac{cx_c}{a + cx_c} = \frac{1}{1 + \beta(x_c)} - \frac{\omega(x_c)x_c\rho'(x_c)}{\gamma\rho(x_c)} \tag{20.40}$$

Comparing this with (20.37) and using the second-order condition, it can be shown that provided $p'(x)$ is one-signed for all x,

$$x_c \gtrless x_e \text{ according as } p'(x) \lessgtr 0 \tag{20.41}$$

With zero pure profit in each case, the points (x_e, p_e) and (x_c, p_c) lie on the same declining average cost curve, and therefore

$$p_c \lessgtr p_e \text{ according as } x_c \gtrless x_e \tag{20.42}$$

Next we note that the *dd* curve is tangent to the average cost curve at (x_e, p_e) and the *DD* curve is steeper. Consider the case $x_c > x_e$. Now the point (x_c, p_c) must lie on a *DD* curve further to the right than (x_e, p_e), and therefore must correspond to a smaller number of firms. The opposite happens if $x_c < x_e$. Thus,

$$n_c \lessgtr n_e \text{ according as } x_c \gtrless x_e \tag{20.43}$$

Finally, (20.41) shows that in both cases that arise there, $p(x_c) < p(x_e)$. Then $\omega(x_c) < \omega(x_e)$, and from (20.34),

$$x_{0c} > x_{0e} \tag{20.44}$$

A smaller degree of intersectoral substitution could have reversed the result, as in Section I.

An intuitive reason for these results can be given as follows. With our large group assumptions, the revenue of each firm is proportional to $xv'(x)$. However, the contribution of its output to group utility is $v(x)$. The ratio of the two is $p(x)$. Therefore, if $p'(x) > 0$, then at the margin each firm finds it more profitable to expand than what would be socially desirable, so $x_e > x_c$. Given the break-even constraint, this leads to there being fewer firms.

Note that the relevant magnitude is the elasticity of utility, and not the elasticity of demand. The two are related, since

$$x \frac{\rho'(x)}{\rho(x)} = \frac{1}{1 + \beta(x)} - \rho(x) \tag{20.45}$$

Thus, if $p(x)$ is constant over an interval, so is $\beta(x)$ and we have $1/(1+\beta) = \rho$, which is the case of Section I. However, if $\rho(x)$ varies, we cannot infer a relation between the signs of $p'(x)$ and $\beta'(x)$. Thus the variation in the elasticity of demand is not in general the relevant consideration. However, for important families of utility functions there is a relationship. For example, for $v(x) = (k + mx)^j$, with $m > 0$ and $0 < j < 1$, we find that $-xv''/v'$ and xv'/v are positively related. Now we would normally expect that as the number of commodities produced increases, the elasticity of substitution between any pair of them should increase. In the symmetric equilibrium, this is just the inverse of the elasticity of marginal utility. Then a higher x would correspond to a lower n, and therefore a lower elasticity of substitution, higher $-xv''/v'$ and higher xv'/v. Thus we are led to expect that $p'(x) > 0$, i.e., that the equilibrium involves fewer and bigger firms than the constrained optimum. Once again the common view concerning excess capacity and excessive diversity in monopolistic competition is called into question.

The unconstrained optimum problem is to choose n and x to maximize

$$u = [nv(x)]^\gamma [1 - n(a + cx)]^{1-\gamma} \tag{20.46}$$

It is easy to show that the solution has

$$p_u = c \tag{20.47}$$

$$\frac{cx_u}{a + cx_u} = \rho(x_u) \tag{20.48}$$

$$n_u = \frac{\gamma}{a + cx_u} \tag{20.49}$$

Then we can use the second-order condition to show that

$$x_u \lessgtr x_c \text{ according as } \rho'(x) \gtrless 0 \tag{20.50}$$

This is in each case transitive with (20.41), and therefore yields similar output comparisons between the equilibrium and the unconstrained optimum.

The price in the unconstrained optimum is of course the lowest of the three. As to the number of firms, we note

$$n_c = \frac{\omega(x_c)}{a + cx_c} < \frac{\gamma}{a + cx_c}$$

and therefore we have a one-way comparison:

$$\text{If } x_u < x_c, \text{ then } n_u > n_c \tag{20.51}$$

Similarly for the equilibrium. These leave open the possibility that the unconstrained optimum has both bigger and more firms. That is not unreasonable; after all the unconstrained optimum uses resources more efficiently.

III Asymmetric cases

The discussion so far imposed symmetry within the group. Thus the number of varieties being produced was relevant, but any group of n was just as good as any other group of n. The next important modification is to remove this restriction. It is easy to see how interrelations within the group of commodities can lead to biases. Thus, if no sugar is being produced, the demand for coffee may be so low as to make its production unprofitable when there are set-up costs. However, this is open to the objection that with complementary commodities, there is an incentive for one entrant to produce both. However, problems exist even when all the commodities are substitutes. We illustrate this by considering an industry which will produce commodities from one of two groups, and examine whether the choice of the wrong group is possible.[7]

Suppose there are two sets of commodities beside the numeraire, the two being perfect substitutes for each other and each having a constant elasticity subutility function. Further, we assume a constant budget share for the numeraire. Thus the utility function is

$$u = x_0^{1-s} \left\{ \left[\sum_{i_1=1}^{n} x_{i_1}^{\rho_1} \right]^{1/\rho_1} + \left[\sum_{i_2=1}^{n_2} x_i^{\rho_2} \right]^{1/\rho_2} \right\}^{s} \tag{20.52}$$

We assume that each firm in group i has a fixed cost a_i, and a constant marginal cost c_i.

Consider two types of equilibria, only one commodity group being produced in each. These are given by

$$\bar{x}_1 = \frac{a_1}{c_1 \beta_1}, \quad \bar{x}_2 = 0$$

$$\bar{p}_1 = c_1(1 + \beta_1)$$

$$\bar{n}_1 = \frac{s\beta_1}{a_1(1 + \beta_1)}$$

$$\bar{q}_1 = \bar{p}_1 \bar{n}_1^{-\beta_1} = c_1(1 + \beta_1)^{1+\beta_1} \left(\frac{a_1}{s} \right)^{\beta_1}$$

$$\bar{u}_1 = s^s (1-s)^{1-s} \bar{q}_1^{-s} \tag{20.53a}$$

$$\bar{x}_2 = \frac{a_2}{c_2 \beta_2}, \quad \bar{x}_1 = 0$$

$$\bar{p}_2 = c_2(1 + \beta_2)$$

$$\bar{n}_2 = \frac{s\beta_2}{a_2(1 + \beta_2)}$$

$$\bar{q}_2 = \bar{p}_2 \bar{n}_2^{-\beta_2} = c_2(1 + \beta_2)^{1+\beta_2} \left(\frac{a_2}{s} \right)^{\beta_2}$$

$$\bar{u}_2 = s^s (1-s)^{1-s} \bar{q}_2^{-s} \tag{20.53b}$$

Equation (20.53a) is a Nash equilibrium if and only if it does not pay a firm to produce a commodity of the second group. The demand for such a commodity is

$$x_2 = \begin{cases} 0 & \text{for } p_2 \geq \bar{q}_1 \\ s/p_2 & \text{for } p_2 < \bar{q}_1 \end{cases}$$

Hence we require

$$\max_{p_2} (p_2 - c_2)x_2 = s\left(1 - \frac{c_2}{\bar{q}_1}\right) < a_2$$

or

$$\bar{q}_1 < \frac{sc_2}{s - a_2} \qquad (20.54)$$

Similarly, (20.53b) is a Nash equilibrium if and only if

$$\bar{q}_2 < \frac{sc_1}{s - a_1} \qquad (20.55)$$

Now consider the optimum. Both the objective and the constraint are such as to lead the optimum to the production of commodities from only one group. Thus, suppose n_i, commodities from group i are being produced at levels x_i each, and offered at prices p_i. The utility level is given by

$$u = x_0^{1-s}\{x_1 n_1^{1+\beta_1} + x_2 n_2^{1+\beta_2}\}^s \qquad (20.56)$$

and the resource availability constraint is

$$x_0 + n_1(a_1 + c_1 x_1) + n_2(a_2 + c_2 x_2) = 1 \qquad (20.57)$$

Given the values of the other variables, the level curves of u in (n_1, n_2) space are concave to the origin, while the constraint is linear. We must therefore have a corner optimum. (As for the break-even constraint, unless the two $q_i = p_i n_i^{-\beta_i}$ are equal, the demand for commodities in one group is zero, and there is no possibility of avoiding a loss there.)

Note that we have structured our example so that if the correct group is chosen, the equilibrium will not introduce any further biases in relation to the constrained optimum. Therefore, to find the constrained optimum, we only have to look at the values of $\bar{u}_i$ in (20.53a) and (20.53b) and see which is the greater. In other words, we have to see which $\bar{q}_i$, is the smaller, and choose the situation (which may or may not be a Nash equilibrium) defined in (20.53a) and (20.53b) corresponding to it.

Figure 20.2 is drawn to depict the possible equilibria and optima. Given all the relevant parameters, we calculate $(\bar{q}_1, \bar{q}_2)$ from (20.53a) and (20.53b). Then (20.54) and (20.55) tell us whether either or both of the situations are possible equilibria, while a simple comparison of the magnitudes of $\bar{q}_1$ and $\bar{q}_2$ tells us which is the constrained optimum. In the figure, the nonnegative quadrant is split into regions in each of which we have one combination of equilibria and optima. We only have to locate the point $(\bar{q}_1, \bar{q}_2)$ in this space to know the

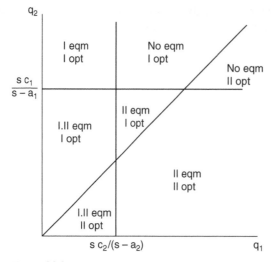

Figure 20.2

Note: Solutions labeled I refer to equation (20.53a): Solutions labelled II refer to equation (20.53b).

result for the given parameter values. Moreover, we can compare the location of the points corresponding to different parameter values and thus do some comparative statics.

To understand the results, we must examine how $\bar{q}_i$, depends on the relevant parameters. It is easy to see that each is an increasing function of a_i and c_i. We also find

$$\frac{\partial \log \bar{q}_i}{\partial \beta_i} = -\log \bar{n}_i \qquad (20.58)$$

and we expect this to be large and negative. Further, we see from (20.9) that a higher β_i corresponds to a lower own-price elasticity of demand for each commodity in that group. Thus $\bar{q}_i$ is an increasing function of this elasticity.

Consider initially a symmetric situation, with $sc_1/(s-a_1) = sc_2/(s-a_2)$, $\beta_1 = \beta_2$ (the region G vanishes then), and suppose the point $(\bar{q}_1, \bar{q}_2)$ is on the boundary between regions A and B. Now consider a change in one parameter, say, a higher own-elasticity for commodities in group 2. This raises $\bar{q}_2$, moving the point into region A, and it becomes optimal to produce commodities from group 1 alone. However, both (20.53a) and (20.53b) are possible Nash equilibria, and it is therefore possible that *the high elasticity group is produced in equilibrium when the low elasticity one should have been.* If the difference in elasticities is large enough, the point moves into region C, where (20.53b) is no longer a Nash equilibrium. But, owing to the existence of a fixed cost, a significant difference in elasticities is necessary before entry from group 1 commodities threatens to destroy the "wrong" equilibrium. Similar remarks apply to regions B and D.

Next, begin with symmetry once again, and consider a higher c_1 or a_1. This increases $\bar{q}_1$, and moves the point into region B, making it optimal to produce the low-cost group alone while leaving both (20.53a) and (20.53b) as possible equilibria, until the difference in costs is large enough to take the point to region D. The change also moves the boundary between A and C upward, opening up a larger region G, but that is not of significance here.

If both $\bar{q}_1$ and $\bar{q}_2$ are large, each group is threatened by profitable entry from the other, and no Nash equilibrium exists, as in regions E and F. However, the criterion of constrained optimality remains as before. Thus we have a case where it may be necessary to prohibit entry in order to sustain the constrained optimum.

If we combine a case where $c_1 > c_2$ (or $a_1 > a_2$) and $\beta_1 > \beta_2$, i.e., where commodities in group 2 are more elastic and have lower costs, we face a still worse possibility. For the point $(\bar{q}_1, \bar{q}_2)$ may then lie in region G, where only (20.53b) is a possible equilibrium and only (20.53a) is constrained optimum, i.e., the market can produce only a low cost, high demand elasticity group of commodities when a high cost, low demand elasticity group should have been produced.

Very roughly, the point is that although commodities in inelastic demand have the potential for earning revenues in excess of variable costs, they also have significant consumers' surpluses associated with them. Thus it is not immediately obvious whether the market will be biased in favor of them or against them as compared with an optimum. Here we find the latter, and independent findings of Michael Spence in other contexts confirm this. Similar remarks apply to differences in marginal costs.

In the interpretation of the model with heterogenous consumers and social indifference curves, inelastically demanded commodities will be the ones which are intensively desired by a few consumers. Thus we have an "economic" reason why the market will lead to a bias against opera relative to football matches, and a justification for subsidization of the former and a tax on the latter, provided the distribution of income is optimum.

Even when cross elasticities are zero, there may be an incorrect choice of commodities to be produced (relative either to an unconstrained or constrained optimum) as Figure 20.3 illustrates. Figure 20.3 illustrates a case where commodity A has a more elastic demand curve than commodity B; A is produced in monopolistically competitive equilibrium, while B is not. But clearly, it is socially desirable to produce B, since ignoring consumer's surplus it is just marginal. Thus, the commodities that are not produced but ought to be are those with inelastic demands. Indeed, if, as in the usual analysis of monopolistic competition, eliminating one firm shifts the demand curve for the other firms to the right (i.e., increases the demand for other firms), if the consumer surplus from A (at its equilibrium level of output) is less than that from B (i.e., the cross hatched area exceeds the striped area), then constrained Pareto optimality entails restricting the production of the commodity with the more elastic demand.

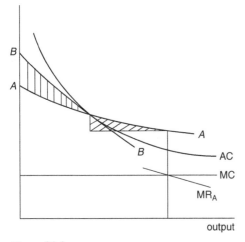

Figure 20.3

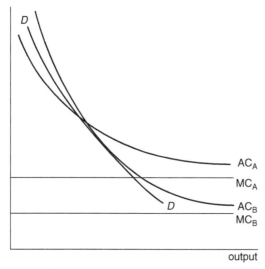

Figure 20.4

A similar analysis applies to commodities with the same demand curves but different cost structures. Commodity *A* is assumed to have the lower fixed cost but the higher marginal cost. Thus, the average cost curves cross but once, as in Figure 20.4. Commodity *A* is produced in monopolistically competitive equilibrium, commodity *B* is not (although it is just at the margin of being produced). But again, observe that *B* should be produced, since there is a large consumer's surplus; indeed, since were it to be produced, *B* would produce at a much higher level than *A*, there is a much larger consumer's surplus. Thus if the government were to forbid the production of *A*, *B* would be viable, and social welfare would increase.

In the comparison between constrained Pareto optimality and the monopolistically competitive equilibrium, we have observed that in the former, we replace some low fixed cost-high marginal cost commodities with high fixed cost-low marginal cost commodities, and we replace some commodities with elastic demands with commodities with inelastic demands.

IV Concluding remarks

We have constructed in this paper some models to study various aspects of the relationship between market and optimal resource allocation in the presence of some nonconvexities. The following general conclusions seem worth pointing out.

The monopoly power, which is a necessary ingredient of markets with nonconvexities, is usually considered to distort resources away from the sector concerned. However, in our analysis monopoly power enables firms to pay fixed costs, and entry cannot be prevented, so the relationship between monopoly power and the direction of market distortion is no longer obvious.

In the central case of a constant elasticity utility function, the market solution was constrained Pareto optimal, regardless of the value of that elasticity (and thus the implied elasticity of the demand functions). With variable elasticities, the bias could go either way, and the direction of the bias depended not on how the elasticity of demand changed, but on how the elasticity of utility changed. We suggested that there was some presumption that the market solution would be characterized by too few firms in the monopolistically competitive sector.

With asymmetric demand and cost conditions we also observed a bias against commodities with inelastic demands and high costs.

The general principle behind these results is that a market solution considers profit at the appropriate margin, while a social optimum takes into account the consumer's surplus. However, applications of this principle come to depend on details of cost and demand functions. We hope that the cases presented here, in conjunction with other studies cited, offer some useful and new insights.

Acknowledgements

Stiglitz's research was supported in part by NSF Grant SOC74-22182 at the Institute for Mathematical Studies in the Social Sciences, Stanford. We are indebted to Michael Spence, to a referee, and the managing editor for comments and suggestions on earlier drafts.

Notes

1 See also the exposition by Michael Spence.
2 A simple exposition is given by Peter Diamond and Daniel McFadden.
3 See p. 21 of John Green.
4 These details and several others are omitted to save space, but can be found in the working paper by the authors, cited in the references.
5 See Edwin Chamberlin, Nicholas Kaldor, and Robert Bishop.
6 See David Starrett.
7 For an alternative approach using partial equilibrium methods, see Spence.

References

R. L. Bishop, "Monopolistic Competition and Welfare Economics," in Robert Kuenne, ed., *Monopolistic Competition Theory*, New York 1967.
E. Chamberlin, "Product Heterogeneity and Public Policy," *Amer. Econ. Rev. Proc.*, May 1950, *40*, 85–92.
P. A. Diamond and D. L. McFadden, "Some Uses of the Expenditure Function In Public Finance," *J. Publ. Econ.*, Feb. 1974, *82*, 1–23.
A. K. Dixit and J. E. Stiglitz, "Monopolistic Competition and Optimum Product Diversity," econ. res. pap. no. 64, Univ. Warwick, England 1975.
H. A. John Green, *Aggregation in Economic Analysis*, Princeton 1964.
H. Hotelling, "Stability in Competition," *Econ. J.*, Mar. 1929, *39*, 41–57.
N. Kaldor, "Market Imperfection and Excess Capacity," *Economica*, Feb. 1934, *2*, 33–50.
K. Lancaster, "Socially Optimal Product Differentiation," *Amer. Econ. Rev.*, Sept. 1975, *65*, 567–85.
A. M. Spence, "Product Selection, Fixed Costs, and Monopolistic Competition," *Rev. Econ. Stud.*, June 1976, *43*, 217–35.
D. A. Starrett, "Principles of Optimal Location in a Large Homogeneous Area," *J. Econ. Theory*, Dec. 1974, *9*, 418–48.
N. H. Stern, "The Optimal Size of Market Areas," *J. Econ. Theory*, Apr. 1972, *4*, 159–73.
J. E. Stiglitz, "Monopolistic Competition in the Capital Market," tech. rep. no. 161, IMSS, Stanford Univ., Feb. 1975.

21 A Disneyland dilemma

Two-part tariffs for a Mickey Mouse monopoly

Walter Y. Oi

A two-part tariff is one in which the consumer must pay a lump sum fee for the right to buy a product. Examples of two-part tariffs are found in the rental of computers and copying machines, country club fees, and the rate structures of some public utilities. The Disneyland economy offers a stylized model of this type of pricing policy. If you are the owner of Disneyland, should you charge high lump sum admission fees and give the rides away, or should you let people into the amusement park for nothing and stick them with high monopolistic prices for the rides? Received theories of monopoly pricing shed little light on this question. The standard model that appears in almost every text assumes that the monopolist sets a single price for his product. The third-degree price discrimination model due to A. C. Pigou still presumes that a single price prevails in each segregated market.[1] Pricing policies that involve tying arrangements (like those examined by M. L. Burstein[2] and W. S. Bowman, Jr.)[3] and the multi-part tariffs of Pigou's first- and second-degree discrimination models come closer to the goal of maximizing the ill-gotten gains of monopoly power. The intricate pricing schemes reported in the antitrust literature are testimony to the fact that the imagination of a greedy entrepreneur outstrips the analytic ability of the economist.

A discriminating two-part tariff is equivalent to Pigou's perfect first-degree price discrimination structure, which globally maximizes monopoly profits by extracting all consumer surpluses. This result was derived by A. Gabor,[4] Burstein,[5] and others. A truly discriminatory two-part tariff is difficult to implement and would probably be illegal. The determination of a nondiscriminatory two-part tariff is presented in Section II. The analysis there implies that in an exceptional case it behooves the monopolist to set price below marginal cost. Finally, attention is directed in Section III to some examples of two-part tariffs and the relationship of this pricing policy to quantity discounts.

I Two-part tariffs and a discriminating monopoly

In the standard textbook model, a monopoly sets price so that marginal cost is equated to marginal revenue. At this price, consumers still enjoy consumer surpluses that are not captured by the firm. Alternative pricing policies, if legal, can always raise monopoly profits above those realized by adopting a single-price tariff.

Suppose that our monopoly is Disneyland, whose product is an amusement park ride. Consumers are assumed to derive no utility from going to the park itself, and all utility derives from consuming a flow of rides X per unit time period. In our model, Disneyland establishes a two-part tariff wherein the consumer must pay a lump sum admission fee of

T dollars for the right to buy rides at a price P per ride. A two-part tariff thus introduces a discontinuity in the consumer's budget equation:

$$XP + Y = M - T \quad [\text{if } X > 0]$$
$$Y = M \quad\quad\quad [\text{if } X = 0]$$

(21.1)

where M is income measured in units of the numeraire, good Y, whose price is set equal to one. The consumer maximizes utility, $U = U(X, Y,)$, subject to this budget constraint. In equilibrium, the consumer who patronizes Disneyland equates the marginal rate of substitution to the price P which forms the variable argument of the two-part tariff:

$$\frac{U_w}{U_v} = P.$$

(21.2a)

A consumer who refuses to pay the admission fee T must specialize his consumption to good Y, thereby attaining a utility index $U_0 = U(X, Y) = U(0, M,)$. This specialization would be optimal if his utility function satisfied the inequality

$$\frac{U_w}{U_v} < P \quad [\text{when } X = 0, Y = M,].$$

(21.2b)

The admission fee is simply a purchase privilege tax that extracts part of the consumer surplus from rides, thereby transferring incomes from consumers to Disneyland.

Under a two-part tariff, the consumer's demand for rides depends on the price per ride P, income M, and the lump sum admission tax T:

$$X = D(P, M - T,).$$

(21.3)

Only the difference $(M - T)$ enters the demand equation because equal increments in income M and the lump sum tax T have no effect on the budget constraint, equation (21.1). Hence, we have

$$\frac{dX}{dM} = -\frac{dX}{dT}.$$

(21.4)

If there is only one consumer, or if all consumers have identical utility functions and incomes, one could easily determine an optimal two-part tariff for the monopoly. Total profits are given by

$$\pi = XP + T - C(X)$$

(21.5)

where $C(X)$ is the total cost function. Differentiation with respect to T yields

$$\frac{d\pi}{dT} = P\left(\frac{dX}{dT}\right) + 1 - c'\left(\frac{dX}{dT}\right) = 1 - (P - c')\left(\frac{dX}{dM}\right)$$

(21.6)

where c' is the marginal cost of producing an additional ride. It can be shown that if Y is a normal good, a rise in T will increase profits.[6] There is, however, a limit to the size of the lump sum tax. An increase in T forces the consumer to move to lower indifference curves as the monopolist extracts more of his consumer surplus. At some critical tax T^*, the consumer would be better off to withdraw from the monopolist's market and specialize his purchases to good Y. The critical tax T^* is simply the consumer surplus enjoyed by the consumer; it can be determined from a constant utility demand curve, $X = \psi(P)$ where utility is held constant at $U_0 = U(0, M,)$. The lower the price per ride P, the larger is the consumer surplus. Hence, the maximum lump sum tax T^* that can be charged by Disneyland while retaining the patronage of the consumer is the larger, the lower is the price P:

$$T^* = \int_P^\infty \psi(P)dP \qquad \frac{dT^*}{dP} = -\psi(P) = -X. \qquad (21.7)$$

In the case of identical consumers, it behooves Disneyland to set T at its maximum value T^*, which in turn depends on P.[7] Hence, profits π can be reduced to a function of only one variable, namely the price per ride P. Differentiating π with respect to P, we get

$$\frac{d\pi}{dP} = X + P\left(\frac{dX}{dP}\right) + \frac{dT^*}{dP} - c'\left(\frac{dX}{dP}\right). \qquad (21.8a)$$

The change in the optimal lump sum admission tax T^* due to a change in P is obtained from equation (21.7). Hence, in equilibrium, the price P satisfies the necessary condition

$$(P - c')\left(\frac{dX}{dP}\right) = 0, \qquad \text{or } P = c' \qquad (21.8b)$$

In equilibrium, the price per ride P (the variable component of a two-part tariff) is equated to marginal cost. The lump sum tax T^* (the fixed component) is then determined by taking the area under the constant utility demand curve $\psi(P)$ above the price P.

In a market of many consumers with different incomes and tastes, a discriminating monopoly could establish an ideal tariff wherein the price per ride P is equated to marginal cost and is the same for all consumers. However, each consumer would be charged a different lump sum admission tax that exhausts his entire consumer surplus.[8] Customers who derive larger surpluses from consuming amusement park rides are thus charged higher purchase privilege taxes. The same global maximum of monopoly profits could have also been achieved by using a Pigovian model of first-degree price discrimination, but a discriminatory two-part tariff provides a simpler scheme for achieving the same end.[9] Although it is discriminatory, this two-part tariff yields Pareto optimality in the sense that the marginal rate of substitution in consumption (U_w/U_v) is equated to that in production $(c'/1)$ where the marginal cost of good Y is assumed equal to one. Admission taxes are nothing more than lump sum transfers of incomes that necessarily put consumers on lower indifference curves. K. J. Arrow has pointed out that there is a unique Pareto optimum for each distribution of income.[10] However, there is nothing in economic theory that allows us unambiguously to compare one Pareto optimum to another.[11]

II Determination of a uniform two-part tariff

The best of all possible worlds for Disneyland would be a discriminating two-part tariff where the price per ride is equated to marginal cost, and each consumer pays a different lump sum tax. The antitrust division would surely take a dim view of this ideal pricing policy and would, in all likelihood, insist upon uniform treatment of all consumers. If Disneyland were legally compelled to charge the same lump sum admission tax T and price per ride P to all customers, how should it proceed to determine an optimum, uniform two-part tariff?[12]

Suppose that there are two consumers whose demands for rides are described by the curves ψ_1 and ψ_2 in Figure 21.1. If the income elasticity is zero, ψ_1 and ψ_2 are constant utility demand curves.[13] If price is equated to marginal cost (here assumed constant at C per ride), the surplus enjoyed by the first consumer is equal to the area of the triangle (ABC), while that of the second individual is $(A'B'C)$. In order to keep both consumers in the market, the lump sum admission tax T cannot exceed the smaller of the two consumer surpluses. No profits are realized from the sale of rides because price is equated to the constant marginal cost C, and all profits derive from admissions:

$$\pi = \pi_1 + \pi_2 = 2(ABC).$$

Profits can, however, be increased by raising price above marginal cost. A rise in P must be accompanied by a fall in T in order to retain the custom of the small consumer. At price P, the first consumer demands $X_1^* = PD$ rides and is willing to pay an admission tax of no more than (ADP). Although the monopolist now obtains some profits from rides, the reduction in the lump sum tax from (ABC) to (ADP) results in a net loss of profits from the small consumer:

$$\Delta\pi_1 = \pi_1^* - \pi_1 = [(ADP)+(PDEC)] - [ABC] = (DBE).$$

Although the second consumer benefits from a lower lump sum tax, he must pay a higher price for rides. The change in profits from sales to the second consumer is thus given by

$$\Delta\pi_2 = \pi_2^* - \pi_2 = [(ADP)+(PD'E'C)] - [ABC] = +(DD'E'B).$$

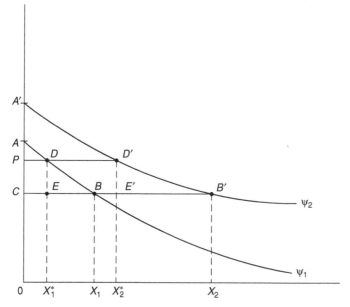

Figure 21.1

Given that the same two-part tariff must be quoted to both consumers, a rise in P accompanied by a fall in T would increase monopoly profits if the area of the quadrangle *(DD'E'B)* exceeded that of the triangle *(DBE)*. Indeed, the optimum price P in this special case of two consumers would maximize the difference in the areas of the quadrangle and triangle.

Before generalizing the model to a market of many consumers, attention is directed to a curious counterexample in which it behooves the monopolist to set price below marginal cost. It is possible to concoct utility functions with the usual convexity properties that would generate the demand curves of Figure 21.2. Income effects are again assumed equal to zero. If price is equated to marginal cost, the uniform lump sum tax cannot exceed the smaller of the two surpluses, which in Figure 21.2 is equal to *(ABC)*. All profits again derive from the tax $T = (ABC)$ from each of the two consumers. Suppose now that price is set below marginal cost, as shown in Figure 21.2. At this price, the first consumer is prepared to pay a tax of *(ADP)* for the right to buy $X_1^* = PD$ rides. The sale of rides at a price below marginal cost leads to a loss, given by the rectangle *(CEDP)*, but part of the loss is offset by a higher lump sum tax. As a result of a lower price P and higher tax T, the net change in profits from the first consumer is given by

$$\Delta \pi_1 = \pi_1^* - \pi_1 = [(ADP) - (CEDP)] - [ABC] = -(BED).$$

By lowering P, the monopolist can raise the lump sum tax to both consumers. If $(A'D'P)$ is greater than (ADP), the second consumer still enjoys some consumer surplus and remains in the market. The increment in the tax *(CBDP)* is, however, larger than the loss in selling

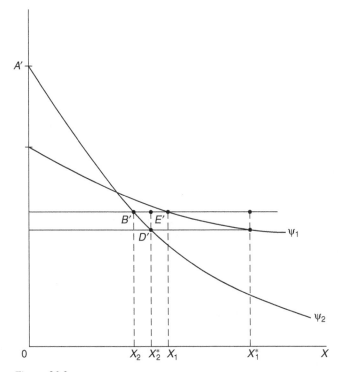

Figure 21.2

PD' rides to the second consumer at a price below marginal cost. More precisely, the net increment in profits from the second consumer is

$$\Delta\pi_2 = \pi_2^* - \pi_2 = [(ADP) - (CE'D'P)] - [ABC] = -(E'BDD').$$

The combined profits at the lower price will be greater if the area $(E'BDD')$ is greater than (BED). In this exceptional case, the first consumer has a smaller consumer surplus even though he demands more rides over the relevant range of prices. The rationale for this exceptional case rests on the fact that the lump sum admission tax can only be raised by lowering the price to retain the custom of the first consumer. Pricing below marginal cost entails a loss in the sale of rides, but this loss is more than offset by the higher admission taxes that could be exacted in this exceptional case.

The establishment of an optimum and uniform tariff in a market of many consumers is complicated by the added problem of determining the number of consumers. It may happen in the two-consumers case that total profits are maximized by forcing the small consumer out of the market. In this event, the solution reverts to that of Section I: namely, set price equal to marginal cost and extract the entire surplus of the remaining large consumer via a lump sum tax. The monopolist's task of arriving at an optimum tariff in a market of many consumers can be divided into two steps.

In the first step, one can imagine that the monopolist tries to arrive at a constrained optimum tariff (consisting of a price per ride P and a lump sum tax T) that maximizes profits subject to the constraint that all N consumers remain in the market. For any price P, the monopolist could raise the lump sum tax to equal the smallest of the N consumer surpluses; this procedure would not only increase profits but would also insure that all N consumers remain in the market. Since all N consumers must be kept in the market in this first step, the tax T must be adjusted whenever the price P is varied. The total profits given by equation 21.9 can thus be reduced to a function of only one parameter, the price per ride P:

$$\pi(N) = XP + NT - C(X) \tag{21.9}$$

where X is the market demand for rides, $T = T_1^*$ is the smallest of the N consumer surpluses, and $C(X)$ is the total cost function. The optimum price for a market of N consumers is then obtained by setting $d\pi/dP$ equal to zero:

$$c' = P\left[1 + \left(\frac{1 - Ns_1}{E}\right)\right] \tag{21.10}$$

where $s_1 = x_1/X$ is the market share demanded by the smallest consumer, and E is the "total" elasticity of demand for rides; details of the mathematical derivation are contained in the Appendix. The price P will exceed marginal cost c' if $(1 - Ns_1) > 0$, meaning that the smallest consumer demands less than $1/N$ of the total market demand. If $(1 - Ns_1) < 0$, the optimum price is below marginal cost; this is precisely the situation in the exceptional case of Figure 21.2. Moreover, the equilibrium price P could occur in an inelastic part of the demand curve since only the term in brackets need be positive.

If the monopolist raises the lump sum tax, the smallest consumer (and possibly others with consumer surpluses only slightly above $T = T_1^*$) would elect to do without the monopolist's product. Having thus decided to contract the number of consumers, the monopolist proceeds to determine a new uniform tariff having a higher lump sum tax and, in most instances, a lower price per ride.[14] One can thus derive a uniform tariff that maximizes profits for any number of consumers n. To ascertain if the expulsion of some consumers is desirable, we need only examine the behavior of constrained monopoly profits, $\pi(n)$, as n is varied.

In the second step, total profits $\pi(n)$ is decomposed into profits from lump sum admission taxes, $\pi_A = nT$, and profits from the sale of rides, $\pi_s = (P - c)X$, where marginal cost is assumed to be constant.[15] A rise in T reduces the number of consumers n who purchase the monopolist's product, and the change in π_A depends on the responsiveness of n to variations in T. The elasticity of the number of consumers with respect to the lump sum tax is ultimately determined by the distribution of consumer surpluses. Plausible assumptions about that distribution would generate a π_A function like the one depicted in Figure 21.3.[16]

A monopolist can obviously limit the size of his market by controlling the magnitude of the tax T. With fewer consumers, it pays to lower the price per ride P in order to capture the larger surpluses of those consumers who continue to buy his product. Consequently, profits from sales, $\pi_s = (P - c)X$, are likely to fall as the size of the market is contracted since both the profit margin $(P - c)$ and the market demand for rides X are likely to decline. In the limit, when only one customer is retained in the market, price is equated to marginal cost, and all profits derive from the lump sum tax. Hence, the π_s function is a monotonically increasing function of the number of consumers n as shown in Figure 21.3.

The optimum and uniform two-part tariff that globally maximizes profits is attained when

$$\frac{d\pi(n)}{dn} = \frac{d\pi_A}{dn} + \frac{d\pi_s}{dn} = 0. \tag{21.11}$$

That optimum is achieved by restricting the market to n' consumers, as shown in Figure 21.3. Recall that at each point on the π_A and π_s curves, the uniform tariff $(P, T,)$ is chosen to maximize profits for a market of precisely n consumers. The optimum number of consumers n' is obtained in the downward sloping portion of the π_A curve where a rise in T would raise profits from admissions even though some consumers would be forced out of the market.

The implementation of a uniform two-part tariff requires considerably more information. The price elasticity of demand ε is the only information needed by a monopoly that adopts

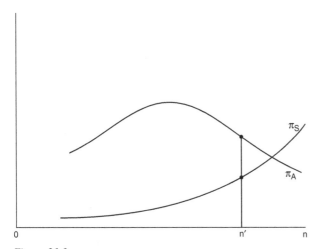

Figure 21.3

the single-price tariff of the textbook model in which marginal revenue is equated to marginal cost. A two-part tariff is a feasible alternative provided that there are impediments to the resale of the product. The monopolist could proceed on a trial and error basis by initially establishing a feasible two-part tariff. The lump sum tax could be raised to see if it drives some consumers out of the market. He could then iterate on the price P to determine if profits are higher or lower. In the final equilibrium, the price per ride exceeds marginal cost but would be lower than the price implied by a textbook, single-price model. However, those customers who purchase the monopolist's product and who pay the lump sum purchase privilege tax would spend a larger fraction of their budget, $(XP + T)/M$, on the good.

The requirement that a uniform tariff must be quoted to all consumers clearly reduces monopoly profits below the level attainable under a discriminating two-part tariff. The welfare implications of a uniform tariff are evident from the two-consumer case of Figure 21.1. The individual with the smallest consumer surplus is fully exploited; he derives no consumer surplus because he is forced to an indifference curve corresponding to a bundle containing none of good X. The other consumer would, however, prefer the uniform tariff to the discriminating tariff that appropriates the consumer surplus via the lump sum tax. In all but the exceptional case of Figure 21.2, price P will exceed marginal cost. Consequently, the size of the consumer surplus that is conceptually amenable to appropriation is smaller than the lump sum tax T_j^* in the tariff of Section I where price was equated to marginal cost.

III Applications of two-part tariffs

A two-part tariff wherein the monopolist exacts a lump sum tax for the right to buy his product can surely increase profits. Yet, this type of pricing policy is rarely observed. That apparent oversight on the part of greedy monopolists can partially be explained by an inability to prevent resale. If transaction costs were low, one customer could pay the lump sum tax and purchase large quantities for resale to other consumers. Resale is precluded in our Disneyland example, where the consumer himself must be physically present to consume the product.[17] In other instances, high transaction costs or freight expenses may provide the requisite impediments preventing resale. I suspect that the latter type of barrier permits firms in the computer and copying machine industries to establish and enforce two-part tariffs.

The pricing policy adopted by IBM can be interpreted as a two-part tariff. The lessee is obliged to pay a lump sum monthly rental of T dollars for the right to buy machine time. If each lessee could be charged a different rental, IBM could behave like the discriminating monopoly of Section I. The price per hour of machine time P would be equated to marginal cost, and all surpluses could be captured by a discriminatory structure of rental charges. If IBM were compelled to quote a uniform tariff, the price per machine hour would exceed marginal cost, but the discrepancy between price and marginal cost would be smaller than that under the single-price tariff of the textbook model.[18]

The IBM price structure introduces an additional twist to a two-part tariff. Every lessee who pays the lump sum rental is entitled to demand up to X^* hours of machine time at no additional charge. If, however, more than X^* hours are demanded, there is a price k per additional hour. The large customers are thus saddled by a volume surcharge. To analyze the rationale for this pricing policy, it is again convenient to deal with two consumers and to neglect income effects. The demand curves of the two consumers are presented in Figure 21.4. At a zero price for machine time, the first customer, ψ_1, is prepared to pay up to $T_1^* = 0AB$ for the right to use IBM equipment. He does not demand his allotment of X^*

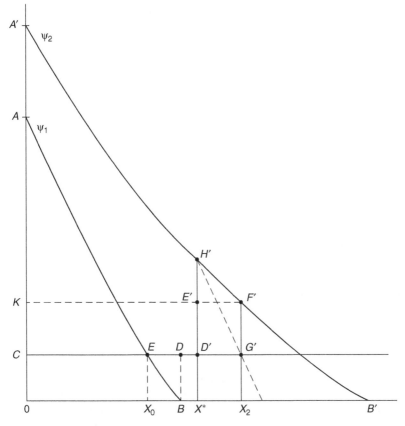

Figure 21.4

hours, but whatever he demands results in a loss from sales so long as there is a positive marginal cost c for machine use. If the monthly rental is set to capture the entire surplus of the small consumer given the zero price, $T = T_1^* = (OAB)$, the profits from this customer are given by

$$\pi_1 = (OAB) - (OCDB).$$

The second customer demands more than X^* hours; his precise demand depends on the surcharge rate k. If the surcharge rate were as high as X^*H, he would be content to pay the monthly rental, $T = (OAB)$, and demand his allotment of X^* hours. At a surcharge rate k, he would demand X_2 hours of machine time and his total outlay for IBM equipment would be $(OAB) + k(X_2 - X^*)$. Although the first X^* hours entail a loss (given a positive marginal cost), the last $(X_2 - X^*)$ hours contribute to IBM's profits. Hence, profit from the second customer is seen to be

$$\pi_2 = (OAB) - (OCD'X^*) + (D'E'F'G').$$

A volume surcharge can thus be interpreted as a device for recapturing part of the larger surplus enjoyed by the second customer. This pricing policy is an optimum only under very special conditions that include (a) the marginal cost of machine time is zero,[19] (b) the spike X^* at which the surcharge rate becomes effective is precisely equal to the maximum demand by the small customer, (c) there is virtually no resale of computer time,[20] and (d) the surcharge rate k is determined in a manner analogous to a single price monopoly tariff.[21] In a market of many consumers, the analytic task of fixing three parameters (a lump sum rental T, the spike X^*, and the surcharge rate k) becomes extremely complicated. However, the principle that a volume surcharge recaptures part of the larger surpluses is still retained.[22]

Pricing policies that involve volume discounts can be analyzed in the context of two-part tariffs. Public utilities, for example, often quote tariffs that embody marginal price discounts. The consumer pays a price P_1 for demands up to X^* units and a lower follow-on price P_2 for demands in excess of X^* units.[23] This type of tariff produces a kink in the consumer's budget constraint:

$$X P_1 + Y = M \qquad \text{[if } 0 < X < X^*\text{]}, \qquad (21.12a)$$

$$X^* P_1 + (X - X^*) P_2 + Y = M \quad \text{[if } X > X^*\text{]}. \qquad (21.12b)$$

For those consumers who have sufficiently large demands to obtain the lower follow-on price, a marginal price discount is equivalent to a two-part tariff. Equation 21.12b can be written

$$X P_2 + Y = M - T \qquad \text{[where } T = X^*(P_1 - P_2), \text{]}. \qquad (21.12c)$$

In a sense, the public utility charges a lump sum purchase privilege tax of $T = X^*(P_1 - P_2)$ for the right to buy X at a price of P_2. This type of quantity discount is thus seen to be a way of appropriating part of the consumer surpluses of large customers, thereby raising monopoly profits.[24] Indeed, a marginal price discount may be preferable to a two-part tariff because it enables the monopolist to retain the custom of those consumers with small demands, $(X < X^*)$.

A second type of volume discount is described by a schedule of average prices. In this case, the consumer still pays a price P_1 for the first block of X^* units. If, however, he demands more than X^* per unit time period, a lower price P_2 applies to all units including the first block of X^* units. The budget constraint exhibits a discontinuity at $X = X^*$, and the consumer who demands enough to get the lower price P_2 is rewarded by getting an implicit rebate of $X^*(P_1 - P_2)$ dollars.[25] In a sense, the firm fails to capture part of the consumer surplus that it could have appropriated by adopting a marginal price discount. It is difficult to explain why some firms have adopted average price discounts with their implicit rebates to large customers, but a detailed analysis of the question is beyond the scope of the present paper.

In summary, the standard monopoly model assumes that the firm establishes a single price that equates marginal revenue to marginal cost. Alternative and more complicated pricing strategies can always increase monopoly profits. Buchanan and Gabor examined the rationale for quantity discounts and block tariffs, while Bowman and Burstein showed that tying arrangements raise profits by appropriating part of the consumer surplus. Those studies fail, however, to come to grips with the actual implementation of these pricing policies and the nature of the equilibrium that would prevail under different pricing policies.[26] In this paper, I have directed attention to a class of pricing policies described by two-part tariffs. A discriminatory two-part tariff, in which price is equated to marginal cost and all consumer surpluses are appropriated by lump sum taxes, is the best of all pricing strategies for a profit-maximizing monopoly. If, however, a uniform tariff must be quoted to all customers, the analysis of Section II outlines how a firm would proceed to determine the parameters of an optimum and uniform two-part tariff. Aside from income redistribution effects, a uniform two-part tariff is preferable to a single monopoly price since the former leads to a smaller discrepancy between marginal rates of substitution in consumption and production. Finally, the analysis of two-part tariffs provides an illuminating interpretation of the rationale for the IBM pricing policy and for volume discounts.

APPENDIX: MATHEMATICAL DERIVATION OF A UNIFORM TWO-PART TARIFF

The task of determining an optimum and uniform two-part tariff in a market of many consumers can be separated into two steps. First, an optimum tariff is determined subject to the constraint that the monopoly retains the patronage of N consumers. It is then possible to derive the constrained monopoly profits corresponding to the optimum tariff for N consumers where N can be varied. The second step then examines how the constrained monopoly profits behave as one varies the number of consumers who are retained in the market.

Suppose initially that the monopoly establishes a feasible tariff (consisting of a price P and lump sum tax T) that insures that all N consumers remain in the market for his product. The profits from this feasible tariff are given by

$$\pi = XP + NT - C(X) \qquad \left[X = \sum_{j=1}^{N} x_j \right]. \qquad (21.A1)$$

Let $\psi_j(P)$ describe the constant utility demand curve of the jth consumer where the utility index is constant for a consumption bundle including *none* of good X. The surplus realized by the jth consumer, T_j^*, is a function of the price P:

$$T_j^* = \int_P^\infty \psi_j(P) dP. \qquad (21.A2)$$

For any price P, profits can be increased by setting the lump sum tax T equal to the smallest of the N consumer surpluses that is assigned to the first consumer; that is, $T = T_1^*$. The demand for rides by the smallest consumer is thus determined by his constant utility demand, $x_1 = \psi_1(P)$. Since the remaining $N - 1$ consumers still enjoy some consumer surplus, their demands for rides depend on the price P and net incomes $(M_j - T)$:

$$x_j = D_j(P, M_j - T,) \qquad [j = 2, 3, \ldots, N]. \qquad (21.A3)$$

In this first step, it is assumed that all N consumers must be kept in the market. Consequently, the tax T must be adjusted whenever the price P is varied in order to keep the smallest consumer in the market. The requisite adjustment is given by equation (21.7) as $(dT/dP) = -x_1$. In this manner, total profits, equation (21.A1), can be reduced to a function of only one parameter, the price per ride P. Setting $(d\pi/dP)$ equal to zero, we get the equilibrium condition for an optimum price P given a market of N consumers:

$$c' = P\left[1 + \left(\frac{1 - Ns_1}{E}\right)\right] \tag{21.A4}$$

where E is the "total" price elasticity of the market demand for rides;

$$E = \left(\frac{P}{X}\right)\left[\sum_{j=1}^{N}\left(\frac{dx_j}{dP}\right) + x_1 \sum_{j=2}^{N}\left(\frac{dx_j}{dM_j}\right)\right] = \epsilon + s_1 \sum_{j=2}^{N} \lambda_j \mu_j \tag{21.A5}$$

where $s_1 = x_1/X$ is the smallest consumer's share of the market demand, $\lambda_j = x_j P/M_j$ represents the budget share devoted to variable outlays for rides, and μ_j is the income elasticity of demand for rides.[27] The optimum price per ride is thus set to satisfy equation (21.A4); by substituting this optimum price in equation (21.A2) for the smallest consumer ($j = 1$), we get the optimum lump sum tax $T = T_1^*$.

This procedure could conceptually be repeated for any number of consumers, n, thereby obtaining an optimum tariff and constrained maximum monopoly profits $\pi(n)$ for a market of n consumers.

Up to now, we have shown how a monopolist can determine an optimum tariff $(P, T,)$ which yields a constrained maximum profit $\pi(N)$ when precisely N consumers are retained in the market. Attention is next directed to the behavior of $\pi(N)$ as the number of consumers N is varied. A rise in T would force the smallest consumer out of the market since $T = T_1^*$ appropriated the smallest of the N consumer surpluses. Having thus decided to ignore the smallest consumer, the monopolist establishes a new price $(P + \Delta P)$, which would maximize profits for a market of $N - 1$ consumers. The equilibrium condition (21.A4) is thus revised to

$$c = (P + \Delta P)\left[1 + \left(\frac{1 - (N - 1)s_2}{E'}\right)\right] \tag{21.A6}$$

where c is marginal cost, s_2 is the market share demanded by the second smallest consumer, and E' is the "total" price elasticity after excluding the smallest consumer. The new lump sum tax, $(T + \Delta T)$, is again set to exhaust the smallest of the remaining surpluses, here assigned to individual 2:

$$\Delta T = \int_P^\infty [\psi_2(P) - \psi_1(P)]dP + \int_{P+\Delta P}^P \psi_2(P)dP. \tag{21.A7}$$

The second integral on the right is the adjustment in the lump sum tax due to a change in the price per ride and can be approximated by $-x_2\Delta P$; consult equation (21.A2) above. If the value of the first integral is denoted by dT, equation (21.A7) can be written

$$\Delta T = dT - x_2\Delta P. \tag{21.A8}$$

If marginal cost is constant, the constrained maximum profits for markets of N and $N-1$ consumers can be written

$$\pi(N)=(P-c)X+NT \tag{21.A9a}$$
$$\pi(N-1)=(P+\Delta P-c)(X+\Delta X)+(N-1)[T+dT-x_2\Delta P] \tag{21.A9b}$$

where ΔX is the change in the market demand for rides.

The change in profits from excluding the smallest consumer (accompanied by the establishment of a new optimum, uniform tariff) can conveniently be separated into changes in profits from admissions $d\pi_A$ and profits from sale of rides $d\pi_s$:

$$d\pi=\pi(N)-\pi(N-1)=d\pi_A+d\pi_s \tag{21.A10a}$$

where

$$d\pi_A=T-(N-1)dT \tag{21.A10b}$$
$$d\pi_s=-[(P-c)\Delta X+(X-(N-1)x_2)\Delta P+\Delta X\Delta P]. \tag{21.A10c}$$

Notice that the revision in the lump sum tax due to a change in the price per ride has been included with the change in profits from sales.

The monopolist limits the number of consumers N by raising the admission tax, thereby inducing some consumer to do without his product. In the discrete case of equation (21.A10b), exclusion of the smallest consumer would raise profits from admissions if

$$dT > \frac{T}{N-1}.$$

If N is large, one can appeal to a continuous approximation; differentiation of $\pi_A=NT$ with respect to N yields

$$\frac{d\pi_A}{dN}=T+N\left(\frac{dT}{dN}\right)=T\left[1+\frac{1}{\eta}\right]$$

$$\text{where }\eta=\left(\frac{T}{N}\right)\left(\frac{dN}{dT}\right). \tag{21.A11}$$

For a fixed marginal price per ride P, the number of consumers N is inversely related to the size of the lump sum tax T. Profits from admissions π_A would fall as N is increased (by reducing T) if $-1<\eta<0$, and would rise if $\eta<-1$. The value of η depends on the distribution of consumer surpluses T_j^*. Plausible assumptions about that distribution would generate a π_A function like that depicted in Figure 21.3.[28]

When individuals with small consumer surpluses are forced out of the market, it behooves the monopoly to establish a new optimum price $(P+\Delta P)$ that satisfies equation (21.A6) given the smaller number of consumers. In general, the optimum price will be lowered as the size of the market is contracted.[29] Profits from the sale of rides π_s will typically fall as the number of consumers is reduced; i.e., $d\pi_s/dN>0$. In the limit, when only one consumer is retained in the market, price would be equated to marginal cost, and profits from sales is a minimum. The global maximum, subject to the contraint that the same two-part tariff is quoted to all customers, is thus attained when $d\pi = d\pi_A + d\pi_s = 0$, and this will occur at the point n' shown in Figure 21.3.[30]

Acknowledgment

I would like to thank my colleagues J. Ferguson, D. F. Gordon, and R. Jackson for their comments on an earlier draft of this paper. The comments by the referee for this article provided a very cogent review and pointed out two serious errors. Financial assistance from the Center for Research in Government Policy and Business is gratefully acknowledged.

Notes

1 A. C. Pigou, *The Economics of Welfare* (London: MacMillan and Co., 1960). See especially Ch. 17, pp. 275–89.
2 M. L. Burstein, "The Economics of Tie-in Sales," *Review of Economics and Statistics*, Vol. 42 (Feb. 1960), pp. 68–73.
3 W. S. Bowman, Jr., "Tying Arrangements and the Leverage Problem," *Yale Law Journal*, Vol. 67 (Nov. 1957), pp. 19–36.
4 A. Gabor, "A Note on Block Tariffs," *Review of Economic Studies*, Vol. 23 (1955), pp. 32–41.
5 *Op. cit.*
6 From the budget constraint, equation (21.1), we have

$$P\left(\frac{dX}{dM}\right) + \left(\frac{dY}{dM}\right) = 1, \qquad \frac{dY}{dM} = 1 - P\left(\frac{dX}{dM}\right).$$

Substitution of this expression into equation (21.6) yields

$$\frac{d\pi}{dT} = \frac{dY}{dM} + c'\left(\frac{dX}{dM}\right).$$

A rising or constant marginal cost curve implies that $c' \geq 0$. In this event, if Y is a normal good meaning $(dY/dM) > 0$, then $d\pi/dT$ will also be positive.
7 The maximum revenue, $R = XP + T^*$, that can be extracted from the consumer increases as P is lowered. This obvious result shows that the "all or none" demand curve defined by M. Friedman (*Price Theory: A Provisional Text*, Chicago: Aldine Publishing Co., 1965, p. 15) is relatively elastic over its entire range because consumer surplus is a monotonically increasing function of the amount consumed.
8 Let $x_j = \psi_j(P)$ be the constant utility demand curve of the jth consumer where utility is constant at U_0, the index corresponding to a consumption bundle containing no rides X. Summation of these constant utility demand curves yields the pertinent market demand curve whose intersection with the marginal cost curve establishes the optimum price per ride P. Having thus fixed P, the optimum lump sum tax T_j^* for the jth consumer is calculated from equation (21.7).
9 The theorem that monopoly profits are truly maximized when the monopolist can extract all consumer surpluses was derived earlier by Gabor, op. cit., P. E. Watts, "Block Tariffs: A Comment," *Review of Economic Studies*, Vol. 23 (1955), pp. 42–45, and Burstein, *op. cit.* In Pigou's language, first-degree price discrimination occurs when a different price is charged for each additional unit demanded by a consumer. The monopolist thus strives to climb down a constant utility demand curve. Implementation of first-degree price discrimination entails the establishment of a complete price-quantity schedule for each consumer. It is evident from the preceding analysis that the same appropriation of consumer surplus could be achieved with a two-part tariff. This equivalence was also derived by Gabor.
10 K. J. Arrow, "Uncertainty and the Welfare Implications of Medical Care," *American Economic Review*, Vol. 53 (Dec. 1963), pp. 941–73.

11 This point deserves further amplification. For any given income distribution A, there is a unique Pareto optimum in which all marginal rates of substitution in consumption are equated to those in production. If, however, another income distribution B applied, there is a corresponding unique, and possibly different, Pareto optimum. Economic theory has very little to say about which income distribution, A or B, is to be preferred. Arrow applied this principle to his analysis of the economics of medical care.

12 Watts recognized the practical problem of quoting a uniform tariff to all consumers, but does not offer a solution.

13 A zero income elasticity means that the demand curve in the $(X, P,)$ plane is invariant to changes in income M or lump sum tax T. J. R. Hicks has shown that in this case the consumer surplus is equal to the area under the demand curve and above the price line (*Value and Capital*, London:, The Clarendon Press, 1961).

14 The lump sum tax is raised to force out individuals with small consumer surpluses. The price P is then revised to satisfy equation (21.10) for a market with fewer consumers. If $(1 - Ns_1) > 0$, as it usually will be, it generally pays the monopolist to lower P when there are fewer consumers in the market.

15 Strictly speaking, π_s includes both the direct profits from selling rides and indirect profits deriving from higher lump sum taxes due to lower prices for rides as the number of consumers is contracted. This point is amplified in the Appendix.

16 Differentiation of $\pi_A = nT$ with respect to n yields

$$\frac{d\pi_A}{dn} = T + n\left(\frac{dT}{dn}\right).$$

Let $f(T)$ denote the frequency density of the number of consumers who enjoy a surplus of T dollars. The number of consumers n who remain in the market is the integral of $f(T)$ to the quoted lump sum tax T. Hence, $(dT/dn) = -1/f(T)$. If $f(T)$ is a unimodal density function, π_A will usually attain a single maximum like the curve shown in Figure 21.3. If, however, $f(T)$ is bimodal, it is possible (though unlikely) that π_A could have two or more local maxima. A clue to the possible shape of the $f(T)$ function is provided by the frequency distribution of sales because x_j would tend to be positively correlated with the size of the consumer surplus.

17 This is just another way of saying that the transaction cost of reselling an amusement park ride is prohibitively high. Most service industries meet this requirement. Night clubs, golf courses, barbers, and bowling alleys can easily prevent resale of their products. Indeed, our theory suggests that a private country club should adopt a two-part tariff consisting of annual membership dues T plus additional prices P per round of golf or per drink. Moreover, the optimum uniform tariff derived in this paper implies that the price per round of golf should be lower at a private club than at a public course of comparable quality even though the total outlay $(XP + T)$ is higher for a member of a private country club. It is also of interest to note that the annual lump sum tax at the University of Rochester faculty club is higher for a full professor than for an assistant professor, who has less income and presumably derives less consumer surplus from the goods vended at the club. Differential lump sum membership dues are, indeed, rational for a profit-maximizing monopoly.

18 The ratio of marginal cost to price, c'/P, is frequently used as a measure of monopoly power. Under a discriminatory two-part tariff, c'/P is equal to unity, implying the complete absence of monopoly power. Yet, in this case, monopoly profits are at an absolute maximum since the monopolist appropriates all consumer surpluses. In short, the ratio of marginal cost to price is *not* a very good measure of monopoly power.

19 It is argued that a volume surcharge is required to pay for the higher maintenance costs resulting from more intensive machine use. The initial allotment X^* corresponded to approximately one shift per week. Maintenance is, however, only a small part of the cost of high-speed computers. If depreciation is mainly a function of use rather than calendar time, the capital cost can properly be allocated to machine hours. On the other hand, if obsolescence is dominant (as it appears to be in the light of rapid technical change), the capital cost would be unrelated to use, and the assumption of zero marginal cost may not be far from the mark, at least for computers.

20 Recent reductions in telephone rates have reduced transaction costs, thereby encouraging more resale via time-sharing arrangements.

21 In the example of Figure 21.4, only the second customer demands additional machine time. In determining an optimum surcharge rate k, the demand curve ψ_2 is translated so that X^* is taken as the origin. The marginal revenue of the truncated demand curve to the right of X^* can be constructed and is depicted by the dashed line in Figure 21.4. The intersection of this constructed marginal revenue with marginal cost then determines the optimum surcharge rate k.

22 According to an alternative hypothesis, the lump sum rental T is a charge for the amortization of the capital cost, while the surcharge reflects the marginal cost of machine time beyond X^* hours. The latter hypothesis suggests that the IBM pricing policy may simply be a competitive price structure. A careful study of the marginal cost of machine time together with the profits of the lessor would enable us to distinguish between the discrimination theory developed in this paper and the amortization argument set forth in this note.

23 In practice, marginal price discount schedules may identify several blocks with their accompanying prices. The essential features of the analysis can, however, be derived in the simplest case involving a single spike at X^* units.

24 To the best of my knowledge, J. M. Buchanan was the first to recognize the point that quantity discounts are devices for appropriating part of the consumer surplus ("The Theory of Monopolistic Quantity Discounts," *Review of Economic Studies*, Vol. 20 (1953), pp. 199–208). This is surely correct, but it has received little attention in the antitrust literature. The equivalence of a two-part tariff and a schedule of marginal prices was demonstrated by Gabor *(op. cit.)*. One can interpret a two-part tariff as a high price T for the first unit and a lower marginal price P for additional units. It should be noticed that the corner of the first block does not have to lie inside of the constant money income demand curve, as was erroneously argued by K. E. Boulding (*Economic Analysis*, New York: Harper and Bros., 1948, p. 543). This is clear if one recalls that the lump sum tax T can be interpreted as the price for a first block of one unit, and T can surely exceed the demand price for precisely one unit of X.

25 Advertising rates, wholesale price schedules, and freight tariffs often involve average price discounts. An interesting implication of price structures with average price discounts is that one should *never* observe demands (sales) in the interval, $\delta X^* < X < X^*$, where $\delta = P_2/P_1$ is the relative price discount. The customer's outlays are $X P_1$ for $X < X^*$, and $X P_2$ for $X > X^*$. Since he can always buy the minimum quantity X^* to get the lower price, he should never buy an amount such that $X P_1 \geqq X^* P_2$ or $X > \delta X^*$, where $\delta = P_2/P_1$. The consumer who would have demanded an amount in the interval, $\delta X^* < X < X^*$, would thus be induced to increase his demand to X^* in order to obtain the lower price. Consequently, the firm would produce a concentration of demands at or slightly above the spike X^*, and it is this concentration of sales that offers the most plausible explanation for average price discounts.

26 Little attention has been devoted to the problem of implementing the pricing policies. In the Burstein model, the monopoly must determine which goods are to be tied to the monopolized tying good as well as the prices of tying and tied goods. Buchanan ("Peak Loads and Efficient Pricing: Comment," this *Journal*, Vol. 80 (Aug. 1966), pp. 463–71) and Gabor ("Peak Loads and Efficient Pricing: Further Comment," this *Journal*, Vol. 80 (Aug. 1966), pp. 472–80) demonstrated that if a public utility adopts marginal price discount schedules (as many actually do) one cannot determine a unique Pareto optimum capacity in the peak load pricing problem. Given the equivalence of two-part tariffs and marginal price discounts, it is conceptually possible to determine a uniform two-part tariff that would maximize the difference between social benefits and costs by solving for the three parameters of a two-part tariff, a price P, a lump sum tax T, and an optimum number of consumers.

27 In differentiating profits π with respect to P, it must be remembered that the market demand X is a function of P and T via equation 21.A3. Hence, we have

$$\frac{d\pi}{dP} = X + P\left[\frac{dX}{dP} + \left(\frac{dX}{dT}\right)\left(\frac{dT}{dP}\right)\right] + N\left(\frac{dT}{dP}\right) - c'\left[\frac{dX}{dP} + \left(\frac{dX}{dT}\right)\left(\frac{dT}{dP}\right)\right].$$

Recall that $(dT/dP) = -x_1$ and that $(dx_j/dT) = -(dx_j/dM_j)$. Thus, we get

$$\left(\frac{dX}{dT}\right)\left(\frac{dT}{dP}\right) = x_1 \sum_{j=2}^{N}\left(\frac{dx_j}{dM_j}\right), \quad \frac{dX}{dP} = \sum_{j=1}^{N}\left(\frac{dx_j}{dP}\right).$$

Collecting terms, we obtain

$$\frac{d\pi}{dP} = (X - x_1 N) + (P - c') \left[\sum_{j=1}^{N} \left(\frac{dx_j}{dP} \right) + x_1 \sum_{j=2}^{N} \left(\frac{dx_j}{dM_j} \right) \right].$$

The "total" price elasticity of the market demand E is defined as follows:

$$E = \left(\frac{P}{X} \right) \left[\sum \left(\frac{dx_j}{dP} \right) + x_1 \sum \left(\frac{dx_j}{dM_j} \right) \right]:$$

The "total" price elasticity thus incorporates the induced change in demand for rides resulting from the requisite adjustment in T when P is varied. If we substitute, we get

$$\frac{d\pi}{dP} = X(1 - s_1 N) + (P - c') \left[\frac{XE}{P} \right].$$

Setting $d\pi/dP$ equal to zero thus yields equation (21.A4). In the expression for the "total" price elasticity, the term ϵ represents the price elasticity unadjusted for the induced effect of changes in T. More precisely,

$$\varepsilon = \left(\frac{P}{X} \right) \sum \left(\frac{dx_j}{dP} \right).$$

28 The shape of the π_A function is determined by the frequency density function of consumer surpluses. In an earlier draft (available upon request from the author), I have developed this relationship. I show there that if the frequency density is a rectangular distribution, the π_A function is a parabola. Although local maxima for the π_A function are possible, they are unlikely.

29 The qualification "in general" is necessitated because different configurations of individual demands could produce situations in which elimination of some consumers would prompt the monopolist to raise P. An example of such a situation is provided by the exceptional case of Figure 21.2, in which the individual with the smaller consumer surplus demands more rides. If the market share demanded by the smallest consumer is less than $1/N$ (i.e., the demand for rides by the smallest consumer $x_1 < X/N$) profits would be maximized by lowering the price P when the smallest consumer is excluded. The mathematical proof of this is contained in the earlier draft of this paper.

30 The anonymous referee's comments on the earlier draft of this paper correctly pointed out that there may not be a unique maximum because the ordering of individuals by the size of consumer surpluses is not invariant to the price per ride. In the example of Figure 21.2, it is possible that the two demand curves intersect twice. I believe, however, that these are pathological cases (including the example of Figure 21.2), and as such should not be viewed as plausible counterexamples.

22 Commodity bundling and the burden of monopoly

William James Adams and Janet L. Yellen

I Introduction

Firms often sell their goods in packages: sporting and cultural organizations offer season tickets; restaurants provide complete dinners; banks offer checking, safe deposit, and travelers' check services for a single fee; and garment manufacturers sell their retailers clothing grab bags comprised of assorted styles, sizes, and colors. We shall refer to the practice of package selling as commodity bundling. A firm that sells goods only in package form has adopted a *pure* bundling strategy. A firm that sells the same goods separately as well as in packages has adopted a *mixed* bundling strategy.

Commodity bundles sometimes include goods that cannot be sold separately in the market place. For example, an automobile can be interpreted as a package of luxury and transport services. The transport services could be offered without luxury (in the form of a stripped down car), but luxury must be sold in conjunction with motive power. Similarly, aspirin can be sold with or without a well-known brand name, but the brand name cannot be sold alone. In general, firms offering several incarnations of the same product, differing in either real or perceived quality, practice mixed bundling.

Commodity bundling also occurs when firms sell the same physical commodity in different container sizes. For example, toothpaste, detergent, and cereal are sold in small and large packages. In such cases, a bundle consists of multiple units[1] of the same commodity. Offering both sizes constitutes mixed bundling, while offering just the large size constitutes pure bundling.[2]

Why is commodity bundling such a prevalent marketing strategy? Some observers focus on the cost savings in production, transactions, and information associated with package selling.[3] Others dwell on the complementarity in consumption of bundle components. We shall demonstrate that commodity bundling can be profitable even when these motivations are absent. In particular, we show that the profitability of commodity bundling can stem from its ability to sort customers into groups with different reservation price characteristics, and hence to extract consumer surplus.[4] We choose to emphasize this rationale for commodity bundling for several reasons.

First, in the real world firms cannot always resort to conventional forms of price discrimination in order to extract consumer surplus: reservation prices of specific customers are typically unknown; even if they were known, laws like the Robinson-Patman Act might prevent a seller from using them in an overtly discriminatory scheme. Commodity bundling can overcome these two practical problems associated with conventional price discrimination. We demonstrate this in Section II. In some circumstances, bundling is just as profitable as Pigouvian price discrimination of the first degree. In most circumstances, it is more profitable than simple monopolypricing.[5]

Second, bundling motivated by price discrimination has distinctive normative consequences. On the one hand, bundling could lead monopolists to oversupply as well as undersupply specific commodities: equilibrium output could fall on *either* side of ideal output. On the other hand, bundling could lead monopolists to sell whatever output is produced to the wrong people, in the sense that potential gains from trade among cusumers would exist in equilibrium. Hence the conditions for distributive efficiency as well as those for allocative efficiency might be violated. Neither Pigouvian first-degree price discrimination nor simple monopoly pricing results in either of these problems. These findings are discussed in Section III.

Third, the existence of commodity bundling seriously complicates public appraisal of monopoly, for it impairs the validity of major tools of applied welfare economics, such as consumer-producer surplus analysis and hedonic price indices. Finally, prohibition of bundling in monopolistic markets, without elimination of monopoly, can either increase or decrease the deadweight loss arising in the relevant markets. This reinforces the desirability of a structural, as opposed to conduct, attack on market power. We discuss these implications of commodity bundling in Section IV.

II The model: positive properties

Consider a model with the following characteristics. Technology is such that Al holds.

A1 (Technology) The marginal cost of supplying each good separately (c_1, c_2) is invariant with respect to output, and the marginal cost of supplying the two goods in a bundle is the sum of the component costs ($c_B = c_1 + c_2$). There are no fixed costs.
   Tastes are such that for all individuals A2 and A3 hold.
A2 (Indivisibility) The marginal utility of a second unit of either commodity is zero.
A3 (Independence) The reservation price for a package comprised of one unit of each commodity (r_B) is equal to the sum of their separate reservation prices (r_1, r_2).[6]

By assumption, therefore, this model excludes both economies in the bundling process and complementarity in consumption. If bundling is found to be profitable, it cannot be explained by these phenomena.

If the monopolist knows the reservation price of each consumer for each commodity, his profit-maximizing strategy is simply Pigouvian first-degree price discrimination with respect to each commodity separately. If the monopolist knows only the distribution of reservation prices in the population, however, or if he is legally prevented from engaging in pure price discrimination, then his ideal pricing strategy is more difficult to establish. Three options open to him are as follows.

1 Set the single price on each commodity separately, (p_1^*, p_2^*), which yields the greatest profits. We call this a pure components strategy, or simple monopoly pricing.
2 Offer the two commodities for sale only in a package comprised of one unit of each at the price p_B^* chosen so as to maximize profits. This is the pure bundling strategy.
3 Combine strategies one and two by offering each commodity separately and a package of both, at a set of prices (p_1^*, p_2^*, p_B^*), which maximizes overall profits. This is the mixed bundling strategy. Since the value of a bundle to consumers is no greater than the value of its components, mixed bundling is a distinct strategy only if the package is sold at a discount relative to its components.

Each of these strategies is easily represented in diagrammatic form.

The reservation price of each consumer for each commodity can be represented as a point in Figure 22.1. If the monopolist adopts the pure components strategy, and sets component prices p_1^* and p_2^* (Figure 22.1), the population is sorted into four groups: individuals with reservation prices at least equal to market prices for both commodities (Area A in Figure 22.1), individuals with reservation prices less than market prices for both commodities (Area C), and individuals with reservation price at least equal to market price for one but not the other commodity (Areas B and D). Those in Area A purchase both goods, those in Areas B and D purchase goods 2 and 1, respectively, and individuals in Area C purchase neither good.

If instead the monopolist adopts the pure bundling strategy, the population is sorted into only two groups: those whose reservation price for the bundle ($r_B = r_1 + r_2$) is at least equal to the bundle's market price, and those for whom the opposite is true. In Figure 22.2 the bundle price appears in reservation price space as a straight line with both intercepts equal to the bundle price p_B^* and hence with a slope of minus one. Those in Area A buy the bundle and hence consume both goods. Those in Area B do not buy the bundle and hence consume neither good.[7]

Finally, if the monopolist adopts the mixed bundling strategy, customers are again sorted into four groups. These appear in Figure 22.3. Individuals in Area $Op_2^* XY p_1^*$ consume nothing. They are characterized by $r_1 \leq p_1^*$, $r_2 p_2^*$, and $r_B \leq p_B^*$. Individuals southeast of $p_1^* YZ$ consume only good 1. They are characterized by $r_1 \geq p_1^*$ and $r_2 \leq p_B^* - p_1^*$. The reason is that $(p_B^* - p_1^*)$ represents the implicit price of good 2 to an individual already prepared to buy good 1.[8] For similar reasons those northwest of $p_2^* XW$ consume only good 2. They are characterized by $r_2 \geq p_2^*$ and $r_1 \leq (p_B^* - p_2^*)$. The last group comprises those northeast of $WXYZ$, who consume the bundle. They are characterized by $r_1 + r_2 \geq p_B^*$, $r_1 > (p_B^* - p_2^*)$, and $r_2 \geq (p_B^* - p_1^*)$. In words, the bundle is consumed by those who not only derive positive

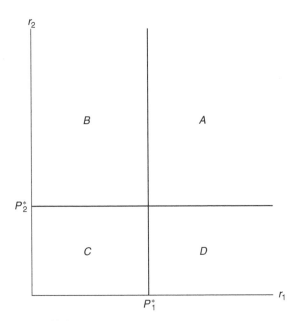

B	A
C	D

r_2

P_2^*

P_1^*

r_1

Figure 22.1

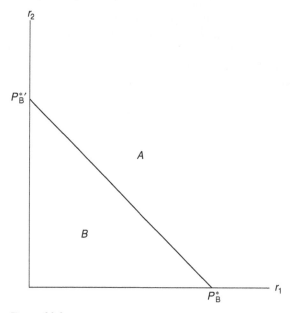

Figure 22.2

consumer surplus from purchase of the bundle but also derive more surplus from the bundle $(r_B - p_B^*)$ than they would from purchase of either component separately $(r_i - p_i^*, i = 1, 2)$.

The profit-maximizing monopolist chooses among these sorting mechanisms by calculating the most remunerative configuration of prices under each strategy and then by comparing the resulting profits. The relative profitability of the three strategies depends on

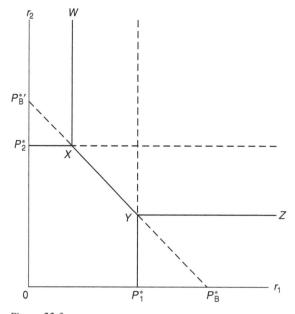

Figure 22.3

the distribution of consumers in reservation price space and the structure of costs. Each conceivable ranking of the three is in fact possible. The reason is that each strategy has both strengths and weaknesses vis à vis its rivals.

In order to assess the virtues and defects of each strategy, a benchmark is required. Since pure price discrimination is known to be the most remunerative pricing strategy available to a firm, it provides a benchmark for appraising the profitability of other pricing schemes. In the context of our model pure price discrimination satisfies three conditions:

C1 (Complete Extraction) No individual realizes any consumer surplus on his purchases.
C2 (Exclusion) No individual consumes a good if the cost of that good exceeds his reservation price for it.
C3 (Inclusion) Any individual whose reservation prices for a good exceeds its cost in fact consumes that good.

   To what extent does simple monopoly pricing, or bundling in some form, also satisfy these conditions?

The pure components strategy never violates Exclusion because within the framework of our model prices in component markets are never set below cost.[9] As we show below, this virtue of simple monopoly pricing is not shared by its bundling rivals. On the other hand, the pure components strategy violates Extraction or Inclusion as long as customers are distributed in reservation price space such that the monopolist faces downward-sloping demand curves in both component markets: the finite elasticity of demand curves implies that monopolists cannot extract all consumer surplus on a particular good without preventing some individuals with valuation in excess of cost from consuming it. This violates Inclusion.

If the bundle demand curve is extremely elastic while the component demand curves are not, pure bundling avoids excessive violation of Inclusion and Extraction. This proposition is illustrated in Figure 22.4. The four consumers – A, B, C, and D – are distributed in reservation price space along a straight line with slope minus one. The value of the bundle is the same to all customers so that the bundle demand curve is perfectly elastic. The relative value of the components differs among customers, however, so that each component demand curve is downward-sloping. If the monopolist knows the common valuation of the bundle by his customers, he can satisfy the extraction and inclusion requirements simultaneously by charging each customer a price equal to that amount for the bundle.[10]

The chief defect of pure bundling is its difficulty in complying with Exclusion. The greater the cost of supplying either good, the greater the possibility of supplying some individuals with commodities for which reservation price falls short of cost. In Figure 22.4, A and D are individuals with $r_i < c_i$ for some commodity. Thus, pure bundling is preferred to simple monopoly pricing only if the greater profits accruing from more complete extraction or inclusion are not outweighed by the lower profits due to less complete exclusion. The more negligible are costs relative to reservation prices, the less of a problem this poses for pure bundling.

The mixed bundling strategy is more profitable than its pure counterpart whenever Exclusion is violated in the pure bundling equilibrium. The reason is that creation of separate component markets adds two categories into which the monopolist can sort his customers. In Figure 22.4, for example, he can charge prices $p_1^* = 90$ and $P_2^* = 90$ in the component markets, thereby inducing individuals A and D to cease consuming the good they value below cost but continue consuming the good they value above cost. In general, *whenever the exclusion requirement is violated in a pure bundling equilibrium, mixed bundling is*

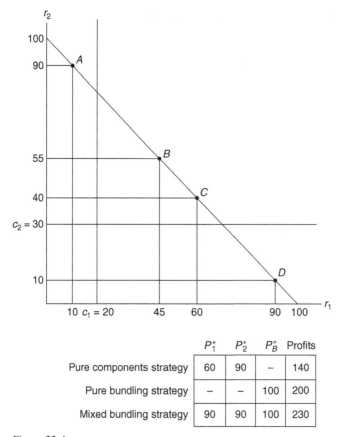

	P_1^*	P_2^*	P_B^*	Profits
Pure components strategy	60	90	–	140
Pure bundling strategy	–	–	100	200
Mixed bundling strategy	90	90	100	230

Figure 22.4

necessarily preferred to pure bundling.[11] That mixed bundling satisfies Exclusion more completely than does pure bundling, however, does not mean that mixed bundling avoids the problem altogether. Rarely does a monopolist find it profitable to exclude every individual whose reservation price for a good falls short of its cost. The reason is apparent in Figure 22.5, which is identical to Figure 22.4 except for the presence of consumers E and F. Mixed bundling is still the most profitable strategy, but Exclusion is unfulfilled in the cases of E and F. To exclude them from the bundle market proves too costly in terms of consumer surplus foregone on A and D. Another way of putting this is that the component demand curves are downward-sloping and hence successive price reductions on a given component usually reduce total revenue in that component market. Like pure bundlers, therefore, mixed bundlers face a trade-off between more complete extraction and more complete exclusion. The dilemma is simply less pronounced in the case of mixed bundling.

   If customers are distributed in reservation price space such that people with high reservation prices for the package exhibit small variance in their valuations of the components, and vice versa, then mixed bundling has another virtue relative to pure bundling: it facilitates the monopolist's attempts to extract the consumer surplus of individuals with high reservation prices for both goods. The reason is that a mixed bundler can charge a high bundle price and yet extract via separates markets the consumer surplus associated with customers valuing one but not both goods highly. This is illustrated in Figure 22.4. The bundle is priced to

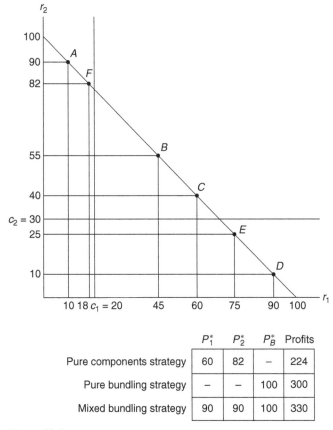

	P_1^*	P_2^*	P_B^*	Profits
Pure components strategy	60	82	–	224
Pure bundling strategy	–	–	100	300
Mixed bundling strategy	90	90	100	330

Figure 22.5

extract all the surplus of B and C, while the separates markets are used to extract the surplus of A and D. If the distribution of consumers in reservation price space is the opposite of that assumed here, however, pure bundling could be preferred to its mixed counterpart.[12]

Turning to comparison of mixed bundling with simple monopoly pricing, if the correlation coefficient linking an individual's valuation of one good to his valuation of the other good is not strongly positive, we can see that the mixed bundling strategy is better able to satisfy Extraction and Inclusion simultaneously. This is possible in Figure 22.7. The monopolist adopting a pure components strategy sets $p_1^* = p_2^* = 10$ in this situation, earning 40 in profits. If he then offers a bundle at $p_B = 16$, without changing the component prices, he entices people currently consuming nothing (i.e., E), as well as people currently consuming just one good (i.e., D, F), to purchase the bundle, while retaining other customers (i.e., A, B, C, G, H, I) in the separates markets. More generally, strong negative correlation helps the monopolist to achieve greater Inclusion by insuring that numerous individuals like F, E, and D exist. In the case at hand, simply adding the bundle at a price of 16 generates profits of 48 rather than 40. Profits are not maximized, however, by leaving component prices at their prebundle level. The bundle option permits the monopolist to raise prices in component markets, in pursuit of more complete extraction, without driving as many customers entirely out of the market. In Figure 22.7, for example, introduction of a bundle at a price of 16 makes it profitable to raise each component price from 10 to 14. This involves sacrifice

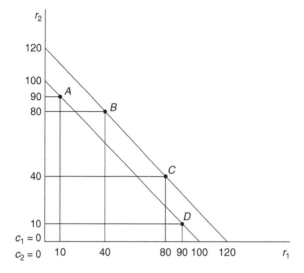

	P_1^*	P_2^*	P_B^*	Profits
Pure components strategy	80	80	–	320
Pure bundling strategy	–	–	100	400
Mixed bundling strategy	90	90	120	420

Figure 22.6

of customers at A and I. Without the bundle, however, D and F would also exit from the market. On balance, introduction of a bundle, when coupled with elevation of component market prices, permits achievement of 54 in profits. These are the highest attainable under any of the three strategies. In effect, negative correlation guarantees the existence of individuals with extreme tastes (e.g., B, C, G, H) who realize substantial consumer surplus in pure components equilibrium.

A major defect of mixed bundling vis à vis simple monopoly pricing is its difficulty in accomplishing Exclusion and Complete Extraction simultaneously. In Figure 22.8, for example, if costs are $c_1 = c_2 = 45$, exclusion is such an important desideratum that pure components pricing is more profitable than mixed bundling. If $c_1 = c_2 = 30$, by contrast, so that exclusion is no longer a serious problem, simple monopoly pricing is less profitable than mixed bundling. This illustrates the general proposition that pure components pricing is a more desirable strategy the greater the cost of violating Exclusion.[13]

In sum, each of the three pricing strategies has both advantages and disadvantages in relation to the other two. Whether one generates more profits than another depends on the prevailing level of costs and on the distribution of customers in reservation price space. In numerous experiments with plausible cost structures and continuous distributions of reservation prices, we found some form of bundling to be more profitable than simple monopoly pricing.[14] Thus, commodity bundling can be expected to occur in the real world under more than the highly particular circumstances discussed here.[15]

We are now in a position to understand why a restaurant might offer complete dinners as well as an à la carte menu. Some people value an appetizer relatively highly (soup on a

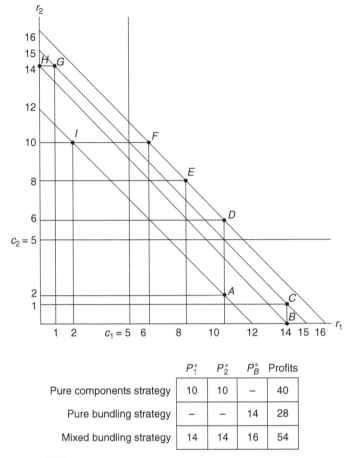

	P_1^*	P_2^*	P_B^*	Profits
Pure components strategy	10	10	–	40
Pure bundling strategy	–	–	14	28
Mixed bundling strategy	14	14	16	54

Figure 22.7

cold day), others may value dessert relatively highly (Baked Alaska, unavailable at home), but all might wish to pay roughly the same amount for a complete dinner. The à la carte menu is designed to capture consumer surplus from those gastronomes with extremely high valuations of particular dishes, while the complete dinner is designed to retain those with lower variance in their reservation prices.

With slight changes in interpretation, our model can be used to explain why products like toothpaste are sold in multiple container sizes. The horizontal axis in such cases measures an individual's reservation price for a first unit of the good, while the vertical axis measures his reservation price for an additional unit of the same good, given that he consumes a first unit. These definitions guarantee that assumptions A1–A3 can be satisfied.[16] Note, however, that what comprises "one unit" of a good is inherently arbitrary. Moreover, customers must lie below the 45-degree line in reservation price space so as to comply with the law of diminishing marginal rates of substitution. Finally, the monopolist must charge the same price in both separates markets. Whenever mixed bundling occurs in toothpaste-type situations, the monopolist is engaging in price discrimination by offering quantity discounts. Individuals with high reservation prices for the first ounce and low reservation prices for the second ounce have lower price elasticities of demand than do those with more equal valuations of

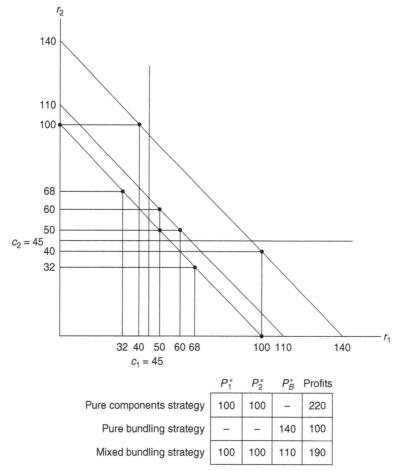

	P_1^*	P_2^*	P_B^*	Profits
Pure components strategy	100	100	–	220
Pure bundling strategy	–	–	140	100
Mixed bundling strategy	100	100	110	190

Figure 22.8

successive units. Offering both one- and two-ounce containers thus induces individuals with inelastic demand to pay a high unit price in the component market, while individuals with elastic demand pay a low unit price in the bundle market.[17]

Our model also provides a plausible explanation of why automobile manufacturers add luxury to at least some of their vehicles. If the horizontal axis of reservation price space is defined as valuation of transport services, while the vertical axis is defined as the valuation of added luxury, assumptions A1–A3 can be satisfied.[18] In such situations the monopolist could offer just a basic car, just a luxury car, or both. Since the last strategy is equivalent to mixed bundling, it is usually the most profitable of the three.[19] That explains why consumer goods' manufacturers typically sell their product in both differentiated and undifferentiated form.[20]

In conclusion, we have shown that commodity bundling is more profitable than simple monopoly pricing in a wide variety of circumstances. The reason is that it often permits more complete extraction of consumer surplus than is possible under a pure components strategy. Price discrimination is another technique designed to achieve that result. What are the relative merits of these two schemes? Package selling has two virtues when compared with price discrimination. First, it requires far less information to implement. For example, Pigouvian first-degree price discrimination could be practiced only if the monopolist knows the reservation prices of each individual for each commodity. Needless to say, individuals have a strong incentive to conceal such information whenever possible. Commodity bundling, on the other hand, can be practiced even if the monopolist knows only the joint distribution of reservation prices in the population. Such information is sufficient to calculate the most profitable bundle and component prices. In a bundling context the price structure is such that individuals automatically sort themselves into distinct reservation price groups and thereby reveal truthful information concerning their tastes. In this sense commodity bundling serves as a self-selection device.[21]

Second, since each person pays the same price for what he consumes as do all others purchasing the same market basket, price discrimination laws based on price differentials alone are not violated. Unlike pure price discrimination, therefore, commodity bundling leaves its practitioner immune from prosecution.

III The model: normative properties

Two requirements of Pareto optimality in the model of Section II are that commodities be distributed among consumers in such a way that no mutual gains from trade are possible, and that output of each commodity be just sufficient to supply all consumers with reservation prices at least equal to the marginal cost of that commodity. It is well known that simple monopoly pricing violates the second but not the first of these requirements. Commodity bundling can violate either or both. Since the precise defects of bundling depend on which case – restaurant, toothpaste, or car – is under consideration, we shall discuss the normative consequences of each case separately.

In cases of the restaurant type, where each component can in principle be disembodied from the bundle, package selling typically results in distributive inefficiency. This is illustrated in Figure 22.9.[22]

Consumers located in the area AHp_1^*E, for example, do not consume good 1, while individuals northeast of $FAEp_1^{*\prime}$ do. And yet, some individuals in the former area (e.g., X) value good 1 more highly than do some individuals in the latter area (e.g., Y). Thus, mutual gains from trade of good 1 for money between X and Y are possible, violating the distributive efficiency criterion. The same reasoning applies to distribution of good 2. Insofar as it leads to distributive inefficiency, commodity bundling shares certain normative properties with (imperfect) price discrimination.[23]

In cases of the restaurant type commodity bundling also results in allocative inefficiency. Unlike simple monopoly pricing, however, bundling can lead to oversupply as well as undersupply of either or both commodities. This, too, is illustrated in Figure 22.9. All consumers located east of $c_1 c_1'$ should consume good 1. In mixed bundling equilibrium, though, it is individuals northeast of $FAEp_1^*$ who in fact consume good 1. If $FABc_1'$ contains more customers than does $c_1BEp_1^*$ then good 1 is oversupplied. If not, the reverse is true. Economically, a necessary if insufficient condition for oversupply of good 1 is that equilibrium prices bear the relationship $p_B^* - p_2^* < c_1$ so that the shadow price of good 1 when consumed in bundles is less than its opportunity cost. By similar reasoning the necessary and sufficient[24] conditions for undersupply of good 1 are $p_1^* > c_1$ and $p_B^* - p_2^* > c_1$. Since the same logic prevails in analyzing good 2, commodity bundling can lead to oversupply of both commodities, undersupply of both commodities, or oversupply of one and undersupply of the other. Figure 22.5 illustrates the first possibility, Figures 22.6 and 22.7 illustrate the second, while

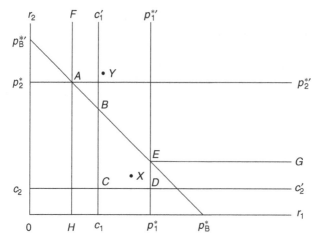

Group	Actually consumes Good I	Should consume Good I	Actually consumes Good 2	Should consume Good 2
$0c_2\,Cc_1$	no	no	no	no
Southeast of $c_2'\,Dp_1^*$	yes	yes	no	no
Northwest of $p_2^*\,AF$	no	no	yes	yes
$c_1'\,BEG$	yes	yes	yes	yes
$c_2\,p_2^*\,ABC$	no	no	no	yes
$c_1\,CDp_1^*$	no	yes	no	no
$GEDc_2'$	yes	yes	no	yes
$FABc_1'$	yes	no	yes	yes
$CBED$	no	yes	no	yes

Figure 22.9

Figure 22.9 could be used to illustrate the last.[25] That monopolists can produce too much as well as too little output implies that the conventional view of monopoly output lacks general validity.

The welfare implications of bundling of the toothpaste variety are identical to those of the restaurant variety: both distributive inefficiency and allocative inefficiency typically occur, and equilibrium output might exceed optimal output. Therefore, no separate treatment of this case is required.

Bundling of the automobile variety, however, does possess distinctive normative characteristics. These can be illustrated in Figure 22.10. If both the basic car and the luxury car are offered at prices p_1^* and p_B^*, respectively, individuals in the area southeast of p_1^*AB consume the basic car, and individuals northeast of $p_1^{*'}AB$ consume the luxury car. Because luxury is valued only by those who also consume transport services, no mutually beneficial trades among potential customers are possible, even though some who do not consume a commodity value it more highly than others who do. For example, X values transport more highly than does Y,

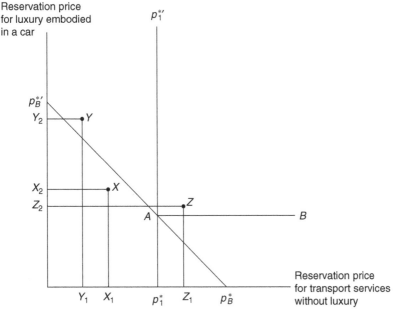

Figure 22.10

and luxury more highly than does Z. Nevertheless, Y would not sell the transport services of his car to X at a price of Y_1, even if he could retain the luxury (e.g., in the form of chrome).[26] For the same reason, X would be unwilling to pay X_2 for the chrome of Z's car if that chrome were disembodied from the vehicle. Thus, no distributive inefficiency results from bundling in the car-type situation.

Allocative inefficiency is possible, however, even if some components cannot be disembodied from the bundle. This can be illustrated in Figure 22.9. In this situation A, B, and C should consume a luxury car, while D, E, and F should consume a basic car. The monopolist's profit-maximizing strategy, however, results in A, B, C, and E consuming the luxury car, F consuming the basic car, and D consuming nothing. Hence luxury is oversupplied, while transport services are undersupplied by the firm. More generally, in cases of the automobile type basic transport is never oversupplied, although the production of luxury can either exceed or fall short of ideal output.

In sum, commodity bundling generally leads to welfare losses when compared with perfect competition. But this does not imply that banning package selling per se decreases the burden of monopoly. In Figure 22.5, for example, mixed bundling is the most profitable strategy. The associated deadweight welfare loss is 7.[27] If bundling were prohibited and the monopolist forced to adopt a pure components strategy, the associated welfare loss would be 60 instead. Thus, prohibition of bundling without more might make society worse off. In fact, within the framework of our model, whenever mixed bundling is equivalent to pure price discrimination, it is Pareto optimal. Simple monopoly pricing never is. The possibility that mixed bundling is Pareto optimal is illustrated in Figure 22.4.

The deadweight loss associated with bundling might also exceed the corresponding loss associated with simple monopoly pricing. This possibility is illustrated in Figure 22.7. The profit-maximizing strategy for a monopolist is mixed bundling. And yet, the deadweight loss associated with that strategy (i.e., 10) exceeds that associated with the most profitable pure

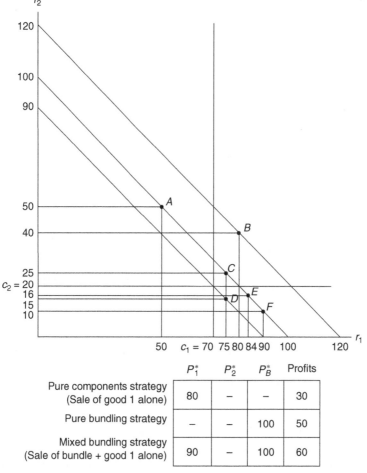

	P_1^*	P_2^*	P_B^*	Profits
Pure components strategy (Sale of good 1 alone)	80	–	–	30
Pure bundling strategy	–	–	100	50
Mixed bundling strategy (Sale of bundle + good 1 alone)	90	–	100	60

Figure 22.11

components strategy (i.e., 8). In this case, therefore, inability to bundle on the part of the monopolist would decrease the burden of monopoly.

IV Implications and conclusion

In the movie *Five Easy Pieces*, Jack Nicholson enters a diner to purchase some toast and coffee. The waitress informs him that toast alone is not available, even though both bread and toaster are on the, premises. Nicholson is forced to order a chicken salad sandwich without chicken, lettuce, or mayonnaise.

Our purpose here has been to explain this and other forms of commodity bundling, such as vacation packages, chrome on cars, and quantity discounts. We have demonstrated that a monopolist's urge to charge customers their reservation prices for each of his products could lead to package selling. We have also demonstrated that bundling is inefficient by Pareto standards: it can lead to oversupply or undersupply of particular goods, and it can lead to the wrong people consuming each good. In this section we present some implications of commodity bundling for public policy analysis.

The first step in social appraisal of monopoly is to ascertain the sources and magnitude of the welfare loss it generates. That is the function of certain tools of applied welfare economics, such as consumer-producer surplus analysis and hedonic price indices. Unfortunately, the reliability of both such tools is seriously jeopardized when monopolists practice commodity bundling.

Looking first at consumer-producer surplus analysis, we estimate the burden of monopoly as

$$\Delta W = \int_0^{z^*} \sum_i D_i(z) \frac{\partial x_i}{\partial z} dz, \tag{22.1}$$

where D_i represents the excess of marginal social benefit over marginal social cost per unit level of activity i, x_i represents the number of units of activity i, and z denotes the extent of monopoly power. In effect, this formula measures the excess of consumer surplus lost over producer surplus gained from simple monopoly, as compared with competitive, pricing.

Where monopolists practice commodity bundling, equation (22.1) has two defects. First, it focuses exclusively on allocative inefficiency, ignoring the distributive inefficiency characteristic of the situation. Second, the formula is inaccurate even in its estimation of allocative inefficiency. To take the simplest and most dramatic example, assume that individuals are uniformly distributed in reservation price space along the line $r_1 + r_2 = 1$, and that both component costs are positive. Suppose also that the monopolist adopts a pure bundling strategy.[28] The profit-maximizing price is $P_B^* = 1$, and all individuals consume the package. Resource misallocation exists, since some consumers have reservation prices below cost for one component, while other consumers have reservation prices below cost for the other component. No distributive inefficiency exists. Yet as long as equation (22.1) is applied at the bundle level, $\partial x_i / \partial z = 0$, so that estimated welfare loss is zero. This follows from the fact that the bundle demand curve is completely inelastic at prices below unity; hence the usual "triangle" measuring the deadweight loss vanishes entirely. In this example the formula not only underestimates welfare loss but fails even to detect its presence.

These defects of the consumer-producer surplus approach have two implications for public policy analysis. First, society may be unaware of the true extent of the burden of monopoly.[29] Second, even if society knows the extent of welfare loss, it may fail to pinpoint its source.[30] This could set governments on the wrong policy track, since distributive inefficiency requires social intervention of a sort different from that designed to eliminate resource misallocation.

Commodity bundling also affects certain conclusions that may be drawn from hedonic price indices. The reason is that practitioners of that art often discuss whether consumers are willing to pay for the quality change they consume. The standard treatment is to suggest that consumers either are willing to pay for improvements they consume, or else are not fully understanding of the costs they bear.[31] Bundling analysis suggests a third explanation of why quality might be consumed. Some people value it highly; others do not. The seller finds it profitable to offer quality in a bundle with characteristics consumers uninterested in quality wish to have. As a result, not everyone who buys quality is willing to pay for it. The normative interpretation of quality indices would accordingly seem ambiguous.

Once the sources and extent of welfare loss have been ascertained, the second step in policy analysis is to determine whether public intervention can reduce the loss. If goods sold in the market place cannot be decomposed for separate purchase, for example, government is powerless to stop the evils of bundling.[32] To the extent that package goods can be decomposed, however, it becomes possible to guarantee that shadow prices on all components are the same for all customers. Hence the distributive inefficiency of bundling could be prevented. Moreover, pure components selling could reduce the waste associated with individuals consuming commodities for which they are unwilling to pay cost. Hence at least some of the allocative inefficiency of bundling could also be prevented.

What specifically, then, should governments do? Clearly they must embark on policies that achieve competitive supply of each decomposable good separately. As some have long, if unpopularly, argued, this might reduce rather than increase the output of firms with market power. The argument that modern industrial societies produce too much product differentiation need not rest on the hypothesis that advertising changes consumer tastes.

In any event public policy must take account of the fact that prohibition of commodity bundling without more may increase the burden of monopoly. This is consistent with the general theorem of second best: when one distortion exists (e.g., monopoly), elimination of other distortions (e.g., bundling) may either enhance or diminish social welfare. The implication is that monopoly itself must be eliminated to achieve high levels of social welfare.

Acknowledgment

We are indebted to Richard Caves, Jerry Green, Zvi Griliches, Rachel McCulloch, and Steven Shavell for their comments. Yellen's research was financed by the National Science Foundation via Grant SOC74-19459.

Notes

1 Whenever a commodity is infinitely divisible, the choice of a "standard unit" is essentially arbitrary.
2 Thus, a telephone company that offers local calling only for a fixed monthly fee is engaged in pure bundling. A telephone company that offers local calling on both a fee for service and a monthly basis is engaged in mixed bundling.
3 This is one implication of the transaction cost literature. See, for example, R. Coase, "The Problem of Social Cost," *Journal of Law and Economics*, III (Oct. 1960), 1–44; and H. Demsetz, "The Cost of Transacting," this *Journal*, LXXXII (Feb. 1968), 33–53.
4 This view was first articulated in G. Stigler, "United States v. Loew's Inc.: A Note on Block Booking," in P. Kurland, *The Supreme Court Review: 1963* (Chicago: University of Chicago Press, 1963), 152–57. See also R. Markovits, "Tie-Ins, Reciprocity and Leverage Theory," *Yale Law Journal*, LXXVI (June 1967), 1397–1472. Several recent papers illustrate the relevance of this phenomenon in a variety of institutional and market settings: R. Parks, "The Demand and Supply of Durable Goods and Durability," *American Economic Review*, LXIV (March 1974), 37–55; S. C. Salop, "The Noisy Monopolist: Imperfect Information, Price Dispersion and Price Discrimination," unpublished manuscript, 1973; J. K. Salop and S. C. Salop, "Self-Selection and Turnover in the Labor Market," paper presented to the Econometric Society Meetings, Toronto, 1972; A. M. Spence, *Market Signaling* (Cambridge, Mass.: Harvard University Press, 1974); A. M. Spence, "Time and Communication in Economic and Social Interaction," this *Journal*, LXXX VII (Nov. 1973), 651–60; and J. Stiglitz, "Monopoly and Imperfect Information: the Insurance Market," unpublished manuscript, 1973. Commodity bundling is not the only sophisticated strategy a monopolist can use to enhance profit and complicate welfare judgments. The most similar practices are full-line forcing and all-or-none offers, although conventional price discrimination, the multipart tariff, and product differentiation are all related. See, respectively, M. Burstein, "The Economics of Tie-In Sales," *Review of Economics and Statistics*, XLII (Feb. 1960), 68–73; and R. Markovits, *op. cit.*; R. Baldwin, "Equilibrium in International Trade," this *Journal*, LXII (Nov. 1948), 748–62; E. Clemens, "Price Discrimination and the Multiple Product Firm," *Review of Economic Studies*, XIX (Jan. 1951), 1–11; W. Oi, "A Disneyland Dilemma: Two-Part Tariffs for a Mickey Mouse Monopoly," this *Journal*, LXXXV (Feb. 1971), 77–96; and E. Chamberlin, *The Theory of Monopolistic Competition* (Cambridge, Mass.: Harvard University Press, 1933).

5 Simple monopoly pricing involves setting those prices for each component that maximize profit. In general, the monopolist must take account of any interdependencies among product demand curves in his computation of these prices. This point is developed in M. Bailey, "Price and Output Determination by a Firm Selling Related Products," *American Economic Review*, XLIV (March 1954), 82–93.

6 We assume here that any individual would be indifferent between consuming both goods 1 and 2 and a package consisting of these two goods. In other words, a package is identical to the sum of its component parts from the consumer's point of view.

7 The sorting of consumers depicted in Figure 22.2 assumes that resale of components is impossible.

8 Note that $p_1^* p_2^*$ must equal $p_1^* Y$, since the slope of $p_B^* P_B^{*'}$ is -1.

9 This follows from assumption A3. If an individual's reservation price for one good depends on the amount of the other he consumes, the profit-maximizing pure components strategy might involve violation of Exclusion. The loss leader is a classic case of this proposition.

10 The pure bundling strategy is analytically equivalent to an all-or-none offer. In both cases a package of commodities is offered to the consumer on a "take it or leave it" basis.

11 The proof of this assertion proceeds as follows. Assume that the monopolist adopts a pure bundling strategy and sets a price of p_B^*. Assume further that there exists some consumer i for whom $r_1 + r_2 \geq p_B^*$ and $r_2 < c_2 - \epsilon$, where $\epsilon > 0$. If the monopolist now adopts a mixed bundling strategy, with prices p_B^* and $p_1 = p_B^* - c_2 + \epsilon$, he necessarily earns more profits than under pure bundling: profits are unchanged on individuals for whom $r_1 + r_2 \geq p_B^*$ and $r_2 > p_B^* - p_1$, since they consume the bundle in both cases. Profits are increased, however, on individuals for whom $r_1 + r_2 > p_B^*$ and $r_2 < p_B^* - p_1$, since they bring in $p_1 - c_1 = p_B^* - c_B + \epsilon$ apiece instead of just $p_B^* - c_B$. Profits are also increased on individuals for whom $r_1 + r_2 < p_B^*$ and $r_1 \geq p_1$, since they previously consumed nothing but now generate $p_1 - c_1$ in profits apiece. All other individuals consume nothing in both cases.

12 For example, if $c_1 = c_2 = 0$ and consumers *A, B, C,* and *D* have reservation prices equal to (30, 90), (40, 60), (60, 40), and (90, 30), respectively, the pure bundling strategy generates profits of 400, while the mixed bundling strategy yields profits of 340. Hence pure bundling could be preferred to mixed bundling.

13 It is also possible, although less probable, that taste considerations alone render pure components pricing more profitable than mixed bundling. This is illustrated by the following example. Assume that five consumers – *A, B, C, D,* and *E* – have reservation prices of (80, 80), (75, 75), (45, 45), (75, 5), and (5, 75). Assume that $c_1 = c_2 = 0$. The pure components strategy with $p_i^* = p_2^* = 75$ generates profits of 450. Although a bundle could be offered at a price of 90 in order to induce C to enter the market, gains from the inclusion of *C* would be outweighed by the loss of revenue on sales to *A* and *B*. Furthermore, increasing prices in components markets in conjunction with introduction of a bundle would not increase profits either. The point of this example is to suggest that there exist some distributions of tastes consistent with any strategy ranking as long as Exclusion is violated by none of the options.

14 To demonstrate this, we explored the profitability of bundling when individual reservation prices for the two components follow the joint normal distribution. Our experiments covered a wide range of parameters of the taste distribution and a wide range of cost structures. Suffice it to say that, for every characterization of tastes we studied, bundling in some form was preferred to pure components pricing for some cost conditions. Less complete explorations of tastes following the uniform and chisquare distributions were consistent with this result.

15 Using attendance data on first-run movies for various cities, Stigler attempted to show that real world tastes are such that the block booking practice of movie distributors can be explained by a model of this type. See Stigler, *op. cit.*

16 Note how this incarnation of the model can be used to treat divisible goods, even though they appear to be excluded by assumption A2. In the limiting case of perfect divisibility, bundling is equivalent to imposing nonlinear budget constraints on consumers. The nonlinearity stems from the fact that the average unit price of toothpaste depends on the quantity of toothpaste consumed. The important point here is that bundling can be profitable in a world of divisible commodities for exactly the reasons set forth here.

17 This point is made in Salop, *op. cit.*

18 Note how this incarnation of the model can be used to treat complementarity even though it appears to be excluded by Assumption A3. Two goods are complements in consumption if an individual's reservation price for a unit of one depends on the quantity consumed of the other. By this definition

luxury and transport services are complements in our model, since we assume that no individual would pay anything for luxury if he does not consume transport. Hence, by defining the vertical axis as we have, it is possible to analyze complementary goods.

19 In this situation it is rarely in the monopolist's interest to offer only a basic car. The reason is that as long as some consumer values luxury in excess of cost, profits can be increased by offering a luxury, as well as a basic, car. The proof is as follows. Assume that the monopolist offers a basic car at price p_1^*. Assume further that there exists an individual with $r_1 \geq p_1^*$ and $r_2 > c_2 + \epsilon, \epsilon > 0$. If the monopolist introduces a luxury car with price $p_B = p_1^* + c_2 + \epsilon$, all consumers with $r_1 \geq p_1^*$ and $r_2 \leq p_B - p_1^*$ continue to purchase only good 1. Profits on these sales are unchanged. All consumers with $r_1 \leq p_1^*$ and $r_2 > p_B - p_1^*$ now purchase the bundle instead of the basic car. Profits on these sales rise from $(p_1^* - c_1)$ to $(p_B - c_1 - c_2 = p_1^* - c_1 + \epsilon)$. In addition, individuals with $r_1 < p_1^*$ and $r_1 + r_2 > p_B$ now consume the bundle instead of nothing. Since $p_B > cB$, greater profits are earned on these individuals. In situations of the car variety pure bundling is likely to be more profitable relative to mixed bundling than in cases of the restaurant type. However, the existence of any consumer in pure bundling equilibrium with $r_2 < c_2$ still suffices to guarantee the superiority of mixed bundling.

20 In the industrial organization literature it is usually argued that product differentiation is profitable because it raises barriers to new competition. Our results suggest that product differentiation might be profitable even if entry barriers are unaffected. On the market structure explanation see W. Comanor and T. A. Wilson, "Advertising, Market Structure and Performance," *Review of Economics and Statistics*, XLIV (Nov. 1967), 423–40.

One major class of automobile-type situations, sometimes discussed in other contexts, involves bundling of a good and a bad. The bad cannot be disembodied from the package. The bad could be the search costs or waiting time required to purchase a commodity. See, respectively, Salop, *op. cit.*; and Spence, "Time and Communication in Economic and Social Interaction."

21 See Spence, "Time and Communication in Economic and Social Interaction;" and Salop and Salop, *op. cit.*

22 The prices and costs depicted in Figure 22.9 were selected to permit simultaneous illustration of all potential sources of welfare loss under commodity bundling.

23 Whenever bundling occurs, the shadow price an individual faces for one commodity depends on his reservation price for the other commodity. Hence shadow prices on particular goods typically differ among consumers. This is what can lead to distributive inefficiency.

24 Sufficient as long as the mixed bundling equilibrium violates Inclusion in any way.

25 In Figure 22.9 good 1 can be either oversupplied or undersupplied, but good 2 must, by construction, be undersupplied.

26 This follows from our assumption that no individual has a positive reservation price for chrome when disembodied from transport services.

27 We calculated welfare loss as follows: the total loss is equal to the difference between consumer surplus in pure competition and the sum of consumer surplus and profits in the monopoly equilibrium.

28 Mixed bundling generates more profits in this situation, but its appraisal via equation (22.1) is more complicated.

29 The Harberger formula provides neither a floor nor a ceiling to the true burden of monopoly; it can be shown that in situations where bundling is profitable, deadweight loss can be overestimated or underestimated by equation (22.1).

30 Conceptually, the loss associated with allocative inefficiency should be measured as the net gain in producer and consumer surplus that results from increasing (decreasing) component outputs to their optimal levels, given the correct distribution of output among individuals. The loss associated with distributive inefficiency should be measured as the net gain in consumer surplus that results from redistribution of existing output.

31 Consider, for example, the stance adopted in F. Fisher, Z. Griliches, and C. Kaysen, "The Costs of Automobile Model Changes Since 1949," *Journal of Political Economy*, LXX (Oct. 1962), 433–51. In discussing consumer expenditures on automobile model changes, they assert that "the model changes of the last decade seem to have been largely those desired by the consuming public, at least until the last years of the horsepower race. There are thus grounds for believing that car owners (at the time of purchase) thought model changes worth most of the cost. The general presumption of consumer sovereignty thus implies that these model changes *were* worth their cost" (p. 450). But they also aver that "the fact that model change costs for the late 1950's (about $700 in the purchase

price per car, or more than 25 percent, and $40 per year in gasoline expenses) will probably seem surprisingly high to consumers is an indication that the costs in question were not fully understood by the consuming public" (p. 450).

32 Where no component can be sold separately, bundling is equivalent to the Lancaster formulation of consumer theory. See K. Lancaster, "A New Approach to Consumer Theory," *Journal of Political Economy*, LXXIV (April 1966) 132–57. Apart from the differences in normative interpretation, our model can be distinguished from Lancaster's in the sense that we provide some explanation for the range of products firms choose to offer in the market place. Our model integrates consumer and producer behavior.

23 Peak loads and efficient pricing

Peter O. Steiner

One of the most pervasive problems affecting the regulated industries is the problem of capacity cost. From an economic standpoint the problem is to find an appropriate price policy that leads to the correct amount of physical capacity and its efficient utilization, and that also covers the full social costs of the resources used. The problem arises, classically, in either of two situations: the case of declining costs, where prices at or near marginal costs imply prices below average costs, and the case of peak loads and the resulting partial underutilization of the total capacity available. It is with the peak load problem, defined more fully below, that this paper is concerned, and to focus on this problem we assume throughout that operating costs are a linear function of output, and that the cost of capacity is a linear function of the number of units of capacity built.[1] In fact, of course, the peak load problem may easily occur in combination with the problem of declining costs.

The phenomenon of peak loads is characteristically found where the product or service is technologically not storable as in services generally and as with electric power and transportation, both inter-and intra-urban; or where the alternative storage costs are high owing to the bulk or other properties of the products, as in the case of pipe line transportation of petroleum.

Particularly with respect to electric power there is a long history of discussion of this problem[2] and a recent revival of this discussion by economists.[3] As Houthakker suggests "the vast literature on electricity tariffs shows so many different views that it would be difficult to be original in proposing tariff changes." But, by the same token, if an optimal solution can be rigorously identified, not all of the various suggestions can be valid. The nonoptimality of various engineering proposals has been adequately demonstrated by the recent literature, but the adequacy of more recent contributions has not been so critically examined. It will appear that Lewis recognizes the correct solution, but perhaps because he merely asserts it, or perhaps because he did not choose to develop its implications, more recent writers (Houthakker and Davidson, in particular) after recognizing his priority appear to be led astray. Davidson explicitly, and Houthakker implicitly are led to the incorrect conclusion that an optimal pricing scheme necessarily lies, not in some scheme of discriminatory pricing,[4] but in a sophisticated application of marginal cost pricing.

A primary purpose of this paper is to demonstrate the nature of the theoretical solution to the peak load problem. This is done rigorously and with some generality in the Appendix, but some treatment of the problem is also given for a simplified case in Section I. It will appear that the optimal prices may require price discrimination. Section II will examine the Houthakker and Davidson solutions. Section III will show an interpretation of cost based (i.e., nondiscriminatory) prices that will uniformly *permit* an optimal solution, but it will appear that this is an unusual, if intriguing, interpretation. But even given this interpretation, we will show that the optimal solution will be reached only under restricted conditions. The paper concludes with some brief comments on implications for public policy.

I

Consider the following simplified problem: suppose a product is to be produced in two time periods of equal length (say, day and night) and to incur only two kinds of costs. Let b be operating costs per unit per period, assumed constant. Let β be the cost of providing a unit of capacity, which is assumed independent of the amount of capacity required. From the long-run (planning) point of view the marginal cost of a unit of output is thus b if there is excess capacity and $b + \beta$ if it requires new capacity. Assume that there is a known demand curve for output in each period, each demand curve being a declining function of the quantity of product in that period alone. Assume further that the two demand curves are not identical, are independent of each other, and that the demand curve for output in the first period lies everywhere above that in the second period.[5] We wish to determine the optimal output in each period, and the prices that will lead buyers to purchase these quantities. The amount of capacity that is required is the maximum output in either period – that is, the maximum (or peak) demand on the system.

A peak load problem will be said to exist at any price, if the quantities demanded in the two periods at that price are unequal.

The social goal implicit in the usual identification of marginal cost pricing with optimal results is the maximization of the excess of expressed consumer satisfaction over the cost of resources devoted to production,[6] and we adopt it here. The private objective is taken to be the maximization of the excess of satisfaction over the prices that must be paid. The problem is to specify a set of prices which will lead buyers to purchase the quantity of output in each period that will lead to the social optimum.

Were it not for the fact that the quantity demanded is a function of the prices charged for output in each period there would be neither difficulty nor interest in the peak load problem. No difficulty because charging $P_1 = b + \beta$ and $P_2 = b$ would recover total costs, would assure that all units sold were paying the full marginal costs of their production, and would assure that no unproduced unit was capable of paying such costs. But if the demands were perfectly inelastic, there would be no effect on output of any change in prices and thus one scheme of prices would be equivalent to any other so far as impact on resource use is concerned.[7]

Figure 23.1 will illustrate the problem. The curves D_1 and D_2 are the demand curves for output in the separate periods from which the operating costs have been subtracted. They are, thus, the effective demands for capacity. (It will be recalled that our problem consists in determining the amount of capacity *ab initio*). The curve D_c, is the *vertical* sum of the positive portions of D_1 and D_2, and can be interpreted as the total effective demand for capacity.[8] Each of the cases pictured is by our definition a peak load problem.

Consider the left hand ("firm peak") case. The total justified capacity is $\bar{x}_1$, (where the demand for capacity equals the marginal cost of providing the capacity), and since the marginal capacity demand is that of users in period 1 only, the appropriate price for period 1 is $P_1 = b + \beta$. This capacity would be justified even if there were no demand in period 2. Hence period 2 users should be permitted to purchase output (or service) as long as they

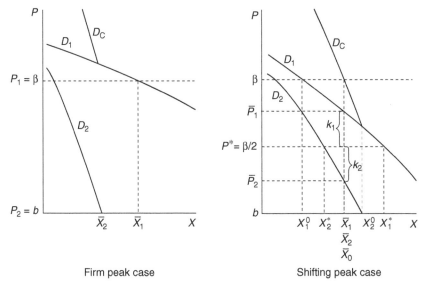

Figure 23.1

cover the operating costs of producing that service. The appropriate quantity is $\bar{x}_2$, and $P_2 = b$. In this case the marginal cost prices,

$P_1 = b + \beta$ (marginal cost including cost of marginal capacity),

$P_2 = b$ (marginal operating cost),

are fully satisfactory. No unproduced unit of output can cover its costs of production, nor does any produced unit fail to do so. The prices while different in the two periods are nondiscriminatory being based wholly on differences in costs.

Application of these same "cost based" prices to the right hand, "shifting peak," diagram leads to quantities x_1^0 and x_2^0 which are less satisfactory. Notice that x_1^0 is less than x_2^0. The off-peak price is charged to units which in fact make the peak demand upon capacity. Capacity cost of only x_1^0 units are recovered, but x_2^0 units of capacity are required. Nor would an "average price" (call it P^*), $P^* = b + \beta/2$ (equal in the diagram to $\beta/2$ because b is taken as the zero axis) be satisfactory. For the resulting outputs (x_1^*, x_2^*) would require x_1^* units of capacity and pay for only $(x_1^* + x_2^*)/2$ units; the marginal units of capacity would not be justified by demand for that capacity (see D_c); nor, given the capacity x_1^*, is it fully utilized in period 2.

To see the correct solution examine the D_c curve. A total amount of capacity equal to $\bar{x}_0$ is justified by the combined demands. Given this capacity the outputs in each period should be extended to this capacity since in each case they exceed the operating costs, b. The optimal quantities $\bar{x}_0 = \bar{x}_1 = \bar{x}_2$ require the prices $\bar{P}_1$ and $\bar{P}_2$ shown in the figure.

To generalize the argument it is essential to recognize that a unit of capacity is justified if and only if (1) it is justified by the demand in any period alone, *or* (2) it is justified by the combined demands in two or more periods. Once the appropriate capacity is determined, output in each period should be extended to that capacity unless additional units of output fail to cover the operating costs at an earlier output. Then given the optimal outputs in each period and the demand curves, it is routine to determine the optimal prices.

The essential feature of the solution to the two period, shifting peak case is that the optimal quantities are equal and the prices unequal. For pedagogic reasons we may write the required prices in terms of a deviation from the average prices as:

$$\bar{P}_1 = b + \beta/2 + k_1,$$
$$\bar{P}_2 = b + \beta/2 + k_2,$$

where, since the sum of the prices is $2b + \beta$, $k_1 + k_2 = 0$. If the demand curves are different at $\bar{x}_o$, the prices are unequal and since this is truly a case of joint costs, unequal prices in the face of equal outputs and joint costs mean discriminatory prices.[9]

These results are easily generalized to more than two periods, which may be mixed in the sense that among some subgroup of periods shifting peak relationships apply, yet between this group and the others a firm peak prevails. Figure 23.2 illustrates a three period case of this sort. Results for an n period case are given in the Appendix, equation (6).[10]

The essence of this solution is the same as for the two period case. The total capacity cost is borne by the periods which make the peak demand upon the capacity, and whose demands collectively justify the marginal unit of capacity. But the capacity charge among these periods is unequal; it is proportional to the strength of the effective demands for capacity. Fundamentally this charge is thus allocated according to demand, and is discriminatory. Output, among these periods, is equal notwithstanding differences in demand. For all other periods output is extended until such point as price equals b, the marginal operating costs.

The nature of the demand curves may occasion comment. It may be argued that responses to price changes are likely to be slow and lagged and thus that use of an instantaneous demand relationship may be misleading. It is common for writers in this field to view the problem of demand response as a series of shifts in short-run demand curves in response to a change in prices. Supposing this to be appropriate we should regard the demand curves as

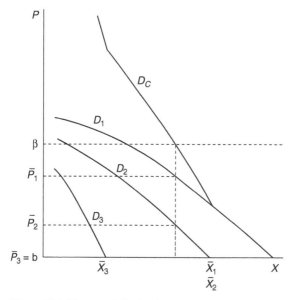

Figure 23.2 Three period mixed case

drawn as being long-run curves embodying the relevant points of a series of instantaneous demand curves, as illustrated in Figure 23.3.

Concerning the significance of the shifting peak case one can not go far on *a priori* reasoning, but two comments seem worth making. Since the ratio of peak to off-peak marginal costs may be large—estimates of the ratio in both England and Baltimore for electric power are of the order of 7:1[11]—it can certainly not be dismissed as trivial without evidence. Further, the restriction of the example to a two period case makes the shifting peak case seem less plausible than in fact it should. Should there be, say a dozen or twenty-four periods (e.g., hours), the relations of the demands among some few of these may well partake of the shifting peak properties even though some subgroup of periods may be a firm peak vis-à-vis the others. It seems not unreasonable that the relevance of shifting peaks may often lie within a broad peak interval.[12]

II

The solution to the peak load problem case presented above provides a framework for discussion of alternative solutions, theoretical and practical. The solution here, of course, is purely theoretical, since it assumes detailed knowledge of the anticipated demand behavior as well as of the nature of costs. The impracticability of a solution resting upon data that would be difficult to come by will be dealt with subsequently. For the moment we digress polemically.

Without exception the able economists who have dealt with this problem have arrived at the correct solution to the firm peak case. With respect to the shifting peak case it is only the proof and implications of the solution given above that claim attention. The solution was succinctly (perhaps overly so) stated by Lewis in 1941 in this sentence: "If there is a good demand for both commodities it is impossible to allocate cost between them; demand alone will decide which part is to be contributed by each."[13] More recent writers have been more explicit but less successful.

Houthakker, in 1951, provided an illuminating discussion of the shifting peak case. In essence his scheme introduced the time-of-day tariff in this form: charge "energy cost" (b in our notation) prices for all periods whose rate of consumption in these periods will not (at this price) exceed the demand in the peak periods;[14] the remaining periods are charged a price which adds to the energy charge the per unit share of the total capacity cost. By this device total capacity costs are always recovered and, as he notes, to achieve this separation of energy and capacity costs "two rates appear to be sufficient".[15] His argument is not limited to the two period case; the need for only two rates is due to the fact that the group of periods

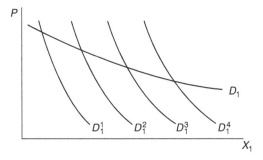

Figure 23.3 Demand for X_1

not receiving the low rate all share the capacity cost on an equal per unit basis. For the two period, shifting peak case Houthakker's rates would be (call them R_1, R_2; other notation unchanged):

$$R_1 = R_2 = b + \frac{x_1 \beta}{x_1 + x_2} = b + \frac{\beta}{1 + x_2/x_1}.$$

Since $x_2 < x_1$ (by definition), the rate for each period is greater than $b + \beta/2$ and too little is consumed in period 2, as output is curtailed short of capacity and before energy costs equal price. The peak price (and thus the amount of capacity required) may be high, low or correct depending upon essentially irrelevant considerations.[16] These prices will thus tend to underutilize the capacity built whether or not they lead to the correct amount of capacity.

Houthakker's own illustration (his Figure 23.4) reduces to a three period case similar to our Figure 23.2. Period 1 is the peak, period 2 is a "potential peak" (if charged the off-peak rate its demand would exceed that in period 1) and period 3 is clearly off-peak. The prices he recommends are:

$$R_1 = R_2 = b + \frac{\beta}{1 + x_2/x_1},$$

$$R_3 = b$$

where, as drawn, $x2 < x3 < x1$ at these prices. Thus period 3 uses more capacity but pays for less than does period 2. As we have seen, the optimal requirement among peak and potential peak periods is equal outputs and unequal prices, not the reverse.

Davidson, in 1955, appears to regard the firm peak case as the basic one, but discusses the shifting peak case explicitly. His solution amounts, in the end, to the same one as Houthakker's, but the exposition has an interesting dynamic element. Letting R_1, R_2 now stand for prices in his two period scheme, but otherwise using the same notation as before,

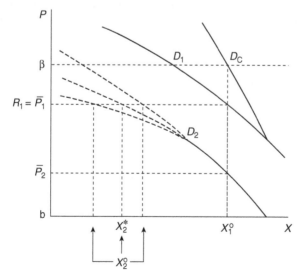

Figure 23.4

his basic prices are:

$$R_1 = b + \beta,$$

$$R_2 = b.$$

If the off-peak quantity threatens to eclipse the peak quantity, the off-peak rate should be increased by an amount (call it a) sufficient to keep the quantity demanded below the peak level. The resulting excess of revenues over off-peak marginal cost should be reflected in a decrease in the peak price. That is:

$$R_2 = b + a; \quad R_1 = b + \beta - \frac{ax_2}{x_1}.$$

How large should a be? This is uncertain, but the limit to a is reached when $R_1 = R_2$.[17] Davidson clearly intends an iterative procedure whereby a is gradually changed in response to lagged demand responses until an equilibrium is reached. Designating x_1^0 and x_2^0 as the equilibrium quantities it is unclear whether at equilibrium $x_1^0 > x_2^0$ and $R_1 = R_2$ or whether $x_1^0 = x_2^0$ and $R1 > R2$.[18] It seems most likely that Davidson regards $R_1 = R_2$ as as implying $x_1^0 = x_2^0$, but of course it does not if the demand curves are separated, as they must be if there is a problem to discuss. Supposing the equilibrium to be reached when $R_1 = R_2$ (for reasons just indicated in note 9), the results are identical to those of the Houthakker scheme and subject to the same limitations.

Can these schemes, which are nonoptimal, be justified in terms of their practicability? Houthakker's proposal clearly requires some demand information (to determine which are the peaks and the potential peaks, and also to permit accurate estimation of the per unit capacity charge), but perhaps less than full knowledge of the demand curves is required. Davidson's iterative scheme has a practical appeal and might be feasible if appropriately modified. A proper gradual procedure would be to start from equal prices (say $= b + \beta/2$) and increase P_1 and decrease P_2 until the quantities were equalized. Of course, if equal price changes are used the total cost of capacity used would not be covered during the transition period. A modified Davidson criterion of unequal price adjustments might avoid the insufficient cost recovery but this requires at least some *ex ante* demand information.[19]

III

Knowing only costs (b and β) can a pricing system be devised that will lead to the optimal results? It should be possible since, when prices are equated with marginal costs private and social costs become identical, and the objective in each case is to maximize the excess of consumer satisfaction (expressed in the demand relationships) over costs. A simple cost based scheme ($P_1 = b + \beta$; $P_2 = b$) failed because the prices appropriate to peak and off-peak periods were assigned to specific periods in advance, and buyers chose to purchase quantities at those prices that led to a different *de facto* peak. These perverse results in the shifting peak case result from buyers taking advantage of the rigidity of *ex ante* labeling of peak and off-peak rather than from any fundamental divergence of private and social optima.

Suppose, however, the following pricing scheme was announced:

peak price $= b + \beta/m,$

off-peak price $= b,$

where m is the number of periods with the maximum demand. These prices would be assessed at the end of the accounting period,[20] based upon actual consumption. The essence of this scheme is to determine the peak *ex post* rather than estimating it *ex ante*. Leaving aside, for the moment, the practicability of such a scheme it would have several advantages:

1 It would require the price-fixing authority to pay attention to nothing but costs, and recorded consumption.
2 It would always recover the full cost of resources used (under the assumption of constant costs). This is so because the peak price always recovers the cost of capacity for the units paying the peak price, and by definition the period(s) of maximum demand pay this price.
3 It would never require more than two prices for any accounting period, notwithstanding m greater than 1.

But would it lead to optimal outputs and optimal capacity? Possibly, but not necessarily. It would if buyers chose to maximize their *collective* welfare. Consider a two period case in which there is a single buyer, who has different demands for output in each period. Under the pricing scheme suggested he cannot avoid paying for any capacity used, and so (if he is assumed to be a maximizer) will (in effect) purchase capacity if it adds more to his satisfactions than to costs. The argument of Figure 23.1 applies directly to him and he will examine the combined demand for capacity of both periods as well as the demand of either. Regarding the shifting peak case of Figure 23.1 he chooses the quantities $\bar{x}_1 = \bar{x}_2 = \bar{x}_0$, because the combined demand for capacity justifies this capacity, and no more. But having purchased this capacity it should be fully utilized. The fact that the monopsonist under this scheme pays an "average" price, $b + \beta/2$ is of no consequence. At those prices he would of course like to buy more in period 1 and less in period 2, but he cannot do so without raising the price (to $b + \beta$) for all units of period 1. This, as is evident, is unwise since it requires him to pay for more capacity than he wants. In like manner a group of individual buyers acting in concert, explicit or implicit, might be expected (given profit sharing) to achieve the same (optimal) result.

But consider the behavior of two buyers, each having demands in both periods, with collusion or communication effectively prohibited. They will not necessarily reach the optimal position for two reasons. First, because under this pricing scheme the marginal cost of capacity to a single buyer may differ from the social marginal cost, and second, because while the combined marginal units of the different buyers may collectively justify a unit of capacity, the individual marginal unit of neither may justify it, and the collective opportunity is thus foregone. Each of these points may be simply illustrated.

To see the first (and probably less important), suppose that two buyers A and B, are purchasing the quantities shown in the following table:

Purchasers	Period	
	1	2
A	1	9
B	9	1
Total	10	10

Under the proposed pricing scheme, each is liable to a capacity charge of 5β.[21] If A considers adding one additional unit in period 2, that period will become the sole peak, and his capacity cost will increase to 10β, resulting in a marginal capacity cost for the additional unit of 5β. Even if the valuation of the tenth unit exceeded $b + \beta$, it might not be profitable to purchase it.[22]

More important perhaps is the problem of underbuilding of capacity that may result from the wide difference between b and β and the nonco-ordination of different buyers' demands. Suppose $b=1$, $\beta=6$ and the following are the valuations placed upon the marginal unpurchased units by the two buyers:

Unit	A in Period 1	B in Period 2
1	6	5
2	5	4
3	4	3
4	3	2

Assuming further that periods 1 and 2 are, at the moment, co-peaks, and that the valuations placed on additional units by A in period 2 and by B in period 1 are ineffective (below b), neither will purchase any additional units since the marginal valuations are below the marginal cost ($=7$). Yet acting together each could profitably add two units if the other did. What is missed (see the shifting peak case in Figure 23.1) is the output to the right of x_1^o which will be the more substantial as the time patterns of preferences of different purchasers are different. But it is precisely such diversified demands that offer the challenge to pricing in peak load situations.

Considerations of this sort immediately suggest the kind of interdependence that characterizes duopoly and oligopoly theory, and also the more recent theory of games. By these pricing rules we have thus converted a quantity-adjusting situation in which all buyers are independent to one of interdependence in which A must take cognizance of B's behavior. Whether this is advantageous depends upon whether we can thereby achieve the optimal results.

If we regard a game theory payoff matrix as nothing more than a convenient way of summarizing the alternative consequences of one "player's" actions in an interdependent situation, our problem cart be instructively treated in this form. The game, however, is nonzero sum, and in the present formulation is a nonco-operative one.

Table 23.1 presents hypothetical values of the "payoffs" to A and B in a situation in which each is supposed to have a choice of only three strategies, each of which corresponds to some combination of (marginal) units purchased in each period.[23] By the payoff is meant the marginal change in the individual's "welfare" of the indicated strategy pair.

Table 23.1 Hypothetical payoff matrixes of nonzero sum game

	A's Payoff				B's Payoff				Combined Payoff		
	B_1	B_2	B_3		B_1	B_2	B_3		B_1	B_2	B_3
A_1	1	7	−5	A_1	1	0	−5	A_1	2	7	−10
A_2	0	2	12	A_2	7	2	3	A_2	7	4	15
A_3	−5	3	8	A_3	−5	12	8	A_3	−10	15	16

Let us define the combination of strategies that maximizes the combined payoff as the "optimal point" which corresponds to the meaning given that term earlier in this paper under the proposed pricing scheme. In the present example the optimal point, A_3B_3, corresponds to A choosing row 3, and B choosing column 3. But in the absences of co-operation or coalition is this result likely? The probable outcome will be a function of the information available to each, his view of the market mechanism, his view of the other player's possible and probable reactions, and, further, any particular structure that may be given to the "game" by permitted or prohibited rules of conduct. The interested reader can explore the possibilities. The conclusion will be that nothing short of full recognition of interdependence and mutual striving for joint maximization will (in general) lead to the optimal point.[24]

This discussion of the game matrix of Table 23.1 is relevant to the suggested *ex post* pricing plan because precisely this type of payoff situation develops in the region where marginal units of capacity are justified by demand for outputs in different periods of different buyers. The critical conclusion is that this pricing scheme, which alone might lead to optimal results using cost-based prices, in fact will do so only if the individuals can somehow be persuaded to pursue collective maximization. Competitive reactions here, as elsewhere, may have adverse effects on resource allocation. It is unlikely that joint maximization will generally prevail, but it is not impossible that the rules of regulatory agencies could be used to structure individual choices toward that end. If, without foreknowledge of demand by the price setter, competitive reactions of individual buyers are to lead to optimal results under a peak load situation it requires the kind of prices suggested *and* some mechanism for structuring individual choice to pursue collective goals. This is not impossible; neither is it easy.

IV

Identification of theoretical optima is hardly sufficient license for policy prescription. Whether it is even necessary is perhaps debatable. But if such optima are used – and economists in this field (as elsewhere) have shown little diffidence – they had best be right. This paper has attempted to show the nature of the optimal solution to the peak load pricing problem (under some restrictive assumptions) and further to explore the conditions under which a purely cost-based (and therefore minimum information) policy would and would not succeed.

Perhaps the most direct interest in the optimal solution given lies in areas where allocation of resources is of direct administrative concern. For example the problem of design and operation of multi-purpose water resource programs is replete with peak load problems some of which are of almost precisely the form of our problem, others of which involve similar reasoning but modified formulation of the problem.[25] But in most regulated industries resource allocation is the indirect result of the pricing scheme employed. It is this that has accounted for the long literature on this problem which was cited earlier in notes 2 and 3.

There is an almost total absence of empirical evidence as to the importance of the potential shifting peak case in the areas where peak loads are a problem. This is partly a matter of definition (the more broadly the peak period is defined, the less shifting there will be) but more basically a matter of empirical fact. Speculation is possible. One would expect, for example, that demand for subway service (and other intra-urban transportation) would be relatively firm peaked, but Vickrey in his study of the New York subway fare problem refuses to assert as much.[26] With respect to electric power, because of the wide difference between peak and off-peak marginal costs, the problem seems potentially important at least within

broadly designated peak periods. In a case like pipe line transportation, where an alternative of storage is available, if expensive, large price differences would almost certainly be
significant. But many factors, most importantly the impact on total costs of given changes
in cost of specific input prices, and the cost and availability of alternatives (if any) are
relevant.

Supposing that the problem is important, and that optimal resource allocation is worth
striving for, and that freedom of choice is to be given at least some role in achieving it,
attention must be devoted to schemes that are conceivable within the limits of data attainable
and that are administratively and dynamically feasible.

Inherently possible is a pricing policy that is based upon an iterative, trial-and-error procedure. Its feasibility would depend not only upon lagged demand responses but also upon the
willingness to change price frequently, and to admit of multiple and discriminatory prices. It
seems likely that considerations of administrative feasibility and equity (which Lewis aptly
characterizes as "the mother of confusion") would be interposed.

An alternative scheme of *ex post* prices would certainly have limited practical appeal
because of the burden of uncertainty placed upon buyers. But it might properly be used
in a case where purchasers were few in number and large in size. The often made suggestion
for common carrier operation of pipe lines would create a peak pricing problem, and the use
of *ex post* prices as a device to encourage advance scheduling negotiations is conceivable.
But the essential requirement is co-ordination of capacity use, and competition here works
badly. It is our central conviction that conscious co-ordination, effectively circumscribed, is
essential to satisfactory settlement of the problem.

Cookenboo's suggested solution to the oil pipe line problem, the compulsory joint venture,
which he favors largely for ideological reasons, takes on added merit when viewed in this
way.[27] It provides almost precisely the kind of incentives for joint cost minimization that are
likely to lead to optimal capacity, and efficient use of that capacity.

Concerning the electrical utilities, the area where the peak pricing problem is most often
raised, the problem of securing conscious co-ordination, is more difficult. Particularly for
domestic users, who are numerous and small, some clearly announced price structure is
essential, and the consequences in terms of their responses to it must be taken as the foundation for other demands. But these users are probably relatively unshiftable in any case,
and, if their demands are firm peaked, they are subject to adequate handling under a price
structure of relatively simple form. Some co-ordination of the demands of industrial users
might be achieved by advance contracting for basic loads, at advantageous rates if complementary to expected domestic requirements; and a system of surcharges, perhaps applied
ex post, for additional demands. This is not the place to propose a detailed pricing scheme.
The problem is more complex than the recent literature suggests, and may be left to another
occasion.

MATHEMATICAL APPENDIX

Definitions:

Let $x_1, x_2, \ldots x_i \ldots x_n$ be quantities of output in periods $1, 2 \ldots i \ldots n$, $x_i \geq 0$ for all i.

Let $P_1, P_2, \ldots P_i \ldots P_n$ be market prices for these quantities.

Let $f_1(x_1), f_2(x_2), \ldots f_i(xi) \ldots f_n(x_n)$ be valuations of the marginal units in the respective periods. Assume $f_i(x_i)$ is continuous and differentiable and $f'(xi) < 0$ for all i.

Let b be the constant operating cost per unit x per period. $b \geq 0$.

Let β be the constant cost of a unit of capacity $\beta > 0$.

Let $F_i(x_i) = \int^{x_i} f_i(x_i)dx_i$.

Let the social net benefit function, Z

$$Z = \sum_{i}^{n} F_i(x_i) - b \sum_{i}^{n} x_i - \beta \max_i(x_i), \quad i = 1, 2, \ldots n,$$

and let buyers, given prices, choose to maximize

$$Y = \sum_{i}^{n} F_i(x_i) - \sum_{i}^{n} P_i x_i.$$

Problem 1a. To find the vector $\bar{P} = \bar{P}_1, \bar{P}_2, \ldots \bar{P}_i \ldots \bar{P}_n$ that will lead to $\bar{x} = \bar{x}_1, \bar{x}_2 \ldots \bar{x}_i \ldots \bar{x}_n$. for which Z is a local maximum. (Demand curves independent.)

Without loss of generality we can assume the x's have been numbered in such a way that

$$\bar{x}_1 = \bar{x}_2 = \ldots \bar{x}_m > \bar{x}_{m+1} \geq \ldots \bar{x}_n,$$

where m is some integer in the range $1, 2 \ldots n$.

Let $x_i = \bar{x}_i + a_i t, t \geq 0, i = 1, \ldots n$.

Since $Z(\bar{x})$ is a local maximum,

$$\left. \frac{dZ}{dt} \right|_{t=0} \leq 0 \quad \text{for all values of } a_1, \ldots a_n;$$

i.e.,

$$\left. \frac{dZ}{dt} \right|_{t=0} = \sum_{i}^{n} f_i(\bar{x}_i)a_i - b \sum_{i}^{n} a_i - \beta \max_i(a_i) \leq 0. \quad i = 1, \ldots m$$

To deduce more specific necessary conditions, apply a number of special values of $a_1, \ldots a_n$.

For notational convenience let $f_i = f_i(\bar{x}_i)$ for all i.

First, let $a_i = 1, i = 1, 2 \ldots m; a_i = 0, i = m + 1, \ldots n$; then

$$\left. \frac{dZ}{dt} \right|_{t=0} = \sum_{}^{m} f_i - mb - \beta \leq 0.$$

Second, let $a_i = -1, i = 1, 2 \ldots m; a_i = 0, i = m + 1, \ldots n$; then

$$\left. \frac{dZ}{dt} \right|_{t=0} = - \sum_{}^{m} f_i + mb + \beta \leq 0.$$

From these two we deduce the necessary condition,

$$\sum_{}^{m} f_i(\bar{x}_o) = mb + \beta \qquad \text{where} \quad \bar{x}_o = \bar{x}_i, \quad i = 1, 2 \ldots m. \tag{23.1}$$

Third, let $a_i = 0$ except for some $j > m$ and $a_j = 1$ [assume $m < n$] then

$$\left. \frac{dZ}{dt} \right|_{t=0} = f_j - b \leq 0.$$

Fourth, let $a_i = 0$ except for some $j > m$ and $a_j = -1$. Then,

$$\frac{dZ}{dt}\bigg|_{t=0} = -f_j + b \leq 0.$$

From these two we deduce the necessary condition,

$$f_j(\bar{x}_j) = b, \tag{23.2}$$

for all j greater than m.

Fifth, let $a_i = 0$ except for some $j \leq m$, $a_j = 1$. Then,

$$\frac{dZ}{dt}\bigg|_{t=0} = f_j - b - \beta \leq 0.$$

Sixth, let $a_i = 0$ except for some $j \leq m$, $a_j = -1$. Then,

$$\frac{dZ}{dt}\bigg|_{t=0} = -f_j + b \leq 0.$$

From these two we deduce the necessary condition,

$$b \leq f_j(\bar{x}_o) \leq b + \beta \quad j = 1, 2 \ldots m. \tag{23.3}$$

Equations (1), (2), (3) are necessary conditions to maximize Z. To see that they are also sufficient, suppose they hold, and suppose, without loss of generality, that

$$a_1 \geq a_j, \quad j = 2, \ldots m. \quad \text{Let } k = m+1, \ldots n.$$

If $m > 1$:

$$\frac{dZ}{dt}\bigg|_{t=0} = a_1\left(mb + \beta - \sum_2^m f_j\right) + \sum_2^m a_j f_j - b\sum_2^m a_j - a_1 b - a_1 \beta,$$

$$+ \sum_{m+1}^n a_k f_b - b\sum_{m+1}^n a_k$$

$$= a_1\left[(m-1)b - \sum_2^m f_j\right] + \sum_2^m a_j(f_j - b) + \sum_{m+1}^n a_k(f_k - b),$$

$$= \sum_2^m a_1(b - f_j) - \sum_2^m a_j(b - f_j) + \sum_{m+1}^n a_k(f_k - b),$$

$$= \sum_2^m (a_1 - a_j)(b - f_j) + \sum_{m+1}^n a_k(f_k - b) \leq 0,$$

since the second summation is zero, and the first nonpositive. If $m = 1$:

$$\left.\frac{dZ}{dt}\right|_{t=0} = a_1(f_1 - b - \beta) + \sum_2^n a_k(f_k - b) = 0.$$

In either case, the conditions are sufficient to a maximum or horizontal Z. But

$$\left.\frac{d^2Z}{dt}\right|_{t=0} = \sum^n a_i^2 f_i' < 0 \quad \text{for all values of } a_i$$

unless $a_i = 0$, all i. Therefore the necessary conditions are sufficient to a local maximum.

These results will become clearer with a further consideration of m. Since we assume $f_i'(x_i) < 0$, all i, it follows from

$$\bar{x}_i < \bar{x}_o, \quad i = m+1, \ldots n \quad \text{and}$$

$$f_i(\bar{x}_i) = b, \quad i = m+1, \ldots n,$$

$$\text{that} \quad f_i(\bar{x}_o) = b, \quad i = m+1, \ldots n.$$

Thus m is the number of functions $f_i(x_i)$ such that $f_i(\bar{x}_o) \geq b$. Where $\bar{x}_o$ is $\max_i(x_i)$ and $\bar{x}$ maximizes Z.

$$i = 1, 2, \ldots n$$

This interpretation of m permits a concise statement of the conditions under which $\bar{x}_o \geq 0$ exists and is unique.

Let $m(x)$ be the number of functions of $f_i(x_i)$ such that $f_i(x) \geq b$.

Let $g_i(x_i) = f_i(x_i) - b$.

Let m_o be the number of functions of $g_i(0)$ for which $g_i(0) \geq 0$.

Let m_* be the number of functions of $g_i(x^*)$ for which $g_i(x^*) \geq 0$, where $m_o, m_* = 0, 1, \ldots n; x* > 0$.

Then, $\bar{x}_o \geq 0$ exists and is unique if, for some x^*,

$$\sum_0^m g_i(0) \geq \beta \geq \sum^m g_i(x^*) \tag{23.4}$$

since $\sum^{m(x)} g_i(x)$ is continuous and $g_i'(x_i) < 0$, all i.

Thus,

$$\sum^m g_i(\bar{x}_o) = \beta,$$

$$0 \leq \bar{x}_o \leq x^*.$$

And

$$\sum^m f_i(\bar{x}_o) = mb + \beta.$$

If the left side of the inequality (4) is violated, zero output is indicated. If the right side is violated for every x^*, there is no rational limit to output in the m. periods.

Having found the maximizing quantities, $\bar{x}$, we inquire what prices are necessary to lead buyers to choose these quantities. Since buyers, given prices, choose to maximize Y, it is necessary that

$$\frac{\partial Y}{\partial x_i} = 0 \quad \text{for all } i;$$

But $\quad \dfrac{\partial Y}{\partial x_i} = f_i(x_i) - P_i = 0,$ and therefore that

$$P_i = f_i(x_i) \quad \text{for all } i. \tag{23.5}$$

Thus the desired $\bar{P} = \bar{P}_1, \bar{P}_2, \ldots \bar{P}_n$, where $\bar{P}_i = f_i(\bar{x}_i)$ and $\bar{x} = \bar{x}_1, \bar{x}_2 \ldots \bar{x}_n$ maximize Z, is

$$\begin{cases} \bar{P}_i = b, \quad i = m+1, \ldots n, \\ \sum_b^m \bar{P}_i = mb + \beta, \quad \text{where } \bar{x}_i = \bar{x}_0, \ i = 1, \ldots m, \\ b \le \bar{P}_i \le b + \beta, \quad i \le m, \end{cases} \tag{23.6}$$

which solves the problem.

For purposes of exposition in the text it proved convenient to express P_i, $i \le m$ as deviations from the average price for the m peak periods, $b + \beta/m$, as:

$$\bar{P}_i = b + \beta/m + k_i \quad i = 1, \ldots m,$$

where

$$k_i = f_i(\bar{x}_0) - (b + \beta/m) \quad i = 1, \ldots m,$$

and

$$\sum_{i=1}^m k_i = 0.$$

We note in passing that, in general, as many as $m+1$ different prices may be required.

The firm peak case in the text corresponds to $m = 1$.

The shifting peak case in the text corresponds to $n \ge m > 1$.

Problem lb. Relaxation of the assumption of independence of the demand curves.

Let $f_i = f_i(x_i, x2, \ldots x_i \ldots x_n)$, all i.

Let $F_i = \int^{x_i} f_i dx_i$.

$$\text{Let } F_i' = \sum_{j=1}^n \frac{\partial F_j}{\partial x_i} = \frac{\partial F_1}{\partial x_i} + \cdots + f_i + \cdots \frac{\partial F_n}{\partial x_i},$$

and proceed with the proof precisely as before. The F'_i replace f_i in every case, and the necessary conditions for maximizing Z become:

$$(1^*) \quad \sum_{i}^{m} F'_i = mb + \beta$$

$$(2^*) \quad F'_j = b \qquad\qquad j \geq m$$

$$(3^*) \quad b \leq F'_j \leq b + \beta \qquad j \leq m$$

$$(5^*) \quad F'_i = P_i \qquad\qquad \text{all } i.$$

Thus the required $\bar{P}$ are formally unchanged, since the F'_i appear symmetrically in $(1^*\text{–}3^*)$ and (5^*). Indirectly, of course, the demand functions are effective in determining m and, in the specific $P_i = b + \beta/m + k_i$, k_i. It should be noted, however, that these conditions may not be sufficient since F''_i may be positive for some i if the demand relationships are complementary.

Problem 2. To compare the capacity required in the Houthakker–Davidson (hereafter, HD) scheme with the optimal capacity.

Let R_1, R_2, x_1^o, x_2^o be the HD equilibrium prices and quantities where

$$R_1 = R_2 \quad \text{and} \quad x_2^o < x_1^o.$$

Let $\bar{P}_1$, $\bar{P}_2$, $\bar{x}_1$, $\bar{x}_2$ be the optimal prices and quantities, where

$$\bar{P}_2 < \bar{P}_1 \quad \text{and} \quad \bar{x}_1 = \bar{x}_2.$$

If the two schemes lead to the same capacity it will be because they have the same peak outputs. That is, because $x_1^o = \bar{x}_1$, which implies $R_1 = \bar{P}_1$. The definitions of R_1 and $\bar{P}_1$ (see the text pp. 590, 593) are as follows:

$$R_1 = b + \frac{\beta}{1 + x_2^o/x_1^o}, \qquad P_1 = b + \beta/2 + k_1.$$

Let x_2^* be the value of x_2^o that would make $R_1 = P_1$. We now determine the conditions under which $x_2^* = x_2^o$.

Since the pricing schemes under discussion precisely recover the total costs of production – both operating and capacity, and since when, as assumed, $\bar{P}_1 = R_1$, the capacity costs are equal, we can equate the revenues available to meet the capacity costs of the HD scheme with those of the optimal prices,

$$R_1(x_1^o + x_2^*) - b(x_1^o + x_2^*) = \bar{P}_1\bar{x}_1 + \bar{P}_2\bar{x}_2 - b(\bar{x}_1 + \bar{x}_2),$$

from which

$$\frac{\bar{P}_1 - b}{\bar{P}_2 - b} = \frac{\bar{x}_2}{x_2^*}.$$

Thus whether the capacity under the HD pricing scheme is optimal depends upon whether x_2^o takes the value x_2^*. Figure 23.4 illustrates that this is determined by the shape of the upper tail of the demand curve in period 2, in a region removed from the optimal quantity to be consumed in period 2. If $x_2^* \neq x_2^o$ then $R_1 \neq \bar{P}_1$. Whether the required capacity is greater or smaller depends upon the direction of inequality and also upon the elasticity of the *horizontally* added demand curves in the neighborhood of $\bar{P}_1$.

Acknowledgment

I gratefully acknowledge the assistance of the Social Science Research Council whose Faculty Research Fellowship made this paper possible. Jack Hirshleifer, Hendrik Houthakker, and Carl Christ raised illuminating objections to an earlier draft. Roger Miller made numerous improvements in the argument. My major debt is to Robert Dorfman whose help at every stage was enormous and whose improvement of the Appendix beggars description. Opinions and errors are my own.

Notes

1 The separate linearity of these two classes of cost (and the consequent constancy of the elements of marginal cost) does not mean that total marginal cost is constant; indeed, it is the variability that is the crux of the problem we treat. Even with this simplification the problem is complex. It should be noted that it is only where average and marginal costs are equal that identification of marginal cost pricing with precise covering of total costs is possible.

2 This literature goes back at least to the famous 1892 paper by John Hopkinson. For reviews of these contributions see P. Schiller, *Methods of Allocating to Classes of Consumers or Load the Demand Related Portion of the Standing Cost of Electricity Supply*, Technical Report K/T 106, British Electrical and Allied Industries Research Association, 1943; and Ralph K. Davidson, *Price Discrimination in Selling Gas and Electricity* (Baltimore, 1955).

3 I date this new discussion from the paper by W. Arthur Lewis, "The Two-Part Tariff," *Economica*, VIII, N.S. (Aug. 1941). This paper is expanded in Lewis' *Overhead Cost* (New York, 1949). See also, H. S. Houthakker, "Electricity Tariffs in Theory and Practice," *The Economic Journal*, LXI (Mar. 1951), 1–25; I .M. D. Little, *The Price of Fuel* (Oxford, 1953); and Davidson, *op. cit.* There is, of course, a long history of theoretical discussion of the problems of overhead cost to which the peak load problem is related.

4 We shall use Davidson's definition of price discrimination: "a seller practices price discrimination if the relative prices he charges for the various units of his...products are disproportionate to the relative costs of production of the units sold." Davidson, *op. cit.* p. 23.

5 A number of these limitations are for expository convenience only and do not affect the results. The Appendix treats the problem more generally, assuming n periods, and placing no restriction on the demand relations other than that they are continuous and declining.

6 The social objective is thus the maximization of the sum of the consumers' and producers' surpluses. This requires the output where the demand curve is cut from below by the marginal cost curve. The private (buyers) objective is the maximization of consumers surplus. Taken together these conditions imply $p = mc$. Where the cost curve is in horizontal sections (our case) the problem is particularly simple since producers surplus is zero (total costs equal total revenues) when $p = mc$. For the further conclusion of optimal resource allocation it is usually, but not universally, argued that price and marginal cost be equal in all sectors of the economy.

7 The linkage between quantities and prices is what chiefly distinguishes the recent economic literature from the earlier discussions. Practically it requires attention to anticipated quantities rather than to quantities observed in the past under a different structure of prices.

8 Demands are added vertically because the demands of the separate periods upon capacity are complementary not competitive. This is the trick. A similar procedure is appropriate in the case of public goods in the theory of public expenditure. See Paul A. Samuelson. "Diagrammatic Exposition of A Theory of Public Expenditure," *Review of Economics and Statistics*, XXXVII (Nov. 1955).

In the vertical addition, attention is restricted to the positive portions of the demands for capacity since ineffective demand (i.e., demand that will not even cover operating costs) is totally irrelevant to the decision.

9 That this is discrimination within the definition used has been questioned by two critics. Hirshleifer suggests that a true representation of marginal cost would have it be a horizontal line (at b) until $\bar{x}_o$ and then rise vertically; in this view the optimal prices are equal to marginal cost (albeit on the vertical section). But, in my view, this neglects the fundamental discontinuity in the marginal cost function of a peak load problem, which leaves marginal cost undefined at $\bar{x}_0$. Further, since we are concerned with a planning cost curve the use of a demand-determined optimal capacity as if it were a "fixed cost" seems wholly unjustified.

   Professor Chamberlin suggests that since periods one and two are separate, the "products" are different and thus the notion of discrimination loses meaning. This view has substantial merit, but it leads away from the meaning generally given to discrimination in this area, and in others. Indeed it virtually annihilates the concept of discrimination.

10 The generalized argument of the Appendix not only covers the "n" period case, but makes no use of the assumption of noncrossing demand curves, and also considers the case of demand curves that are interdependent. The essentials of the simplified two period case are unchanged.

11 See Houthakker *op. cit.* pp. 22–23; and Davidson *op. cit.* p. 194.

12 A peak interval is defined as some group of consecutive periods among which shifting peak relationships occur. I have assumed throughout that the periods occur in a recurring cycle and that the full cycle takes a fairly short interval (e.g., days, or months). Roger Miller has called my attention to the fact that if there is a significant time interval between time zero and the first peak, and if there is a carrying cost of capital, the amount of optimal capacity takes on a dynamic aspect. One must then also consider the right time path of capacity construction, and an interim pattern of short-run utilization. This is a good point, but I will continue to neglect it for simplicity.

13 *Economica, op. cit.* p. 251. The expanded version of this paper leaves little doubt that Lewis saw the correct solution as far as the producer's optimum is concerned. He appears to rely upon competitive pressure to force prices down to the level of marginal costs. For regulated (and, presumably, insufficiently competitive) industries public policy must assume the role of the competitive force.

14 This is my interpretation of his statement (p. 16) that "the low-rate periods were defined by the condition that their maximum demand was equal to the maximum demand in the high-rate periods."

15 Houthakker *op. cit.* pp. 15–17.

16 See the Mathematical Appendix, problem 2.

17 Cf. Davidson, *op. cit.* pp. 120–23, 194–95.

18 It is unclear for two reasons. First because it is impossible to be sure what Davidson intends since his several verbal formulations say quite different things. Second because the dynamics of the iterative process involved presents problems. Each will be considered briefly.

   The most important reason for supposing that Davidson believes the equilibrium to occur at $R_1 = R_2$ is his stress on the nondiscriminatory nature of the proposed prices. The pricing scheme he proposes is at the heart of his nondiscriminatory scheme which he argues is clearly superior to systems of discrimination. But consider also: "Rates for such hours where a new peak developed should be raised sufficiently to flatten out the peak and keep the quantity demanded below the annual peak level." (p. 194) "If the rate of consumption during U (off peak period) continues to threaten to exceed the peak rate of consumption during T (peak period), the price charged for energy consumed during U should continue to be increased and the rate for energy consumed during T decreased until the point is reached where the rate per unit of energy consumed during both periods is equal" (p. 122).

   But, despite all of the above, I may misinterpret him. If so, and if an equilibrium is reached where $x_1^o = x_2^o$, the results while discriminatory are optimal. But will such an equilibrium be reached?

   Suppose a uniform price system is replaced by the prices $R_1 = b + \beta$, $R_2 = b$ in a two period, shifting peak situation where the initial quantity sold in the first period exceeds that in the second, but where the equilibrium quantities at the new prices will be greater in period 2 than in period 1. Now change prices gradually following Davidson's formula. Eventually as a is increased, R_1 will equal R_2. But what happens to quantities? In the absence of any further change in prices, x_1 will fall and x_2 rise, but the effect of the price changes will be to inhibit both of these changes, quite possibly stopping them short of equality. It is not possible to say whether this iteration will lead to equal quantities before the limiting price equality is reached without knowing a good deal about the dynamics of the lagged demand responses and the elasticities of both long-run demand curves.

   There is a further dynamic problem: should prices be gradually changed in response to every shift in the quantities x_1, x_2? If so, even clearly off-peak periods will have prices raised above the optimal level of marginal operating cost, b; if not, when does one start the process?

Since $R_1 = R_2$,

$$b + a = b + \beta - \frac{ax_2}{x_1},$$

$$a = \frac{\beta}{1 + x_2/x_1},$$

and therefore Davidson's $b + a$ is identical with Houthakker's

$$b + \frac{\beta}{1 + x_2/x_1}.$$

19 When speaking of cost recovery, it is evident that the most that can be achieved is cost of capacity actually used, including, of course, any standby capacity required for continuity of service in the face of repairs. Whether a solution (such as this one) that would leave some previously built capacity idle, deserves to be called optimal, is debatable. If secular growth in the demand for capacity is anticipated, or if resources are reasonably free to exit and the durability of capacity is fairly short, a revision of the pricing system looking toward an optimal pricing scheme seems clearly worthwhile. Under other conditions the problem should be modified to consist of optimal utilization of existing capacity, the cost of which is irrelevant.

20 Which is longer than a full cycle of periods within which demands vary. For daily variations, the accounting period might be a month.

21 By "capacity charge" is meant the excess of the total amount paid under the pricing system over $b(x_1 + x_2)$, the total operating cost.

22 In a similar vein one might argue that in this example A could profitably buy one more unit in period 1, and thereby reduce his capacity charge from 5β to 5β or, alternatively reduce by one his purchase in period 2 and thereby reduce his capacity charge to β. But either of these changes would impinge directly upon B, and he could reverse their effect by a parallel move. That is, even with communication forbidden one would expect duoposonists to make some recognition of their interdependence. (A more general discussion is pursued below.) Given reasonable respect for B's ability to protect himself, A would be unwise to act using a *ceteris paribus* assumption for B's behavior, in a case where B is so vulnerable. But the inhibiting effect on output expansion discussed in the text remains, since B would have no incentive to offset such action.

23 This limitation on the available strategies is for convenience. It is, however, not so limiting as might be supposed, for maximum and minimum purchases of each "player" are determined solely by reference to his own demand relationships. He will always buy an additional unit in both periods if the sum of his own valuations therefore is $2b/\beta$; he will generally buy an additional unit in either period if its valuation is $b + \beta$; and he will never purchase a unit if its valuation is below b. All that is at issue are the units that are possibly justified only by the joint demands of both "players." In addition, the cost uncertainty faced by A is a function of the difference between his purchases in the two periods, not their level, which limits the number of alternatives whose payoffs are a function of the game that he must consider. Finally mixed strategies can be interpreted as linear interpolations between listed pure strategies, and if the net benefits of a player can be viewed as a series of linear segments, it is necessary only to consider the corners as available pure strategies.

24 It is impractical, even in a note, to survey all possibilities, but some of the alternative possibilities are as follows:

As a formal problem in nonzero sum, nonco-operative game theory this matrix presents no difficulties. The central notion, due to Nash, ("Non Cooperative Games", *Annals of Mathematics*, Vol. 54, Sept. 1951) is that of an equilibrium point, defined to be a point such that no unilateral change in strategy by either player can improve his payoff. In this case there is a unique equilibrium point, $A_1 B_1$. While the payoff to each player is positive, compared with the optimal combination, (and even with several of the nonoptimal combinations of strategies), it is poor indeed. Yet it is possible to imagine a situation in which this, relatively unprofitable, set of strategies might be used. Suppose each player to be a shortsighted maximizer, who given any strategy by the other player chooses to maximize his payoff assuming no change in the other's strategy. If we permit recontracting, the resting place would be the equilibrium point. This psychology is analogous to that underlying the Cournot, Bertrand, and Edgeworth duopoly analyses, and also that of the quantity-adjusting pure competitor. But here, also, there is no necessary reason to accept that outcome as the only admissible one.

Suppose, given full knowledge of the matrixes, B is a mere quantity adjuster, but A is prepared to look at the consequences of his own actions although he recognizes that B will not. Looking at B's payoffs he sees that B will choose strategy B_s if A selects either A_1 or A_2, and B_2 in response to A_3. The most favorable of these combinations to A is the combination A_3B_2 with a payoff of "3." This is preferable (in terms of payoff to each player) to the equilibrium point solution and we shall designate it as a quasi-equilibrium point for A. This outcome is analogous to the Stackelberg leadership solution in which A is the leader, and B the follower. It may also resemble the kind of price leadership associated with a dominant firm in an industry with a competitive fringe, in which the large seller maximizes his profits while granting his competitors the share of the market they choose as quantity adjusters. There is, of course, a quasi-equilibrium for B, which may or may not differ from A's. If it coincides, the quasi-equilibrium points are also equilibrium points, but even then it need not be an optimal point. Returning to A's quasi-equilibrium, A could assure this result without any co-operation or negotiation with B simply by announcing or contracting to follow strategy A_3.

The purely game-theoretic features of this problem occasion these parenthetic comments: That the equilibrium point is not the optimal point is perhaps not surprising. That the optimal point can occur in a dominated strategy seems more damaging. (In the example the third strategies of each player are dominated by a linear combination of the first two.) Even more damaging (to game theory as a source of help) is the fact that points, designated as "quasi-equilibrium points" are superior to the equilibrium point in payoff to each player, yet can be reached without any co-operation whatever. Yet *these* points may well occur in dominated strategies and thus be eliminated from consideration if the usual game theory procedures of solution are adopted.

Other outcomes can be enumerated. For example, suppose that each player knows only his own payoff matrix and fears taking losses. An outcome in which he chose his second strategy might result, as the second strategies are alone lossproof. A similar result might occur with full knowledge of the matrixes if each player imputed irrationality or vindictiveness to the other. (This is maximin behavior, which is generally irrelevant in a nonconstant sum game.

Note, finally, that to reach the optimal point, mere recognition of interdependence by both players may not suffice. For example, A may hope to bluff B into B's quasi-equilibrium if he (A) can gain a higher payoff there than at the optimal point. And similarly for B.

25 I have been privileged to meet during 1956–57 with the Water Resources Planning and Development Project, Graduate School of Public Administration, Harvard University. A chief lesson of this experience is that the problems encountered, both theoretical and practical, are vastly more complex than meet the eye. At this point I therefore merely suggest one potential application of this theoretical solution. Some of the most challenging problems in the water resource field arise from the complementarity (with respect to use of capacity) of different outputs whose valuations are central to efficient project design and operation. Given variable demands (over time) for different outputs (e.g., electric power, irrigation, water supply, flood control) a peak load problem arises in which the additional units of (storage) capacity may be justified by several of the uses. There are, of course, other complications: to mention just one, some uses are partially or wholly competitive with one another. A fuller discussion is beyond the scope of the present paper.

26 Vickrey, "A Proposal For Revising New York's Subway Fare Structure," *Journal of the Operations Research Society of America*, Vol. 3 (Feb. 1955), pp. 38–68 (reprinted in McCloskey and Copinger, *Operations Research for Management*, Vol. II, 1956). While himself proposing a time-of-day fare, he limits himself to estimating the responsiveness of demand to a change in the *uniform* rate of fare. Recognizing the other problem he says "indeed there is no direct evidence as to how great such a shift (induced by a differential rate structure) would be." (*Journal*, p. 54).

27 See Leslie Cookenboo Jr., *Crude Oil Pipelines* (Cambridge, Mass., 1955).

24 Bundling as an entry barrier

Barry Nalebuff

Introduction

In this paper we look at the case for bundling in an oligopolistic environment. We show that bundling is a particularly effective entry-deterrent strategy. A company that has market power in two goods, A and B, can, by bundling them together, make it harder for a rival with only one of these goods to enter the market. Bundling allows an incumbent to defend both products without having to price low in each. While it is still possible to compete by offering a rival bundle, a monopolist can significantly lower the potential profits of a one-product entrant without having to engage in limit pricing prior to entry.

We also show that bundling continues to be an effective pricing tool even if entry deterrence fails (or if there is already an existing one-product rival). A company with a monopoly in product A and a duopoly in product B makes higher profits by selling an A–B bundle than by selling A and B independently. Leveraging market power from A into B and accepting some one-product competition against the bundle is better than using the monopoly power in good A all by itself. Since bundling mitigates the impact of competition on the incumbent, an entrant can expect the bundling strategy to persist, even without any commitment.

The traditional explanation for bundling that economists have given is that it serves as an effective tool of price discrimination by a monopolist (see Stigler [1968], Adams and Yellen [1976]), Schmalensee [1982, 1984], McAfee, McMillan, and Whinston [1989], and Bakos and Brynjolfsson [1999]). Typically, a firm has to charge one price to all consumers. In these cases, variability in customer valuations frustrates the seller's ability to capture consumer surplus. Thus, a tool that helps reduce heterogeneity in valuations will help a monopolist earn greater profits. This advantage of bundling is especially apparent when the values of A and B are perfectly negatively correlated: offering an A–B bundle leads to homogeneous valuations among consumers, and thus the monopolist can capture 100 percent of the consumer surplus. Even if A and B have independent valuations, McAfee, McMillan, and Whinston [1989] show that a monopolist still does better by selling A and B as a bundle rather than independently.

Although price discrimination provides a reason to bundle, the gains are small compared with the gains from the entry-deterrent effect. Our baseline model has two goods, where consumer valuations are independent and uniformly distributed over [0, 1]. In this environment, price discrimination through bundling raises a monopolist's profits from 0.50 to approximately 0.544, a gain of about 9 percent. Certainly worthwhile. But the same act of bundling cuts an entrant's potential profits by 60 percent. If this deters entry, profits are more than doubled. Even if this is not enough to deter entry, bundling is still of great value – post-entry profits to the incumbent are more than 50 percent higher with a bundle offering compared with when the goods are sold independently.

The literature on bundling as a price discrimination tool emphasizes that it works best when the bundled goods have a negative correlation in value. This is when bundling most reduces the dispersion in valuations and allows the monopolist to capture the lion's share of consumer surplus. Bundling still works when the valuations are independent, but the gain from bundling disappears with perfect positive correlation.

The opposite is true when bundling is used as an entry deterrent or monopoly extension strategy. It is most effective when the bundled goods are positively correlated in value. Even with independent valuations, bundling is still an effective tool, but it loses its effectiveness when the goods are perfectly negatively correlated in value. The reason is that a one-product entrant has everything its consumers want when the valuations for A and B are negatively correlated. The markets for A and B are essentially different groups of consumers. In contrast, when A and B are positively correlated, the same group of consumers is buying both A and B and, thus, a one-product entrant cannot satisfy its customers.

Price discrimination and entry deterrence are only two of many reasons to offer a bundled product. Creating cost savings is another (see Salinger [1995]) as is creating a more valuable product.[1] In a larger sense, almost everything is a bundled product. A car is a bundle of seats, engine, steering wheel, gas pedal, cup holders, and much more. An obvious explanation for many bundles is that the company can integrate the products better than its customers can. For simplicity, we start with the case in which there is no complementarity in creating the bundle, either in consumption or in production. On the consumption side, that means Value $(A + B$ together$) =$ Value $(A$ alone$) +$ Value $(B$ alone$)$. Similarly, there is no complementarity in producing the bundle: Cost $(A + B$ together$) =$ Cost $(A$ alone$) +$ Cost $(B$ alone$)$.[2]

The motivating example for this paper is Microsoft Office, in which Word, Excel, Power-Point, and Exchange are bundled together into a software suite. The consumer could just as well assemble his or her own bundle. In fact, many consumers may feel that they could do an even better job of assembling a bundle using "best-of-breed" components, perhaps combining Microsoft's PowerPoint with Corel's Word Perfect, IBM's Lotus 123, and Qualcomm's Eudora for email. Since not all of its products are best-of-breed, how does Microsoft gain an advantage by selling its office products as a bundle?

Certainly there are synergies between the software applications in Microsoft Office. The commonality of commands and the ability to create links between applications make the products easier to use. A single telephone number to call for help also makes the package more attractive. On the supply side, it is cheaper to include multiple products on a single CD disc than to package each one individually. We will show that even absent these synergistic gains, a monopolist concerned about competition would have a strong incentive to sell these products as a bundle rather than individually.

While bundled products are common in many sectors of the economy, the software suite is a particularly good example of the power of bundling because the marginal cost of software is zero. As marginal costs rise, bundling becomes less attractive. Bundling creates an inefficiency in that some consumers are "forced" to buy the bundle even though they value one of its components at below production cost (see Adams and Yellen [1976]). Thus, it is not surprising that software is especially conducive to bundling since this countervailing force does not arise. The potential for very large scale bundling of information goods is demonstrated in Bakos and Brynjolfsson [1999] who consider the limiting case of bundling together an infinite number of information goods.[3]

Remarkably few papers examine the role of bundling as an entry deterrent device or as a competitive tool to use against a rival with a limited product line. One explanation for this is that the Chicago School has largely succeeded in discrediting the idea of leveraging monopoly power (see, for example, Director and Levi [1956] and Schmalensee [1982] for a more formal argument). A company with a monopoly in good A gains no advantage by only selling A as part of a bundle with a competitively supplied product B.[4] The reason is that good B is freely available at its marginal cost. Thus, consumers evaluate an A–B bundle by whether or not A is worth more than the incremental cost of the bundle over B alone. Anyone who buys the bundle would also be willing to buy A alone, at the same profit margin for the monopolist. In fact, the monopolist would typically do even better by selling A alone as some customers who would buy A alone would not choose to buy the bundle.[5]

Whinston [1990] was the first to reexamine and resurrect the role of tying as an entry deterrent. He recognized that the Chicago School's criticism of leveraging monopoly power from market A to market B applies only if market B is perfectly competitive. Whinston demonstrates the advantages of tying when one firm has a monopoly in A and faces a competitor in B with a differentiated product. In his model, tying commits the monopolist to being more aggressive against an entrant, and this commitment discourages entry. Of course, if entry occurs, the incumbent would then prefer to abandon his bundling strategy. We, too, find a reason to leverage monopoly power, although the model and the mechanism of action are quite different. For example, we find that bundling reduces the entrant's potential profits while mitigating the profit loss to an incumbent if entry occurs. Thus, bundling is credible even without any commitment device.

Choi and Stefanadis [2001] also rely on a commitment to bundle as a way to deter entry. In their model, A and B are only of any value when consumed together. Thus, an incumbent bundle completely forecloses a one-product entry Innovation has a lower expected payoff as success in both the A and B good is required to gain access to the market.

Carlton and Waldman [2002] show how bundling can be used to deny an entrant scale and thus deter entry. One case they consider involves an entrant with a superior complementary product that might subsequently enter the original product market. If this firm can only enter the complements market, then its entry will increase industry profits, some of which will go to the original producer and entry will be welcomed. The problem arises if the rival might later enter the original market, in which case the incumbent's profits fall. Forcing a bundle product on consumers denies the entrant sales when it only has the complement product and this reduction in sales can be enough to make entry unprofitable. However, note that if entry were to occur, forcing a bundle would depress profits, and thus there is a commitment issue (which might be resolved through technical bundling). In our paper bundling arises without commitment. Even without complementarity, we find that bundling leaves little opportunity for a one-product firm to enter the market.

The plan of the paper is to first present the main results in as simple a model as possible. We begin with the case of independent valuations, a neutral ground on which to compare the price-discrimination effect with the entry deterrent or market-power effect. Conveniently, this is also the most mathematically tractable case. Then, in an extensions section, we show that the results are quite general. The extensions include nonuniform value distributions, three or more good bundles, nonzero production costs, positive and negative correlation in valuations, and complementarity among the products. We also demonstrate that the power of bundling extends to a game against an existing one-product rival or to the game where an incumbent responds to entry. The proofs for most propositions are in an Appendix.

A model

Consider a market with two goods, labeled A and B. Consumers are interested in purchasing exactly one unit of A or one unit of B or both. A consumer of type α values A at α_a and B at α_b. We normalize the total market to be of size 1 and assume that budget constraints are not an issue. We further assume that the distribution of consumers is uniform over the unit square.[6] This implies that the valuations of A and B are independent and uniform over $[0, 1]$.

The two strategic players in the game are an incumbent and a potential challenger. The incumbent produces both goods A and B, each at zero marginal cost. The challenger is assumed to have a perfect substitute product for one of A or B, also produced at zero marginal cost. Whether the challenger will have a rival A product or a rival B product is random, and each outcome is equally likely. The incumbent's challenge is to prepare against possible entry in either A or B without knowing which flank the entrant will attack.[7]

Even though a challenger has a rival product, it need not enter the game. The entry decision will be based on whether the expected profits in the game cover its costs of entry. The entry costs are determined by the environment and known to all players.

It is reasonable to ask what an entrant will expect prices to be following entry. In the subgame perfect approach, the preentry price is irrelevant, except, perhaps, as an indication of the incumbent's costs.[8] But as Bain [1949] argued "the supposition that the potential entrant's judgment of industry demand and rivalry he will meet is entirely unrelated to current price or profit in the industry, however, probably goes too far. Even if he does not believe the observed price will remain there for him to exploit, he may nevertheless regard this price as an indicator both of the character of industry demand and of the probable character of rival policy after his entry." We do not imagine that an entrant expects the incumbent not to react at all to entry – rather that the post-entry price will be somewhere between the incumbent's preentry price and the result of post-entry competition. If an entrant cannot justify entry costs at the prevailing preentry prices, then this is a persuasive argument not to enter the market.

Moreover, the entrant may employ a judo strategy by entering into the market with a limited capacity. If the incumbent is constrained to charge one price to all its customers (perhaps by a most-favored customer clause), it may not be worthwhile to reduce price in order to regain the limited number of customers that were stolen away.[9]

For these reasons, we first assume that the incumbent sets its prices prior to the challenger's entry decision. The incumbent's prices are then fixed for the rest of the game. This approach is generally favorable toward an entrant.[10] If an incumbent can deter entry without being able to lower prices post entry, then even a myopic entrant would be deterred from coming into the market.

The result that entry is made difficult via bundling does not rely on holding prices fixed. Later in the paper, we extend the results to include a Bertrand-Nash pricing equilibrium post entry. An entrant will also expect to make low profits when the incumbent responds. The surprise is how low an entrant's potential profits are without any price response. Profits are low primarily because a one-product entrant has difficulty capturing market share against a bundle, even when charging half the bundle price. By first employing a Stackelberg approach, we are able to illustrate this effect with simple mathematics.

As an entrant considers the incumbent's potential response, the most relevant question is not whether the incumbent will respond immediately in terms of pricing. The most relevant question is whether the incumbent will continue to bundle in response to entry. If the incumbent can revert to selling its goods individually, then Bertrand-Nash post-entry pricing is a very powerful entry deterrent tool. (Pricing and profits on the good with entry would fall to zero, and entry would be costlessly deterred.) In fact, akin to a nuclear bomb, unbundled pricing is too powerful. We show that it is not credible to respond to entry by pricing goods individually when bundling is an option. Thus, an entrant can expect that an incumbent will bundle absent entry and will continue to bundle post entry.[11] This underscores the need to understand the nature of bundling.

Independent pricing

As a baseline, we consider the case in which A and B are only sold separately. If the incumbent were alone in the market and priced the two goods independently, profits would be maximized at $p_a = p_b = 0.5$. The incumbent's profits would be $0.25 + 0.25 = 0.50$.

This pricing makes it particularly easy for a challenger to enter the market. The challenger comes in with a price of $0.5 - \epsilon$ and steals all the market in whichever product he has. If this happens, the entrant earns 0.25, and the incumbent's profits are reduced by half to 0.25.

The incumbent can also engage in limit pricing. For example, if the incumbent lowers the price of A, this would reduce a challenger's potential profits. Symmetrically, if it made sense for the incumbent to lower the price of A, it would also make sense for it to lower the price of B. Since the challenger can make essentially all of the profits of an incumbent in whichever market it enters, if an incumbent has preentry profits of Z, the entrant can make $Z/2$. Thus, instead of choosing a price directly, it is easier to think of the incumbent's strategy as choosing a profit level, which translates back into a price.

To deter a challenger with entry costs of E requires the incumbent to price at a point p such that its profits are no more than $2E$. This is because the entrant can take half of the incumbent's market and profits. If the incumbent chooses not to deter entry, it should charge $(1/2, 1/2)$, the optimal price absent entry. This is because the firm will lose one of two markets. In the remaining market, the firm does best to maximize profits, which occurs when price is $1/2$.

Thus, the incumbent's choice is between deterring entry and earning profits of $2E$ or accepting entry and earning profits of $1/4$. The incumbent will deter entry if $E > 1/8$ and accept entry otherwise.

Pure bundling

Here we assume that the incumbent can sell A and B only as a bundle. If the incumbent prices the bundle at 1, the sum of the monopoly prices for A and B, it would sell to half the market, and its profits would remain unchanged at $1/2$. However, the marginal consumers are now more valuable (as price is 1, not $1/2$), and this creates an incentive to cut price.[12] Absent entry, the profits of an incumbent with bundle price x are $x * (1 - x^2/2)$, for $x \leq 1$, which is maximized at $x = \sqrt{2/3}$. (Since the optimal monopoly bundled price is below 1, henceforth we will restrict our attention to the case of $x \leq 1$.)

Having presented the basic mathematics of monopoly bundling, we are now ready to explain how bundling makes entry much less profitable without lowering the profits of the incumbent if entry is deterred. The advantages come from two channels, what we call (i) the pure bundling effect and (ii) the bundle discount effect.

The pure bundle effect examines the case in which the incumbent and challenger simply translate their independent pricing strategy into the bundled case without reoptimizing. Call this "equivalent prices." If the bundle is priced at 1, the incumbent makes the exact same amount as it would selling the two products independently, assuming no entry. The entrant considers coming into the market with a price of 0.50, essentially the same price it would charge against an incumbent selling A and B each for 0.50. (Of course, neither the incumbent's bundled price of 1 nor the entrant's contemplation of 0.50 is an optimal strategy – these simple translations from the independent case are used to demonstrate the pure bundling effect.)

Pure bundling effect.   At equivalent prices, the act of putting two independent products into a bundle reduces the entrant's profits by 50 percent.

Assume that the entrant has product B. An entrant who comes in to the B market with independent pricing can steal the entire market with a marginal discount and thereby earn 0.25. Consider, in contrast, what happens when an entrant comes into a market against an incumbent with a bundle priced at 1. If the entrant prices at 0.50, it sells only to people who value B at above 0.50 and A at less than 0.50. A consumer who values A at more than 0.50 would be better served by buying the bundle. Consequently, the entrant only sells to 25 percent of the market, and its profits are cut by 50 percent.

The second channel that provides additional entry deterrence is the "bundle discount effect." As the bundle price is reduced and the bundle is sold at a discount relative to the original component prices, entry becomes even less profitable. This is low-cost or even costless deterrence, as absent considerations of entry an incumbent would choose to price its bundle at below 1.

Bundling discount effect.   Selling the bundle at a discount to the optimal independent pricing provides an opportunity to raise the incumbent's profits absent entry, while making entry even less profitable. Reductions below the profit-maximizing bundle price have a second-order loss to the incumbent and a first-order loss to the entrant.

Recall that the optimal bundled price for an uncontested monopoly is $\sqrt{2/3} \approx 0.8$. Lowering the incumbent's bundle price from 1 to 0.8 reduces the potential profits of an entrant, while raising profits if entry is deterred. Reducing the bundled price below 0.8 further reduces the potential profits of an entrant, while also lowering profits if entry is deterred. However, the incumbent's price is near an optimum, and so profits fall slowly while the entrant's profits continue to fall rapidly.

Table 24.1 shows the incumbent's profits alongside the opportunities presented to an entrant. These calculations are all based on the optimal price response by an entrant, as shown by Proposition 1 in the Appendix.[13]

If the incumbent charges 0.8, its profits absent entry rise from 0.50 to 0.544. Meanwhile, the entrant's potential profits fall by 30 percent, from 0.148 to 0.105.

The incumbent can push things even further at little cost. For example, a move down to a bundled price of 0.68 reduces the incumbent's profits absent entry to 0.523, or by about 2 percent. The entrant's potential profits are reduced by another 23 percent, down to 0.081.

Table 24.1

Incumbent's price	Incumbent profits/no entry	Entrant's potential profits
1.00	0.500	0.148
0.80	**0.544**	0.105
0.68	0.523	0.081
0.41	0.375	0.034

Further prices begin to impose first-order costs on the incumbent. For example, if the bundle price falls to 0.41, the incumbent's profits fall to 0.375, about a 25 percent reduction. The entrant's potential profits fall almost 60 percent, all the way down to 0.034.[14]

The cumulative effect of these price cuts is impressive. Taking the bundled price down from 1 to 0.68 results in an inconsequential loss to the incumbent, while reducing the entrant's profits by 45 percent. Going all the way down to a bundled price of 0.41 reduces the incumbent's profits by 25 percent, but leaves the entrant with potential profits of only 0.034, a 77 percent reduction from its profits against a bundle priced at 1 and a fall of 86 percent compared with its potential profits of 0.25 when the incumbent sells the goods independently.[15]

Post-entry protection

Up until this point, we have focused on the reduction in potential profits to an entrant. A further benefit to the incumbent is that, if entry should occur, the loss to the incumbent is significantly reduced relative to the independent pricing case.

Take the case in which the incumbent charges $x = 1$ for the bundle and the entrant comes in selling B at $p_e = 0.5$. Instead of losing all of its B sales, the incumbent loses sales only to its customers who value the bundle at above 1, but value A at less than 0.50. In fact, this is only one-quarter of the incumbent's market – but, since it loses the bundled sale, this is like losing half the sales on one of the products.

This, of course, understates the cost of entry. Against a bundle price of 1, the entrant would charge $1/3$, not $1/2$, and capture $(2/3)(2/3) = 4/9$ of the market. When $x = 1$, it is always the case that the incumbent loses half of what the entrant captures. Thus, the incumbent loses $2/9$ the of the market. Since the incumbent was charging a price of 1 for the bundle, this also represents its lost profits. In comparison, when the challenger came into the market with independent pricing, the incumbent lost all of the B market and half of its profits, or 0.25.

Anticipating entry, the incumbent can do much better by charging a price below 1. $\Pi_I |$ *entry* is maximized at $x = 0.68$, which leads to profits of 0.374. In response to this price, the entrant would charge 0.27 and earn 0.081.

Since the incumbent can earn 0.374 by allowing entry, the incumbent should attempt to deter entry only if doing so leads to profits above 0.374. Recall that the incumbent's profits without entry are given by $x(1 - x^2/2)$. As seen in Table 24.2, a bundle price of 0.41 translates to incumbent profits of 0.375, absent entry. Facing a bundle price of 0.41, an entrant can earn only 0.034.

Putting this all together, the incumbent should charge 0.68 and accept entry if the rival's entry costs are below 0.034. Otherwise, the incumbent should engage in "limit pricing" and set a bundled price just low enough to deter the rival from entering. The incumbent follows

Table 24.2

Incumbent's price	Incumbent profits/no entry	Incumbent profits/entry
1.00	0.500	0.278
0.80	0.544	0.361
0.68	0.523	**0.374**
0.41	0.375	0.309

this policy from a bundle price of 0.41 all the way up to a price of $\sqrt{2/3} \approx 0.8$, at which point there is no further gain from raising price.

The results about bundling can all be summarized in Figures 24.1 and 24.2. In Figure 24.1 the top curve shows the incumbent's profits as a monopolist. The middle curve traces the incumbent's profits if entry occurs, while the bottom curve illustrates the entrant's potential profits for each bundle price. The incumbent can always achieve the maximum of its profits-with-entry curve (profits of 0.374). Therefore, it deters entry only when the top curve lies above 0.374.

The results of Figure 24.1 can be incorporated into a new graph (Figure 24.2) in which the horizontal axis now reflects entry costs.

The price-discrimination effect on which previous authors have focused is evidenced by the fact that the bundle line reaches profits of 0.54 as opposed to 0.50. The ability of bundling to deter entry is reflected in the fact that entry occurs only when entry costs are below 0.034, compared with 0.25 in the case with independent pricing. It is remarkable that once entry costs are above 0.10, the incumbent can pick its unconstrained monopoly price and not be concerned about entry.

The result that entry is less costly to the incumbent is reflected in the fact that when entry occurs, the incumbent's profits are 0.374 versus 0.25, a 50 percent improvement. Thus, bundling mitigates the cost of entry. For this reason, it is in the incumbent's self-interest to maintain the bundle post entry. There is no issue of credibility or commitment.[16]

The rapidly rising profits in the curved section, where entry costs are between 0.034 to 0.1, demonstrate that bundled pricing is an efficient way to deter entry. When entry costs are 0.1, an incumbent that bundles earns 0.54, more than double the profits of an incumbent that sells its products independently. The take away message demonstrated by Figure 24.2 is that the price discrimination effect offered by bundling is valuable, but the largest gains come from the entry-mitigation effect and the efficient entry-deterrence.

There is a side benefit to bundling that is hard to quantify. This benefit arises when entry costs are so low (below 0.034) that entry is not profitably deterred. When the entrant comes into the market, its profits are only 0.08, which is 68 percent less than when it enters against unbundled pricing.[17] Once the decision to accommodate entry has been made, there is no reason in our model for the incumbent to be concerned with a competitor's profits. Even so, we recognize that most firms would feel less threatened when their rivals are less profitable.

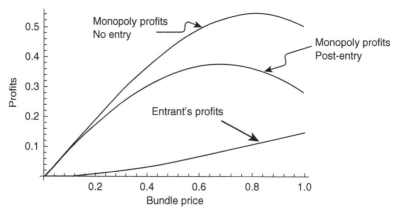

Figure 24.1

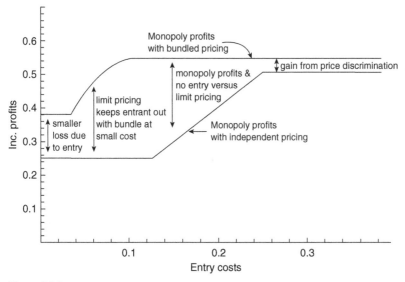

Figure 24.2

Extensions

In this section we first develop the basic model along several lines. We begin with some simple extensions to include mixed bundling, uncertain entry costs, nonzero production costs, and nonuniform distribution of valuations.[18]

We then explore in more depth the advantages of bundling more than two items together and the effect of positive and negative correlations in value. Positive correlation amplifies the gains to bundling while negative correlation makes it less valuable. The intuition for positive and negative correlation is often better captured by the existence of complementarity between the bundled goods, and we turn to this topic next. When the bundled products are complements, bundling is an even more powerful tool. The value does not disappear with substitutes, although it is diminished.

Finally, we consider the issue of commitment in the post-entry Bertrand-Nash pricing game. We show that the incumbent has an incentive to persist with a bundled offering following entry. Even if the incumbent can adjust prices post entry, we demonstrate there are still significant advantages to competing with a bundled offering. Bundling mitigates the impact of entry. Although an entrant's potential profits would be even lower if the incumbent could commit not to bundle following entry, we find there is little room for an entrant to earn profits against a bundle offering.

Simple extensions

An uncontested monopolist, selling a mixed bundle – *A*, *B*, and an *A*–*B* bundle – could always achieve higher profits. However, mixed bundling is less effective in the presence of a rival than in the pure monopoly model. The reason is that the incumbent has to be concerned that a rival with one product, say *B*, will use the incumbent's other product, A, to create a rival bundle and thereby steal all of the incumbent's bundle sales. Thus, the individual items need to be priced very high relative to the bundle, and so the individual items in the mixed bundle generate relatively few additional sales. Given the limited potential for this approach to increase profits, we do not pursue it further.

Our analysis was made under the assumption that the incumbent knows the precise entry cost of the challenger and thus can fine-tune its entry deterrent strategy. The same analysis can be used to illustrate the advantages of bundling when the potential challenger's entry costs are uncertain. In this case the incumbent deters the entrant with some probability. With bundling, the optimal probability of entry deterrence is much higher and is done at a lower cost [Nalebuff 1999].

Selling two or more goods together will create inefficiencies when production costs are no longer zero at the margin. As shown in the working paper version, significant gains from bundling persist, even for moderate costs [Nalebuff 1999].

Extending the model to nonuniform distribution of valuations strengthens the results. Over the entire class of symmetric, single-peaked densities, the uniform density is the *least* favorable to the pure bundling effect.

Pure bundling effect with nonuniform densities.   If the density of consumer types is symmetric and unimodal, then at equivalent prices, the act of putting two products into a bundle reduces the entrant's profits by at least 50 percent.

Proof of pure bundling effect with nonuniform densities. See the Appendix.

The intuition for the result is that the entrant only sells to customers who value its one good, say B, at more than p_e and good A at less than its monopoly price, $\hat{p}_a$. With a uniform distribution, $\hat{p}_a = 1/2$, and the entrant loses half of its potential market. With a more general symmetric unimodal density of preferences, $\hat{p}_a \leq 1/2$, and this makes it harder for the entrant to attract customers for its single B product.

Bundling three or more goods

It might be tempting to extrapolate and predict that if bundling two items together is a good idea, then putting three together would be even better. It turns out that there are advantages of adding more goods to the bundle, but they are smaller than one might expect given our preceding analysis. The discrete gains that come from the act of bundling two goods do not continue to grow when more goods are added to the bundle. There is a gain from creating a very large bundle, but that gain is primarily due to a third effect, the law of large numbers.

More precisely, Proposition 2 below shows that the pure bundling effect remains constant for any number of products in the bundle. Assume that a one-product entrant prices at $1/2$. Its sales will be $1/2$ against a monopolist with independent pricing, but only $1/4$ against a two-product bundle priced at 1. In fact, the entrant's sales *remain* at $1/4$ against a three-product bundle priced at 1.5, a four-product bundle priced at 2, a one-hundred-product bundle priced at 50, and so on.

PROPOSITION 1 *For all $n \geq 2$, with $x = n/2$ and $p_e = 1/2$, the challenger has sales of $1/4$ units and revenue of $1/8$.*

Proof of Proposition 2. See the Appendix.

The intuition for this result is as follows: if a one-product entrant offers its product at $1/2$ against a 100-product bundle priced at 50, whether consumers will buy the single product or the bundle depends on whether they value the other 99 products above or below 49.50. Half do, and half do not. Thus, the entrant's demand is cut by 50 percent, just as in the two-product bundle.

The advantage of adding more products to the bundle is the incremental gain from the bundle discount effect. The price-discount effect gets stronger as the dimensionality of the bundle increases. By the time there are ten goods in the bundle, the entrant gets only one-third as many customers at its optimal entry price compared with its optimal entry against a two-good bundle (see Nalebuff [1999]).

In a recent series of papers, Bakos and Brynjolfsson [1999, 2000] examine the effect of bundling at a very large scale. Their first paper [1999] demonstrates that bundling an infinite number of goods together allows a monopolist to achieve perfect price discrimination. Along with being a super-effective price-discrimination tool, bundling also creates a significant barrier to entry [2000]. Because the monopolist is able to sell its bundle to 100 percent of consumers, an entrant can sell its individual products only for their incremental value. When all the entrant's potential customers have already purchased the incumbent's *B* product, the entrant's price is thus limited by the extent to which its product is differentiated and viewed as superior by a subset of consumers.

Our focus lies at the other end of the spectrum, namely small bundles, mostly two goods. Although two-good bundles are not that effective at price discrimination, they are surprisingly effective at entry deterrence.

When it is feasible to create super-large bundles, this will clearly be an effective strategy, both for price-discrimination and entry deterrence reasons. There are several constraints that may prevent this. First, as the size of the bundle grows, the i.i.d. assumption implies that the bundle will also become increasingly valuable – and expensive. Although AOL might bundle thousands of information goods together in its package, the value of the bundle does not seem to grow proportionately. Nor does the distribution in valuations appear to converge. One likely reason is that valuations across goods are typically positively correlated, so that dispersion remains. This would be the case if valuations depend on some common factors, such as personal or business use. As we will observe below, bundling as an entry deterrent continues to work – is even enhanced – with positive correlation while the price discrimination effect is diminished.

Upon reflection, when the scope of bundling is modest, the strongest argument for adding another good to a bundle is to keep one step ahead of a potential entrant. An incumbent with a three-good bundle has less to fear from a potential entrant who can put together a two-good package. The third good prevents the incumbent from competing head-to-head and makes it harder for the entrant to gain share.

Positive and negative correlation in values

Looking at most bundles, especially software bundles, it appears that the items are positively correlated in value. At first glance, this is somewhat of a puzzle. Positive correlation in values lowers a monopolist's profits as it makes price discrimination more difficult. The gain from bundling must lie elsewhere. With positive correlation, entry against a bundle is even less profitable. However, if entry should occur, the entrant is forced to come in with a very low price, and profits are correspondingly very low. Thus, positive correlation in values is helpful to the incumbent to the extent that it makes entry deterrence more effective. But if entry cannot be prevented, then positive correlation in values ends up hurting the incumbent as the resulting entry is more costly. Conversely, a negative correlation in values makes entry easier, but also less costly to the incumbent.

We begin by considering the pure bundling effect with correlated values. For comparison purposes we want to keep the marginal density for each individual good unchanged and thus the optimal independent price at 1/2.

When the two values are perfectly correlated, all of the individuals lie along the 45-degree line, $\alpha_a = \alpha_b$. Similarly, when the two values are perfectly negatively correlated, all of the individuals lie along the opposite diagonal, $\alpha_a + \alpha_b = 1$. The way we model intermediate levels of correlation is to take a weighted average of the uniform density and either the diagonal density or the off-diagonal density. The correlation between A and B is denoted by $\rho \in [-1, 1]$.

Pure bundling effect with correlation.   At equivalent prices, the act of putting two independent products into a bundle reduces the entrant's profits by $(1 + p)/2$.

At perfect negative correlation there is no pure bundling effect, while at perfect positive correlation the pure bundling effect reduces the entrant's profits to zero. Consider what happens when an entrant comes into a market against an incumbent with a bundle priced at 1. If the entrant prices at 0.50, it sells only to people who value B at above 0.50 and A at less than 0.50. Consequently, the entrant only sells to 25 percent of the uniformly distributed market. There is no overlap with the 45-degree line so none of the perfectly positively correlated consumers will go to the entrant. Conversely, half of the off-diagonal consumers lie in the lower right quadrant. Thus, with $p = 1$, the entrant's sales are zero while with $p = -1$ sales are 0.50. Intermediate cases lie linearly in between.

The full analysis is more complicated as the optimal response of the entrant is influenced by the correlation; details can be found in Nalebuff [1999].

Bundling complements

Often the products in a bundle complement each other. This is separate from and potentially in addition to the existence of positive correlation in the value of the bundled products. Thus, a high valuation for Excel may indicate a high income or a business use, and this correlation would suggest a high value for Power-Point. With complementarity, the value of PowerPoint plus Excel is higher than PowerPoint alone plus Excel alone. In the case of the components of Microsoft Office, we suspect that both positive correlation and complementarities are present.

We say that A and B are complements if $V_{a+b} = (1 + \delta)(V_a + V_b)$, $\delta > 0$. If $\delta < 0$, then A and B are substitutes.

Complementarities, similar to positive correlation, amplify the advantages of bundling. Intuitively, consumers are less attracted to a one-product offering since that means giving up on the bundle bonus. Nalebuff [1999] demonstrates the following.

Pure bundling effect with complementarity.   At equivalent prices, the act of putting two complementary products into a bundle reduces the entrant's profits from 1/4 to $1/8(1/(1 + \delta))[1 - 3\delta/2]$, where δ is the measure of complementarity.

Thus, if $\delta = 0$, the reduction in profits is 50 percent, from 0.25 to 0.125. This is our original pure bundling result. If $\delta = 0.10$, then profits are reduced to 40 percent of their previous level, from 0.25 to 0.10. If $\delta = 0.25$, then profits are reduced to 25 percent of their previous level, from 0.25 to 0.0625.

Conversely, if the two products are substitutes, bundling is less effective. If $\delta = -0.10$, then profits are reduced by 36 percent, from 0.25 to 0.16. If $\delta = -0.25$, then profits are only reduced by 12 percent, from 0.25 to 0.22.

An anonymous referee suggested the possibility that the complementarity might not be symmetric. Here we consider the case where $V_{a+b} = (V_a + V_b)$ if the two goods are purchased together, but $V_b = 0$ if good B is purchased alone. To say this another way, the only way to get the value from good B is to also buy good A. One might think of B as software that runs on an operating system and thus has no value on its own but serves to enhance the value of the operating system.

In that case, the optimal pricing strategy for an incumbent is the same as first presented. Because the incumbent sells a bundle, consumer valuations are still $(V_a + V_b)$.

Entry is a bit different. Since good A is not sold on its own, there is no value in entering the good B market by itself. No consumers will buy B without A. As for entering with good A, that follows as in the original analysis. A more sophisticated analysis of this case is considered in Heeb [2003], who adds an element of product differentiation between the incumbent's and entrant's B goods. He provides conditions that lead all consumers to purchase of one of the B goods, in which case bundling is an optimal strategy.

Bertrand-Nash pricing or competition against an existing rival

In this subsection we show how the earlier results generalize to the case of a Nash pricing game post entry. This can also be understood as the expected outcome of competition between two companies, each established in the market, where one has two products and the other has only one.

Company 1 sells both products A and B, and company 2 sells only product B. The question is whether company 1 (with its monopoly in good A) should extract all of its monopoly rents in good A directly, or, would it do better by leveraging that monopoly and selling an A–B bundle?

We demonstrate that the benefits to bundling continue to hold when we consider the Nash equilibrium in the pricing game. Bundling is a credible strategy. Firm 1 becomes more aggressive in its bundle price, since raising price no longer leads firm 2 to follow suit. Yet, firm 1's profits are still nearly 50 percent higher than what it can extract by simply exploiting its monopoly in good A and competing head-to-head on good B. Bundling prevents the price of good B from being driven to marginal cost, and firm 1 is able to capture most of the demand for good B as part of its bundle.

The case in which the two goods are sold independently is straightforward. The two B goods are perfect substitutes, and so the Bertrand-Nash equilibrium price is 0. As for good A, the monopoly price is 1/2, and profits are 1/4. Thus, total profits of firm 1 are 1/4, and profits of firm 2 are 0.

Next, we consider the Nash equilibrium when firm 1 sells only an A–B bundle and firm 2 sells B. Firm 2's optimal response to a bundle price of x is the same as in the Stackelberg case. As demonstrated in Proposition 1 in the Appendix, its profits are maximized when it charges p_b^*:

$$p_b^* = \frac{1+x}{3} - \frac{1}{3}\sqrt{1-x+x^2}.$$

Firm 1's profits given a price of p_b for good B are

$$\Pi_i | entry = x * (1 - x + p_b - p_b^2/2).$$

Profits are maximized at

$$1 - 2x + p_b - p_b^2 = 0 \quad \text{or} \quad x^* = (1 + p_b - p_b^2)/2.$$

The Nash equilibrium is $x^* = 0.59$, $p_b^* = 0.24$. Equilibrium profits are 0.366 for firm 1 and 0.064 for firm 2. With two goods, firm 1 makes nearly six times the profits of its one-good rival. In that sense, bundling triples the advantage a two-good firm has over a one-good rival while protecting most of the incumbent's profits in the process.

PROPOSITION 2 *In the post-entry Nash equilibrium pricing game between a two-product incumbent and a one-product rival, bundled pricing is the subgame perfect equilibrium.*

Proof of Proposition 3. As just demonstrated, the incumbent makes profits of 0.366 in the event it continues to bundle and 0.25 in the event it sells its two products separately. When compared with independent pricing, the gain in profits is 46.8 percent for firm 1 and an infinite percent for firm 2 (which previously made 0). In absolute terms, it is the incumbent who has the greater gain, by almost two to one.[19]

In this setting, the gains from bundling come from mitigating the effects of competition. Thus, it is interesting to note that the result is more efficient than the outcome with independent pricing.

PROPOSITION 3 *In the post-entry Nash equilibrium pricing game between two-product incumbent and a one-product rival, total surplus is greater under bundling than when A and B are sold independently.*

Proof of Proposition 4. See the Appendix.

The intuition for this result is as follows: bundling leads to an increase in the price of good B from 0 to 0.24. Initially, this price increase only results in a second-order welfare loss. With a bundle priced at 0.59 and B priced at 0.24, the marginal price of A is 0.35. Thus, the price of A falls from 0.50 to 0.35 to those customers who are prepared to buy B, and this increase in sales leads to a first-order welfare gain. While the gain is 60 percent bigger than the loss in this case, the net result may still depend on the specific distribution of preferences.

We note that the results in the Nash equilibrium game are sensitive to the details in the model setup. For example, Whinston [1990] considers a similar problem, a monopoly in product A and a duopoly in product B. In his initial setup the two B goods are differentiated, but all customers have identical valuations for A. As a result, if the rival were to get any B customers, the incumbent would lose *all* of its A customers. This is because all customers have the same extra value from getting a bundle with A. Thus, in a second-stage pricing game, the incumbent has a great incentive to price the bundle low so as to preserve the value it creates in the A market. The end result is that a potential rival finds it hard to beat the A–B bundle and chooses not to enter the market.

In Whinston's model, the pure bundling effect not only disappears, it is reversed. Assume that the common value of A is $1/2$ and that the value of B is uniformly distributed on $[0, 1]$. Against a bundle price of 1, an entrant who comes in at $1/2$ (minus epsilon) sells to half the market, up from $1/4$. And, instead of taking away only $1/4$ of the incumbent's sales, it takes away 100 percent of the incumbent's sales.

With a common value for good A, bundling does not help the incumbent defend itself once the entrant is in the market – quite the contrary. However, this weakness is turned into strength as an entry deterrent.[20] The only way that the incumbent can earn any money is to ensure that the entrant makes zero sales. Even an entrant with a cost advantage (or superior product) in B is deterred, as the incumbent uses its value in good A to cross-subsidize the B good in the bundle and thereby deny the entrant any sales.[21] This approach requires the incumbent to make a credible commitment to selling its products only as part of a bundle; if entry occurs, the incumbent would prefer not to bundle.[22]

Credibility is not an issue in our approach, even in the Nash game, because the incumbent's post-entry profits are higher with a bundle than without. This is because we allow for heterogeneity in consumer values of A.[23] As a result, the entrant can take a small number of customers without threatening all of the incumbent's sales. Second, the entrant does not have a cost advantage in B, and so the entrant is not forced to cross-subsidize the bundle price. Of course, in Whinston's model if the incumbent does not have a cost disadvantage in B, then it can fight the entrant better when the goods are sold independently, and so there is no gain from bundling. We saw this in the previous section. When all costs are zero, the entrant's profits rise from 0 with independent pricing to 0.064 when the incumbent bundles.

While bundling may be less effective at deterring entry than an independent pricing strategy, it has the advantage of being ex post credible. In that sense it may be useful to have a powerful, if imperfect, tool that does not require any commitment. It is to be expected that the Nash pricing game post entry will lead to lower profits for both the incumbent (0.375 down to 0.366) and the entrant (0.081 down to 0.064) compared to the Stackelberg game.[24] But, the difference in profits is relatively small. This suggests that most of the effect is due to the *pure bundle effect* and the *bundle discount effect* identified earlier in the paper. A potential entrant cannot expect to make much profit against an incumbent who can bundle, whether the incumbent responds or even if it does not.

Conclusions

Bundling is a credible tool to protect a multigood monopolist against entry. In this case, bundling is not used to leverage a monopoly from one market to another. The incumbent is starting from a position of two monopolies. By bundling these two goods together, the incumbent is able to use each of the monopolies to protect the other one. What makes this strategy remarkable is that unlike most entry deterrent strategy (such as limit pricing) it can actually raise profits absent entry.

A firm that has only some components of a bundle will find it hard to enter against an incumbent who sells a package solution at a discount. This will be especially true when the consumers have positively correlated values for the components of the package or when the components are complements. Bundling also softens the harm done by a one-product (or limited line) competitor. The rival takes fewer customers away, and prices do not fall as far.

A monopolist, even without fear of entry, has incentives to bundle, either as a way to achieve better price discrimination (when values have a negative correlation) or to help save costs (when valuations are positively correlated). But most important to a firm with market power is preserving that power, by deterring a potential entrant or reducing the impact of a one-product rival. It is in this role that bundling truly shines. Entry is more easily deterred, in which case profits are more than doubled. And when entry deterrence fails, postprofits are still more than 50 percent higher when products are sold as a bundle.

APPENDIX

Pure bundling effect with nonuniform densities.   If the density of consumer types is symmetric and unimodal, then at equivalent prices, the act of putting two products into a bundle reduces the entrant's profits by at least 50 percent.

Proof of pure bundling effect with nonuniform densities.   Let $f(\cdot)$ represent the symmetric and unimodal density of consumer types a over the unit square. Let $f_a(\cdot)$ and $f_b(\cdot)$ represent the marginal density functions for the valuations of goods A and B, and $F_a(\cdot)$ and $F_b(\cdot)$ represent the marginal cumulative densities. Without loss of generality, we assume that the entrant comes into the B market.

Absent bundling, we denote the optimal monopoly prices of incumbent firm 1 as $\hat{p}_a$, and $\hat{p}_b$. We then compare a potential entrant's profits at a price of $p_e = \hat{p}_b - \epsilon$ when the incumbent does not bundle with the entrant's profits at a price of $\hat{p}_b$, against a bundle at price $x = \hat{p}_a + \hat{p}_b$.

If the incumbent does not bundle, firm 2 can earn $\hat{p}_b[1 - F_b(\hat{p}_b)]$.

If the incumbent does bundle, then at an entry price of $\hat{p}_b$ the marginal cost of buying the bundle (and getting product A) over just buying B from the entrant is $\hat{p}_a$. Thus, the entrant's demand, denoted by D_b, is

$$D_b(\hat{p}_b) = \int_0^{\hat{p}_a} \int_{\hat{p}_b}^1 f(\alpha_a, \alpha_b) d\alpha.$$

The entrant only attracts customers who value B at above $\hat{p}_b$ and A at below $\hat{p}_a$.

Assume that $\hat{p}_a \leq 1/2$. Then

$$D_b(\hat{p}_b) \leq \int_0^{1/2} \int_{\hat{p}_b}^1 f(\alpha_a, \alpha_b) d\alpha.$$

$$= \left(\frac{1}{2}\right) \int_0^1 \int_{\hat{p}_b}^1 f(\alpha_a, \alpha_b) d\alpha$$

$$= \left(\frac{1}{2}\right)[1 - F_b(\hat{p}_b)],$$

where the middle step follows as $f(a, b) = f(1 - a, b)$. This would complete the proof as the entrant's demand (and hence profits) is reduced by at least $1/2$.

Thus, we need only show that $\hat{p}_a \leq 1/2$. In choosing its optimal individual prices, firm A maximizes

$$\hat{p}_a[1 - F_a(\hat{p}_a)].$$

Since the density is symmetric on $[0, 1]$, we know that at $p = 1/2$, $F_a(1/2) = 1/2$ and the first-order condition is $[1 - F_a(1/2)] - (1/2)f_a(1/2) = (1/2)[1 - f_a(1/2)]$. Since the density is maximized at $1/2$, it must be the case that $f_a(1/2) \geq 1$ (as otherwise the cumulative density could not integrate up to 1). Thus, the first-order condition is weakly negative at $p = 1/2$. Moreover, for $p \geq 1/2$, the second-order condition is $-2f_a(p) + pf_a'(p)$. Since $f(p)$ is single-peaked and maximal at $p = 1/2$, for $p \geq 1/2$, $f_a'(p) \leq 0$, and the profit function is clearly concave for $p \geq 1/2$. Thus, the maximum must arise at some $\hat{p}_a \leq 1/2$.

PROPOSITION 4 *The entrant maximizes profits at*

$$p_e^* = \frac{1+x}{3} - \frac{1}{3}\sqrt{1-x+x^2}.$$

Proof of Proposition 1. The entrant's profits are $\Pi_e = p_e * (1 - p_e) * (x - p_e)$. Differentiating the profit function, the first-order condition is $(1 - 2p)(x - p) - p(1 - p) = 0$. Rearranging and applying the quadratic formula leads to the result.

COROLLARY 1 $x/3 \leq p_e^* < x/3 + 0.045$.

The first inequality, $p_e^* \geq x/3$, follows from the fact that $(1 - x + x^2) \leq 1$ for $0 \leq x \leq 1$; the second inequality, $p_e^* < x/3 + 0.045$, follows as $1 - x + x^2$ is minimized at $x = 0.5$.

Corollary 1 implies that the elasticity of the entrant's profits with respect to the incumbent's price is at least 150 percent.

COROLLARY 2 $\partial \log(\Pi_e)/\partial \log(x) \geq 3/2$.

This follows as $(\partial \log(\Pi_e))/(\partial \log(x)) = x/(x - p_e)$ and $x/(x - p_e) \geq 3/2$ as $p_e \geq x/3$.

PROPOSITION 5 *For all $n \geq 2$, with $x = n/2$ and $p_e = 1/2$, the challenger has sales of $1/4$ units and revenue of $1/8$.*

Proof of Proposition 2. Without loss of generality, assume that the entrant offers product 1. A consumer buys from the entrant if and only if $\alpha_1 - 1/2 \geq \alpha \cdot 1 - n/2$. Rearranging this inequality leads to $\sum_2^n \alpha_i \leq (n-1)/2$. It follows from this directly that the challenger's sales always equal $1/4$. Among the population that values good 1 at more than $1/2$, the challenger sells to half the population, and the incumbent sells to the other half.

PROPOSITION 6 *In the post-entry Nash equilibrium pricing game between two-product incumbent and a one-product rival, total surplus is greater under bundling than when A and B are sold independently.*

Proof of Proposition 3. With independent pricing, all consumers purchase good B. The surplus from this transaction is 0.5, as this is the mean valuation of good B. As for the surplus from the sale of A, only half the market, namely those consumers with valuations above 0.5, purchase A. Their mean value for A is 0.75. Thus, 0.5 purchases with a mean value of 0.75 adds 0.375 to the 0.5 surplus from the B sales for a total of 0.875.

With bundling, the mean valuation for B among the consumers who buy only B is $(1 + 0.24)/2 = 0.62$. Sales are 0.266, which generates a surplus of $0.62 * 0.266 = 0.165$. The average value of the bundle among those who purchase the bundle from firm 1 is 1.21. Bundle sales are 0.62, which leads to a total surplus of 0.75 on bundled sales. Combining this with the 0.165 surplus from B sales results in aggregate surplus of 0.915 which exceeds 0.875 without bundling.

Acknowledgment

My heartfelt thanks go to Kyle Bagwell, Adam Brandenburger, Meghan Busse, Jeremy Bulow, Aaron Edlin, Rena Henderson, Roger Howe, Michael Riordan, Marius Schwartz, Philip Williams, an anonymous referee, and seminar participants at the Federal Trade Commission, Massachusetts Institute of Technology, Melbourne Business School, and Yale University.

Notes

1 Salinger [1995] recognizes that cost synergies from bundling are most valuable when consumer valuations are positively correlated. Thus, if most consumers would buy both (or neither) A and B when sold separately, then any cost savings from selling them together will create an incentive for a monopolist to sell bundled products when valuations are positively correlated.

2 This assumption rules out such topical bundles as Microsoft Windows and Explorer as Value (Windows + Explorer) > Value (Windows) + Value (Explorer). This is because the value of Explorer by itself is essentially zero since it needs an operating system on which to run. The case of bundling complements is considered later in the extensions section and in Cournot [1838], Matutes and Regibeau [1992], Spiller and Zelner [1997], Nalebuff [2000], Economides [1998], Carlton and Waldman [2002], and Heeb [2003].

3 Bakos and Brynjolfsson [2000] apply this result to show how large bundles make entry especially difficult.

4 In this paper we will focus on creating an A–B bundle of fixed proportions. More generally, as the Chicago School has recognized, tying the sale of A to B but allowing for variable proportions creates the possibility of profitable price discrimination or metering.

5 A customer who has a small surplus for A but who values B below its production cost might prefer to purchase nothing than purchase an A–B bundle.

6 Note that the assumption of a uniform density is not just a mathematical simplification. As shown in the extensions section, over the entire class of symmetric quasi-concave densities – such as the multivariate normal – the uniform density minimizes the pure bundling effect. Thus, we can put aside issues of realism as the uniform density is chosen to be conservative rather than for its simplicity.

7 The model also applies to the more traditional setting where there is potential entry into only one market. In fact, the use of bundling as an entry deterrent strategy is unchanged whether the incumbent is defending market A or B or both. One of the attractive features of bundling is this very feature, that it allows an incumbent to defend both flanks at once.

8 The status quo price of the incumbent is relevant to an entrant when it can be taken as a signal of the incumbent's cost structure. Here, all the costs are known, and there is no private information and, hence, nothing to signal.

9 In a similar vein, the entrant might be able to approach some customers and offer them a better deal before the incumbent can react. Once the incumbent reacts, the ensuing price war might destroy subsequent profitability; however, the short-term profits that arise during the period prior to discovery could be enough to cover entry costs. Here, we are not considering the repeated game and the incentives this might create to engage in a price war to deter future entry.

10 Over a small range of parameters, a sophisticated entrant might expect the incumbent to raise price post entry (to the Nash equilibrium level), as a commitment to a low price is used to deter entry.

11 This is the reverse of the Whinston [1990] result where the firm needs to commit to bundle in order to deter entry. We compare these two approaches and the different assumptions behind them in our section on the Nash pricing game.

12 The intuition of bundling as a more cost-effective way to discount comes from McAfee, McMillan, and Whinston [1989].

13 In response to an incumbent price of 1, the optimal entry price is $1/3$; in response to an incumbent price of 0.8, the optimal entry price is approximately 0.29. Thus, the entrant's potential profits fall from $(1/3)(2/3)(2/3) = 0.148$ at $x = 1$ to $(0.29)(0.71)(0.51) = 0.105$ at $x = 0.8$ or a further 30 percent at no cost, and even some gain, to the incumbent.

14 As we show later on, the optimal bundle price in the subgame following entry is 0.59. If prices below 0.59 are not considered credible, then an entrant's potential profits can be held to 0.064.

15 At $x = 0.68$, $p_e = 0.27$, and $\Pi_e = (0.27)(0.73)(0.41) = 0.081$. At $x = 0.41$, $p_e = 0.18$, and $\Pi_e = (0.18)(0.82)(0.23) = 0.034$, a fall of 86 percent.

16 In contrast, in Whinston [1990] bundling is used as a way to commit to *greater* post-entry competition. This lowers the entrant's profits along with the incumbent's. Thus, the credibility of this commitment will be an issue.

17 In the case of independent pricing, firm 1 charges 0.5 for both A and B. Firm 2 comes in at a penny less for its product, say B, and earns $1/4$ (minus ϵ). When firm 1 employs bundling, the low-cost entrant faces a bundle price of 0.68 against which it would charge 0.265 and earn 0.08.

18 We do not consider entry by multiple firms as once there is a rival A and B good available, then we have bundle versus bundle competition and in the present model that would result in zero profits.

19 In this context, bundling might be viewed as a facilitating device in that it raises the post-entry profits of both the incumbent and the entrant. This perspective is explored further in Carbajo, De Meza, and Seidman [1990] and Chen [1997].

20 There is the old saying: my enemy's enemy is my friend. In a two-stage game, weakness in the second stage often translates into strength in the first. When the post-entry market is more competitive, then there is less incentive to enter the market (see, for example, Bernheim [1984]).

21 For example, imagine that the incumbent can produce A at a cost of 0.20 while all consumers value it at $1/2$. The rival can only produce good B, but can do so at a cost advantage – the rival's unit cost is 0.10 while the incumbent's unit cost is 0.30. With independent sales, the price of B would be 0.30, and the rival would expect to earn a margin of 0.20 on sales of 0.70. If the incumbent only sold A as part of a bundle, it would be forced to sell the bundle at a price of 0.60 in order to make any sales. It would use 0.20 of the surplus it generates in sales of A to subsidize its cost disadvantage in B. The result is that the entrant would not be able to attract any customers and, anticipating this, would not enter the market.

22 A commitment to bundling also changes an incumbent's incentives to innovate, as shown by Choi [2003]. Bundling gives the monopolist a greater incentive to engage in cost-cutting R&D and thus helps preserve and extend its advantageous position.

23 Whinston also considers the case in which there is heterogeneity in the valuation of A. He finds that a high dispersion in the value of good A and a low differentiation in B goods are necessary for bundling to raise the entrant's profits.

24 The Nash pricing can sometimes lead to higher entrant profits. Potential entrants with costs between 0.034 and 0.064 will enter in the Nash game and earn 0.064 but will not enter in the Stackelberg game. The difference arises as the incumbent is able to commit to a limit price below 0.59 in order to deter entry.

References

Adams, Williams J., and Janet L. Yellen, "Commodity Bundling and the Burden of Monopoly," *Quarterly Journal of Economics*, XC (1976), 475–498.

Bain, Joe, "A Note on Pricing in Monopoly and Oligopoly," *American Economic Review*, XXXIX (1949), 448–464.

Bakos, Yannis, and Eric Brynjolfsson, "Bundling Information Goods: Pricing, Profits, and Efficiency," *Management Science*, VL (1999), 1613–1630.

Bakos, Yannis, and Eric Brynjolfsson, "Bundling and Competition on the Internet: Aggregation Strategies for Information Goods," *Marketing Science*, XIX (2000), 63–82.

Bernheim, B. Douglas, "Strategic Deterrence of Sequential Entry into an Industry," *Rand Journal of Economics*, XV (1984), 1–11.

Carbajo, Jose, David De Meza, and Daniel J. Seidman, "A Strategic Motivation for Commodity Bundling," *Journal of Industrial Economics*, XXXVIII (1990), 283–298.

Carlton, Dennis W., and Michael Waldman, "The Strategic Use of Tying to Preserve and Create Market Power in Evolving Industries," *RAND Journal of Economics*, XXXIII (2002), 194–220.

Chen, Yongmin, "Equilibrium Product Bundling," *Journal of Business*, LXX (1997), 85–103.

Choi, Jay Pil, "Tying and Innovation: A Dynamic Analysis of Tying Arrangements," *Economic Journal* (2003).

Choi, Jay Pil, and Christodoulos Stefanadis, "Tying, Investment, and the Dynamic Leverage Theory," *RAND Journal of Economics*, XXXII (2001), 52–71.

Cournot, Augustin, *Recherches sur les principes mathématiques de la théorie des richesses* (Paris: Hachette, 1838), English translation: (N. Bacon, trans.), *Research into the Mathematical Principles of the Theory of Wealth* (Mountain Center, CA: James and Gordon, 1995).

Director, Aaron, and Edward Levi, "Law and the Future: Trade Regulation," *Northwestern University Law Review*, LI (1956), 281–296.

Economides, Nicholas, "Raising Rival's Costs in Complementary Goods Markets: LECs Entering into Long Distance and Microsoft Bundling Internet Explorer," Discussion Paper EC-98–03 NYU Stern School, 1998.

Heeb, Randal, "Innovation and Vertical Integration in Complementary Markets," *Journal of Economics and Management Strategies*, XII (2003), 387–417.

Matutes, Carmen, and Pierre Regibeau, "Compatibility and Bundling of Complementary Goods in a Duopoly," *Journal of Industrial Economics*, XL (1992), 37–54.

McAfee, R. Preston, John McMillan, and Michael D. Whinston, "Multiproduct Monopoly, Commodity Bundling, and Correlation of Values," *Quarterly Journal of Economics*, CIV (1989), 371–384.

Nalebuff, Barry, "Bundling," Working paper, available online at Social Science Research Network, http://papers.ssrn.com, 1999.

——, "Competing against Bundles," in *Incentives, Organization, and Public Economics*, Peter Hammond and Gareth Myles, eds. (New York, NY: Oxford University Press, 2000).

Salinger, Michael A., "A Graphical Analysis of Bundling," *Journal of Business*, LXVIII (1995), 85–98.

Schmalensee, Richard, "Commodity Bundling by Single-Product Monopolies," *Journal of Law and Economics*, XXV (1982), 67–71.

——, "Gaussian Demand and Commodity Bundling," *Journal of Business*, LVII (1984), 58–73.

Spiller, Pablo T., and Bennet A. Zelner, "Product Complementarities, Capabilities and Governance: A Dynamic Transaction Cost Perspective," *Industrial and Corporate Change*, VI (1997), 561–594.

Stigler, George J., "A Note on Block Booking," in G. J. Stigler, ed., *The Organization of Industries* (Homewood, IL: Irwin, 1968), pp. 165–170.

Whinston, Michael D., "Tying Foreclosure, and Exclusion," *American Economic Review*, LXXX (1990), 837–859.

25 What really matters in auction design

Paul Klemperer

Auctions have become enormously popular in recent years. Governments are now especially keen, using auctions to sell mobile-phone licenses, operate decentralized electricity markets, privatize companies and for many other purposes. The growth of e-commerce has led to many business-to-business auctions for goods whose trade was previously negotiated bilaterally.

Economists are proud of their role in pushing for auctions; for example, Coase (1959) was among the first to advocate auctioning the radio spectrum. But many auctions – including some designed with the help of leading academic economists – have worked very badly.

For example, six European countries auctioned off spectrum licenses for "third-generation" mobile phones in 2000. In Germany and the United Kingdom, the spectrum sold for over 600 euros per person ($80 billion in all, or over 2 percent of GDP). But in Austria, the Netherlands, Italy, and Switzerland, the revenues were just 100, 170, 240 and 20 euros per person, respectively. To be sure, investors became more skeptical about the underlying value of the spectrum during 2000 (and they are even more skeptical today). But this is just a fraction of the story. The Netherlands auction was sandwiched between the U.K. and German auctions, and analysts and government officials predicted revenues in excess of 400 euros per person from the Italian and Swiss auctions just a few days before they began (Michelson, 2000; Roberts, 2000; Total Telecom, 2000; Klemperer, 2002). These other auctions were fiascoes primarily because they were poorly designed.

So what makes a successful auction?

What really matters in auction design are the same issues that any industry regulator would recognize as key concerns: discouraging collusive, entry-deterring and predatory behavior. In short, good auction design is mostly good elementary economics.

By contrast, most of the extensive auction literature (as summarized in, for example, Klemperer, 1999a, 2000a) is of second-order importance for *practical* auction design. The auction literature largely focuses on a fixed number of bidders who bid noncooperatively, and it emphasizes issues such as the effects of risk aversion, correlation of information, budget constraints and complementarities. Auction theorists have made important progress on these topics from which other economic theory has benefited, and auction theory has also been fruitfully applied in political economy, finance, law and economics, labor economics, and industrial organization, often in contexts not usually thought of as auctions (Klemperer, 2003). But most of this literature is of much less use for actually designing auctions.

This paper will list and give examples of some critical pitfalls in auction design and discuss what to do about them. We show that ascending and uniform-price auctions are both very vulnerable to collusion and very likely to deter entry into an auction. We consider including a final sealed-bid stage into an otherwise-ascending auction to create an

"Anglo-Dutch" auction, and we emphasize the need for stronger antitrust policy in auction markets.

Collusion

A first major set of concerns for practical auction design involves the risk that participants may explicitly or tacitly collude to avoid bidding up prices. Consider a multiunit (simultaneous) *ascending* auction. (This is just like the standard auction used, for example, to sell a painting in Sotheby's or Christies – the price starts low, and competing bidders raise the price until no one is prepared to bid any higher, and the final bidder then wins the prize at the final price bid. However, in this case, several objects are sold at the same time, with the price rising on each of them independently, and none of the objects is finally sold until no one wishes to bid again on any of the objects.) In such an auction, bidders can use the early stages, when prices are still low, to signal who should win which objects and then tacitly agree to stop pushing up prices.

For example, in 1999, Germany sold ten blocks of spectrum by a simultaneous ascending auction with the rule that any new bid on a block had to exceed the previous high bid by at least 10 percent. Mannesman's first bids were 18.18 million deutschmarks per megahertz on blocks 1–5 and 20 million DM per MHz on blocks 6–10; the only other credible bidder – T-Mobil – bid even less in the first round. One of T-Mobil's managers then said (Stuewe, 1999, p. 13): "There were no agreements with Mannesman. But [T-Mobil] interpreted Mannesman's first bid as an offer." The point is that 18.18 plus a 10 percent raise equals approximately 20. It seems T-Mobil understood that if it bid 20 million DM per MHz on blocks 1–5, but did not bid again on blocks 6–10, the two companies would then live and let live with neither company challenging the other on the other's half. Exactly that happened. So the auction closed after just two rounds with each of the bidders acquiring half the blocks for the same low price (Jehiel and Moldovanu, 2001; Grimm, Riedel and Wolfstetter, 2001).

Ascending auctions can also facilitate collusion by offering a mechanism for punishing rivals. The threat of punishment may be implicit; for example, it was clear to T-Mobil that Mannesman would retaliate with high bids on blocks 1–5 if T-Mobil continued bidding on blocks 6–10. But an ascending auction can also allow more explicit options for punishment.

In a multilicense U.S. spectrum auction in 1996–1997, U.S. West was competing vigorously with McLeod for lot number 378: a license in Rochester, Minnesota. Although most bids in the auction had been in exact thousands of dollars, U.S. West bid $313,378 and $62,378 for two licenses in Iowa in which it had earlier shown no interest, overbidding McLeod, who had seemed to be the uncontested high bidder for these licenses. McLeod got the point that it was being punished for competing in Rochester and dropped out of that market. Since McLeod made subsequent higher bids on the Iowa licenses, the "punishment" bids cost U.S. West nothing (Cramton and Schwartz, 1999).

A related phenomenon can arise in one special kind of sealed-bid auction, namely a *uniform-price* auction in which each bidder submits a sealed bid stating what price it would pay for different quantities of a homogenous good, like electricity (that is, it submits a demand function), and then the good is sold at the single price determined by the lowest winning bid. In this format, bidders can submit bids that ensure that any deviation from a (tacit or explicit) collusive agreement is severely punished: each bidder bids very high prices for smaller quantities than its collusively agreed share. Then, if any bidder attempts to obtain more than its agreed share (leaving other firms with less than their agreed shares), all bidders will have to pay these very high prices. However, if everyone sticks to their agreed shares, then these very high prices will never need to be paid. As a result, deviation from the collusive agreement is unprofitable.[1]

The electricity regulator in the United Kingdom believes the market in which distribution companies purchase electricity from generating companies has fallen prey to exactly this kind of "implicit collusion" (Office of Gas and Electricity Markets, 1999, pp. 173–174). "Far from being the success story trumpeted around the world, the story of the U.K. generation market and the development of competition has been something of a disaster," reported *Power U.K.* (1999; see also von der Fehr and Harbord, 1998; Newbery, 1998; Wolfram, 1998, 1999). In addition, a frequently repeated auction market such as that for electricity is particularly vulnerable to collusion, because the repeated interaction among bidders expands the set of signaling and punishment strategies available to them and allows them to learn to cooperate (Klemperer, 2002).

Much of the kind of behavior discussed so far is hard to challenge legally. Indeed, trying to outlaw it all would require cumbersome rules that would restrict bidders' flexibility and might generate inefficiencies, without being fully effective. It would be much better to solve these problems with better auction designs.

Entry deterrence and predation

The second major area of concern of practical auction design is to attract bidders, since an auction with too few bidders risks being unprofitable for the auctioneer (Bulow and Klemperer, 1996) and potentially inefficient. Ascending auctions are often particularly poor in this respect, since they can allow some bidders to deter the entry, or depress the bidding, of rivals.

In an ascending auction, there is a strong presumption that the firm that values winning the most will be the eventual winner, because even if it is outbid at an early stage, it can eventually top any opposition. As a result, other firms have little incentive to enter the bidding and may not do so if they have even modest costs of bidding.

Consider, for example, Glaxo's 1995 takeover of the Wellcome drugs company. After Glaxo's first bid of 9 billion pounds, Zeneca expressed willingness to offer about 10 billion pounds if it could be sure of winning, while Roche considered an offer of 11 billion pounds. But certain synergies made Wellcome worth a little more to Glaxo than to the other firms, and the costs of bidding were tens of millions of pounds. Eventually, neither Roche nor Zeneca actually entered the bidding, and Wellcome was sold at the original bid of 9 billion pounds, literally a billion or two less than its shareholders might have received. Wellcome's own chief executive admitted "there was money left on the table" (Wighton, 1995a, b).

While ascending auctions are particularly vulnerable to lack of entry, other auction forms can result in similar problems if the costs of entry and the asymmetries between bidders are too large.

The 1991 U.K. sale of television franchises by a sealed-bid auction is a dramatic example. While the regions in the South and Southeast, Southwest, East, Wales and West, Northeast and Yorkshire all sold in the range of 9.36 to 15.88 pounds per head of population, the only – and therefore winning – bid for the Midlands region was made by the incumbent firm and was just one-twentieth of one penny (!) per head of population. Much the same happened in Scotland, where the only bidder for the Central region generously bid one-seventh of one penny per capita. What had happened was that bidders were required to provide very detailed region-specific programming plans. In each of these two regions, the only bidder figured out that no one else had developed such a plan.[2]

Another issue that can depress bidding in some ascending auctions is the "winner's curse." This problem applies when bidders have the same, or close to the same, actual value for a prize, but they have different information about that actual value (what auction theorists call the "common values" case). The winner's curse reflects the danger that the winner of an auction is likely to be the party who has most greatly overestimated the value of the prize. Knowing about the winner's curse will cause everyone to bid cautiously. But weaker firms must be especially cautious, since they must recognize that they are only likely to win when they have overestimated the value by even more than usual. Therefore, an advantaged firm can be less cautious, since beating very cautious opponents need not imply one has overestimated the prize's value. Because the winner's curse affects weak firms much more than strong ones, and because the effect is self-reinforcing, the advantaged bidder wins most of the time. And because its rivals bid extremely cautiously, it also generally pays a low price when it does win (Klemperer, 1998).

The bidding on the Los Angeles license in the 1995 U.S. auction for mobile-phone broadband licenses illustrates this problem. While the license's value was hard to estimate, it was probably worth similar amounts to several bidders. But Pacific Telephone, which already operated the local fixed-line telephone business in California, had distinct advantages from its database on potential local customers, its well-known brand-name and its familiarity with doing business in California. The auction was an ascending one. The result was that the bidding stopped at a very low price. In the end, the Los Angeles license yielded only $26 per capita. In Chicago, by contrast, the main local fixed-line provider was ineligible to compete, and it was not obvious who would win, so the auction yielded $31 per capita even though Chicago was thought less valuable than Los Angeles because of its lower household incomes, lower expected population growth and more dispersed population (Klemperer, 1998; Bulow and Klemperer, 2002). For formal econometric evidence for the FCC auctions more broadly, see Klemperer and Pagnozzi (2002).

Of course, the "winner's curse" problem exacerbates the problem that weaker bidders may not bother to participate in an ascending auction. GTE and Bell Atlantic made deals that made them ineligible to bid for the Los Angeles license, and MCI failed to enter this auction at all. Similarly, takeover battles are essentially ascending auctions, and there is empirical evidence that a firm that makes a takeover bid has a lower risk of facing a rival bidder if the firm has a larger shareholding or "toehold" in the target company (Betton and Eckbo, 2000).

Because outcomes in an ascending auction can be dramatically influenced by a seemingly modest advantage, developing such an advantage can be an effective predatory strategy. An apparent example was the 1999 attempt by BSkyB (Rupert Murdoch's satellite television company) to acquire Manchester United (England's most successful soccer club). The problem was the advantage this would give BSkyB in the auction of football television rights. Since Manchester United receives 7 percent of the Premier League's television revenues, BSkyB would have received 7 percent of the price of the league's broadcasting rights, whoever won them. So BSkyB would have had an incentive to bid more aggressively in an ascending auction to push up the price of the rights, and knowing this, other potential bidders would have faced a worse "winner's curse" and backed off. BSkyB might have ended up with a lock over the television rights, with damaging effects on the television market more generally. Largely for this reason, the U.K. government blocked the acquisition.[3]

A strong bidder also has an incentive to create a reputation for aggressiveness that reinforces its advantage. For example, when Glaxo was bidding for Wellcome, it made it clear that it "would almost certainly top a rival bid" (Wighton, 1995b). Similarly, before bidding for the California phone license, Pacific Telephone announced in the *Wall Street Journal* that "if somebody takes California away from us, they'll never make any money" (Cauley and Carnevale, 1994, p. A4). Pacific Telephone also hired one of the world's most prominent auction theorists to give seminars to the rest of the industry to explain the winner's curse argument that justifies this statement, and it reinforced the point in full-page ads that ran in the newspapers of the cities where its major competitors were headquartered (Koselka, 1995, p. 63). It also made organizational changes that demonstrated its commitment to winning the Los Angeles license.

Predation may be particularly easy in repeated ascending auctions, such as in a series of spectrum auctions. A bidder who buys assets that are complementary to assets for sale in a future auction or who simply bids very aggressively in early auctions can develop a reputation for aggressiveness (Bikhchandani, 1988). Potential rivals in future auctions will be less willing to participate and will bid less aggressively if they do participate (Klemperer, 2002).

Finally, because an ascending auction often effectively blocks the entry of "weaker" bidders, it encourages "stronger" bidders to bid jointly or to collude; after all, they know that no one else can enter the auction to steal the collusive rents they create. In the disastrous November 2000 Swiss sale of four third-generation mobile-phone licenses, there was considerable initial interest from potential bidders. But weaker bidders were put off by the auction form – at least one company hired bidding consultants and then gave up after learning that the ascending-bidding rules would give the company very little chance against stronger rivals. Moreover, the government permitted last-minute joint-bidding agreements – essentially officially sanctioned collusion. In the week before the auction, the field shrank from nine bidders to just four bidders for the four licenses! Since no bidder was allowed to take more than one license, the sale price was determined by the reserve price, which was just one-thirtieth of the U.K. and German per capita revenues and one-fiftieth of what the Swiss had once hoped for!

Other pitfalls

Reserve prices

Many of the disasters above were greatly aggravated by failure to set a proper reserve price (the minimum amount the winner is required to pay). Take the previous example. It was ridiculous for the Swiss government to set its reserve at just one-thirtieth of the per capita revenue raised by the German and U.K. governments for similar properties. Since the government's own spokesman predicted just five days prior to the auction that twenty times the reserve price would be raised, what was the government playing at?

Inadequate reserve prices also increase the incentives for predation and may encourage collusion that would not otherwise have been in all bidders' interests. A stronger bidder in an ascending auction has a choice between either tacitly colluding to end the auction quickly at a low price or forcing the price up to drive out weaker bidders. The lower the reserve price at which the auction can be concluded, the more attractive is the first option. This factor may have been an important contributor to several of the fiascoes we have discussed.

Political problems

Serious reserve prices are often opposed not only by industry groups, but also by government officials for whom a very embarrassing outcome is that the reserve price is not met, the object is not sold, and the auction is seen as a "failure."

Similarly, standard (first-price) sealed-bid auctions – in which the bidders simultaneously make "best and final" offers, and the winner pays the price he bid – can sometimes be very embarrassing for bidders, as BSCH (Spain's biggest bank) found out when Brazil privatized the Sao Paulo state bank Banespa. When the bids were opened, BSCH's managers were horrified to learn that their bid of over 7 billion reals ($3.6 billion) was more than three times the runner-up's bid and that they were therefore paying 5 billion reals ($2.5 billion) more than was needed to win. In other auctions, meanwhile, losers who have just narrowly underbid the winners have found it equally hard to explain themselves to their bosses and shareholders. So firms, or at least their managers, can oppose first-price auctions.

On the other hand, a *second-price* sealed-bid auction – in which the winner pays the runner-up's bid – can be embarrassing for the auctioneer if the winner's actual bid is revealed to be far more than the runner-up's, even if the auction design was both efficient and maximized expected revenue. McMillan (1994) reports a second-price New Zealand auction in which the winner bid NZ $7 million but paid the runner-up's bid of NZ $5,000. New Zealand should have set a minimum reserve price that the winner had to pay, but even if that had been politically possible, the winner would probably have bid more than it had to pay, so this might have been an economically but not politically sensible auction.

Loopholes

In some cases, the auction rules may leave gaping loopholes for behavior to game the auction. In 2000, Turkey auctioned two telecom licenses sequentially, with an additional twist that set the reserve price for the second license equal to the selling price of the first. One firm then bid far more for the first license than it could possibly be worth if the firm had to compete in the telecom market with a rival holding the second license. But the firm had rightly figured that no rival would be willing to bid that high for the second license, which therefore remained unsold, leaving the firm without a rival operating the second license!

As another example, McMillan (1994) reports an Australian auction for satellite-television licenses in which two bidders each made large numbers of different sealed bids on the same objects and then, after considerable delays, defaulted on those bids they did not like after the fact – since the government had neglected to impose any penalties for default. More recently, the U.S. spectrum auctions have been plagued by bidders "winning" licenses and subsequently defaulting on their commitments, often after long delays. (Spectrum auctions in India also recently fell into the same trap.) If default costs are small, then bidders are bidding for *options* on prizes rather than the prizes themselves. Furthermore, if smaller, underfinanced firms can avoid commitments through bankruptcy, then an auction actually favors these bidders over better-financed competitors who cannot default.

Credibility of the rules

It may not be credible for the auctioneer to punish a bidder violating the auction rules when just one bidder needs to be eliminated to end an auction, because excluding the offending bidder would end the auction immediately, and it might be hard to impose fines large enough to have a serious deterrent effect. Fines of hundreds of millions or even billions of dollars might have been required to deter improper behavior in some of the European third-generation mobile-phone license auctions. In the Netherlands sale, for example, six bidders competed for five licenses in an ascending auction in which bidders were permitted to win just one license each. One bidder, Telfort, sent a letter to another, Versatel, threatening legal action for damages if Versatel continued to bid! Telfort claimed that Versatel "believes that its bids will always be surpassed by [others' ... so it] must be that Versatel is attempting to either raise its competitors' costs or to get access to their ... networks." Many observers felt Telfort's threats against Versatel were outrageous. However, the government took no action – not even an investigation. As a result, Versatel quit the auction, and the sale raised less than 30 percent of what the Dutch government had forecast based on the results of the United Kingdom's similar auction just three months earlier.

Ascending auctions are particularly vulnerable to rule breaking by the bidders, since they necessarily pass through a stage where there is just one or a few excess bidders, and the ascending structure allows a cheat time to assess the success of its strategy (Klemperer, 2001, 2002). Sealed-bid auctions, by contrast, may be more vulnerable to rule changing by the auctioneer. For example, excuses for not accepting a winning bid can often be found if losing bidders are willing to bid higher. The famous RJR-Nabisco sale went through several supposedly final sealed-bid auctions (Burrough and Helyar, 1990). But if, after a sealed-bid auction, the auctioneer can reopen the auction to higher offers, the auction is really an ascending-bid auction and needs to be recognized as such. In fact, genuine sealed-bid auctions may be difficult to run in takeover battles, especially since a director who turns down a higher bid for his company after running a "sealed-bid auction" may be vulnerable to shareholder lawsuits.

Sealed-bid auctions can also be especially hard to commit to if the auctioneer has any association with a bidder, as, for example, would have been the case in the U.K. football television rights auction discussed earlier if BSkyB (a bidder) had taken over Manchester United (an influential member of the football league, which was the auctioneer).

Committing to future behavior may be a particular problem for governments. For example, it may be difficult to auction a license if the regulatory regime may change, but binding future governments (or even the current government) to a particular regulatory regime may prove difficult.

The credibility of reserve prices is of special importance. If a reserve price is not a genuine commitment not to sell an object if it does not reach its reserve, then it has no meaning, and bidders will treat it as such. For example, returning to the Turkish tale of woe, the government is now considering new arrangements to sell the second license, but at what cost to the credibility of its future auctions?[4]

Market structure

In some auctions, for example, of mobile-phone licenses, the structure of the industry that will be created cannot be ignored by the auction designer. It is tempting simply to "let the market decide" the industry structure by auctioning many small packages of spectrum, which individual firms can aggregate into larger licenses. But the outcome of an auction is driven by bidders' profits, not by the welfare of consumers or society as a whole.

The most obvious possible distortion is that since firms' joint profits in a market are generally greater if fewer competitors are in the market, it is worth more to any group of firms to prevent entry of an additional firm than the additional firm is willing to pay to enter. As a result, too few firms may win a share of spectrum, and these winners may each win too much, in just the same way as a "hands-off' policy to merger control will tend to create an overly concentrated industry. The Turkish fiasco discussed earlier was a spectacular example of how an auction can be biased toward generating a monopoly.[5]

But this outcome is not the only socially suboptimal possibility. A firm with a large demand may prefer to reduce its demand to end the auction at a low price, rather than raise the price to drive out its rivals, even when the latter course would be socially more efficient

(Ausubel and Cramton, 1998). There can also be too many winners if firms collude to divide the spoils at a low price. In the Austrian third-generation mobile spectrum sale, for example, six firms competed for twelve identical lots in an ascending auction and, not surprisingly, seemed to agree to divide the market so each firm won two lots each at not much more than the very low reserve price. Perhaps six winners was the efficient outcome. But we certainly cannot tell from the behavior in the auction. It was rumored that the bidding lasted only long enough to create some public perception of genuine competition and to reduce the risk of the government changing the rules.

Thus, it may sometimes be wiser to predetermine the number of winners by auctioning off fewer larger licenses, but limiting bidders to one license apiece, rather than to auction many licenses and to allow bidders to buy as many as they wish.

When is auction design less important?

The fact that collusion, entry deterrence and, more generally, buyer market power is the key to auction problems suggests that auction design may not matter very much when there is a large number of potential bidders for whom entry to the auction is easy. For example, though much ink has been spilt on the subject of government security sales, auction design may not matter much for either price or efficiency in this case. Indeed, the U.S. Treasury's recent experiments with different kinds of auctions yielded inconclusive results (Simon, 1994; Malvey, Archibald and Flynn, 1996; Nyborg and Sundaresan, 1996; Reinhart and Belzar, 1996; Ausubel and Cramton, 1998), and the broader empirical literature is also inconclusive. Of course, even small differences in auction performance can be significant when such large amounts of money are involved, and collusion has been an issue in some government security sales, so further research is still warranted.[6]

Solutions

Making the ascending auction more robust

Much of our discussion has emphasized the vulnerability of ascending auctions to collusion and predatory behavior. However, ascending auctions have several virtues, as well. An ascending auction is particularly likely to allocate the prizes to the bidders who value them the most, since a bidder with a higher value always has the opportunity to rebid to top a lower-value bidder who may initially have bid more aggressively.[7] Moreover, if there are complementarities between the objects for sale, a multiunit ascending auction makes it more likely that bidders will win efficient bundles than in a pure sealed-bid auction in which they can learn nothing about their opponents' intentions. Allowing bidders to learn about others' valuations during the auction can also make the bidders more comfortable with their own assessments and less cautious, and it often raises the auctioneer's revenues if information is "affiliated" in the sense of Milgrom and Weber (1982).

A number of methods to make the ascending auction more robust are clear enough. For example, bidders can be forced to bid "round" numbers, the exact increments can be pre-specified, and bids can be made anonymous. These steps make it harder to use bids to signal other buyers. Lots can be aggregated into larger packages to make it harder for bidders to divide the spoils, and keeping secret the number of bidders remaining in the auction also makes collusion harder (Cramton and Schwartz, 2000; Salant, 2000). Ausubel's (1998) suggested modification of the ascending auction mitigates the incentive of bidders to reduce their demands to end the auction quickly at a low price. Sometimes it is possible to pay bidders to enter an auction; for example, "white knights" can be offered options to enter a takeover battle against an advantaged bidder.

But while these measures can be useful, they do not eliminate the risks of collusion or of too few bidders. An alternative is to choose a different type of auction.

Using sealed-bid auctions

In a standard sealed-bid auction (or "first-price" sealed-bid auction), each bidder simultaneously makes a single "best and final" offer. As a result, firms are unable to retaliate against bidders who fail to cooperate with them, so collusion is much harder than in an ascending auction. Tacit collusion is particularly difficult since firms are unable to use the bidding to signal. True, both signaling and retaliation are possible in a series of sealed-bid auctions, but collusion is still usually harder than in a series of ascending auctions.

From the perspective of encouraging more entry, the merit of a sealed-bid auction is that the outcome is much less certain than in an ascending auction. An advantaged bidder will probably win a sealed-bid auction, but it must make its single final offer in the face of uncertainty about its rivals' bids, and because it wants to get a bargain, its sealed-bid will not be the maximum it could be pushed to in an ascending auction. So "weaker" bidders have at least some chance of victory, even when they would surely lose an ascending auction (Vickrey, 1961, appendix III). It follows that potential entrants are likely to be more willing to enter a sealed-bid auction than an ascending auction.

A sealed-bid auction might even encourage bidders who enter only to resell, further increasing the competitiveness of the auction. Such bidders seem less likely to enter an ascending auction, since it is generally more difficult to profit from reselling to firms one has beaten in an ascending auction.

Because sealed-bid auctions are more attractive to entrants, they may also discourage consortia from forming. If the strong firms form a consortium, they may simply attract other firms into the bidding in the hope of beating the consortium. So strong firms are more likely to bid independently in a sealed-bid auction, making this auction much more competitive.

Consistent with all this, there is some evidence from timber sales that sealed-bid auctions attract more bidders than ascending auctions do and that this makes sealed-bid auctions considerably more profitable for the seller, and this seems to be believed in this industry (Mead and Schneipp, 1989; Rothkopf and Engelbrecht-Wiggans, 1993), even though conditional on the number of bidders, sealed-bid auctions seem only slightly more profitable than ascending auctions (Hansen, 1986).

Furthermore, in the "common values" case that bidders have similar actual values for a prize, the "winner's curse" problem for a weaker bidder is far less severe in a sealed-bid auction. Winning an ascending auction means the weaker bidder is paying a price that the stronger rival is unwilling to match – which should make the weaker bidder very nervous. But the weaker player has a chance of winning a sealed-bid auction at a price the stronger rival *would* be willing to match, but didn't. Since beating the stronger player isn't necessarily bad news in a sealed-bid auction, the weaker player can bid more aggressively. So auction prices will be higher, even for a given number of bidders (Klemperer, 1998; Bulow, Huang, and Klemperer, 1999).[8]

But while sealed-bid auctions have many advantages, they are not without flaws. Mainly, by giving some chance of victory to weaker bidders, sealed-bid auctions are less likely than ascending auctions to lead to efficient outcomes. Moreover, in standard sealed-bid auctions in which winners pay their own bids, bidders need to have good information about the distribution of their rivals' values to bid intelligently (Persico, 2000). By contrast, in an ascending or uniform-price auction the best strategy of a bidder who knows its own value is just to bid up to that value, and winners' payments are determined by the bids of non-winners. So "pay-your-bid" sealed-bid auctions may discourage potential bidders who have only small amounts to trade and for whom the costs of obtaining market information might not be worth paying. For example, in March 2001, the U.K. electricity regulator replaced the problematic uniform-price auction we described earlier by an exchange market followed by a "pay-your-bid" sealed-bid auction, which makes collusion harder, because bids can no longer be used as costless threats. But a major concern is that the new trading arrangements may deter potential entrants from investing the sunk costs necessary to enter the electricity market.[9]

However, the entry problem in many-unit auctions is much less serious if small bidders can buy from larger intermediaries who can aggregate smaller bidders' demands and bid in their place, as, for example, occurs in auctions of Treasury bills. And the entry problem is also alleviated if smaller bidders are permitted to make "noncompetitive bids," that is, to state demands for fixed quantities for which they pay the average winning price, as is also the case in some Treasury bill auctions.

The Anglo-Dutch auction

A solution to the dilemma of choosing between the ascending (often called "English") and sealed-bid (or "Dutch") forms is to combine the two into a hybrid, the "Anglo-Dutch," which often captures the best features of both and was first described and proposed in Klemperer (1998).

For simplicity, assume a single object is to be auctioned. In an Anglo-Dutch auction, the auctioneer begins by running an ascending auction in which price is raised continuously until all but two bidders have dropped out. The two remaining bidders are then each required to make a final sealed-bid offer that is not lower than the current asking price, and the winner pays the winning bid. The process is much like the way houses are often sold, although, unlike in many house sales, the procedure the auctioneer will follow in an Anglo-Dutch auction is clearly specified in advance.

Another auction with similar features – and probably similar motivations to the Anglo-Dutch – is W. R. Hambrecht's *OpenBook* auction for corporate bonds. The early bidding is public and ascending, but bidders can make final sealed bids in the last hour. Although all bidders are permitted to make final bids, higher bidders in the first stages are given an advantage that is evidently large enough to induce serious bidding early on (Hall, 2001, p. 71).

The process also has some similarity to auctions on eBay (by far the world's most successful e-commerce auctioneer), which are ascending auctions, but with a fixed ending time so that many bidders often bid only in the last few seconds in essentially sealed-bid style. eBay attracts far more bidders than its rival, Yahoo, which runs a standard ascending auction with a traditional "going, going, gone" procedure that does not close the auction until there have been no bids for 10 minutes.

The main value of the Anglo-Dutch procedure arises when one bidder (for example, the incumbent operator of a license that is to be reauctioned) is thought to be stronger than potential rivals. Potential rivals might be unwilling to enter a pure ascending-bid auction against the strong bidder, who would be perceived to be a sure winner. But the sealed bid at the final stage induces some uncertainty about which of the two finalists will win, and entrants are attracted by the knowledge that they have a chance to make it to this final stage. So the price may easily be higher even by the end of the first ascending stage of the Anglo-Dutch auction than if a pure ascending auction were used.

The Anglo-Dutch should capture the other advantages of the sealed-bid auction discussed in the previous section. Collusion will be discouraged because the final sealed-bid round allows firms to renege on any deals without fear of retaliation and because the Anglo-Dutch auction eliminates the stage of the ascending auction when just one excess bidder remains, at which point the rules against collusion and predation may not be credible.

Consortium formation will also be discouraged. Imagine there are two strong bidders for an item. In an ascending auction they are unlikely to be challenged if they form a consortium, so they have an incentive to do so. But in an Anglo-Dutch auction, forming the consortium would open up an opportunity for new entrants who would now have a chance to make it to the final sealed-bid stage. So the strong firms are much less likely to bid jointly.

But the Anglo-Dutch should also capture much of the benefit of an ascending auction. It will be more likely to sell to the highest valuer than a pure sealed-bid auction, both because it directly reduces the numbers allowed into the sealed-bid stage and also because the two finalists can learn something about each other's and the remaining bidders' perceptions of the object's value from behavior during the ascending stage.

When the Anglo-Dutch auction is extended to contexts in which individual bidders are permitted to win multiple units and there are complementarities between the objects, the ascending stage makes it more likely that bidders will win efficient bundles than in a pure sealed-bid auction.

Finally, I conjecture that the ascending stages of the Anglo-Dutch auction may extract most of the information that would be revealed by a pure ascending auction, raising revenues if bidders' information is "affiliated," while the sealed-bid stage may do almost as well as a pure sealed-bid auction in capturing extra revenues due to the effects of bidders' risk aversion, budget constraints and asymmetries. This suggests the Anglo-Dutch auction may outperform ascending and sealed-bid auctions even if it attracts no additional bidders.

In short, the Anglo-Dutch auction often combines the best of both the ascending and the sealed-bid worlds.

Antitrust

Effective antitrust is critical to fighting collusion and predation in auctions. But antitrust enforcement in the context of auctions seems much lighter than in "ordinary" economic markets.

The U.S. Department of Justice has pursued some auction signaling cases, but the legal status of many of the kinds of behavior discussed in this article remains ambiguous, and collusion in takeover battles for companies is legal in the United States.

European antitrust has been even weaker, as evidenced by T-Mobil's willingness to confirm explicitly the signaling behavior described earlier. True, when apparently similar behavior was observed in the more recent German third-generation spectrum auction, firms refused to confirm officially that they were signaling to rivals to end the auction. Even so, the *Financial Times* reported that "[o]ne operator has privately admitted to altering the last digit of its bid in a semi-serious attempt to signal to other participants that it was willing to accept [fewer lots to end the auction]" (Roberts and Ward, 2000, p. 21). This kind of signaling behavior could perhaps be challenged as an abuse of "joint dominance" under European law. But European regulators have showed no interest in pursuing such matters.

Firms are also permitted to make explicit statements about auctions that would surely be unacceptable if made about a "normal" economic market. For example, before the Austrian third-generation spectrum auction, Telekom Austria, the largest incumbent and presumably the strongest among the six bidders, said it "would be satisfied with just two of the 12 blocks of frequency on offer" and "if the [5 other bidders] behaved similarly it should be possible to get the frequencies on sensible terms," but "it would bid for a third frequency block if one of its rivals did" (Crossland, 2000). It seems inconceivable that a dominant firm in a "normal" market would be allowed to make the equivalent offer and threat that it "would be satisfied with a market share of just one-sixth" and "if the other five firms also stick to one-sixth of the market each, it should be possible to sell at high prices," but "it would compete aggressively for a larger share, if any of its rivals aimed for more than one-sixth."[10]

Just as damaging has been the European authorities' acceptance of joint-bidding agreements that are, in effect, open collusion. Combinations that are arranged very close to the auction date (as in the example of Switzerland discussed earlier) should be particularly discouraged since they give no time for entrants to emerge to threaten the new coalition. One view is that auction participants should generally be restricted to entities that exist when the auction is first announced, although exceptions would clearly be necessary.

The antitrust agencies' response to predation in auction markets has also been feeble. Dominant bidders such as Glaxo and Pacific Telephone in the examples above are apparently allowed to make open threats that they will punish new entrants. For example, Glaxo's letting it be known that it "would almost certainly top a rival bid," would roughly translate to an incumbent firm in a "normal" economic market saying it "would almost certainly undercut any new entrant's price."[11]

Regulators should take such threats seriously and treat auction markets more like "ordinary" economic markets.

Tailoring auction design to the context

Good auction design is *not* "one size fits all." It must be sensitive to the details of the context. A good example of this lesson – and of our other principles – is afforded by the recent European third-generation (UMTS) mobile-phone license auctions.

The United Kingdom, which ran the first of these auctions, originally planned to sell just *four* licenses.[12] In this case, the presence of exactly four incumbent operators who had the advantages of existing brand names and networks suggested that an ascending auction might deter new firms from bidding strongly in the auction or even from entering at all. So the government planned an Anglo-Dutch auction. An ascending stage would have continued until just five bidders remained, after which the five survivors would have made sealed bids, required to be no lower than the current price level, for the four licenses.[13] The design performed extremely well in laboratory experiments in both efficiency and revenue generation.

But when it became possible to sell *five* licenses, an ascending auction made more sense. Because no bidder was permitted to win more than one license, at least one license had to be sold to a new entrant. This would be a sufficient carrot to attract several new entrants in the U.K. context in which it was very unclear which new entrant(s) might be successful.[14] Because licenses could not be divided, bidders could not collude to divide the market without resort to side payments. As a result, the problems of collusion and entry deterrence were minimal, and a version of an ascending auction was therefore used for efficiency reasons. The auction was widely judged a success; nine new entrants bid strongly against the incumbents, creating intense competition and record-breaking revenues of 22.5 billion pounds.

The Netherlands sale came next. Their key blunder was to follow the actual British design when they had an equal number (five) of incumbents and licenses. It was not hard to predict (indeed, prior to the auction, an early draft of this paper, quoted in the Dutch press and Maasland, 2000, *did* predict) that very few entrants would show up. Netherlands antitrust policy was as dysfunctional as the auction design, allowing the strongest potential entrants to make deals with incumbent operators. In the end, just one weak new entrant (Versatel) competed with the incumbents. As we have already discussed, with just one excess bidder in an ascending auction, it was unsurprising when the weak bidder quit early amid allegations of predation, at less than 30 percent of the per capita U.K. prices. Six months later, the Dutch parliament began an investigation into the auction process.

A version of the Anglo-Dutch design would probably have worked better in the Netherlands context. There are reasons to believe Versatel would have bid higher in the sealed-bid stage than the price at which it quit the ascending auction. In addition, the fear of this would have made the incumbents bid higher. Furthermore, the "hope and dream" that a sealed-bid stage gives weaker bidders might have attracted more bidders and discouraged the formation of the joint-bidding consortia.

The Italian government thought it had learned from the Netherlands fiasco. It also chose roughly the U.K. design, but stipulated that if there were no more "serious" bidders (as defined by prequalification conditions) than licenses, then the number of licenses could, and probably would, be reduced. At first glance, this seemed a clever way to avoid an uncompetitive auction, but (as I and others argued) the approach was fundamentally flawed. First, it is putting the cart before the horse to create an unnecessarily concentrated mobile-phone market to make an auction look good. Second, our earlier discussion demonstrates that a rule that allows the possibility that there will be just one more bidder than license does *not* guarantee a competitive ascending auction! Also, it was clear that the number of likely entrants into an ascending auction was much smaller than it had been for the United Kingdom, in large part because weaker potential entrants had figured out from the earlier auctions that they were weaker and that they therefore had little chance of winning such an auction. In the event, just six bidders competed for five licenses, and the auction ended amid allegations of collusion after less than two days of bidding with per capita revenues below 40 percent of the U.K. level, about half the amount the government was expecting. Again, an Anglo-Dutch or pure sealed-bid design would probably have performed better.

Klemperer (2001, 2002) discusses the 2000–2001 European spectrum auctions in much more detail.

Conclusion

Much of what we have said about auction design is no more than an application of standard antitrust theory. The key issues in both fields are collusion and entry. The signaling and punishment strategies that support collusion in auctions are familiar from "ordinary" industrial markets, as are firms' verbal encouragement to collude and the predatory threats they make. Our point that even modest bidding costs may be a serious deterrent to potential bidders is analogous to the industrial-organization point that the contestability of a market is nonrobust to even small sunk costs of entry. We also argued that because an ascending auction is more likely than a sealed-bid auction to be won by the strongest firm, the ascending auction may therefore be less attractive to bidders and may therefore be less profitable than a sealed-bid auction; this is just an example of the standard industrial organization argument that a market that is in principle more competitive (for example, "Bertrand" rather than "Cournot") is less attractive to enter and so may in fact be less competitive. A particular feature of auction markets is that "winner's curse" effects may mean that sealed-bid and Anglo-Dutch auctions not only attract more firms than ascending auctions, but may also lead to better outcomes for the auctioneer for a given number of firms. But there is no justification for the current feebleness of antitrust policy in auction markets: regulators should treat them much more like "ordinary" economic markets.

However, none of our examples of auction failures should be taken as an argument against auctions in general. Most auctions work extremely well. Occasionally – for example, when there are too few potential bidders or large costs of supplying necessary information to bidders – a form of structured negotiations may be better, but an auction is usually more attractive to potential buyers, who are crucial to a sale's success (Bulow and Klemperer, 1996). Even relatively unsuccessful auctions, such as the Netherlands and Italian spectrum auctions, were probably more successful than the "beauty contest" administrative hearings used to allocate third-generation spectrum in several other European countries. For example, the Spanish beauty contest yielded just 13 euros per head of population, but generated considerable political and legal controversy and a widespread perception that the outcome was both unfair and inefficient, all problems that are typical of such procedures (Binmore and Klemperer, 2002; Klemperer, 2000b). The difficulties with the French beauty contest mean that France has not only missed its government's originally planned date for allocation of the spectrum (already by a year at the time of writing), but also missed European Union deadlines.

In conclusion, the most important features of an auction are its robustness against collusion and its attractiveness to potential bidders. Failure to attend to these issues can lead to disaster. Furthermore, anyone setting up an auction would be foolish to follow past successful designs blindly; auction design is *not* "one size fits all." While the sealed-bid auction performs well in some contexts, and the Anglo-Dutch auction is ideal in other contexts, the ascending auction has also frequently been used very successfully. In the practical design of auctions, local circumstances matter, and the devil is in the details.

Acknowledgment

I was the principal auction theorist advising the U.K. government's Radiocommunications Agency, which designed and ran the recent U.K mobile-phone license auction described here, and have advised several other U.K. government agencies, but the views expressed here are mine alone. Although some observers thought some of the behavior described above warranted investigation, I do not intend to suggest that any of it violates any applicable rules or laws. I am very grateful to many colleagues, including Sushil Bikhchandani, Nils-Henrik von der Fehr, Tim Hanford, Emiel Maasland, Margaret Meyer, Mike Rothkopf, David Salant, Rebecca Stone, Timothy Taylor, Chuck Thomas, Tommaso Valletti, Michael Waldman, Mark Williams, and especially my coauthors Jeremy Bulow and Marco Pagnozzi, for helpful advice.

Notes

1 Since, with many units, the lowest winning bid in a uniform-price auction is typically not importantly different from the highest losing bid, this auction is analogous to an ascending auction (in which every winner pays the runner-up's willingness-to-pay). The "threats" that support collusion

in a uniform-price auction are likewise analogous to the implicit threats supporting collusion in an ascending auction. Collusion in a uniform-price auction is harder if supply is uncertain, since this reduces the number of points on the bid schedule that are inframarginal and can be used as threats (Klemperer and Meyer, 1989; Back and Zender, 1993, 1999).

2 While I have advised the U.K. government on several auctions, I have never had anything to do with television licenses!

3 Although the term "toehold effect," coined by Bulow, Huang, and Klemperer (1999) and Klemperer (1998) in the related context of takeover battles (see above), entered the popular press, and these papers were cited by the U.K. Monopolies and Mergers Commission (1999) report, which effectively decided the issue, neither I nor my coauthors had any involvement in this case.

4 Reauctioning with a lower reserve price after a delay may sometimes be sensible, to allow further entry if there are high costs of entering the auction (Burguet and Sakovics, 1996; McAfee and McMillan, 1988), but in this case the auctioneer should make clear in advance what will happen if the reserve is not met.

5 Similarly, the recent July 2001 Greek second-generation spectrum auction led to a more concentrated telecom market than seems likely to be socially efficient.

6 These views are personal. I have advised U.K. government agencies on the related issue of the sale of gold. See Klemperer (1999b) for more discussion.

7 This applies in many "common values" and "private values" settings (Maskin, 1992), but is not necessarily the same as maximizing efficiency. When bidders are firms, it ignores consumer welfare (which is likely to favor a more widely dispersed ownership than firms would choose), and, of course, it ignores government revenue. We assume governments (as well as other auctioneers) care about revenue because of the substantial deadweight losses (perhaps 33 cents per dollar raised) of raising government funds through alternative methods (Ballard, Shoven, and Whalley, 1985). Resale is not a perfect substitute for an efficient initial allocation, because even costless resale cannot usually ensure an efficient outcome in the presence of incomplete information (Myerson and Satterthwaite, 1983; Cramton, Gibbons, and Klemperer, 1987).

8 In Milgrom and Weber's (1982) model, sealed-bid auctions are less profitable than ascending auctions if signals are "affiliated." But they assume symmetric bidders, and the effect does not seem large in practice (Riley and Li, 1997). Sealed-bid auctions are generally more profitable if bidders are risk averse or budget constrained (Klemperer, 2000a).

9 Also, the new arrangements may not fully resolve the collusion problem anyway since the market is so frequently repeated (Klemperer, 1999b).

10 Similarly, during the German third-generation spectrum auction, MobilCom told a newspaper that "should [Debitel] fail to secure a license [it could] become a 'virtual network operator' using MobilCom's network while saving on the cost of the license" (Benoit, 2000, p. 28). This translates roughly to a firm in a "normal" market saying it "would supply a rival should it choose to exit the market," but MobilCom's remarks went unpunished.

11 Similarly, Pacific Telephone's remark that "if somebody takes California away from us, they'll never make any money" seems to correspond to threatening that "if anyone tries to compete with us, we'll cut the price until they lose money." Further, Pacific Telephone's hiring of an auction theorist to explain the winner's curse to competitors might correspond to hiring an industrial economist to explain the theory of the difficulties of entering new markets to potential entrants.

12 I was the principal auction theorist advising the U.K. government's Radiocommunications Agency, which designed and ran the recent U.K. mobile-phone license auction. Ken Binmore had a leading role and supervised experiments testing the proposed designs. Other academic advisors included Tilman Borgers, Jeremy Bulow, Philippe Jehiel, and Joe Swierzbinski.

13 It was proposed that all four winners would pay the fourth-highest sealed bid. Since the licenses were not quite identical, a final simultaneous ascending stage would have followed to allocate them more efficiently among the winners. The sealed-bid stage could be run using an ascending mechanism that would hide the actual bids even from the auctioneer, if this would reduce political problems. See Klemperer (1998, 2001, 2002), Radiocommunications Agency (1998a, b), and Binmore and Klemperer (2002) for more details.

14 In large part, this was because the United Kingdom ran the first third-generation auction. Going to market first was a deliberate strategy of the auction team, and the sustained marketing campaign was also important. The U.K. auction attracted 13 bidders who then learnt about others' strengths, and none of the eight subsequent auctions had more than seven bidders.

References

Ausubel, Lawrence M. 1998. "An Efficient Ascending-Bid Auction for Multiple Objects." Mimeo, University of Maryland.

Ausubel, Lawrence M. and Peter Cramton. 1998. "Demand Reduction and Inefficiency in Multi-Unit Auctions." Mimeo, University of Maryland.

Ausubel, Lawrence M., Peter Cramton, Preston McAfee, and John McMillan. 1997. "Synergies in Wireless Telephony: Evidence from the Broadband PCS Auction." *Journal of Economics and Management Strategy*. Fall, 6:3, pp. 497–527.

Back, Kerry and Jaime F. Zender. 1993. "Auctions of Divisible Goods." *Review of Financial Studies*. Winter, 6:4, pp. 733–64.

Back, Kerry and Jaime F Zender. 1999. "Auctions of Divisible Goods with Endogenous Supply." Working Paper, Washington University in St. Louis and University of Arizona.

Ballard, Charles L., John B. Shoven, and John Whalley. 1985. "General Equilibrium Computations of the Marginal Welfare Costs of Taxes in the United States." *American Economic Review*. March, 75:1, pp. 128–38.

Benoit, Bertrand. 2000. "Bidders Warned in German 3G Phone Auction." *Financial Times*. August 2, p. 28.

Betton, Sandra and Espen B. Eckbo. 2000. "Toeholds, Bid Jumps, and Expected Payoffs in Takeovers." *Review of Financial Studies*. Winter, 13:4, pp. 841–82.

Bikhchandani, Sushil. 1988. "Reputation in Repeated Second-Price Auctions." *Journal of Economic Theory*. October, 46:1, pp. 97–119.

Binmore, Ken and Paul D. Klemperer. 2002. "The Biggest Auction Ever: The Sale of the British 3G Telecom Licences." *Economic Journal*.

Bulow, Jeremy I. and Paul D. Klemperer. 1996. "Auctions versus Negotiations." *American Economic Review*. March, 86:1, pp. 180–94.

Bulow, Jeremy I. and Paul D. Klemperer. 2002. "Prices and the Winner's Curse." *Rand Journal of Economics*.

Bulow, Jeremy I., Ming Huang, and Paul D. Klemperer. 1999. "Toeholds and Takeovers." *Journal of Political Economy*. June, 107:3, p. 427–54.

Burguet, Roberto and Jozsef Sakovics. 1996. "Reserve Prices Without Commitment." *Games and Economic Behavior*. August, 15:2, pp. 149–64.

Burrough, Brian and John Helyar. 1990. *Barbarians at the Gate: The Fall of RJR Nabisco*. London: Arrow.

Cauley, Leslie and Mary Lu Carnevale. 1994. "Wireless Giants, Some Surprise Players to Seek New Generation of Licenses." *Wall Street Journal*. October 31, p. A4.

Coase, Ronald H. 1959. "The Federal Communications Commission." *Journal of Law and Economics*. October, 2, pp. 1–40.

Cramton, Peter and Jessie A. Schwartz. 1999. "Collusive Bidding in the FCC Spectrum Auctions." Working Paper, University of Maryland.

Cramton, Peter and Jesse A. Schwartz. 2000. "Collusive Bidding: Lessons from the FCC Spectrum Auctions." *Journal of Regulatory Economics*. May, 17:3, pp. 229–52.

Cramton, Peter, Robert Gibbons, and Paul D. Klemperer. 1987. "Dissolving a Partnership Efficiently." *Econometrica*. 55:3, pp. 615–32.

Crossland, David. 2000. "Austrian UMTS Auction Unlikely to Scale Peaks." *Reuters*. October 31. Available at (http://www. totaltele.com).

Fehr, Nils-Henrik von der and David Harbord. 1998. "Competition in Electricity Spot Markets: Economic Theory and International Experience." Memorandum No. 5/1998, Department of Economics, University of Oslo.

Grimm, Veronika, Frank Riedel and Elmar Wolfstetter. 2001. "Low Price Equilibrium in Multi-Unit Auctions: The GSM Spectrum Auction in Germany." Working Paper, Humboldt Universitat zu Berlin.

Hall, Robert E. 2001. *Digital Dealing*. New York: W. W. Norton.

Hansen, Robert G. 1986. "Sealed-Bid versus Open Auctions: The Evidence." *Economic Inquiry*. January, 24:1, pp. 125–42.

Jehiel, Phitsppe and Benny Moldovanu. 2001. "The UMTS/IMT-2000 License Auctions." Working Paper, University College London and University of Mannheim.

Klemperer, Paul D. 1998. "Auctions With Almost Common Values: The 'Wallet Game' and its Applications." *European Economic Review*. May, 42:3–5, pp. 757–69.

Klemperer, Paul D. 1999a. "Auction Theory: A Guide to the Literature." *Journal of Economic Surveys*. 13:3, pp. 227–86. Also reprinted in *The Current State of Economic Science*, Volume 2. 1999. Shri Bhagwan Dahiya, ed. Rohtak, India: Spellbound, pp. 711–66.

Klemperer, Paul D. 1999b. "Applying Auction Theory to Economics." Oxford Department of Economics Discussion Paper, April.

Klemperer, Paul D. ed. 2000a *The Economic Theory of Auctions*. Cheltenham, U.K.: Edward Elgar.

Klemperer, Paul D. 2000b. "Spectrum on the Block." *Wall Street Journal (Asia)*. May 10, p. 8. Also at (http://www.paulklemperer.org).

Klemperer, Paul D. 2003. "Why Every Economist Should Learn Some Auction Theory." Forthcoming in *Advances in Economics and Econometrics: Invited Lectures to Eighth World Congress of the Econometric Society*. M. Dewatripont, L. Hansen and S. Turnovksy, eds. Cambridge, U.K.: Cambridge University Press. Also at (http://www. paulklemperer.org).

Klemperer, Paul D. 2001. "What Really Matters in Auction Design." Working Paper version, Nuffield College, Oxford University Discussion Paper. Also at (http://www.paulklemperer.org).

Klemperer, Paul D. 2002." How (Not) to Run Auctions: The European 3G Telecom Auctions." *European Economic Review*. 46: 4–5, pp. 829–45. Also at (http://www.paulklemperer.org).

Klemperer, Paul D. and Margaret A. Meyer. 1989. "Supply Function Equilibria in Oligopoly Under Uncertainty." *Econometrica*. November, 57:6, pp. 1243–77.

Klemperer, Paul D. and Marco Pagnozzi. 2002. "Advantaged Bidders and Spectrum Prices: An Empirical Analysis."

Koselka, Rita. 1995. "Playing Poker with Craig McCaw." *Forbes*. July 3, pp. 62–3.

Maasland, Emiel. 2000. "Veilingmiljarden Zijn een Fictie (Billions from Auctions: Wishful Thinking)." *Economisch Statistische Berichten*. June 9, p. 479. Translation available at (http://www.paulklemperer.org).

Malvey, Paul F., Christine M. Archibald and Sean T. Flynn. 1996. "Uniform-Price Auctions: Evaluation of the Treasury Experience." Working Paper, U.S. Treasury.

Maskin, Eric S. 1992. "Auctions and Privatization," in *Privatization*. H. Siebert, ed. Tubingen: Mohr, pp. 115–36.

McAfee, R. Preston and John McMillan. 1988. "Search Mechanisms." *Journal of Economic Theory*. February, 44:1, pp. 99–123.

McMillan, John. 1994. "Selling Spectrum Rights." *Journal of Economic Perspectives*. Summer, 8:3, pp. 145–62.

Mead, Walter J. and Mark Schneipp. 1989. "Competitive Bidding for Federal Timber in Region 6, An Update: 1983–1988." Community and Organization Research Institute, University of California, Santa Barbara, Contractor Report, USDA Award No. 40-3187-8-1683, June.

Michelson, Marcel. 2000. "Swiss 3G Auction Set to Become Battle of Giants." *Reuters*. November 9. Available at (http://www.totaltele.com).

Milgrom, Paul R. and Robert J. Weber. 1982. "A Theory of Auctions and Competitive Bidding." *Econometrica*. September, 50:5, pp. 1089–122.

Myerson, Roger B. and Mark A. Satterthwaite. 1983. "Efficient Mechanisms for Bilateral Trading." *Journal of Economic Theory*. April, 29:2, pp. 265–81.

Newbery, David M. 1998. "Competition, Contracts, and Entry in the Electricity Spot Market." *RAND Journal of Economics*. 29:4, pp. 726–49.

Nyborg, Kjell and Suresh Sundaresan. 1996. "Discriminatory versus Uniform Treasury Auctions: Evidence from When-Issued Transactions." *Journal of Financial Economics*. September, 42:1, pp. 63–104.

Office of Gas and Electricity Markets. 1999. "The New Electricity Trading Arrangements, July." At (http://www.open.gov.uk/offer/reta.htm).

Persico, Nicola. 2000. "Information Acquisition in Auctions." *Econometrica*. 68:1, pp. 135–48.

Power U.K. 1999. "The Problems with the Pool." August 31, 66, p. 14.

Radiocommunication Agency. 1998a. "UMTS Auction Design." UMTS Auction Consultative Group Paper 14 of 1998. Available as UACG(98)14 at (http://www.spectrumauctions.gov.uk).

Radiocommunication Agency. 1998b. "UMTS Auction Design 2." UMTS Auction Consultative Group Paper 16 of 1998. Available as UACG(98)16 at (http://www.spectrumauctions.gov.uk).

Reinhert, Vincent and Gregory Belzer. 1996. "Some Evidence on Bid Sharing and the Use of Information in the U.S. Treasury's Auction Experiment." Working Paper, Board of Governors of the Federal Reserve System.

Riley, John G. and Huagang Li. 1997. "Auction Choice: A Numerical Analysis." Mimeo, University of California at Los Angeles.

Roberts, Dan. 2000. "Phone Numbers that Could Well Result in Panic." *Financial Times*. October 19, p. 38.

Roberts, Dan and Andrew Ward. 2000. "Little Gold at the End of the Spectrum." *Financial Times*. November 3, p. 21.

Rothkopf, Michael H. and Richard Engelbrecht-Wiggans. 1993. "Misapplications Reviews: Getting the Model Right: The Case of Competitive Bidding." *Interfaces*. May, 23:3, pp. 99–106.

Salant, David. 2000. "Auctions and Regulation: Reengineering of Regulatory Mechanisms." *Journal of Regulatory Economics*. May, 17:3, pp. 195–204.

Simon, David P. 1994. "The Treasury's Experiment with Single-Price Auctions in the Mid-1970s: Winner's or Taxpayer's Curse?" *Review of Economics and Statistics*. November, 76:4, pp. 754–60.

Stuewe, Heinz. 1999. "Auktion von Telefonfrequenzen: Spannung bis zur letzten Minute." *Frankfurter Allgemeine Zeitung*. October 29.

Total Telecom. 2000. "Italy's UMTS Auction to Start October." *Reuters*. October 12. Available at (http://www.totaltele.com).

U.K. Monopolies and Mergers Commission 1999. *British Sky Broadcasting Group and Manchester United: A Report on the Proposed Merger*. Cm 4305. London: The Stationery Office.

Vickrey, William. 1961. "Counterspeculation, Auctions, and Competitive Sealed Tenders." *Journal of Finance*. 16, pp. 8–37.

Wighton, David. 1995a. "Wellcome Accepts Glaxo Bid and Criticises Trust." *Financial Times*. March 8, p. 27.

Wighton, David. 1995b. "Wellcome Still Smarting Over Handling of Trust's Stake." *Financial Times*. March 8, p. 32.

Wolfram, Catherine D. 1998. "Strategic Bidding in a Multiunit Auction: An Empirical Analysis of Bids to Supply Electricity in England and Wales." *RAND Journal of Economics*. 29:4, pp. 703–25.

Wolfram, Catherine D. 1999. "Measuring Duopoly Power in the British Electricity Spot Market." *American Economic Review*. September, 89:4, pp. 805–26.

26 Network externalities (effects)

S. J. Liebowitz and S. E. Margolis

What are network effects?

Network externality has been defined as a change in the benefit, or surplus, that an agent derives from a good when the number of other agents consuming the same kind of good changes. As fax machines increase in popularity, for example, your fax machine becomes increasingly valuable since you will have greater use for it. This allows, in principle, the value received by consumers to be separated into two distinct parts. One component, which in our writings we have labeled the autarky value, is the value generated by the product even if there are no other users. The second component, which we have called the synchronization value, is the additional value derived from being able to interact with other users of the product, and it is this latter value that is the essence of network effects.

An illustration: As this article was being written, commentators are speculating on whether the Apple computer will survive, since its network (base of users) is shrinking, some think, below a minimum acceptable level. Since the actual quantity of Apple computers sold is still among the very largest of personal computer manufacturers which should allow Apple to take advantage of economies of scale in production, and the computers are not thought to be deficient in terms of quality, any lack of viability must be due to the fact that the network of Apple computer users is small. In other words, the synchronization value of Apple computers is thought to be too low.

First a definitional concern: Network effects should not properly be called network externalities unless the participants in the market fail to internalize these effects. After all, it would not be useful to have the term 'externality' mean something different in this literature than it does in the rest of economics. Unfortunately, the term externality has been used somewhat carelessly in this literature. Although the individual consumers of a product are not likely to internalize the effect of their joining a network on other members of a network, the owner of a network may very well internalize such effects. When the owner of a network (or technology) is able to internalize such network effects, they are no longer externalities. This distinction, first discussed in Liebowitz and Margolis (1994) now seems to be adopted by some authors (e.g. Katz and Shapiro 1994) but has not been universally adopted.

Putting aside definitional concerns, the import of network effects comes largely from the belief that they are endemic to new, high-tech industries, and that such industries experience problems that are different in character from the problems that have, for more ordinary commodities, been solved by markets (Katz and Shapiro 1985, Farrell and Saloner 1985, Arthur 1996). The purported problems due to network effects are several, but the most arresting is a claim that markets may adopt an inferior product or network in the place of some superior alternative. Thus if network effects are a typical characteristic of modern technologies, the theory suggests that markets may be inadequate for managing the fruits of such technologies.

The concept of network externality has been applied in the literature of standards, where a primary concern is the choice of a correct standard (Farrell and Saloner 1985, Katz and Shapiro 1985, Besen and Farrell 1994, Liebowitz and Margolis 1996). The concept has also played a role in the literature of path dependence (Arthur 1989, 1990, David 1985, Liebowitz and Margolis 1990, 1995a.).

The literature has identified two types of network effects. Direct network effects have been defined as those generated through a direct physical effect of the number of purchasers on the value of a product (e.g. fax machines). Indirect network effects are "market mediated effects" such as cases where complementary goods (e.g. toner cartridges) are more readily available or lower in price as the number of users of a good (printers) increases. In early writing, however, this distinction was not carried into models of network effects. Once network effects were embodied in payoff functions, any distinction between direct and indirect effects was ignored in developing models and drawing conclusions. However, our 1994 paper demonstrates that the two types of effects will typically have different economic implications. It is now generally agreed (Katz and Shapiro 1994) that the consequences of internalizing direct and indirect network effects are quite different. Indirect network effects generally are pecuniary in nature and therefore should not be internalized. Pecuniary externalities do not impose deadweight losses if left uninternalized, whereas they do impose (monopoly or monopsony) losses if internalized. An interesting aspect of the network externalities literature is that it seemed to ignore, and thus repeat, earlier mistakes regarding pecuniary externalities. (For the resolution of pecuniary externalities see Young (1913), Knight (1924), and Ellis and Fellner (1943).)

Concern about marginal adjustment of the level of network activity has not been the primary focus of the network externality literature. Instead, this literature has focused primarily on selection among competing networks. Our discussion below follows this relative emphasis. We briefly consider the issue of levels of network activities, then turn to the choice of networks.

Levels of network related activities

Harvey Liebenstein's work on bandwagon and snob effects (1950) anticipates much of the argument regarding network effects. His main result is that demand curves are more elastic when consumers derive positive value from increases in the size of the market.

One branch of the modern network literature would easily fit in the Liebenstein framework. Such research has reexamined various economic models with network effects introduced. For example, an analysis of the impacts of unauthorized software copying will change when network effects are introduced. Copying increases the size of a network, increasing the value to authorized users, so that any harm from unauthorized copying will likely be mitigated.

The difference between a network effect and a network externality lies in whether the impact of an additional user on other users is somehow internalized. Since the synchronization effect is almost always assumed to be positive in this literature, the social value from another network user will always be greater than the private value. If network effects are not internalized, the equilibrium network size may be smaller than is efficient. For example, if the network of telephone users were not owned, it would likely be smaller than optimal since no agent would capture the benefits that an additional member of the network would impose on other members. (Alternatively, if the network effects were negative, a congestion externality might mean that networks tend to be larger than optimal.) Where networks are owned, this effect is internalized and under certain conditions the profit maximizing network size will also be socially optimal. (For which see our paper, 1995b.)

Perhaps surprisingly, the problem of internalizing the network externality is largely unrelated to the problem of choice between competing networks that is taken up in the next section. In the case of positive network effects, all networks are too small. Therefore, it is not the *relative* market shares of two competing formats, but rather, the overall level of network activity that will be affected by this difference between private and social values. This is completely compatible with the literature on conventional externalities. For reasons that we will expand on below, this is a far more likely consequence of uninternalized network effects than the more exotic cases of incorrect choices of networks, standard, or technologies.

Network size is a real and significant issue that is raised by network effects. Nevertheless, this issue has received fairly little attention in the contemporary literature of network externality, perhaps because it is well handled by more conventional economic models.

Choice among competing networks under increasing returns

The literature on network externalities challenges economists' traditional use of decreasing returns and grants primacy to economies to scale. Positive network effects, which raise the value received by consumers as markets get larger, have impacts that are very similar to conventional firm-level economies of scale. If we start an analysis with the assumption that firms produce similar but incompatible products (networks), and that the network effects operate only within the class of compatible products, then competitors (networks) with larger market shares will have an advantage over smaller competitors, *ceteris paribus*. If larger competitors have a forever widening advantage over smaller firms, we have entered the realm of natural monopoly, which is exactly where most models that address network and standards choices find themselves.

It is critical to note, however, that network effects are not in general *sufficient* for natural-monopoly-type results. In cases where average production costs are falling, constant, or nonexistent, network effects would be sufficient for a result of natural monopoly. Many, if not most, models in this literature ignore production costs and thus with any assumption of positive network effects are unavoidably constructed as instances of natural monopoly. But notice that if production costs exhibit decreasing returns, and if these decreasing returns overwhelm the network effects, then natural monopoly is not implied, and competing incompatible networks (standards) will be possible.

Though economists have long accepted the possibility of increasing returns, they have generally judged that except in fairly rare instances, the economy operates in a range of decreasing returns. Some proponents of network externalities models predict that as newer technologies take over a larger share of the economy, the share of the economy described by increasing returns will increase. Brian Arthur has emphasized these points to a general audience: "[R]oughly speaking, diminishing returns hold sway in the traditional part of the economy – the processing industries. Increasing returns reign in the newer part – the knowledge-based industries ... They call for different management techniques, strategies, and codes of government regulation. They call for different understandings" (Arthur 1996: 101)

If the choice of a standard or network is dominated by natural monopoly elements, then only one standard will survive in the market. It thus is of great importance that the standard that comes to dominate the market also be the best of the alternative standards available. Traditionally it has been assumed that the natural monopolist who comes to dominate a market will be at least as efficient as any other producer, but this assumption is specifically questioned in the newer literature. Specifics differ across the many versions of this problem that appear in the literature. The recurring issue, however, is that we lose the usual assurances that the products that prevail in markets are the ones that yield the greatest surpluses.

The mere existence of network effects and increasing returns is not sufficient to lead to the choice of an inferior technology. For that, some additional assumptions are needed. One common assumption that can generate a prediction of inefficient network choice is that the network effect differs across the alternative networks. In particular, it is sometimes assumed that the network type that offers the greatest surplus when network participation is large is the one that offers the smallest surplus when participation is small. This condition, however, is not likely to be satisfied, since synchronization effects are likely to be uniform. For example, if there is value in a cellular telephone network becoming larger, this should be equally true whether the network is digital or analog. Similarly, the network value of an additional user of a particular videorecorder format is purported to be the benefits accrued by having more opportiunities to exchange video tapes. But this extra value does not depend on the particular format of videorecorder chosen. If network effects are the same for all versions of a given product, it is very unlikely that the wrong format would be chosen if both are available at the same time.

Common restrictions in network effects models

As we have noted, network externality models often feature particular outcomes: Survival of only one network or standard, unreliability of market selection, and the entrenchment of incumbents. In formal models, these results follow inevitably from assumptions that are common simplifications in economic theory and that appear to be relatively unrestrictive. As applied in these network models, however, these assumptions are both critically responsible for the results and unappealingly restrictive.

Two important limitations of many network externalities models are the assumptions of constant marginal production cost and network value functions that rise without limit (see, for example, Chou and Shy (1990: 260), Church and Gandal (1993: 246), Katz and Shapiro (1986: 829), and Farrell and Saloner (1992: 16)). Matutes and Regibeau (1992) consider issues of duopoly and compatibility under a similar structure. Such assumptions install an inexhaustible economy of large-scale operation. If a network size can reach a point where additional participation does not provide additional value to participants, increases in scale would no longer be advantageous and it would then be possible for multiple networks to compete on an even basis.

Without investigation, it is unreasonable to accept that the law of diminishing marginal product is somehow suspended in new-technology industries. While the scale properties of a technology pertain to the simultaneous expansion of all inputs, it seems evident that resource limitations do ultimately restrain firm size. Economists have long supposed that limitations of management play a role in this, a relationship formalized in Radner (1992). The capacity constraints evident in the crisis at America On-Line in early 1997 exemplifies the influence of resource limitations on the performance of a network.

Another limitation is the common assumption that consumers are identical in their valuations of competing networks. Once heterogeneous tastes are allowed it becomes feasible for competing networks to coexist with one another even though each exhibits natural monopoly characteristics (e.g. if some computer owners much prefer Macintoshes and others much prefer the PC, they could both coexist).

A further restriction is the symmetric value received by consumers when another consumer joins a network. If economists, for example, much prefer to have other economists join their network as opposed to, say, sociologists, then it would be possible for economists to form a coalition that switches to a new standard even if the new standard failed to attract many sociologists. This latter point will prove to be of great importance when examining empirical examples of choosing the wrong standard, where large entities such as multinational firms and governments play an important role.

The empirical relevance of network effects and increasing returns

The confluence of network effects, increasing returns, and market outcomes may be spurious. Although many technologies have tended to evolve into single formats (e.g. home-use VCRs are almost all of the VHS variety) some portion of these may actually have evolved for reasons having little to do with either network effects *or* increasing returns. We should not be surprised to find that where there are differences in the performance of various standards, one may prevail over the others simply because it is better suited to the market.

First of all, the extent (and symmetry) of network effects may be much more limited than is commonly assumed. For example, in the case of spreadsheets and word processors, it may be quite important for a small group of collaborators to use identical software so as to be perfectly compatible with each other. Similarly, compatibility may be important for employees within a firm. But compatibility with the rest of the world may be relatively unimportant, unimportant enough to be overwhelmed by differences in preferences, so that multiple networks could survive. Networks that serve niche markets well (such as wordprocessors specializing in mathematical notation), might not be significantly disadvantaged by network effects.

As an illustration, consider the empirical examples of tax software and financial software. By far the dominant firm is Intuit, with its Turbo-Tax products and Quicken financial software. This market seems to have tilted strongly toward a single producer. Yet network effects should be virtually nonexistent for these products. Consumers do *not* exchange this type of information with one another. A better explanation that is consistent with the product reviews in computer magazines is that these products are just *better* than the alternatives.

Similarly, for large firms, compatibility within the firm should be of great importance, but compatibility outside of the firm should be of little consequence. For many products where the majority of customers are large firms, producers will not encounter natural monopoly elements since there may be little or no network advantage in selling to multiple firms.

Regarding increasing returns in production, it is true that the past decades have evidenced a number of technologies that have experienced enormous declines in prices and tremendous growth in sales. Nevertheless, it is not clear that this is the result of increasing returns. Since bigger has been cheaper, it has often been assumed that bigger causes cheaper. But an available alternative explanation is that as technologies have advanced with time, the average cost curves are shifting down. If that is the case, the implied causality is reversed: Cheaper causes bigger. Consider for example, the history of old technologies, such as refrigerators and automobiles. These industries, currently thought to exhibit conventional decreasing returns, experienced tremendous cost decreases, along with tremendous increases in utilization, early in their histories. (For a discussion of an earlier episode of this confusion, see Stigler 1941).

Policy implications

The theory of network externality is currently playing a role in several antitrust actions, the most prominent of which are the investigations of Microsoft by the Justice Department over various aspects of Microsoft's behavior including its attempted purchase of Intuit, the inclusion of the Microsoft Network as an icon in Windows 95, Microsoft's attempt to wrest control of the web browser market from Netscape and so forth. The claim seems to be that since markets cannot be relied upon to choose the best standards or bring about the right networks, governments might wish to investigate and control firms' efforts to make standards or establish networks. Several of the theorists involved in this literature have consulted for parties involved with these investigations. For example, Brian Arthur and Garth Saloner were two of the authors in the *amicus curiae* brief against Microsoft presented by four anonymous parties (thought to be four well-known and generally well-heeled competitors of Microsoft).

Clearly the potential to misuse such antitrust theories by competitors unable to win in the marketplace is very great, not unlike various theories of predation. Since the empirical support for this theory is so weak, it appears at best to be premature and at worst simply wrong to use this theory as the basis for antitrust decisions.

In a related vein, for those cases where network effects are important, the role of copyright and patent law may be cast in a new light. First, networks are likely to be too small if network effects are not internalized. Intellectual property laws are one means by which such network effects can be internalized, since ownership is an ideal method of internalization.

The possibility that networks can compete with each other suggests a further consideration regarding intellectual property law. Where one standard is owned and another is not, we can have less confidence that an unowned but superior standard will be able to prevail against an owned standard, since the owner of a standard can appropriate the benefits of internalizing any network effects. Although we do not have any evidence that inferior standards have prevailed against superior standards, this may be in large part because most standards are supported by companies who have some form of ownership such as patent, copyright, or business positioning. The greatest chance for some form of third-degree path dependence to arise would be if an unowned standard with dispersed adherents were to engage in competition with a standard that had well defined ownership. Further research in this area is needed before any firm conclusions can be drawn, however.

Conclusions

Network effects are undoubtedly real and important phenomena. The popular and very compelling example is the telephone network. Who would deny that the value of phone service depends heavily on the number of other people who have phone service? Contemporary technologies expand that example enormously.

The enthusiasm for recognizing and understanding these phenomena should not, however, lead us to inappropriate or premature conclusions. As we have noted above, there are distinctions and reservations that ought to be maintained. The first and broadest is that between network effects and network externalities. A further distinction is between pecuniary externalities and real ones. Even for the set a real externalities, it is important to note the distinction between the problem of network size and that of network choice, the boundedness of the network effect, the likely symmetry of network effects for alternative products, the ability of large consumers to self-internalize network effects, and differences in tastes.

Finally, we would urge some reservation about the empirical validity of economies of production scale for many high tech products. If these products have diseconomies of scale at some production level, these production costs may overturn other natural monopoly elements. Improvements in production costs, as with many other economic results, may have more to do with being smarter than with being bigger.

References

Arthur, W. B. 1989. Competing technologies, increasing returns, and lock-in by historical events. *Economic Journal* 99: 116–31.

Arthur, W. B. 1990. Positive feedbacks in the economy. *Scientific American* 262: 92–9.

Arthur, W. B. 1996. Increasing returns and the new world of business. *Harvard Business Review*: 100–9.

Besen, S. M. and Farrel, J. 1994. Choosing how to compete: Strategies and tactics in standardization. *Journal of Economic Perspectives* 8: 117–31.

Chou, D. and Shy, O. 1990. Network effects without network externalities. *International Journal of Industrial Organization* 8: 259–70.

Church, J. and Gandal, N. 1993. Complementary network externalities and technological adoption. *International Journal of Industrial Organization* 11: 239–60.

David, P. A. 1985. Clio and the economics of QWERTY. *American Economic Review* 75: 332–37.

Ellis H. S. and Fellner, W. 1943. External economies and diseconomies. *American Economic Review* 33: 493–511.

Farrell J. and Saloner, G. 1985. Standardization, compatibility, and innovation. *Rand Journal* 16: 70–83.

Farrell J. and Saloner, G. 1992. Converters, compatibility, and control of interfaces. *Journal of Industrial Economics* 40: 9–36.

Katz M. L., and Shapiro C. 1985. Network externalities, competition, and compatibility. *American Economic Review* 75: 424–40.

Katz, M. L., and Shapiro, C. 1986. Technology adoption in the presence of network externalities. *Journal of Political Economy* 94: 822–41.

Katz, M. L. and Shapiro, C. 1994. Systems competition and network effects. *Journal of Economic Perspectives* 8: 93–115.

Knight, F. H. 1924 Some fallacies in the interpretation of social cost. *Quarterly Journal of Economics* 38: 582–606.

Leibenstein, H. 1950. Bandwagon, snob, and Veblen effects in the theory of consumer's demand. *Quarterly Journal of Economics* 64: 183–207.

Liebowitz, S. J. and Margolis, S. E. 1990. The fable of the keys. *Journal of Law and Economics* 33: 1–26.

Liebowitz, S. J. and Margolis, S. E. 1995a. Path dependence, lock-in and history. *Journal of Law, Economics and Organization* 11: 205–26.

Liebowitz, S. J. and Margolis, S. E. 1995b. Are network externalities a new source of market failure? *Research In Law And Economics* 17: 1–22.

Liebowitz, S. J. and Margolis, S. E. 1996. Market processes and the selection of standards. *Harvard Journal of Law and Technology* 9: 283–318.

Matutes, C. and Regibeau, P. 1992. Compatibility and bundling of complementary goods in a duopoly. *Journal of Industrial Economics* 40: 37–54.

Radner, R. 1992. Hierarchy: The economics of managing. *Journal of Economic Literature* 30: 1382–1415.

Stigler, G. J. 1941. *Production and Distribution Theories*, New York: Macmillan Company.

Young, A. A. 1913. Pigou's *Wealth and Welfare. Quarterly Journal of Economics* 27: 672–86.

Part V

Labor compensation theory

Introduction

Labor economics is another branch of microeconomics where there has been consider-able progress beyond the simple analysis of decades past, when labor was treated as little more than another type of "factor of production," with labor productivity and prod-uct price being the key variables in hiring decisions. One significant advance in recent years is a better understanding of the way employers compensate their workers, and how this compensation (pecuniary and otherwise) affects workers' productivity. The balance of research has also tilted toward firm-level analysis, as opposed to market-level analysis, although there is still mentioning of "internal labor market" as if it is a counterpart of the external labor market. Indeed, at the micro level, labor economics has become "personal economics."

The new personal economics starts with two observations: (a) Labor is multidimensional: effort, pace, thoroughness ..., and (b) an employee's contribution to a firm varies a great deal, depending not only on skills and experience, but also on how motivated the employee is in his/her job.

The challenge for the employer (and the employee knows this!) is how to measure these separate attributes (effort, pace, thoroughness) of the employee. Indeed, many of these attributes may not be observable at all. This problem is linked with the problem of moni-toring cost, and thus with transaction costs. The compensation package must be designed to minimize monitoring cost, and deal with observability. Moreover, the fact that each worker rarely works alone raises issues of rivalry, cooperation and the likes. Intertemporal strategic behavior (e.g., if I take this action today, what will be my options tomorrow?) should also be considered.

The question, then, is how to motivate the workers. There are four major ways: piece rates, tournaments, efficiency wages, and team incentives. The oldest method is probably *piece rates*, where each worker is paid his/her observed output. In *tournaments system*, workers are paid according to their rankings within a group. *Efficiency wages* rely on the idea that workers should be paid according to their efficiency, which in turn depends on how they are paid. *Team incentives* (for example, profit-sharing) are to reward the whole team rather than to each individual based on his/her own output.

In theory, it is possible to find the correct incentive if the employee's behavior could be accurately assessed. Indeed, the new view is that labor markets cannot be understood without understanding information imperfections (and agency problems). Consider the four schemes listed above: Some would require accurate information that is impossible to obtain. Some would encourage free-riding (when each worker tends to "let others do the work"), some would create the opposite effect of discouraging cooperation among team members. A perfect compensation package remains elusive.

Spence (1973) opened up a new way to look at the role of education in the labor market. A diploma, for example, is as much an information-carrying "signal" as an accumulation of human capital. Job market signaling models (Spence, 2001) are built on this insight.[1]

Labor market and macroeconomics

Not surprisingly, given the central role of labor markets in macroeconomics, many works in labor economics are inspired by macroeconomic problems, specifically unemployment.

According to efficiency wage theory, the firm should aim not only at compensating for the workers' innate productivity but also at giving him the optimal incentive to work hard. This theory typifies the works in labor economics that have served as the microfoundation for macroeconomics. Interestingly, its precursor is Leibenstein's, which has its run-in with pure Chicago-type micro-theory in his theory of X-efficiency[2] and bandwagon effects.

Part V has four articles. Rosen (1981) is a classic in labor compensation theory, analysing a common but so far not well understood phenomenon, that of "superstars", wherein relatively small numbers of people earn huge amounts of money and dominate the activities in which they engage. Why are they paid such unbelievably high compensation? Dixit (1987) is representative of the type of model which brings rivalry among workers into labor compensation and in so doing, alleviates the problem of information, since relative ranking is easier to determine than absolute measurement of effort. In his model, workers compete for fixed prizes, with the highest prize awarded to the person with the most output. The classic paper on tournament model is Rosen and Lazear (1981). As these authors put it: "The essence of tournament theory is that individuals can be motivated simply by comparison with their peers or by comparison to some standard." Spence (1973) shows how information can be manipulated and used in the labor market and various consequences. Stiglitz (1987) takes on the dependence of quality on price, but it has special implications for the labor market. Not surprisingly, Stiglitz is also the originator of efficiency wage theory.

Notes

1 As defined by Spence: "Market signals are activities or attributes of individuals in a market which, by design or accident, alter the beliefs of, or convey information to other individuals in the market" (1973, p. 1).
2 See Leibenstein (1966).

References

Dixit, A. (1987) "Strategic Behavior in Contests," *American Economic Review* 77(5), pp. 891–8.
Leibenstein, H. (1966) "Allocative Efficiency v. 'X-efficiency'," *American Economic Review* 56, 392–415.
Rosen, S. (1981) "The Economics of Superstars," *American Economic Review* 71, pp. 845–58.
Rosen, S. and Lazear, E. P. (1981) "Rank-order Tournaments as Optimal Labor Contracts," *Journal of Political Economy* 89, pp. 841–64.
Spence, A. M. (1973) "Job Market Signaling," *Quarterly Journal of Economics* 87, pp. 355–74.

Spence, A. M. (2001) "Signaling in Retrospect and the Informational Structure of Markets," *Nobel Lecture.*

Stiglitz, J. E. (1987) "The Causes and Consequences of The Dependence of Quality on Price," *Journal of Economic Literature* 25, pp. 1–48.

27 The economics of Superstars

Sherwin Rosen

The phenomenon of Superstars, wherein relatively small numbers of people earn enormous amounts of money and dominate the activities in which they engage, seems to be increasingly important in the modern world. While some may argue that it is all an illusion of world inflation, its currency may be signaling a deeper issue.[1] Realizing that world inflation may command the title, if not the content of this paper, quickly to the scrap heap, I have found no better term to describe the phenomenon. In certain kinds of economic activity there is concentration of output among a few individuals, marked skewness in the associated distributions of income and very large rewards at the top.

Confidentiality laws and other difficulties make it virtually impossible to obtain systematic data in this field. However, consider the following:

(i) Informed opinion places the number of full-time comedians in the United States at approximately two hundred. This is perhaps a smaller number than were employed in vaudevillian days, though it hardly can be maintained that the demand for (intended) comic relief is in a state of secular decline. Some of the more popular performers today earn extraordinary sums, particularly those appearing on television. The capacity for television to produce high incomes is also manifest in the enormous salaries paid to network news broadcasters.

(ii) The market for classical music has never been larger than it is now, yet the number of full-time soloists on any given instrument is also on the order of only a few hundred (and much smaller for instruments other than voice, violin, and piano). Performers of first rank comprise a limited handful out of these small totals and have very large incomes. There are also known to be substantial differences in income between them and those in the second rank, even though most consumers would have difficulty detecting more than minor differences in a "blind" hearing.

(iii) Switching to more familiar territory, sales of elementary textbooks in economics are concentrated on a group of best sellers, though there exists a large number of very good and highly substitutable alternatives in the market (the apparent inexhaustable supply of authors willing to gamble on breaking into the select group is one of the reasons why so many are available). A small number of graduate schools account for a large fraction of Ph.Ds. A relatively small number of researchers account for a large fraction of citations and perhaps even articles written.

Countless other examples from the worlds of sports, arts and letters, and show business will be well known to readers. Still others can be found in several of the professions. There are two common elements in all of them: first, a close connection between personal reward and the size of one's own market; and second, a strong tendency for both market size and reward to be skewed toward the most talented people in the activity. True, standard theory suggests that those who sell more generally earn more. But that principle applies as well to shoemakers as to rock musicians, so something more is involved. In fact the competitive model is virtually silent about any special role played by either the size of the total market or the amount of it controlled by any single person, because products are assumed to be undifferentiated and one seller's products are assumed to be as good as those of any other.

The elusive quality of "box office appeal," the ability to attract an audience and generate a large volume of transactions, is the issue that must be confronted. Recognition that one's personal market scale is important in the theory of income distribution has a long history, but the idea has not been developed very extensively in the literature.[2] I hope to fill in some of the gaps in what follows.

The analytical framework used is a special type of assignment problem, the marriage of buyers to sellers, including the assignment of audiences to performers, of students to textbooks, patients to doctors, and so forth. Rest assured that prospective impresarios will receive no guidance here on what makes for box office appeal, sometimes said to involve a combination of talent and charisma in uncertain proportions. In the formal model all that is taken for granted and represented by a single factor rather than by two, an index q labeled talent or quality. The distribution of talent is assumed to be fixed in the population of potential sellers and costlessly observable to all economic agents. Let p be the price of a unit of service (for example, a performance, a record, a visit, etc.) and let m be the size of the market, the number of "tickets" sold by a given seller. Then an overall market equilibrium is a pair of functions $p(q)$ and $m(q)$ indicating price and market size of sellers of every observable talent and a domain of q such that: (a) all sellers maximize profit and cannot earn larger amounts in other activities, and (b) all buyers maximize utility and cannot improve themselves by purchasing from another seller.

Properties of sellers' maximum net revenue functions, $R(q)$, will have special interest. Specifically, convexity of this function describes much of the observable consequences of Superstars. Since $R(q)$ is the transformation that takes the distribution of talent to the distribution of rewards, convexity implies that the income distribution is stretched out in its right-hand tail compared to the distribution of talent. Hence a genuine behavioral economic explanation is provided for differential skew between the distributions of income and talent, a problem that has been an interesting and important preoccupation of the literature on income distribution down through the years.[3] Convexity of $R(q)$ literally means that small differences in talent become magnified in larger earnings differences, with great magnification if the earnings-talent gradient increases sharply near the top of the scale. This magnification effect is characteristic of the phenomenon under consideration.

Convexity of returns and the extra skew it imparts to the distribution of earnings can be sustained by imperfect substitution among different sellers, which is one of the hallmarks of the types of activities where Superstars are encountered. Lesser talent often is a poor substitute for greater talent. The worse it is the larger the sustainable rent accruing to higher quality sellers because demand for the better sellers increases more than proportionately: hearing a succession of mediocre singers does not add up to a single outstanding performance. If a surgeon is 10 percent more successful in saving lives than his fellows, most people would be willing to pay more than a 10 percent premium for his services. A company involved in a $30 million law suit is rash to scrimp on the legal talent it engages.

Imperfect substitution alone implies convexity and provides a very general explanation of skewed earnings distributions which applies to myriad economic service activities. However, preferences alone are incapable of explaining the other aspect of the Superstar phenomenon, the marked concentration of output on those few sellers who have the most talent. This second feature is best explained by technology rather than by tastes.[4] In many instances rendering the service is described as a form of joint consumption, not dissimilar to a public good. Thus a performer or an author must put out more or less the same effort whether 10 or 1,000 people show up in the audience or buy the book. More generally, the costs of production (writing, performing, etc.) do not rise in proportion to the size of a seller's market.

The key difference between this technology and public goods is that property rights are legally assigned to the seller: there are no issues of free riding due to nonexclusion; customers are excluded if they are unwilling to pay the appropriate admission fee. The implied scale economy of joint consumption allows relatively few sellers to service the entire market. And fewer are needed to serve it the more capable they are. When the joint consumption technology and imperfect substitution features of preferences are combined, the possibility for talented persons to command both very large markets and very large incomes is apparent.

A theory of the assignment of buyers to sellers is required to make these ideas precise. The demand and supply structure of one such model is set forth in Sections I and II. The nature of market equilibrium and its implications for income and output distributions are discussed in Sections III and IV. Comparative static predictions of the model are sketched in Section V and conclusions appear in Section VI.

I Structure of demand

Imperfect substitution among quality differentiated goods in the same product class arises from indivisibilities in the technology of consumption. No satisfactory analytical specification exists in the literature, because indivisibilities lead to nonadditivities in preference relations which are analytically intractable.[5] Yet some specific model is required to make any progress on this problem. My solution to this dilemma is to adopt a smooth quantity-quality substitution technology and introduce the indivisibility through a fixed cost of consumption per unit of quantity. Consumers' attempts to minimize consumption costs gives an extra competitive advantage to higher quality sellers. However, it is a surprising implication of the analysis that this form of indivisibility is not crucial to the central conclusions, so that true nonadditivities would only strengthen the argument.

Assume the consumer has a well-behaved weakly separable utility function $u = u(x, g(n, z))$, where x is a composite commodity and $y = g(n, z)$ has the natural interpretation of consumption of "services" of the type in question. n is the quantity purchased, a measure of exposure to a seller, such as a patient visit, a performance, etc.; and z is the quality of each unit of exposure. Quantity-quality substitution requires that $g(\cdot)$ is increasing in both of its arguments and that $\partial^2_g / \partial_n \partial_z > 0$.

This specification has the virtue of being simple, at the cost of ignoring some details and not being perfectly general. The definitions of markets are left somewhat vague: for example, for some purposes it is sufficient to think about the market for novels as a whole and for others distinguishing between mysteries, romances, and so forth is necessary. This is simply treated by allowing y to be a vector and is therefore ignored. There are several dimensions to quantity in any specific application which might be treated in a similar manner. For example, most people do not purchase more than one copy of an author's book but may buy several different books written by the same author. Or there may be preferences for variety. But these considerations are less than compelling in markets for professional services where direct personal contact between buyers and sellers is required. Preferences for variety per se cannot be treated in a quantity-quality substitution model, and since the generalization of increasing the dimensionality of exposure is clear enough in any given case, it is ignored too. It is doubtful whether the general nature of the results are greatly affected by these simplifications.

A cardinal measure of quality or talent must rely on measurement of actual outcomes. Taken to extreme, this view would define the talent distribution as the realized output or income distribution. However, that goes too far because it ignores the fact that more talented people typically command greater cooperating resources in producing observed outcomes and it refers to all consumers as a group rather than to any one of them. The service flow y is a natural personal outcome measure in this case and is the prime candidate for scaling talent, so long as n is held constant in the imputation to obtain the right *ceteris paribus* conditions. Still, the measure is strongly dependent on n unless $g(n, z)$ is multiplicatively separable. To avoid ambiguity I restrict $g(n, z)$ to the form $zf(n)$, so that relative talent is defined independently of n (since y is the product of a function of n and another function of z, talent can always be rescaled to be the function of z itself, for example, if $y = f_1(z') f_2(n)$, change the scaling of z' by defining $z \equiv f_1(z')$). The properties of $f(n)$ play no important role in this analysis, so it is assumed to be linear. Therefore $y = nz$, which is the familiar efficiency units specification. This is a very strong form of substitution which obviously works in the direction of spreading sales around all qualities of sellers, not concentrating them among the top, and is a weak specification in that sense.

The cost of one unit of service of a given quality is its price $p(z)$ plus a fixed cost s. For example, if each unit requires t hours and the wage rate is w, then $s = tw$. Measuring prices in units of x, the budget constraint is

$$I = x + (p+s)n = x + [(p+s)/z]y = x + vy \qquad (27.1)$$

where I is full income and v is the full price of services directly implied by the multiplicative specification $y = nz$ (herein lies the analytical value of that assumption).

Marginal conditions for consumer choice are

$$u_y/u_x = dp(z)/dz \quad \text{for } z \qquad (27.2)$$
$$u_y/u_x = (p+s)/z \quad \text{for } n$$

Combining these two, choice of z solves

$$dp/dz = p'(z) = (p+s)/z \qquad (27.3)$$

Choice of n follows from the requirements that the marginal rate of substitution between y and x equals the relative marginal cost $v = (p+s)z$. The schedule $p(z)$ is the same for all buyers. It maps the talent of a seller into the unit price charged for that quality of service. Therefore optimal choice of z in (27.3) depends only on s and not on the form of the utility function under the separability assumption. Condition (27.3) balances larger direct costs of greater talent against larger indirect costs of greater quantity and lesser talent. For example, customers with larger s prefer more talented sellers to economize on consumption time in this specification. Finally, all effects of intensity of preferences are absorbed in choice of the quantity consumed, given the optimum value of z determined by condition (27.3).

Because it plays an important role in the analysis below, suppose the equality in (27.3) held for all possible values of z, not just for one of them. Evidently that occurs only if

$p(z)$ happens to follow a definite functional form; the one satisfying (27.3) interpreted as a differential equation for all z. Integrating and simplifying equation (27.3) yields

$$p(z) = vz - s \qquad (27.4)$$

The full price v is the constant of integration, since $v = (p + s)/z$ by definition. If market prices line up as in (27.4), the consumer is indifferent among all values of z that appear on the market, since (27.3) is an identity. Therefore (27.4) must be a price-talent indifference curve, an equalizing difference function, showing the maximum amount the customer is willing to pay for alternative values of z at a given utility index. The larger is v, the smaller the utility index. Finally, if (27.4) does in fact hold true in the market, too, then both equations in (27.2) reduce to $u_y/u_x = v$, so that y is uniquely determined for the consumer even though z and n are not.

II Structure of supply: external and internal diseconomies

The economic activities under consideration invariably involve direct contact of buyers with the seller in one way or another. If a competitive market was ever impersonal, this surely is not it. The seller's choice of market size (volume of transactions) amounts to determining the number of contacts to make with buyers. In many cases the technology admits a certain kind of duplication in which the seller delivers services to many buyers simultaneously, as a form of joint consumption. Once the author tells his tale to the publisher, it can be duplicated in writing as many times as desired. A performer appearing on television literally clones his performance to whomever happens to tune in. The services rendered by any seller become more like a kind of public good the more nearly the technology allows perfect duplication at constant cost.

Just as it is difficult to find practical examples of pure public goods in public finance, so too it is difficult to find them here. In fact services of this type are analogous to local public goods, due to ultimate limitations on joint consumption economies. To the extent that the technology is subject to congestion, that is, to external diseconomies of scale, the required analytical apparatus is the theory of clubs rather than the theory of pure public goods.[6] These external diseconomies reflect a type of degradation of services a seller supplies to each of his customers as the number of contacts expands. There are two fundamental reasons for this:

First, in cases where duplication is possible, market expansion ultimately requires using inferior techniques to render the service. It is preferable to hear concerts in a hall of moderate size rather than in Yankee Stadium. Recordings are a superior way of reaching a large audience, but are inferior in quality to live performances with smaller audiences. Furthermore, many of the activities in question involve certain creative elements so the ultimate negative impact of market sizes sometimes can be interpreted as the effect of overexposure and repetition.

Second, the analysis should not be constrained to only those activities where some form of cloning is possible. The general model also applies to cases of one-on-one buyerseller contact, as is true of professional services. Here the negative effects of personal market scale are caused by limitations on the seller's time. As a doctor's patient load increases, the amount of direct contact time available to any person decreases, waiting time between appointments and in the office increases, and so forth. Nevertheless patients may be willing to trade off service time against quality of service per unit time.

In both cases the quality of service z that appears in consumers' preferences is itself pro-duced by both the quality and size of the market of the seller with whom transactions occur: $z = h(q, m)$, where q is an index of seller talent or quality and $m = m(q)$ is the total num-ber of units sold by a seller of type q. The arguments above imply $\partial z/\partial q = h_q > 0$ and $\partial z/\partial m = h_m > 0$. Furthermore, I assume that $h_{qm} \geq 0$: superior talent stands out and does not deteriorate so rapidly with market size as inferior talent does. The importance of this assumption will emerge later on.

Preferences are structured on service flows, which in turn depend upon q and m. Therefore $p = p(q, m)$ is the unit price charged by a seller of quality q selling m units. Competition in the market for services implies that the *function* $p(q, m)$ is taken as given by a seller. This market is competitive even though a seller affects the unit price charged by choosing m. The reason for competition in markets of this type is that each seller is closely constrained by other sellers offering similar services. Though sellers of different quality are imperfectly substitutable with each other, the extent of substitution decreases with distance. In the limit very close neighbors are virtually perfect substitutes. Assume there is a regular distribution of talent in the population $\phi(q)dq$. Then potential substitution is generated by both the density ϕ in the neighborhood dq of q and by degradation through larger market size of better quality sellers some distance above q, and the opposite for those some distance below q.

In addition to market size effects on demand, the other factor influencing the output deci-sion is direct cost of production. Let $C(m)$ be out of pocket costs of producing m units, with $C' \geq 0$ and $C'' \geq 0$. There are non-decreasing (marginal) costs of production – internal dis-economies – for the usual reasons, including the fact that here the seller must work harder as m increases. Assume also that all sellers have opportunity cost K of working in this sector compared with the next best alternative, with K independent of q.

A seller of type q chooses $m(q)$ to maximize net revenue

$$R(q) = p(q, m)m - C(m) \tag{27.5}$$

Therefore $m(q)$ is chosen to satisfy

$$mp_m(q, m) + p(q, m) - C'(m) = 0 \tag{27.6}$$

so long as

$$2p_m + mp_{mm} - C'' < 0 \tag{27.7}$$

and R exceeds K. Equation (27.6) determines the intensive margin. If $R(q)$ is monotone in q, then free entry determines an extensive margin as well; the value of q, denoted q, which satisfies both $R(q_1) = K$ and (27.7) simultaneously.

In context a more elaborate return specification decomposes the internal margin above into two additional components, one being the size of each act of joint consumption, m_1, and the other being the number of such acts, m_2. In that case the revenue function is

$$m_2[m_1 p(q, m_1, m_2) - C_1(m_1)] - C_2(m_2) \tag{27.8}$$

where $m_1 p - C_1$ are the "gate" receipts for each event and $C_2(m_2)$ is the cost of increasing the number of events. This avoids some of the dimensionality or units ambiguities in (27.5), as noted in Section I. If all external diseconomies reside in m_1 alone and not m_2 (so that

$p = p(q, m_1)$), then (27.8) and (27.5) have very similar implications; only the diseconomy associated with each event is somewhat overcome by expanding their number in formulation (27.8). This carries over to a case where the external diseconomy of m_2 is small. Otherwise, precise results depend on whether the effect on performance services of m_1 are stronger than those of m_2 and on their interaction. It is simplest to merely think of m in (27.5) as the product of m_1 and m_2, in those cases where this type of decomposition is applicable.

III Market equilibrium

A complete closed market solution is available if all buyers have the same fixed cost s, though possibly different marginal rates of substitution between y and x. In that case it is possible to aggregate total services in a single market, with a unique implicit market price v which contains all the relevant information and acts as a "sufficient statistic." The unit price p charged by a seller of type q is then constrained to follow (27.4) independent of market supply conditions. Though n and z are not uniquely determined for any consumer, each one has a regular demand function for services y which depends only upon v. These demands in turn can be summed across consumers to obtain the total market demand for services $\sum y \equiv Y^d = F(v)$. Since consumers are indifferent between n and z, the composition of services between qualities and quantities is determined completely by sellers, who maximize profit according to condition (27.6). Individual supply choices may be aggregated too, this time by integrating the optimum value of zm, the total services a seller supplies to the market, over those values of q which are actually found in the market, weighted by the number of sellers of type $q, \phi(q)$. This sum represents total services supplied to the market, $Y^S = G(v)$. The intersection of supply and demand determines v itself. Given this equilibrium, the internal cross-section price, output, and income distributional structure may be examined in detail.

To find the supply decision of each seller at a given value of v, substitute $z = h(q, m)$ into the equalizing difference function (27.4). Applying (27.6) and (27.7) yields

$$vmh_m(q, m) + vh(q, m) - s - C'(m) = 0 \tag{27.9}$$
$$2vh_m + vmh_{mm} - C'' < 0 \tag{27.10}$$

Differentiate (27.9) with respect to q:

$$\partial m/\partial q = -v(h_q + mh_{qm})/(2vh_m + vmh_{mm} - C'') > 0 \tag{27.11}$$

Market size increases with q if $h_{qm} > 0$. Next differentiate net revenue $R(q)$ in (27.5) with respect to q, at its maximized value. By the envelope property

$$R'(q) = vmh_q > 0 \tag{27.12}$$

Net revenue is monotonically increasing in talent, since $h_q > 0$. Finally, differentiate (27.12) with respect to q and simplify to obtain

$$R''(q) = v(h_q + mh_{qm})(\partial m/\partial q) + vmh_{qq} \tag{27.13}$$

where $\partial m/\partial q$ is defined by equation (27.11). So long as h_{qq} is not sufficiently negative, reward is convex in q.

The market supply of services is easily calculated. Let $m(q; v)$ be the solution to (27.9). Then the amount of service supplied to the market by a seller of quality q is $h(q, m(q; v))m(q; v)$ and the total amount supplied to the market by all active sellers is

$$Y^s(v) = \int_{q_1(v)}^{\infty} h(q, m(q; v))m(q; v)\phi(q)dq$$

where $q_1(v)$ is the extensive margin. Differentiate with respect to v:

$$dY^s/dv = -h(q_i, m')m'\phi(q_1)(dq_1/dv)$$
$$+ \int_{q_1}^{\infty} h\left[1 + \frac{m}{h}\left(\frac{\partial h}{\partial m}\right)\right]\left(\frac{\partial m}{\partial v}\right)\phi(q)dq$$

where $m^1 = m(q_1; v)$. Condition (27.9) implies that $1 + (m/h)h_m$ is positive. Therefore the second (integral) term in dY/dv is positive. The fact that R is increasing in both q and v from (27.12) implies that $dq_1/dv < 0$, so that the first term is positive as well. Hence there is rising supply price in the service market. It is obvious from Section I that there is falling demand price for services, so a conventional equilibrium is obtained and v is uniquely determined.

Internal diseconomies

The cross-section structure of the market equilibrium is most easily established in the case where there are no effects of a seller's market size on service quality.[7] In that case m is not an argument of $h(\cdot)$ and talent is scaled so that $z = h(q) = q$. Now the model has a Ricardian flavor, with differential rent sustained by talent induced product differentiation.

Since $z \equiv q$ the unit price charged by sellers of talent q is increasing linearly in q at rate v, from (27.4); and since price is higher for the better sellers and cost conditions no less favorable, more talented sellers produce more and have larger markets.[8] Application of (27.11) to this case yields $\partial m/\partial q = v/C'' > 0$. From (27.12), $R'(q) = vm > 0$, and $R''(q) = v^2/C'' > 0$, from (27.13). Not only does rent reward increase in talent, but marginal rent reward increases in talent as well. $R(q)$ is convex because both price and quantity increase in q. To see the powerful force of convexity in producing skewness, consider an example where $s = 0$ and $C(m)$ is quadratic. Then $m \propto vq$ and both price and quantity increase linearly in q. Therefore, revenue increases in the square of q. In fact $R \alpha v^2 q^2/2$. A person who is twice as talented as another earns four times more money in this example.[9]

This case is important in showing that the tendency toward skewed rewards arising from convexity of revenues holds under very general circumstances: individuals who, by virtue of superior talent and ability in an activity, can sell their services for higher prices have strong incentives to produce more so long as costs are not perfectly correlated with talent. The increase in both price and quantity with quality implies that talent has a multiplicative effect on reward. It is surprising that the tendency toward skewed rewards is not necessarily dependent on indivisibilities and occurs in the linear efficiency-units case, perhaps the weakest possible specification. However, no relative skew is implied in the distribution of output in this case because there are no interactive effects in that dimension of the problem.

Pure joint consumption

The effect of scale economy on seller concentration is strikingly seen in the extreme case when internal and external diseconomies vanish, when $C(m) \equiv 0$ (nonzero constant marginal costs will do also) and $h_m \equiv 0$, so $z = h(q) = q$. Then there literally is public goods technology and a single seller services the total market in equilibrium. That person is the most talented of all potential sellers. Even though there is one seller, essentially competitive market conditions are maintained by threats of potential entry.

Let $N = N(p, q)$ denote the total market demand for quantity at price p and talent q. If there were several potential sellers of the same talent, only one of them is required to provide the service efficiently, so $m \equiv N$. This is seen in Figure 27.1. Free entry implies that total revenue pN must be driven down to opportunity cost K in equilibrium. This equation, $pN = K$, is the rectangular hyperbola in Figure 27.1. It is competitive supply price. Market equilibrium occurs where demand intersects supply from above. Suppose the seller were to charge price p_1. Then the value of sales exceeds K and rents are nonzero. Therefore another seller would enter and charge a slightly lower price, attracting all business away from the initial seller. By continuation, price must be driven down in equilibrium to p^*, rents are driven to zero, there is one seller and potential entry maintains that situation indefinitely.

What happens when sellers have different talents? The demand function facing a more able seller is different from the one in Figure 27. 1 because q is an argument of demand, $N(p, q)$. Whether N_q is positive or negative, less talented sellers are driven out of the market. To see this, note that $R(q) = p. N(p, q)$ in this case. Therefore

$$R'(q) = N[1 + (p/N)\partial N/\partial p]\partial p/\partial q + p(\partial N/\partial q) \tag{27.14}$$

Given the structure of demand above, equation (27.4) implies that $\partial p/\partial q = v$. Furthermore, it is easy to show that the price and quality elasticities of demand for quantities are related

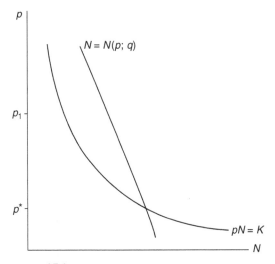

Figure 27.1

to the full price elasticity of services as follows:

$$(p/N)\partial N/\partial p = \theta(v/Y)\partial Y/\partial v$$
$$(q/N)\partial N/\partial q = -[1+(v/Y)\partial Y/\partial v]$$

where $\theta = p/(p+s)$ is the share of full price accounted for by nonfixed costs and $Y = \sum y$ with the sum extending over individual consumers. The quality elasticity of demand for quantity is negative if the full price elasticity of demand for services is inelastic. Substituting these relations into (27.14) and simplifying yields

$$R'(q) = Nv(1-\theta) > 0 \qquad (27.15)$$

Consider the following two cases:

(i) Assume $\phi(q)$ is dense on the interval $[q_0, q]$, where q_0 is the least talented and q the most talented potential seller. Equation (27.15) shows that R is increasing in both q and v. For a given value of v all sellers for whom $R(q) - K > 0$ would choose to enter and, since $R' > 0$, they must be selected from the upper tail of $\phi(q)$. But in equilibrium there is only one seller. Therefore v must adjust so that $R(\bar{q}) - K = 0$ and all people for whom $q < \bar{q}$ rationally choose the alternative occupation. There is no rent in equilibrium when ϕ is dense even though there is a single seller, because someone is waiting in the wings who is imperceptably different from that supplier.

(ii) Assume $\phi(q)$ basically the same as before, with the addition of outlier q^* a finite distance ϵ above $\bar{q}$: $q^* = \bar{q} + \varepsilon$. The Superstar is perceptibly different from the closest rival and earns rent on this unique talent. Now it is q^* who supplies the service. Equilibrium v must be slightly smaller than in case (i) so that people for whom $q \leq \bar{q}$ choose not to compete. q^* charges price $p^* = vq^* - s$ (see equation (27.4), whereas $\bar{q}$ would charge $\bar{p} = v\bar{q} - s$. The price differential $p^* - p = v\varepsilon$ is the unit rent accruing to q^*. This is a small number if ε is small. Yet the total rent received by q^* is $Nv\varepsilon$, which can be very large if N is large. Though unit rent is limited by the equalizing difference (27.4) and the supply (distance) of close competitors, scale economies can make total rent very large in equilibrium.[10]

External diseconomies

External diseconomies support a nondegenerate equilibrium distribution of sellers. The spatial structure of the market is illustrated in Figure 27.2. Given the market full price v, prices charged by sellers of different talent must satisfy (27.4) and $z = h(q, m)$. Therefore a seller of talent q must solve the following constrained maximum problem:

$$\max_m [pm - C(m)] \qquad (27.16)$$

subject to $p = vh(q, m) - s$.

To examine the pure effect of externalities assume no internal diseconomies, $C(m) \equiv 0$. Two families of curves are shown in Figure 27.2, one corresponding to the objective function, and the other to the constraint at alternative values of q. A seller of given talent q_1 is constrained by both consumer preferences and sellers of other talents to charge prices along the curve, marked $vh(q_1, m) - s$; seller q_2 is constrained by the presence of q_1 and others to

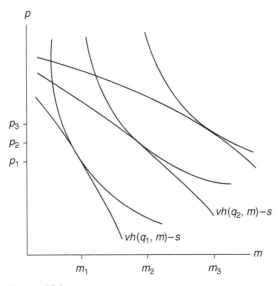

Figure 27.2

operate along $vh(q_2 m) - s$, etc. The isorevenue curves are rectangular hyperbolas. Points of tangency between the two represent the solution to (27.9) and (27.10) or to (27.16) for each value of q. Thus q_1 charges price p_1 and has a market size m_1; q_2 charges p_2 and sells m_2 units, etc.

The importance of the crowding condition $h_{qm} > 0$ is now apparent. Since the services produced by more talented sellers are less contaminated by crowding, the quantity-price gradient grows as talent increases. Therefore the better sellers can and do handle much larger crowds in equilibrium. Equation (27.11) demonstrates that the market size gradient increases with q when h_{qm} is positive. To see what effect this has on prices, differentiate the constraint in (27.16) with respect to q:

$$dp/dq = vh_q + vh_m(\partial m/\partial q) \tag{27.17}$$

The first term is positive, but the second is negative if $\partial m/\partial q > 0$, which it must be if $h_{qm} > 0$. The extra crowding and dilution of unit service of high quality sellers constrains unit prices from rising with quality as much as they would without it. Figure 27.2 shows market size increasing with quality to a much larger extent than the price-quality gradient. It is definitely not irrational for better sellers to have a great deal of business, but prices that are not much higher than those with lesser talents. The market may impel them to act that way, to become relatively "crowded out" in equilibrium.

With only internal diseconomies, the multiplicative effect of both positive price and quantity gradients with respect to quality implies convexity of the return function $R(q)$. In this case the quantity gradient tends to be larger and the price gradient tends to be smaller. Nevertheless, there are strong forces working toward convexity. Substitute (27.11) into (27.13) to obtain

$$R''(q) = -v^2(h_q + mh_{qm})^2/(2vh_m + vmh_{qm} - C'') + vmh_{qq} \tag{27.18}$$

Since the first term in (27.18) is positive, $R(q)$ is convex so long as h_{qq} is not sufficiently negative. In fact, given the caveat about h_{qq}, $R''(q) > 0$ independent of the sign of h_{qm}. When $h_{qm} < 0$ the constraint functions in Figure 27.2 become steeper as q increases, tending to stretch out the equilibrium price-quality gradient and to compress the quantity-quality gradient, just the opposite of the case where $h_{qm} > 0$. Symmetry of the reward function in p and m implies similarity of $R(q)$ in either case.

The effects of external diseconomies are illustrated by the following example. Let $z = h(q,m) = q - a(q/m)^{-b}$ where a and b are constants. Here adulteration depends on the talent-audience ratio and the unadulterated service satisfies $z = h(q,0) = q$. Assuming $s = 0$, it is readily verified that $p(q)$ is proportional to q, $m(q)$ to $q^{1+1/b}$ and $R(q)$ to $q^{2+1/b}$. Suppose $b = 1$. Then p is linear in q, m is quadratic in q, and R is a cubic in q. A seller that is twice as talented has a market that is four times larger and earns eight times more money. If $b = 1/2$ market size grows with the cube of talent and incomes by powers of four: a seller who is twice as talented earns sixteen times more, but only charges prices that are twice as large.[11]

IV Heterogeneous consumers

Consumer differences in intensity of demand for services are unrestricted in Section III, though much use is made of the assumption that s is identical among them. How should the equilibrium be described when s is distributed in the population of customers? That analysis is more complex because there is no longer a single equilibrium market price for services, v, that summarizes all the information. Nevertheless, differences in s imply restrictions on market outcomes that actually strengthen the qualitative results. I do not attempt a full analysis here, but the reason is that the market assignment of customers to sellers may force the relationship between p and z to be convex. Therefore the more talented sellers receive even greater rents and service even larger markets than when p is linear in z as in (27.4).

That $p(z)$ must be convex can be sketched as follows: Figure 27.3 shows the equalizing difference function (27.4) for two types of customers, s_1 and s_2, at alternative values of v. Each line represents the willingness to pay for z at a given utility index. At the same value of v the functions are parallel and s_1 type consumers outbid s_2 types at all values of z. In equilibrium the relevant v (the negative of the utility index) for type s_2 must exceed that for type s_1. Otherwise the former group would not purchase the service at all. Consequently the observed market relation must be the envelope of functions such as $p = v_1 z - s_1$ and $p = v_2 z - s_2$, the heavier curve in Figure 27.3. The envelope is convex. Evidently the main features of the analysis above hold for each linear piece of $p(z)$ in Figure 27.3. There are, however, additional implications of sorting between segments. First, the more talented sellers gravitate to that segment of the market with the largest value of v, precisely the reason why the convexity implications of the previous analysis are strengthened. Second, consumers with smaller values of s buy from less talented sellers. This is quantity-quality substitution at work: buyers with smaller values of s find quantity relatively cheaper and economize on quality, while those with large values of s demand greater quality and economize on quantity. Adding more types of consumers smooths the locus of equilibrium points in Figure 27.3 without affecting the general principles.[12]

V Comparative statics

Since Section IV indicated that the qualitative results are not affected, it is convenient to exploit the assumption of common s in the consuming population. Demand and supply shifts are considered in turn.

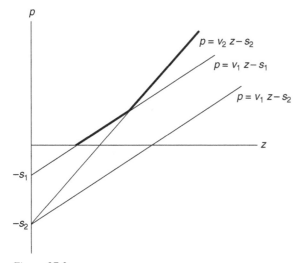

Figure 27.3

Demand shifts

An increase in the number of consumers or in the intensity of their demands for y increases the market demand for services. Market equilibrium price v rises due to rising supply price. Hence unit prices, $p(q)$, of all sellers increases. Since $R(q)$ increases everywhere, less talented people enter. At the same time, existing sellers expand their scales of operations. Though average quality of sellers falls, all previous entrants earn larger rents than before, and the largest increases accrue to the most talented persons (see the effect of v in equation (27.13) or (27.18)). Therefore the distribution of reward becomes more skewed than before.

The important practical implication is that it is monetarily advantageous to operate in a larger overall market; and it is increasingly advantageous the more talented one is. No wonder that the best economists tend to be theorists and methodologists rather than narrow field specialists, that the best artists sell their work in the great markets of New York and Paris, not Cincinnati, or that the best writers are connected with the primary literary centers such as New York or London. The best doctors, lawyers, and professional athletes should be found more frequently in larger cities. For a given place in the distribution of talent, it is more lucrative to be a violinist than an accordianist, a heavyweight than a flyweight, a rock musician than a folk singer, a tennis player than a bowler, or a writer of elementary texts rather than of monographs.

Supply shifts

The interesting experiments are changes in internal and external diseconomies. Lesser diseconomies increase the market supply of services, reduce the equilibrium value of v, and make consumers better off. The effects on the distributions of talents and rents are less obvious and complicated by the presence of two opposing forces: the reduction in v lowers unit prices of all sellers, tending to decrease individual output and reward; whereas the reduction in costs or congestion tends to increase them. The balance between the two depends on the elasticity of demand for services.

If demand for services is sufficiently elastic, then cost reducing effects swamp the decline in unit prices and rents of sellers increase. The rent-talent gradient increases as well and there is greater concentration in the distribution of rewards among the most talented. A reduction in the internal diseconomy induces entry at the extensive margin, and the average seller becomes less talented. However, a reduction of the external diseconomy, if large enough, can actually reduce the number of sellers, kicking out the less talented and increasing the average quality of those remaining. If demand is inelastic, then the number of sellers declines and, since those leaving are selected from the lower tail, the average remaining talent rises. Effects on the return function $R(q)$ are ambiguous in this case, though sufficient reductions in the costs of congestion still can imply increases in both $R(q)$ and $R'(q)$. However, that is a less likely outcome than when demand is elastic.

The practical importance of all this is related to technical changes that have increased the extent of scale economies over time in many activities. Motion pictures, radio, television, phono reproduction equipment, and other changes in communications have decreased the real price of entertainment services, but have also increased the scope of each performer's audience. The effect of radio and records on popular singers' incomes and the influence of television on the incomes of news reporters and professional athletes are good cases in point. And there are fine gradiations within these categories. Television is evidently a more effective medium for American football and basketball than it is for bowling, and incomes reflect it. Nonetheless, television has had an enormous impact on the incomes of the top bowlers, golfers, and tennis players, because their markets have expanded. The "demise" of the theatre is more a complaint about competition from the larger scale media; and incomes of the top performers in the theatre, motion pictures, and television certainly are closely geared to audience size. These changes are not confined to the entertainment sector. Undoubtedly, secular changes in communications and transportation have expanded the potential market for all kinds of professional and information services, and allowed many of the top practitioners to operate at a national or even international scale. With elastic demands there is a tendency for increasing concentration of income at the top as well as greater rents for all sellers as these changes proceed over time.

Interactions

A change in s shifts the supply of services, not demand, even though it is a consumer parameter. This has no counterpart in standard theory. Demand is not directly affected because v embodies all relevant information for the consumption decision. Supply is shifted because s affects unit prices (see (27.4)). An increase in s reduces unit prices at any value of v and reduces market supply. Therefore the equilibrium service price v increases and the rent distribution is altered in favor of the more talented sellers. The less talented leave the market. Both the increase in average quality of sellers and greater concentration in rewards at the top reflect customers' substitution of quality for quantity as s rises.

Since important components of s are time and effort costs, time-series changes are correlated with consumer earnings. Therefore market demand increases at the same time that supply is reduced, resulting in an even greater increase in v and additional skew. It can even push the extensive margin down rather than up. The incentives for investments in time saving innovations that tend to reduce s as earnings rise, for example, consumption at home, have been well remarked upon in the literature.[13]

VI Conclusion

In discussing the general influence of economic progress on value, Alfred Marshall wrote:

> The relative fall in the incomes to be earned by moderate ability ... is accentuated by the rise in those that are obtained by many men of extraordinary ability. There never was a time at which moderately good oil paintings sold more cheaply than now, and ... at which first-rate paintings sold so dearly. A business man of average ability and average good fortune gets now a lower rate of profits... than at any previous time, while the operations, in which a man exceptionally favoured by genius and good luck can take part, are so extensive as to enable him to amass a large fortune with a rapidity hitherto unknown.
>
> The causes of this change are two; firstly, the general growth of wealth, and secondly, the development of new facilities for communication by which men, who have once attained a commanding position, are enabled to apply their constructive or speculative genius to undertakings vaster, and extending over a wider area, than ever before.
>
> It is the first cause... that enables some barristers to command very high fees, for a rich client whose reputation, or fortune, or both, are at stake will scarcely count any price too high to secure the services of the best man he can get: and it is this again that enables jockeys and painters and musicians of exceptional ability to get very high prices.... But so long as the number of persons who can be reached by a human voice is strictly limited, it is not very likely that any singer will make an advance on the £10,000 said to have been earned in a season by Mrs. Billington at the beginning of the last century, nearly as great as that which the business leaders of the present generation have made on those of the last.
>
> [pp. 685–6]

Even adjusted for 1981 prices, Mrs. Billington must be a pale shadow beside Pavarotti.[14] Imagine her income had radio and phonograph records existed in 1801! What changes in the future will be wrought by cable, video cassettes, and home computers?

Acknowledgments

I am indebted to the National Science Foundation for financial support, and to Gary Becker, David Friedman, Robert J. Gordon, Michael Mussa, Edward Prescott, and George Stigler for helpful discussion and comments.

Notes

1 That escalation is not confined to wars and prices is established by the fact that Stars would have sufficed not long ago. Academics have a certain fondness for Giants, while businessmen prefer Kings. Obviously there is a fair bit of substitution among all these terms in depicting related data in different contexts.
2 Albert Rees is a good introduction to the size distribution of income. The selectivity effects of differential talent and comparative advantage on the skew in income distributions are spelled out in my 1978 article, also see the references there. Melvin Reder's survey touches some of the issues raised here. Of course social scientists and statisticians have had a long standing fascination with rank-size relationships, as perusal of the many entries in the *Encyclopedia of the Social Sciences* will attest.
3 Few economic behavioral models exist in the literature. On this see Harold Lydall. Jacob Mincer has shown that investment can produce skewness through the force of discounting, and established that as an important source of skewness empirically. Learning is not treated here because those issues are well understood, whereas the assignment problem has received little attention. Some recent works,

but with different focus and emphasis than is discussed here, are Gary Becker (1973), David Grubb, and Michael Sattinger.

4 Milton Friedman proposed a model based on preferences for risk taking, but did not explain why or how the market sustains the equilibrium *ex post* with few sellers earning enormous incomes (for example, why the losers in the lottery rest content with such low incomes if they have the same talents as the winners). Issues of uncertainty that make these elements of supply more interesting are abstracted from here. A model of prizes based on effort-incentive monitoring and the principal agency relation is found in my article with Edward Lazear.

5 Some of the thorny issues of primitives in problems of product differentiation are discussed from the point of view of the theory of measurement by Manuel Trajtenberg.

6 That a doctor's patients or a performer's fans might be considered as a club has intuitive plausibility. The original reference in the theory of public finance is James Buchanan. Eitan Berglas, and Berglas and David Pines present elegant developments of that model.

7 This version of the model has a strong family resemblance to a class of problems previously considered in my 1974 article.

8 Throughout this paper I make the usual club theory assumptions and ignore indivisibilities requiring an integer number of sellers. This can be problematic when the number of sellers is very small, and raises well-known problems in industrial organization about which I have nothing to contribute. The magnitude of the rent of the lowest rent seller (extensive margin) is the issue. That must be sufficiently small for this analysis to apply.

9 The two functions $m(q)$ and $R(q)$ are the transforms from the distribution of ability to the distribution of output and reward. Inverting and computing the Jacobians, the distribution of output is $(1/v)\phi(m/v)$, the same form as the distribution of talent because $m(q)$ is linear. The distribution of rent is $(v(8R)^{1/2})\phi((2R/v)^{1/2})$, which is skewed to the right relative to ϕ.

10 The equilibrium concept used in this particular example is the same as the notion of sustainability in natural monopoly. The equilibrium in Figure 27.1 is inefficient. This inefficiency vanishes when the externality is bounded sufficiently by either internal or external diseconomies. Those bounds are implicitly assumed in all other portions of this paper.

11 Notice that with imperfect information the effect of a reputation and fixed costs creates a type of scale economy which broadens the scope of this result. If two scholars write on the same subject, the one with the better track record is much more likely to be read and subsequently cited. Similarly, a firm with a fine reputation is more likely to get the business than one that is of unknown quality. While a reputation has many of the elements of a public good, the analogy is not quite complete because this discussion ignores the dynamics of how reputations are established. An "epidemic model" is an intriguing possibility.

12 Reder points out that the market is less concentrated if there are differences of opinion on who is the most talented. This raises subtle questions of the definition of markets that remain to be solved. An approximate solution in the analysis here is to adjust the density of $\phi(q)$: if several sellers are thought by different customers to have the same value of q, that is nearly the same as more mass in ϕ at that value.

13 See Becker (1965).

14 The entries for Elizabeth Billington in the eleventh edition of the *Encyclopedia Britannica* and *Grove's Musical Dictionary* indicate that she earned somewhere between £10,000 and £15,000 in the 1801 season singing Italian Opera in Covent Garden and Drury Lane. She is reported to have had an extraordinary voice and was highly paid throughout her professional life, but there is a hint that the 1801 sum was unusual even for her. No information is given on endorsements.

References

G. Becker, "A Theory of the Allocation of Time," *Econ. J.,* Sept. 1965, 73, 493–508.

—, "A Theory of Marriage: Part *I*," *J. Poht. Econ.,* July/Aug. 1973, 81, 813–46.

E. Berglas, "On the Theory of Clubs," *Amer. Econ. Rev. Proc.,* May 1976, 66, 116–121.

—, and D. Pines, "Clubs as a Case of Competitive Industry with Goods of Variable Quality," Tel Aviv University, 1980.

J. M. Buchanan, "An Economic Theory of Clubs," *Economica,* Feb. 1965, 32, 1–14.

M. Friedman, "Choice, Chance and the Personal Distribution of Income," *J. Polit. Econ.,* Aug. 1953, 61, 277–90.

D. Grubb, "Power and Ability in the Distribution of Earnings," Centre for Labour Economics, London School of Economics, 1980.

E. Lazear and S. Rosen, "Rank-Order Tournaments as Optimum Labor Contracts," *J. Polit. Econ.,* 1981.

Harold Lydall, *The Structure of Earnings*, Oxford 1968.

Alfred Marshall, *Principles of Economics*, 8th ed., New York: MacMillan, 1947.

Jacob Mincer, *Schooling, Experience and Earnings*, New York: Columbia University Press, 1974.

M. Reder, "A Partial Survey of the Income Size Distribution," in Lee Soltow, ed., *Six Papers on the Size Distribution of Wealth and Income*, New York: Columbia University Press, 1969.

Albert Rees, *The Economics of Work and Pay*, New York: Harper and Row, 1973.

S. Rosen, "Hedonic Prices and Implicit Markets: Product Differentiation in Pure Competition," *J. Polit. Econ.,* Jan./Feb. 1974, 82, 34–55.

—, "Substitution and Division of Labor," *Economica*, Aug. 1978, 45, 235–50.

M. Sattinger, *Capital and the Distribution of Labor Earnings*, Amsterdam: North-Holland, 1980.

M. Trajtenberg, "Aspects of Consumer Demand for Characteristics," Maurice Falk Institute, Jerusalem, 1979.

28 Strategic behavior in contests

Avinash Dixit

This chapter considers the effect of precommitment in contests where the rivals expend effort to win a prize. With two asymmetric players, it is found that the favorite will commit effort at a higher level than that in a Nash equilibrium without commitment, and the underdog at a lower level. With many players, the absence of an odds-on favorite among rivals is sufficient to ensure overcommitment by any one player. Applications to sports, oligopoly, and rent seeking are discussed.

Many economic and social games are contests where the players expend effort to increase their probability of winning a given prize. Examples include: (*i*) inter-firm or international *R&D* rivalry for a profitable innovation; (*ii*) bribery to secure a lucrative license or contract from a government; and (*iii*) the Wimbledon final or the Super-bowl. Economists have studied such games in many contexts. Glenn Loury, 1979, Partha Dasgupta and Joseph Stiglitz, 1980, and Tom Lee and Louis Wilde, 1980, have examined *R&D* rivalry. Gordon Tullock, 1980, has analyzed rent seeking. John Riley, 1979, and Barry Nalebuff and Riley, 1985, have dealt with wars of attrition. Ed Lazear and Sherwin Rosen, 1981, Jerry Green and Nancy Stokey, 1983, Bengt Holmstrom, 1982, Nalebuff and Stiglitz, 1983, and Sherwin Rosen, 1986, have looked at contests from the viewpoint of incentive design. Dale Mortensen, 1982, has studied a general model with different interpretations and applications.

In all of that literature, the focus is on the existence and the characterization of Nash equilibria. In this paper I examine a different aspect. Suppose one of the players is given the opportunity to make a strategic pre-commitment to the level of effort. This may be done directly by imposing an order of moves (Stackelberg leadership), or indirectly through some other variable that will influence the *ex post* choice of effort (such as capacity or tax-subsidy policy in industrial games), or merely by psyching oneself up (or down) in sporting contests. The question I address is: What governs whether a player will choose an effort level that is higher or lower than the Nash equilibrium level without precommitment?

I find that in a perfectly symmetric two-player game, there is no *local* incentive for any strategic manipulation of the effort level. Analysis of the case in which the players have asymmetric prospects requires special forms of the function governing the probabilities of winning. For the two specifications most commonly used in the literature, namely logit and probit, there is a remarkably simple answer. The player who is the favorite (in the sense of having a probability of winning greater than 1/2 in the Nash equilibrium) has the incentive to overcommit effort, and the other has the opposite incentive. Section I sets up the model and establishes these results.

Section II introduces several contestants, of whom one is given the opportunity to pre-commit effort. For the logit specification, there is a simple sufficient condition for strategic overcommitment of effort by this player: there should be no odds-on favorite among the rest.

Therefore it appears that overexertion is the likely case in most contests of several players in practice. Section III examines some applications and extensions of the basic model.

I The two-person case

Let K be the prize, x_i, x_2 the two players' effort levels in units commensurate with the prize, and $p(x_i, x_2)$ the probability that player 1 wins. Then the players' expected payoffs are

$$\pi_1 = Kp(x_1, x_2) - x_1 \tag{28.1}$$

and

$$\pi_2 = K[1 - p(x_1, x_2)] = x_2. \tag{28.2}$$

To ensure a positive but diminishing marginal effect of each player's effort on his own probability of winning, I assume

$$p_1 > 0, \quad p_{11} < 0, \quad p_2 < 0, \quad p_{22} > 0, \tag{28.3}$$

where subscripts denote partial derivatives and the arguments (x_i, x_2) are omitted for brevity. The first-order conditions for Nash equilibrium are

$$\frac{\partial \pi_1}{\partial x_1} \equiv Kp_1(x_1, x_2) - 1 = 0 \tag{28.4}$$

and

$$\frac{\partial \pi_2}{\partial x_2} \equiv -Kp_2(x_1, x_2) - 1 = 0. \tag{28.5}$$

The assumptions (3) also ensure that an increase in each player's effort level harms the other, and therefore makes it strategically desirable for each to precommit his effort level in such a way as to induce a lower effort from the other in response. Whether this means a commitment at a higher or a lower level of one's own effort depends on whether the other's best response function has a negative or positive slope. The general significance of the slopes of reaction functions is discussed by Drew Fudenberg and Jean Tirole, 1984, Jeremy Bulow *et al.*, 1985, and Jonathan Eaton and Gene Grossman, 1986.

Formally, if x_i can be precommitted,[1]

$$d\pi_1/dx_1 = \partial \pi_1/\partial x_1 + \partial \pi_1/\partial x_2 \cdot dx_2/dx_1,$$

where the first term on the right-hand side is zero in Nash equilibrium, $\partial \pi_1/\partial x_2 = Kp_2$ is negative, and dx_2/dx_i is the slope of player 2's best response function. Differentiating along his first-order condition (28.5), we have

$$\frac{dx_2}{dx_1} = -\frac{\partial^2 \pi_2/\partial x_2 \partial x_1}{\partial^2 \pi_2/\partial x_2^2} = \frac{-Kp_{12}}{-\partial^2 \pi_2/\partial x_2^2}. \tag{28.6}$$

The denominator is positive by the second-order condition. Then

$$\frac{d\pi_1}{\partial x_1} = \frac{\partial \pi_1}{\partial x_2} \cdot \frac{K p_{12}}{\partial \pi_2 / \partial x_2^2}. \qquad (28.7)$$

This is positive, giving player 1 an incentive to overcommit to effort, if and only if P_{12} is positive.

Likewise, if player 2 can precommit,

$$\frac{dx_1}{dx_2} = -\frac{\partial^2 \pi_1 / \partial x_1 \partial x_2}{\partial^2 \pi_1 / \partial x_1^2} = \frac{-K p_{12}}{-\partial^2 \pi_1 / \partial x_1^2} \qquad (28.8)$$

and

$$\frac{d\pi_2}{dx_2} = \frac{\partial \pi_2}{\partial x_1} \cdot \frac{K p_1 2}{-\partial^2 \pi_2 / \partial x_2^2}. \qquad (28.9)$$

Therefore, player 2 has an incentive to overcommit to effort if and only if P_{12} is *negative*.

We see that the two players' strategic incentives are necessarily in opposite directions, except when $P_{12} = 0$, in which case neither has a strategic incentive for precommitment to effort locally away from the Nash level. I will show that the latter must occur when there is perfect symmetry, and then explore the consequences of asymmetry.

Perfect symmetry between the players means that if their effort levels were interchanged, so would the probabilities. Therefore,

$$p(x_2, x_1) = 1 - p(x_1, x_2). \qquad (28.10)$$

Differentiating with respect to x_i,

$$p_2(x_2, x_1) = -p_1(x_1, x_2). \qquad (28.11)$$

In particular, for any x,

$$p_2(x, x) = -p_12(x_1, x_2).$$

Looking at the first-order conditions (28.4), (28.5), we see that under the usual mild restrictions there is a symmetric Nash equilibrium, defined by $K p_i(x, x) = 1$. Now differentiate (28.11) with respect to x_2:

$$p_2 1(x_2, x_1) = -p_12(x_1, x_2).$$

Therefore, for any x,

$$p_2 1(x, x) = -p_12(x, x).$$

But

$$p_2 1(x, x) = p_12(x, x).$$

So both must be zero in the symmetric Nash equilibrium. This proves the result.

Without perfect symmetry, little can be said about p_{12} in general. Therefore, I will consider special functional forms. There are two natural possibilities. The first is the logit form used in models of discrete choice; see Daniel McFadden, 1973. It is used for contests by Rosen, 1986, and Mortensen, 1982, and in a special case by Tullock, 1980. It also arises in a modified way (because of discounting) in models of patent races; see Loury, 1979, and Dasgupta and Stiglitz, 1980. We have

$$p(x_1, x_2) = \frac{f_1(x_1)}{f_1(x_1) + f_2(x_2)}, \tag{28.12}$$

where f_1 and f_2 are increasing functions. It is a routine matter to verify that

$$p_{12} = f_1' f_2'(f_1 - f_2)/(f_1 + f_2)^3. \tag{28.13}$$

Therefore, $p_{12} > 0$ if and only if $f_1 > f_2$, that is, $p > 1/2$.

The second special form, the probit, arises in some of the literature on contests as incentive schemes. Suppose efforts x_1 and x_2 yield sure components of outcomes $f_1(x_i)$ and $f_2(x_2)$,[2] but the full outcomes also contain noise components e_l and e_2. Then player 1 wins if and only if

$$f_1(x_1) + \epsilon_1 > f_2(x_2) + \epsilon_2$$

or

$$\epsilon_2 - \epsilon_1 < f_1(x_1) - f_2(x_2).$$

Let G be the cumulative distribution function of $(\varepsilon_2 - \varepsilon_l)$. Then

$$p(x_1, x_2) = G(f_1(x_1) - f_2(x_2)). \tag{28.14}$$

Differentiating this twice, we have

$$p_{12} = -g'(f_1(x_1) - f_2(x_2)) \times f_1'(x_1) f_2'(x_2), \tag{28.15}$$

where g is the density corresponding to G. If the noise effects are symmetric between players, we have g symmetric about zero. Assume it is unimodal, as will usually be the case. Then $p_{12} > 0$ if and only if $f_1(x_1) - f_2(x_2) > 0$, that is, $p > 1/2$.

For both specifications, we have found that the player favored to win is the one who has the strategic incentive to overexert, and the underdog, to ease up. The intuition behind this result is explained in Figure 28.1. This is based on the logit model; the probit case can be explained similarly. In panel (a) of Figure 28.1, the curve TT shows the total gross return to player 2, $[1 - p(x_i, x_2)]K$, as a function of his effort x_2, for a fixed level of x_1. In panel (b), the curve MM is the corresponding marginal. A slight increase in x_1 shifts these curves to $T'T'$ and $M'M'$, respectively. The marginals cross at the point P. To its left, an increase in x_1 reduces the marginal return to x_2, which leads 2 to reduce x_2 if x_1 is precommitted. If player 1 is the favorite, $(1 - p)$ is low, and x_2 lies to the left of P. Therefore,

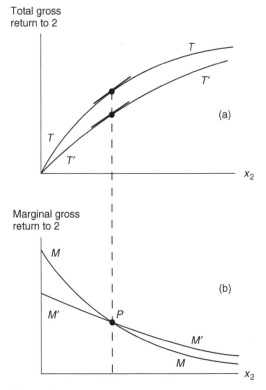

Figure 28.1

it is in 1's strategic interest to commit to overexertion. The opposite holds if player 1 is the underdog.

Figure 28.2 develops the corresponding intuition using "reaction" or "best response" functions. Player 1 is the favorite. In a neighborhood of the Nash equilibrium N, the favorite's best response function (R_1) is upward sloping and that of the underdog (R_2) is downward sloping. Then player 1 has the incentive to make a strategic precommitment to a higher x_1, moving the outcome from N to S_i. Player 2 gains if he can commit to a lower x_2, and move the outcome from N to S_2. When precommitment is made by means of a separate variable y_1 (respectively, y_2), the effect is to shift the best response function R_1 to R_1 to R_1' (respectively, $R2$ to R_2'), thereby achieving the desired shift of the outcome. If both players can precommit to variables y_1 and y_2, in the perfect equilibrium of the two-stage game there is a tendency to shift R_1 and R_2 in the directions indicated. Depending on the relative magnitudes of the shifts, *either* x_i will be higher and x_2 lower than at N, or both will be lower.

The perfectly symmetric case is shown in Figure 28.3. Here R_1 is vertical and R_2 horizontal at the Nash equilibrium. Therefore, there is no local incentive for strategic manipulation of effort. The possibility of gain from large shifts depends on the relative *curvatures* of the other player's best response function and one's own payoff contours. That matter is going to be too context-specific to be settled theoretically.

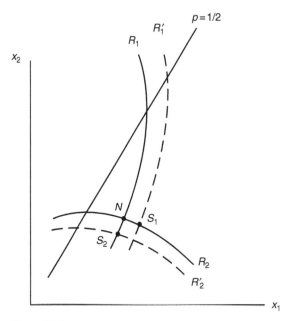

Figure 28.2

II Many players

Index the players $i = 1, 2, \ldots, n$, and suppose player 1 can precommit his effort level. I choose the logit specification for the probability of a win for player i:

$$p_i = f(x_i)/S, \quad i = 1, 2, \ldots, n, \tag{28.16}$$

where

$$S = \sum_{j=1}^{n} f_j(x_j). \tag{28.17}$$

The functions f_i are assumed to be increasing, and concave. The latter is sufficient for second-order conditions.

The payoffs are given by

$$\pi_i = K p_i - x_i, \quad i = 1, 2, \ldots, n. \tag{28.18}$$

Given x_1, the remaining players achieve a Nash equilibrium in their effort levels. The first-order conditions are

$$\frac{\partial \pi_i}{\partial x_i} = \frac{K \partial p_i}{\partial x_i} - 1 = 0 \quad i = 2, 3 \ldots, n. \tag{28.19}$$

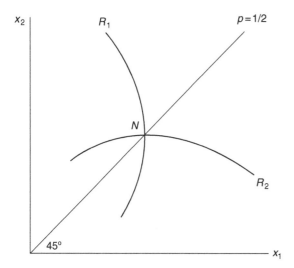

Figure 28.3

These define $(x_2, x_3, \ldots, X_n)$ as functions of x_1. Then player 1's calculation of the payoff to precoimnitment is

$$\frac{d\pi_1}{dx_1} = \frac{\partial \pi_1}{\partial x_1} + \sum_{j=2}^{n} \frac{\partial \pi_1}{\partial x_j} \frac{dx_j}{dx_1}. \qquad (28.20)$$

The first term is zero in the full Nash equilibrium of all players. The other terms give the strategic effect of manipulating the other players' effort levels.

Introduce the notation, for $i = 1, 2, \ldots, n$,

$$q_i = f_i'(x_i)/S,$$
$$r_i = f_i''(x_i)/S \qquad (28.21)$$

Then it is routine to verify that

$$\frac{\partial p_i}{\partial x_i} = q_i(1 - p_i),$$

$$\frac{\partial p_i}{\partial x_i^2} = (1 - p_i)(r_i - 2q_i^2) \qquad (28.22)$$

and for $j \neq i$

$$\frac{\partial p_i}{\partial x_j} = -p_i q_j,$$

$$\frac{\partial_2 p_i}{\partial x_i \partial x_j} = q_i q_j (1 - 2p_i). \qquad (28.23)$$

Using (28.23), we can write (28.20) as

$$\frac{d\pi_1}{dx_1} = -Kp_i \sum_{j=2}^{n} q_j \frac{dx_j}{dx_1}. \tag{28.24}$$

To find the right-hand side, differentiate the first-order conditions (28.19) totally, using (28.22) and (28.23). This gives, for $i = 2, 3, \ldots, n$,

$$(1 - p_i)(r_i - 2q_i^2)dx_i - q_i(1 - 2p_i) \sum_{j \neq i}^{n} q_j dx_j = 0$$

or

$$[(1 - p_i)(r_i - 2q_i^2) + q_i^2(1 - 2p_i)]dx_i - q_i(1 - 2p_i) \sum_{j \neq i}^{n} q_j dx_j = 0$$

or

$$q_i dx_i = -\theta_i \sum_{j=1}^{n} q_j dx_j, \tag{28.25}$$

where

$$\theta_i = -\frac{q_i^2(1 - 2p_i)}{(1 - p_i)r_i - q_i^2}. \tag{28.26}$$

Then

$$\sum_{i=2}^{n} q_i dx_i = -\left\{\sum_{i=2}^{n} \theta_i\right\}\left\{\sum_{j=1}^{n} q_j dx_j\right\}$$

or

$$\left\{\sum_{i=2}^{n} q_i dx_i\right\}\left\{1 + \sum_{i=2}^{n} \theta_i\right\} = -\left\{\sum_{i=2}^{n} \theta_i\right\}q_1 dx_1$$

or

$$\sum_{i=2}^{n} q_i dx_i = -\left\{\sum_{i=2}^{n} \theta_i\right\}q_1 dx_1 \bigg/ \left\{1 + \sum_{i=2}^{n} \theta_i\right\}. \tag{28.27}$$

Substituting in (28.24), we finally have

$$d\pi_1/dx_1 = Kp_1q_1\left\{\sum_{i=2}^{n} \theta_i\right\} \bigg/ \left\{1 + \sum_{i=2}^{n} \theta_i\right\}. \tag{28.28}$$

To determine the sign of this, examine the definition (28.26) of θ_i. Each denominator is negative since each r_i is nonpositive. If each $p_i < 1/2$, then each numerator is positive. Then each θ_i is positive, and so is $d\pi_i/dx_i$. Thus the absence of an odds-on favorite among the remaining players is a sufficient condition for commitment to overexertion by player 1. In particular, the favorite is sure to overexert given an opportunity to precommit.

If $n = 2$, the right-hand side becomes

$$Kp_1q_1\theta_2/(1+\theta_2) = -Kp_1q_1q_2^2(1-2q_2)/(1-p_2)(r_2-2q_2^2),$$

and $p_2 < 1/2$ becomes necessary as well as sufficient for $d\pi/dx_i > 0$. Thus the model contains the analysis of Section II as a special case, as of course it should.

III Applications and extensions

The two-person result of Section I finds support in many sports events where one player or team is clearly favored to win. Such a player, or the manager of such a team, often declares that "since he is expected to win, he must try all the harder." The underdog, on the other hand, is " under no pressure, and is just going to enjoy the occasion." There is some objective truth to these assertions, but to a considerable extent the pressure on a favorite is of his own making, as is the relaxed mood of an underdog. Therefore, these can be seen as ways of altering one's own preferences in advance, that is, as instruments of commitment that will credibly alter future behavior.

The result runs counter to the popular belief that No. 2's "try harder." But that statement never clarifies " than what or whom." My comparison is between the same player's uncommitted and precommitted effort levels. An underdog may be making more effort than the favorite; $p > 1/2$ is compatible with $x_1 < x_2$ if the two players' functions A and f_2 are suitably different. It is also believed that underdogs use riskier strategies, or that favorites play too safely, but such questions need a different model.

Next consider rent seeking. Suppose a contract or an import license is being awarded. The two contenders are not equally efficient, and the bureaucrats or the politicians pay *some* attention to this aspect. Let x_1, x_2 be the bribes offered by the two, and let $p(x_1, x_2)$ be *either* the probability that player 1 gets the whole contract (license) *or* his share. Then the result says that the more efficient user, if given first access to the bureaucrat or the politician, will bribe more than he would in the case of simultaneous access.

One case of oligopoly fits the model directly, namely a homogeneous product with unit-elastic demand. Then we can interpret K as the total market revenue and $p(x_i, x_2)$ as firm 1's market share.

Patent races are more natural settings, especially in the international arena where countries make commitments to $R\&D$ programs. If one thinks of the U.S.–Japan rivalry in this way, one would use the above result to conclude that since the United States was favored over Japan in the late 1970's, therefore Japan should have committed to under-exertion. It clearly did not. However, an explanation may be found in the model of Section II. The United States was not a single player, but a group of separate firms in which no one was an odds-on favorite.

Discounting influences the result in the same direction. In the model of Loury, 1979, and Dasgupta and Stiglitz, 1980, the research effort x_i of firm i is expected at time 0, and buys a conditional probability of success (hazard rate) $f_i(x_i)$ in a Poisson process. Let K be the capitalized royalties from the innovation. Then we find

$$\pi_i = Kf_i(x_i)/S - x_i \tag{28.29}$$

where

$$S = f_i(x_1) + f_2(x_2) + r, \tag{28.30}$$

r being the discount rate. Now

$$\frac{\partial_2 \pi_1}{\partial x_1 \partial x_2} = \frac{K f_1' f_2 (f_1 - f_2 - r)}{(f_1 + f_2 + r)^3} \tag{31i}$$

and

$$\frac{\partial_2 \pi_2}{\partial x_1 \partial x_2} = \frac{K f_1' f_2' (f_1 - f_2 - r)}{(f_1 + f_2 + r)^3}. \tag{31ii}$$

Compare these with (28.13). The introduction of discounting makes both of these negative in more cases, and therefore favors a commitment to overexertion by both players. Mathematically, the discount rate is just like having a third player whose response function happens to be totally inelastic.

In conclusion, I should point out some issues that were not addressed here. The commitments considered were unconditional, that is, they amounted to a first-mover advantage. Conditional commitments can achieve more. In a sense they can achieve too much, for player 1 can drive player 2 out of the game by committing himself to choosing a destructively large x_l if x_2 is positive. As usual, the crucial question is the credibility of such conditional commitments, and it is better studied in a context-specific way.

Another question is that of efficiency of the outcome. In rent seeking, it may be socially desirable to have the minimum total investment. Then the underdog briber should go first. In *R&D* races, we may be concerned with the industry's total expected profit, or may want to add on some spillover benefit to society. In both cases, it is of interest to compare the Nash equilibrium with a leader-follower outcome. But once again, the general answers are so vague that the question is best addressed specifically in each application.

Acknowledgments

I thank Barry Nalebuff for valuable discussions, Carl Shapiro, Robert Solow, and the referee for helpful comments, and the National Science Foundation for research support under grant no. SES8509536.

Notes

1 The same qualitative results are obtained if we introduce an indirect instrument y_i for precommitment. Of course a separate variable is essential if one wants to study a two-stage Nash game when both players use precommitment.
2 Nalebuff and Stiglitz (1983) and several others take what I call $f_1(x_1)$ and $f_2(x_1)$ as the choice variables; then asymmetries show up in the costs of effort for the two players. The two methods are, of course, formally equivalent. In econometric uses of the probit, ε_l and ε_2 are assumed to be normally distributed. Weaker assumptions stated later suffice for my purpose.

References

Bulow, Jeremy, Geanakoplos, John and Klemperer, Paul, "Multimarket Oligopoly: Strategic Substitutes and Complements," *Journal of Political Economy*, June 1985, 93, 488–511.

Dasgupta, Partha and Stiglitz, Joseph, "Uncertainty, Industrial Structure, and the Speed of *R&D*," *Bell Journal of Economics,* Spring 1980, 11, 1–28.

Eaton, Jonathan and Grossman, Gene, "Optimal Trade and Industrial Policy Under Oligopoly," *Quarterly Journal of Economics,* May 1986, 101, 383–406.

Fudenberg, Drew and Tirole, Jean, "The Fat-Cat Effect, the Puppy-Dog Ploy, and the Lean and Hungry Look," *American Economic Review Proceedings*, May 1984, 74, 361–66.

Green, Jerry and Stokey, Nancy, "A Comparison of Tournaments and Contracts," *Journal of Political Economy*, June 1983, 91, 349–64.

Holmstrom, Bengt, "Moral Hazard in Teams," *Bell Journal of Economics*, Autumn 1982, 13, 324–40.

Lazear, Edward and Rosen, Sherwin, "Rank Order Tournaments as Optimum Labor Contracts," *Journal of Political Economy*, October 1981, 89, 841–64.

Lee, Tom and Wilde, Louis, "Market Structure and Innovation: A Reformulation," *Quarterly Journal of Economics*, March 1980, 94, 429–36.

Loury, Glenn, "Market Structure and Innovation," *Quarterly Journal of Economics*, August 1979, 93, 395–410.

McFadden, Daniel, "Conditional Logit Analysis of Qualitative Choice Behavior," in Paul Zarembka, ed., *Frontiers in Econometrics*, New York: Academic Press, 1973, 105–42.

Mortensen, Dale T., "Property Rights and Efficiency in Mating, Racing, and Related Games," *American Economic Review*, December 1982, 72, 968–79.

Nalebuff, Barry and Riley, John, "Asymmetric Equilibria in the War of Attrition," *Journal of Theoretical Biology*, July 1985, 113, 517–27.

——, and Stiglitz, Joseph, "Prizes and Incentives: Toward a General Theory of Compensation and Competition," *Bell Journal of Economics*, Spring 1983, 14, 21–43.

Riley, John, "Evolutionary Equilibrium Strategies," *Journal of Theoretical Biology*, January 1979, 76, 109–23.

Rosen, Sherwin, "Prizes and Incentives in Elimination Tournaments," *American Economic Review*, September 1986, 76, 701–15.

Tullock, Gordon, "Efficient Rent Seeking," in J. Buchanan, R. Tollison, and G. Tullock, eds., *Toward a Theory of the Rent-Seeking Society*, College Station: Texas A&M University Press, 1980.

29 Job market signaling

Michael Spence

Introduction

The term "market signaling" is not exactly a part of the well-defined, technical vocabulary of the economist. As a part of the preamble, therefore, I feel I owe the reader a word of explanation about the title. I find it difficult, however, to give a coherent and comprehensive explanation of the meaning of the term abstracted from the contents of the essay. In fact, it is part of my purpose to outline a model in which signaling is implicitly defined and to explain why one can, and perhaps should, be interested in it. One might accurately characterize my problem as a signaling one, and that of the reader, who is faced with an investment decision under uncertainty, as that of interpreting signals.

How the reader interprets my report of the content of this essay will depend upon his expectation concerning my stay in the market. If one believes I will be in the essay market repeatedly, then both the reader and I will contemplate the possibility that I might invest in my future ability to communicate by accurately reporting the content of this essay now. On the other hand, if I am to be in the market only once, or relatively infrequently, then the above-mentioned possibility deserves a low probability. This essay is about markets in which signaling takes place and in which the primary signalers are relatively numerous and in the market sufficiently infrequently that they are not expected to (and therefore do not) invest in acquiring signaling reputations.

I shall argue that the paradigm case of the market with this type of informational structure is the job market and will therefore focus upon it. By the end I hope it will be clear (although space limitations will not permit an extended argument) that a considerable variety of market and quasi-market phenomena like admissions procedures, promotion in organizations, loans and consumer credit, can be usefully viewed through the conceptual lens applied to the job market.

If the incentives for veracity in reporting anything by means of a conventional signaling code are weak, then one must look for other means by which information transfers take place. My aim is to outline a conceptual apparatus within which the signaling power of education, job experience, race, sex, and a host of other observable, personal characteristics can be determined. The question, put crudely, is what in the interactive structure of a market accounts for the informational content, if any, of these potential signals. I have placed primary emphasis upon (i) the definition and properties of signaling equilibria, (ii) the interaction of potential signals, and (iii) the allocative efficiency of the market.

Hiring as investment under uncertainty

In most job markets the employer is not sure of the productive capabilities of an individual at the time he hires him.[1] Nor will this information necessarily become available to the employer immediately after hiring. The job may take time to learn. Often specific training is required. And there may be a contract period within which no recontracting is allowed. The fact that it takes time to learn an individual's productive capabilities means that hiring is an investment decision. The fact that these capabilities are not known beforehand makes the decision one under uncertainty. To hire someone, then, is frequently to purchase a lottery.[2] In what follows, I shall assume the employer pays the certain monetary equivalent of the lottery to the individual as wage.[3] If he is risk-neutral, the wage is taken to be the individual's marginal contribution to the hiring organization.

Primary interest attaches to how the employer perceives the lottery, for it is these perceptions that determine the wages he offers to pay. We have stipulated that the employer cannot directly observe the marginal product prior to hiring. What he does observe is a plethora of personal data in the form of observable characteristics and attributes of the individual, and it is these that must ultimately determine his assessment of the lottery he is buying. (The image that the individual presents includes education, previous work, race, sex, criminal and service records, and a host of other data.) This essay is about the endogenous market process whereby the employer requires (and the individual transmits) information about the potential employee, which ultimately determines the implicit lottery involved in hiring, the offered wages, and in the end the allocation of jobs to people and people to jobs in the market.

At this point, it is useful to introduce a distinction, the import of which will be clear shortly. Of those observable, personal attributes that collectively constitute the image the job applicant presents, some are immutably fixed, while others are alterable. For example, education is something that the individual can invest in at some cost in terms of time and money. On the other hand, race and sex are not generally thought to be alterable. I shall refer to observable, unalterable attributes as *indices*, reserving the term *signals* for those observable characteristics attached to the individual that are subject to manipulation by him.[4] Some attributes, like age, do change, but not at the discretion of the individual. In my terms, these are indices.

Sometime after hiring an individual, the employer will learn the individual's productive capabilities. On the basis of previous experience in the market, the employer will have conditional probability assessments over productive capacity given various combinations of signals and indices. At any point of time when confronted with an individual applicant with certain observable attributes, the employer's subjective assessment of the lottery with which he is confronted is defined by these conditional probability distributions over productivity given the new data.

From one point of view, then, signals and indices are to be regarded as parameters in shifting conditional probability distributions that define an employer's beliefs.[5]

Applicant signaling

For simplicity I shall speak as if the employer were risk-neutral. For each set of signals and indices that the employer confronts, he will have an expected marginal product for an individual who has these observable attributes. This is taken to be the offered wage to applicants with those characteristics. Potential employees therefore confront an offered wage schedule whose arguments are signals and indices.

There is not much that the applicant can do about indices. Signals, on the other hand, are alterable and therefore potentially subject to manipulation by the job applicant. Of course, there may be costs of making these adjustments. Education, for example, is costly. We refer to these costs as *signaling costs*. Notice that the individual, in acquiring an education, need not think of himself as signaling. He will invest in education if there is sufficient return as defined by the offered wage schedule.[6] Individuals, then, are assumed to select signals (for the most part, I shall talk in terms of education) so as to maximize the difference between offered wages and signaling costs. Signaling costs play a key role in this type of signaling situation, for they functionally replace the less direct costs and benefits associated with a reputation for signaling reliability acquired by those who are more prominent in their markets than job seekers are in theirs.

A critical assumption

It is not difficult to see that a signal will not effectively distinguish one applicant from another, unless the costs of signaling are negatively correlated with productive capability. For if this condition fails to hold, given the offered wage schedule, everyone will invest in the signal in exactly the same way, so that they cannot be distinguished on the basis of the signal. In what follows, we shall make the assumption that signaling costs are negatively correlated with productivity. It is, however, most appropriately viewed as a *prerequisite* for an observable, alterable characteristic to be a persistently informative signal in the market. This means, among other things, that a characteristic may be a signal with respect to some types of jobs but not with respect to others.[7]

Signaling costs are to be interpreted broadly to include psychic and other costs, as well as the direct monetary ones. One element of cost, for example, is time.

Information feedback and the definition of equilibrium

At this point it is perhaps clear that there is informational feedback to the employer over time. As new market information comes in to the employer through hiring and subsequent observation of productive capabilities as they relate to signals, the employer's conditional probabilistic beliefs are adjusted, and a new round starts. The wage schedule facing the new entrants in the market generally differs from that facing the previous group. The elements in the feedback loop are shown in Figure 29.1.

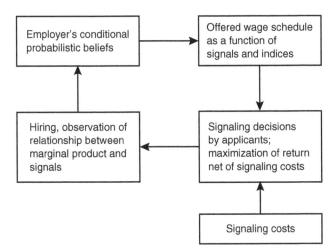

Figure 29.1 Informational feedback in the job market

It is desirable to find a way to study this feedback loop in the market over time. To avoid studying a system in a continual state of flux, it is useful to look for nontransitory configuration of the feedback system. The system will be stationary if the employer starts out with conditional probabilistic beliefs that after one round are not disconfirmed by the incoming data they generated. We shall refer to such beliefs as self-confirming. The sense in which they are self-confirming is defined by the feedback loop in Figure 29.1.

A signaling equilibrium

As successive waves of new applicants come into the market, we can imagine repeated cycles around the loop. Employers' conditional probabilistic beliefs are modified, offered wage schedules are adjusted, applicant behavior with respect to signal choice changes, and after hiring, new data become available to the employer. Each cycle, then, generates the next one. In thinking about it, one can interrupt the cycle at any point. An equilibrium is a set of components in the cycle that regenerate themselves. Thus, we can think of employer beliefs being self-confirming, or offered wage schedules regenerating themselves, or applicant behavior reproducing itself on the next round.[8]

I find it most useful to think in terms of the self-confirming aspect of the employer beliefs because of the continuity provided by the employer's persistent presence in the market.[9] Thus, in these terms an equilibrium can be thought of as a set of employer beliefs that generate offered wage schedules, applicant signaling decisions, hiring, and ultimately new market data over time that are consistent with the initial beliefs.

A further word about the definition of equilibrium is in order. Given an offered wage schedule, one can think of the market as generating, via individual optimizing decisions, an empirical distribution of productive capabilities given observable attributes or signals (and indices). On the other hand, the employer has subjectively held conditional probabilistic beliefs with respect to productivity, given signals. In an equilibrium the subjective distribution and the one implicit in the market mechanism are identical, *over the range of signals that the employer actually observes.*[10] Any other subjective beliefs will eventually be disconfirmed in the market because of the employer's persistent presence there.

Indices continue to be relevant. But since they are not a matter of individual choice, they do not figure prominently in the feedback system just described. I shall return to them later.

Properties of informational equilibria: an example

I propose to discuss the existence and properties of market signaling equilibria via a specific numerical example.[11] For the time being, indices play no part. The properties of signaling equilibria that we shall encounter in the example are general.[12]

Let us suppose that there are just two productively distinct groups in a population facing one employer. Individuals in Group I have a productivity of 1, while those in Group II have a productivity of 2.[13] Group I is a proportion q_1 of the population; Group II is a proportion of $1 - q_1$. There is, in addition, a potential signal, say education, which is available at a cost. We shall assume that education is measured by an index y of level and achievement and is subject to individual choice. Education costs are both monetary and psychic. It is assumed that the cost to a member of Group I of y units of education is y, while the cost to a member of Group II is $y/2$.

We summarize the underlying data of our numerical example in Table 29.1.

Table 29.1 Data of the model

Group	Marginal product	Proportion of population	Cost of education level y
I	1	q_1	y
II	2	$1 - q_1$	$y/2$

To find an equilibrium in the market, we guess at a set of self-confirming conditional probabilistic beliefs for the employer and then determine whether they are in fact confirmed by the feedback mechanisms described above. Suppose that the employer believes that there is some level of education, say y^* such that if $y < y^*$, then productivity is one with probability one, and that if $y \geqslant y^*$, then productivity will be two with probability one. If these are his conditional beliefs, then his offered wage schedule, $W(y)$, will be as shown in Figure 29.2.

Given the offered wage schedule, members of each group will select optimal levels for education. Consider the person who will set $y < y^*$. If he does this, we know he will set $y = 0$ because education is costly, and until he reaches y^*, there are no benefits to increasing y, given the employer's hypothesized beliefs. Similarly, any individual who sets $y > y*$ will in fact set $y = y^*$, since further increases would merely incur costs with no corresponding benefits. Everyone will therefore either set $y = 0$ or set $y = y^*$. Given the employer's initial beliefs and the fact just deduced, if the employer's beliefs are to be confirmed, then members of Group I must set $y = 0$, while members of Group II set $y = y^*$. Diagrams of the options facing the two groups are shown in Figure 29.3.

Superimposed upon the wage schedule are the cost schedules for the two groups. Each group selects y to maximize the difference between the offered wages and the costs of education. Given the level of y^* in the diagram, it is easy to see that Group I selects $y = 0$, and Group II sets $y = y^*$. Thus, in this case the employer's beliefs are confirmed, and we have a signaling equilibrium. We can state the conditions on behavior by the two groups, in order that the employer's beliefs be confirmed, in algebraic terms. Group I sets $y = 0$ if

$$1 > 2 - y^*.$$

Group II will set $y = y^*$ as required, provided that

$$2 - y^*/2 > 1.$$

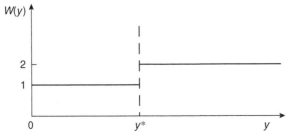

Figure 29.2 Offered wages as a function of level of education

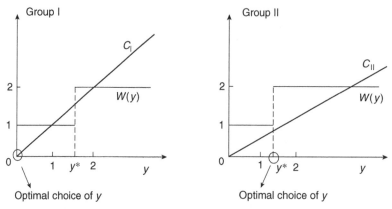

Figure 29.3 Optimizing choice of education for both groups

Putting these two conditions together, we find that the employer's initial beliefs are confirmed by market experience, provided that the parameter y^* satisfies the inequality,

$$1 < y^* < 2.$$

It is worth pausing at this point to remark upon some striking features of this type of equilibrium. One is that within the class of employer expectations used above, there is an infinite number of possible equilibrium values for y^*. This means that there is an infinite number of equilibria. In any one of the equilibria the employer is able to make perfect point predictions concerning the productivity of any individual, having observed his level of education. The reader will realize that this property is special and depends, at least in part, upon the assumption that education costs are perfectly negatively correlated with productivity. However, even in this case, there are equilibria in which the employer is uncertain, as we shall shortly see.

The equilibria are not equivalent from the point of view of welfare. Increases in the level of y^* hurt Group II, while, at the same time, members of Group I are unaffected. Group I is worse off than it was with no signaling at all. For if no signaling takes place, each person is paid his unconditional expected marginal product, which is just

$$q_1 + 2(1 - q_1) = 2 - q_1.$$

Group II may also be worse off than it was with no signaling. Assume that the proportion of people in Group I is 0.5. Since $y^* > 1$ and the net return to the member of Group II is $2 - y^*/2$, in equilibrium his net return must be below 1.5, the no-signaling wage. Thus, everyone would prefer a situation in which there is no signaling.

No one is acting irrationally as an individual. Coalitions might profitably form and upset the signaling equilibrium.[14] The initial proportions of people in the two groups q_1 and $1 - q_1$ have no effect upon the equilibrium. This conclusion depends upon this assumption that the marginal product of a person in a given group does not change with numbers hired.

Given the signaling equilibrium, the education level y^*, which defines the equilibrium, is an entrance requirement or prerequisite for the high-salary job – or so it would appear from the outside. From the point of view of the individual, it is a prerequisite that has its source in a signaling game. Looked at from the outside, education might appear to be productive. It is productive for the individual, but, in this example, it does not increase his real marginal product at all.[15]

A sophisticated objection to the assertion that private and social returns differ might be that, in the context of our example, the social return is not really zero. We have an information problem in the society and the problem of allocating the right people to the right jobs. Education, in its capacity as a signal in the model, is helping us to do this properly. The objection is well founded. To decide how efficient or inefficient this system is, one must consider the realistic alternatives to market sorting procedures in the society.[16] But notice that even within the confines of the market model, there are more or less efficient ways of getting the sorting accomplished. Increases in y* improve the quality of the sorting not one bit. They simply use up real or psychic resources. This is just another way of saying that there are Pareto inferior signaling equilibria in the market.

It is not always the case that all groups lose due to the existence of signaling. For example, if, in the signaling equilibrium, $y^* < 2q_1$, then Group II would be better off when education is functioning effectively as a signal than it would be otherwise. Thus, in our example if $q_1 > \frac{1}{2}$ so that Group II is a minority, then there exists a signaling equilibrium in which the members of Group II improve their position over the no-signaling case. Recall that the wage in the no-signaling case was a uniform $2 - q_1$ over all groups.

We may generalize this bit of analysis slightly. Suppose that the signaling cost schedule for Group I was given by $a_1 y$ and that for Group II by $a_2 y$.[17] Then with a small amount of calculation, we can show that there is a signaling equilibrium in which Group II is better off than with no signaling,[18] provided that

$$q_1 > a_2/a_1.$$

How small a "minority" Group II has to be to have the possibility of benefiting from signaling depends upon the ratio of the marginal signaling costs of the two groups.[19]

Before leaving our education signaling model, it is worth noting that there are other equilibria in the system with quite different properties. Suppose that the employer's expectations are of the following form:

If $y < y^*$: Group I with probability q_1,

   Group II with probability $1 - q_1$;

If $y \geqslant y^*$: Group II with probability 1.

As before, the only levels of y that could conceivably be selected are $y = 0$ and $y = y^*$. The wage for $y = 0$ is $2 - q_1$, while the wage for $y = y^*$ is simply 2. From Figure 29.4 it is easy to see that both groups rationally set $y = 0$, provided that $y^* > 2q_1$. If they both do this, then the employer's beliefs are confirmed, and we have an equilibrium.

It should be noted that the employer's beliefs about the relationship between productivity and education for are $y \geq y^*$ confirmed in a somewhat degenerate, but perfectly acceptable, sense. There are no data relating to these levels of education and hence, by logic, no disconfirming data. This is an example of a phenomenon of much wider potential importance. The employer's beliefs may drive certain groups from the market and into another labor market. We cannot capture this situation in a simple one-employer, one-market model. But when it happens, there is no experience forthcoming to the employer to cause him to alter his beliefs.[20]

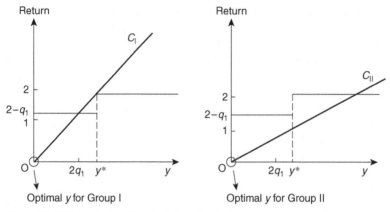

Figure 29.4 Optimal signaling decisions for the two groups

Education conveys no information in this type of equilibrium. In fact, we have reproduced the wages and information state of the employer in the no-signaling model, as a signaling equilibrium.

Just as there exists a signaling equilibrium in which everyone sets $y = 0$, there is also an equilibrium in which everyone sets $y = y^*$ for some positive y^*. The requisite employer beliefs are as follows:

> If $y < y^*$: Group I with probability 1;
>
> If $y \geqslant y^*$: Group I with probability q_1,
>
> Group II with probability $1 - q_1$.

Following our familiar mode of analysis, one finds that these beliefs are self-confirming in the market, provided that

$$y^* < 1 - q_1.$$

Again, the education level conveys no useful information, but in this instance individuals are rationally investing in education. If they as individuals did not invest, they would incur lower wages, and the loss would exceed the gain from not making the educational investment. The implication of this version of the signaling equilibrium is that there can be stable prerequisites for jobs that convey no information by virtue of their existence and hence serve no function.

It is interesting to note that this last possibility does not depend upon costs being correlated with productivity at all. Suppose that the signaling costs *for both groups* were given by the one schedule y. And suppose further that employer beliefs were as described above. Then everyone will rationally select $y = y^*$, provided that

$$y^* < 1 - q_1.$$

The outcome is the same. But the interesting thing is that, because of the absence of any correlation between educational costs and productivity, education could *never* be an effective signal, in the sense of conveying useful information, in an equilibrium in this market.

We have dwelt enough upon the specifics of this model to have observed some of the effects the signaling game may have upon the allocational functioning of the market. The numerical example is not important. The potential effects and patterns of signaling are.

An alterable characteristic like education, which is a potential signal, becomes an actual signal if the signaling costs are negatively correlated with the individual's unknown productivity. Actually, the negative correlation is a necessary but not sufficient condition for signaling to take place. To see this in the context of our model, assume that the only values y can have are one and three. That is to say, one can only get units of education in lumps. If this is true, then there is no feasible value of y^* that will make it worthwhile for Group II to acquire an education. Three units is too much, and one unit will not distinguish Group II from Group I. Therefore, effective signaling depends not only upon the negative correlation of costs and productivities, but also upon there being a "sufficient" number of signals within the appropriate cost range.[21]

An equilibrium is defined in the context of a feedback loop, in which employer expectations lead to offered wages to various levels of education, which in turn lead to investment in education by individuals. After hiring, the discovery of the actual relationships between education and productivity in the sample leads to revised expectations or beliefs. Here the cycle starts again. An equilibrium is best thought of as a set of beliefs that are confirmed or at least not contradicted by the new data at the end of the loop just described. Such beliefs will tend to persist over time as new entrants into the market flow through.

Multiple equilibria are a distinct possibility. Some may be Pareto inferior to others. Private and social returns to education diverge. Sometimes everyone loses as a result of the existence of signaling. In other situations some gain, while others lose. Systematic overinvestment in education is a distinct possibility because of the element of arbitrariness in the equilibrium configuration of the market. In the context of atomistic behavior (which we have assumed thus far) everyone is reacting rationally to the market situation. Information is passed to the employer through the educational signal. In some of our examples it was perfect information. In other cases this is not so. There will be random variation in signaling costs that prevent the employer from distinguishing perfectly among individuals of varying productive capabilities.

In our examples, education was measured by a scalar quantity. With no basic adjustment in the conceptual apparatus, we can think of education as a multidimensional quantity: years of education, institution attended, grades, recommendations and so on. Similarly, it is not necessary to think in terms of two groups of people. There may be many groups, or even a continuum of people: some suited to certain kinds of work, others suited to other kinds. Nor need education be strictly unproductive. However, if it is too productive relative to the costs, everyone will invest heavily in education, and education may cease to have a signaling function.

The informational impact of indices

In the educational signaling model we avoided considering any observable characteristics other than education. In that model education was a signal. Here we consider what role, if any, is played by indices. For concreteness I shall use sex as the example. But just as education can stand for any set of observable, alterable characteristics in the first model, sex can stand for observable, unalterable ones here. The reader may wish to think in terms of race, nationality, size, or in terms of criminal or police records and service records. The latter is potentially public information about a person's history and is, of course, unalterable when viewed retrospectively from the present.[22]

Table 29.2 Data of the model

Race	Productivity	Education costs	Proportion within group	Proportion of total population
W	1	y	q_1	$q_1(1-m)$
W	2	$y/2$	$1-q_1$	$(1-q_1)(1-m)$
M	1	y	q_1	$q_1 m$
M	2	$y/2$	$1-q_1$	$(1-q_1)m$

Let us assume that there are two groups, men and women. I shall refer to these groups as W and M. Within each group the distribution of productive capabilities and the incidence of signaling costs are the same. Thus, within M the proportion of people with productivity one and signaling (education) costs of y is q_1. The remainder have productivity two and signaling costs $y/2$. The same is true for group W. Here m is the proportion of men in the overall population of job applicants.

Given the assumptions the central question is, "how could sex have an informational impact on the market?" The next few paragraphs are devoted to arguing that indices do have a potential impact and to explaining why this is true. We begin by noting that, under the assumptions, the conditional probability that a person drawn at random from the population has a productivity of two, given that he is a man (or she is a woman), is the same as the unconditional probability that his productivity is two. Sex and productivity are uncorrelated in the population. Therefore, by *itself*, sex could never tell the employer anything about productivity.

We are forced to the conclusion that if sex is to have any informational impact, it must be through its interaction with the educational signaling mechanism. But here again we run up against an initially puzzling symmetry. Under the assumptions, men and women of equal productivity have the same signaling (education) costs. It is a general maxim in economics that people with the same preferences and opportunity sets will make similar decisions and end up in similar situations. We may assume that people maximize their income net of signaling costs so that their preferences are the same. And since signaling costs are the same, it would appear that their opportunity sets are the same. Hence, again we appear to be driven to the conclusion that sex can have no informational impact. But the conclusion is wrong, for an interesting reason.

The opportunity sets of men and women of comparable productivity are *not* necessarily the same. To see this, let us step back to the simple educational signaling model. There are externalities in that model. One person's signaling strategy or decision affects the market data obtained by the employer, which in turn affect the employer's conditional probabilities. These determine the offered wages to various levels of education and hence of rates of return on education for the next group in the job market. The same mechanism applies here, with a notable modification. If employers' distributions are conditional on sex as well as education, then the external impacts of a man's signaling decision are felt only by other men. The same holds for women.

If at some point in time men and women are not investing in education in the same ways, then the returns to education for men and women will be different in the next round. In short, their opportunity sets differ. In what follows, we demonstrate rigorously that this sort of situation can persist in an equilibrium. The important point, however, is that there are externalities implicit in the fact that an individual is treated as the average member of the group of people who look the same and that, as a result, and in spite of an apparent sameness the opportunity sets facing two or more groups that are visibly distinguishable may in fact be different.

The employer now has two potential signals to consider: education and sex. At the start he does not know whether either education or sex will be correlated with productivity. Uninformative potential signals or indices are discarded in the course of reaching an equilibrium. As before we must guess at an equilibrium form for the employer's expectations and then verify that these beliefs can be self-confirming via the market informational feedback mechanisms. We will try beliefs on the following form.

If W and $y < y^*_W$, productivity $= 1$ with probability 1.
If W and $y \geqslant y^*_W$, productivity $= 2$ with probability 1.
If M and $y < y^*_M$, productivity $= 1$ with probability 1.
If M and $y \geq y^*_M$, productivity $= 2$ with probability 1.

These lead to offered wage schedules $W_w(y)$ and $W_M(y)$ as shown in Figure 29.5.

Because groups W and M are distinguishable to the employer, their offered wages are not connected at the level of employer expectations. Applying the reasoning used in the straightforward educational signaling model, we find that the required equilibrium conditions on y^*_W and y^*_M are

$$1 < y^*_W < 2$$

and

$$1 < y^*_M < 2.$$

No logical condition requires that y^*_W equals y^*_M in an equilibrium.

Essentially we simply have the educational signaling model iterated twice. Because sex is observable, the employer can make his conditional probability assessments depend upon sex as well as education. This has the effect of making signaling interdependencies between two groups, W and M, nonexistent. They settle into signaling equilibrium configurations in the market independently of each other. But in the first model there was not one equilibrium, there were many. Therefore, there is at least the logical possibility that men and women will settle into *different* stable signaling equilibria in the market and stay there.

As we noted earlier, the signaling equilibria are not equivalent from the point of view of social welfare. The higher that y^*_W (or y^*_M) is, the worse off is the relevant group or,

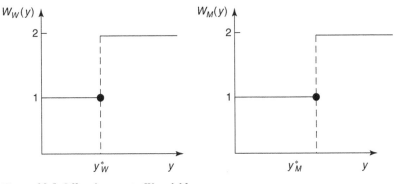

Figure 29.5 Offered wages to W and M

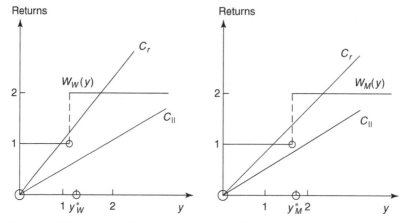

Figure 29.6 Market equilibrium with sex as an index

more accurately, the high-productivity portion of the group. One example of an asymmetrical equilibrium would be given by $y_M^* = 1.1$ and $y_M^* = 1.9$. In this case high-productivity women have to spend more on education and have less left over to consume in order to convince the employer that they are in the high-productivity group.

Notice that the proportions of high- and low-productivity people in each group do not affect the signaling equilibrium in the market. Hence, our initial assumption that the groups were identical with respect to the distribution of productive characteristics and the incidence of signaling costs was superfluous. More accurately, it was superfluous with respect to this type of equilibrium. As we saw in the educational signaling model, there are other types of equilibrium in which the proportions matter.

Since from an equilibrium point of view men and women really are independent, they might settle into different types of equilibrium. Thus, we might have men signaling $y = y_M^* = 1.1$ if they are also in the higher productivity group, while other men set $y = 0$. On the other hand, we may find that all women set $y = 0$. In this case all women would be paid $2 - q_1$, and the upper signaling cutoff point y_M^* would have to be greater than $2q_1$. Notice that all women, including lower productivity women, would be paid more than low-productivity men in this situation.[23] High-productivity women would, of course, be hurt in

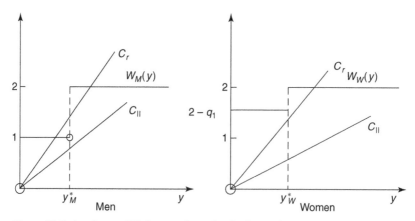

Figure 29.7 Another equilibrium configuration in the market

terms of wages received. It is conceivable, however, that returns net of signaling would be higher for women with productivity of two. In other words, it is possible that

$$2 - q_1 > w - y^*_{M/2}.$$

This will occur when

$$2q_1 < y^*_M.$$

Looking at this situation from outside, one might conclude that women receive lower wages than some men because of a lack of education, which keeps their productivity down. One might then go looking outside the job market for the explanation for the lack of education. In this model the analysis just suggested would be wrong. The source of the signaling and wage differentials is in the informational structure of the market itself.[24]

Because of the independence of the two groups, M and W, at the level of signaling, we can generate many different possible equilibrium configurations by taking any of the educational signaling equilibria in our first model and assigning it to W and then taking any education equilibrium and assigning it to M. However, an exhaustive listing of the possibilities seems pointless at this stage.

We have here the possibility of arbitrary differences in the equilibrium signaling configurations of two or more distinct groups. Some of them may be at a disadvantage relative to the others. Subsets of one may be at a disadvantage to comparable subsets of the others. Since the mechanism that generates the equilibrium is a feedback loop, we might, following Myrdal and others, wish to refer to the situation of the disadvantaged group as a vicious cycle, albeit it an informationally based one. I prefer to refer to the situation of the disadvantaged group as a lower level equilibrium trap, which conveys the notion of a situation that, once achieved, persists for reasons endogenous to the model. The multiple equilibria of the education model translate into arbitrary differences in the equilibrium configuration and status of two groups, as defined as observable, unalterable characteristics.

Conclusions

We have looked at the characteristics of a basic equilibrium signaling model and at one possible type of interaction of signals and indices. There remains a host of questions, which can be posed and partially answered within the conceptual framework outlined here. Among them are the following:

1 What is the effect of cooperative behavior on the signaling game?
2 What is the informational impact of randomness in signaling costs?
3 What is the effect of signaling costs that differ systematically with indices?
4 How general are the properties of the examples considered here?
5 In a multiple-market setting, does the indeterminateness of the equilibrium remain?
6 Do signaling equilibria exist in general?
7 What kinds of discriminatory mechanisms are implicit in, or interact with, the informational structure of the market, and what policies are effective or ineffective in dealing with them?

I would argue further that a range of phenomena from selective admissions procedures through promotion, loans and consumer credit, and signaling status via conspicuous consumption lends itself to analysis with the same basic conceptual apparatus. Moreover, it may be as important to explain the absence of effective signaling as its presence, and here the prerequisites for effective signaling are of some use.

On the other hand, it is well to remember that the property of relative infrequency of appearance by signalers in the market, which defines the class signaling phenomena under scrutiny here, is not characteristic of many markets, like those for consumer durables, and that, as a result, the informational structures of these latter are likely to be quite different.

Acknowledgements

This work is based on the author's doctoral dissertation ("Market Signalling: The Informational Structure of Job Markets and Related Phenomena," Ph.D. thesis, Harvard University, 1972), forthcoming as a book entitled *Market Signaling: Information Transfer in Hiring and Related Screening Processes* in the Harvard Economic Studies Series, Harvard University Press. The aim here is to present the outline of the signaling model and some of its conclusions. Generalizations of the numerical examples used for expositional purposes here are found in *ibid.* and elsewhere.

I owe many people thanks for help in the course of the current study, too many to mention all. However, I should acknowledge explicitly the magnitude of my debts to Kenneth Arrow and Thomas Schelling for persistently directing my attention to new and interesting problems.

Notes

1 There are, of course, other informational gaps in the job market. Just as employers have less than perfect information about applicants, so also will applicants be imperfectly informed about the qualities of jobs and work environments. And in a different vein neither potential employees nor employers know all of the people in the market. The resulting activities are job search and recruiting. For the purpose of this essay I concentrate upon employer uncertainty and the signaling game that results.

2 The term "lottery" is used in the technical sense, imparted to it by decision theory.

3 The certain monetary equivalent of a lottery is the amount the individual would take, with certainty, in lieu of the lottery. It is generally thought to be less than the actuarial value of the lottery.

4 The terminological distinction is borrowed from Robert Jervis *(The Logic of Images in International Relations* (Princeton, N.J.: Princeton University Press, 1970)). My use of the terms follows that of Jervis sufficiently closely to warrant their transplantation.

5 The shifting of the distributions occurs when new market data are received and conditional probabilities are revised or updated. Hiring in the market is to be regarded as sampling, and revising conditional probabilities as passing from prior to posterior. The whole process is a learning one.

6 There may be other returns to education. It may be a consumption good or serve as a signal of things other than work potential (status for example). These returns should be added to the offered wage schedule.

7 The reason is that signaling costs can be negatively correlated with one type of productive capability but not with another.

8 In pursuing the properties of signaling equilibria, we select as the object for regeneration whatever is analytically convenient, but usually employer beliefs or offered wage schedules.

9 The mathematically oriented will realize that what is at issue here is a fixed point property. A mapping from the space of conditional distributions over productivity given signals into itself is defined by the market response mechanism. An equilibrium can be thought of as a fixed point of this mapping. A mathematical treatment of this subject is contained in Spence, *op. cit.*

10 In a multi-market model one faces the possibility that certain types of potential applicants will rationally select themselves out of certain job markets, and hence certain signal configurations may never appear in these markets. When this happens, the beliefs of the employers in the relevant market are not disconfirmed in a degenerate way. No data are forthcoming. This raises the possibility of persistent informationally based discrimination against certain groups. The subject is pursued in detail in *ibid.*

11 Obviously, an example does not prove generality. On the other hand, if the reader will take reasonable generality on faith, the example does illustrate some essential properties of signaling equilibria.

12 See Spence, *op. cit.*

13 For productivity the reader may read "what the individual is worth to the employer." There is no need to rely on marginal productivity here.

14 Coalitions to change the patterns of signaling are discussed in Spence, op. *cit.*

15 I am ignoring external benefits to education here. The assertion is simply that in the example education does not contribute to productivity. One might still claim that the social product is not zero. The signal cost function does, in principle, capture education as a consumption good, an effect that simply reduces the cost of education.

16 This question is pursued in Spence, op. *cit.*

17 It is assumed that $a_2 < a_1$.

18 Notice that the statement is that there exists a signaling equilibrium in which Group II is better off. It turns out that there always exists a signaling equilibrium in which Group II is worse off as well.

19 The calculation is straightforward. Given these signaling costs groups will make the requisite choice to confirm the employer's beliefs provided that

$$1 > 2 - a_1 y^*$$

and

$$2 - a_2 y^* > 1.$$

These translate easily into the following condition on y^*:

$$\frac{1}{a_2} < y^* < \frac{1}{a_1}.$$

Now, if Group II is to be better off for some signaling equilibrium, then

$$2 - \frac{a_2}{a_1} > 2 - q_1,$$

or

$$q_1 > \frac{a_2}{a_1}.$$

This is what we set out to show.

20 This is discussed in detail in Spence, *op. cit.*

21 In *ibid.* it is argued that many potential signals in credit and loan markets effectively become indices because the "signaling" costs swamp the gains, so that characteristics that could be manipulated in fact are not. House ownership is an example of a potential signal that, in the context of the loan market, fails on this criterion and hence becomes an index.

22 It is, or ought to be, the subject of policy decisions as well.

23 I have not assumed that employers are prejudiced. If they are, this differential could be wiped out. Perhaps more interestingly laws prohibiting wage discrimination, if enforced, would also wipe it out.

24 Differential signaling costs over groups are an important possibility pursued in Spence, *op. cit.*

30 The causes and consequences of the dependence of quality on price

Joseph E. Stiglitz

If the legal rate . . . was fixed so high . . . , the greater part of the money which was to be lent, would be lent to prodigals and profectors, who alone would be willing to give this higher interest. Sober people, who will give for the use of money no more than a part of what they are likely to make by the use of it, would not venture into the competition.

(Adam Smith, *Wealth of Nations*, 1776)

A plentiful subsistence increases the bodily strength of the laborer and the comfortable hope of bettering his condition and ending his days perhaps in ease and plenty animates him to exert that strength to the utmost.

(Adam Smith, *Wealth of Nations*, 1776)

Low wages are by no means identical with cheap labour. From a purely quantitative point of view the efficiency of labour decreases with a wage which is physiologically insufficient . . . the present-day average Silesian mows, when he exerts himself to the full, little more than two-thirds as much land as the better paid and nourished Pomeranian or Mecklenburger, and the Pole, the further East he comes from, accomplishes progressively less than the German. Low wages fail even from a purely business point of view wherever it is a question of producing goods which require any sort of skilled labour, or the use of expensive machinery which is easily damaged, or in general wherever any greater amount of sharp attention of of initiative is required. Here low wages do not pay, and their effect is the opposite of what was intended.

(Max Weber, *The Protestant Ethic and the Spirit of Capitalism* (Scribner, New York, 1925, p. 61))

. . . highly paid labour is generally efficient and therefore not dear labour; a fact which though it is more full of hope for the future of the human race than any other that is known us, will be found to exercise a very complicating influence on the theory of distribution.

(Alfred Marshall, *Principles of Economics*, 1920)

. . . the landlord who attempted to exact more than his neighbour . . . would render himself so odious, he would be so sure of not obtaining a metayer who was an honest man, that the contract of all the metayers may be considered as identical, at least in each province, and never gives rise to any competition among peasants in search of employment, or any offer to cultivate the soil on cheaper terms than one another.

(J. C. L. Simonde de Sismondi, *Political Economy*, 1814, cited in John Stuart Mill, *Principles of Political Economy*, 1848)

Conventional competitive economic theory begins with the hypothesis of price-taking firms and consumers, buying and selling homogeneous commodities at well-defined marketplaces. In many situations, these assumptions are implausible: in insurance markets, firms know that some risks are greater than others (some individuals' life expectancy is greater than others'; some individuals are more likely to have an automobile accident than others), but cannot tell precisely who is the greater risk, even within fairly narrowly defined risk categories. In labor markets, firms know that some workers are better than others, but at the time they hire and train the worker, they cannot tell precisely who will turn out to be the more productive. In product markets, consumers know that some commodities are more durable than others, but at the time of purchase, they cannot ascertain precisely which are more durable. In capital markets, banks know that the probability of bankruptcy differs across loans, but cannot tell precisely which loans are better.

This heterogeneity has important consequences, some of which have long been recognized. There are strong incentives to sort, to distinguish the high risk from the low risk, the more able from the less able. This sorting can be done on the basis of observable characteristics (say, sex or age) or the (inferences made from) actions undertaken by individuals, e.g., the job for which the individual applies (George Akerlof 1976), the wage structure chosen by the individual (Joanne Salop and Steven Salop 1976), or the quantity of insurance purchased (Michael Rothschild and Joseph Stiglitz 1976). In these models, the choices made convey information; individuals know this, and this affects their actions.

Willingness to trade may itself serve as a sorting device. In insurance markets, firms have recognized that as the price of insurance increases, the mix of applicants changes *adversely*. Akerlof (1970) has shown how such adverse selection effects may also arise in other markets, including the market for used cars (see Charles Wilson 1979, 1980). His analysis has subsequently been applied to the labor market (Bruce Greenwald 1986) and to capital markets (Greenwald, Stiglitz, and Andrew Weiss 1984; Stewart Myers and Nicholas S. Majluf 1984). In each of these instances, the uninformed party (the seller of insurance, the used car buyer, etc.) forms rational expectations concerning the quality mix of what is being offered on the market; the price serves as a signal or as a screening device. The fact that an employee is willing to work for $1 an hour suggests that she knows of no better offers; others who have looked at her have evidently decided that she is worth no more than $1 an hour.

Insurance firms have also long recognized that the terms at which they write insurance contracts may affect the actions undertaken by individuals; that is, the likelihood of the insured against an event occurring is an *endogenous* variable, which the insurance firm can hope to affect. The fact that individuals can undertake unobservable actions that affect the likelihood of an accident is referred to as the *moral hazard* problem. The term has come to be used to describe a wide range of incentive problems. In particular, employers know that the incentives workers have to work hard may be affected by the wage paid; and the incentives borrowers have to undertake risky projects may be affected by the interest rate charged on the bank's loan. Thus, the characteristics of what is being traded again depend on the price at which the trade is consummated, though now because of *incentive* effects rather than *selection* effects.

These are instances in which price serves a function in addition to that usually ascribed to it in economic theory: It conveys information and affects behavior. Quality depends on price. Of course, in standard economic theory, higher-quality items will sell at higher prices: Prices depend on quality. But here, beliefs about quality, about what it is that is being traded, depend (rationally) on price.[1]

This dependence of beliefs about quality on price has some fundamental implications. Firstly, demand curves, may under quite plausible conditions, not be downward sloping. When the price of some security is higher, uninformed buyers may infer that the expected return is higher, and their demand may increase (Jerry Green 1973; Sanford Grossman and Stiglitz 1976, 1980). An increase in the wage may so increase the productivity of the workers that the demand for labor may actually increase. A decrease in the price of used cars results in a decrease in the average quality of those being offered and this may decrease demand (Akerlof 1970). In each of these instances, one can think of the change in the price as having two effects: a movement along a fixed-information demand curve, and a shift in the demand curve from the change in information (beliefs).

Secondly, one may not be able to separate out neatly the analysis of demand and supply. Individuals' demands are based on inferences they are making from prices, and these inferences are critically dependent on the nature of the supply responses. Thus, any alteration, say, in the probability distribution of supply characteristics will, in general, lead to an alteration in the demand functions.

Thirdly, markets may be thin. At the equilibrium price of insurance, some risk averse individuals choose not to purchase insurance, even though with perfect information, they would have. The marginal person buying insurance is, in effect, subsidizing other purchasers; he is not obtaining actuarially fair insurance, as he would in a (risk neutral) competitive market with full information.[2]

These models, while departing from the traditional paradigm in denying the validity of the hypothesis of homogeneous markets, retain the assumption of price-taking firms and consumers. In many situations, firms are not price or wage takers. Banks do not simply take the interest rate that they charge on loans as given.

This paper is concerned with situations where firms not only recognize the dependence of quality on price (of productivity on wages, of default probability on the interest rate charged), but also attempt to use what control they have over price (wages, interest rates) to increase their profits. The recognition of this possibility has important implications for economic theory, which have recently been explored in a large number of papers in several disparate fields. The objective of this paper is to survey these papers and to draw out the central themes of this literature.

This paper is divided into four parts In Part I, we discuss the most important implications of the dependence of quality on price for competitive equilibrium theory – the repeal of the law of supply and demand (Part I.1), the repeal of the law of the single price (Part 1.2), the existence of discriminatory equilibria (Part 1.3), the comparative static consequences (Part 1.4), and the inefficiency of market equilibria (Part 1.5). Part II discusses alternative explanations for the dependence of quality on price in labor, capital, and product markets. Part III explains more precisely how these models differ from standard competitive models and from other models with imperfect information. Finally, Part IV discusses some of the more important applications of the theory, including those in macroeconomics (Part IV.1) and in development economics (Part IV.2).

I The fundamental implications of the dependence of quality on price

1 Repeal of the law of supply and demand

No law in economics has such standing as the "Law of Supply and Demand." There is an old joke about being able to teach a parrot to be an economist – and a good economist at that – simply by teaching it to repeat the words "demand and supply." The law holds that competitive market equilibrium is characterized by demand equaling supply. It asserts that the way to analyze changes in market equilibrium is to isolate the changes in the demand function and in the supply function.

When quality depends on price, market equilibrium may be characterized by demand not equaling supply.[3]

Consider the labor market. Assume there is an excess supply of labor. The conventional story is that in the face of excess supply, unemployed workers go to potential employers and offer their services at lower wages. The wage is bid down. As the wage decreases, the demand for labor increases and the supply decreases. This process continues until the wage is bid down to the level where supply equals demand.

If, however, the firm believes that the workers who offer their services at a lower wage are less productive, then – if they are sufficiently less productive – it will not hire the lower-wage workers, for the cost per effective unit of labor service will actually be higher with the lower-wage worker.

Thus, in Figure 30.1 we have depicted the cost per effective unit of labor service as initially falling as the wage is increased. There is a wage, w^*, at which wage costs per effective unit of labor service are minimized. This is referred to as the *efficiency wage*. For this section, we assume the same costs per efficiency unit schedule faces all firms and characterizes all workers. (In the following sections we shall consider the consequences of differing costs per efficiency unit schedules.)

If, at the efficiency wage, there is an excess supply of laborers, no firm has an incentive to lower its wage, or to hire a worker who offers his services at a lower wage, for to do so simply increases labor costs. Thus, when at w^*, the supply of labor equals or exceeds the demand, w^* is the equilibrium wage.

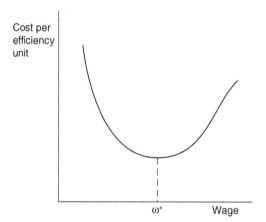

Figure 30.1

Note: Cost per efficiency unit is minimized at wage w^*

This curve, giving the relationship between the cost per effective unit of labor and the wage rate, is derived from the more fundamental *wage productivity curve*, giving the productivity of the representative worker hired at a particular wage. The curve depicted in Figure 30.2 shows λ, the productivity of the worker, increasing with the wage; the essential feature of this productivity curve is that there is initially a region of increasing returns, where an increase in the wage leads to a more than proportionate increase in the productivity. Many of our results depend critically on the existence of some region for which this is true; in the models that we investigate in detail, we establish that this is in fact the case.

In Figure 30.2, the cost per efficiency unit (cost per effective unit of labor) is given by the (inverse of the) slope of a line through the origin to a point on the wage productivity curve. Because the slope is increasing as we increase the wage from 0 to w^*, the cost per effective unit of labor is decreasing. Beyond w^* the slope decreases and hence the cost per effective unit of labor increases. It is clear, then, that the wage-productivity curve generates a cost per effective unit of labor curve of the form depicted in Figure 30.1.

The existence of wage-productivity relationship has long been recognized, as the quotations at the beginning of this article indicate. The more recent revival of interest may be attributed to Harvey Leibenstein (1957) who discussed it in the context of less developed countries and the subsequent developments by James Mirrlees (1975) and Stiglitz (1976b). There, however, the relationship is based on nutritional considerations.[4] Near subsistence, workers are not very productive; increases in wages may lead to marked increases in efficiency. Though our analysis focuses on alternative explanations of the relationship, the consequences are very similar.

Exactly the same analysis applies to the capital market (Stiglitz and Weiss 1981). Assume that as the bank increases the interest rate, the "quality" of those who apply decreases; that is, those who apply have, on average, a higher probability of defaulting, of not repaying their loans. The safest borrowers are unwilling to borrow at high interest rates. Then, the expected return on a loan, ρ, may actually decrease as the interest rate, r, increases, as depicted in Figure 30.3; r^* is the efficiency interest rate. If, at r^*, there is an excess demand for loans (credit is rationed), r^* is still an equilibrium. The bank will refuse to lend to anyone offering to borrow at a higher interest rate; its expected return would be lower than what it obtains by lending at r^*.

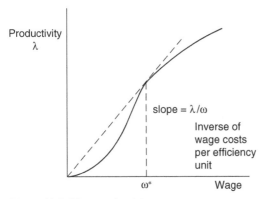

Figure 30.2 Wage productivity curve

Note: $\frac{\lambda}{w}$ increases as w increases to w^*, and then decreases.

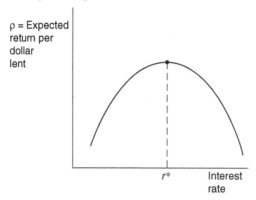

Figure 30.3

Note: Expected return per dollar lent is maximized at r^*.

The curve in Figure 30.3 may be derived from the default curve. The probability of a default is postulated to increase with the rate of interest charged. Let $p =$ probability that the loan is repaid; we assume, for simplicity, that when the loan is not repaid the lender receives nothing. Thus, the expected return to a lender is

$$\rho = p(1+r).$$

In Figure 30.4, we have plotted $1/p$ as a function of $1+r$. Thus, the slope of any line from the origin to the default curve is $1/(1+r)p$. The bank wishes to maximize $p(1+r)$, i.e., find the point on the default curve with the lowest slope; this is clearly just the point of tangency of a line through the origin with the default curve. Note that the slope decreases as r increases up to $1+r^*$ (i.e., ρ increases) and decreases thereafter (i.e., ρ decreases), just as depicted in Figure 30.3. (We postpone until later a justification for the shape of the default curve.)

Again, the conventional story for why there cannot be credit rationing in equilibrium is that those who are willing to borrow at the given interest but denied credit go to the bank and

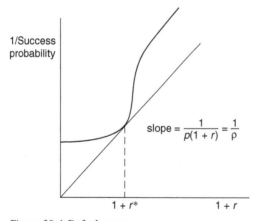

Figure 30.4 Default curve

Note: $p(1+r)$ increases as r increases to r^*, and then decreases.

offer it a higher interest rate; this bids up the interest rate. As the interest rate is bid up, the supply of credit is increased and demand decreases. The process continues until equilibrium is reached at the point where the demand for loans equals the supply; there is no credit rationing. But now, the bank realizes that if it charges a higher interest rate, the probability of default increases; and it may increase so much that the expected return to the bank actually decreases. Thus, no bank will ever charge an interest rate above r^*.[5,6]

In each of these cases, the story is the same: Because quality (labor efficiency, bankruptcy probability) changes as the price (wage, interest rate) changes, excess supply or demand may persist without any tendency for price (wages, interest rates) to move to correct the market imbalance.

General formulation.   In each of the instances described above, an individual (firm) sets the terms of the contract with another individual or firm to maximize its utility (profits), subject to offering terms that make the contract acceptable; under the circumstances described, the optimal contract will be such that the constraint on acceptability is not binding. That is, if $U[p, x, q(p, x)]$ is the utility of the buyer, paying a price p, and offering nonprice terms[7] of the contract x, where $q(p, x)$ represents a description of the (expected value of the) quality of the object (service) being purchased, a function of p and x, then the individual chooses p and x to

$$\underset{(p, x)}{Max} U \tag{30.1}$$

subject to the constraint of being able to obtain the item, i.e., if $V[p, x, q(p, x)]$ is the (expected) utility of an individual (firm) selling an item of quality q and V^* represents the reservation utility level,[8] then

$$V[p, x, q(p, x)] \geq V^* \tag{30.2}$$

In a variety of circumstances, the solution to this problem may entail the constraint (30.2) not being binding, at least for some potential sellers.[9] When that happens, market equilibrium will be characterized by demand not equaling supply.[10]

2 Repeal of the law of the single price

The law of supply and demand is of course, only one of the fundamental "laws" of conventional economics. Another central aspect of the traditional paradigm is codified in the "Law of the Single Price." This law holds that all objects with the same observable characteristics should sell at the same price. When there is a relationship between quality and price, the price itself becomes a relevant characteristic; market equilibrium may be characterized by a price distribution (or a wage distribution, or a distribution of interest rates) for objects that cannot be distinguished (before purchase) other than by price.

It has been widely observed that some firms have a high-wage policy; others pursue a low-wage policy. It is important to bear in mind that the differences we are concerned with here are not differences in whether the firm hires those with more education or less education, those with more work experience or those with less work experience. Rather, we are comparing the wages paid by firms for workers with a *given* set of observable qualifications.

There are several reasons that economies in which productivity depends on wages (or more generally quality on prices) may be characterized by a wage (price) distribution.

Differences in firms.   If the wage-productivity relationship differs across firms, as in Figure 30.5, the efficiency wage may differ. More generally, firms where net productivity is more sensitive to wages (with higher turnover costs, higher monitoring costs, or where shirking workers can do more damage) will find it desirable to pay higher wages for workers of identical characteristics (Steven Salop 1973). This is consistent with the observation that more capital intensive firms tend to pay higher wages, because the "damage" a worker can do in such jobs may be higher. If monitoring costs are higher in firms employing large numbers of workers, one might expect to see such firms paying higher wages (other things being constant).

Wage distributions when costs per effective unit are not monotonic.   Wage (price, or interest rate) distributions also arise when costs per effective unit are not monotone, as we suggested that they might not be.

Assume, in particular, that the reason that productivity increases with wage is nutritional;[11] though productivity always increases with wage, it may increase more or less than proportionately. When it increases more than proportionately, labor costs per efficiency unit decline with wage increases. Thus, if over some ranges, say, for very low wages and for an intermediate range of wages, productivity increases more than proportionately with wages, one would obtain a curve describing wage per efficiency unit as in Figure 30.6.

We define the Walrasian wage, $\bar{w}$, as that wage at which demand for labor equals the supply. However, the Walrasian wage is not the equilibrium wage whenever there exists a wage higher than the Walrasian wage with a lower cost per efficiency unit. For it would pay any firm to increase its wage. Assume, in Figure 30.6, that the Walrasian equilibrium occurred at some wage between $\hat{w}$ and w^{**}. One might be tempted to suggest that w^{**}, the wage greater than the Walrasian wage at which costs per efficiency unit are minimized, is the market equilibrium; but at w^{**}, there is unemployment; and by lowering their wage enough (to any wage between $\hat{w}$ and w^*), workers can be hired with a cost per efficiency unit that is lower than at w^{**}. The equilibrium now entails full employment with a wage distribution; some workers are hired at w^{**} and others at $\hat{w}$. Costs per efficiency unit are exactly the same.

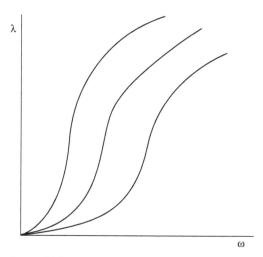

Figure 30.5

Note: The wage-productivity relationship may differ across firms. Different firms may find it optimal to pay different wages.

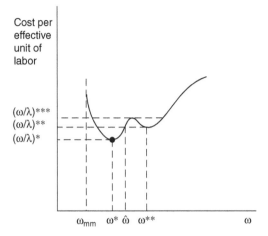

Figure 30.6 Wage distribution

Note: Market equilibrium is characterized by excess supply of labor whenever Walrasian wage is lower than w^*. When Walrasian wage is between $\hat{w}$ and w^{**}, some workers are hired at w^{**}, and other workers are hired at $\hat{w}$.

If all workers were paid a wage of $\hat{w}$, there would be (by assumption) an excess demand for labor; that is why $\hat{w}$ is not an equilibrium. If all workers were paid w^{**}, there would be an excess supply of laborers. There is a particular proportion of workers hired at $\hat{w}$ and w^{**} at which demand is equal to supply for the low-wage jobs, though there is excess supply of labor at the high-wage firms.

Similar arguments apply to other markets.

Wage distributions when costs per effective unit are minimized at several different wages. The previous subsection considered a situation where the cost per effective unit was not monotonic. Equilibrium wage distributions also arise when the curve describing the cost per effective unit of labor, depicted earlier, has several peaks, and all of the peaks generate exactly the same level of costs per effective unit of labor, as illustrated in Figure 30.7. Such a configuration would seem to be an anomaly. Even if there is no reason that the productivity curve has a single peak, why should the peaks occur at the same level? One can show that this may, in fact, occur quite easily. The curve that we have depicted is the curve facing a

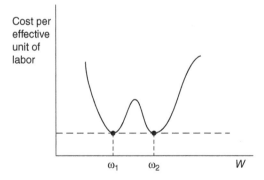

Figure 30.7

Note: Wage distribution where cost per effective unit of labor is the same at w_1 and w_2.

particular firm, *given* the wages paid by all other firms. Stiglitz (1974b, 1985) shows, in the context of the labor-turnover model, that there is a wages distribution (and in fact many such distributions) with the property that the productivity curve has many peaks, each of which yields exactly the same cost per effective unit of labor. The reason for this is that the turnover costs facing any firm are a function of the fraction of firms paying a higher wage, which itself is an endogenous variable. The low-wage firm faces a higher turnover. The fraction of high-wage firms is such that the total labor costs – wages plus turnover costs – are the same at low-wage firms and high-wage firms (see also Phillip Dybvig and Gerald Jaynes 1980).

Similar results can be obtained in the context of selection models. If different individuals have different costs associated with queuing, or with not selling their commodity (their labor), then high-wage firms may find that they face a longer queue and a higher quality of applicants. In these models, high-wage labor looks (in terms of observable characteristics) the same as low-wage labor, but in fact it is more productive with differences in productivity corresponding (in equilibrium) precisely to differences in wages. Wages together with queues are acting as self-selection devices.[12] (See Barry Nalebuff and Stiglitz 1982 and Stiglitz 1976a.)

3 Discrimination

It has long been noted that, in the absence of perfect information, there may be statistical discrimination: Members of a group will be paid the mean marginal product of the group, or will be charged an interest rate corresponding to the mean default probability of their group or charged an insurance premium corresponding to the mean probability of accident, illness, or death of their group. But the traditional theory of statistical discrimination (see, e.g., Dennis Aigner and Glen Cain 1977 or Rothschild and Stiglitz 1982) has not provided an explanation of job discrimination or red lining – the differential access to certain jobs or credit of certain groups. The theories we are concerned with here do this.

Assume that in the labor market there are a number of different identifiable groups, each with its own "cost per effective unit of labor" curve, as depicted in Figure 30.8. Then, equilibrium will be characterized by all groups hired having the same cost per effective labor unit; those with lower costs per effective labor service at any wage are paid a higher wage. (There is, thus, wage discrimination.) But there are some groups, such as Group C in Figure 30.8, for whom the cost per labor service, at the optimum wage, and hence at any wage, exceeds

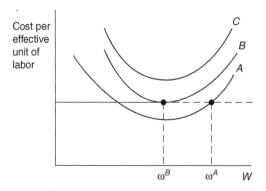

Figure 30.8

Note: Group *C* is excluded from labor market.

that of the market equilibrium; such workers will not be hired. "Discrimination" takes the form not of paying the workers in group C a lower wage, but of refusing to hire them.

While all of those in category A will be hired, and none of those in category C, in general only some of those in category B will be hired. *Other apparently identical workers will not be employed.*

When productivity depends on the unemployment rate, there may be large differences in equilibrium in group specific unemployment rates as well as wage rates.[13]

The theory not only predicts that some groups may be rationed out of the market, but also suggests that the brunt of changes in the demand for labor (aggregate demand) will be felt by some groups in increased job rationing. Moreover, some versions of the theory predict which groups will be rationed out of the market. In particular, in the incentive version of the model (Carl Shapiro and Stiglitz 1984), the wage that must be paid to a worker to induce him not to shirk depends on the cost of being fired. This cost is likely to be lower for part-time workers, for those close to retirement, and for secondary participants in the labor force (e.g., low-wage workers with high-income spouses).

Exactly the same phenomenon can occur in credit markets. Assume that the function relating the expected return to the interest rate differs across individuals who differ in certain observable characteristics, as depicted in Figure 30.9. There will be an equilibrium rate of return on a loan; loans to all categories that are offered yield the same expected return.[14] The interest rate charged for categories of loans, such as A, whose maximal expected return exceeds ρ^*, are charged lower interest rates ($r_A < r_B$). On the other hand, loan category C is such that at no interest rate does it yield a return equal to p^*; all those in this category are simply denied loans. The practice of denying credit to certain categories of potential borrowers is called red-lining. (Some of those in category B, where the maximal expected return is equal to ρ^*, receive loans, while others do not.)

4 Comparative statics

With "normally" shaped demand and supply curves, an increase in supply (that is, a shift in the supply curve such that at every price a greater quantity of the good is supplied) leads

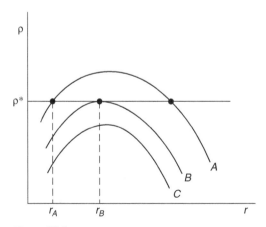

Figure 30.9

Note: Group *C* is excluded from labor market.

to an equilibrium with a lower price and a greater quantity traded. Similarly, a decrease in demand (that is, a shift in the demand curve such that at every price a smaller quantity of the good is demanded) leads to an equilibrium with a lower price and a lower quantity traded. Now, in the class of models being examined in this paper, the major effect of such a shift may be a change in the magnitude of rationing, with little effect on prices. Thus, in the labor market, when there is an equilibrium with excess supply of labor, a small increase in the demand for labor has no effect on the wage rate, but increases employment. An increase in the supply of credit available may have no effect on interest rates, but may simply lead to more loans (less credit rationing) at the old interest rates (Figure 30.10).

In markets where there are many groups in the population, a decrease in the demand for labor may result in some groups being completely excluded from the market, with only a slight lowering of the wage of those remaining. This is distinctly different from the conventional models, in which the wage for all workers would be reduced, and no group of workers would be excluded (though some groups of workers may decide to drop out of the labor market) (Figure 30.11(a)).

Similarly, in markets with credit rationing, a decrease in the supply of available credit may result in some groups being excluded from the credit market, with relatively small increases in the interest rates charged to those who are not excluded (Figure 30.11(b)).[15]

Shifts in the productivity curves.   The other important source of changes in the equilibrium comes from changes in the productivity (or return) curves. In the labor market, a change in technology may result in a change in the efficiency wage, as depicted in Figure 30.12(a). If the efficiency wage increases markedly, but the cost per effective unit of labor decreases only slightly, as in Figure 30.12(b), then the new equilibrium may be characterized by a lower level of employment and a higher wage.

Similarly, if banks' expectations of defaults increase, then the expected return, at any interest rate, will decrease. This will normally result in a decrease in the supply of credit; the effect on the extent of credit rationing will depend on how the changed expectations affect the demand for credit. But there are no clear implications for the interest rate charged by the bank; it may either increase or decrease (Figure 30.13).[16]

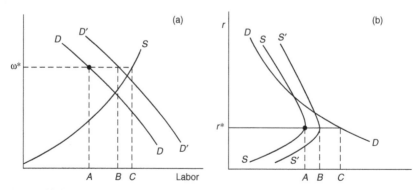

Figure 30.10

Note: (a) An increase in the demand for labor may leave wage rate unchanged, but simply increase employment. (b) An increase in the supply of credit may leave interest rate unchanged, but simply decrease extent of credit rationing.

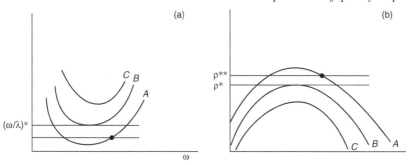

Figure 30.11

Note: (a) A decrease in the demand for labor may lead to a decrease in the equilibrium cost per effective unit of labor, resulting in exclusion of some groups from the labor market. (When wage per efficiency unit falls from just above $(w/\lambda)^*$ to just below it, group B is excluded.) (b) A decrease in supply of credit may lead to an increase in the equilibrium return, resulting in the exclusion of some groups from the credit market.

5 Implications for welfare economics

One of the crowning achievements of competitive equilibrium theory during the past half century has been the proof of the fundamental theorem of welfare economics – providing a precise statement of the meaning of Adam Smith's invisible hand conjecture.

An implicit assumption in the standard proofs of the Fundamental Theorem of Welfare Economics is that there is perfect information.[17] Obviously, economies with perfect information are likely to function better than economies with imperfect information:[18] That is an irrelevant comparison. The relevant question is, in a market characterized by incomplete information, are there interventions that can attain a Pareto improvement? Is the market, in other words, constrained Pareto efficient, taking into account the imperfections of information and costs of obtaining more information?

Greenwald and Stiglitz (1986a) have shown that competitive economies with incomplete markets and/or imperfect information are essentially never constrained Pareto efficient.

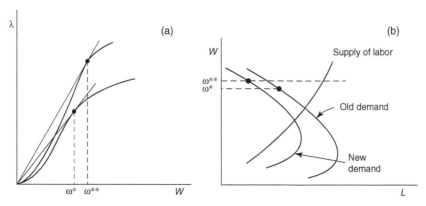

Figure 30.12

Note: (a) A change in technology may result in a large change in wages, but a relatively small change in the cost per efficiency unit of labor. (b) A technological change may lead to a higher wage and less employment.

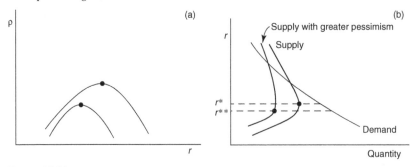

Figure 30.13

Note: (a) More pessimistic expectations may lower expected return and lower interest rate charged. (b) More pessimistic expectations may result in more credit rationing and lower interest rates.

These authors develop a general framework within which a variety of informational imperfections can be analyzed. They limit themselves to tax and subsidy interventions. They apply their analysis to one of the models that are the subject of discussion in this paper, namely, the Akerlof adverse selection model, where the quality offered is a function of the price but markets clear. In the context of the labor market, they show that a welfare improvement can be attained by subsidizing commodities whose consumption increases the mean quality of labor sold on the market and by taxing commodities whose consumption decreases the mean quality. The mean quality of labor offered on the market resembles the mean quality of air: There is an important externality in each individual's decision.

Their earlier paper was limited to economies with market clearing. In a sequel (Greenwald and Stiglitz 1986b), they identify the inefficiencies that arise in economies in which quality is dependent on prices and markets do not clear. There are inefficiencies both in setting wages (interest rates) and determining the level of employment (the number of loans of different types).

A direct consequence of the Fundamental Theorem of Welfare Economics is the decentralizability of efficient resource allocations; and a direct consequence of the failure of the Fundamental Theorem – of the externalities we have noted – is that the scope for decentralization may be limited.[19]

Some rationing may be consistent with Pareto efficiency. Assume the government has no more information about the quality of workers or potential borrowers than do firms (or banks). It has to allocate workers to different jobs. It has to allocate capital among different firms. The wage at which workers are willing to work or the interest rate at which firms are willing to borrow conveys information to the government, just as it does to the employer or the bank, and it will, in general, wish to use this information, even though to use it necessitates rationing – unemployment or credit rationing. But the objectives of the government, what it wishes to glean from the information, are different from those of firms and banks in the private market equilibrium. The latter are simply concerned with maximizing their own profits. Thus, in choosing a wage, the government would be concerned with ascertaining that those with a comparative advantage in a job get assigned to that job; the firm is simply concerned with cost per efficiency unit. (Similarly, the bank is not concerned with how its actions affect the profitability of investors, only with how it affects the profitability of the bank.)

Private firms will not only set the wage incorrectly; they will also hire an incorrect number of workers. Because all workers whose opportunity cost is less than the wage offer themselves for work, the mean opportunity cost of an individual randomly hired by a firm is less than the wage. Thus firms will not hire workers up to the point where the wage equals the mean opportunity costs, as a government concerned with maximizing national income would.

The inefficiencies we noted above are not the only inefficiencies associated with private market allocations and there may be other grounds for government intervention. Taxes and subsidies may affect the consumption vector of individuals, and thus indirectly the effort exerted by the worker (or the wage required to induce the worker not to shirk). Such taxes and subsidies may thus be welfare enhancing (Arnott and Stiglitz 1985).

Shapiro and Stiglitz (1984) point out a variety of other inefficiencies that arise in their model where high wages are used to reduce shirking. These relate to the intensity of monitoring and policies that affect quits and shirking. For instance, if workers are very risk averse, unemployment insurance may be desirable even though in their model private firms will never supply unemployment insurance; if there is an excess supply of labor, firms can obtain the desired labor force at the going wage; any increases in unemployment compensation simply increase the wage that a firm must pay to induce workers not to shirk.[20]

These models also have some more basic implications for how we think about the welfare properties of market economies. One of the important consequences of the Fundamental Theorem of Welfare Economics was that it enabled a neat separation of efficiency and equity issues. In particular, whether the economy is or is not Pareto efficient did not depend on the distribution of wealth. In the models under examination, this is not true, for two reasons. First, the inefficiencies with which we have been concerned arise because of the asymmetric information between two parties to a transaction – between landlord and worker, or between worker and capitalist. But whether these transactions arise is, at least partly, determined by the distribution of wealth. For instance, sharecropping arises largely because of the concentration of wealth. Secondly, the distribution of ownership of factors determines whether it is, in fact, feasible to design Pareto improvements. In the Shapiro-Stiglitz model, for instance, national income can be increased by taxing capital and subsidizing wages; if wealth were equally distributed, the losses individuals would suffer qua capitalists would be more than offset by the gains that would be received qua workers. But if there are two distinct groups in the population, capitalists and workers, there may be no way of improving the welfare of the workers without simultaneously hurting the capitalists – the market equilibrium, while not maximizing net national product, is Pareto efficient (see Shapiro and Stiglitz 1984; Dasgupta and Ray 1986).

II Explanations for the dependence of quality on price

In the introduction, we described two broad classes of models giving rise to a dependence of quality on price based on incentive and selection effects. In the preceding sections, we showed that if the dependence of quality on price took on particular forms (e.g., the cost per effective unit had an interior minimum) then there might exist an equilibrium in which demand did not equal supply, or in which there might be, in equilibrium, a price (wage, interest rate) distribution. We now consider in more detail not only why quality may depend on price in certain situations, but why the dependence should take on a form that may give rise to nonmarket-clearing equilibria and/or wage/price/interest rate distributions.

The analysis is divided into three sections, describing selection models, incentive models, and nutritional models.

1 Selection models

Labor market.   The reasons for the presence of adverse selection in the labor market are clear (Stiglitz 1976b; Weiss 1976, 1980; Greenwald 1979, 1986). One of the inferences I can make from the fact that a worker is willing to work for me for 50 cents an hour is that he does not have (know of) a better offer elsewhere.[21] If other firms are screening workers, keeping high-productivity workers and letting go of low-productivity workers, or adjusting their wages to reflect their lower productivity, the fact that no other firm has offered the worker a wage in excess of 50 cents an hour conveys a considerable amount of information. (Obviously, the inferences I make depend on a number of details of the surrounding circumstances; if the worker is a newly arrived worker to the United States, the fact that he is willing to accept a job at 50 cents an hour is more likely to reflect his limited opportunities for search and his lack of knowledge of the job market; if a job has a number of extremely attractive nonpecuniary advantages, the inferences I make should take that into account.)

More productive workers are likely to have better wage offers from other firms, but even if they are self-employed, they are likely to be more productive (that is, if those who are more able in one production task are more able, on average, in other production tasks as well).

In the simplest formulation of the adverse selection-labor model, a worker whose reservation wage is v has a productivity of $a(v)$; if all workers whose reservation wage v is less than or equal to w apply for a job with wage w,[22] then the mean productivity of the applicants is

$$\sum a(v)f(v)/F(v)$$

where $F(v)$ is the distribution function of the population by reservation wages, and $f(v)$ the density function. It is clear that if $a' > 0$, then mean productivity will increase with w. To see that it may have the shape depicted in Figure 30.1, consider a two group model; low-productivity individuals with productivity a_1 have a reservation wage of v_1 while high-productivity individuals with productivity a_2, have a reservation wage of V_2. $\bar{a}$ is the mean productivity; obviously, at high wages, when everyone is willing to work, $a = \bar{a}$. The resulting productivity curve is depicted in Figure 30.14(a).

A variant of this model arises when there are job-specific skills and positive search costs; the larger the applicant pool, the higher the expected productivity, simply because the firm can find a larger number of individuals that fit in well with the needs of the firm.

Capital market.   The intuitive reasons for the presence of adverse selection in the capital market follow along parallel lines to those in the labor market (Stiglitz and Weiss 1981).

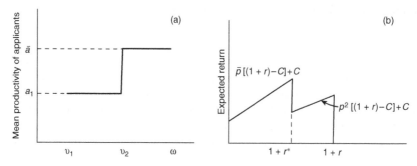

Figure 30.14 (a) Wage productivity curve in two group model (b) Expected return as function of interest rate change: two group model

The fact that an individual is willing to borrow from a bank at a 25 percent interest rate implies that he has found no one else willing to lend to him at lower interest rate, and this fact conveys considerable information. Moreover, even if the individual had not been turned down by other banks, those who are undertaking very risky projects, with little prospect of repaying the loan, are likely to be less concerned about the interest rate they have promised to pay (when they do not default) than those who are undertaking safe projects and will always repay.

More formally, Stiglitz and Weiss (1981) consider a set of projects that the bank has identified as "similar." They all yield the same mean return, and require the same amount of bank finance. They show (*a*) the riskier projects[23] yield a lower return to the bank; (*b*) at any interest rate charged by the bank, firms with riskier projects apply, those with safer projects do not; and (*c*) as the bank increases the interest rate charged there is an adverse selection effect, with firms with the best projects (the least risky, i.e., those yielding the bank the highest expected return) no longer applying.[24] They show that the adverse selection effect may outweigh the direct gain from an increase in the interest rate. This may be seen most easily in the case where there are only two kinds of firms; each project costs B dollars, and is entirely bank financed. The firm is required to put up c dollars worth of collateral per dollar loaned, which it forfeits in the event of a default. The projects of type i firm yield a return of R^i if successful, and nothing otherwise; the probability of success is p^i. The expected return to the bank per dollar loaned from a loan to a firm of type i is just $p^i(1+r)+(1-p^i)c$, where r is the interest rate charged. Thus, if $p^1 > p^2$, one is the safe project and yields a higher return to the bank, provided $c < (1+r)$, which it always would be (otherwise, the bank faces no risk).

The expected return to a firm of type i is $p^i[R^i - B(1+r)B] - cB(1-p^i)$. It follows then that if the two projects have the same mean return, the riskier project yields the higher return to the firm. The safe firms no longer apply when

$$p^1[R^1 - (1+r)B] - cB(1-p^1) = 0$$

Thus, for interest rates below $[p^1R^1 - cB(1-p^1)]/p^1B - 1 = r^*$, both types of firm apply; for higher interest rates, only the risky firms apply. Even if at r^* there is an excess demand for funds, banks may not raise the interest rate (see Figure 30.14(b)).

2 Incentive effects

We are concerned here with the variety of circumstances under which the quality of the product (the likelihood of bankruptcy, the productivity of a worker) is affected by actions of the seller (borrower, worker), and those actions are affected by the price (interest rate, wage). Two broad categories of models will be discussed, depending on whether there is or is not a long-term relationship. The latter are of particular interest; bad performance is (in these models) often punished by a termination of the relationship. For the threat of termination to be an effective incentive, the terms of the contract (relationship) must be such as to make that contract strictly better than that of the next best opportunity; e.g., price must be in excess of marginal cost or the wage paid must be higher than the minimum wage required to recruit the worker.

We now describe in greater detail the effects of wages, prices, or interest rates on economic incentives.

Capital markets.   An increase in the interest rate charged on a loan may induce the borrower to undertake greater risks, lowering the expected return to the lender (William R. Keeton 1980; Stiglitz and Weiss 1981). This may be seen most simply in the case where the firm has two projects that it can undertake, each of which costs B. As before, project i has a return, if successful, of R^i, and the probability of success is p^i; if unsuccessful, the project yields no return. For simplicity, we ignore collateral. Then, the expected return to the firm of undertaking project i when the interest rate is r is

$$p^i[R^i - (1+r)B].$$

As Figure 30.15 illustrates, the safe project 1 has a higher expected return to the firm for $r \leq r^*$, where

$$(1+r^*)B = (p^1 R^1 - p^2 R^2)/(p^1 - p^2)$$

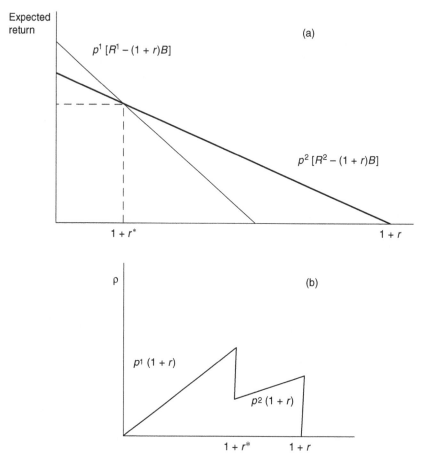

Figure 30.15

Note: (a) Firm chooses safe project if and only if $r \leq r^*$. (b) Expected returns are maximized at r^*.

Thus, the bank will not raise the interest rate above r^*, even if there is an excess demand for funds at r^*, because to do so would induce firms to undertake the risky project, lowering the bank's return.

This is an example of what has come to be called a *principal agent* problem.[25] The principal (here the bank) can exert only indirect control over the actions of the agent (the firm) and, he does so through the design of the payoff schedule. Changing the nominal price (here the interest rate) may have adverse (in terms of the interests of the principal) effects on the actions undertaken by the agent.

The discussion so far has focused on a single period model. Stiglitz and Weiss (1983) have extended the analysis to a multi (two) period model. They establish that the threat of *terminating* the credit relationship may have beneficial incentive effects and that terminations are a better incentive device than threats to charge higher interest rates (pay lower wages).

Their analysis is similar to the explanation of why the expected return may decrease with the rate of interest charged provided by the models of Jonathan Eaton and Mark Gersovitz (1980, 1981a, 1981b), Eaton (1985), and Franklin Allen (1980, 1981, 1983). They are concerned with situations where contracts are not enforceable. We might say that there are implicit contracts, which have to be designed to be self-enforcing. The terms of the contract determine whether, and under what circumstances, it will pay a borrower to refuse to repay a loan (for a sovereign to repudiate his debt).[26]

In these models, it is again the threat of termination of the relationship that induces the borrower to repay the loan. (In the Eaton-Gersovitz model, access to international capital markets enables the country to smooth out income variability.) For any given amount loaned, the higher the rate of interest charged, the more likely it is that the loan will be repudiated.[27]

Labor markets. There are several different explanations for why the wage might affect the productivity of workers and the profitability of the firm.

(a) Shirking. (Walter J. Wessels 1979, 1985; Guillermo Calvo 1979; Calvo and Phelps 1977; Calvo and Stanislaw Wellisz 1979; Shapiro and Stiglitz 1984; Samuel Bowles 1985;[28] Stiglitz and Weiss 1983; Steve Stoft 1982.) If there were no unemployment and if all firms paid the market-clearing wage, then the threat of being fired would not lead individuals to reduce their shirking: they would know that they could costlessly obtain another job. But if the firm pays wages in excess of that of other firms, or if there is unemployment (so that a fired worker must spend a period in the unemployment pool before he again obtains a job) then workers have an incentive not to shirk; there is a real cost to being fired.[29] One of the immediate consequences, then, of costly monitoring is that equilibrium must be characterized by unemployment and/or wage dispersion.

It also implies that the productivity of the worker hired by the *i*th firm, λ_i, is a function of the wage it pays, the wage paid by all other firms, w_{-i}, and the unemployment rate, U:

$$\lambda_i = \lambda_i(w_i, w_{-i}, U).$$

In the simplest version of the shirking model, workers either work or shirk; there is a critical wage below which the worker shirks. This critical wage is an increasing function of the employment level or of the wage differential between this firm and other firms. In the case where all firms pay the same wages, the so-called no-shirking constraint, giving the minimum wage below which shirking occurs, is depicted in Figure 30.16(a). The demand for labor, given that workers do not shirk, is a decreasing function of the wage.

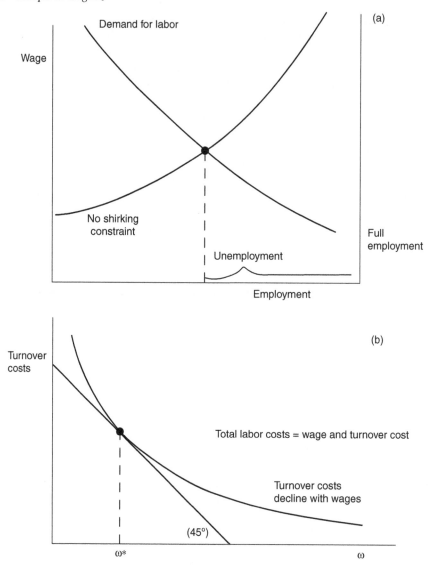

Figure 30.16 (a) Shirking model (b) Labor turnover model

Note: (a) High wages and unemployment are necessary to induce workers not to shirk. (b) Total labor costs are minimized at w^*.

Equilibrium, at the intersection of the demand curve and the no-shirking constraint, always entails unemployment.

(b) Labor turnover. (John Pencavel 1972; Wessels 1979; Stiglitz 1974b, 1974c, 1985; Robert Hall 1975; Salop 1973, 1979; Dybvig and Jaynes 1980; Ekkehart Schlicht 1978.) A second important way that workers' behavior affects the productivity of firms is through labor turnover.[30] In most jobs, there are costs to hiring and training that are specific to the firm. So long as individuals do not pay their full costs at the moment they are hired (recouping them later in the form of higher wages)[31] then the greater the quit rate, the greater the

firm's expenditures on training and hiring costs. Increasing the wage rate (relative to wages paid by other firms) will, in general, lead to a reduction in the quit rate; there is a wage that minimizes total labor costs of the firm (Figure 30.16(b)). Moreover, the greater the unemployment rate, the less likely it is that the worker will find a better job. Because the effect of higher quit rates is to decrease the "net" productivity (net of turnover costs), we obtain a productivity wage relationship of the above form.

(c) Morale effects. (James E. Annable 1977, 1980, 1985; Stiglitz 1973, 1974a; Pencavel 1977; Akerlof 1984; Whiteside 1974.) Employers often allege that paying higher wage results in higher productivity, and not simply because of the greater penalty associated with being fired. A worker who believes he is being treated more than fairly may not only get more job satisfaction from his job, but also may put out more for his employer. And notions of fairness are closely related to how one *perceives* others of similar ability being treated. Thus, we can postulate that an individual's efforts depend not only on his own wage, but on the wage of others in his reference group, ev, the monitoring intensity, m, and the cost of being fired (the unemployment rate):[32]

$$e_i = e(w_i, \hat{w}, m, U).$$

The formal analysis of this model follows closely along the lines of that of the shirking model.[33] (It may, in fact, be possible to derive at least some variants of this morale model from a standard utility maximizing model, in which utility depends not only on effort and wages, but on relative wages.[34] Obviously, quit rates too will depend on morale effects: Individuals may spend more resources searching for a better job if they believe that they are being unfairly treated on their present job.)

Sharecropping. (Stiglitz 1974d; David Newbery and Stiglitz 1979; Avishay Braverman and T. N. Srinivasan 1981; Braverman and Stiglitz 1982, 1986; Allen 1985a). It has long been recognized that increasing the share provided to the tenant worker could have beneficial effects on his work incentives, and thus could actually increase the receipts of the landlord.[35,36] It is possible that at the share at which the landlord's expected income is maximized, there is an excess supply of tenants.[37,38]

Product Markets. (Joseph Farrell 1979, 1980; Shapiro 1983; Dybvig and Chester Spatt 1983; Allen 1984; Ben Klein and Keith B. Leffler 1981).

In the product market, incentive effects similar to those described earlier arise: Buyers often cannot ascertain the quality of a commodity before they purchase it. Earlier, we noted that the penalty associated with a worker caught shirking and who is thereupon fired depended on the wage relative to the wage paid by other firms and the cost of getting another job (which depends, in part, on the unemployment rate). Similarly, the penalty a customer levies on a firm that has cheated him is to terminate the relationship; and the penalty associated with this depends on how high the price is relative to the production costs (the profit the firm attains from the relationship) and how hard it is to recruit another, similar customer.

The essential insights are provided by the following simple model. Assume that the cost of production for a high-quality commodity is c^h, for a low-quality commodity is c^l, and the price is p. Assume that when a customer observes a bad-quality commodity, he infers that the seller will always continue to sell a bad quality. The bad quality commodity is worth nothing to the customer, so if he believes that the commodity is bad, he will terminate the relationship. Then, the value to the firm of continuing to produce good-quality commodities is

$$(1+r)(p-c^h)Q/r$$

where Q is the quantity sold, r the rate of interest. The value of cheating and producing a bad quality commodity is

$$(p-c^l)Q.$$

Thus, for it to be worthwhile for the firm to produce good-quality commodities,

$$(1+r)(p-c^h)/r > p - c^l$$

or

$$p > (1+r)c^h - rc^l = p^*.$$

Accordingly, any individual who saw a firm attempting to sell a commodity for less than p^* would infer that that commodity was a low-quality commodity.[39]

3 Nutritional models

This paper focuses on the dependence of quality on price arising from imperfect information (adverse selection, moral hazard). But, as we noted, in one of the earliest sets of efficiency-wage models the quality of labor depended on the wage for nutritional reasons. How are these nutritional models related to the information models?

If the output of workers were perfectly observable, then presumably all workers would be paid on a piece rate basis. In equilibrium, some workers would be employed (at the efficiency wage), and other identical workers would be unemployed. Assume that workers get zero disutility from work, up to 40 hours per week, and infinite disutility thereafter (there is no disutility associated with effort up to a critical level λ, and infinite disutility thereafter) and that the output per unit time with the maximum effort level e is a function of nutrition. Then the number of labor units supplied will be a function of the wage rate. There is no way of obtaining any labor at a cost per efficiency unit of less than $w^*/\lambda(w^*)$. At wages in excess of w^* effective labor supply increases, as depicted in Figure 30.17. Although, by assumption at w^*, each worker supplies either zero effective labor units or $\lambda(w^*)$, all workers strictly prefer to supply the latter; at w^* there is an excess supply of labor.

Although nutritional models can give rise to unemployment even if workers are paid on a piece rate basis, they obviously can also give rise to unemployment when piece rates are not feasible; thus, in the example given above, there are no incentive problems, whether workers are paid on a piece rate basis or not.[40]

Thus, the nutritional efficiency-wage models, while differing in fundamental ways from the informational efficiency-wage models in their microfoundations, yield similar conclusions: They generate similar reduced form relationships between productivity and the wage paid by the firm, wages paid by other firms, and the unemployment rate. It is worth noting, however, that in one polar form of the efficiency-wage model, where individuals do not share any of their income with others, productivity depends only on the absolute value of the wage

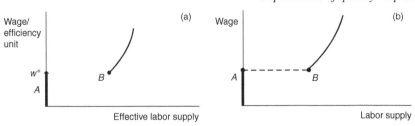

Figure 30.17

Note: (a) At wages below w^*, the effective labor supply is zero; at w^* it increases discontinuously. (b) With nonconvexities in preferences, labor supply may be discontinuous, but with continuum of individuals equilibrium exists.

paid by the firm; accordingly the equilibrium wage will be independent of the unemployment rate. (This stands in contrast with several versions of the informational efficiency-wage model, where relative wages and the unemployment rate are the primary determinants of productivity.)

III The implications of the dependence of quality on price for economic theory

1 Differences between economies in which the law of supply and demand is repealed and those where it still holds

It is useful to clarify the differences between the assumptions in our analysis and those that are (often implicit) in the traditional competitive paradigm, e.g., of the model of Arrow and Debreu. Arrow and Debreu assume that each employer has perfect information concerning the quality of his labor, that each buyer of a commodity has perfect information concerning the quality of the commodities which he purchases, and that each lender has perfect information concerning the characteristics of those to whom he lends. Thus, when they speak of a market for a commodity, they have in mind a market for a collection of objects, all of which are identical, at least in all relevant aspects. The person buying a commodity or hiring on the market is completely indifferent about which commodity he obtains; the firm hiring a worker is indifferent about which worker he obtains, and no additional information would change his indifference.

This assumption of a competitive market for homogeneous commodities is neither plausible nor innocuous. Markets in which commodities are completely homogeneous – with respect to location and the date as well as other characteristics – are almost inherently sufficiently thin so that the postulate of perfect competition is inapplicable. Markets that are sufficiently "thick" to be competitive are almost always nonhomogeneous. Consider the market for labor. If we define a sub-market, say, J. E. Stiglitz's labor, then it may be homogeneous, but hardly competitive; if we take a broader definition of the market, say, those with PhDs in economics, it may be fairly competitive, but it is hardly homogeneous.

The problems with which we are concerned are central in capital markets and insurance markets. Both markets are essentially intertemporal: In the capital market, the lender lends the borrower money today, in return for a promise to repay $\$(1+r)$ next period, provided the borrower can; in the insurance market, the insurer agrees today to pay the insured a given amount next period if a particular event occurs. The lender cares about the likelihood that the borrower will default; the insurer cares about the likelihood that the insured against event will occur. Borrowers (the insured) differ, but lenders (insurers) cannot tell who is more likely to default (to have an accident).

Moreover, the probability of default (of an accident) can be affected by the actions of the borrower (insured).

The Arrow-Debreu model does not actually require perfect information. What it does require is that the nature of the "commodity" be fixed (i.e., that the average quality of labor be unaffected by prices or wages and that average default (accident) probability be unaffected by the terms of the loan (insurance policy)). There can be neither adverse selection or moral hazard effects; that is, if all individuals (commodities) are not identical, at least the mix of types is fixed *and* any actions which they might take that affect their productivity (or default, or accident, probabilities) are observable.

Many economic relationships involve an element of insurance and/or loan. This is the case, for instance, with most employment and rental arrangements.

There is one set of circumstances under which a firm does not care about the characteristics of those it hires. If the firm can perfectly and costlessly monitor the *actions*[41] of its employees, and pay the employee for the services performed, and there are no fixed costs associated with hiring a worker, then the firm is unconcerned whether the worker is a low-ability worker pulling out three medium sized weeds a day, or a high-productivity worker pulling out three hundred a day. It pays a fixed price per medium sized weed pulled out.

In fact, relatively few workers are paid even partially on a piece rate basis (which is not to say that performance goes unrewarded, either in terms of promotions or salary). The literature on compensation schemes details a number of reasons for this, all of which attest to the importance of the informational concerns that are the center of our analysis (Stiglitz 1975) but are completely ignored in the traditional competitive paradigm.[42]

Because most workers are not paid a piece rate equal to the value of their marginal product, and because there are costs associated with hiring workers, some of which are borne by the firm, firms are concerned both about the quality of the workers they hire, their productivity on the job, and their turnover rate.[43] The wage affects all of these variables. And so long as that is the case, the possibilities with which we have been concerned here – that equilibrium will be characterized by an excess supply of labor, and/or by a wage distribution – are real possibilities.[44]

It should be noted that most of the issues with which we have been concerned here would arise so long as individuals are not paid on a piece rate, regardless of the reason. Similarly, if the firm must pay a uniform wage to all workers, even though it knows which workers are more productive, it will worry about the adverse selection effects of lowering wages.

The conventional models assume not only that there is not imperfect information concerning what is being bought, but also, in trades which occur over time, that there are no *enforcement* problems. In fact, of course, there are important enforcement problems, arising both from the incompleteness of contracts and from the costs of enforcing the contract terms that are explicit.[45]

The nutritional efficiency wage models can give rise to unemployment even without informational problems, as we have already noted. These models differ from the conventional Arrow-Debreu model in two technical respects, which turn out to be important: There is a non-convexity associated with the productivity wage relationship, and in equilibrium individuals are on the boundary of their feasible set.[46]

2 Alternative equilibrium concepts

In Section I we argued that when quality depends on price, equilibrium may be characterized by markets not clearing. In traditional economic theory, equilibrium is defined as market clearing. Clearly, different notions of equilibrium are being employed. Indeed, even within the literature recognizing the dependence of quality on price, more than one equilibrium notion has been employed, with contrasting results. In this section, we review and contrast several of the more important equilibrium concepts that have been used.

Walrasian versus rationing equilibria. In models where quality depends on price, there may exist a market-clearing price, for instance, a wage at which demand equals supply. We referred to this as the Walrasian equilibrium, but this may *not* be a market equilibrium. Whenever in the labor market there is a region where cost per effective labor unit decreases with an increase in the wage, or in the capital market there is a region where the expected return decreases with an increase in the interest rate, there may exist an equilibrium with excess supply of labor or excess demand for capital. Indeed, there always exists some level of demand for labor or supply of funds for which this is true.[47]

It is important to emphasize that we are not arguing here that equilibrium is *never* characterized by the equality of demand and supply, only that it may not be.[48]

The Walrasian wage (interest rate). Is the market equilibrium if and only if there exists no higher wage *(lower interest rate)* at which costs per efficiency unit *(expected returns)* are lower *(higher)*.[49]

The choice of appropriate equilibrium concepts. Our analysis thus differs from the standard Arrow-Debreu model not only in its informational assumptions, but also in its definition of equilibrium. Traditional theory has taken the equality of supply and demand to be part of the definition of equilibrium. This, I think, is wrong.

Equilibrium is defined, loosely, as a state where no economic agents have an incentive to change their behavior. Whether a particular configuration of the economy is an equilibrium depends, then, on agents' perceptions of the consequences of changes in their behavior. If employers believed that at a lower wage they would obtain exactly the same quality of laborers as they obtained at a higher wage, then clearly, if a worker offered to work for a wage lower than that of existing workers, the firm would hire him (assuming there were no further repercussions of what might be viewed by other workers as antisocial behavior).[50] Under these circumstances, equilibrium would be characterized by demand equaling supply.

The fact that under these circumstances equilibrium is characterized by demand equaling supply is thus a theorem (admittedly trivial) to be proven; the equality of demand and supply should not be taken as a definition of equilibrium, but rather as a consequence following from more primitive behavioral postulates. What we have established in this paper is that, under plausible behavioral postulates, equilibrium may not be characterized by demand equaling supply. At the same time, it should be emphasized that our economy is competitive in the conventional sense in which that word is used: We are concerned with atomistic equilibria, in which all agents are small relative to the market though in spite of this they are not price takers.[51]

Passive versus active sellers and buyers. While the models presented here differ from the conventional competitive paradigm both in informational assumptions and in the equilibrium concept, these models differ from Akerlof's analysis of adverse selection only with respect to the equilibrium concept. In Akerlof's model, as in the traditional perfect information model, however, both buyers and sellers act completely passively. For instance, although firms know the statistical relationship between the wage paid and the productivity of the workers they hire, they do not try to use this knowledge to increase their profits, e.g., by setting wages at other than a market-clearing level. We would argue that there is, in most situations, no persuasive reason to limit out uninformed agents to the passive role that conventional theory has assigned to them.

Nonprice rationing.   A number of writers have argued that when, in the capital market, interest rates cannot fall, there are other methods by which markets can be made to clear; similarly, in labor markets, when wages cannot fall, there are other methods by which markets can be made to clear. In markets with imperfect information, contractual arrangements involve more than a single term; and it must be shown that none of these can adjust in a way as to restore market clearing. There may be adverse selection and incentive effects from changes in each of the contract terms.

In the capital market, emphasis has been placed on the role of collateral. Increasing collateral does induce firms to undertake less risky projects, but may have adverse selection effects (Stiglitz and Weiss 1981; Hildegard Wette 1983; Gerhard E. Clemenz 1984, 1985; Chang-Ho Yoon 1984, 1985). Several authors (e.g., Helmut Bester 1985) have constructed models in which, if banks can design contracts with varying interest rates and collateral, there will be no credit rationing.

It is important to recall that our contention has been not that equilibrium would always be characterized by credit rationing, but that it may be, under plausible conditions. Indeed, it is easy to construct examples in which equilibrium is not characterized by credit rationing. Bester (1985) and David Besanko and Anjan Thakor (1984) provide examples with the peculiar property in that bankers can obtain, through offering a set of con tracts, perfect information concerning their borrowers. By contrast, Stiglitz and Weiss (1986a, 1986b) argue that as long as there is a residual of imperfect information there may be scope for credit rationing.[52]

In the Stiglitz-Weiss models, each borrower borrows the same amount. Another term of the contract that can adjust is the amount lent. Under certain circumstances, reducing the amount lent reduces the risk faced by the bank. Thus, adjustments in the loan size can eliminate credit rationing (H. Milde and John Riley 1984). Again, the issue is not whether one can construct examples in which rationing does not occur, but rather, are there alternative, plausible structures under which it does. In a multiperiod context, Stiglitz and Weiss (1981) have shown that reducing the size of the loan may have an adverse effect on the risks undertaken by the borrower; they undertake projects that in effect, "force" the lender to ante up more money in subsequent periods, if they are to recover their initial loans (see also Martin Hellwig 1977).

In the labor market, discussions have focused on the role of bonding and "job" purchases. That is, a worker could put down a sum of money that he surrenders in the event of being caught shirking. Bonding, it is argued, can alleviate the incentive problems. B. Curtis Eaton and William White (1982), Shapiro and Stiglitz (1984, 1985a), Edward Lazear (1982), and Stoft (1985) have argued against this on several grounds: Firstly, they note that with young individuals having limited capital there is, at least for these workers, incomplete bonding, so that firms are, in fact, concerned with the relationship between wages and productivity. (Though they could borrow to put up the bond, this simply shifts who bears the risk that the worker fails to perform, from the firm to the lender. Though non-vested pensions can be viewed as a form of bonding, it takes individuals a number of years to accumulate enough within their pension fund to serve as a sufficiently effective bond to eliminate the need for firms to be concerned with whether their workers shirk.) Secondly, they note the "double moral hazard" problem, the incentive of the firm to declare that the worker has shirked when he has not. This may be alleviated by making the bond forfeiture go to a third party: again, the empirical relevance may be questioned; moreover such arrangements are sensitive to complicity by two of the parties against the third.[53] Thirdly, they note that many individuals may not have funds to post a bond; to borrow the funds would entail all the adverse effects noted earlier in our discussion of capital markets; and to restrict applicants to those who could finance the bond themselves would have the adverse selection effects noted earlier in connection with collateral.

Similar problems arise with job purchases (or, what is equivalent, in the context of labor turnover, with requiring individuals to pay for their full costs of training).[54]

Advocates of the efficiency wage models claim, in the end, that the central point is that firms do care about quit rates, they do care about the incentives of their workers, and they do use wage policies to affect the net profitability of their employees.

Other imperfect information models

The last two decades have seen a burgeoning in imperfect information models. It is worth noting the relationships between the models that are the center of discussion here and some of these other models.

Prices versus quantities. Earlier literature (Rothschild and Stiglitz 1976; Akerlof 1976; Michael Spence 1974) stressed the role of *quantities* in conveying information; the literature this paper is concerned with stresses the role of prices in conveying information.

The quantity of education obtained by an individual conveys information because it is more costly for a less able individual to acquire education than for a more able individual. But it is no more costly for a less able individual to announce that he is willing to work only at a higher wage than a more able individual. How then can workers (informed sellers) use prices to convey information about themselves? There must be some cost to announcing a higher reservation price: The price is the lower probability of being employed (or selling one's commodity). Stiglitz (1976a) and Nalebuff and Stiglitz (1982) have constructed models in which higher-quality workers are willing to face a higher probability of not obtaining a job because their fallback wage is higher. (Wilson [1979, 1980] has constructed a similar model for the product market.)[55] Thus, if there are two types of workers, whose reduced form utility function can be represented by $U_i = U_i(w, g)$, where g is the probability of obtaining a job, then equilibrium may be characterized by both groups obtaining wages commensurate with their abilities (though employers cannot observe them directly), but with the low-ability individuals having a probability g^* just large enough to induce the low-ability not to apply, i.e., letting superscript 1 denote the low-ability workers

$$U^1(w^1, 1) = U^1(w^2, g^*)$$

(See Figure 30.18).[56, 57]

In the simple model's analyzing the dependence of quality on price, quantity variables are not observable. (There is no variable, like education, to reveal the individual's true ability.) But all that is required for wages/prices/interest rates to play a role in conveying quality

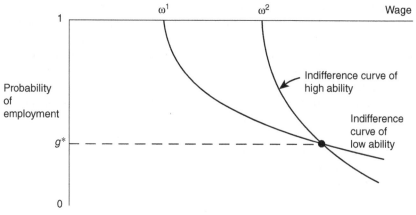

Figure 30.18

Note: Wage and probability of employment acting as self-selection device.

information given whatever variables that are observable is that there remains some residual uncertainty of either the adverse selection or moral hazard sort.[58]

Information revealing prices in the capital market.   There is a closely related literature to that discussed here, where prices also convey information. In capital markets, the price at which a security sells may convey information concerning the expected return of the security (or the likelihood of the occurrence of various states). (See Green 1973; Grossman and Stiglitz 1976, 1980; Margaret Bray 1981; Roy Radner 1979.) In structure, these models are most like the Akerlof "Lemons" (1970) model, in which both sellers and buyers act non-strategically: They take prices, and the information conveyed by the price, as given. They differ in that, while there is only one seller (and usually only one buyer) of any particular automobile, or any particular person's labor services, there are many potential buyers and sellers of any particular security. (Indeed, in the absence of transactions costs, with risk aversion and imperfectly correlated securities, virtually everyone is a buyer or seller.) Thus, while the price of a car sold at an auction reflects the valuation placed on it by those who value it most highly, in a security market, those who believe that a security is overpriced will sell it short, and their beliefs are, accordingly, reflected in the market equilibrium price.

IV Applications

1 Implications for macroeconomics

These models have direct and important implications for macroeconomics.[59]

This section is divided into four subsections, dealing respectively with labor markets, capital markets, product markets, and the relationship of these theories to other recently advanced theories.

Labor markets.   The fact that these theories have yielded competitive market equilibrium in which wages do not fall in the face of unemployment, in which there is an equilibrium level unemployment, immediately suggests the possibility that these theories may provide an important part of the explanation of involuntary unemployment. This is an area of active ongoing research and controversy. What I wish to do here is to explain why some economists

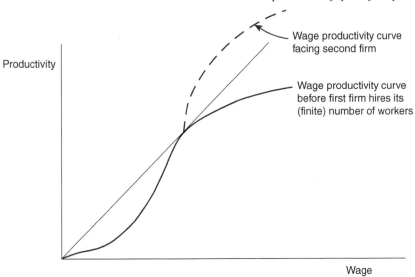

Figure 30.19 The advantages of being late

find these models more persuasive than at least several of the competing theories, and to present what appear to be at the present time the major issues, both the criticism and the defenses, pointing to certain unsettled controversies.

(a) The pattern and form of unemployment. A theory purporting to explain cyclical fluctuations in unemployment should not only show that it can generate unemployment, but also explain the pattern and form of unemployment. This efficiency-wage theories do.[60] Less productive workers – those for whom the minimum wage per efficiency unit is below some critical level – cannot get jobs, though they might at higher levels of effective demand. (These may include young workers, part-time workers, or others for whom the total surplus from work is small, so that the no-shirking wage, at any unemployment level, is high.)

Moreover, there is no work sharing, with the associated income reductions, for this would simply reduce the quality (productivity) of the labor force. In the incentive efficiency-wage model, it is the total surplus (the amount by which the value of wage payments exceeds the foregone leisure) that determines whether workers shirk; in the turnover model, it is the total surplus (relative to that offered by other firms) that determines whether a worker quits; in the selection models, it is again the total surplus that determines the individual's choice of one job over another. Work sharing reduces the surplus available to any individual, and thus adversely affects the effort (quality, labor turnover). See, for example, Arnott, Hosios, and Stiglitz (1983) or Michael Hoel and Bent Vole (1986).

(b) Criticisms. Critics have raised several objections, concerning both the quantitative significance of the efficiency wage effects and the consistency of the theory with certain observed macroeconomic phenomena.

1 Can efficiency wage theory explain involuntary unemployment? Perhaps the most widely cited criticism is that, unless efficiency wage considerations are important in all sectors, the theory cannot explain unemployment; that is, if there is some sector (such as agriculture) where workers can be paid on a piece rate basis, and the piece rate is flexible, then that sector should absorb all workers laid off from those sectors where efficiency-wage

considerations are important. Thus, efficiency-wage theory might be able to explain wage differentials (the secondary labor market), but not unemployment. (Note that this objection can be raised against implicit contract theory explanations of unemployment as well.)[61]

Several of the efficiency-wage models have attempted to incorporate a flexible wage sector. In Stiglitz (1974c), for instance, the agricultural sector has flexible wages, while efficiency-wage considerations are important in the industrial sector. Individuals must choose in which sector to locate (mobility between the sectors is not costless and instantaneous). Unemployment in the urban sector is such as to equilibrate expected income (of the marginal migrant) in that sector to that in the rural sector.[62]

Jeremy Bulow and Larry Summers (1985) assume that individuals can search for a (high-wage) job only while unemployed, and thus even if individuals could have obtained a low-wage job, they choose not to do so.[63]

Greenwald has provided several alternative explanations for why individuals may not accept a low-wage job, based on information theoretic considerations: Accepting a low-wage job may convey information about the individual's ability; with high-ability individual's expecting to get a "good" job sooner than a low-ability individual, an individual who readily accepts a low-wage job signals that he thinks of himself as low-ability, and this signal will lower his future wages.[64] Moreover, accepting a job creates an information asymmetry – the firm's new employer will know more about the individual's ability than other prospective employers. Just as Akerlof showed that these information asymmetries lead to thin markets for used cars, Greenwald has shown that they result in thin markets for "used labor."[65] Finally, he has attempted to relate unemployment to capital market imperfections, which themselves can be explained by information theoretic concerns. There are, in general, some training costs that firms must bear when they hire a worker; moreover, hiring a worker represents a risky investment. With imperfect capital markets, firms cannot divest themselves of this risk; as a result, the implicit cost of capital may be very high in a recession, and hence it is possible that in a recession, firms are willing to hire workers only if the lifetime wages are lower than they would be if the worker were hired in a later period, when the risks faced by the firm are less.

Critics might say at this juncture, "Aha, so unemployment is really voluntary." We think little is gained from a semantic debate over whether unemployment is, in this sense, voluntary or involuntary. What is critical is (a) in the market equilibrium, some individuals, with a given set of characteristics, have a distinctly higher level of (expected) utility than other similar individuals; (b) the equilibrium has, for one reason or another, some individuals in the unemployment pool who, under other circumstances, would be working; and (c) the market equilibrium is not (constrained) Pareto efficient.

2 Are there alternative mechanisms for ensuring quality? A second criticism is that if these efficiency-wage considerations were really important, alternative mechanisms would be found that would not be anywhere near as socially costly as the unemployment to which it gives rise. There are several answers to this objection: Firstly, the fact of the matter is that firms are concerned about the quality of their labor force and their rates of turnover. Secondly, we have already detailed some reasons why at least some of the proposed alternatives that would eliminate unemployment (credit rationing) may be ineffective. Some of these arguments may hold with more force for some groups of workers or for some industries than for others. Thus, consider the argument that bonding is not employed because workers have insufficient capital. This argument seems more applicable to young workers and to low-wage (unskilled) workers than to older workers, and therefore might suggest

that the effort-efficiency wage model is more relevant for these workers than for other groups of laborers.[66]

Finally, we note that because of the presence of the important externalities discussed in Part I.5, the private costs of pursuing, say, high-wage policies (leading to unemployment) and of not employing alternative strategies of sorting and providing incentives may be much less than the social costs. This has been stressed by Akerlof and Janet Yellen (1985).[67] In particular, if firms are risk averse[68] then they may not revise their wages or may not change other policies even in the presence of some disturbance to the economy which leads to an excess supply of labor, even if were they to do so would be welfare enhancing.

3 Can efficiency wage theory explain nominal as well as real wage rigidities? Although the criticism that these models provide an explanation of real-wage rigidities, not of nominal-wage rigidities, is valid against most versions of the efficiency-wage models – as it is against most versions of implicit contract theory (where, in principle, contracts should be indexed) – it is worth noting that the labor-turnover efficiency-wage model is also consistent with money-wage rigidities: The turnover rate facing any firm depends on the wages set by other firms; if each firm believes that other firms will leave the wages unchanged in nominal terms, it pays it to leave its wage unchanged in nominal terms. The Akerlof (1984) morale model is also consistent with nominal-wage rigidities.

4 Can efficiency wage theory explain rationing among several groups? Simpler versions of the efficiency-wage theory yielded rationing for only one group in the population. For all other groups, either no one was hired or there was full employment. But with more general specifications, with productivity depending on (each group's) unemployment rate then in equilibrium, there may be unemployment among several groups. And even if there were a continuum of groups, with only one group rationed, the discontinuity in utility (between similar groups) would remain. It is this discontinuity – with similar individuals being treated discretely differently – which is so much at odds with standard competitive theory.

5 Can efficiency wage theory explain wage and employment dynamics? The final criticism[69] is that while the efficiency-wage theory may provide an explanation of the "natural unemployment rate," it does not provide an explanation of cyclical movements in real wages. This criticism takes on two forms. First, it is observed, that in a recession, increases in unemployment (reductions in relevant opportunities, including self-employment income) should result in lower wages in the effort-efficiency wage models. Whether this is in fact the case is debatable; if the quality of workers laid off in a recession is, on average, lower than those retained (a pattern that itself is consistent with efficiency-wage theory), then even if the average product wage does not fall much, the quality adjusted product wage may. Moreover, what is relevant for the incentive-based efficiency-wage theory is the lifetime return from holding a job; with low discount rates and long lifetimes, disturbances to the economy may leave this relatively unaffected. Though the value of alternative opportunities may decrease in a recession, thus enabling a myopic firm to lower its wage without inducing shirking, nonmyopic firms will realize that the value of the job is enhanced by the implicit insurance provided through income smoothing.[70,71] (On the other hand, because unemployment benefits are typically lengthened during recessions, and the stigma associated with being laid off is decreased, it may actually be worthwhile for firms to raise wages in recessions.)

Still, the criticism that the efficiency-wage theories have yet to provide a dynamic theory is, for the most part, valid: The models constructed to date have been static. At a heuristic level, these models do provide an explanation for why when there is a sudden shift in, say, the demand for labor, it is not quickly reflected in a change in the wage, but rather is reflected in a decrease in employment; the new equilibrium may entail unemployment, but even if in the long run equilibrium entails full employment of labor, the adjustment process may entail unemployment as part of the transition.

The intuitive reason for this is easy to see. Under a variety of conditions, the quality of the workers obtained (or their productivity on the job) depends on the wage paid by the given firm relative to that of other firms. Thus, if the different firms in the economy do not simultaneously adjust their wages, given the high wages of other firms, it will not pay any single firm to lower its wage very much.[72]

Our analysis of dynamics stands in marked contrast to the standard kind of dynamics, which simply assumes slowness in the adjustment of wages and prices, and thus derives the transitional unemployment as a consequence of the ad hoc dynamic adjustment assumptions.

Consider, for instance, the staggered wage contract model (Taylor 1980). The *assumption* of nonsynchronous long-term contracts explains why wages at any particular firm do not fall instantaneously in the face of a decrease in the demand for labor, and why average wages fall only gradually But in the absence of some kind of efficiency-wage story, staggered contracts cannot explain the persistence, even for a short while, of unemployment: At the first instance at which a contract comes up for renewal, the wage should fall to the market-clearing level.

Moreover, the explanation of the process by which wages change is markedly different from the conventional story. We have argued that in general the quality of the labor force (its productivity) depends on the unemployment rate as well as the wage. At higher unemployment levels, the efficiency wage may be lower. For a variety of reasons, firms may be slow to fire workers, and thus the unemployment rate increases only slowly in response to a decrease in the "long-run" demand for workers. In such circumstances, the fall in the wage rate can be viewed both as a consequence of the increased unemployment and as mitigating the extent to which unemployment increases. But in this theory the wage does not fall because of the "pressure" of excess supply directly on the labor market, but only because of the indirect effect, through the effect on the efficiency wage.

Capital markets.   We have already noted how the theory we have presented provides a theory of credit rationing. Credit rationing, in turn, may provide both an explanation of why, and the mechanism by which, government policy affects the macroeconomic equilibrium (Alan Blinder and Stiglitz 1983), and a part of the explanation of why the effective cost of capital actually rises in the recession (Greenwald and Stiglitz 1986c, 1986d).[73]

Information concerning the nature of borrowers is firm-specific and not easily transferable. Accordingly, when the monetary authorities reduce the supply of high-power money, banks reduce the credit that they make available. Monetary policy, in this view, has effects not through the rate of interest (variations in real rates of interest until recently have been too small to account for much of the variability in investment or savings), but through its effects on the supply of credit. This theory agrees with the monetarists that the quantity of money may, as a result, play a more important role than the interest rate, but unlike the monetarists, provides a plausible mechanism by which these effects are realized.[74,75]

The increased uncertainty, for example, associated with recessionary periods, results in some groups being rationed out of the market who previously had not been. Moreover, other groups anticipate that the likelihood that they may be rationed out of the market sometime in the future has increased. Firms face, or anticipate facing, a liquidity crisis, one that may result in their bankruptcy: For them the effective cost of capital has increased. Thus, recessionary periods may be characterized by high effective interest rates (in contrast to low nominal interest rates, emphasized in the traditional literature); high effective interest rates can partly explain many of the anomolous features of the business cycle, including patterns of inventory accumulation (with a low shadow price on labor and low interest rates, there should be much more production smoothing than does in fact occur) and some aspects of pricing policies.[76]

Product markets.   Allen (1985b) has emphasized an alternative explanation for why firms may not lower prices in the face of a downward shift in the demand for their products: To do so could be interpreted as a signal of a deterioration of quality.

Relationship to other macrotheories.   We have already discussed briefly some of the contrasting implications of efficiency-wage theory and implicit contract theory.

(a) Insider–Outsider theory. Another important recent development is commonly called insider–outsider theory (Lindbeck and Snower 1984a, 1984b, 1986, 1987; Robert Solow 1985). This theory stresses the asymmetries between insiders (the firm's current employees) and outsiders (potential employees). These theories provide alternative explanations for why net profits of the firm might be reduced if a firm hired new workers at much lower wages; for example, the current workers, recognizing the threat that these workers pose to them, may refuse to provide them training. These theories are thus perfectly consistent with efficiency-wage theories.[77]

(b) Fixed price models and efficiency wage theories. One of the reasons for interest in the efficiency-wage theories is that they provide an explanation of wage and price rigidities, which play such a central role in the fixed wage-price models that have enjoyed such popularity during the past decade. Though the two approaches are, to that extent complementary,[78] the efficiency-wage models can also be seen as providing a critique of the fixed-wage models, or at least of the relevance of those models for policy purposes. Though wages do not fall to a market-clearing level, government policies can affect the level of wages and thus the equilibrium level of employment. (In contrast, the fixed-wage price models simply assume that wages and prices will remain unchanged.)

(c) Multipliers. Multipliers have had a long and noble history in macroeconomic analysis. It has not been widely recognized how difficult it is to obtain multipliers in conventional models: Usually price responses in stable systems dampen the effect of any initial disturbance. It is precisely because of price rigidities that traditional macroeconomic models yield multipliers. Our analysis provides the microfoundations of these price rigidities.[79]

2 Implications for development economics

We noted earlier that much of the recent interest in the unemployment consequences of the dependence of productivity on wages originated in the development literature, where the relationship was attributed to nutritional considerations. Since than a large literature has explored a variety of other causes and consequences of the wage-productivity nexus within LDCs.[80]

Mirrlees (1975) and Stiglitz (1976b) showed that wage-productivity relations of the form depicted in Figure 30.2 would give rise, even within utilitarian families (maximizing the sum of the utility of the members of the family) to inequality in consumption; some members would receive a low consumption level, others a high consumption level; those with a low consumption level would have a low productivity. What they consumed would exceed their marginal product, but be less than their marginal product plus a pro rata share of the rents. Conversely for the high consumers. Indeed, even if the family is Rawlsian (maximizes the welfare of the worst off individual) there may be consumption inequality.

Because productivity depends on consumption, individuals with landholdings will be more productive than landless workers, and will, accordingly, receive higher wages. Dasgupta and Ray (1986a, 1987) have explored the implications of inequality in land ownership for wages and output. In particular, they note that the very poor, those with very small landholdings, may be completely excluded from the market because their minimum wage costs per efficiency unit is too high. In their model, whether the economy is in an unemployment regime or a full employment regime will depend on the aggregate land supply (relative to the labor supply), in effect, on whether the Walrasian wage is below or above the efficiency wage; it may also depend on the distribution of land. A land reform may thus have a significant effect on national output.

The dependence of productivity on wages in the urban sector results in urban wages being set at levels in excess of the rural wage. This, by the familiar Harris-Todaro migration mechanism (Todaro 1968, 1969; Harris and Todaro 1970) and its generalizations (Stiglitz 1974c; Gary Fields 1975; Raaj Sah and Stiglitz 1984, 1985), results in urban unemployment. As noted earlier (Part I.5 above) the wage and employment levels set by private firms do not maximize national income (and are not Pareto efficient). On the other hand, even if the government could directly control the urban wage, it would not set it at the rural wage: Some level of unemployment is optimal. Moreover, policy prescriptions to reduce the real wage indirectly, through increasing the prices of commodities, are, at best, misguided. For private firms would respond, say, to an increase in the price of food by increasing the wage. Indeed, if productivity is more sensitive to the consumption of food than to the consumption of other commodities, government should subsidize the consumption of food.[81] In this context, specific and ad valorem wage subsidies have distinctly different effects on wage setting and employment policies. Because there are two objectives that the government wishes to achieve (the correct wage level and the correct urban employment level), it requires two instruments; the two forms of wage subsidies/taxes provide the requisite instruments.

The wage-productivity nexus also has important implications for the determination of the shadow wage of labor (particularly in the context of models with Harris-Todaro and related migration mechanisms). The opportunity cost of labor is not zero (in spite of the presence of unemployment) or even the rural wage. In some central cases, the shadow wage is the urban wage, independent of attitudes toward future generations; in other cases, it lies between the urban wage and the rural wage (see Stiglitz 1982a).

3 Further applications

The dependence of quality on price has a large number of other implications, two of which we briefly note here.

Technological change and competitive entry.   The fact that a lower price is associated with lower quality has important implications for technological change. Normally, we argue that if a firm develops a cheaper way of making a mousetrap it will be able to undercut its rivals, and thus to capture the whole market for itself. When prices convey information, the firm may not be able to undercut its rivals; lowering the price may simply lead potential customers to believe that it is selling a lower-quality mousetrap. (Farrell [1984, 1985] has discussed the entry barriers that arise in these models.)

The consequences of the wage-quality relationship in noncompetitive markets. The analysis so far has been confined to competitive markets. But similar results apply to noncompetitive markets as well.

The standard theory maintains that a monopsonist would never ration. For at the given price, if there is an excess demand he can increase his profits simply by increasing his price. Similarly, a monopsonist in the labor market would never pay a wage in excess of the minimum wage required to hire the number of workers he wishes; there would never be an excess supply of workers (though the number of workers hired may be less than in a competitive market-clearing equilibrium). But if the firm recognizes that by raising the wage it increases the quality of its labor force, it may minimize its wage costs by paying a wage that is above the minimum required to obtain the amount of labor that it wishes to obtain. Similarly, in the capital market, a monopoly bank may charge an interest rate below the market-clearing level, recognizing that in doing so it increases its expected returns.

Earlier, we showed how, in a competitive market, wages cum queues would screen individuals; more able individuals might be willing to take the risk of applying for a high-wage job, with a low probability of getting the job, when an (observationally identical) individual of lesser ability would not. The monopsonist would similarly attempt to use wages cum queues to differentiate among workers.

Still, it should be emphasized that the motives for differentiating among individuals (customers or workers) are markedly different under monopoly than under competition: Under competition, the motive is simply to identify workers who differ in productivity, while under monopoly, the motive is to discriminate, to capture as much of the consumer surplus from each worker/customer as possible.

V Concluding remarks

There is little doubt that the observation that quality may depend on price (productivity on wages; default probability on interest rates) has provided a rich mine for economic theorists: A simple modification of the basic assumptions results in a profound alteration of many of the basic conclusions of the standard paradigm. The Law of Supply and Demand has been repealed. The Law of the Single Price has been repealed. The Fundamental Theorem of Welfare Economics has been shown not to be valid.

More than that, the theories that we describe here provide the basis of progress toward a unification of macroeconomics and microeconomics. They provide an explanation of unemployment and credit rationing, derived from basic microeconomic principles. It is a theory in which the extensive idleness that periodically confronts society's resources, human and capital, is seen as but the most obvious example of market failures that pervasively and persistently distort the allocation of resources.

Several caveats should, however, be borne in mind. Firstly, the repeal of the Law of Supply and Demand (and the Law of the Single Price) is a selective repeal: We have not contended that equilibrium is never described by the equality of demand and supply, only that it need not be, and will not be in some important circumstances.

Secondly, though the basic outlines of the general theory appear now to be well established, there remain several important extensions and developments. We have referred to several of these within the text. The models presented here were, for the most part, static; it is imperative to develop an explicitly dynamic model if these theories are to provide part of the foundations of a theory explaining cyclical fluctuations in employment. Moreover, on several occasions we contrasted efficiency-wage theory with implicit contract theory, arguing that efficiency-wage theory provides a far better explanation of unemployment than does implicit contract theory. In fact, individuals do have long-term implicit contract relationships with their employers; these relationships are affected in fundamental ways by efficiency-wage considerations. The integration of implicit contract theory and efficiency-wage theory thus is a second important topic for a research agenda.

We have also noted that the problems with which we have been concerned are mitigated, but not eliminated, by monitoring and bonding (among other instruments that may be available to the firm). The limitations on monitoring and bonding have, however, received only limited theoretical scrutiny. Finally, we have, for the most part, analyzed incentive models and selection models in isolation from each other.[82] We have noted, however, that there may be important interactions between the two, and these require further study.

Thirdly, we have focused our attention on the burgeoning theoretical literature (but have made no pretense of being even complete within the scope of the topics covered). This is partly a consequence of the author's comparative advantage, but partly a consequence of the fact that the models presented here have not been the subject of extensive empirical testing.[83] We hope, in fact, that this survey will spur continuation of efforts in that direction.

This paper has, however, attempted to show how similar ideas have found application in the analysis of labor, capital, and product markets. These models provide an explanation of several phenomena within these markets that cannot be easily explained within the more conventional paradigm.

Acknowledgments

I am greatly indebted to my several coauthors, with whom I have worked on the analysis of the causes and consequences of the dependence of quality on price: Carl Shapiro, Barry Nalebuff, Andy Weiss, and Bruce Greenwald. I am also indebted to helpful conversations with George Akerlof, Janet Yellen, Franklin Allen, Bill Rogerson, Mark Gersovitz, Jonathan Eaton, Partha Dasgupta, among others. Larry Summers and Gary Fields provided helpful comments on an earlier draft.

The opening quotations were supplied by Michael Perelman, Gavin Wright (second and fourth quotation), Graciela Chichilnisky, and Franklin Allen.

Gavin Wright has drawn my attention to the fact that there was a large literature in the eighteenth and nineteenth centuries arguing for a link between wages and productivity. For instance, he cites the former U.S. Secretary of State Thomas F. Bayard's "Introductory Letter" to Jacob Schoenhof (in *The Economy of High Wages*, New York, 1893) as saying, "The facts you have adduced and your deductions irresistibly establish the proposition that low wages do not mean cheap production, and that the best instructed and best paid labor proves itself to be the most productive . . . " Similarly, Thomas Brassey, Jr., is quoted by John H. Habbakuk (*American and British Technology in the Nineteenth Century*, 1962) as saying, "The cheap labour at the command of our competitors seems to exercise the same enervating influence as the delights of Caphua on the soldiers of Hannibal" (*Work and Wages*, 1872, p. 142).

Some of this earlier literature is reviewed by Gregory Clark, in "Productivity Growth without Technical Change: European Agriculture before 1850" (1986), and by A. W. Coats, in

"Changing Attitudes to Labour in the Mid-eighteenth Century," *Economic History Review* (August 1958, 2(11), pp. 35–51). Coats traces the idea that high wages lead to high productivity back to Jacob Vanderlint, in *Money Answers All Things* (London, 1734).

Financial support from the Hoover Institution and the National Science Foundation is gratefully acknowledged.

Notes

1 Some 40 years ago, Tibor Scitovsky (1945) wrote a brief but important paper discussing the consequences of the habit of judging quality by price. Another antecedent of the recent literature is Alvin Klevorick and Roger Alcaly (1970), who explore the implications for the traditional theory of consumers' behavior.

2 Akerlof (1970) investigated a case where equilibrium entailed no trade. As the price of cars decreased, supply decreased and demand decreased (the deterioration in car quality was so great that the quality-adjusted price actually increased): Intersection occurred only at zero trade. But this is a special case which arises primarily because of the limited incentives to trade in his model. The effect he noted in the used car market is the same as had long been recognized in insurance markets. As the price of insurance increases, the adverse selection effect implies that the mix of applicants changes adversely; thus the premium required for the insurance firms to break even must increase. Nonetheless, there may exist insurance markets in which trade occurs.

3 And as we have already noted, because the inferences that can be drawn from observing a given price – and hence the demand at a given price – depend on the nature of supply, it may not be possible in some cases to isolate demand and supply disturbances.

4 For discussions of the validity of this relationship, see Christopher Bliss and Nicholas Stern (1978, 1981). See also P. H. Prasad (1970), G. B. Rodgers (1975), and Dasgupta and Ray (1986b).

5 A cartoon appeared in several newspapers in the early eighties, when interest rates were soaring, in which a banker is seen leaning over his desk, asking the loan applicant, "What kind of person would be willing to borrow at the interest rates we charge?"

6 Note too that in the circumstances with which we have just been concerned, where quality depends on price, the quantity demanded at any price depends on the quality supplied: Thus, for instance, a change in the mix of loan applicants will affect the supply of loans available at any interest rate; a change in the mix of job applicants will affect the demand for labor at any wage.

7 Nonprice terms in credit markets include collateral requirements, specifications of circumstances under which credit is terminated, etc.

8 The reservation utility level also may vary across sellers.

9 In the incentive (moral hazard) versions, q is a result of an action taken by the individual; the action taken is a function of the terms of the contract. In the selection version, q is the average quality of those offering goods (services) at the price p and x; the constraint (30.2) is to be read as saying that at least one item is offered for sale at the given terms. In general, in adverse selection models, the constraint (30.2) is binding for only some individuals offering to sell the commodity.

10 It is worth noting that while (30.2) may be viewed, from the perspective of the buyer, as what has come to be called the "individual rationality constraint," V^* is in general itself endogenously determined (it represents the individual's best alternative opportunity); and in the adverse selection models, (30.2) also can be viewed as a self-selection constraint, differentiating between those for whom the job (loan) is acceptable and those for whom it is not.

11 We choose this example because in more general models, with adverse selection or incentive effects, the productivity of a worker at one firm depends on the wages paid at other firms and on the unemployment rate. We wish to avoid these complications in this simple exposition.

12 Note, however, that the length of queue is not chosen by the firm, but is an endogenous property of the equilibrium. In this respect, these models differ in an important way from those in which the terms of the contract are determined either by the uninformed agent or the informed agent.

13 If the productivity of group λ_i is a function of its wage w_i, and its unemployment rate, U_i, then in equilibrium, for all groups hired (for which $U_i < 1$)

$$\lambda_i(w_i, U_i)/w_i$$

is the same, and

$$\lambda_i(w_i, U_i)/w_i = \lambda_i(w_i, U_i)/w_i.$$

14 Assuming that bankers are risk neutral, and thus care only about the expected return of the loan.

15 Indeed, in some circumstances a decrease in supply may actually lead to a decrease in the weighted mean interest rate charged. See Stiglitz and Weiss (1986a, 1986b).

16 In the simple models presented here, only one group in the population is rationed; those above the critical cutoff level receive all the credit they wish, or can sell all the labor they wish, while others are completely excluded from the market. But it is easy to construct models in which rationing is extended to many groups. See Barry Nalebuff and Stiglitz (1982) and Stiglitz and Weiss (1986a, 1986b, 1987).

17 The analyses can be extended to situations where there is uncertainty, provided there is a complete set of risk markets, and provided that the nature of the commodity being traded (the quality of labor, the probability of bankruptcy, etc.) does not change as prices (wages, interest rates) change. It is the latter which concerns us here.

18 This section focuses on the welfare economics of the imperfect information models. For a discussion of the welfare economics of the nutrition-based efficiency wage models, see Partha Dasgupta and Debraj Ray (1986a).

19 One should perhaps distinguish between two situations: that where the decentralized allocation *without* government intervention is inefficient, but government intervention, in the form of taxes and subsidies, can induce a decentralized efficient allocation; and those where even with this form of intervention, a decentralized allocation, cannot attain certain Pareto efficient allocations. Both problems may arise here.

20 This assumes that the firm cannot treat quits and fires differentially. There are good reasons for this: If quits are treated preferentially, a worker who knows he is about to be fired will quit. For a more extended discussion, see Shapiro and Stiglitz (1985a).

21 Unless a worker's productivity is completely firm-specific, then no information is conveyed to one firm by another firm's refusal to hire him.

22 More generally, the reservation wage of an individual will depend on his fallback (self-employment) income and the probability that he will obtain a higher wage, and this depends on the probability distribution of abilities and wage offers in the population, on the nature of the search technology, and on the costs of quitting a job once it has been accepted. See Nalebuff and Stiglitz (1982). Schlicht (1986) argues for a link between reservation wage and productivity based on the shorter expected duration of holding a job by less competent individuals.

23 A project is said to be riskier than another if its return is a mean preserving spread of that of the other.

24 The first result is a direct consequence of the concavity of the payoff function of the bank (in the absence of collateral, this is $\max[R, (1+r)B]$, where R is the return to the project, $(1+r)B$ the amount the firm has promised to repay); the second result is a direct consequence of the convexity of the payoff function of the borrower ($\min[R - (1+r)B, 0]$ in the absence of collateral); the third result is an immediate consequence of the second.

25 A vast literature has developed on the principal agent problem since the early papers by Steve Ross (1973), Mirrlees (1974), and Stiglitz (1974d). We make note of only those papers that are directly relevant to the subject of this review, the dependence of quality on price.

26 In the Stiglitz and Weiss (1983) analysis, contracts are explicit, but enforceable only if it is in the interests of at least one party to the contract to do so. In the papers discussed in this paragraph, there is no legal enforcement mechanism. "Moral hazard" issues arise both in the compliance with the contract, and in the actions borrowers take which affect the likelihood they will wish to comply.

27 Repudiation could always be avoided if the repayments could be made state dependent, and if all states were perfectly observable and verifiable by both parties. For a more general discussion, see Eaton, Gersovitz, and Stiglitz (1986).

28 There is a large "radical" literature emphasizing the effect of the employment relationship on worker productivity. Other contributions to this literature include Herbert Gintis and Tsuneo Ishikawa (1987), Tom Weisskopf, Bowles, and David Gordon (1983), Gerry Oster (1980), and Geoff Hodgson (1982). The distinction between this literature and the nonradical literature is not always readily

apparent. For instance, the Bowles (1985) and Shapiro and Stiglitz (1984) models appear to be essentially identical; some of the interpretations given to the model, and the lessons drawn, differ.

29 These models are thus long-term models. The "punishment" is provided "publicly" by the period of unemployment (rather than privately, through reduced wages or other means). Stiglitz and Weiss (1983) provide conditions showing that termination is in fact the optimal punishment.

These models are constructed with identical individuals so there is no reputation effect associated with being fired. In any case, it is often hard to distinguish among voluntary and involuntary termination, in which case, the reputation effect of separations may be minimal (Shapiro and Stiglitz 1985a).

30 The importance of this had, of course, long been recognized by labor economists. See Sumner Slichter (1919).

31 Richard Arnott and Stiglitz (1985) and Shapiro and Stiglitz (1985a) provide explanations for why individuals do not bear the full costs of training; these have to do with worker risk aversion, incomplete insurance, and imperfect capital markets (though these market imperfections in turn, can be related to information imperfections).

32 These effects have, of course, long been discussed by labor economists. For an early formalization of the notion of interdependence, see Dan Hamermesh (1975).

33 The observation that it is individuals' perceptions of whether they are being treated fairly that affects behavior has one important consequence. The productivity curve of a group that believes it is being treated unfairly will (if our argument is correct) lie below that of groups of identical abilities that do not believe they are being treated unfairly. Such individuals either will not be hired, or will be hired at lower wages than someone of the *same* ability (let alone someone of the ability that they believe that they have). The fact that they are hired at lower wages reconfirms their belief they are not being treated fairly. The employer who pays the lower wage does not believe he is discriminating, only that he is paying wages that are in accord with productivity, which depends both on (statistical projections of) ability and effort.

34 Akerlof (1980, 1982) and Schlicht (1981a, 1981b) develop alternative theories of the employer-employee relationship in which psychological and sociological considerations lead to a dependence of productivity on wages. Akerlof (1984) describes some experiments in which different workers are assigned identical jobs and paid identical wages, but believe that they are either being under-or overpaid. These perceptions affect productivity.

35 Obviously, if the landlord could monitor the actions of the tenant, the share contract would specify the level of work required, and these incentive effects would not arise. See Steve Cheung (1969).

36 Braverman and Srinivasan (1981) have identified circumstances in which in equilibrium there *cannot* exist an excess supply of labor.

37 If part of the fixed payment is paid after the crop, then it is as if the landlord lent the funds to the worker; an increase in the amount to be paid has precisely the same effects as an increase in the rate of interest detailed earlier. An increase in the fixed fee can, accordingly, adversely affect the expected return of the landlord (-cum-lender) (D. Gale Johnson 1950). Allen (1985a) has shown that at low shares, tenants may have an incentive to "cheat" on the contract, absconding with the entire produce of the land.

38 The quotation from Sismondi in the introduction to this paper makes it clear that selection effects may also arise in the context of sharecropping.

39 These beliefs are "rational"; given the beliefs of the individual, it would not pay the firm to produce a high-quality commodity, if it ever produced a low-quality commodity; and given that the firm indeed produces a low-quality commodity, the beliefs of individuals are consistent with firm behavior. More formally, the equilibrium can be shown to be a perfect equilibrium. See Dybvig and Spatt (1983).

This is a "reputation" model based solely on incentive considerations. Other reputation models entail a mixture of incentive and adverse selection effects. There are good producers and bad producers. When a buyer purchases a commodity that turns out to be a low-quality commodity, then he infers that the seller must be a low-quality seller. It is their concern about being so labeled that induces good producers to produce high-quality commodities. One does not necessarily need many "bad" firms to induce good behavior on the part of the good firms, as David Kreps and Robert Wilson (1982) show in a rather different context.

40 It is straightforward to construct models that incorporate both incentive and nutritional effects.

41 Where "actions" are sufficiently precisely specified to imply a particular outcome in a particular situation, regardless of who performed the action.

42 The monitoring required by piece rate systems is costly; for it to be effective, there can be little variation in the quality of what is produced, or it needs to be easy to write a contract that specifies the relationship between quality and price, and then to observe and verify the quality of what is produced.

Moreover, as technology changes, the piece rate needs to change; but this is often a contentious process. If, of course, there were no costs of labor mobility (no costs of hiring workers and no costs to the worker of moving to another firm) then if the firm offered too low a piece rate, resulting in an income below the worker's opportunity cost, then the worker would simply quit; exit would replace voice, to use Albert Hirschman's insightful terminology. But labor mobility is costly, and thus workers and firms are concerned about how the piece rate is set; it determines the division of the "*ex post* surplus" – given that the workers are working for the firm, the difference between the worker's income and his opportunity cost; and the difference between the profits of the firm from the current employees and what the profits would be if the employer had to replace them.

43 To the extent that firms bear these turnover costs or pay workers not solely on the basis of their actions, firms can be thought of as providing insurance.

44 There is one other situation where moral hazard problems do not arise in labor markets: When workers are risk neutral (so there is no need for an insurance component in the relationship), then they can rent the machines on which they work (rent the land); because they receive all the residual, they will have "correct incentives"; and because what the capitalist (landlord) receives is independent of the action of the worker, he is indifferent to the actions they undertake. But even this is not correct if the worker cannot pay the rent ahead of time; then there is some probability that he will fail to pay the promised rent, and the likelihood of this is, in general, a function of the actions he undertakes: There is still a moral hazard problem. When rents are paid *ex post*, then it is as if the owner lent the money to the renter (see Johnson 1950; Stiglitz and Weiss 1981). Moreover, if how the worker uses the machine affects its future productivity and if it is difficult to verify whether the deterioration in the machine is due to misuse, there is a further moral hazard problem limiting the extent of rental markets. The contractual arrangements between the parties will try to limit these moral hazard problems, by stipulating restrictions on the use of the rented property. Thus, a landowner may stipulate what crops are to be planted, and he may impose restrictions on grazing. These moral hazard problems can be avoided by selling the machine; but this increases the risk of the worker; and it is even less likely that he will have the resources to pay for the purchase than to rent.

45 These enforcement problems are, of course, central both in international lending, in implicit contract theory, in sharecropping markets, and in product markets.

46 Thus what appears to be a technical assumption in Gerard Debreu's *Theory of Value* becomes of central importance in this analysis. Loosely speaking, to prove the existence of a market-clearing equilibrium, one must show that the supply correspondences are continuous, and to do this one must show that the budget sets are continuous functions of prices. To recast the nutritional efficiency-wage model in standard terms, we let $w\#$ denote the wage per efficiency unit. While at $w\# = w^*/\lambda^*$, the individual supplies λ^* efficiency units of labor, and at higher wages, the individual can supply, say, up to $\lambda(w)$ units of labor, at lower values of $w\#$ the feasible set shrinks to zero.

Note that while with nonconvex preferences, say, for leisure, the supply of labor correspondence might look as in Figure 30.17(b), with the individual being indifferent between points A and B; with the efficiency wage model, the labor supply correspondence appears as in Figure 30.17(a); the individual strictly prefers B to A. This explains why, with nonconvex preferences, an equilibrium exists with a continuum of individuals, but a market-clearing equilibrium does not exist in the efficiency-wage model. Moreover, while with standard nonconvexities those who supply labor and those who do not have the same level of utility, this is not true in our model. For a more extended discussion, see Dasgupta and Ray (1986a).

47 The demand curve is derived as follows. Assume the firm's production function is $Q = F[\lambda(w)L]$. It chooses w and L to maximize $Q - wL$ where we have chosen output as the numeraire. From the first-order conditions, $\lambda/\lambda' = w$ meaning that the wage is chosen to minimize labor costs per unit of effective labor (the efficiency wage). Employment is chosen so that, at the efficiency wage, the real wage equals the value of the marginal product of labor: $w = F'(w)\lambda$.

48 In particular, if the Walrasian wage exceeds the efficiency wage, the market equilibrium is the Walrasian wage, and the law of supply and demand holds. Any firm that attempted to lower the wage to the efficiency wage would not be able to obtain any labor.

49 In this example, the cost per effective unit of labor curve has taken on a simple shape: At wages below w^*, cost per effective labor unit is decreasing, and at wages greater than w^*, it is increasing. There is no intrinsic reason why the cost per effective unit of labor curve should take on such a simple shape as we have already noted (see Figure 30.6). Then, there will be an excess supply of labor if the Walrasian wage is below w^* or between w and w^{**}. It always pays the firms to pay the wage in excess of the Walrasian wage, which minimizes cost per effective unit of labor. Thus, for Walrasian wages in the interval between $\hat{w}$ and w^{**} it pays the firm to increase the wage to w^{**}. (In these circumstances, equilibrium may be characterized by a wage distribution, as we noted earlier.)

50 These repercussions have been at the center of recent literature focusing on the distinction between insiders and outsiders. See Assar Lindbeck and Dennis Snower (1984a).

51 The concept of equilibrium employed by Dasgupta and Ray (1986a) in their analysis of the nutritional efficiency wage model corresponds to a quasi-equilibrium in Debreu (1959) and to the concept of a compensated equilibrium in Kenneth Arrow and Frank Hahn (1971).

52 They constructed a simple model in which they combine incentive and selection effects; there are two groups in the population, and each group has two activities (a safe and a risky project). Even though the bank is able to sort individuals perfectly, it cannot raise interest rates, because to do so would induce greater risk taking. Hence, they show that there may be credit rationing at one or both credit contracts. Credit rationing may also arise if individuals differ in more than one dimension, e.g., with respect to risk aversion and wealth.

53 These problems would also be ameliorated if firms could establish a reputation.

Another mechanism for providing incentives for workers that does not suffer from the "double moral hazard" problem are contests (Lazear and Sherwin Rosen 1981; Green and Nancy Stokey 1983; Halebuff and Stiglitz 1983b; Sudipto Bhattacharya 1983). They do impose some risk for workers, and workers have to believe that the contests are fairly administered, and that they are evenly matched with their competitors. Intrafirm contests may also have deleterious morale effects.

54 Some of the "problems" with job purchases explain why the price for jobs would be low (e.g., workers' risk aversion, limitations on workers' access to the capital market), but not why the market for jobs does not clear.

55 Similarly the probability of consummating a deal may serve as a self-selection device within a bargaining model.

56 Technically this analysis should be contrasted with that of Rothschild and Stiglitz (1976), where each firm (uninformed agent) sets the price and quantity; here firms set only the price; the unemployment rate is determined as part of the equilibrium. This is also true of the Stiglitz-Weiss (1986a) model of the capital market.

Some questions have been raised about the relevance of this particular model for the description of labor markets; it may have more to do with the number of hours worked by a Harley Street doctor than it does with unemployment among the low skilled. It is important to note, however, that in this model "unemployment" does not have the same interpretation that it does in the national income statistics: It means that the individual is not employed by others. For the low skilled, this may indeed correspond to unemployment; for the high skilled, it may correspond to self-employment.

57 This model has been extended by Nalebuff and Stiglitz (1982) to the case where individuals can apply for several jobs. In that case, the nature of the equilibrium depends critically on whether contracts are binding – whether once a job has been accepted, the worker can quit when he is offered a better job. If contracts are binding, the opportunity cost of accepting a low-wage job is the foregone possibility of a high-wage job, the likelihood of which depends on both the job offers of different firms and the behavior of other individuals (how high they set their reservation wages). They show that there exists a particular wage distribution, such that when all workers rationally set their reservation wages, the cost-per-efficiency unit of the firm is the same for all firms. (In their equilibrium, while the quality of those who apply at each wage are, in fact, different, it is only the wage-cum-unemployment rate that distinguishes them: in all other respects the workers look the same. Moreover, at each wage, except the lowest, there is an excess supply of applicants.)

By contrast, if the first firm to enter the market had simply hired at what it thought was the efficiency wage, because it would have hired only lower-ability workers, those with reservation wages below the efficiency wage, the "new" efficiency-wage schedule facing the later entrant would

588   *Joseph E. Stiglitz*

lie above the old one, for $w > w^*$, and hence there would be an advantage to being late. See Lewis Guasch and Weiss (1980).

58 Thus, models in which there are only limited sources of imperfect information may be very misleading. For instance, if individuals differ only in one dimension, then education may serve to sort individuals perfectly: There will be no residual imperfect information, and hence no need to lower wages to improve the mix of laborers. But if individuals differ in several dimensions, then education alone will not suffice to provide complete information. Similarly, in the capital market, if borrowers differ only in one dimension, and there is no moral hazard problem, there may exist a fully revealing self-selection equilibrium, and there will be, as a consequence, no role for credit rationing. But if borrowers differ in several dimensions and/or there are moral hazard problems, there may exist credit rationing. Though self-selection devices may reveal some information, they will not be perfectly revealing.

59 It is important to emphasize that although we believe that these models provide an important part of the microfoundations for macroeconomics, they do not provide the whole story: Other models (many of them also based on considerations of imperfect information) are required.

This section owes much to the comments of Bruce Greenwald and Larry Summers.

60 This should be contrasted with the standard implicit contract theories (e.g., Costas Azariadis 1983; Grossman and Oliver Hart 1981; for recent surveys, see Azariadis and Stiglitz 1983; and Hart 1983) which, at best, provide an explanation of work sharing (see Stiglitz 1986). Arnott, Arthur Hosios, and Stiglitz (1983) incorporate some aspects of efficiency-wage theory in their analysis of labor contracts with costly labor mobility.

61 Including theories of staggered contracts (Taylor 1980), which need to explain why labor is not absorbed into those sectors whose contracts are up for negotiation.

62 John Harris and Michael Todaro (1970) have developed a similar analysis to explain urban unemployment in LDCs. The major difference between the Harris-Todaro model and the Stiglitz model is that in the former, the wage is exogenous and in the latter – as in all the work under examination here – it is endogenous. Robert Hall (1975) has used a similar model to explain differences in unemployment rates in different urban areas.

63 Similarly, Arnott, Hosios and Stiglitz (1985) assume that the costs of search for the unemployed and the employed may be different and show that optimal contracts may then entail some individuals being layed off even if it means a finite probability of being unemployed for a period.

64 As is often the case, there may be another equilibrium in which accepting a low-wage job does not signal one's ability: When there are significant transactions costs, it is more plausible that the acceptance of a low-wage job will serve as a signal. Alternatively, the argument to be given next serves to explain why accepting a job would lower one's lifetime wage prospects quite apart from signaling considerations: Signaling considerations would then serve to strengthen the magnitude of the effect of the acceptance of a low-wage job on lifetime income.

65 This result depends, in part, on the firm's not being able to commit itself to paying higher wages in the future. Those commitments themselves are, at best conditional on the firm's surviving. Thus, a worker who accepts a low wage now from a firm in bad financial straits with the promise of a high wage in the future takes, in effect, an equity position in the firm. The reasons why workers may not be willing to do so have been set forth in Greenwald, Stiglitz and Weiss (1984).

66 This argument was put forward by Robert Hall in his discussion of Yellen's survey of efficiency-wage models at the San Francisco meetings of the American Economic Association, December 1984.

67 This is in fact a general property of economies that are not (constrained) Pareto efficient. There then exist large classes of perturbations to the economy that effect Pareto improvements. If the firm sets its wage in a privately optimal way, there exist some pertubations of this wage that have a second order effect on the profits of the firm but have a first order effect on the welfare of other agents in the economy. See Greenwald and Stiglitz (1986a).

68 Again, the fact that firms behave in a risk averse manner can be explained in terms of certain capital market imperfections which, in turn, can be related to imperfect information.

69 This list of criticisms is not meant to be exhaustive. Another objection is that these models require not only that productivity increase with wages, but also that there be a range of wages over which increases in wages lead to more than proportionate increases in productivity. This objection has been dealt with where we showed how several simple models exhibiting these properties can be constructed. It then becomes an empirical question whether in practice the wage-productivity

relationship has the required shape. Unfortunately, there is insufficient empirical evidence to date to provide a convincing answer.

70 This formulation entails, in effect, a synthesis of implicit contract theory with efficiency-wage theory. A firm that cheats on the implicit contract will find that their workers leave later, when job opportunities become better. In this view, the appropriate time unit for the analysis of the worker-employer relationship is longer than just a month or even a year.

Moreover, selection (quality-efficiency wage) considerations may strengthen these concerns, because it is likely to be the better workers who will have the easiest time finding alternative opportunities and will have the highest propensity to quit.

71 Moreover, wages are affected not only by demand disturbances but also by any shock that affects the no-shirking constraint. Thus, the expectation of an upturn in the economy would shift the no-shirking constraint upward, necessitating an increase in today's wage and a decrease in current employment.

72 The analysis is somewhat more subtle than this suggests: Each firm's wage is dependent not only on other firms' wages, but also on the unemployment rate; nevertheless, in at least some versions of the efficiency-wage model, the unemployment effect is dominated by the wage effect, and wages do not fall, or fall only slowly in the face of a downward shift in the demand curve for labor.

73 This analysis can also be related to the recent studies (Robert Barro 1974; Stiglitz 1982c, 1983; Neil Wallace 1981) arguing for the irrelevance of public financial policies. A critical assumption in these analyses is that public and private borrowing are perfect substitutes for each other; in particular, individuals are assumed to have unlimited access to the capital market. If they do not (and the theories presented here explain why they do not), then public financial policies are not irrelevant.

74 For this to be a cogent explanation of the cyclical variability in investment, one must explain why firms do not turn to other sources of funds. The explanation for this is provided in Greenwald, Stiglitz, and Weiss (1984), where they argue that asymmetries of information make the cost of raising capital on the equity market very high, prohibitively high for many firms. (Their model is essentially a direct application of the Akerlof-Lemons model to the equity market; their result on the thinness of equity markets corresponds to Akerlof 's results on the thinness of used car markets.)

Equity rationing can give rise to investment fluctuations, even without credit rationing; for the absence of futures markets combined with limitations on the ability to sell equity imply that a decision to produce forces managers/owners to absorb risk. A reduction in their working capital will thus lead to a reduction in their equilibrium production levels. If, as is in fact the case, debt is not indexed, monetary shocks can have real effects through their effects on working capital.

75 For other studies of monetary policy in the presence of credit rationing, see Jackman and John Sutton (1982), Smith (1983), Vale (1986), and Lindbeck (1963).

76 As Edmund Phelps and Sidney Winter (1970) emphasized, there may be a trade-off involved in recruiting customers today by lowering prices, with higher future profits, but lower current profits. An increase in the effective cost of capital tilts the tradeoff toward higher current profits, i.e., higher prices today.

77 They emphasize, however, at least one important aspect to which efficiency-wage theory has paid insufficient attention: The worker may not be able to commit himself to receiving low wages in the future; after he is trained he may be in a position to extract a high wage. What is relevant, of course, for the firm's decision is the relationship between lifetime wages and productivity. (Notice that while Greenwald has emphasized the consequences of the inability of firms to commit themselves to pay high wages in the future, insider-outsider theory has emphasized the consquences of the inability of workers to commit themselves to accepting low wages in the future.)

78 For an explicit attempt to integrate the two approaches, see Karl Moene (1985).

79 The externalities associated with incomplete markets and imperfect information also give rise to multipliers. These multipliers should not be confused with the welfare multipliers that arise whenever the economy is not (constrained) Pareto efficient. Then there always exist some perturbations to some individual or firm that have a second order effect on the welfare of the individual or firm but a first order effect on social welfare (see Greenwald and Stiglitz 1986b).

80 In this section, we focus our discussion on the consequences of the nutritional-wage productivity nexus for LDCs. For a discussion of alternative explanations, see Stiglitz (1982b, 1974c).

81 Firms would, in such circumstances, find it in their interests to subsidize the consumption of food; but unless the subsidy is provided for on-premise consumption, workers could resell the subsidized food, and the firm would thus not directly gain from the food subsidy.

For an analysis of optimal taxation and subsidies in the presence of productivity effects, see Sah and Stiglitz (1984).

82   An exception is the Stiglitz and Weiss (1986a, 1986b) studies.

83   There have, however, been numerous studies addressing particular aspects of the theories described in this paper. For an early investigation of the price-quality relationship, see Gabor and Granger (1966). For a recent examination of the empirical evidence on whether the labor market clears, see Thomas Kniesner and Arthur Goldsmith (1985). For a recent discussion of the relationship between productivity and wages, see, for example, James Medoff and Katharine Abraham (1981). Macroeconomic analyses of the relationship between unemployment and productivity include James Rebitzeer (1985), and Weisskopf, Bowles, and Gordon (1983).

There is a growing literature attempting to test the credit-rationing models. See, for instance, Charles Calomiris and R. Glenn Hubbard (1985), Leonard Nakamura (1985), and P. Kugler (1985).

References

Aigner, Dennis and Cain, Glen. "Statistical Theories of Discrimination in Labor Markets," *Ind. Lab. Relat. Rev.*, Jan. 1977, *30*(2), pp. 175–87.

Akerlof, George A. "The Market for 'Lemons': Qualitative Uncertainty and the Market Mechanism," *Quart. J. Econ.*, Aug. 1970, *84*(3), pp. 488–500.

——. "The Economics of Caste and of the Rat Race and Other Woeful Tales," *Quart. J. Econ.*, Nov. 1976, *90*(4), pp. 599–617.

——. "A Theory of Social Custom, of Which Unemployment May Be One Consequence," *Quart. J. Econ.*, June 1980, *94*, pp. 749–75.

——. "Labor Contracts as Partial Gift Exchange," *Quart. J. Econ.*, Nov. 1982, *97*(4), pp. 543–69.

——. "Gift Exchange and Efficiency Wage Theory: Four Views," *Amer. Econ. Rev.*, May 1984, *74*(2), pp. 79–83.

Akerlof, George A. and Stiglitz, Joseph. "Capital, Wages and Structural Unemployment," *Econ. J.*, June 1969, *79*(314), pp. 269–81.

Akerlof, George A. and Yellen, Janet. The Macroeconomic Consequences of Near Rational Rule of Thumb Behavior." Mimeo, U.C. Berkeley, 1983.

——. "A Near-rational Model of the Business Cycle, with Wage and Price Inertia," *Quart, J. Econ.*, Supp. 1985, *100*(5), pp. 823–38.

Allen, Franklin. "Loans, Bequests and Taxes Where Abilities Differ: A Theoretical Analysis Using a Two-ability Model." D. Phil. thesis, Oxford, 1980.

——. "The Prevention of Default," *J. Finance*, May 1981, *36*(2), pp. 271–76.

——. "Credit Rationing and Payment Incentives," *Rev. Econ. Stud.*, Oct. 1983, *50*(4), pp. 639–46.

——. "Reputation and Product Quality," *Rand J. Econ.*, 1984. *15*(3), pp. 311–27.

——. "On the Fixed Nature of Sharecropping Contrasts," *Econ. J.*, Mar. 1985a, *95*(377), pp. 30–48.

——. "A Theory of Price Rigidities When Quality Is Unobservable." Mimeo, U. of Pennsylvania, 1985b.

Annable, James E., Jr. "A Theory of Downward-Rigid Wages and Cyclical Unemployment," *Econ. Inquiry*, July 1977, *15*(3), pp. 326–44.

——. "Money Wage Determination in Post Keynesian Economics," *J. Post Keynesian Econ.*, Spring 1980, *2*(3), pp. 405–19.

——. "Another Auctioneer is Missing." Mimeo, Economics Department, The First National Bank of Chicago, 1985 (earlier version presented at meetings of the International Atlantic Economic Association, Rome, 1985).

Arnott, R.; Hosios, A. and Stiglitz, J. "Implicit Contracts, Labor Mobility and Unemployment." Mimeo, Princeton U., 1983 (revised version of a paper presented at NBER-NSF conference, Dec. 1980).

Arnott, R. and Stiglitz, J. "Labor Turnover, Wage Structures and Moral Hazard," *J. Labor Econ.*, 1985, *3*(4), pp. 434–62.

——. "Moral Hazard and Optimal Commodity Taxation," *J. Public Econ.*, Feb. 1986, *29*, pp. 1–24.

Arrow, Kenneth J. and Hahn, F. H. *General competitive analysis*. Edinburgh: Oliver and Boyd, 1971.

Azariadis, C. "Employment with Asymmetric Information," *Quart. J. Econ.*, Supplement 1983, *98*(3), pp. 157–72.

Azariadis, C. and Stiglitz, J. E. "Implicit Contracts and Fixed Price Equilibria," *Quart. J. Econ.* Supplement, 1983, *98*(3), pp. 1–22.

Baltensperger, Ernst and Milde, Hellmuth. "Loan Rate Flexibility and Asymmetric Default Information," *Geld, Banken and Versicherungen*, 1982, pp. 1165–78.

Barro, Robert. "Are Government Bonds Net Wealth?" *J. Polit. Econ.*, Nov./Dec. 1974, *82*(6), pp. 1095–1117.

Becker, Gary S. and Stigler, George J. "Law Enforcement, Malfeasance, and Compensation of Enforcers," *J. Legal Stud.*, Jan. 1974, *3*(1), pp. 1–18.

Besanko, David and Thakor, Anjan. "Collateral and Rationing: Sorting Equilibria in Monopolistic and Competitive Markets." Northwestern University Discussion Paper, 1984.

Bester, Helmut. "Screening vs. Rationing in Credit Markets with Imperfect Information, *"Amer. Econ. Rev.*, Sept. 1985, *75*(4) pp. 850–55.

Bhattacharya, Sudipto. "Tournaments, Termination Schemes and Forcing Contracts." Mimeo, U. of California, Berkeley, June 1985.

Blinder, A. and Stiglitz, J. E. "Money, Credit Constraints and Economic Activity," *Amer. Econ. Rev.*, May 1983 *73*(2), pp. 297–302.

Bliss, Christopher J. and Stern, Nicholas. "Productivity, Wages and Nutrition," *J. Devel. Econ.* Dec. 1978, *5*(4), pp. 331–97.

——. *Palanpur-studies in the economy of a North Indian village.* New Delhi: Oxford U. Press, 1981.

Bowles, Samuel. "The Production Process in a Competitive Economy: Walrasian, Neo-Hobbesian, and Marxian Models," *Amer. Econ. Rev.*, Mar 1985, *75*(1), pp. 16–36.

Braverman, Avishay and Srinivasan, T. N. "Credit and Sharecropping in Agrarian Societies," *J. Devel. Econ.*, Dec. 1981, *9*(3), pp. 289–312.

Braverman, Avishay and Stiglitz, Joseph E. "Sharecropping and the Interlinking of Agrarian Markets," Amer. *Econ. Rev.*, Sept. 1982, *72*(4), pp. 695–715.

——. "Landlords, Tenants and Technological Innovations," *J. Devel. Econ.*, 1986.

Bray, Margaret. "Futures Trading, Rational Expectations, and the Efficient Markets Hypothesis," *Econometrica*, May 1981, *49*(3), pp. 575–96.

Bulow, Jeremy I. and Summers, Lawrence H. "A Theory of Dual Labor Markets with Application to Industrial Policy, Discrimination and Keynesian Unemployment." NBER Working Paper No. 1666, July 1985.

Calomiris, Charles and Hubbard, Robert Glenn. "Price Flexibility, Credit Rationing, and Economic Fluctuations: Evidence from the U.S., 1979–1914." Mimeo, Northwestern U., Oct. 1985.

Calvo, Guillermo. "Quasi-Walrasian Theories of Unemployment," *Amer. Econ. Rev.*, May 1979, *69*(2), pp. 102–07.

Calvo, Guillermo and Phelps, Edmund. "Indexation Issues: Appendix: Employment Contingent Wage Contracts," in *Stabilization of the domestic and international economy.* Vol. 5. Eds.: Karl Brunner and Allan H. Meltzer. Carnegie-Rochester Conference Series on Public Policy. *J. Monet. Econ.*, Suppl., Series 1977, *5*, pp. 160–68.

Calvo, Guillermo and Wellisz, Stanislaw. "Hierarchy, Ability and Income Distribution," *J. Polit. Econ.*, Part 1, Oct. 1979, *87*(5), pp. 991–1010.

Cheung, S. N. S. *The theory of share tenancy.* Chicago: U. of Chicago Press, 1969.

Clark, Gregory. "Productivity Growth without Technical Change: European Agriculture before 1850." Unpub. ms., 1986.

Clark, Kim and Summers, Laurence. "Labor Market Dynamics and Unemployment: A Reconsideration," *Brookings Pap. Econ. Act.*, 1979, *1*, pp. 13–60.

Clemenz, G. "Credit Rationing in the Absence of Direct Observability of Efforts and Abilities of Borrowers." Institut fur Wirtschaftswissenschaften der Universität Wien, Working Paper No. 8405, June 1984.

——. "Credit Markets with Asymmetric Information and the Role of Collateral." Mimeo, U. Wien, 1985.

Dasgupta, Partha and Ray, Debraj. "Inequality as a Determinant of Malnutrition and Unemployment: Theory," *Econ. J.*, Dec. 1986a, *96*.

——. "Adapting to Undernourishment: The Clinical Evidence and Its Implications." Mimeo, U. of Cambridge, 1986b.

——. "Inequality as a Determinant of Malnutrition and Unemployment: Policy," Mar. 1987, *97*.

Debreu, Gerard. *Theory of value.* NY: John Wiley, 1959.

Devinney, Timothy M. "Incentives and Multi-Period Rationing in Loan Contracts, in *Geld, Banken and Versicherungen*, Eds.: Hermann Goppl and Rudof Henn, VVW Karlsruhe, pp. 629–46.

Dybvig, Philip H. and Jaynes, G. "Output-supply, Employment and Intra-Industry Wage Dispersion," Cowles Foundation Discussion Paper No. 546, 1980.

Dybvig, Philip H. and Spatt, Chester S. "Does It Pay to Maintain a Reputation? Consumer Information and Product Quality." Working paper, 1983.

Eaton, B. Curtis and White, William D. "Agent Compensation and the Limits of Bonding," *Econ. Inquiry*, July 1982, *20*(3), pp. 330–43.

Eaton, Jonathan. "Lending with Costly Enforcement of Repayment and Potential Fraud." *J. Banking and Finance*, 1986, *10*, pp. 281–93.

Eaton, Jonathan and Gersovitz, Mark. "LDC Participation in International Financial Markets: Debt and Reserves," *J. Devel. Econ.*, Mar. 1980, *7*(1), pp. 3–21.

——. "Debt with Potential Repudiation: Theoretical and Empirical Analysis," *Rev. Econ. Stud.*, Apr. 1981a, *48*(2), pp. 289–309.

——. "Poor Country Borrowing and the Repudiation Issue." Princeton Studies in International Finance No. 47, Princeton, NJ, June 1981b.

Eaton, Jonathan; Gersovitz, Mark and Stiglitz, J. E. "The Pure Theory of Country Risk," *European Econ. Rev.*, 1986, *30*(3), pp. 481–513.

Farrell, Joseph. "Prices as Signals of Quality." M. Phil. dissertation, Oxford, 1979.

——. "Repeat Sales, Quality and Prices." Mimeo, M.I.T., Dec. 1980.

——. "Moral Hazard in Quality, Entry Barriers, and Introductory Offers," M.I.T. Working Paper, May 1984.

——. "Moral Hazard and an Entry Barrier." *Rank J. Econ.*, Fall 1986, *17*, pp. 440–49.

Fields, Gary. "Rural-Urban Migration, Urban Unemployment and Underemployment, and Job-Search Activity in LDCs," *J. Devel. Econ.*, June 1975, *2*(2), pp. 165–87.

Fitzroy, F. "Contests." Mimeo, International Institute of Management, West Berlin, 1981.

Freimer, Marshall and Gordon, M. J. "Why Bankers Ration Credit," *Quart. J. Econ.*, Aug. 1965, *79*, 397–416.

Friedman, Benjamin M. "The Roles of Money and Credit in Macroeconomic Analysis." in *Macroeconomics, prices, and quantities: Essays in memory of Arthur M. Okun.* Ed.: James Tobin. Washington, DC: Brookings Inst., 1983, pp. 161–89.

Gabor, Andre and Granger, C. W. J. "Price as an Indicator of Quality: Report of an Inquiry," *Economica*, N.S., Feb. 1966, *33*, pp. 43–70.

Gintis, Herbert and Ishikawa, Tsuneo. "Wages, Work Discipline and Macroeconomic Equilibrium," in *J. Japanese and International Economies.* 1987, *1*, pp.195–228.

——. "The Theory of Production and Price in Contingent Renewal Markets." Mimeo, U. of Massachusetts, Nov. 1985.

Green, Jerry. "Information, Efficiency and Equilibrium." Harvard Institute of Economic Research, Discussion Paper No. 284, Mar. 1973.

Green, Jerry and Stokey, Nancy. "A Comparison of Tournaments and Contracts," *J. Polit. Econ.*, June 1983, *91*(3), pp. 349–64.

Greenwald, Bruce. *Adverse selection in the labor market.* NY: Garland, 1979.

——. "Adverse Selection in the Labour Market," *Rev. Econ. Stud.*, July 1986, *53*(3), pp. 325–47.

Greenwald, Bruce and Stiglitz, Joseph. "Externalities in Economics with Imperfect Information and Incomplete Markets," *Quart. J. Econ.*, May 1986a, *101*(2), pp. 229–64.

Greenwald, Bruce and Stiglitz, J. "Externalities in Economies with Information," *Quart. J. Econ.*, Feb. 1986a.

——. "The Inefficiency of Competitive Equilibria with Rationing." Mimeo, 1986b.

——. "Information, Finance Constraints and Business Fluctuations." Paper prepared for the Seminar on Monetary Theory, Taipei, Jan. 3–8, 1986c.

"Money, Imperfect Information, and Economic Fluctuations." Paper parpared for the Seminar on Monetary Theory, Taipei, Jan. 3–8, 1986d.

Greenwald, Bruce; Stiglitz, Joseph and Weiss, Andrew. "Informational Imperfections and Macroeconomic Fluctuations," *Amer. Econ. Rev.*, May 1984, *74*(2), pp. 194–99.

Grossman, Sanford and Hart, Oliver. "Implicit Contracts, Moral Hazard, and Unemployment," *Amer. Econ. Rev.*, May 1981, *71*(2), pp. 301–07.

Grossman, Sanford and Stiglitz, Joseph E. "Information and Competitive Price Systems," *Amer. Econ. Rev.*, May 1976, *66*(2), pp. 246–53.

——. "On the Impossibility of Informationally Efficient Markets," *Amer. Econ. Rev.*, June 1980, *70*(3), pp. 393–408.

Guasch, Luis and Weiss, Andrew. "Adverse Selection by Markets and the Advantage of Being Late," *Quart. J. Econ.*, May 1980, *94*(3), pp. 453–66.

Hall, Robert. "The Rigidity of Wages and the Persistence of Unemployment," *Brookings Pap. Econ. Act.*, 1975, *2*, pp. 301–49.

——. "Employment Fluctuations and Wage Rigidity," *Brookings Pap. Econ. Act.*, 1980, *1*, pp. 91–123.

Hamermesh, Daniel S. "Interdependence in the Labour Market," *Economica*, Nov. 1975, *42*(168), pp. 420–29.

Harberger, A. C. "On Measuring the Social Opportunity Cost of Labour," *Int. Lab. Rev.*, June 1971, *103*(6), pp. 559–79.

Harris, John R. and Todaro, Michael P. "Migration, Unemployment & Development: A Two-Sector Analysis," *Amer. Econ. Rev.*, Mar. 1970, *60*(1), pp. 126–42.

Hart, Oliver. "Optimal Labour Contracts Under Asymmetric Information: An Introduction," *Rev. Econ. Stud.*, Jan. 1983, *50*(1), pp. 3–35.

Heal, Geoffrey. "Do Bad Products Drive Out Good?" *Quart. J. Econ.*, Aug. 1976, *90*(32), pp. 499–502.

Hellwig, Martin F. "A Model of Borrowing and Lending with Bankruptcy," *Econometrica*, Nov. 1977, *45*, pp. 1879–1906.

Hodgson, Geoff. "Theoretical and Political Implications of Variable Productivity," *Cambridge J. Econ.*, Sept. 1982, *6*(3), pp. 213–26.

Hoel, M. and Vale, Bent. "Effects of Reduced Working Time in an Economy Where Firms Set Wages," *Eur. Econ. Rev.*, 1986, *30*, pp. 1097–1104.

Holmström, Bengt. "Equilibrium Long-Term Labor Contracts," *Quart. J. Econ.*, 1983, *98*(5), pp. 23–54.

Jackman, R.; Layard, R. and Pissarides, C. "Policies for Reducing the Natural Rate of Unemployment," in *Keynes economic legacy*. Eds.: J. L. Butkiewicz, K. J. Koford and J. B. Miller. Praeger, 1986, pp. 111–52.

Jackman, Richard and Sutton, John. Imperfect Capital Markets and the Monetarist Black-Box: Liquidity Constraints, Inflation, and the Asymmetric Effects of Interest Rate Policy," *Econ. J.*, Mar. 1982, *92*(365), pp. 108–28.

Jaffee, Dwight and Russell, Thomas. Imperfect Information, Uncertainty, and Credit Rationing," *Quart. J. Econ.* Nov. 1976, 90(4), pp. 651–66.

Johnson, D. Gale. "Resource Allocation Under Share Contracts," *J. Polit. Econ.*, Apr. 1950, *58*, pp. 111–23.

Keeton, William R. *Equilibrium credit rationing.* NY: Garland, 1980.

Klein, Benjamin and Leffler, Keith B. The Role of Market Forces in Assuring Contractual Performance,"*J. Polit. Econ.*, Aug. 1981, *89*(4), pp. 615–41.

Klevorick, Alvin K. and Alcaly, Roger E. "Judging Quality by Price, Snob Appeal, and the New Consumer Theory," *Z. Nationalökon.*, 1970, *30*(1–2), pp. 53–64.

Kniesner, Thomas and Goldsmith, Arthur H. "Does the Labor Market Clear? A Survey of the Evidence for the U.S.," *Res. Labor Econ.*, 1985, *7*, pp. 209–56.

Kreps, David M. and Wilson, Robert. "Reputation and Imperfect Information," *J. Econ. Theory*, Aug. 1982, *27*(2), pp. 253–79.

Kugler, P. "Credit Rationing: Evidence from Disequilibrium Interest Rate Equations." U. Basel Working Paper No. 32, 1985.

Lazear, Edward P. "Agency, Earnings Profiles, Productivity and Hours Restrictions,"*Amer. Econ. Rev.*, Sept. 1982, *71*(4), pp. 606–20.

Lazer, Edward P. and Rosen, Sherwin. Rank Order Tournaments as Optimum Labor Contracts," *J. Polit. Econ.*, Oct. 1981, *89*(5), pp. 841–64.

Leibenstein, Harvey. *Economic backwardness and economic growth.* NY: Wiley, 1957.

Lindbeck, Assar. A *study in monetary analysis.* Stockholm: Almquist and Wiksell, 1963.

Lindbeck, Assar and Snower, Dennis. Involuntary Unemployment as an Insider-Outsider Dilemma." Seminar Paper No. 282, Institute for International Economic Studies, U. of Stockholm, 1984a. Revised as "Wage Rigidity, Union Activity and Unemployment," in *Wage rigidity and unemployment.* Ed.: Wilfred Beckerman. Duckworth and Johns Hopkins U. Press, 1986, ch. 5.

——. "Labor Turnover, Insider Morale and Involuntary Unemployment." Seminar Paper No. 310, Institute for International Economic Studies, U. of Stockholm, 1984b.

——. "Explanations of Unemployment," *Oxford Rev. Econ. Policy*, 1986, *1*(2), pp. 34–59.

——. "Efficiency Wages Versus Insiders and Outsiders," *Eur. Econ. Rev.*, 1987, (Paper presented at EEA Congress, Vienna, Aug. 1986).

Malcolmson, James. "Unemployment and the Efficiency Wage Hypothesis," *Econ. J.*, Dec. 1981, *91*(364), pp. 848–66.

Manove, Michael. "Job Responsibility and Promotion: An Efficiency-Wage Analysis." Mimeo, Dept. of Economics, Boston U., Boston, MA, Apr. 2, 1986.

Marshall, Alfred. *Principles of economics.* 8th ed. London: Macmillan, 1920.

Medoff, James L. and Abraham, Katharine. "Are Those Paid More Really More Productive?" J. *Human Res.*, Spring 1981, *16*(2), pp. 186–216.

Melnik, A. and Plaut, S. "Loan Commitment Contracts, Terms of Lending, and Credit Allocation," *J. Finance*, June 1986, *41* pp. 425–35.

Milde, Hellmuth and Riley, John. Signaling in Credit Markets," UCLA Working Paper 334, 1984.

Mill, J. S. *Principles of political economy.* London: J. W. Parker, 1848.

Mirrlees, James. "Notes on Welfare Economics, Information, and Uncertainty," in *Contributions to economic analysis.* Eds.: M. S. Balch, D. L. Mcfadden and S. Y. Wu. Amsterdam: North-Holland, 1974.

——. "A Pure Theory of Underdeveloped Economies," in *Agriculture in development theory.* Ed.: L. A. Reynolds. New Haven: Yale U. Press, 1975, pp. 84–106.

Miyazaki, Hajime. "Work Norms and Involuntary Unemployment." *Quart. J. Econ.*, May 1984, pp. 297–311.

Moene, Karl O. "A Note on Keynesian Unemployment as a Worker Discipline Device," *Econ. Lett.* 1985, *18*(1), pp. 17–19.

Mookherjee, Dilip. "Involuntary Unemployment and Worker Moral Hazard." Stanford U., Graduate School of Business, May 1985.

Myers, Stewart C. and Majluf, Nicholas S. "Corporate Financing and Investment Decisions When Firms Have Information that Investors Do Not Have," *J. Finan. Econ.*, June 1984, *13*(2), pp. 187–221.

Nakamura, Leonard Isamu. "Customer Credit, Financial Intermediaries and Real Income: Preliminary Evidence That Credit Matters." Mimeo, Dept. of Economics, Rutgers, Oct. 1985

Nalebuff, Barry T. and Stiglitz, Joseph E. "Quality and Prices." Econometric Research Program Memorandum No. 297, Princeton U., May 1982.

——. "Information, Competition and Markets," Amer. *Econ. Rev.*, May 1983, *73*(2), pp. 278–83.

——. "Prizes and Contests: Towards a General Theory of Compensation and Competition," *Bell J. Econ.*, Spring 19836, *14*, pp. 21–43.

Newbery, David and Stiglitz, Joseph E. "Share-cropping, Risk Sharing and the Importance of Imperfect Information," in *Risk, uncertainty and agricultural development.* Eds.: J. A. Roumasset, J. M. Boussard, and I. Singh. Searca, A/D/C, 1979, pp. 311–41.

——. *The theory of commodity price stabilization: A study in the economics of risk.* Oxford: Clarendon Press, 1981.

Oster, Gerry. "Labour Relations and Demand Relations: A Case Study of the 'Unemployment Effect,'" *Cambridge J. Econ.*, Dec. 1980, *4*(4), pp. 337–48.

Pencavel, J. H. "Wages, Specific Training, and Labor Turnover in U.S. Manufacturing Industries," *Int. Econ. Rev.*, Feb. 1972, 13(1), pp. 53–64.

——. "Industrial Morale," in *Essays in labor market analysis in memory of Yochanan Peter Comay.* Eds.: O. Ashenfelter and Wallace E. Oates. NY: Wiley, 1977, pp. 129–46.

Phelps, Edmund S. and Winter, Sidney G. "Optimal Price Policy Under Atomistic Competition," in *Microeconomic foundations of employment and inflation theory.* Ed.: Edmund S. Phelps. NY: Norton, 1970, pp. 309–37.

Prasad, P. H. *Growth with full employment.* Bombay: Allied Publishers, 1970.

Radner, Roy. "Rational Expectations Equilibrium: Generic Existence and the Information Revealed by Prices," *Econometrica*, May 1979, *47*(3), pp. 655–78.

Rebitzeer, James B. "Unemployment, Long-term Employment Relations, and Labor Productivity Growth." Mimeo. U. of Texas, Nov. 1985.

Repullo, Rafael. "A Simple Model of Interest Rate Deregulation." Mimeo, London School of Economics and Bank of Spain, Nov. 1985.

Riley, J. and Zeckhauser, R. "When to Haggle, When to Hold Firm," *Quart. J. Econ.*, 1983, *98*(2), pp. 267–89.

Rodgers, G. B. "Nutritionally Based Wage Determination in the Low Income Labour Market," *Oxford Econ. Pap.*, Mar. 1975, *27*(1), pp. 61–81.

Ross, Stephen A. "The Economic Theory of Agency: the Principal's Problem," *Amer. Econ. Rev.*, May 1973, *63*(2), pp. 134–39.

Rothschild, Michael and Stiglitz, J. E. "Equilibrium in Competitive Insurance Markets: An Essay on the Economics of Imperfect Information," *Quart. J. Econ.*, Nov. 1976, *90*(4), pp. 630–49.

——. "A Model of Employment Outcomes Illustrating the Effect of the Structure of Information on the Level and Distribution of Income," *Econ. Letters*, 1982, *10*, pp. 231–36.

Sah Raaj Kumar and Stiglitz, Joseph. "Taxation and Pricing of Agricultural and Industrial Goods." National Bureau of Economic Research, Working Paper No. 1338, Cambridge, 1984. In *The theory of taxation for developing countries*. Eds.: D. Newbery and N. Stern. Oxford U. Press.

——. "The Social Cost of Labor and Project Evaluation: A General Approach," *J. Public Econ.*, Nov. 1985, *28*(2), pp. 135–63.

Salop, Joanne and Salop, Steven. "Self-Selection and Turnover in the Labor Market," *Quart. J. Econ.*, Nov. 1976, *90*(4), pp. 619–27.

Salop, Steven C. "Wage Differentials in a Dynamic Theory of the Firm." *J. Econ. Theory*, Aug. 1973, *6*(4), pp. 321–44.

——. "A Model of the Natural Rate of Unemployment," *Amer. Econ. Rev.*, Mar. 1979, *69*(1), pp. 117–25.

Schlicht, Ekkehart. "Labour Turnover, Wage Structure and Natural Unemployment," *Z. ges. Staatswiss.*, June 1978, *134*(2), pp. 337–46.

——. "Reference Group Behaviour and Economic Incentives: A Remark," *Z. ges. Staatswiss.*, Mar. 1981a, *137*, pp. 125–27.

——. "Reference Group Behaviour and Economic Incentives: A Further Remark," *Z. ges. Staatswiss.*, Dec. 1981b, *137*(4), pp. 733–36.

——. "Dismissal vs. Fines as a Discipline Device: Comment on Shapiro-Stiglitz." Mimeo, Institute for Advanced Study, Princeton, NJ, Dec. 1985.

——. "A Link Between Reservation Wage and Productivity." Mimeo, Institute for Advanced Study, Princeton, NJ, Feb. 1986.

Scitovsky, Tibor. "Some Consequences of the Habit of Judging Quality by Price," *Rev. Econ. Stud.*, 1945, *12*(2), pp. 100–05.

Shapiro, Carl. "Premiums for High Quality Products as Returns to Reputations," *Quart. J. Econ.*, Nov. 1983, *98*(4), pp. 659–79.

Shapiro, Carl and Stiglitz, Joseph E. "Equilibrium Unemployment as a Worker Discipline Device," *Amer. Econ. Rev.*, June 1984, *74*(3), pp. 433–44.

——. "Equilibrium Unemployment as a Worker Discipline Device: A Reply," *Amer. Econ. Rev.*, Sept. 1985a, *75*(4), pp. 892–93.

——. "Can Unemployment be Involuntary: Reply?" *Amer. Econ. Rev.*, Dec. 1985b, *75*(5), 121–157.

Simonde De Sismondi, J. C. L. *Political economy.* NY: Kelley, [1814] 1966.

Slichter, Sumner H. *The turnover of factory labor* NY: Appleton, 1919.

Smith, Bruce. "Limited Information, Credit Rationing, and Optimal Government Lending," *Amer. Econ. Rev.*, June 1983, *73*(3), pp. 305–18.

Solow, Robert. "Another Possible Source of Wage Stickiness,"*J. Macroecon.*, Winter 1979, *1*(1), pp. 79–82.

——. "On Theories of Unemployment," *Amer. Econ. Rev.* Mar. 1980, *70*(1), pp. 1–11.

——. "Insiders and Outsiders in Wage Determination," *Scand. J. Econ.*, 1985, *87*(2), pp. 411–28.

Spence, A. Michael. *Market signaling: Informational transfer in hiring and related processes.* Cambridge, MA: Harvard U. Press, 1974.

Stiglitz, Joseph E. "Approaches to the Economics of Discrimination," *Amer. Econ. Rev.*, May 1973, *3*(2), pp. 287–95.

——. "Theories of Discrimination and Economic Policy," *in Patterns of racial discrimination.* Ed.: Von Furstenberg. Lexington, MA: Lexington, 1974a, pp. 5–26.

——. "Equilibrium Wage Distributions." IMSSS Technical Report No. 154, Stanford U., 1974b. *Econ. J.*, Sept. 1985, *95*(379), pp. 595–618.

——. "Alternative Theories of Wage Determination and Unemployment in L.D.C.s: The Labor Turnover Model," *Quart. J. Econ.*, May 1974c, *88*(2), pp. 194–227.

——. "Incentives and Risk Sharing in Sharecropping," *Rev. Econ. Stud.*, Apr. 1974d, *41*(2), pp. 219–55.

——. "Incentives, Risk and Information: Notes Towards a Theory of Hierarchy," *Bell J. Econ. Management Sci.*, Autumn 1975, *6*(2), pp. 552–79.

——. "Prices and Queues as Screening Devices in Competitive Markets." IMSSS Technical Report No. 212, Stanford U. Aug. 1976a.

——. "The Efficiency Wage Hypothesis, Surplus Labour and the Distribution of Income in L. D.C.s," *Oxford Econ. Pap.*, July 1976b, *28*(2), pp. 185–207.

——. "Lectures in Macro-economics." Mimeo, Oxford U., 1978.

——. "The Wage-Productivity Hypothesis: Its Economic Consequences and Policy Implications." Paper presented at the New York Meetings of the American Economic Association, 1982a. *Modern developments in public finance: Essays in honor of Arnold Harberger.* Ed.: M. Boskin. Oxford: Basil Blackwell, 1987.

——. "Alternative Theories of Wage Determination and Unemployment: The Efficiency Wage Model," in *The theory and experience of economic development's essays in honor of Sir W. Arthur Lewis.* Eds.: Mark Gersovitz et al. London: Allen & Unwin, 1982b, pp. 78–106.

——. "On the Relevance or Irrelevance of Public Financial Policy." Paper presented to a conference at Rice University, NBER Working Paper No. 1057, Apr. 1982c.

——. "On the Relevance or Irrelevance of Public Financial Policy: Indexation, Price Rigidities and Optimal Monetary Policy," in *Inflation, debt and indexation.* Eds.: Rudiger Dornbusgh and Mario Simonsen. Paper presented to a conference at Rio de Janeiro, Dec. 1981. Cambridge, MA: MIT Press, 1983, pp. 183–222.

——. "Theories of Wage Rigidity," in *Keynes' economic legacy.* Eds.: J. Butkiewicz, K. Koford, and J. Miller. NY: Praeger, 1986, pp. 153–221 (also available as NBER Working Paper 1442).

Stiglitz, Joseph E. and Weiss, Andrew. "Credit Rationing in Markets With Imperfect Information," *Amer. Econ. Rev.*, June 1981, *71*(3), pp. 393–410.

——. "Incentive Effects of Terminations: Applications to the Credit and Labor Markets," *Amer. Econ. Rev.*, Dec. 1983, *73*(5), pp. 912–27.

——. "Credit Rationing and Collateral," in *Recent developments in corporate finance.* Eds.: Jeremy Edwards, Julian Franks, Colin Mayer and Stephen Schaefer. NY: Cambridge U. Press, 1986a, pp. 101–35.

——. "Macroeconomic Equilibrium and Credit Rationing." Mimeo. Bellcore, 1986b.

——. "Credit Rationing With Many Borrowers," *Amer. Econ. Rev.*, Mar. 1987, *77*(1).

Stoft, Steven. "Cheat Threat Theory: An Explanation of Involuntary Unemployment." Mimeo, Boston U., 1982.

——. "Wages, Unemployment and Piece Rate: Double Asymmetric Information." Boston U. Discussion Paper No. 113, July 1985.

Strand, Jon. "Efficiency Wages, Implicit Contracts and Dual Labor Markets: A Theory of Work Habit Formation." Mimeo, Dept. of Economics, U. of Oslo, 1986.

Tan, Tommy Chin-Chiu and Da Costa Werlang, Sergio Ribeiro. "Life Cycle Credit Rationing." Mimeo, U. of Chicago, June, 1985.

Taylor, John B. "Aggregate Dynamics and Staggered Contracts," *J. Polit. Econ.*, Feb. 1980, *88*(1), pp. 1–23.

Todaro, Michael. The Urban Employment Problem in Less Developed Countries: An Analysis of Demand and Supply," *Yale Econ. Essays*, 1968, *8*(2), pp. 331–402.

——. "A Model for Labor Migration and Urban Unemployment in Less Developed Countries," *Amer. Econ. Rev.*, Mar. 1969, *59*(1), pp. 138–48.

Vale, B. "Effects of Bank Reserve Requirements with 'Grey' Credit Markets Under Asymmetric Information." Mimeo No. 15, U. of Oslo, Aug. 19, 1986.

Wallace, Neil. "A Modigliani-Miller Theorem for Open Market Operations," *Amer. Econ. Rev.*, June 1981, *71*(3), pp. 267–74.

Weiss, Andrew. "A Theory of Limited Labor Markets." Ph.D. dissertation, Stanford U., 1976.

——. "Job Queues and Layoffs in Labor Markets with Flexible Wages," *J. Polit. Econ.*, June 1980, *88*(3), pp. 526–38.

Weisskopf, Thomas E. Bowles, Sumner and Gordon, David M. "Hearts and Minds: A Social Model of U.S. Productivity Growth," *Brookings Papers Econ. Act.*, 1983, 2, pp. 381–450.

Wessels, Walter J. The Contribution by Firms to Unemployment: A Dynamic Model," *Southern Econ. J.*, Apr. 1979, *45*(4), 1130–50.

——. "The Uses and Limits of Unemployment as a Disciplining Device in the Efficiency Wage Model." Mimeo. North Carolina State U., Nov. 1986.

Wette, Hildegard. "Collateral in Credit Rationing in Markets with Imperfect Information: Note," *Amer. Econ. Rev.*, June 1983, *73*(3), pp. 442–45.

Whiteside, Harold D. "Wages: An Equity Approach," *J. Behav. Econ.*, 1974, *3*(1), pp. 64–84.

Wilson, Charles A. "Equilibrium and Adverse Selection," *Amer. Econ. Rev.*, May 1979, *69*(2), pp. 313–17.

——. "The Nature of Equilibrium in Markets with Adverse Selection," *Bell J. Econ.*, 1980, *11*(1), pp. 108–30.

Yellen, Janet. "Efficiency Wage Models of Unemployment," *Amer. Econ. Rev.*, May 1984, *74*(2), pp. 200–05.

Yoon, Chang-Ho. "A Reexamination of the Theory of Credit Rationing." Mimeo, Stanford U., 1984a.

——."On the theory of Credit Rationing: Further Analysis." Mimeo, Stanford U., 1984b.

Index